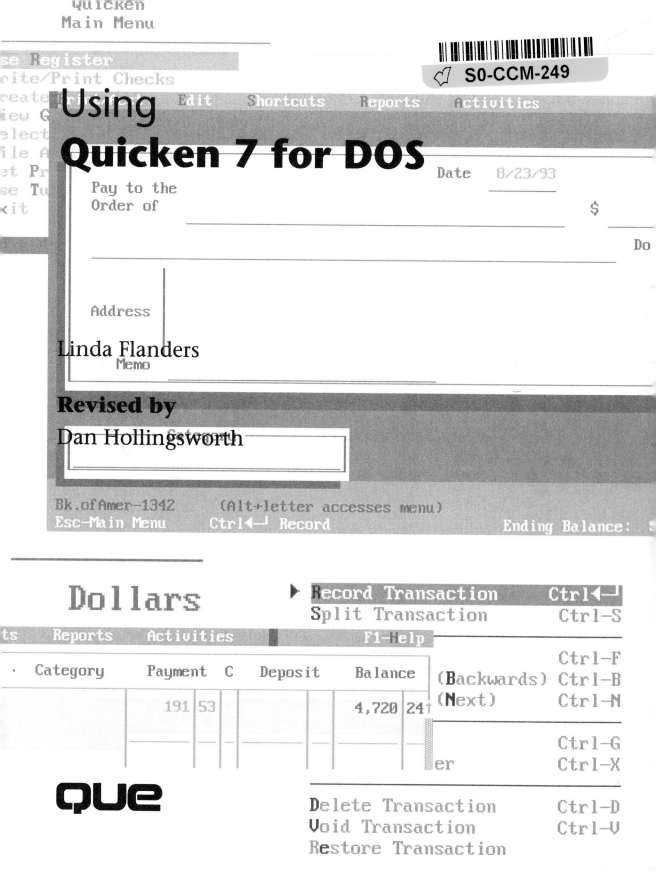

Quicken
Main Menu

se Register
rite/Print Checks
reate
iew G
elect
ile A
et Pr
se Tu
xit

Edit   Shortcuts   Reports   Activities

Using
Quicken 7 for DOS

S0-CCM-249

Pay to the
Order of

Date   8/23/93

$

Do

Address

Linda Flanders
Memo

Revised by

Dan Hollingsworth

Bk.of Amer—1342   (Alt+letter accesses menu)
Esc—Main Menu   Ctrl⏎ Record   Ending Balance:

Dollars

▶ Record Transaction   Ctrl⏎
  Split Transaction   Ctrl-S

ts   Reports   Activities   F1-Help

· Category   Payment C Deposit   Balance

191 53   4,720 24↑

(Backwards) Ctrl-F
            Ctrl-B
(Next)   Ctrl-N

            Ctrl-G
er   Ctrl-X

que

Delete Transaction   Ctrl-D
Void Transaction   Ctrl-V
Restore Transaction

Using Quicken 7 for DOS

Library of Congress Catalog No.: 93-86243

ISBN: 1-56529-462-9

95 94 93   4 3 2 1

Interpretation of the printing code: the rightmost double-digit number is the year of the book's printing; the rightmost single-digit number, the number of the book's printing. For example, a printing code of 93-1 shows that the first printing of the book occurred in 1993.

This book is based on Quicken Version 7 for DOS.

Publisher: David P. Ewing

Director of Publishing: Michael Miller

Managing Editor: Corinne Walls

Publishing Manager: Don Roche, Jr.

Dedication

To my good friend and mentor Brian, who convinced me that I could and should write.

Dan Hollingsworth

Credits

Marketing Manager
Ray Robinson

Acquisitions Editor
Nancy Stevenson

Product Director
Joyce J. Nielsen

Development and Production Editor
Jill D. Bond

Technical Editor
Scott Avery

Book Designer
Amy Peppler-Adams

Proofreading/Indexing Coordinator
Joelynn Gifford

Production Analyst
Mary Beth Wakefield

Production Team
Angela Bannan
Paula Carroll
Karen Dobson
Brook Farling
Carla Hall
Heather Kaufman
Shelley Palma
Caroline Roop
Tina Trettin
Michelle Worthington
Lillian Yates

Graphic Image Specialists
Teresa Forrester
Tim Montgomery
Dennis Sheehan
Sue VandeWalle

Indexers
Jennifer Eberhardt
Johnna VanHoose

Composed in *Stone Serif* and *MCPdigital*
by Que Corporation.

About the Authors

Linda A. Flanders is a Certified Public Accountant with a Bachelor of Science degree in accounting from Indiana University. She has worked in public accounting for Arthur Andersen & Co. and in corporate taxation for Mayflower Group, Inc. She is the author of *Using QuickBooks for Windows*, *Using TurboTax*, *Using Microsoft Money 2.0*, and several other Que books.

Dan Hollingsworth is a Certified Public Accountant based in Reno, Nevada. He holds a Master of Business Administration degree from the University of Arkansas at Fayetteville and has over 20 years experience in accounting and financial management. He currently operates an individual tax and consulting practice. He has performed technical edits on several books for Que Corporation, including *Using TurboTax: 1993 Edition* and *Using Microsoft Money 2.0*.

Trademarks

All terms mentioned in this book that are known to be trademarks or service marks have been appropriately capitalized. Que cannot attest to the accuracy of this information. Use of a term in this book should not be regarded as affecting the validity of any trademark or service mark.

Quicken is a registered trademark of Intuit, Inc.

Contents at a Glance

Table of Contents

5 **Using the Register**   **119**

6 **Automating the Register**   **143**

Introduction

If you're like most people, your personal bookkeeping takes you hours and hours each month. You probably sit down three to four times a month to pay bills, each time gathering paperwork, writing checks, entering checks and deposits into your checkbook register, calculating your bank account balance, and addressing envelopes. Then, when your monthly bank statement arrives, you have to sit down once more to perform the tedious task of balancing your checkbook by checking off cleared transactions, adding outstanding deposits and checks, and performing the reconciling calculations. After you've endured all these ordeals, heaven forbid if *your* bank account balance does not agree with the bank's! That crisis means spending even more time trying to detect the error(s). All of these tasks just to keep your financial records in some semblance of order. But keeping your financial records in order is a task that *cannot* be overlooked nor trusted to a financial system that is outdated or ineffective.

If you invest your money in any type of securities, then you absolutely must keep track of your investments or you won't know if your investment strategies are paying off. If your focus is on income-producing investments, you need to monitor those investments to make sure that the income yields are maximized. If your focus is on growth investments, you need to monitor those investments to make sure that they are growing at a satisfactory level. No matter what your focus, you need to monitor your investments to make sure they don't dwindle away. Of course, you can entrust this process to your investment advisor or broker, but you'll want to be on top of things to make sure the experts are doing their job with *your* money.

Quicken is your solution to the boring and long process of bookkeeping and financial management and the necessary, but sometimes complex task of monitoring your investments. With Quicken, you can speed up your record-keeping activities and have a little fun, too. By using screens that resemble what you're used to seeing on the desktop (checks and check Registers), you can quickly and easily enter your financial transactions, print checks, reconcile your bank account, create budgets, and generate reports so that you can analyze your finances more easily. Quicken's investment features help you track each of your investments so that you can easily manage your portfolio.

To truly have a handle on your finances, you must keep track of your income and expenses so that you know how much money is coming in and how much is going out. Quicken helps you do that. In order to make informed decisions about spending, you must know exactly where you are (financially) at any given time. If you want to take a vacation to Europe or buy a new car, for example, you immediately know what you can afford. Quicken helps you make these decisions by presenting the financial data that you need in a format that is meaningful to you. That's what this book is really about: making better financial decisions by using financial information—financial information that Quicken can help you collect, store, and use.

In this age of super technology, almost anything you do behind a desk can be accomplished with a computer. Bookkeeping and financial management are no exception. With a well-designed software package, you can perform all your financial activities, including tracking your investments, in far less time and with far less frustration.

If you are considering the installation of a personal or small-business accounting package like Quicken, if you have decided to install Quicken and want a little extra help, or if you already have begun using Quicken and want a reference source that goes beyond the information provided in the user's manual, *Using Quicken 7 for DOS* will help. This text includes a wealth of information about Quicken Version 7 and about managing your personal or small-business finances.

After you read this Introduction, you will know what Quicken Version 7 is and whether the program suits your needs. This Introduction also identifies the contents of each chapter.

What Is Quicken?

Quicken is a computer-based bookkeeping system you can use to manage your personal or business finances. Used in the simplest way, Quicken maintains your check register for you by deducting payments and adding deposits to your checking account balance. Quicken eliminates the possibility of you overdrawing your account because of an arithmetic error.

The real value of Quicken, however, stems from several other features the program provides. First, Quicken enables you to use your computer and printer to generate checks, which is a real time-saver if you find yourself writing many checks at home every month. Second, Quicken enables you to use the information stored in your Check Register to report on your income and expenses, track tax deductions, and compare your actual income and expenses to what you originally budgeted. Third, you can use Quicken to perform bookkeeping for most personal and business assets and liabilities, including personal investments, business receivables, personal credit lines and mortgages, and business payables. With these extra features, individuals can track and manage their finances closely, and many small businesses can use Quicken as a full-fledged accounting package. (Quicken enables you to generate personal and business income statements, balance sheets, and cash-flow statements.)

New Features in Quicken 7

If you've used earlier versions of Quicken, you'll want to know what Quicken 7 has in store for you. The following is a list of the new features in Quicken 7:

Printing graphs: Now you can print your graphs on a graphical printer. Refer to Chapter 17, "Creating Graphs," to learn more about printing graphs.

QuickZoom for graphs: Use QuickZoom to investigate the underlying details for amounts in your graphs. Refer to Chapter 17, "Creating Graphs," to learn more about QuickZoom.

Investments: Investments have a whole new look. The new Portfolio views provide comprehensive analysis of your investment performance and value. The new investment forms simplify entering transactions. Refer to Chapter 16, "Monitoring Your Investments," to learn more about these new features.

QuickReport: In an account register, QuickReport enables you to zoom out from an individual field in a transaction to see historical transaction information about the entry in that field, without setting up a report or modifying your regular layout. Refer to Chapters 5, 10, and 11 for discussions on QuickReport.

QuickMath: Now you can do basic calculations without a calculator for numeric fields in the register and many other Quicken windows. Refer to Chapter 2, "Getting Around in Quicken," to see how this option works.

Improved QuickFill: QuickFill is available in more places to speed up your data entry. See Chapters 6, 8, and 20 for discussions on QuickFill.

Scheduled Transactions: Put all your bill paying on auto pilot. Quicken's scheduled transactions feature uses a familiar calendar format to let you schedule and view future transactions. Then Quicken reminds you of each transaction as it comes due, or simply records it for you automatically. Refer to Chapter 6 "Automating the Register," to learn more about scheduled transactions.

Calendar Notes: Quicken enables you to create and save notes on your Calendar to remind you of key dates and events (financial or otherwise). Refer to Chapter 2 "Getting Around in Quicken," to see how this new feature works.

New Reports: Comparison reports enable you to compare dollar amounts between two defined time periods. New percentage columns in Summary and Comparison reports let you view the allocation of your income or expenses as a percentage of your total income or expenses. Refer to Chapter 12, "Creating and Printing Reports," to learn how to use these reports.

Named date ranges: Quicken provides you with a pop-up menu in the Report date range field in any report setup window. You choose from descriptive text names such as: Current Quarter, Year to Date, Last Month, and Last Year. This means that you don't have to enter dates manually when creating reports. Refer to Chapter 12, "Creating and Printing Reports," to see how this feature works.

AutoCreate budgets: Now you can use AutoCreate for individual categories without overwriting your entire budget. Refer to Chapter 15, "Budgeting with Quicken," to learn how to use this feature.

Named Budgets: Quicken enables you to save and retrieve multiple budget scenarios that you can use with any Quicken file. See Chapter 15, "Budgeting with Quicken," to learn more about this feature.

New Budget views: You can still see your budget in the standard view that shows dollar amounts in each field, or you can choose one of the new percentage views to see the amounts in each field as a percentage of total income or total expenses. Refer to Chapter 15, "Budgeting with Quicken," to see how this option works.

AutoInflate budgets: You can inflate or deflate your budget amounts by a specified percentage to adjust for changing circumstances. Refer to Chapter 15, "Budgeting with Quicken," to learn how to utilize this feature.

Qcards: Qcards appear on-screen to help you enter the correct information in windows. When Qcards are turned on, they appear automatically as you move from field to field in a window. See Chapter 2 "Getting Around in Quicken," to learn about the benefits of this feature.

Loans with balloon payments: Now you can set up an amortized loan to include a balloon payment. See Chapter 10, "Tracking Your Net Worth, Other Assets, and Liabilities," to learn how to use this feature.

When to Use Quicken

Answering the question *When should I use Quicken?* depends on whether you are using the program for personal or small-business purposes. If you are considering Quicken for personal use, four factors indicate that Quicken represents a good investment of your time and money:

- When check-writing and checking-account recordkeeping take more time than you want to spend. Quicken does most of the work related to keeping your checkbook: recording transactions, writing checks, reconciling account balances, and maintaining the check register. Because Quicken does the work for you, the program saves you a tremendous amount of time.

- When you need to track your tax deductions carefully. Quicken tracks the amounts you spend on tax-deductible items. At the end of the year, totaling your charitable contribution deductions is as simple as printing a report.

- When you want to budget income and expense amounts and compare what you earn and spend with what you budgeted. Budgets, contrary to their reputation, are not equivalent to financial handcuffs that prevent you from enjoying life. Budgets are tools that enable you to identify your financial priorities. They help you monitor your progress in organizing your financial life so that you can meet your financial objectives. Quicken makes budgeting easy.

- When you want to monitor and track personal assets (such as investments) and personal liabilities (such as your mortgages and credit card debt).

If you are considering Quicken for business, three factors indicate that Quicken represents a good investment of your time and money and a reasonable accounting alternative:

- You do not need or want to use a small-business accounting package that requires double-entry bookkeeping. Bookkeeping for a small business should involve double-entry accounting to accurately record the activity of the business, however. Packages such as DacEasy, Peachtree, and others require that you use double-entry bookkeeping. Although this procedure is a powerful and valuable tool, if you are not familiar with double-entry bookkeeping, you probably can better spend your time in ways other than learning accounting methods. Quicken provides a single-entry, easy-to-use accounting system. Quicken's category and transfer accounts provide an easy way to meet this requirement without the added difficulty of entering transactions in journals and then posting transactions to a general ledger.

- You do not need a fancy billing and accounts receivable system. Quicken enables you to perform recordkeeping for accounts receivable. If you have fewer than two dozen transactions a month, Quicken provides a satisfactory solution. If your transaction volume exceeds this amount, however, you may want to consider a full-fledged accounts receivable package that prepares invoices, calculates finance charges, and easily handles high volumes of customer invoices and payments. You may want to use QuickBooks, Intuit's new software for small businesses.

■ You do not need an automated inventory recordkeeping system. Although Quicken enables you to track other assets, such as inventory, the program does not enable you to track the number of units of these other assets—only the dollars. With inventory, however, you not only need to know the dollar value of inventory, you need to know the number of units of inventory. Suppose that you sell snow skis. You need to know how many pairs of skis you have as well as the dollar value of your ski inventory.

What This Book Contains

Using Quicken 7 for DOS is divided into 5 parts and 22 chapters. If you read the book from cover to cover, you may notice a little repetition in some places; repetition is inevitable because the book also serves as a reference.

Part I, "Learning Quicken," includes nine chapters that, as the title implies, help you learn the basics of Quicken so that you can perform most tasks.

Chapter 1, "Preparing To Use Quicken," guides you through the steps you need to take before you start using Quicken, including ordering any pre-printed forms you will need, learning to use the system, choosing a starting date, and setting up Quicken to work with your printer. Chapter 1 describes each of these steps in detail.

Chapter 2, "Getting Around in Quicken," gives you a quick introduction to the mechanics of actually working with the program. You learn how to start the program, select menu options, tap Quicken's on-line help feature, use the built-in calculator, and learn about the new calendar feature. If you already have started using Quicken, you may want to skim this material.

Chapter 3, "Defining Your Accounts," walks you through the steps to set up your second and subsequent bank accounts. This chapter also describes a few basic concepts you need to know from the start if you will be using Quicken for more than just a single bank account.

Chapter 4, "Organizing Your Finances," discusses one of Quicken's optional and most powerful features—the capability to categorize and classify your income and expenses. The categories make it easy to determine tax deductions, the amounts spent for various items, and the types of income that go into your bank accounts. The classes also enable you to look at specific groups of categories, such as expenses relating to specific clients, jobs, or properties. Chapter 4 defines Quicken's categories and classes, describes why and when you should use them, shows the predefined categories provided within Quicken, and explains how to use these categories. This chapter also outlines the steps for adding, deleting, and modifying your own categories and classes.

Chapter 5, "Using the Register," explains the steps for using Quicken's fundamental feature: its Register. This chapter doesn't assume that you know anything about Quicken. Rather, you read a complete explanation of what the Register is, what information it contains, and how you use it. If you're a new user of Quicken or think you can use a little help with the basics, you'll get a lot out of this chapter.

Chapter 6, "Automating the Register," describes some of the special menu options, which, although not essential, can make the Quicken Register easier to use. When you're comfortable with the information covered in Chapter 5, spend some time in Chapter 6. Your time investment should pay rich dividends.

Chapter 7, "Writing and Printing Checks," describes one of Quicken's core features—the capability to print checks. This chapter includes instructions for completing the Write Checks screen, where you provide the information Quicken needs to print a check. You also learn how to record, review, edit, and print checks. Not everyone wants or needs to use Quicken to print checks, but if you do, Chapter 7 is the place to start after you understand the Quicken Register.

Chapter 8, "Automating Check Writing," describes how to use the special menu options available on the Write Checks screen to speed up the check-writing process. Although the information in Chapter 8 is not essential to writing checks, it will make writing and printing checks even faster.

Chapter 9, "Reconciling Your Bank Account," discusses one of the important steps you can take to protect your cash and the accuracy and reliability of your financial records. This chapter first reviews the reconciliation process in general terms and then describes the steps for reconciling your accounts in Quicken, correcting and catching errors, and printing and using the reconciliation reports that Quicken creates.

Part II, "Getting the Most," shows you how to use Quicken to its maximum potential.

Chapter 10, "Tracking Your Net Worth, Other Assets, and Liabilities," describes some of the special features that Quicken Version 7 provides for personal use. You can track cash and other assets (such as real estate), as well as liabilities (such as a mortgage). Chapter 10 also describes how to use the loan calculator and Quicken 7's features to amortize variable rate loans and loans that you have made prepayments on.

Chapter 11, "Managing Your Credit Cards," explains how to use Quicken's Credit Card Register to record credit card purchases and payments and reconcile your account against your credit card statements. And if you have a Quicken VISA card, Chapter 11 will show you how to set up an IntelliCharge account so that you can receive your credit card statements on disk or by modem.

Chapter 12, "Creating and Printing Reports," shows you how to sort, extract, and summarize the information contained in the Quicken Registers by using the Reports menu options. Quicken's reports enable you to gain better control over and insight into your income, expenses, and cash flow.

Chapter 13, "Paying Bills Electronically," describes how you can use Quicken to pay your bills electronically by using the CheckFree service. Electronic payment isn't for everybody, but if you're a Quicken user, you should at least know what's involved and whether it makes sense for you. Chapter 13 gives you this information.

Chapter 14, "Using Quicken To Prepare for Income Taxes," is a short chapter, but an important one. This chapter tells you how to make sure that the financial records you create with Quicken provide the information you will need to prepare your federal and state income tax returns. This chapter also briefly discusses the general mechanics of exporting Quicken data to an income tax preparation package, such as TurboTax.

Part III, "Analyzing Your Finances," shows you how to use Quicken beyond the basics to help you analyze your finances through budgeting, monitoring investments, graphing financial results, and financial planning.

Chapter 15, "Budgeting with Quicken," discusses one of Quicken's most significant benefits—budgeting and monitoring your success in following a budget. This chapter reviews the steps for budgeting, describes how Quicken helps with budgeting, and provides some tips on how to budget more successfully. If you are not comfortable with the budgeting process, Chapter 15 should give you enough information to get started. If you find budgeting an unpleasant exercise, the chapter also provides some tips on making budgeting a more positive experience.

Chapter 16, "Monitoring Your Investments," describes the Investment Register feature that Quicken provides for investors. If you want to monitor your investments better, read through Chapter 16 to see the tools and options that Quicken provides specifically for managing investments.

Chapter 17, "Creating Graphs," describes the new Quicken 7 graph feature. If you want to see relationships between your income and expenses, assets and liabilities, actual and budget amounts, and investment portfolios, read Chapter 17 to learn about the various graphs that you can create on-screen.

Chapter 18, "Financial Planning with Quicken," explains how to use Quicken's financial calculators: the investment planning calculator, the retirement planning calculator, the college planning calculator, and the refinance calculator. Quicken's financial calculators help you play out *what-if* scenarios to quickly see results.

Part IV, "Managing Quicken," shows you how to manage your Quicken files and customize the Quicken program.

Chapter 19, "Managing Your Quicken Files," describes how to take care of the files that Quicken uses to store your financial records. Chapter 19 describes how to back up and restore your Quicken files, how to make copies of the files, and how to purge from the files information you no longer need.

Chapter 20, "Customizing Quicken," describes the two ways you can customize, or fine-tune, Quicken's operation. One way is to use the commands under the Main Menu option Set Preferences. The other way is to start Quicken with parameters. This chapter describes both approaches.

Part V, "Putting Quicken To Use," moves away from the mechanics of using Quicken's features and talks about how to use Quicken as a financial-management tool.

Chapter 21, "Using Quicken for Home Finances," discusses how you can use Quicken for personal financial recordkeeping. Using any software, and particularly a financial-management program, is more than mechanics. This chapter answers questions about where Quicken fits in for home users, how Quicken changes the way you keep your personal financial records, and when you should use Quicken options.

Chapter 22, "Using Quicken in Your Business," covers some of the special techniques and procedures for using Quicken in business accounting. This chapter begins by discussing the overall approach to using Quicken in a business. Next, the following six basic accounting tasks are detailed: tracking receivables, tracking payables, tracking inventory, accounting for fixed assets, preparing payroll, and job costing.

Using Quicken 7 for DOS also provides two appendixes.

Appendix A, "Installing Quicken," discusses the hardware and software requirements to use Quicken and shows you how to install the Quicken program on your hard disk.

Appendix B, "Using QuickPay with Quicken," briefly describes the QuickPay payroll utility, how the utility works, and when it is an appropriate business solution. If you're preparing payroll by using Quicken, review this appendix to learn whether you should acquire the QuickPay program.

Conventions Used in This Book

The conventions used in this book have been established to help you learn how to use Quicken quickly and easily.

Because you can use the keyboard or the mouse when executing Quicken commands and options, the text is not specific unless you must type or press keys. Keys you press and text you type are indicated by **boldface type**. You can access a menu option by clicking the menu and then the option with the mouse. Many times, Quicken offers keyboard shortcuts that enable you to access the command using only the keyboard. These keyboard shortcuts appear as **F10** to continue or **Enter**. You also can use the menu hot keys that are indicated in bold, such as choose Print from the File menu by pressing **Alt-F** to access the File menu and **P** to access the Print command.

Words and text that appear on-screen are in a `special font`.

Italics are used for new terms.

This book also contains special tips, notes, cautions, and CPA tips. Tips are instructions for improving your performance with a particular feature. Notes are blocks of text you should find especially useful. Cautions are warnings about what can happen if particular actions are performed, and CPA Tips are accounting information that will help you when budgeting, calculating taxes, writing reports, and so on.

Part I

Learning Quicken

Quicken
Main Menu

Use Register
Write/Print Checks
Create Print/Acct   Edit   Shortcuts   Reports   Activities
View G
Select
File A
Set Pr
Use Tu
Exit

                                        Date   8/23/93

        Pay to the $
        Order of

        Address

        Memo

        Category

Bk.ofAmer-1342   (Alt+letter accesses menu)
Esc-Main Menu   Ctrl⏎ Record   Ending Balance:

Dollars   ▶ Record Transaction   Ctrl⏎
                         Split Transaction   Ctrl-S

cuts   Reports   Activities   F1-Help
                                                           Ctrl-F
no · Category   Payment C   Deposit   Balance   (Backwards) Ctrl-B
                                                      (Next)   Ctrl-N
ss   191 53   4,720 24↑

                                                           Ctrl-G
                                                     er   Ctrl-X

                                       Delete Transaction   Ctrl-D
                                       Void Transaction   Ctrl-V
                                       Restore Transaction

Chapter 1

Preparing to Use Quicken

Preparing to use Quicken is not difficult. If you are new to computers, however, a little hand-holding and emotional support never hurts. Chapter 1 walks you through the steps for preparing to use Quicken. Don't worry that you may not know enough about computers, Quicken, or computer-based accounting systems. Simply follow the instructions and steps described in this chapter.

Choosing a Conversion Date

Choosing a conversion date is another critical decision you must make before you can enjoy the advantages of an automated accounting system. The *conversion date* is the day on which you stop using your old manual system and begin using your new Quicken system. The less frequently you expect to use Quicken, the less important is the conversion date.

If you intend to use Quicken to organize your income tax deductions, calculate business profits, or plan budgets, designate a clean accounting cutoff point for the date you begin keeping records with Quicken. From the conversion date forward, Quicken handles all your accounting information. Before the conversion date, your old accounting system still provides your accounting information. Choose a natural cutoff date that makes switching from one system to another easy. Often the best time to begin a new accounting system is at the beginning of the year. All income and expense transactions for the new year then are recorded in the same place. Choosing a good cutoff date may seem trivial, but having all your tax deductions for one year recorded and summarized in one place can save you much time and effort.

In this chapter, you learn how to do the following:

- Choose a conversion date (the best date to start using Quicken to automate your finances)

- Start Quicken 7 for the first time and set up your Quicken system

- Set up Quicken to print to your printer

- Order checks and other supplies from Intuit

If you cannot start using Quicken at the beginning of the year, the next best time is at the beginning of a month. If you do start at the beginning of a month, you must combine your old accounting or record-keeping information with Quicken's information to get totals for the year. When calculating tax deductions, for example, you must add the amounts Quicken shows to whatever your old system shows.

CPA TIP

If you use data from both your manual system and your Quicken system to complete your income tax return, make sure that you keep adequate worksheets and documentation for any items you deduct. If audited, you want your documentation to show clearly that you added amounts from your manual system to your Quicken system to arrive at your deductions.

To start using Quicken at the beginning of the month, first take time to summarize your accounting information from the old system. Make sure that you don't record the same transaction (income received or an expense paid) twice or forget any altogether.

Caution

Two common errors are possible after you choose an accounting cutoff date: You may record the same income or expense transaction in both systems and therefore count the transaction twice when you combine the two systems to get your annual totals. Or, you may neglect to record a transaction in one system because you think that you recorded it in the other system. Your records will be wrong if you make either error.

The worst time to begin using Quicken is in the middle of a month. With no natural cutoff point, you are even more likely than at the beginning of a month to count some transactions on both systems and to forget to record others in either system.

Perhaps you don't intend to use Quicken to summarize income and expense transactions or to monitor how closely you are sticking to a budget; all you really want is a tool to help you maintain your checkbook and produce checks. If so, the conversion date isn't as important.

Starting Quicken 7 the First Time

To start Quicken, press **Q** at the DOS prompt. The Quicken Main Menu appears (see fig. 1.1). You then can choose commands from the Main Menu.

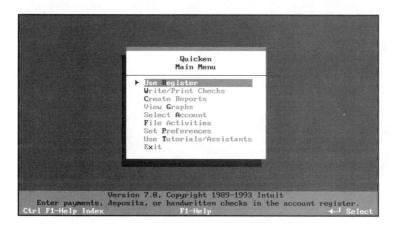

If you're a new user of Quicken, you should take the time to go through Quicken's ten minute tutorial titled "See Quicken Overview." The overview is a series of sample Quicken windows that contain explanations of what Quicken is and shows you how the program works. To take the tutorial, follow these steps:

1. From the Quicken Main Menu, choose Use Tutorials/Assistants. Quicken displays the Use Tutorials/Assistants menu (see fig. 1.2).

2. Choose See Quicken Overview. Quicken displays the Run Quicken Overview window (see fig. 1.3). Press **Enter** to run the tutorial.

Fig. 1.3

The Run Quicken Overview window.

To stop the overview after it starts, press **Esc** twice. Quicken displays the Main Menu. Quicken also displays the Main Menu after you complete the Overview.

Setting Up Your Quicken System

You already may have set up your financial records. If so, you can skip this section. If you haven't, you must set up the file, accounts, and categories you need to store and organize your financial records.

If you're new to Quicken, you can set up your records by using a Quicken assistant or by using the Select/Set Up File command from the File Activities menu. If you have been using an earlier version of Quicken, you simply can convert your old Quicken data files. The sections that follow describe the steps for performing each task.

> **Note**
>
> You can use a mouse to select menu options and perform operations in Quicken 7. Using a mouse is explained in Chapter 2, "Getting Around in Quicken."

Setup for New Quicken Users

New users of Quicken have a choice of two methods for creating a data file in which to store financial records: a Quicken assistant called the File Assistant and the Select/Set Up File command. The File Assistant takes a tutorial approach to help you set up a file, an account, and the categories you want to use within that file. Based on information you enter in the initial assistant windows, Quicken sets up your file, account, and categories for you. Quicken requires more effort on your part when you use the Select/Set Up File command to create a data file.

The following steps describe how to set up a new file using the File Assistant:

1. From the Quicken Main Menu, choose Use Tutorials/Assistants. Quicken displays the Use Tutorials/Assistants menu.

2. Select Create New File. Quicken displays the Create New File Assistant window (see fig. 1.4).

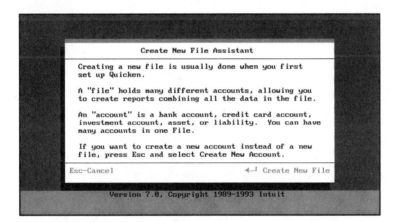

Fig. 1.4
The Create New File Assistant window.

3. Press **Enter** to continue past the Create New File Assistant window. Quicken displays the Set Up an Account window (see fig. 1.5). You must enter specific information about the account you want to set up before you enter information to create the new file. Quicken accounts are similar to the accounts used in your finances, such as bank accounts, credit card accounts, and cash accounts. You learn more about accounts in Chapter 3, "Defining Your Accounts."

   The Set Up an Account window provides two fields you must fill with information: an account name and an account type.

4. In the Choose an Account Type field, indicate whether the account is a bank account, a credit card account, or a cash account. If you are setting up a bank account, the account type is 1. Bank accounts are used

to record transactions in a checking account or another type of account where you deposit and withdraw funds. Press **Enter** to move to the Enter a Name for the Account field.

Fig. 1.5

The Set Up an Account Window.

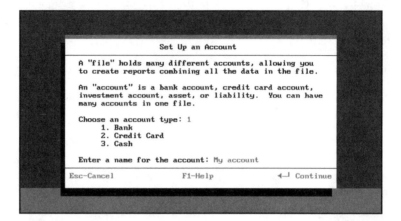

5. Enter a description of the account in the Enter a Name for the Account field. The description can be up to 15 characters long and you can use any characters (including spaces) except the following:

    [ ] / :

> ### CPA Tip
>
> In describing your bank account, you may want to abbreviate the bank name and use the last four digits of the account number in order to distinguish among various accounts at the same bank. Standard Bank of Washington, account 9173526471, for example, becomes StdWash 6471. Standard Bank of Oregon, account 7386427389, becomes StdOre 7389. Standard Bank of Washington, account 9173533721, becomes StdWash 3721. This procedure enables you to separate different accounts at the same bank.

6. After you enter the account name and type, press **Enter** to display the Account Balance and Date window (see fig. 1.6). Enter the starting account balance in the Balance field. If you are creating a bank account file, this amount is your current account balance according to your bank statement. You must enter a balance, even if it is 0.

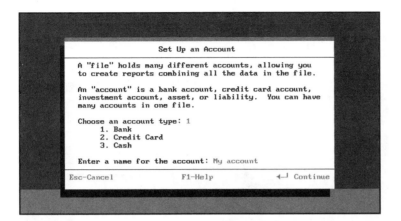

Fig. 1.6
The Account
Balance and Date
window.

Caution

When you enter the ending balance from your last bank statement as the starting balance in your bank account, you must include all uncleared transactions. In other words, you must include all transactions that have not cleared through your bank account by the current date (the date you start Quicken). If you overlook these transactions, you will have difficulty reconciling your account. You learn how to enter transactions in Chapter 5, "Using the Register."

7. Enter the date in the As Of field. The *as of* date is the day on which the balance you entered is correct. If you use the ending balance from your last bank statement, enter the bank statement date in the As Of field.

CPA TIP

Notice that in the Account Balance and Date window shown in figure 1.6, Quicken tells you to enter the total of all the cleared transactions in your check register if you don't have your latest bank statement. You should go back in your checkbook register to the last check cleared through the bank. Enter that balance in the Balance field. Then enter the date of the last cleared check in the As Of field.

8. When you finish entering information for the Account Balance and Date window, press **Enter**.

Quicken now displays the File Assistant window (see fig. 1.7). The File Assistant window identifies the account type, the account name, the account balance, and the as of date.

Fig. 1.7

The File Assistant window.

9. If any information that appears in the File Assistant window is incorrect, move the cursor to the field you want to correct, and then replace the incorrect information by typing the correct entry.

10. When the information in the File Assistant window is correct, press **Enter** if the cursor is positioned in the last field (the As Of field). If the cursor is positioned in any other field, press **Ctrl-Enter** or **F10**.

You haven't actually created a file yet. Rather, you have collected the information necessary for creating your first account in the Quicken file you are about to create. Quicken now displays the File Assistant Note window (see fig. 1.8). In the screens that follow, Quicken prompts you for the information needed to create a new file.

To create a new file, follow these steps:

1. From the File Assistant Note window, press **Enter**. Press **Enter** at each on-screen message until the Set Up New File window appears (see fig. 1.9).

   Quicken creates an eight-character name for the DOS file in which it stores your financial records. This name is based on the user name you gave during installation. The name entered was D HOLLINS, so Quicken created a default file named D_HOLLINS—a shortened version of a long name.

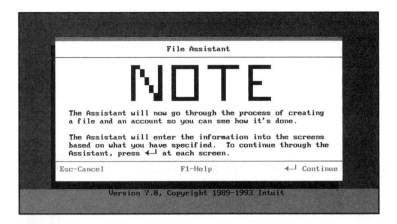

Fig. 1.8
The File Assistant
Note window.

Fig. 1.9
The Set Up New
File window.

> **Note**
>
> If you want, you can enter a different file name. The name you enter here,
> however, must be a valid DOS file name. If you are unsure about DOS file-
> naming conventions, refer to your DOS user's manual.

2. When the file name is correct, press **Enter** to move the cursor to the
Location for File field.

By default, Quicken stores the file in the Quicken program directory—
QUICKEN, unless you specified a different directory name when you
installed the program.

3. To specify another directory in which to locate the new file, enter the
complete path name of the directory you want.

If you're a new computer user, don't worry about specifying some other file name or directory—the defaults work fine.

4. After you specify the location of the new file, press **Enter**.

5. Press **Enter** again at the on-screen message that follows, which tells you to select categories. Quicken displays the Standard Categories window (see fig. 1.10).

Fig. 1.10
The Standard Categories window.

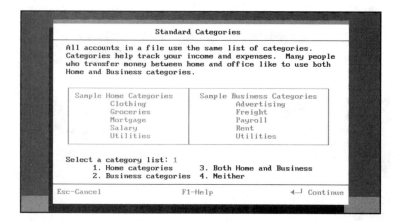

Now you must decide whether to use the standard categories defined by Quicken or to define your own categories. A *category* describes and summarizes common business and personal income and expenses, such as salary, insurance, utilities, and so on. Categories group your income and expenses so that Quicken can classify your transactions for reporting, budgeting, and income tax purposes. In simple terms, categories describe where your money comes from and where it goes. (Chapter 4, "Organizing Your Finances," describes Quicken's categories in more detail.)

Quicken includes two predefined sets of categories: *Home* and *Business*. If you want to use Quicken's categories, you can instruct Quicken to use one of or both the predefined category lists.

6. Choose **1** if you want to use Quicken's Home categories. Choose **2** if you want to use Quicken's Business categories. If you want to use both, choose **3**. If you don't want to use either category, choose **4** to select neither. When you select neither of the standard category lists, you must create your own list if you plan to use categories to classify your

transactions in Quicken. Chapter 4, "Organizing Your Finances," explains how to add categories.

> **Caution**
>
> Now is the only time that you can choose to use one of the predefined categories. After your data file is created, you cannot go back and select or change to another of these category lists. Be sure to select the category list that works best for you. If you plan to use Quicken in your business, make certain that you select Business categories instead of Home categories so that you don't need to completely modify the list to make it appropriate for business use.

7. After you select the categories you want to use, press **Enter**. The File Assistant is ready to create the file.

8. To direct the File Assistant to create the account for your file, press **Enter**. Quicken's File Assistant then executes the Quicken commands that create the account according to the information the program has collected. Simultaneously, the File Assistant explains each step it performs and prompts you to press **Enter** to continue. When the File Assistant finishes creating the new account, the program returns you to a File Assistant window suggesting further actions.

After you create a file and your first account with the File Assistant, you may not need as much help the next time you set up a file. Instead, you can use the Select/Set Up File command. To set up a new file using this command, follow these steps:

1. From the Quicken Main Menu, choose File Activities. Quicken displays the File Activities menu (see fig. 1.11).

2. Choose Select/Set Up File. Quicken displays the Select/Set Up New File window (see fig. 1.12).

3. Highlight the <Set Up New File> line in the window, and then press **Enter**. Quicken displays the Set Up New File window (see fig. 1.13).

4. In the Enter Name for File field, enter the name you want to use for your financial records file. This name must be a valid DOS file name.

Fig. 1.11
The File Activities
menu.

Fig. 1.12
The Select/Set Up
New File window.

Fig. 1.13
The Set Up New
File window.

5. When the file name is correct, press **Enter** or **Tab** to move the cursor to
the Location for File field. By default, Quicken stores data files in the

Quicken program directory. If you want the file stored in a different directory, enter that directory and path name.

6. After you specify the file location you want, press **Enter**. Quicken displays the Standard Categories window (see fig. 1.14).

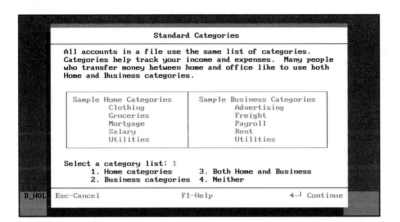

Fig. 1.14
The Standard
Categories
window.

7. Press **1** to use Quicken's Home categories. Press **2** to use Quicken's Business categories. To use both, press **3**. If you don't want to use either category, press **4**. When you select neither of the standard category lists, you must create your own list if you plan to use categories to classify your transactions in Quicken. Chapter 4, "Organizing Your Finances," explains how to add categories.

8. After you identify the categories you want, press **Enter**. Quicken redisplays the Select/Set Up New File window.

9. Use the arrow keys to highlight the new file you just created, and then press **Enter**. Quicken displays the Set Up New Account window superimposed over the Select Account to Use window (see fig. 1.15).

10. In the Account Type field, indicate whether the account is a bank account, credit card account, cash account, other asset account, other liability account, or an investment account by pressing the number listed for the account type you want to set up. (See Chapter 3, "Defining Your Accounts," for more information about these account types.) To set up a bank account, for example, press **1**. Press **Enter** to move to the Name for This Account field.

Fig. 1.15
The Set Up New
Account window.

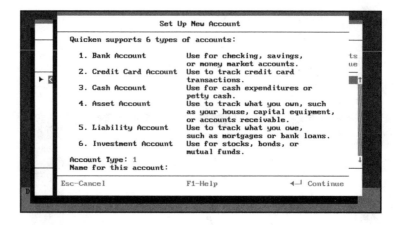

11. Enter a description of the account in the Name for This Account field. The description can be up to 15 characters long and can use any characters (including spaces) except the following:

    [ ] / :

12. Press **Enter** to display the Starting Balance and Description window (see fig. 1.16).

Fig. 1.16
The Starting Balance and Description window.

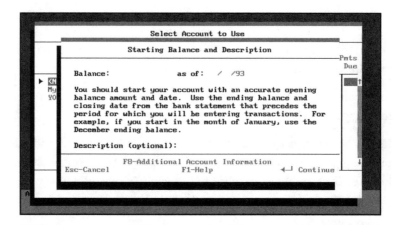

13. Enter the starting account balance. If you are creating a bank account file, this amount is your current account balance according to your records. For best results, use the ending balance from your last bank statement as the starting account balance. You must enter a balance, even if it is 0.

CPA TIP

When you enter the ending balance from your last bank statement as the starting balance in your bank account, you must enter all uncleared transactions in the Bank Account Register. In other words, you must include all transactions that have not cleared through your bank account by the current date (the date you start using Quicken). If you overlook these transactions, you will have difficulty reconciling your account. You learn how to enter transactions in Chapter 5, "Using the Register."

14. Enter the date in the As Of field. The *as of date* is the day on which the balance you entered is correct. If you use the ending balance from your last bank statement, enter the statement date in the As Of field.

15. (Optional) Fill in the Description field to provide an additional 21 characters of account description.

16. To personalize the account further, press **F8** to display the Additional Account Information window (see fig. 1.17). The information recorded in this window is in the form of memo data, meaning that it doesn't appear on any reports. After completing the form, press **Enter** and you return to the Starting Balance and Description window.

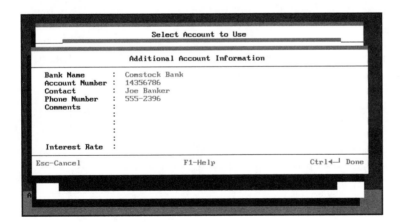

Fig. 1.17
The Additional Account Information window.

17. If you are setting up a credit card account, Quicken displays the Specify Credit Limit window so that you can enter your current credit limit for the account you set up. Specifying your credit limit is optional. If you are setting up any other type of account, Quicken adds the account and goes to the Select Account to Use window (see fig. 1.18).

18. Press **Esc** three times to return to the Quicken Main Menu.

Fig. 1.18
The Select Account
to Use window.

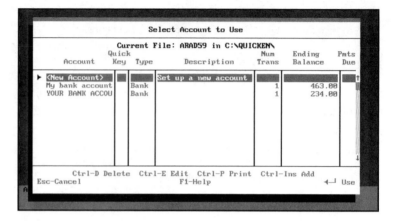

Setup for Current Quicken Users

If you have been using Quicken 5 or 6, your existing files are automatically updated when you install Quicken 7. When you install Quicken, the install program searches for your old data files on your hard disk drive or drives. It then passes the information about the location of the existing data files on to Quicken 7.

If you have been using Quicken 3 or 4, you can update your existing data and use it to create your Quicken 7 data file.

> **Note**
>
> You can update your Quicken 1 or 2 data also, but you need a special file-conversion utility from Intuit. Contact Intuit's customer service department and request the Quicken 2 Copy and Update utility.

To update a Quicken 3 or 4 file for use with Quicken 7, follow these steps:

1. From the Main Menu, choose File Activities. Quicken displays the File Activities menu.

2. Choose Select/Set Up File. Quicken displays the Select/Set Up New File window.

3. If the Quicken 3 or 4 file does not appear in the Select/Set Up New File window, press **F9**. Quicken displays the Set File Location window (see fig. 1.19).

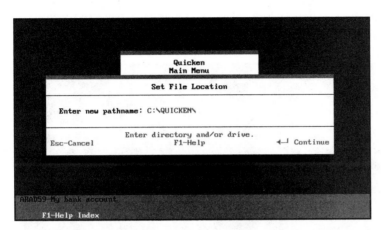

Fig. 1.19
The Set File Location window.

Enter the path for the Quicken 3 or 4 file in the Set File Location window. If the Quicken 4 file you want to convert to a Quicken 7 file is stored in the QUICKEN4 directory on the C drive, for example, type **quicken4** in the Enter New Pathname field, and then press **Enter**. Quicken redisplays the Select/Set Up New File window and lists the Quicken files in the specified directory.

4. Highlight the Quicken 3 or 4 file you want to convert to a Quicken 7 file, and then press **Enter**. The About to Update Data window appears. Quicken asks whether you want to back up your data before updating (see fig. 1.20).

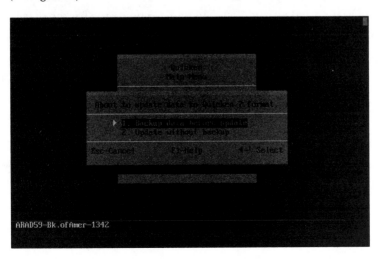

Fig. 1.20
The About to Update window.

5. To backup a copy of your Quicken 3 or 4 data file before converting it to Quicken 7, choose 1.

6. Quicken displays the Select Backup Drive window (see fig. 1.21). Specify the drive or floppy drive to which you want Quicken to back up your Quicken 3 or 4 data file.

Fig. 1.21
The Select Backup
Drive window.

7. Insert your backup disk and type the appropriate drive letter. Press **Enter** to back up your Quicken 3 or 4 data file.

If you select option 2 at the About to Update Data to Quicken 7 Format window (Update without backup), Quicken displays a warning message stating that you will not be able to use your data file in Quicken 3 or 4 after it is updated to Quicken 7. If you're sure you want to update your Quicken 3 or 4 data file without backing it up, type **yes** and press **Enter**. To make a backup, press **Esc** to return to the About To Update Data to Quicken 7 window, and then choose **1** to choose the Backup data before update option.

Quicken converts your Quicken 3 or 4 data file to Quicken 7 and displays the File Updated window (see fig. 1.23). Quicken tells you which categories weren't used in your Quicken 3 or 4 data file by placing an asterisk next to each unused category category list. You learn about categories in Chapter 4, "Organizing Your Finances."

8. Press **Enter**. Quicken next displays the Select Account to Use window for the Quicken 3 or 4 file you just updated.

Learning Quicken

Fig. 1.22
The File Updated
window.

9. Highlight the account you want to use, and then press **Enter**. Quicken
   displays the Register screen for the selected account. You now are ready
   to begin using your Quicken 3 or 4 data file in Quicken 7. Refer to
   Chapter 5, "Using the Register," to learn how to enter transactions in
   the Register.

Setting Your Printer

You want to be sure to set up Quicken for your printer before you go any
further. If you identified your printer during installation, all you need to
do is to describe how your computer and printer connect.

Specifying Printer Settings

To describe how your printer and computer connect, follow these steps:

1. From the Main Menu, choose Set Preferences. Quicken displays the Set
   Preferences menu.

2. Choose Printer Settings. Quicken displays the Printer Settings menu
   (see fig. 1.23).

   With Quicken, you can maintain four sets of printer configuration settings: one setting for printing checks, a primary setting for printing
   reports, an alternate setting for printing reports, and a setting for printing graphs.

3. Highlight the printer configuration setting you want to modify, and
   then press **Enter**. If you choose Settings for Printing Checks from the

Printer Settings menu, for example, Quicken displays the Check Printer Settings screen with the Select Check Printer window and Available Styles window overlaid on-screen (see fig. 1.24).

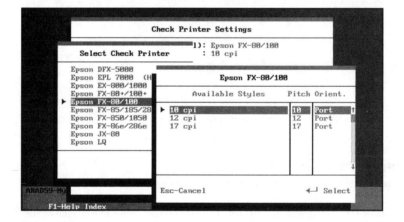

If you choose any of the other settings from the Printer Settings menu, Quicken displays the appropriate windows to select report printing options.

Each printer configuration setting identifies the printer, describes the printer-to-computer connection, and controls how the printer operates.

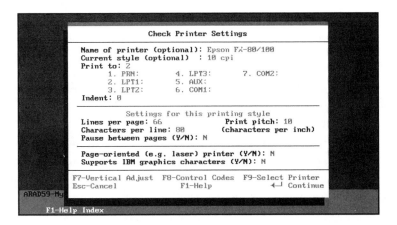

Fig. 1.25
The Check Printer
Settings screen.

4. Press **Esc** twice to remove the Select Check Printer and Available Styles windows. With these two windows gone, the full Check Printer Settings screen shows, as in figure 1.25.

5. Move the cursor to the Print To: field. This field tells Quicken which communications port to use to send checks and reports to the printer. The PRN, LPT1, LPT2, and LPT3 options refer to parallel ports. The AUX, COM1, and COM2 options refer to serial ports.

6. Press the number that identifies the correct communications port. Press 1 to select PRN, for example. If you aren't sure which port your printer uses, follow the printer cable to the back of your computer. The socket the printer cable plugs into may be labeled.

7. To save the printer settings, press **Enter** when the cursor is positioned in the Supports IBM Graphics Characters field. Or, press **Ctrl-Enter** or F10 when the cursor is positioned in any other field in the Check Printer Settings screen. Quicken redisplays the Set Preferences menu. Press **Esc** to return to the Main Menu.

If you selected an undefined printer (None, Other Dot-Matrix, Other Laser, or Other PostScript from the Select Check or Report Printer window), you must follow these additional steps before saving your printer settings:

1. Enter the name of the printer in the Name of Printer: field.

2. Move the cursor to the Print To: field. Press the number that identifies the communications port that connects your printer and computer.

Tip
If you can choose how your printer and computer communicate, choose a parallel port. Parallel connections enable the printer and computer to talk to each other at the same time-in parallel. This capability usually results in faster communication.

When you use a serial port, the computer can send information to the printer only when the printer is not sending information back to the computer and vice versa. With a serial port, your computer and printer take turns communicating with each other.

3. Move the cursor to the Indent field. Use this field to instruct Quicken how many characters from the left margin of the form or paper to begin printing.

   Each time Quicken begins printing a line, the copy starts that many characters to the right. Enter a number from 0 to 80, but be careful not to enter a number so large that Quicken doesn't have room to print. If you have a laser printer, you can use an indent setting equal to 0. If you own an impact printer, you can start with an indent setting equal to 0 also; you may need to increase this setting, however, if Quicken prints too close to the left side of your paper. If Quicken prints off the page on the right side of the paper, reduce your indent setting.

4. Move the cursor to the Lines per Page field. Use this field to instruct Quicken how many lines you want printed on a page. Quicken assumes that 6 lines equal an inch. If you use 11-inch paper, therefore, set this value to 66. If you use 14-inch paper, set this value to 84.

   To determine whether the Lines per Page setting is correct, compare where Quicken begins printing on successive pages. If the print doesn't start at the same distance from the top of each page, you must adjust the Lines per Page setting. The setting is too high if Quicken starts printing lower on the second page than on the first. The setting is too low if Quicken starts printing higher on the second page than on the first.

5. Move the cursor to the Print Pitch field. Use this field to tell Quicken how many characters your printer prints per inch. Typical pitch, or characters per inch, settings are 10, 12, and 15. Check your printer manual to determine your printer's pitch. You also can use a ruler to measure the number of characters, including blank spaces, printed in 1 inch on a sample of the printer's output.

6. Move the cursor to the Characters per Line field. Use this field to tell Quicken how many characters fit in a line. This setting usually equals 80 if your pitch setting is 10, or 96 if your pitch setting is 12.

7. Move the cursor to the Pause between Pages field. Use this field to tell Quicken whether to stop after printing a full page so that you can insert a new piece of paper or adjust the printer. Press **Y** for Yes or **N** for No.

8. Move the cursor to the Page-Oriented Printer field. To Quicken, printers that use individual sheets of paper are page-oriented, such as laser or inkjet printers. Use the Page-Oriented Printer field to tell Quicken whether your printer uses individual sheets of paper. Press **Y** for Yes or **N** for No.

9. Move the cursor to the Supports IBM Graphics Characters field. Use this field to tell Quicken whether your printer supports the extended IBM character set. If this set is available on your printer, Quicken uses IBM graphics characters in the extended character set in headings on your reports. Press **Y** for Yes or **N** for No.

10. Press **F8** to access the Printer Control Codes window. Figure 1.26 shows the Printer Control Codes window for setting print configurations for check printers. The control codes vary, depending on whether you set the print configurations to print reports or checks. You use the Printer Control Codes window to enter the special sequences of letters, numbers, and other keyboard characters that instruct your printer to perform in a specific manner or print in a certain style, such as condensed print.

To determine which printer control codes are appropriate for your printer, look them up in your printer manual. Enter the control code Quicken must initially send to your printer in the Before Printing field. Move the cursor to the Start of Page field, and enter the control code Quicken must send to your printer as it starts a new page.

11. Move the cursor to the After Printing field, and enter the control code Quicken must send to your printer when it finishes printing. Move the cursor to the Form-Feed field, and enter the control code Quicken must send to advance your printer to the top of the next page. Move the cursor to the Half Line-Feed field, and enter the control code Quicken must send to advance your printer one line.

The last field on the Printer Control Codes window for printing checks tells Quicken how you feed single check forms through your printer. Choose **P** to feed the check form through the printer in normal portrait fashion. Choose **C** to feed the check form through the printer in centered landscape fashion. Choose **L** to feed the check form through the printer in left-aligned landscape fashion.

Fig. 1.26

The Printer
Control Codes
window for Check
Printer Settings.

12. Press **Enter** or **F10** to return to the Check or Report Printer Settings screen.

13. To save the printer settings, press **Enter** when the cursor is positioned in the Supports IBM Graphics Characters field in the Check Printer Settings screen. Or, press **Ctrl-Enter** or **F10** when the cursor is positioned in any other field. Quicken redisplays the Set Preferences menu. Press **Esc** to return to the Main Menu.

Identifying a New Printer

If you connect a different printer to your computer after the initial installation, you must identify the new printer. Follow these steps to identify your new printer to Quicken:

1. From the Main Menu, choose Set Preferences. Quicken displays the Set Preferences menu.

2. Choose Printer Settings. Quicken displays the Printer Settings menu.

    With Quicken, you can maintain four sets of printer configuration settings: one setting for printing checks, a primary setting for printing reports, an alternate setting for printing reports, and a setting for printing graphs.

3. Highlight the printer configuration setting you want to modify, and then press **Enter**.

If you select the Settings for Printing Checks configuration from the Printer Settings menu, for example, Quicken displays the Check Printer Settings screen with the Select Check Printer window and Available Styles window overlaid on-screen.

4. Press **Esc** once so that just the Select Check Printer window appears (see fig. 1.27).

Fig. 1.27
The Check Printer Settings screen with the Select Check Printer window displayed.

5. Highlight the name of your printer, or type the first letter of your printer name to move quickly to the first printer name that starts with the same letter. Then use the down-arrow key to highlight your printer. Press **Enter**. Quicken displays the Available Style window.

6. Highlight the print style, pitch, and page orientation you want. If your printer has a variety of *fonts* (character sets), *pitches* (number of characters-per-inch horizontally), and *orientations* (direction in which text is printed on paper), highlight the exact style you want from the choices listed in the Print Style window. Press **Enter** to select that style. Quicken displays the Check Print Settings screen without the Select Printer and Available Style windows.

7. To save the printer settings, press **Enter** when the cursor is positioned in the Supports IBM Graphics Characters field, or press **Ctrl-Enter** or **F10** when the cursor is positioned in any other field in the Check Printer Settings screen. Quicken redisplays the Set Preferences menu. Press **Esc** to return to the Main Menu.

Ordering Check Forms and Other Supplies

You don't need to print your checks with Quicken in order to benefit from the program, but Quicken's check-writing feature is a time-saver. The time saved, however, does not come cheaply. Expect to pay between $50 and $90 for 250 computer check forms. Usually, you will spend more for check forms in the course of a year than you originally spent for Quicken. Obviously, you want to make sure that you make the right decision about ordering checks. Two situations merit the expense of check forms: You write a great many checks at home or at work (more than two dozen each month), or you plan to use Quicken for a business and want the professional appearance of computer-printed checks.

Tip
You will continue to use manual checks—those you write by hand—even if you choose to use Quicken check forms. Home users, for example, need manual checks for trips to the grocery or the department store. And business owners need manual checks for unexpected deliveries that require immediate cash payments (when access to a computer is not available).

If you decide to use Quicken to print checks, you must order preprinted check forms for every bank account for which you want computer-printed checks. The cheapest and easiest source of preprinted check forms is Intuit, the manufacturer of Quicken. Intuit offers both laser and continuous-feed checks. You can order from Intuit other supplies that you may need, such as deposit slips, double-window envelopes, stationery, and so on.

Complete and mail the order form included in the Quicken package; Intuit prints checks with your name and address at the top of the check and the bank and account information at the bottom.

CPA TIP

When choosing a starting number for your computer checks, consider two points: First, start the computer-printed check form numbers far enough away from your manual check numbers so that the numbers don't overlap or duplicate; duplications may cause confusion in your record-keeping and reconciliations. Second, start your computer-printed checks with a number that quickly shows you whether you wrote a check manually or with Quicken.

Deciding Which Checks to Use

When you order preprinted checks, you make choices about size, style, or color, and you decide whether the check is multipart or has voucher stubs. Table 1.1 summarizes your options.

You are on your own when selecting the color, size, and lettering style of your check forms. The following discussion, however, offers some hints about choosing the number of parts your check form can have and about deciding whether you want a voucher stub (or a remittance advice) on your checks.

Name	Colors	Form Size (inches)	Number of Parts	Comments
Table 1.1 Summary of Quicken Check Form Options				
Antique Standard	Tan	3 1/2 x 8 1/2	1	*Antique* refers to parchment background; printed three to a sheet.
Prestige Standard	Gray	3 1/2 x 8 1/2	1 or 2	You can choose blue, green, or maroon accent strip; printed three to a sheet.
Prestige Voucher	Gray	7 x 8 1/2	1 or 2	You can choose blue, green, or maroon accent strip; larger form size due to voucher stub.
Classic Standard	Blue or Green	3 1/2 x 8 1/2	1, 2, or 3	8 1/2 x 10 1/2 sheets—each with three check forms—fit into printer paper tray.
Classic Voucher	Blue or Gray	7 x 8 1/2	1, 2, or 3	Larger form size due to voucher stub.
Laser Voucher	Blue or Green	3 1/2 x 8 1/2	1 or 2	8 1/2-by-11-inch sheets—each with one check form—fit into printer paper tray.
Classic Wallet-Size	Blue or Green	2 5/6 x 6	1 or 2	Has a 2 1/2-inch check stub so that overall form width is 8 1/2 inches.

(continues)

Learning Quicken

Table 1.1 Continued				
Name	**Colors**	**Form Size (inches)**	**Number of Parts**	**Comments**
Antique Wallet-Size	Tan	2 5/6 x 6	1 or 2	Has a 2 1/2-inch check stub so that overall form width is 8 1/2 inches.

The *number of parts* in a check refers to the number of printed copies. With a one-part check, only the actual check form that you sign is printed. With a two-part check, a copy is printed at the same time as the original. With a three-part check, you get two copies plus the original.

Multipart checks probably aren't necessary for most home uses. In a business, however, the second parts can be attached to paid invoices as a fast and convenient way of keeping track of which checks paid which invoices. The third copy of a check can be placed in a numerical sequence file to help you identify the payee more quickly than you can by using the check number alone.

If you use multipart checks, keep in mind that the check forms may wear out your impact printer's *head* (the points that strike the printer ribbon and cause characters to be printed). Check your printer's multipart form rating by referring to your printer manual. Verify that your printer is rated for at least the number of parts you want to print.

The *voucher stub*, also called the *remittance advice*, is the blank piece of paper, about the same size as the check form, attached to the form. Voucher stubs give you extra space to describe, or *document*, the reason for the check. You can use this area to show any calculations involved in arriving at the total check amount. You may use the voucher stub space to describe how an employee's payroll amount was calculated, for example, or to define the invoices for which that check was issued. As with multipart checks, voucher stubs probably make more sense for business use rather than home use.

Printing the Product Order Form

Before you print the Product Order form, make sure that Quicken is set up to work with your printer. When you installed Quicken 7, you told it which printer you use (see Appendix A). If you specified an undefined printer when you installed Quicken 7, you now must set up Quicken for your printer. See the earlier section in this chapter, *Setting Your Printer*.

To print the Product Order form, follow these steps:

1. From the Quicken Main Menu, choose Use **R**egister or **W**rite/Print Checks. The Order Supplies option is available only from the Register or the Write Checks screen.

2. From the Register or the Write Checks screen, choose **A**ctivities. The Activities menu appears (see fig. 1.28).

Fig. 1.28
The Activities menu.

3. From the Activities menu, choose Order **S**upplies. The Print Supply Order Form window appears (see fig. 1.29).

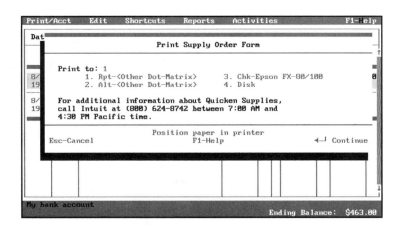

Fig. 1.29
The Print Supply Order Form window.

4. In the Print To field, choose the number that matches that of the printer setting you want to use to print your Product Order form. Choose **1**, for example, to print using the primary setting for reports. You can print your order to a disk file rather than to your printer by choosing **4**. If you choose to print to disk, Quicken requests three additional pieces of information: the file name, the number of lines to be printed on a page, and the width of the page. For more information about printing to disk, refer to Chapter 12, "Creating and Printing Reports."

5. Press **Enter** to print the Product Order form.

After you print your Product Order form, you must complete it manually. It is three pages long and is self explanatory. You then can mail it to Intuit. Be sure to enclose your check or money order if you are paying by either method.

Summary

This chapter described the steps you take in preparing to use Quicken: choosing the conversion date, starting Quicken the first time, setting up your Quicken system, setting your printer for Quicken, and ordering checks and supplies. Now you are ready to begin using the system. Before you start entering actual checks and deposits, writing checks, or reconciling accounts, however, take a few minutes to peruse the next chapter. Chapter 2 covers the basics of using Quicken and makes getting the most from Quicken that much easier.

Chapter 2

Getting Around in Quicken

Starting Quicken

In Chapter 1, "Preparing to Use Quicken," you learned how to start Quicken for the first time. You start subsequent Quicken sessions the same way, but you don't have to set up a new file or account each time. To start Quicken, follow these steps:

1. At the C:\ prompt, type **Q**.

2. Press **Enter**.

Quicken loads and displays the Quicken Main Menu, as shown in figure 2.1. The Main Menu is always your starting point when you begin a new Quicken session.

Using Quicken Menus

You instruct Quicken to perform various activities through the use of menus. The Quicken Main Menu lists the program's main areas and activities, called *options*. Following are the available Main Menu options and their functions:

Main Menu Option	Function
Use Register	Displays the Register for the account you currently are using. See Chapter 5, "Using the Register," for more about Register screens.

(continues)

Quicken isn't difficult to use, especially if you begin with the operations described in this chapter. In this chapter, you learn how to do the following:

- Start Quicken

- Select menu options and move around in Quicken, using the keyboard and a mouse

- Use the Quicken screens to collect financial information

- Access the on-screen Help system

- Use Quicken's Calculator and Calendar

(continued)

Main Menu Option	Function
Write/Print Checks	Displays the Write Checks screen, where you write and print checks or write and transmit electronic payments. Refer to Chapter 7, "Writing and Printing Checks," for more about the Write Checks screen. See Chapter 13, "Paying Bills Electronically," for more about writing and transmitting payments.
Create Reports	Displays the Reports menu so that you can select the type of report you want to create and print.
View Graphs	Displays various graphs menus so that you can create graphs of your income and expenses, net worth, budgeted and actual amounts, and investments. See Chapter 17, "Creating Graphs," for more about this option.
Select Account	Displays the list of accounts in the current file. You can select an account from this list, or you can add, edit, or delete accounts from the current file. See Chapter 3, "Defining Your Accounts," for more about working with accounts.
File Activities	Enables you to select/create files, back up/restore data, or change the location of data.
Set Preferences	Enables you to change Quicken's settings (including printer settings, screen settings, passwords, and so on) or to select another Quicken file. Preferences are covered in various chapters in *Using Quicken 7 for DOS*.
Use Tutorials/Assistants	Provides an on-screen overview of the Quicken program and assists you in initiating first-time setup; creating new files, accounts, and payroll support; exporting tax information; amortizing loans; and setting up investment accounts. Using tutorials and assistants is explained in this chapter.
Exit	Saves your Quicken data in the current file and exits the program. Exiting Quicken is covered later in this chapter.

Selecting Menu Options

Quicken gives you four ways to select menu options:

- Pressing the highlighted letter in the option name

- Clicking the left mouse button when the mouse pointer is positioned on the option name (see the *Using a Mouse To Move Around in Quicken* section, later in this chapter)

■ Highlighting the option and pressing **Enter**

■ Using the shortcut keys

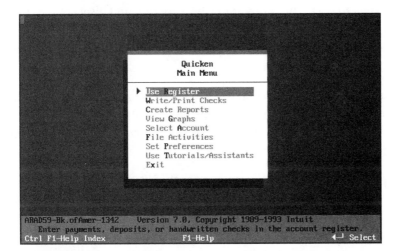

Fig. 2.1
The Quicken Main
Menu.

The first way you can choose an option from a menu is to press the letter that
identifies the option. If you want to choose **Write/Print Checks** option from
the Main Menu, for example, press **W**. Quicken displays the Write Checks
screen (see fig. 2.2). To exit the screen and return to the Main Menu, press
Esc.

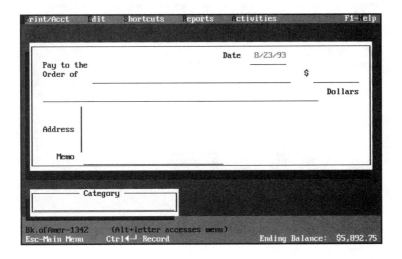

Fig. 2.2
The Write Checks
screen.

The second way you can choose an option from a menu is to click the left mouse button when the mouse pointer is positioned on the option name. At the Main Menu, position the mouse pointer on the **Write/Print Checks** option name to select the Write/Print Checks option and display the Write Checks screen. To exit the screen and return to the Main Menu, click the right mouse button. (In Quicken, clicking the right mouse button is the same as pressing Esc on the keyboard.)

The third way to select menu options is to use the cursor-movement keys to highlight the appropriate selection. If you press the up- and down-arrow keys, the highlight bar moves up and down, respectively. When the bar high-lights the option you want to select, press **Enter**.

Tip

The Write Checks screen also contains a Help menu you can access by pointing and clicking F1-**Help** with the mouse, pressing **Alt-H**, or pressing **F1**.

At the top of each data-entry screen, such as the Write Checks screen, Quicken gives you access to other menus (refer to fig. 2.2). The Write Checks screen, for example, features a Print/Acct menu, an Edit menu, a **S**hortcuts menu, a **R**eports menu, and an Activities menu. Select one of these menus, and Quicken displays a list of menu options. The selection techniques de-scribed previously apply to these menus also. First, however, you must acti-vate the menus and display the menu you want: Press **Alt** and the first letter of the menu name. To select the Edit menu, for example, press **Alt-E**. The Edit menu appears (see fig. 2.3). To activate menus using a mouse, position the mouse pointer on the menu name and click the left mouse button.

Fig. 2.3

The Edit menu.

The fourth way to select menu options is to use a shortcut key combination. Quicken displays the shortcut keys (Ctrl-D to Delete Transaction, for ex-ample) to the right of each option on certain menus. Not every menu option has a shortcut key, but most options you use regularly do. To execute a shortcut, press and hold down the Ctrl key and press the appropriate letter key. One way to delete a check or deposit in the Register, for example, is to highlight the Delete Transaction option from the Edit menu and press **Enter** to confirm that you want the transaction deleted (refer to fig. 2.3). Or you can simply press **Ctrl-D** to accomplish the same thing. (Chapter 6, "Automating the Register," describes the Delete Transaction option in detail.)

Tip

After you activate any menu, you can use the left- and right-arrow keys to display the other menus. If the Edit menu is displayed, for example, pressing the right-arrow key displays the Shortcuts menu (see fig. 2.4).

> **Note**
>
> You can use a few shortcut keys from the Main Menu to select options or perform other tasks. Refer to Table 2.1 for a list of those keys.

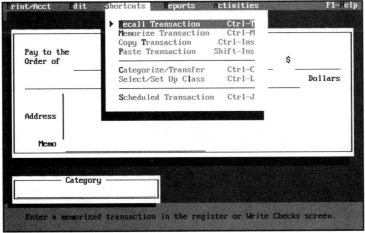

Fig. 2.4
The Shortcuts menu.

Table 2.1 lists and describes the shortcut keys for performing Quicken functions or selecting Quicken menu options. Many shortcut keys are available from any Noninvestment Register, the Write Checks screen, and report screens. A *Noninvestment Register* is any register used for accounts other than investment accounts. Investment accounts are explained in Chapter 16, "Monitoring Your Investments." Other shortcut keys are available only from the Investment Register. Some shortcut keys access other screens or perform Quicken functions from the Main Menu. The appropriate chapters of this book more fully describe the menu options accessed by shortcut keys. For now, remember that shortcut keys are another way to execute menu options and that using these keys can save time.

Table 2.1 Shortcut Keys To Perform Quicken Functions or Access Menu Options

Main Menu Shortcut Keys

Shortcut Key	Function
Ctrl-A	Displays the Select Account To Use screen
Ctrl-B	Backs up all files and remains in Quicken
Ctrl-E	Backs up all files and exits Quicken
Ctrl-F or Ctrl-G	Goes to the Select/Set Up New File screen
Ctrl-O	Displays the Quicken Calculator
Ctrl-W	Displays the Write Checks screen

Noninvestment Registers, the Write Checks Screen, and Report Screens Shortcut Keys

Shortcut Key	Function
Ctrl-C	Selects or sets up a category or transfer
Ctrl-D	Deletes transaction or item
Ctrl-E	Edits account, category, class, or files
Ctrl-F	Finds transaction
Ctrl-B	Repeats Find (backwards)
Ctrl-N	Repeats Find (next)
Ctrl-G	Goes to Date
Ctrl-H	Accesses field-specific Help
Ctrl-I	Inserts a transaction
Ctrl-J	Selects or sets up a transaction Group
Ctrl-K	Displays Quicken's Calendar
Ctrl-L	Selects or sets up a class
Ctrl-M	Memorizes a transaction or report
Ctrl-O	Displays the Quicken Calculator

Shortcut Key	Function
Ctrl-P	Print
Ctrl-Q	Changes view of Register
Ctrl-R	Displays the Register
Ctrl-S	Splits a transaction
Ctrl-T	Recalls a memorized transaction
Ctrl-V	Voids a transaction
Ctrl-W	Displays the Write Checks screen
Ctrl-X	Displays the transfer transaction
Ctrl-Z	Uses QuickZoom or redoes the last report
Ctrl-Ins	Copies a transaction
Shift-Ins	Pastes the copied transaction

Investment Register Shortcut Keys

Shortcut Key	Function
Ctrl-A	Selects account
Ctrl-C	Selects or sets up a category or transfer
Ctrl-D	Deletes transaction
Ctrl-E	Edits securities
Ctrl-F	Finds transaction
Ctrl-B	Repeats find (backwards)
Ctrl-N	Repeats find (next)
Ctrl-G	Displays date
Ctrl-H	Displays price history
Ctrl-I	Inserts a transaction
Ctrl-J	Selects or sets up a transaction group
Ctrl-K	Displays Quicken's Calendar
Ctrl-L	Selects action

(continues)

Table 2.1 Continued

Investment Register Shortcut Keys

Shortcut Key	Function
Ctrl-M	Memorizes a transaction
Ctrl-O	Displays the Quicken Calculator
Ctrl-P	Print
Ctrl-R	Displays Investment Register
Ctrl-T	Recalls a memorized transaction
Ctrl-U	Updates prices
Ctrl-W	Displays the Write Checks screen
Ctrl-X	Displays the transfer transaction
Ctrl-Y	Displays Security list
Ctrl-Z	Redoes last report
Ctrl-Ins	Copies a transaction
Shift-Ins	Pastes the copied transaction

Changing the Menu Access

If you used Version 1, 2, 3, or 4 of Quicken before switching to Quicken 7, you know that you selected Quicken menu options in those versions differently than in the current version. (Quicken 5 and 6 use the same menu style as Quicken 7.) In versions prior to Quicken 5, you selected Main Menu options by pressing numbers, and you selected pull-down menus from data-entry screens by pressing function keys. This type of menu access is called *function-keys access*. To select the Use Register option from the Main Menu of an earlier version of Quicken, for example, you pressed 1; to select the Edit pull-down menu from the Write Checks screen, you pressed F3. The default method used in Quicken 7 to select menu options is the Alt-*key* access because you press letters to select menu options from menus and you press the Alt key to access pull-down menus.

If you feel more comfortable selecting menu options as you did in an earlier Quicken version, you can change the way Quicken 7 displays its menus to

resemble that of the old method. To change Quicken 7's menu access, follow
these steps:

1. From the Quicken Main Menu, choose Set Preferences. Quicken
    displays the Set Preferences menu (see fig. 2.5).

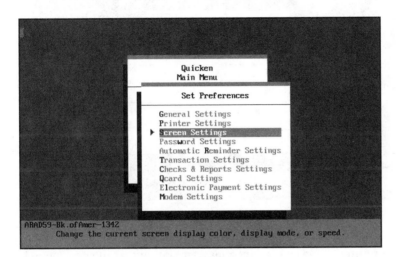

Fig. 2.5
The Set Preferences
menu.

2. From the Set Preferences menu, choose Screen Settings. The Screen
    Settings menu appears (see fig. 2.6).

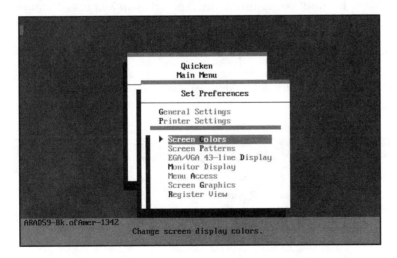

Fig. 2.6
The Screen Settings
menu.

3. From the Screen Settings menu, choose Menu Access. Quicken displays the Menu Access window (see fig. 2.7).

Fig. 2.7
The Menu Access window.

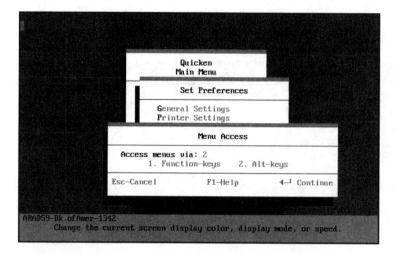

4. Choose 1 to choose the function-keys menu access option, and then press **Enter**. Quicken displays a message stating that the new menu display takes effect the next time you start Quicken. Press **Enter** to remove the message.

5. Choose Esc until you return to the Quicken Main Menu, and choose Exit to exit the program.

6. Restart Quicken by pressing **Q** at the C:\QUICKEN> prompt.

When Quicken restarts, the Main Menu appears in function-key access style, as shown in figure 2.8.

> **Note**
>
> When you install Quicken 7, the Alt-*key* method is the default menu-access method. If you are upgrading to Quicken 7 from Version 3 or 4, Quicken 7 also uses the Alt-*key* menu-access method as the default. If you changed the menu access in Version 5 or 6 of Quicken to function keys, when you install Quicken 7, however, the function-keys menu access method remains in use.

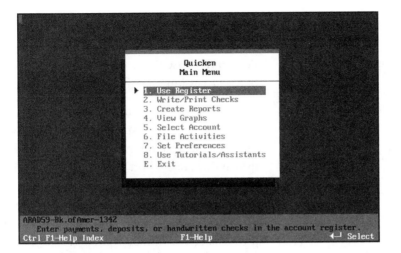

Fig. 2.8
The Quicken Main
Menu in function-
key access style.

Using a Mouse to Move Around in Quicken

You can use a mouse in Quicken to move around screens and to choose
menu options. First, however, you must know the basic procedures of using a
mouse.

Quicken works with any Microsoft-compatible mouse. If your mouse is installed properly, you should see a mouse *pointer* (cursor) on your screen. If
you don't see the mouse pointer on your screen, check for the following
problems:

- Improper installation of your mouse. Test your mouse with other programs to see whether the mouse pointer appears on-screen and works
  properly. If not, reinstall the mouse with the mouse software.

- The cable connections may not be securely fastened to the correct port
  on your computer. Check your mouse manual to determine which port
  to use, and then check the connection. Make any necessary adjustments.

- Your PATH statement may not include the directory in which you installed your mouse software. Check your PATH statement and edit as
  necessary. (Refer to your DOS manual for information on how to edit
  PATH statements.)

As you move the mouse on your desktop or on a mouse pad, the mouse
pointer moves in the same direction on your screen. After you move the
mouse pointer where you want it, you can perform one of the following
procedures:

Click	Press and release the left or right mouse button once.
Double-click	Press and release the left mouse button twice in quick succession.
Drag	Hold down the left mouse button and move the mouse on your desktop or mouse pad. You use dragging to scroll through the Register, a list window, or a report screen using the vertical scroll bar. When you drag the scroll box within a vertical scroll bar, it moves the scroll box up or down so that your position within the Register, list window, or report screen changes. To drag the scroll box, click and hold down the left mouse button and move the mouse. Then release the mouse button to place the scroll box you are "dragging" in the place you want it in the vertical scroll bar. The scroll bar and scroll box are explained next.

To scroll up and down in Quicken with a mouse, use the vertical scroll bar that appears on the right side of the screen (see fig. 2.9). The shaded scroll box indicates your location within a screen. If the scroll box appears in the middle of the scroll bar, for example, you are in the middle of a Register, screen, or report. The arrow at the top and bottom of the scroll bar (the *up* and *down scroll arrows*) control movement by one line or one transaction. To move up one transaction in a Register, for example, click the up scroll arrow. To move down one transaction, click the down scroll arrow.

In report screens, Quicken also displays a horizontal scroll bar (see fig. 2.10). The horizontal scroll bar enables you to move across wide reports that cannot fit on one screen. Like the vertical scroll bar, the horizontal scroll bar includes a shaded scroll box. A right scroll arrow and a left scroll arrow control movement right or left, respectively, by column.

To execute commands, position the mouse pointer on the command that appears at the bottom or top of a screen and click. Position the mouse pointer on F1-**Help**, for example, and click to execute this command.

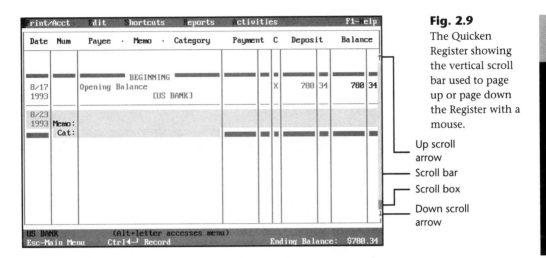

Fig. 2.9
The Quicken Register showing the vertical scroll bar used to page up or page down the Register with a mouse.

Up scroll arrow

Scroll bar

Scroll box

Down scroll arrow

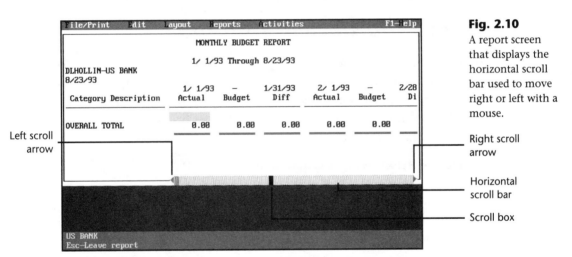

Fig. 2.10
A report screen that displays the horizontal scroll bar used to move right or left with a mouse.

Left scroll arrow

Right scroll arrow

Horizontal scroll bar

Scroll box

To move around Quicken screens, use the following mouse procedures:

■ To move up or down the screen, click the vertical scroll bar above or below the scroll box.

■ To move up one transaction or line, click the up scroll arrow.

■ To move down one transaction or line, click the down scroll arrow.

■ To scroll a list, Register, or Help screen, drag the scroll box towards the bottom or the top of the vertical scroll bar. Alternatively, you can position the mouse pointer on the up or down scroll arrow and click and hold down the left mouse button.

- To move right or left in a report screen, click the horizontal scroll bar to the right or left of the scroll box.

- To move to a different position in the Register, list window, or report screen, drag the scroll box to a different position on the scroll bar.

Note

Throughout this book, most Quicken activities are explained in terms for either the mouse or the keyboard. If you have a mouse, use the techniques described in the preceding section to select menu options and commands and to move around screens and windows.

Entering Data in Quicken

Collecting data on-screen involves moving between fields, entering and editing fields, and saving your work. Quicken gives you many ways to accomplish these tasks. These methods are explained in the following sections. To follow along on your computer, go to the Write Checks screen by choosing Write/Print Checks from Quicken's Main Menu.

Moving Between and Within Fields

Quicken gives you several ways to move between fields: You can move from field-to-field by pressing **Enter**. You can move to the next field by pressing Tab or to the preceding field by pressing **Shift-Tab**. You can move to different fields (as well as within the same field) by using the arrow keys; pressing **Ctrl** ← moves the cursor to the beginning of the preceding field, and pressing **Ctrl** → moves the cursor to the beginning of the next field. You can move to any field by positioning the mouse pointer within the field and clicking the left mouse button. You also can use keys from the keyboard to move within a field, such as moving to the beginning of the current field or the end.

Table 2.2 summarizes the cursor-movement keys used to move between fields, as well as those used to move within a field. To practice using the cursor-movement keys in the Write Checks screen, try each key or key combination listed in Table 2.2.

Table 2.2 Cursor-Movement Keys for Moving Between and Within Fields	
Key	**New Cursor Placement**
Enter	Next field
Tab	Next field
Shift-Tab	Preceding field
← or →	One space to the left or right, according to the arrow
Ctrl-←	Beginning of preceding word within field
Ctrl-→	Beginning of next word within field
Home	Beginning of current field
End	End of current field
Home, Home	First field
End, End	Last field

Entering and Editing Data On-Screen

Entering data in a field or editing an existing field of data is as easy as moving between and within fields. To enter data into a field, simply type the appropriate characters. Whether Quicken accepts only numeric or alphabetic and numeric characters depends on the field in which you are entering the data. Refer to the chapters pertaining to the different screens for more information.

You usually enter dollar amounts as numeric data by using the number keys on your keyboard or your numeric keypad; however, because Quicken adds these symbols for you, you do not need to enter the dollar symbol or commas. If an amount represents a negative number, however, do precede the number with a minus sign, as in -1.47. Quicken assumes that the number is an even dollar amount unless you use a decimal when entering the numerals. The entry *1245*, for example, appears as $1,245.00, and *12.45* displays as $12.45. Quicken does not place dollar signs before amounts in the Register, however.

If you make an error entering an amount, use the arrow keys to position the cursor on the numbers you want to change. You also can click the characters you want to change. You can use the Home and End keys to move the cursor within a field, too. Press **Home** to move the cursor to the start of a field; press

End to move the cursor to the end of a field. To delete numbers, use the Backspace or Delete key. The Backspace key removes the number preceding the cursor location; the Delete key removes the number at the cursor location. To delete the entire field, press **Ctrl-Backspace**.

Most of the remaining data stored in Quicken (that is, data other than dollar amounts) can be alphabetic, numeric, or both. Where alphabetic characters are allowed, you can use either upper- or lowercase characters. Practice typing the name of someone to whom you frequently write checks, such as your cleaning person. You can use spaces, capital letters, numbers, and whatever else you want or need.

You can edit or change any entry in a text field. Retype the field's contents, or use the arrow keys or click the mouse to position the cursor on the characters you want to change. To delete characters, use the Backspace or Delete key. To add characters to existing text, press the Insert key and type the new characters. To add characters to the end of existing text, use the right-arrow key or the mouse to position the cursor at the end of the text and type the remaining characters. As with numeric data, you can clear the field to start over by pressing **Ctrl-Backspace**.

Quicken has a special editing capability for changing date fields. By pressing the + (plus) key, you can add one day to the date; by pressing the - (minus) key, you can subtract one day. Try this feature by entering 9/1/93 in the Date field. Pressing + changes the date to 9/2/93 and pressing - changes the date to 8/31/93. If the date shows the month and year only—as in some places in the Quicken system—you can move the date ahead one month by pressing the + key and back one month by pressing the - key.

Quicken provides several tools to help you enter dates quickly. By pressing **T**, you enter the current system date. By pressing **M**, you enter the first date of the current month. By pressing **H**, you enter the last date of the current month. By pressing **Y**, you enter the first date of the year. Finally, by pressing **R**, you enter the last date of the year. The month and day of the Date field must be blank, however, for you to use these date-entering keys.

Table 2.3 summarizes the keys you can use to enter or edit date fields.

Note

You can use Quicken's on-screen calendar to enter a date in a Date field. See the *Using Quicken's Calendar* section, later in this chapter, for information about using Calendar to enter dates.

Table 2.3 Keys To Enter Dates or Edit Date Fields

Key	Function
+ (plus)	Adds one day to the current date or one month to the current month/year shown.
- (minus)	Subtracts one day from the current date or one month from the current month/year shown.
T	Enters the current system date.
M	Enters the first day of the current month.
H	Enters the last day of the current month.
Y	Enters the first day of the current year.
R	Enters the last day of the current year.

Saving Your Work

When you finish entering data on-screen and want to keep the data, Quicken provides the following four ways to save your work:

- Press **F10**

- Press **Enter** from the last field on-screen

- Press **Ctrl-Enter**

- Position the cursor on Ctrl ↵ Record and click the left mouse button.

After you record a check, Quicken displays a blank Write Checks screen for you to enter another check. After you record a transaction in the Register, Quicken displays the next empty transaction line in the Register for you to record another transaction.

Using Help

Quicken provides extensive on-screen assistance. If you encounter a problem carrying out any procedure, Quicken's Help system usually provides a solution. Help screens assist with Quicken menu options, screens, and specific fields.

Accessing the Help System

Think of Quicken's Help feature as a user's manual stored in your computer's memory. You can access this manual anywhere in Quicken by pressing **F1**, **Alt-H**, or clicking the F1-Help menu that appears in the upper right corner of the Register or Write Checks screen. Quicken's Help feature is *context-sensitive*; that is, Help not only provides the manual but also opens it to the correct page. If you access F1-**Help** from Quicken's Main Menu, for example, you receive information about the Main Menu options (see fig. 2.11).

Fig. 2.11
Help for Quicken's
Main Menu.

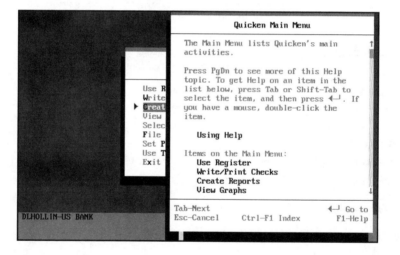

Often, the information that appears when you access Help requires more than one screen. Use the PgDn and PgUp keys to access, respectively, the following or preceding pages of information. A Help screen usually refers the user to other Help topics, too. Quicken identifies these topics by displaying the topic name in black rather than blue letters. The Help screen for Quicken's Main Menu, for example, refers you to **Using Help**, **Use Register**, **Write/Print Checks**, and so on. To view the Help screens for a referred topic, double-click the topic or highlight it and press **Enter**. After you read the Help information, choose **Esc** to return to the program. Quicken returns you to the place you were when you accessed Help.

Learning Quicken

Using the Help Index and Table of Contents

Pressing **F1** twice anywhere in Quicken except from a Help file screen accesses the Help Table of Contents screen, which organizes topics into related groups (see fig. 2.12). Pressing **F1** from any Help screen accesses the Help Table of Contents screen.

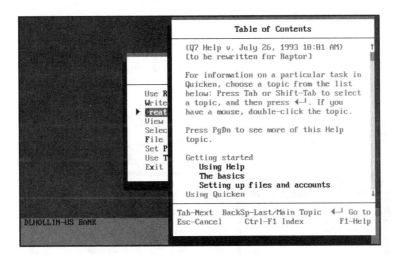

Fig. 2.12
The Help Table of
Contents screen.

Pressing **Ctrl-F1** from anywhere in Quicken, including the Help Table of Contents screen, accesses the Help Index screen, which lists all the Help topics available (see fig. 2.13). To choose a topic, highlight the topic, and press **Enter**. To access the Help Table of Contents screen from the Help Index, press **F1**.

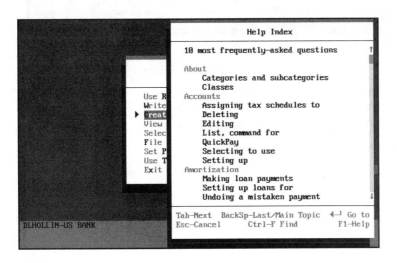

Fig. 2.13
The Help Index
screen.

Getting Field-Specific Help

Quicken 7 provides context-sensitive Help that enables you to access information for a particular field. This feature is called *field-specific Help*. You can access it from any Quicken screen or window containing three or more data-entry fields.

To get help for a field, follow these steps:

1. Position the cursor on the field for which you want field-specific Help.

2. Choose F1-Help. Quicken displays a Help screen with information that pertains to that field only.

Figure 2.14 shows the Category field help screen after you choose F1-Help from the Category field in the Write Checks screen.

Fig. 2.14

The field-specific Help screen for the Category field in the Write Checks screen.

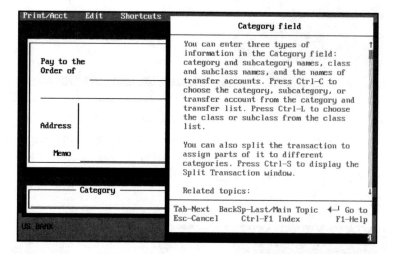

At the bottom of each field-specific Help screen, Quicken lists any related topics you can access for more information. Highlight a related topic in the Help screen, and press **Enter**. From the field-specific Help screen, you also can access Help for the entire screen in which the field is located. Press **Backspace**, and Help appears for the entire screen.

Exiting Help Screens

After you finish viewing a Help screen, choose **Esc** to remove the screen. You return to the screen or window in which you were working before you accessed Quicken's Help system.

Using the Quicken Tutorials and Assistants

As you learned in Chapter 1, "Preparing To Use Quicken," Quicken's tutorials and assistants give you an overview of the Quicken program; help you set up your Quicken system; and help you create new files, new accounts, and payroll support.

Quicken 7 features assistants to help you export tax information, amortize loan payments, set up your first investment account, enter investment transactions, and create payroll accounts. To use Quicken's tutorials and assistants, follow these steps:

1. From the Quicken Main Menu, choose Use Tutorials/Assistants. Quicken displays the Use Tutorials/Assistants menu (see fig. 2.15).

Fig. 2.15
The Use Tutorials/
Assistants menu.

2. From the Use Tutorials/Assistants menu, highlight the menu option that identifies the area of Quicken you want to review, and then press **Enter**. Quicken begins the tutorial or displays the assistant screens.

3. To discontinue a tutorial or an assistant screen, choose **Esc** to return to the Main Menu.

Finding Other Resources

Quicken usually is easy to use, but sometimes you may find yourself perplexed. To minimize the hassles and headaches that can come from learning a new program, consider the following additional resources.

For a solid foundation in the program, read both the Quicken user's manual and this book—at least those chapters that apply to the program features you intend to use.

Talk to other Quicken users. They may be working through problems similar to yours and find helpful solutions. Formal and informal users' groups often are excellent support systems. Among those who may be able to direct you to Quicken users' groups are the people at the store where you purchased Quicken, the store or computer consultant who helps you with your hardware and software, or the CPA who prepares your tax return or annual financial statements.

Spend some time experimenting with the software. Try different transactions, explore the menus and screens, and study the reports. Such experimentation increases your confidence in the system; gives you experience working with actual business or family data; and, most important, confirms which operations accomplish which tasks.

Using the Calculator

Another of Quicken's tools is its on-screen calculator. You access the calculator from the Register or Write Checks screens by choosing Calculator from the Activities menu. You also can press **Ctrl-O**. Figure 2.16 shows the Calculator screen. Quicken's calculator is accessible from any Register screen, the Write Checks screen, or the report screens. You can access the calculator during bank account reconciliation and from the Quicken Main Menu as well.

Fig. 2.16
The Calculator screen before entering numbers.

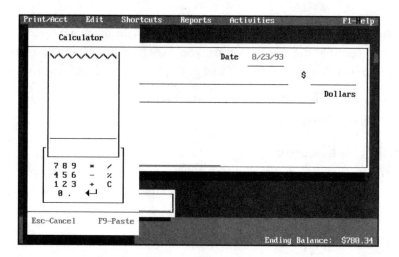

Quicken verifies that Num Lock (*number lock—a* key on the keypad) is on when you access the calculator so that you can use the numeric keypad to enter numbers. If the Num Lock key is off, Quicken temporarily toggles on the key while you use the calculator.

Using the Calculator's Math Functions

Use the on-line calculator as you do a regular calculator. To add three invoices for $12.87, $232.01, $49.07 and subtract a $50 credit memo, for example, enter the following:

> + 12.87 + 232.01 + 49.07 - 50

Press **Enter** or the equal sign on the keyboard. Quicken performs the calculation and displays the results of $243.95, as shown in figure 2.17. The calculator "tape" shows both the numbers and the math operators. To clear the calculator tape, press C. (If you do not clear the calculator tape, Quicken saves the numbers and the math operators, and they reappear the next time you access the calculator.) When subtracting numbers, choose the minus sign or use the minus key on the regular keyboard or the numeric keypad.

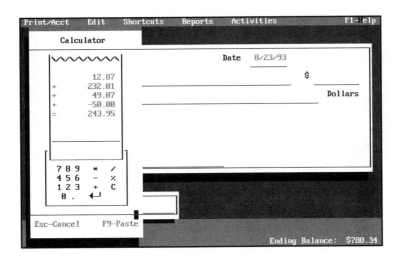

Fig. 2.17
The Calculator tape displaying the numbers and the math operators.

To multiply numbers, click the asterisk or press the asterisk on the numeric keypad or the keyboard. To multiply $232.01 by .25, for example, enter the following:

> 232.01 * .25

Press **Enter** or the equal sign on the keyboard to perform the calculation and give the answer of $58.0025.

Tip

If you paste the results to a numeric field, Quicken rounds to $58.00 for you. For more information about pasting calculator results in a field, see the following section.

To divide numbers, click the / (slash) or press the slash key on the keyboard or numeric keypad. To divide $527.32 by 2, for example, enter the following:

527.32 / 2

Press **Enter** or the equal sign on the keyboard to perform the calculation and give a result of $263.66.

The on-line calculator can add or subtract percentages also. To add 25 percent to 200 (add 25% of 200 to 200), for example, enter **200 + 25%** and press **Enter**. Quicken calculates and displays the result of 250.00 as shown in figure 2.18. Choose **Esc** to exit the on-line calculator.

Fig. 2.18
The Quicken calculator calculates percentages for you.

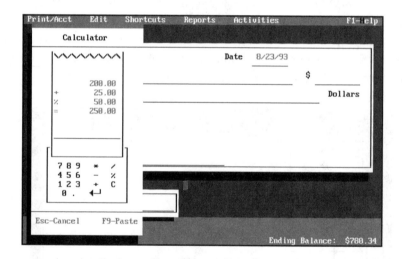

Pasting Calculator Results into Fields

If you are calculating an amount with Quicken's calculator to enter as a value in a field, you can paste the result from the calculator to that field. Pasting results from the calculator is the same as copying the result from the calculator into an amount field in Quicken.

To paste or copy a calculation from the calculator into a field, follow these steps:

1. Position the cursor in the field for which you want to calculate a value.

2. Choose Calculator from the Activities menu, or press **Ctrl-O**. The on-screen calculator appears.

3. Perform the calculation you want.

4. Choose **F9-Paste**. Quicken removes the calculator from the screen and pastes the result into the field in which the cursor was located when you accessed the calculator.

Using QuickMath

QuickMath, a new feature in Quicken 7, is a streamlined version of the calculator. It enables you to calculate and place results in a numeric field without displaying the calculator on-screen. You cannot use the mouse in QuickMath, however.

To use the QuickMath feature, follow these steps:

1. Move the cursor to the numeric field in which you want to perform the calculation.

2. Press = (equal) or a number followed by an equal sign. Quicken displays an equation bar in which you can enter an equation (see fig. 2.19).

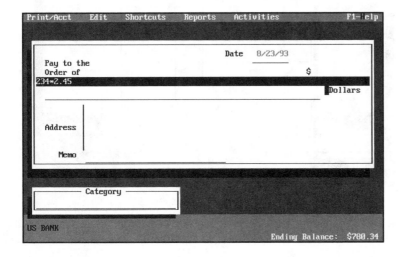

Fig. 2.19
The QuickMath equation bar.

3. Type an equation using the plus sign for addition (+), the minus sign for subtraction (-), the asterisk for multiplication (*), and the slash for division (/). You also can use a percent sign (%) when calculating percentages.

4. Press **Enter** or = (equal) to place the result of the calculation in the field you were when you started the calculation.

Using Quicken's Calendar

Another feature of Quicken 7 is Calendar, which is an on-screen calendar. You can use Calendar to review dates, to enter or paste a date into the Date field of the Register or the Write Checks screen, to write yourself notes, or to find a specific transaction.

You also can use the Calendar when using scheduled transactions. You learn more about schedules transactions in Chapter 6, "Automating the Register."

To access Calendar from the Register or the Write Checks screen, choose Calendar from the Activities menu, or press **Ctrl-K** (see fig. 2.20). When you access Calendar, Quicken highlights the current date in the calendar.

Fig. 2.20
The Quicken
Calendar.

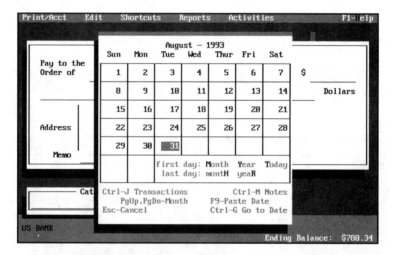

> **Note**
>
> You cannot access Calendar from the Quicken Main Menu, from a Help screen, or from any window in Quicken that displays a list.

To exit Calendar and remove it from the screen, choose **Esc**. Quicken returns to the Register or screen in which you were working before you accessed Calendar.

Selecting Dates in Calendar

To select a specified date in Calendar, simply move the highlight bar (by moving the cursor) to the date you want. To move the highlight bar within the current month in Calendar, click the date you want or use the up-, down-, right-, and left-arrow keys. To change the month in Calendar, choose PgDn to scroll through future months or PgUp to scroll through past months.

Use the following keys to quickly select dates in Calendar:

Key	Moves To
T	Today's date
M	First day of current month
Y	First day of current year
H	Last day of current month
R	Last day of current year

Finding Transactions with Calendar

If you need to find a transaction made on a specific date, you can use Calendar to locate and move to that transaction from the Register or the Write Checks screen.

To find a transaction using Calendar, follow these steps:

1. From the Register or the Write Checks screen, choose Calendar from the Activities menu, or press **Ctrl-K**.

2. If the transaction you want to find was made in the current month, select the date of the transaction by highlighting it. If the transaction took place in a month other than the current one, choose PgUp or PgDn to change to the correct month, and then highlight the date.

3. Choose Go to Date or press **Ctrl-G**. Quicken goes to the first transaction with the selected date that is listed in the Register or at the Write Checks screen.

Pasting Calendar Dates into Fields

You can use Calendar to paste dates into the Date field in the Register or the Write Checks screen. To paste a date into a date field, follow these steps:

1. From the Register or the Write Checks screen, choose Calendar from the Activities menu, or press **Ctrl-K**.

Tip

Choosing PgUp and PgDn to change the month in Calendar may seem backwards. To move forward one month, you choose PgDn; to move backward one month, you choose PgUp. If this gets confusing, think of the calendar as a continuous-roll calendar. Future months are below the current month; therefore, you choose PgDn to display a future month. Past months are above the current month; therefore, you select PgUp to display a past month.

2. Choose the date you want to paste into the Date field.

3. Choose **F9**-Paste Date. Quicken removes Calendar from the screen and pastes the date from Calendar into the Date field.

Creating Calendar Notes

Quicken 7 offers another new feature that enables you to create and save notes on your calendar. These notes remind you of key dates and events (financial or otherwise).

To create notes for Calendar, follow these steps:

1. From the Register or the Write Checks screen, choose Calendar from the Activities menu, or press **Ctrl-K**.

2. Choose **Ctrl-N** Notes to display the Notes Window for the current month as shown in figure 2.21.

Fig. 2.21
The Calendar Notes window.

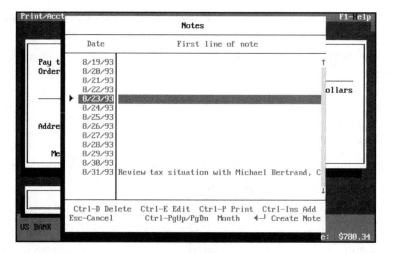

3. Select the date you want to use. To write a note in a month other than the current one, choose **Ctrl-PgUp/PgDn**.

4. When you begin typing your note, the Quick Note window appears (see fig. 2.22).

5. When you finish typing your note, choose **Ctrl ↵** Done to record it. Quicken returns you to the Notes window.

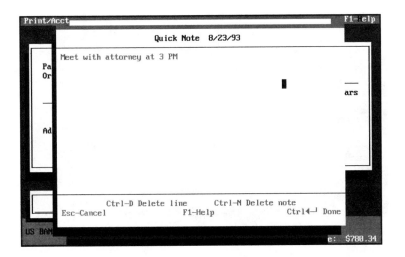

Fig. 2.22
The Calendar
Quick Note
window.

The first line of your note appears in the Notes window and an N marks the
note date on the calendar. Quicken also tells you about past months' notes at
the beginning of the current month and about future months' notes at the
end of the current month in the Notes window (refer to fig. 2.21).

Using Qcards

Quicken 7 has a new feature called *Qcards*. If you are a new Quicken user,
Quicken displays help messages automatically (called Qcards) for seven activities where you may need some help. Qcards tell you what type of information to enter in a field or what type of action is appropriate. A new Qcard
appears each time you move to another field in the window.

To use Qcards, follow these steps:

1. From the Main Menu, choose Set Preferences. The Set Preferences menu
   appears.

2. Choose Qcard Settings. Quicken displays the Qcard Settings menu (see
   fig. 2.23). Choose Yes or No one at a time for the seven areas where
   Quicken provides Qcards or press **F9** to toggle between on or off for all
   seven options.

3. Choose **Enter** when finished or press **Esc** twice to return the Main
   Menu.

Fig. 2.23

The Qcard Settings menu.

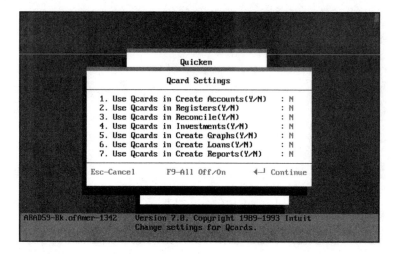

If you turned on the Qcards options, each time you access the Register or one of the other six areas Qcards cover, a Qcard will appear (see fig. 2.24).

Fig. 2.24

The Register with an active Qcard.

The Qcard shown in figure 2.24 is for the date field in the Register. The top part of the Qcard displays a message to help you enter information. If more information (such as a tip or a shortcut) is available, you can press **Ctrl-F7** to see it. You also can shrink the Qcard to get it out of your way by pressing **Ctrl-F8** or **Ctrl-F9** to eliminate it completely. By pressing **Ctrl-F9**, you can toggle off and on the Qcards feature for the Register. The other six Qcard areas are not affected.

Using DOS from Quicken

While in Quicken, you may need to access DOS to format a floppy disk for backup or to list files in a directory. Rather than ending your Quicken session, you can access DOS directly from the Quicken program and return to Quicken afterward.

To access DOS from Quicken, follow these steps:

1. From the Register or the Write Checks screen, choose Activities. The Activities menu appears.

2. Select Use DOS. Quicken exits to DOS, where you can use DOS commands, such as FORMAT or DIR.

3. To return to Quicken after you finish in DOS, type **exit** at the C:> prompt.

> **Caution**
>
> Do not load a memory-resident utility while using DOS from Quicken; the utility may interfere with your Quicken files. A *memory-resident* utility is a program that remains in your computer's memory while you are working in other programs, such as Quicken.

Exiting Quicken

When you exit Quicken, it saves your work in the data file you are in when you leave the program. To exit Quicken, follow these steps:

1. Press **Esc** repeatedly until you return to the Main Menu.

2. From the Main Menu, choose Exit. Quicken saves your data file and returns you to the DOS prompt.

> **Caution**
>
> If you turn off your computer before exiting Quicken through the Main Menu, you may lose some of your data. Although Quicken reconstructs some files the next time you use the program, complete reconstruction of interrupted data files is not possible.

> **Note**
>
> Be sure to keep backup copies of all your financial data to prevent losses due to system failure or power outages. Quicken's reminder system can help you remember to back up your files each time you exit Quicken. See Chapter 19, "Managing Your Quicken Files," to learn about Quicken's reminder system and about backing up your Quicken data.
>
> To back up your Quicken data file before you exit Quicken, press **Ctrl-B** from the Main Menu. Also, from the Register or the Write Checks screen, you can access the Print/Acct menu and then choose the Back Up File option. Backing up your files before you exit also is explained in Chapter 19.

Summary

This chapter describes the basics of getting around in Quicken: selecting menu options; using the mouse; entering data on-screen; and using Help, the Calculator, QuickMath, the Calendar including writing notes, as well as accessing DOS from Quicken. This chapter also provides additional tips for learning to use Quicken.

If you need to define more than one bank account to use with Quicken, you now should read Chapter 3. If you need only one bank account defined, you are ready to learn the fundamentals of actually working in Quicken: using categories and classes, writing and printing checks, using Quicken's Register, and reconciling your bank account. These operations are covered starting in Chapter 4.

Chapter 3

Defining Your Accounts

If you followed the steps outlined in Chapter 1, "Preparing To Use Quicken," you already have defined one bank account as part of setting up your Quicken system, but you may want to define other bank accounts. You may, for example, have more than one checking account, one or two savings accounts, and even certificates of deposit for which you will keep records with Quicken. If you want to use Quicken to track more than one account, you need to define these accounts in Quicken. You then can use Quicken to record transactions in the accounts and track transfers between accounts.

You can add other Quicken account types (Credit Card, Cash, Other Asset, Other Liability, and Investment Accounts) to your Quicken file so that you can record and track all your financial activity—not just transactions that occur in a bank account. These account types are explained in general later in this chapter, and more specifically in later chapters. This chapter also gives you some tips on creating accounts—information that should make working with multiple accounts easy.

In this chapter, you learn how to do the following:

- Add another bank account to your Quicken file

- Edit and delete accounts

- Select an account to use

Defining Account Types

Before you go any further, you should learn a little more about accounts and the types of accounts that you can use in Quicken. A Quicken account is similar to the accounts you use to keep track of your transactions, such as checking, savings, credit card accounts, and so on. You use other types of accounts to track the value of your assets and investments or the principal balance of your liabilities or debts. The types of accounts you can add and use in Quicken follow:

- *Bank accounts:* This is the most commonly used account type. Use bank accounts to set up your checking, savings, or money market accounts.

■ *Credit card accounts:* These accounts keep track of your credit card activity, including purchases, payments, other credits, finance charges, and credit card fees. With Quicken 7, you can set up an IntelliCharge account to electronically track your Quicken VISA card activity. See Chapter 11, "Managing Your Credit Cards," to learn more about credit card accounts.

■ *Cash accounts:* Cash accounts keep track of your cash expenditures, such as the cash you spend on vacations or dining out, or your business's petty cash fund. See Chapter 10, "Tracking Your Net Worth, Other Assets, and Liabilities," for more information on how to use cash accounts.

■ *Other asset accounts:* Use this account type to record and track the value of the things you own, such as your home or auto, or your business's accounts receivable and fixed assets. You learn more about other asset accounts in Chapter 10, "Tracking Your Net Worth, Other Assets, and Liabilities."

■ *Other liability accounts:* Use this account type to record and track the debts you owe, such as the mortgage on your home or the outstanding loan balance on your auto. For businesses, the other liability account type can be used to track accounts payable or a credit line with the bank. Refer to Chapter 10, "Tracking Your Net Worth, Other Assets, and Liabilities," for more on other liability accounts.

■ *Investment accounts:* Use investment accounts to track your investments, such as stocks, bonds, and mutual funds. The investment account is an advanced feature in Quicken; therefore, you should be sure to read Chapter 16, "Monitoring Your Investments," and use the Quicken assistants from the Use Tutorials/Assistants menu to learn about these accounts. Using the Quicken assistants is explained in Chapter 2, "Getting Around in Quicken."

Adding Another Account

You need to define or identify accounts for each account you want to track with Quicken. You defined only one bank account as part of setting up your

Quicken system, but you can have as many as 255 accounts in a file, and you can have multiple files. (Files are discussed in more detail in Chapter 19, "Managing Your Quicken Files.")

This chapter explains how to add another account by using the Select Account option from the Quicken Main Menu. You also can use the Create New Account command on the Use Tutorials/Assistants menu, however.

To set up another bank account, choose Select Account from Quicken's Main Menu (see fig. 3.1). Quicken displays the Select Account to Use window shown in figure 3.2. This window shows the bank account you defined as part of setting up your Quicken system.

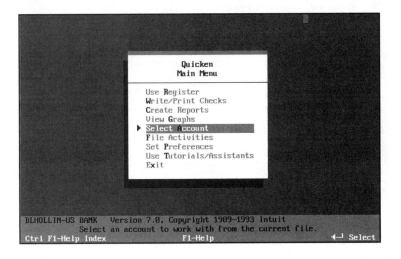

Fig. 3.1
The Quicken Main Menu with the Select Account option high-lighted.

Fig. 3.2
The Select
Account to Use
window.

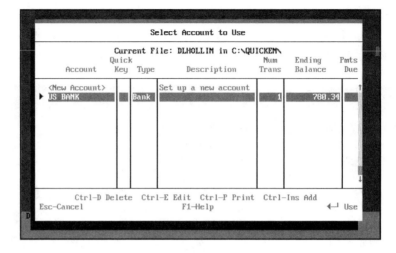

Tip
You can access the
Select Account to
Use window from
other screens in
Quicken by press-
ing **Ctrl-A**.

To add another account, follow these steps:

1. Highlight the <New Account> line in the Select Account to Use window
and press **Enter**. The Set Up New Account window appears (see fig. 3.3).
You also can choose **Ctrl-Ins Add** to access the Set Up New Account
window.

Fig. 3.3
The Set Up New
Account window.

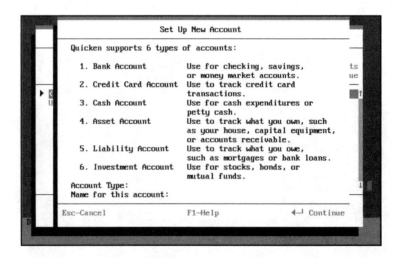

2. With the cursor in the Account Type field, choose **1** to select Bank Account. If you're adding another account type, just select the number
next to the account type that you want to add.

3. Move the cursor to the Name for This Account field. Type a name or short description of the account in the field. Use characters, letters, spaces, and any symbols except brackets ([]), a slash (/), or a colon (:).

> **Note**
>
> Remember that you have only 15 spaces for the account name. Use an abbre-viation of the bank's name; First National could become 1stNatl, for example. This leaves room for the last four digits of the account number. You then can distinguish accounts easily, as shown by the following example:
>
> 1stNatl-1234 for a checking account
>
> 1stNatl-3272 for a savings account
>
> 1stNatl-7113 for CDs

4. When the Set Up New Account window is complete, choose **Enter**. Quicken displays the Starting Balance and Description window as shown in figure 3.4.

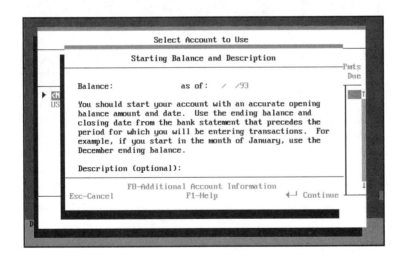

Fig. 3.4
The Starting Balance and Description window.

5. In the Balance field, type the ending balance from your last bank state-ment, and then choose **Enter**. Do not use commas or dollar signs when you enter the balance. If the starting balance for an account is zero, you must enter 0.

6. Type the date of the balance amount in the As Of field using the MM/DD/YY format. If you entered the ending balance from your last bank statement in step 5, you should enter the bank statement date (the ending or cut-off date) in the As Of field. Remember that you can use the + (plus) and - (minus) keys to move the date ahead and back one day.

7. (Optional) Move the cursor to the Description field. Type a further description of the account, such as the account number.

Note

Although you can enter a starting balance for an account from any source, not just your bank statement, Quicken recommends that you use the ending balance from your last bank statement as your starting balance. Make sure, however, that you reconciled your account with that statement before you rely on the amount the bank states that you have in your account.

Caution

When you enter the ending balance from your last bank statement as the starting balance in your bank account, you must enter all uncleared transactions in your Quicken Bank Account Register. In other words, you must enter all transactions that have not been cleared through your bank account as of the current date (the date that you start Quicken). If you don't enter these transactions, you will have difficulty reconciling the account. You learn how to enter transactions in Chapter 5, "Using the Register."

---

8. To return to the Select Account to Use window, press **Enter**. The bank account you just added now is listed in the Select Account to Use window.

To add more accounts, repeat steps 1 through 8.

Deciding Which Accounts to Add

When you first set up accounts for Quicken, adding accounts can get out of hand. You might define Quicken accounts for every checking account you have, regardless of whether the account is active. You also may define

Quicken accounts for each of your savings accounts, credit unions, money market accounts, and perhaps even accounts for certificates of deposit. Rather than indiscriminately defining accounts for every bank account you have, consider a few ideas and rules for determining which of your bank accounts also should be Quicken accounts:

- If you want to write checks on the account by using Quicken, you must define a Quicken account.

- If you want to use Quicken's reconciliation feature to explain differences between your records and the bank's, credit union's, or brokerage house's statement, you must define a Quicken account.

- If you have transactions in an account that you want to include in Quicken's tax deduction summaries or profit and loss statements, you must define a Quicken account. You may have charitable contributions or mortgage interest transactions in other bank accounts, for example.

Other factors may indicate that you probably do not need to define a bank, credit union, or brokerage house account as a Quicken account:

- If you do not have any deposits into or withdrawals from the account other than interest income or bank service fees, your monthly statement will suffice for your financial records, unless you want the comprehensive balance sheet.

- If you have only a handful of transactions a month (fewer than a dozen) and none represents an account transfer from or to an account for which you will use Quicken, you probably do not need to track the account in Quicken. This choice, however, is a matter of personal preference.

- If you otherwise would not track an account, you probably should not bother to put the account into Quicken—even if you have the best of intentions about becoming more diligent in your recordkeeping.

Editing Existing Accounts

You also can use the Select Account to Use window to edit the names and descriptions of existing accounts. You might do this if you originally described the account incorrectly. Or, you may want to edit an account name

Tip
If you want to measure your *net worth* (assets minus liabilities), add a Quicken account for each account you have that represents an asset. You might have an account with only a few transactions per month, but with a large account balance, for example. If you don't set up a Quicken account for this account, the account balance, which represents an asset, will not be reflected in your net worth in Quicken Net Worth reports.

and description if you have transferred the account in total to a new account number or even a new bank. Maybe you moved from Denver to San Francisco and are using the same bank, but a different branch. Quicken does not, however, enable you to change the account type, balance, or as of date after you add the account. If these dates are wrong, you need to delete and then re-create the account.

To edit an account, follow these steps:

1. From the Quicken Main Menu, choose Select Account. The Select Account to Use window appears. You also can press **Ctrl-A** from the Register or the Write Checks screen.

2. Highlight the account you want to edit.

3. Press **Ctrl-E**. The Edit Account Information window appears, filled with the current information for the account (see fig. 3.5).

Fig. 3.5

The Edit Account Information window.

4. (Optional) Edit the bank account name in the Account Name field by typing over the existing characters or using the Backspace or Delete key to remove characters.

5. (Optional) Move the cursor to the Description field to edit the bank account description.

6. (Optional) If you want to assign a quick key that you can use to move easily to another account, move the cursor to the Quick Key Assignment field. Choose a number from 1 to 9 and press **Enter**.

> **Note**
>
> The Edit Account Information window also enables you to attach a tax schedule and tax schedule line number to an account. If you do this, transactions that are transfers to and from an account are summarized so that you can more easily complete a particular line of a particular tax schedule. You can attach a tax schedule and line to an account by pressing **F9** to display the list of tax schedules. Refer to Chapter 14, "Using Quicken To Prepare for Income Taxes," for more information on attaching tax schedules to accounts and collecting income tax return data using Quicken.

Tip

If you assign a quick key to an account, you can switch to that account from the Main Menu, any Register, or the Write Checks screen. To switch to the account, press the Ctrl key in combination with the number that you assigned to the account in the Edit Account Information window. When you assign a quick key to an account, the quick key number appears next to the account name in the Select Account to Use window (see fig. 3.2).

7. Press **Enter** to save your changes to the account and return to the Select Account to Use window.

To edit additional accounts, repeat steps 1 through 7.

Deleting Accounts

You can use the Select Account to Use window to delete accounts you no longer use. Perhaps you closed an account or decided that an account wasn't worth tracking with Quicken. To delete an account, follow these steps:

1. From the Quicken Main Menu, choose Select Account. The Select Account to Use window appears. You also can press **Ctrl-A** from the Register or the Write Checks screen.

2. Highlight the account you want to delete.

3. Press **Ctrl-D**. The Deleting Account window appears, providing the name of the account to be deleted and alerting you to the permanence of the deletion (see fig. 3.6).

4. Type **yes** and then press **Enter** to delete the selected account. If you do not want to delete the account, press **Esc**.

> **Caution**
>
> When you delete an account, you delete the account description and any transactions you have recorded in the account. Be sure that you really want to delete the account before taking the steps to do so.

Learning Quicken

Fig. 3.6

The Deleting Account window.

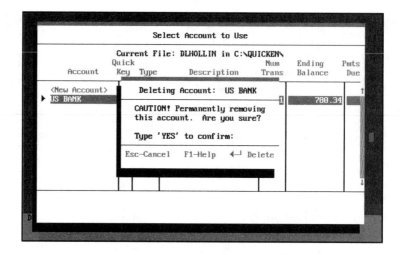

Selecting an Account to Use

When you start working with multiple accounts, you need to tell Quicken which account you want to use. Suppose that you decide to use Quicken to track a savings and a checking account. Whenever you enter a savings account deposit, be sure to record the deposit in the savings account and not in the checking account. Similarly, if you withdraw money from the checking account, you need to make sure that the withdrawal is recorded correctly in your checking account and not in the savings account. To record account activity correctly, you first must select the appropriate Quicken account to use.

Tip

Entering all transactions for an account at one time is more efficient than entering them randomly. Consider collecting several transactions for an account and then recording them at one time.

To select an account to use, follow these steps:

1. From the Quicken Main Menu, choose Select Account. The Select Account to Use window appears. You also can press **Ctrl-A** from the Register or the Write Checks screen.

2. Highlight the account you want to use.

3. Press **Enter**.

Summary

In this chapter, you learned how to add other accounts—specifically bank accounts—and how to edit and delete existing Quicken accounts. You also learned how to select the account you want to use in your Quicken file.

With the information in the first three chapters, you should be ready to use Quicken. In essence, these first three chapters covered the details of getting started with Quicken—the things you need to do before you actually start working with the program.

The next six chapters in Part I, "Learning Quicken," describe the basics of using Quicken and cover such tasks as using categories and subcategories, recording financial transactions with Quicken, printing Registers, writing and printing checks, and reconciling your bank account. These chapters don't cover as much about business and personal accounting topics as they do about using the Quicken system. When you finish reading the chapters in this part of *Using Quicken 7 for DOS*, you will be well acquainted with the mechanics of using the Quicken program. That knowledge is essential to turning Quicken into a tool you can use for business or personal financial management.

Chapter 4

Organizing Your Finances

Previous chapters in this book mention Quicken's categories. *Categories* enable you to summarize the information in a Register, track tax deductions, and monitor the money flowing into and out of accounts.

This chapter goes into depth on the subject of categories and how you can use categories to organize your finances and track your income and expenses. This chapter describes—and tells you why and when to use— categories, and shows the predefined categories Quicken provides for business and home use.

This chapter also describes the steps for adding, deleting, and editing categories you create and how to take categories one step further by creating subcategories. A *subcategory* further divides a category into smaller categories that provide a more detailed accounting of your income and expenses.

Finally, this chapter covers a related tool, Quicken's *classes* and *subclasses*. Classes and subclasses add a second dimension to categories by enabling you to classify which project, job, client, and so on, that a particular income or expense item belongs to.

More specifically, in this chapter, you learn how to do the following:

- Add categories and subcategories to the Category and Transfer list

- Specify categories as tax-related

- Edit and delete, and merge categories and subcategories

- Assign subcategories and classes to transactions

- Change categories to subcategories and vice versa

- Add, edit, and delete classes and subclasses

Working with Categories

To review briefly, categories enable you to group *income* and *expense* items that flow into and out of accounts. Income or deposits into an account may stem from earned wages from a full-time job, interest income, dividends, revenues from a part-time business, and so on. Expenses or payments can stem from rent, food, transportation, clothing, part-time business expenses, and so on. By grouping each payment from and each deposit into an account, Quicken easily adds the totals for each kind of payment and deposit. You then can see exactly how much each category contributes to the cash flow. You may find, for example, that cash flows into and from your account are like the cash flows summarized in Table 4.1.

Table 4.1 Personal Cash Flows	
Deposits	**Amount**
Wages from job	$35,000
Interest	$500
Dividends	$500
Business revenue	$4,300
Total Deposits	$40,300
Withdrawals	**Amount**
Housing	$18,000
Food	$4,000
Transportation	$3,000
Clothing	$2,500
Business Expenses	$1,500
Total Withdrawals	$29,000
Cash Flows	$11,300

The information shown in Table 4.1 is valuable because categorizing your inflows and outflows is the first step in beginning to manage personal or business finances. Categories enable you to do the following:

■ Track and tally income tax deductions for individual retirement accounts, mortgage interest deductions, charitable contributions, and so on.

■ Break down checking account deposits and payments into groups of similar transactions so that you can summarize income and expenses.

■ Budget income and expenses and compare budgeted amounts with actual amounts.

CPA TIP

Not all cash inflows represent income and not all cash outflows represent an expense. If you sell stock, for example, the proceeds from the sale are not considered income. Income from the sale is determined by subtracting the cost basis of the stock from the net sales proceeds (if the result is negative, you incur a loss). Medical insurance reimbursements also are not considered income, but rather they offset your medical expense. If you pay $100 to a doctor, for example, you enter a transaction in the Register for $100 and assign the Medical category to the transaction. If you later receive $80 reimbursement from your medical insurance company, the $80 is not income, but rather it offsets the $100 medical expense transaction that you previously entered. Your net medical expense is $20 ($100 - $80).

If you pay $15,000 cash for a car, this is not considered an expense. You should enter a transaction in your Bank Account Register for the $15,000 check you write to the car dealer, but assign an account to the transaction rather than a category. In this example, you probably would set up an Other Asset account for your new automobile (perhaps called *Auto*) and enter the Other Asset account in the Category field. In essence, this transaction transferred funds from your bank account to another asset account (the account called *Auto*). Transfer transactions like this are explained in Chapter 5.

If you want to use Quicken for a business, the predefined categories enable you to prepare most of the reports you need for managing business finances. These reports include the following:

- A business profit and loss statement that resembles and performs most of the calculations required to complete the federal income tax form Schedule C. The Schedule C form reports the profits or losses from a business or profession that is organized as a sole proprietorship.

- Income and cash-flow statements on a monthly and annual basis that enable you to understand cash flows and measure business profits or losses.

- Employee payroll checks and payroll reports.

If any of the reports listed look like benefits you want to enjoy as part of using Quicken, you will want to use Quicken's categories. How involved or complicated the use of these categories becomes depends on your goals.

Note

The Quicken program does not require you to assign a category to transactions. If you want to make sure that you do assign a category to all your transactions so that your income and expenses are accurately accounted for, you can turn on the Warn If a Transaction Has No Category transactions setting. When this transaction setting is turned on, Quicken displays a message each time you attempt to record a transaction in the Register or Write Checks screen without a category. You must confirm that you do not want to assign a category to the transaction before you can record the transaction. To learn how to turn on the Warn If a Transaction Has No Category transaction setting, refer to Chapter 20, "Customizing Quicken."

Building a List of Categories

The information you want to track determines the various categories you will want to use to group similar payments or deposits. Three basic rules apply when building a list of categories:

- If you want to use categories for tallying and tracking income tax deductions, you need a category for each deduction.

- If you want to use categories to summarize cash inflows and outflows, you need a category for each income or expense account you want to use in the summaries.

- If you want to use categories to budget—so that at a later date, you can compare what you budgeted and what you actually spent—you need a category for each comparison you want to make.

Creating Categories for Tax Deductions. If you want to use categories for tallying and tracking income tax deductions, you need a category for each deduction. If you deduct contributions to your IRA (Individual Retirement Accounts), mortgage interest, and state and local taxes, you need categories for each of these deductions. The following list shows the itemized deductions you may want to track to prepare a personal income tax return more easily. The list is based on the Federal Income Tax Form 1040, Schedule A.

Sample Personal Tax Deduction Categories

Medical and dental*

Medical and dental-other*

State and local income taxes

Real estate taxes

Other taxes, including personal property taxes

Deductible home mortgage interest paid to financial institutions

Deductible home mortgage interest paid to individuals

Deductible points

Deductible investment interest

Contributions by cash or check

Contributions other than by cash or check

Casualty or theft losses

Moving expenses**

Unreimbursed employee expenses**

Union dues, tax preparation fees, investment publications, and fees

Individual retirement account contributions

Other miscellaneous expenses

* The first medical expense category includes prescription medicines and drugs, insulin, doctors, dentists, nurses, hospitals, and medical insurance premiums. The second includes items like hearing aids, dentures, eyeglasses, transportation, and lodging.

** This itemized deduction must be supported by an additional tax form. Therefore, you also want to consider setting up the individual amounts that need to be reported on that form as categories.

The following list shows the income and deduction categories you may want to use to prepare a business income tax return. This list is based on Schedule C of Federal Income Tax Form 1040.

Income Categories

Gross receipts or sales

Sales returns and allowances

Cost of goods sold*

Rental/interest

Other income

* The cost of goods sold must be calculated or verified by using Part III of Schedule C.

Deduction Categories

Advertising

Bad debts from sales or services

Bank service charges

Car and truck expenses

Commissions

Depletion

Depreciation**

Dues and publications

Employee benefit programs

Freight

Insurance

Interest-mortgage

Interest-other

Laundry and cleaning

Legal and professional services

Office expense

Pension and profit-sharing plans

Rent on business property

Repairs

Supplies

Taxes (payroll and business)

Travel

Meals and entertainment

Utilities and telephone

Wages

Wages-job credit

Other deductions

** This deduction amount must be supported by an additional tax form; consider setting up as categories the individual amounts reported on the second form.

CPA TIP

If you plan to take the home office deduction on IRS form 8829, be sure that you have adequate support for the expenses that you show on the form. The rules have recently become much more restrictive and you should check with your CPA before deducting a home office. Consider using split transactions to allocate utilities, mortgage or rent payments, cleaning, and so on between business and personal use. Once you determine the percentage that applies to your home office, you can split transactions using percentages as explained in Chapter 6, "Automating the Register."

Creating Income and Expense Categories. If you want to use categories to summarize cash inflows and outflows, you need a category for each income or expense account you want to use in the summaries. To account for your work expenses and a spouse's work expenses, you need categories for both sets of expenses.

Creating Budget Categories. If you want to use categories to budget—so that at a later date, you can compare what you budgeted with what you actually spent—you need a category for each comparison you want to make. To budget entertainment expenses and clothing expenses, you need categories for both.

Completing the List. By applying these three rules, you can build a list of the categories you want to use. As an aid in creating the list, you can access the category list that Quicken provides for home use by pressing **Ctrl-C**. To access the category list Quicken provides for business use, choose Set up Business categories at the Standard Categories screen from Select/Set Up New File, and then access Categories List (Business). To print either one of these category lists, press **Ctrl-P** at the Category List screen.

Consider these lists as starting points. The predefined Personal, or Home, category list provides a long list of income and expense categories that you may find useful for your home finances. Depending on the situation, some categories you don't need may be provided, and other categories you do need may be missing. Similarly, the predefined Business list provides income and expense categories you may find useful in business accounting. If you apply the rules described previously for devising categories, you may have no problem when using the predefined lists as starting points for constructing a category list that works well for you.

After you complete the list, review the categories for any redundancies produced by two of the rules calling for the same category. For home use of Quicken, for example, you can add a category to budget for monthly individual retirement account (IRA) contributions. You also can add a category to tally IRA payments because these payments represent potential tax deductions. Because both categories are the same, cross one category off the list.

Sometimes, however, overlapping or redundant categories are not as easy to spot. A tax deduction you need to calculate may be only a small part of a budgeting category, or a budgeting amount you need to calculate may be only a portion of a tax-deduction category. You need to detail categories so that each represents separate tax deduction or budgeting categories.

Categories act as building blocks you use to classify data the way you want it. You can use the following categories to calculate the tax-deduction amounts and the budgeted amounts shown in Table 4.2:

Mortgage interest

Mortgage principal

Mortgage late-payment fees

Credit card late-payment fees

Property taxes

Table 4.2 Personal Budget and Tax Amounts

Amounts	Categories Used
Late fees (a budgeted amount)	Mortgage late-payment fees Credit card late-payment fees
Housing (a budgeted amount)	Mortgage principal Mortgage interest Property taxes
Mortgage interest (deduction)	Mortgage interest Mortgage late-payment fees
Property taxes (deduction)	Property taxes

Setting Up Categories

When you create files, you can choose to use the defined Home or Business categories from the Standard Categories window as the foundation of the Category and Transfer list (see fig. 4.1).

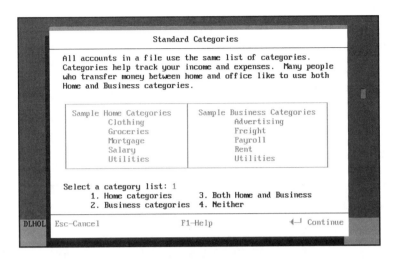

Fig. 4.1
The Standard Categories window.

If you select Home categories, Quicken copies its predefined list of Home categories to the Category and Transfer list in your file. If you select Business categories, Quicken copies its predefined list of Business categories to your list. Even if you select to use one of the predefined category lists, however, you may need to modify the category list.

CPA TIP

Quicken enables you to specify which categories are tax-related (a taxable income item or a tax-deductible expense). To help you identify tax-related items, review last year's tax return. Taxable income items usually are found on page 1 of Form 1040 (Federal Individual Income Tax Return). Schedule A of Form 1040 lists deductible itemized expenses, including medical expenses, mortgage interest, charitable contributions, moving expenses, investment expenses, and so on. You learn how to use Quicken to identify tax-related items in Chapter 14, "Using Quicken to Prepare for Income Taxes." Call a CPA if you have specific questions when trying to identify a potential tax-deductible expense.

Adding Categories

Quicken enables you to add categories in two ways:

- Access the Category and Transfer list and select the <New Category> line.

- Type the new category name in the Category field while entering a transaction.

Both methods are described here, and you can use the method you find most convenient.

Using the Category and Transfer List. To add categories from the Category and Transfer list, follow these steps:

1. From the Register or Write Checks screen, choose Categorize/Transfer from the Shortcuts menu. The Category and Transfer list appears (see fig. 4.2).

Fig. 4.2
The Category and Transfer List window.

2. Highlight the <New Category> line, and then press **Enter**. Quicken displays the Set Up Category window (see fig. 4.3). You also can press **Ctrl-Ins** to display the Set Up Category window.

Fig. 4.3
The Set Up Category window.

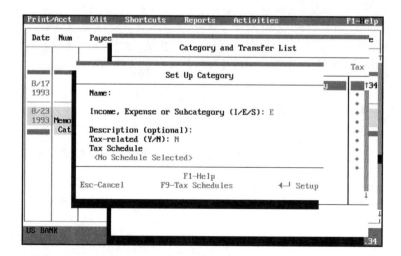

Learning Quicken

> **Note**
>
> The Category and Transfer list is where Quicken stores all the categories, subcategories, and transfer accounts in your Quicken file. Quicken provides a separate Category and Transfer list for each file.
>
> The Category and Transfer list not only lists the categories, subcategories, and transfer accounts, but also shows the category type (income or expense), the account type (bank, cash, investment, and so on), the category or account description, and whether the category or subcategory is tax-related.
>
> You can use the Category and Transfer list to select a category, subcategory, or transfer account to assign to a transaction. You also can use the list to add, edit, or delete categories and subcategories, change a category to a subcategory (and vice versa), and print a hard copy of the Category and Transfer list.

Tip

You can access the Category and Transfer List by pressing **Ctrl-C** from the Register or Write Checks screen, or click the abbreviation **Cat:** from the Register screen or the word **Category** from the Write Checks screen.

3. Type the category name you want to use in the Name field. Category names can contain up to 15 characters, and can include any character except the following:

   [ ] : /

4. Move the cursor to the Income, Expense, or Subcategory field. Choose **I** if the category that you are adding represents an income category, or **E** if the category is for an expense item. If you're adding a subcategory, choose **S** (adding subcategories is covered later in this chapter).

5. (Optional) Move the cursor to the Description field. You can use up to 25 characters to describe the category.

6. (Optional) Move the cursor to the Tax-Related field. The Tax-Related field determines whether the category that you are adding is a taxable income or tax-deductible expense item. If you specify that a category is tax-related by selecting **Y** from the Tax-Related field, Quicken includes that category in tax reports. Tax reports then can be used to accumulate transactions that are assigned to tax-related categories to help you prepare your personal or business income tax return. If you specify a category as tax-related, go to step 7; otherwise, skip to step 8.

7. (Optional) If you are setting up a category to report a specific kind of taxable income or tax deduction, press **F9**. The Tax Schedule window appears, listing two dozen common tax schedules (see fig. 4.4). Highlight the tax schedule to which the category pertains. If you're adding a category for an itemized deduction, such as tax preparation fees, highlight Schedule A in the Tax Schedule window and press **Enter** to select it.

Fig. 4.4

The Tax Schedule
window.

After you select a tax schedule, Quicken displays the Tax Line window so
that you can indicate on which line of the schedule the category will
appear (see fig. 4.5). The items in the Tax Line window depend on the tax
schedule selected. Highlight the line you want to select and press **Enter**.
In the example, you would select the Tax preparation fees option.

For some tax schedules, such as Schedule C, Schedule K-1, and Form W-2,
Quicken lists a tax line for your spouse. Also, these schedules and forms
can be filed in duplicate. If, for example, you and your spouse own separate businesses and therefore file separate Schedule Cs to report the income and expenses of the businesses, you can assign certain categories to
one copy of Schedule C and others to another copy of Schedule C. When
you select one of these schedules or forms from the Tax Schedule window
and then select a tax line, Quicken displays the Schedule Copy Number
window shown in figure 4.6. Indicate which copy of the schedule or form
(1 to 16) that the category you are adding relates to.

After you select a tax schedule and tax line for a tax-related category,
Quicken returns to the Set Up Category window you saw in figure 4.3.

8. When the Set Up Category window is complete, press **Ctrl-Enter** or **F10**
to save the category information and add the category to the Category
and Transfer list. Quicken inserts the new category name in its proper
alphabetical order.

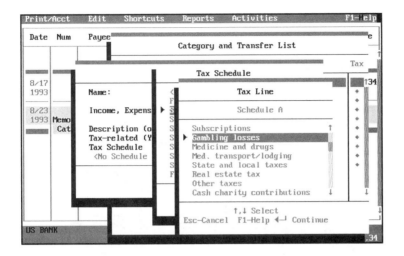

Fig. 4.5
The Tax Line window.

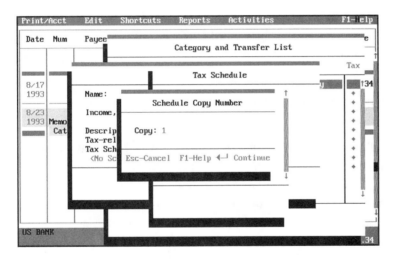

Fig. 4.6
The Schedule Copy Number window.

Adding a Category as You Enter a Transaction. You can shortcut the entire process of adding a category by typing the new category in the Category field as you are entering a transaction. To add a category using this shortcut method, follow these steps:

1. Move the cursor to the Category field in the Write Checks screen, the Register screen, or the Split Transactions window (**Ctrl-S**).

2. Type the new category name in the Category field. If the category doesn't already exist, the Category Not Found window appears (see fig. 4.7).

Fig. 4.7

The Category Not Found window.

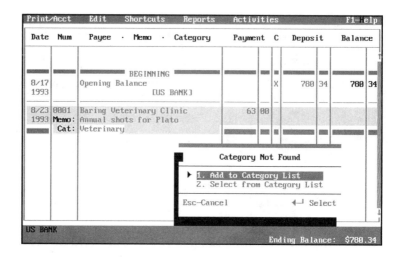

3. To add the category, choose **1** to select Add to Category List. The Set Up Category window appears, which you complete as discussed in steps 4 through 9 of the preceding procedure.

If you choose the Select from Category List option, Quicken displays the Category and Transfer list that you saw in figure 4.2 and highlights the category that comes closest to the name you entered.

Generally, you have plenty of room for as many categories as you need. The precise maximum number, however, depends on the computer's available memory, the length of the category names and descriptions, and the other information stored in memory. You usually have room for about 150 categories with 384K of memory and more than 1,000 categories with 512K of memory.

Deleting a Category

You also may want to delete categories—because you don't use a particular category or because you added the category incorrectly. Deleting categories is even easier than adding categories.

To delete a category, follow these steps:

1. From the Write Checks or Register screen, choose Categorize/Transfer from the Shortcuts menu, or press **Ctrl-C**. Quicken displays the Category and Transfer list.

2. Highlight the category you want to delete. Pressing **Home** moves you to the beginning of the list; pressing **End** moves you to the end of the list.

3. When the item you want to delete is highlighted, press **Ctrl-D**. A warning message appears, telling you that you are about to permanently delete a category.

4. To remove the category from the category list, press **Enter**. If you don't want to remove the category, choose Esc.

After you delete a category, you cannot use the category unless you add the category again. If you assigned previous transactions to the deleted category, Quicken removes the category from the Category field (the Category field becomes blank). You need to return to the Register and assign a new category to any blank Category field. (Chapters 5 and 6 explain how to use the Register.)

Editing a Category

You also can edit a category. Suppose that you run a business and use Quicken to account for, among other things, the wages you pay. Further, suppose that the Wages category always was used for employees working in Washington state. If you create a new category named *OR_WAGES* to account for the wages you pay to employees working in Oregon, you may want to change the name of the Wages category to *WA_WAGES* to reflect the change in the significance of the account.

The steps for editing a category roughly parallel the steps for adding one. To edit a category, follow these steps:

1. From the Write Checks or Register screen, choose Categorize/Transfer from the Shortcuts menu, or press **Ctrl-C**. Quicken displays the Category and Transfer list.

2. Highlight the category that you want to edit. Pressing **Home** moves you to the beginning of the list; pressing **End** moves you to the end.

3. Press **Ctrl-E**. The Edit Category window appears, as shown in figure 4.8.

4. (Optional) Retype or edit the category name you want to use in the Name field.

5. (Optional) Move the cursor to the Income, Expense, or Subcategory field. If necessary, change the Income, Expense, or Subcategory field by choosing **I** for income, **E** for expenses, or **S** for subcategory.

6. (Optional) Move the cursor to the Description field. If necessary, retype or edit the existing description.

Fig. 4.8

The Edit Category window.

7. (Optional) Move the cursor to the Tax-Related field. If necessary, change the Tax-Related field.

8. (Optional) Press **F9** to display the Tax Schedule window. Highlight the appropriate schedule, and then press **Enter**. Quicken displays the Tax Line window. Highlight the appropriate line of the schedule and press **Enter**. Next, if this is a schedule that allows multiple copies, type the schedule number (1 to 16) in the Schedule Copy Number window. Press **Enter** to return to the Edit Category window.

9. To save the changes to the category, press **Ctrl-Enter** or **F10**.

Using Subcategories

If you decide to use categories as building blocks to classify your income and expenses, you need to know about subcategories. Taking the first row of the data from Table 4.2, suppose you create a category called *LateFees* to track late-payment fees. You then can set up two subcategories of the category *LateFees* called *LMortgage* for late mortgage fees and *LCredit* for late credit card fees (the *L* stands for *late*.) Then, when you record a transaction to pay late fees on your mortgage, you can assign the subcategory *LMortgage* to the transaction. When you record a transaction for late fees on your credit card, assign the subcategory *LCredit* to the transaction. You can design reports so that all your subcategories are shown or just the categories.

When only categories are shown, Quicken shows the sum of all transactions assigned to their subcategories as the category total. In the example, you could show a subcategory line for *LMortgage* and *LCredit* to see just how much was spent on late fees for each, or you could lump both the *LMortgage* and *LCredit* subcategories together and show their total in the category line *LateFees*. Figure 4.9 shows a cash flow report where subcategories were used.

Assigning Subcategories to Transactions

Subcategories are assigned to transactions in much the same way that categories are assigned in the Category field of the Register or Write Checks screen. When you assign a subcategory, however, you first must enter the category that the subcategory falls under.

To assign a subcategory to a transaction, follow these steps:

1. At the Register or Write Checks screen, move the cursor to the Category field.

```
                          Cash Flow Report 3
                        8/ 1/93 Through 8/31/93
        ARAD59-Bank, Cash, CC Accounts                          Page 1
        9/22/93
                                              8/ 1/93-
                     Category Description      8/31/93

        INFLOWS
           Interest Income                        2.18
           Professional Fees                  6,000.00

        TOTAL INFLOWS                          6,002.18

        OUTFLOWS
           Automobile Expenses:
              Auto Fuel                96.57
              Auto Loan Payment       315.67
              Auto Service             31.00

           Total Automobile Expenses              443.24
           Bank Charge                              7.50
           Credit Card                            533.00
           Dues                                   200.00
           Education                              198.35
           Entertainment                          271.66
           Insurance                               50.00
           Miscellaneous                            6.50
           Mortgage Interest Exp                  750.00
           Mortgage                               100.00
           Postage                                 25.00
           Taxes:
              Property Tax           100.00

           Total Taxes                            100.00
           Telephone Expense                       34.65
           Water, Gas, Electric:
              Gas and Electricity     64.98
              Water                   23.95

           Total Water, Gas, Electric              88.93

        TOTAL OUTFLOWS                          2,808.83

        OVERALL TOTAL                           3,193.35
```

Fig 4.9

Using subcategories gives you the capability of showing greater detail.

2. Enter the primary income or expense category. Enter the category by typing the first few characters, and QuickFill takes over and fills in the rest of the category name. QuickFill is explained in Chapter 6 "Automating the Register." If the category that QuickFill enters is not the one you want, press **Ctrl-+** (plus) or **Ctrl-–** (minus) to enter the next or preceding category from the Category and Transfer list. You also can press **Ctrl-C** to display the Category and Transfer list, highlight the category that you want to assign to the transaction, and press **Enter**.

3. After the appropriate category is entered in the Category field, type a colon after the category name. QuickFill fills in the first subcategory for the category that you entered. If the subcategory that QuickFill enters is not the one you want, type the first few letters of the subcategory name or press **Ctrl-+** (plus) to enter the next subcategory. You also can type the subcategory name or press **Ctrl-C** to display the Category and Transfer list, highlight the subcategory that you want to assign, and press **Enter**.

4. If the rest of the transaction is complete, press **Ctrl-Enter** to record the transaction and the category and subcategory assigned to the transaction.

Figure 4.10 shows a recorded transaction with a subcategory assigned in the Category field.

Fig. 4.10
A recorded transaction with a subcategory assigned in the Category field.

Adding Subcategories

You add a subcategory to the Category and Transfer list in much the same way you add a category. You can add the subcategory directly to the Category and Transfer list, or you can type the new subcategory name in the Category field of a transaction and choose the Add to Category List option that Quicken presents when it doesn't find the subcategory in the list.

Using the Category and Transfer List. To add a subcategory to the Category and Transfer list, follow these steps:

1. From the Write Checks or Register screen, choose Categorize/Transfer from the Shortcuts menu, or press **Ctrl-C**. Quicken displays the Category and Transfer list.

2. Highlight the category that you want to add a subcategory to. Press **Ctrl-Ins** to display the Set Up Category window.

3. Type the subcategory name you want to use in the Name field. Subcategory names can include up to 15 characters and can include any character except the following:

    [ ] : /

4. Move the cursor to the Income, Expense, or Subcategory field. Choose **S** for Subcategory.

5. (Optional) Move the cursor to the Description field. You can use up to 25 characters to describe the subcategory.

6. (Optional) Move the cursor to the Tax-Related field. The Tax-Related field determines whether the subcategory that you are adding is a taxable income or tax-deductible expense item. If you specify that a subcategory is tax-related, Quicken includes that subcategory in tax reports. Tax reports then can be used to accumulate transactions that are assigned to tax-related categories and subcategories to help you prepare your personal or business income tax return.

7. (Optional) If you are setting up a subcategory to report a specific kind of taxable income item or tax deduction, press **F9**. The Tax Schedule window appears, listing two dozen common tax schedules. Highlight the tax schedule to which that the category pertains. Press **Enter** to select it.

    After you select a tax schedule, Quicken displays the Tax Line window so that you can indicate which line of the schedule the subcategory will be shown on in your return. The items in the Tax Line window depend on the tax schedule selected. Highlight the line you want to select and press **Enter**.

Learning Quicken

For some tax schedules, such as Schedule C, Schedule K-1, and Form W-2, Quicken lists a tax line for your spouse. Also, these schedules and forms can be filed in duplicate. When you select one of these schedules or forms from the Tax Schedule window and then select a tax line, Quicken displays the Schedule Copy Number window. Indicate which copy of the schedule or form (1 to 16) that the subcategory you are adding relates to.

After you select a tax schedule and tax line for a tax-related subcategory, Quicken returns to the Set Up Category window.

8. When the Set Up Category window is complete, press **Enter** or **F10** to save the subcategory information and add the subcategory to the Category and Transfer list. Quicken inserts the new subcategory name in its proper alphabetical order under its parent category.

Adding a New Subcategory as You Enter a Transaction. To add a subcategory from the Category field as you are entering a transaction, follow these steps:

1. Move the cursor to the Category field in the Write Checks screen, the Register screen, or the Split Transactions window (**Ctrl-S**).

2. Enter the category to which you want to add a subcategory. Enter a colon after the category name.

3. Type the name of the new subcategory. Because the subcategory doesn't already exist, the Category Not Found message appears.

4. To add the subcategory, choose 1 to select the Add to Category List option. The Set Up Category window appears, which you complete as discussed in steps 4 through 9 of the procedure for adding subcategories.

If you choose the Select from Category List option, Quicken displays the Category and Transfer list and highlights the subcategory that comes closest to the name you entered.

Editing and Deleting Subcategories

You can edit a subcategory at any time. When you change a subcategory name, all previous transactions assigned to that subcategory also are changed. To edit a subcategory, follow the same steps for editing a category as explained earlier in this chapter.

You also can delete a subcategory if you no longer need it. When you delete a subcategory, Quicken permanently removes it from the Category and Transfer list. Previous transactions assigned to the subcategory that you subsequently delete are merged into the parent category. If, for example, you assign transactions to the subcategory *Movies*, under the category *Entertainment*, and then delete the subcategory, Quicken assigns all those transactions to the category *Entertainment*.

To delete a subcategory, follow the same steps for deleting a category as explained earlier in this chapter.

Rearranging Categories and Subcategories

After you establish your category list and added categories and subcategories, you can change categories to subcategories and vice versa. The Move option from the Category and Transfer list enables you to change a category to a subcategory (*demote* a category), change a subcategory to a category (*promote* a subcategory), or move a subcategory underneath another category (so that it has a different parent category). You may decide to make the category *Auto Fuel* a subcategory of the category *Auto*, for example. The Move option enables you to make this change, and Quicken changes the previous transactions assigned to these categories.

Changing a Category to a Subcategory

To change a category to a subcategory (demote a category), follow these steps:

1. From the Write Checks or Register screen, choose Categorize/Transfer from the Shortcuts menu, or press **Ctrl-C**. Quicken displays the Category and Transfer list.

2. Highlight the category that you want to change to a subcategory.

3. Press **F8** to select the Move option. Quicken moves the category to the top of the Category and Transfer list and places a colon (:) in front of the category name to show that it now can be moved (changed).

4. Highlight the category name (target category) for which it is to be a subcategory. Quicken displays the category name next to the target category name. In the preceding example, after completing this step, the category will appear like this:

    ```
    Auto : Auto Fuel
    ```

5. Press **Enter** to change the category to a subcategory. Quicken places the new subcategory beneath the target category name in the Category and Transfer list.

Changing a Subcategory to a Category

To change a subcategory to a category (promote a subcategory), follow these steps:

1. From the Write Checks or Register screen, choose Categorize/Transfer from the Shortcuts menu, or press **Ctrl-C**. Quicken displays the Category and Transfer list.

2. Highlight the subcategory that you want to change to a category.

3. Press **F8** to select the Move option. Quicken moves the subcategory name to the same line as its parent category name, separated by a colon (:) to show that the subcategory can be moved or changed.

4. Press **Home** or use the scroll bar to move the subcategory to the top of the Category and Transfer list.

5. Press **Enter**, and Quicken changes the subcategory to a category and positions the new category alphabetically in the Category and Transfer list.

Merging Categories and Subcategories

You can merge one category or subcategory into another. You may want to merge the Int Inc (Interest income) category into the Invest Inc (Investment income) category if you find that you are not really using the former category, for example.

When you merge two categories or subcategories, Quicken assigns the category or subcategory name that you retain (in this case, Invest Inc) to each transaction that was assigned to the merged category or subcategory (Int Inc).

Before you can merge a category into another category, you first must change the category that you want to merge to a subcategory. To merge a subcategory into another subcategory, make the subcategory that you want to merge a subcategory of the subcategory that you want to retain. If, for example, you have a subcategory named *Condo Exp* and want to merge it with a subcategory named

Condo Repairs, you first must make the subcategory *Condo Exp* a subcategory of *Condo Repairs*. Figure 4.11 shows how categories and subcategories are listed in the Category and Transfer list. Notice how categories and subcategories appear in outline format with a category listed first, followed by its subcategory (indented to the right). A subcategory of a subcategory is indented to the right a little farther.

Fig. 4.11
Categories and subcategories appear in outline format in the Category and Transfer List.

To merge a category or subcategory, follow these steps:

1. From the Write Checks or Register screen, choose Categorize/Transfer from the Shortcuts menu, or press **Ctrl-C**. Quicken displays the Category and Transfer list.

2. Highlight the category or subcategory that you want to merge into another category or subcategory.

3. If you want to merge a category into another category, you first must change the category that you want to merge to a subcategory. If you want to merge a subcategory into another subcategory, make the subcategory that you want to merge a subcategory of the one you want to retain. Follow the steps explained in the preceding section to change a category or subcategory to a subcategory.

4. After the category or subcategory you want to merge changes to a subcategory of the category or subcategory that you want to retain, delete it by pressing **Ctrl-D**.

Quicken displays the warning message that you are about to delete a subcategory and that all transactions currently assigned to the subcategory will be merged into the parent category or subcategory.

5. Press **Enter** to delete the subcategory and merge it into its parent category or subcategory.

Printing a Category and Transfer List

When you select Categorize/Transfer from the Shortcuts menu, a list of categories and accounts appears. Occasionally, you may want a printed copy of this list. You also may want to review the list with a tax advisor at his office to verify that you are tracking all tax deduction categories, or you may want to keep a paper copy of the list as an aid to entering transactions.

To print a copy of the Category and Transfer list, follow these steps:

1. From the Write Checks or Register screen, choose Categorize/Transfer from the Shortcuts menu, or press **Ctrl-C**. Quicken displays the Category and Transfer list.

2. Press **Ctrl-P**. The Print Category and Transfer List window appears, as shown in figure 4.12. This window, which resembles the Print Register window, provides fields to select the printer settings you want to use.

Fig. 4.12

The Print Category and Transfer List window.

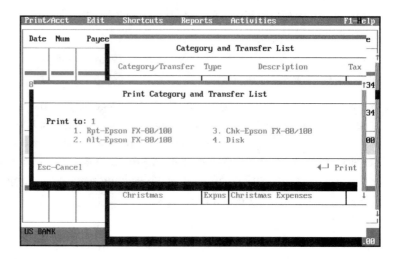

3. Indicate the printer settings you want to use by choosing **1** for the first setting, **2** for the second setting, and so on.

4. Press **Enter**. Quicken prints a copy of the Category and Transfer list.

For help in completing the Print Category and Transfer List window, refer to the discussion in Chapter 5 on printing a Register. The Print Register window, which you use to print a Register, works the same way as the Print Category and Transfer List window.

Working with Classes

Categories and subcategories group revenues and expenses by the type of transaction. Income transactions may be categorized as gross sales, other income, and so on, for example. Expense transactions may be categorized as car and truck expenses, supply expenses, utilities, and so on. But you may want to slice the data in other ways. You also may want to see income or expenses by job or project, by salesperson or product line, and by geographic location or functional company areas.

Classes add a second dimension to the income and expense summaries that categories provide. Nonbusiness use of Quicken probably does not require this second dimension. Business owners, however, can find Quicken's classes a powerful way to view financial data from a second perspective.

Besides using two categories—Product and Service—to track income, you can use classes to determine which salespeople actually are booking the orders. With three salespeople, use these three classes: Joe, Bill, and Sue. Besides seeing the sales of company products and company services, you also can see things such as the sales Bill made, the product sales Joe made, and the service sales Sue made. In effect, you have two perspectives on this income—the kind of income (which appears as a product or service) and salespeople (which appears as Joe, Bill, or Sue). Table 4.3 shows these perspectives.

Table 4.3 Two Perspectives on Income			
Type of Income	**Salespeople Booking Orders**		
	Joe	**Bill**	**Sue**
Product	Joe's product sales	Bill's product sales	Sue's product sales
Service	Joe's service sales	Bill's service sales	Sue's service sales

Defining a Class

The first step in using classes is to define the classes you want to use. The classes you choose depend on how you need or want to view the financial data you collect with Quicken. Unfortunately, giving specific advice on choosing appropriate classes is difficult and Quicken does not provide predefined lists of classes (as it does for categories). Classes usually are specific to the particular personal or business finances. You can, however, follow one rough rule of thumb: Look at the types of questions you currently ask but cannot answer by using categories alone. A real estate investor may want to use classes that correspond to individual properties. A law firm may want to use classes that represent each of the partners or each client. Other businesses have still different views of financial data. After you define the classes you want to use, you are ready to add the classes in Quicken. You can add as many classes as you want.

To add classes, follow these steps:

1. From the Write Checks or Register screen, choose Select/Set Up Class from the **Shortcuts** menu, or press **Ctrl-L**. The Class list appears (see fig. 4.13).

Fig. 4.13

The Class List.

2. Highlight the <New Class> line at the top of the list and press **Enter**. The Set Up Class window appears (see fig. 4.14).

3. Type the name you want to use for the class. Class names can contain up to 15 characters, including spaces. You cannot use the following characters:

: [ ] /

4. (Optional) Move the cursor to the Description field. Type a description for the class.

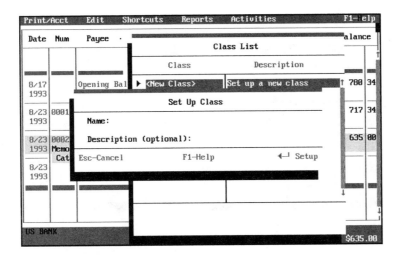

Fig. 4.14
The Set Up Class window.

5. To save the class, press **Enter** or **F10**. Quicken adds the class to the Class list in alphabetical order.

Editing and Deleting Classes

If you start defining classes, you also need to know how to edit and delete these classes. The classification scheme you use undoubtedly can change over time. Suppose that you are a real estate investor and you use classes to track properties. You probably buy and sell properties over a period of time. Alternatively, if you are a bookkeeper for a law firm, the lawyers working at the firm probably change over a period of time. Both of these examples indicate a need for editing classes. The steps for editing and deleting are simple and familiar if you previously edited or deleted categories.

To edit a class, follow these steps:

1. From the Write Checks or Register screen, choose Select/Set Up Class from the Shortcuts menu, or press **Ctrl-L**. The Class list appears (see fig. 4.13).

2. Highlight the class you want to edit.

3. Press **Ctrl-E**. Quicken displays the Edit Class window (see fig. 4.15).

4. (Optional) If necessary, retype or edit the class name.

5. (Optional) Move the cursor to the Description field. If necessary, retype or edit the class description.

6. To save the changes to the class, press **Ctrl-Enter** or **F10**.

Fig. 4.15
The Edit Class window.

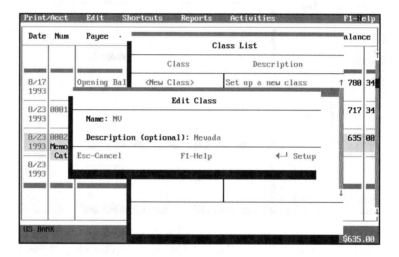

To delete a class, follow these steps:

1. From the Write Checks or Register screen, choose Select/Set Up Class from the Shortcuts menu, or press **Ctrl-L**. The Class list appears (see fig. 4.13).

2. Highlight the class that you want to delete.

3. Press **Ctrl-D**. Quicken warns you that you are about to permanently delete a class.

4. Press **Enter** to complete the deletion, or choose **Esc** to cancel the deletion.

Using Subclasses

Tip
Subclasses are helpful for sales taxes based on a state, county, or city with different tax rates for each jurisdiction, or if you must report sales within each jurisdiction.

If you use classes to add another dimension to the reporting and recording process, you also may want to use subclasses. *Subclasses* are classes within classes. If you use a geographical scheme to create classes, the classes may be states. Within each state, you may choose to use subclasses corresponding to portions of the state. *Washington*, a class, may have the subclasses *Eastern Washington* and *Western Washington*, for example. *California*, another class, may have the subclasses *Northern California* (excluding the Bay Area), *Bay Area*, *Southern California* (excluding Los Angeles County), and *Los Angeles County*. You enter, edit, and delete subclasses by following the same procedures as for classes.

Assigning Classes and Subclasses to Transactions

You use the Category field in the Write Checks or Register screen or Split Transaction window to assign classes to transactions. Quicken does not prompt you to assign classes to transactions, so if you want to use classes, be sure to remember to assign them after you assign a category.

To assign a class to a transaction, follow these steps:

1. After the category or subcategory is entered into the Category field, type / (slash).

2. Type the class name or press **Ctrl-L** to display the Class list and select a class from the list. If, for example, you want to record the income category **SALES** and the California class **CAL** for a transaction, type **SALES/ CAL** in the Category field. The same QuickFill feature noted previously in this book also applies to classes. If you enter enough of a class name for Quicken to identify the class, QuickFill completes the entry for you.

3. If the rest of the transaction is complete, press **Enter** or **F10** to record the transaction and the class assignment.

If you use subclasses, enter the primary class, a colon, and then the subclass. If, for example, the class *CAL* has the subclass *NORTH*, you can record sales for Northern California by typing **SALES/CAL:NORTH** in the Category field.

If you have more than one subclass—classes within classes within classes— you also separate the additional subclasses with colons.

CPA TIP

The Quicken user's manual describes a series of ways you can use classes. For the most part, the ideas are good. Some accounting problems exist with many of the manual's suggestions. From the start, think about these problems so that you don't go to a great deal of work and then find you wasted time. The basic problem with classes is that they don't give you a way to budget. You cannot, for example, budget by classes. This may not seem too important to you right now, but before you begin to use classes, read Chapter 15, "Budgeting with Quicken." Business users also will probably benefit by reading Chapter 22, "Using Quicken in Your Business."

Summary

Quicken's categories and classes give you a means to organize your finances to give you the information that you need. This chapter described how you can modify Quicken's defined categories; how to add, edit, and delete categories; and how you use subcategories. This chapter also defined classes; described when to use the class features; and detailed the steps for adding, editing, and deleting classes.

In the next chapter, you learn how to access the register to record checks, deposits, other withdrawals, transfers between accounts, and enter uncleared transactions. You also learn how to review and edit register transactions, postdate transactions, and to print the register.

Chapter 5

Using the Register

Your checkbook, or check register, is your most fundamental financial tool. You probably agree that your check register largely summarizes your financial life. Money flows into your checking account in the form of wages for a household or sales collections for a business. Money flows out of the checking account to pay expenses.

Moving your check register to Quicken provides two major benefits. First, Quicken does the arithmetic of deducting checks and withdrawals and adding deposits—a trivial contribution until you remember the last time an error in your arithmetic caused you to bounce a check. Second, Quicken records each of your checking account transactions in the Register so that you can use Quicken's Reports feature to summarize and extract information from the Register—information that helps you plan and control your finances more effectively.

Quicken's Register is the program's major component. Every other program feature—writing checks, reconciling accounts, and printing reports—depends on the Register. Every user works with Quicken's Register directly by entering transactions into the Register and indirectly by using the information stored in the Register. In fact, any of the financial transactions you record can be entered directly into the Quicken Register.

This chapter describes the basics of using Quicken's Register, including the following:

- Understanding the Register screen

- Recording transactions in the Register

- Reviewing and editing Register transactions

- Printing the Register

Note

If you want to use Quicken to write and print checks, the Write/Print Checks option provides a convenient format for collecting the information Quicken needs to print checks.

Chapter 6, "Automating the Register," describes Quicken features that you can use to speed up your work in the Register and make using the Check Register even easier. Chapter 10, "Tracking Your Net Worth, Other Assets, and Liabilities," describes how you can use the Register to track other assets and even to track liabilities such as your mortgage or other bank loans. Chapter 16, "Monitoring Your Investments," describes a special set of tools that Quicken provides for managing your investments. To track and monitor your investments, Quicken provides the Investment Register.

Accessing the Register

You choose Use **R**egister from Quicken's Main Menu to access the Register screen. You use this screen to record most of your checking account transactions, such as manual checks, deposits, interest, bank fees, and so on, that affect your checking account (see fig. 5.1).

Fig. 5.1
The Register
screen.

```
Print/Acct    Edit    Shortcuts    Reports    Activities           F1-Help

Date  Num    Payee  ·  Memo  ·  Category      Payment  C  Deposit    Balance

8/22         Baldwin Environmental                         6,000 00   6,147 33
1993         Consulting Fee   Prof. Fees

8/22 0005    A-1 Transmissions                     31 00             6,116 33
1993         Change Trans. F→Auto:Service

8/22 0006    Sierra Pacific Power Company           64 98             6,051 35
1993         July              Utilities:Gas →

8/22 0007    Nevada Bell                            34 65             6,016 70
1993         July              Telephone

8/22 0008    City of Reno                           23 95             5,992 75
1993         July              Utilities:Water

8/22         Deposit to Savings                    100 00             5,892 75
1993  Memo:
      Cat: [Acme]

Bk.ofAmer-1342    (Alt+letter accesses menu)
Esc-Main Menu    Ctrl↵ Record              Ending Balance:  $5,892.75
```

Tip
You can access the
Register from the
Write Checks
screen by pressing
Ctrl-R.

Understanding the Register Screen

The Register screen looks similar to the manual check register you use. The Register includes a transaction line with fields to enter the following information:

Field	Records
Date	The date of the transaction.
Num	The check number. Or, you can use this field to enter *ATM* for *automatic teller machine transaction* or any other descriptive term for transactions that don't involve checks.
Payee	The person or firm you are paying. Or, in the case of a deposit, the source of the deposit.
Memo	An optional field to enter a check memo or description of the transaction.
Category	The category or subcategory assigned to the transaction. You learn about categories in Chapter 4, "Organizing Your Finances."
Payment	The amount of the check or withdrawal.
C (Cleared)	Indicates whether the transaction has cleared the bank. You learn more about cleared transactions in Chapter 9, "Reconciling Your Bank Account."
Deposit	The amount of the deposit or bank credit.
Balance	Quicken calculates the balance in your account after the current transaction and enters the result here. You cannot make an entry in the Balance field.

If you don't print checks using Quicken, you probably will enter all of your checking account transactions in the Register. If you do print checks with Quicken, you should enter check information in the Write Checks screen. You can print checks from information entered in the Register as well, however. When you enter and record a check in the Write Checks screen, Quicken records the transaction in the Register and updates the account balance. The steps for entering check information in the Write Checks screen are outlined in Chapters 7 and 8. The steps you take to record a transaction in the Register screen are described in the next section.

The Register screen can be broken down into three parts: the *menu bar* at the top of the screen, the actual *Check Register*, and the *information lines* at the bottom of the screen.

The menu bar shows the menus you can use from the Register screen to access commands: Print/Acct, Edit, Shortcuts, Reports, and Activities.

The second part of the Register screen is the actual Check Register you use to record account transactions. Take a minute to review the Register—it probably resembles the register you now use to record checks manually. (The fields are described later in the chapter.)

The third part of the Register screen contains the information lines at the bottom. These lines show the bank account name (checking) that you are using, information on what the Esc and Enter keys do, and the ending balance in the account.

Before you start recording transactions in the Register, you can use the information at the bottom of the Register screen to make sure you have selected the correct account and to gauge the effect of the transactions you want to record (do you have enough money in your account to cover the checks that you need to write?).

Changing the Register View

Tip

To toggle between one-line and two-line Register views, press **Ctrl-Q**.

When you start using Quicken, the Register appears using two lines of text for each transaction (other than the highlighted transaction). You can change the Register view so that each transaction takes up only one line in the Register. When you change the Register view, Quicken compresses each transaction line into one line. Don't worry, your data is safe, some of it is just hidden from view.

To change the Register view, follow this step:

From the Register, choose **Register View** from the Activities menu, or press **Ctrl-Q** (see fig. 5.2).

Fig. 5.2

The Activities menu.

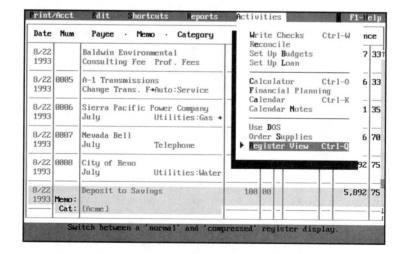

Quicken changes the Register view so that each transaction takes up only one line of text (see fig. 5.3).

Fig. 5.3
Changing the Register view to one line per transaction.

Note

You cannot change the Register view in the Register for an investment account.

Moving Around the Register

As you get up to speed with Quicken, you will want to move through the Register quickly so that you can enter transactions as fast as possible or review prior transactions without having to move through the Register line by line. Use the following keys to help you move quickly and easily around the Register:

Press	To Move
↑	Up one transaction
↓	Down one transaction
PgUp	Up one screen of transactions
PgDn	Down one screen of transactions
Ctrl-PgUp	To the beginning of the preceding month
Ctrl-PgDn	To the beginning of the next month
Ctrl-Home, or Home, Home, Home	To the beginning of the Register
Ctrl-End, or End, End, End	To the end of the Register

To use the mouse to move around the Register, you use the *scroll bar*. The scroll bar is the vertical bar along the right edge of the Register with arrows at both ends. Using the scroll bar gives you three additional ways to move through the Register. To move to the preceding page of Register transactions, for example, you can click the up arrow at the top of the scroll bar. To move to the next page of Register transactions, you can click the down arrow at the bottom of the scroll bar.

You can move the portion of the Register that is on-screen by dragging the *scroll box*. The scroll box is the dark square on the scroll bar that shows you approximately which portion of the Register is currently displayed. To drag the scroll box, press the left mouse button and drag the scroll box up or down. You also can move to the preceding or next page of Register transactions by clicking the scroll bar above the scroll box to see the preceding page of transactions. Click the scroll bar below the scroll box to see the following page of transactions.

If you want to find a specific transaction, such as a check written to a particular payee or a check written on a certain date, Quicken includes Find and Go to Date options that enable you to locate transactions in the Register quickly without needing to scroll through months of transactions. To learn about these features, refer to Chapter 6, "Automating the Register."

Recording a Check

Recording a check in the Quicken Register closely parallels recording a check by hand in a paper checkbook register. The Register screen, however, makes the whole process easier. You can record any check in the Register, including checks you want to print. Typically, however, you record checks you have written previously by hand directly into the register. You record checks you want to print using Write/Print Checks option, which is described in Chapter 7, "Writing and Printing Checks."

To record a check, follow these steps:

1. Choose Use **Register** from Quicken's Main Menu if the Register is not displayed already. Quicken displays the Register screen. If you are working with more than one account, you may need to select the account first (see Chapter 3, "Defining Your Accounts").

2. Enter the check date in the Date field in the MM/DD/YY format.

Note

You can change the way dates are entered and displayed by changing the transaction setting option called Enter Dates as MM/DD/YY or DD/MM/YY. By default, Quicken displays dates as MM/DD/YY; however, you can change the way dates are displayed (to DD/MM/YY) by changing this transaction setting option. If you change the transaction setting option, for example, dates are entered and displayed with the day first, followed by the month. August 18, 1993, for example, is entered and displayed as 18/08/93 rather than 08/18/93. See Chapter 20, "Customizing Quicken," to learn how to change this transaction setting.

The first time you use Quicken, the program fills the Date field with the system date. After you record your first transaction in the Register screen, Quicken fills the Date field with the last date you used. To edit the date, you have two choices. First, you can move the cursor to the month, day, or year you want to change and type over what already is showing on-screen. Or, you can use the special date-entry keys, such as the + (plus) and - (minus) keys, and the T, M, H, W, and R keys. (For more information on how these keys work, refer to Chapter 2, "Getting Around in Quicken.")

CPA TIP

Businesses and individuals often receive discounts for paying bills early. Consider early payment in setting the check date. Not taking early payment discounts is an extremely expensive way to borrow money from the vendor. Suppose that a vendor normally requires payment within 30 days but allows a 2 percent discount for payments received within 10 days. If you pay within 30 rather than 10 days, you essentially pay the vendor a 2 percent interest charge for paying 20 days later. Because one year contains roughly 18 20-day periods, the 2 percent for 20 days equals approximately 36 percent annually.

Although you may need to "borrow" this money, you probably can find a much cheaper lender. As a rule of thumb, if a vendor gives you a 1 percent discount for paying 20 days early, you are borrowing the vendor's money at about an 18 percent annual interest rate if you do not pay early. A 3 percent discount works out to a whopping 54 percent a year.

3. Move the cursor to the Num field. Enter the number of the check in this field. Checks you recorded in the Write Checks screen but have not printed show asterisks as check numbers.

If you want to enter a check that you will want to print later, you can enter the check number as asterisks. The Write/Print Checks screen and option, however, provide a more convenient method of writing and printing checks. Refer to Chapter 7 for detailed information on Quicken's Write/Print Checks feature.

4. Move the cursor to the Payee field. Enter the name of the person or business to which you are writing the check. You have space for up to 31 characters.

5. Move the cursor to the Payment field. Enter the check amount, using up to 10 characters for the amount. You can enter a check as large as $9,999,999.99. The decimal point counts as one of the 10 characters, but the commas do not.

6. Move the cursor to the Cleared (C) field, which shows whether a transaction has been recorded by the bank. Use this field as part of *reconciling*, or explaining the difference between your check register account balance and the balance the bank shows on your monthly statement. To mark a transaction as cleared, enter an asterisk (*), the only character Quicken accepts here, in the C field. During reconciliation, Quicken changes the asterisk to an X (see Chapter 9, "Reconciling Your Bank Account").

7. (Optional) Move the cursor through the Deposit field and to the Memo field. Use the Memo field to describe a transaction. You can use up to 31 characters to describe a transaction. If you are making several payments a month to the bank, the Memo field enables you to specify the house payment, the school loan, the hot tub, the boat, and so on.

8. (Optional) Move the cursor to the Category field. You use this field to assign a category to a transaction. The category is used to classify expenses, such as utilities expense, interest expense, or entertainment. (Categories also are used to classify income, such as dividend income, interest income, wages, and so on.) Access the Category and Transfer list (press **Ctrl-C**), or click Cat:, which contains the existing categories provided by Quicken or those you have added previously (see fig. 5.4). Highlight the category you want to assign to the check transaction, and press **Enter** or double-click the category with the mouse.

Tip

You can use the + (plus) key to enter the next check number or the - (minus) key to enter the check number before the last check number used. If the check number from the preceding transaction was 1892, for example, press the + (plus) key to enter 1893 as the check number in the next transaction line or press the - (minus) key to enter 1891 as the check number.

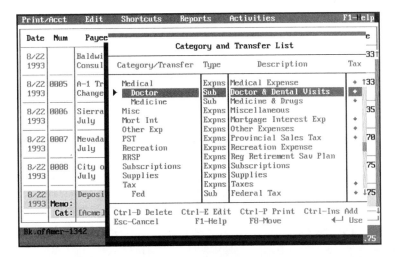

Fig. 5.4
The Category and Transfer List.

Note

You can assign more than one category to a single transaction. This is called *splitting a transaction*. You may need to do this if you are writing one check to a department store, for example, to pay for clothing, computer supplies, and cosmetics. Obviously, no one category that describes these different expenses exists. By splitting the transaction, you can assign three categories to the check transaction so that each expense is properly classified in your records. You learn how to split a transaction in the next chapter.

You also can use the Category field to describe the class into which a transaction falls. Categories and classes were described in Chapter 4, "Organizing Your Finances." Figure 5.5 shows a check to the Sierra Pacific Power Company. The category is Utilities.

Fig. 5.5
A sample check entered in the Register.

Print/Acct	Edit	Shortcuts	Reports	Activities		F1-Help

Date	Num	Payee · Memo · Category	Payment	C	Deposit	Balance
8/22 1993		Baldwin Environmental Consulting Fee Prof. Fees			6,000 00	6,147 33
8/22 1993	0005	A-1 Transmissions Change Trans. F→Auto:Service	31 00			6,116 33
8/22 1993	0006	Sierra Pacific Power Company **Memo:** July **Cat:** Utilities:Gas & Electric	64 98			6,051 35
8/22 1993	0007	Nevada Bell July Telephone	34 65			6,016 70
8/22 1993	0008	City of Reno July Utilities:Water	23 95			5,992 75
8/22 1993		Deposit to Savings [Acme]	100 00			5,892 75

Bk.of Amer—1342   (Alt+letter accesses menu)
Esc-Main Menu   Ctrl⏎ Record   Ending Balance: $5,892.75

9. Record the transaction by pressing Enter when the cursor is on the last field, Category, or record the transaction while the cursor is on any transaction field by pressing **Ctrl-Enter** or **F10**. If you're using a mouse, record the check transaction by clicking the words Ctrl-Record at the bottom of the screen, in the information line.

> ### Note
>
> Quicken provides a feature known as *QuickFill*, which you can use when you know the category name. If you type enough of the category name to uniquely identify that name and press Enter, QuickFill types the rest of the category name for you.
>
> Suppose that you have a category named *Utilities*, and it is the only category name that starts with the letter *U*. If you type a **U** in the Category field and press Enter, QuickFill types the remaining letters of the word—**tilities**. The only trick to the QuickFill feature is that you need to type enough of the category name to uniquely identify it from other categories in the Category and Transfer list.
>
> Refer to Chapter 6, "Automating the Register," for more information on QuickFill.

If you press Enter when the cursor is in the last field (Category), Quicken displays a prompt asking you to confirm that you want to record the transaction. If you select Record Transaction, the transaction is recorded.

When you record a transaction, a flashing message in the lower left-hand corner of the screen says RECORDING. (If your computer is very fast, you can hardly read the message.) When Quicken finishes recording the transaction, your computer beeps and an empty row is added to the bottom of the Register, with the cursor positioned at the empty Date field. Because Quicken arranges checking account transactions by date, it rearranges transactions if you enter them in an order other than the order of their dates.

Quicken also calculates the new Balance field when you record a transaction (see fig. 5.6). If the balance is too large for a positive or negative number to display, Quicken displays asterisks in the Balance field. Quicken uses negative numbers to indicate that you have overdrawn your account. If you have a color monitor, Quicken displays negative amounts in a different color.

```
Print/Acct    Edit    Shortcuts    Reports    Activities              F1-Help

 Date   Num    Payee  · Memo  · Category    Payment  C  Deposit     Balance

 8/19  0004  FMCC                            315 67                  147 33
 1993                      Auto:Loan

 8/22        Baldwin Environmental                    6,000 00     6,147 33
 1993 Memo: Consulting Fee
      Cat: Prof. Fees
 8/22  0005  A-1 Transmissions               31 00               6,116 33
 1993        Change Trans. F→Auto:Service

 8/22  0006  Sierra Pacific Power Company    64 98               6,051 35
 1993        July             Utilities:Gas  →

 8/22  0007  Nevada Bell                     34 65               6,016 70
 1993        July             Telephone

 8/22  0008  City of Reno                    23 95               5,992 75
 1993        July             Utilities:Water

Bk.of Amer-1342    (Alt+letter accesses menu)
Esc-Main Menu      Ctrl◄─┘ Record                   Ending Balance:  $5,892.75
```

Fig. 5.6
The Register showing the new balance after a check is recorded.

Recording a Deposit

As you may expect, recording a deposit in the Quicken Register is like recording a deposit in your checkbook's paper register. To record a deposit in the Quicken Register, follow these steps:

> **Note**
>
> Quicken enables you to turn off the beep that you hear when you record a transaction. This is particularly attractive if you're entering several transactions at a time and are becoming annoyed with the constant beeping. To turn off the beep sound, choose Set Preferences from the Main Menu. From the Set Preferenes menu, choose Transaction Settings. Move to the Beep When Recording and Memorizing field and press N. To learn how to access transaction settings and turn off the beep sound, see Chapter 20, "Customizing Quicken."

1. Choose Use Register from Quicken's Main Menu if the Register is not displayed already. Quicken displays the Register screen. If you are working with more than one account, you may need to select the account first (see Chapter 3, "Defining Your Accounts").

2. Enter the deposit date in the Date field in MM/DD/YY format. Remember that you can use the + (plus) and – (minus) keys to change the date one day at a time.

Learning Quicken

3. (Optional) Move the cursor to the Num field. Enter the receipt number of the deposit in this field. Remember that you also can use the + (plus) and – (minus) keys to change the Num field one number at a time.

4. Move the cursor to the Payee field. Enter a description of the deposit transaction. You have space for up to 31 characters. A business recording a deposit from a customer, for example, may describe the deposit by using the customer name, such as *Acme Manufacturing*. A home user recording a payroll deposit may describe the deposit as *Payroll Check*. Interest may be described as *October Interest Income*.

5. Move the cursor through the Payment and C fields to the Deposit field. As with the Payment field, Quicken enables you to enter only numbers, with amounts under $9,999,999.99.

6. (Optional) Move the cursor to the Memo field. Use this field to describe the transaction. You can use up to 31 characters to describe a transaction. A business, for example, may note the invoice number that a customer's deposit relates to. A home user may indicate the payroll period covered by a payroll check.

7. (Optional) Move the cursor to the Category field to assign a category to the deposit transaction, such as *gross sales, wages,* or *interest income.* Press **Ctrl-C** to access the Category and Transfer list, which includes the existing categories provided by Quicken or those you have previously added. Highlight the category you want to assign to the deposit transaction.

   You also can use the Category field to describe the class into which a transaction falls. Categories and classes were described in Chapter 4, "Organizing Your Finances." Figure 5.7 shows a deposit transaction for recording interest income.

8. Record the transaction by pressing **Enter** when the cursor is on the last field, Category, or record the transaction while the cursor is in any field by pressing **Ctrl-Enter** or **F10**. If you're using a mouse, record the transaction by clicking **Ctrl-Record** at the bottom of the screen in the information line.

If you press Enter when the cursor is in the last field (Category) Quicken displays a prompt asking you to confirm that you want to record the transaction. If you select Record Transaction by choosing 1, the transaction is recorded.

```
 Print/Acct    Edit    Shortcuts    Reports    Activities           F1-Help
┌────────────────────────────────────────────────────────────────────────┐
│ Date  Num    Payee  ·  Memo  ·  Category    Payment  C  Deposit   Balance │
├────────────────────────────────────────────────────────────────────────┤
│ 8/19 0004  FMCC                             315 67               147 33↑ │
│ 1993                   Auto:Loan                                         │
│                                                                          │
│ 8/22       Baldwin Environmental                      6,000 00  6,147 33 │
│ 1993 Memo: Consulting Fee                                                │
│      Cat:  Prof. Fees                                                    │
│ 8/22 0005  A-1 Transmissions                 31 00              6,116 33 │
│ 1993       Change Trans. F→Auto:Service                                  │
│                                                                          │
│ 8/22 0006  Sierra Pacific Power Company      64 98              6,051 35 │
│ 1993       July              Utilities:Gas →                            │
│                                                                          │
│ 8/22 0007  Nevada Bell                       34 65              6,016 70 │
│ 1993       July              Telephone                                   │
│                                                                          │
│ 8/22 0008  City of Reno                      23 95              5,992 75 │
│ 1993       July              Utilities:Water                            │
└────────────────────────────────────────────────────────────────────────┘
 Bk.of Amer-1342      (Alt+letter accesses menu)
 Esc-Main Menu     Ctrl←┘ Record                  Ending Balance:  $5,892.75
```

Fig. 5.7
A sample deposit recorded in the Register.

Recording Other Withdrawals

The steps for recording other withdrawals, such as automated teller machine transactions, wire transfers, and automatic payments, parallel the steps for recording a check. You enter the date, number, payee, payment amount, and, optionally, a memo description and a category. Record the withdrawal by pressing **Enter** when the cursor is in the Category field or by selecting **Ctrl-Enter** or **F10** when the cursor is in any other transaction field.

CPA TIP

Consider the monthly service fees a bank charges when choosing a bank and in keeping minimum balances. Most banks charge monthly service fees of about $5. Some banks waive the $5 fee if you keep an average balance of $200 at all times in your account. The $5 a month translates into $60 a year. Because $60 in fee savings equals $60 in interest, the interest rate the bank pays people who keep their minimum balance at $200 is $60/$200 or 30 percent. The return is even better than that for most people because the interest income gets taxed, but the fee savings do not. Probably no other $200 investment in the world is risk-free and pays 30 percent interest.

Recording Transfers Between Accounts

You can use the Category field to record transfers from one account to another. Suppose that you are recording a check drawn on your checking account for deposit to your credit union account with the Acme Credit Union. The check is not an expense, so it should not be categorized as utilities, medical, insurance, or something else. It is a transfer of funds from one account to another. You can identify such transfers by entering the account name in brackets, as shown in figure 5.8.

Fig. 5.8

The Category field completed to record a transfer between accounts.

```
 Print/Acct     Edit     Shortcuts    Reports    Activities          F1-Help
┌──────┬─────┬──────────────────────────────────┬─────────┬─┬─────────┬──────────┐
│ Date │ Num │  Payee  ·  Memo  ·  Category     │ Payment │C│ Deposit │ Balance  │
├──────┼─────┼──────────────────────────────────┼─────────┼─┼─────────┼──────────┤
│ 8/22 │0005 │A-1 Transmissions                 │  31 00  │ │         │ 6,116 33↑│
│ 1993 │     │Change Trans. F→Auto:Service      │         │ │         │          │
│ 8/22 │0006 │Sierra Pacific Power Company       │  64 98  │ │         │ 6,051 35 │
│ 1993 │     │July            Utilities:Gas  →   │         │ │         │          │
│ 8/22 │0007 │Nevada Bell                       │  34 65  │ │         │ 6,016 70 │
│ 1993 │     │July            Telephone         │         │ │         │          │
│ 8/22 │0008 │City of Reno                      │  23 95  │ │         │ 5,992 75 │
│ 1993 │     │July            Utilities:Water   │         │ │         │          │
│ 8/22 │0009 │Deposit to Savings                │ 100 00  │ │         │ 5,892 75 │
│ 1993 │Memo:│                                  │         │ │         │          │
│      │Cat: │[Acme]                            │         │ │         │          │
│ 8/23 │     │                                  │         │ │         │          │
│ 1993 │     │                                  │         │ │         │          │
│      │     │            END                   │         │ │         │          │
└──────┴─────┴──────────────────────────────────┴─────────┴─┴─────────┴──────────┘
 Bk.of Amer-1342    (Alt+letter accesses menu)
 Esc-Main Menu    Ctrl◄┘ Record              Ending Balance:  $5,892.75
```

Be sure that the account has been set up first before you try to transfer to or from the account. Quicken enables you to add categories, but not accounts, while you are using the Register. If you enter a transaction and find that it needs a new account, simply record the transaction without a category; set up the new account, and then come back to place the account the Category Transfer field.

> **Note**
>
> When you click Cat: or press **Ctrl-C**, Quicken lists categories as well as accounts in the Category and Transfer list. Quicken lists categories first (income categories, then expense categories) followed by accounts. Accordingly, you also can click Cat: (Ctrl-C) to see accounts for transfers. Because the accounts are located at the end of the Category and Transfer List, you can access them more quickly by pressing the End key to reach the end of the list. Then highlight the proper account, press **Enter**, and Quicken inserts the account name (enclosed in brackets, such as [Acme]) in the Category field in the Register.

If you record a transfer transaction, Quicken records the transaction in the Registers for both accounts. In the transaction shown in figure 5.8, a payment of $100 is recorded in the checking account and, at the same time, a deposit of $100 is recorded in the Acme savings account. Figure 5.9 shows the Register for the Acme savings account with the $100 deposit. You can toggle between the two Registers by pressing **Ctrl-X**.

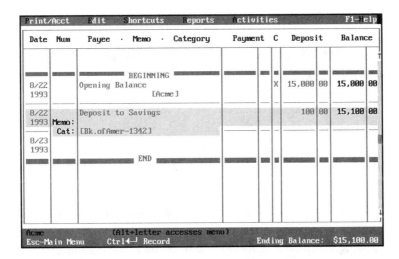

Fig. 5.9

The other part of the transfer transaction shown in Figure 5.8.

Entering Uncleared Transactions

You learned in Chapters 1 and 3 that you should enter the ending balance from your last bank statement as the starting balance in your Quicken bank account. This makes reconciling easy the next time you receive your bank statement and start to reconcile your bank account with Quicken.

Using the balance from your last bank statement, however, doesn't account for transactions that have occurred (before you started using Quicken) but have not been cleared through your bank. In order to accurately reflect your account balance in Quicken, you must enter all uncleared transactions from the date of your last bank statement to the date that you start using Quicken. If your last bank statement was dated 09/15/93, for example, and you started using Quicken on 10/01/93, you must enter all transactions that occurred between 09/15/93 and 10/01/93 in addition to those transactions that occurred prior to 09/15/93 but did not show up on your last statement.

This chapter shows you how to enter check, deposit, and other withdrawal transactions in the Register, which is all you need to know to enter uncleared transactions. Just move to the last empty line in the Register and begin entering uncleared transactions the way you enter any other transaction. Be sure you enter the correct date, check number, or deposit number for each transaction. After you record the transaction by pressing **Ctrl-Enter** or **F10** (or press **Enter** from the Category field of a transaction), Quicken sorts your transactions in the Register and places the transactions you just entered in order by date.

Reviewing and Editing Register Transactions

You can review and edit transactions by accessing the Register at any time. You may want to review a transaction to make sure that you recorded the transaction correctly. You also may want to review a transaction to see whether you received a deposit or to see whether you remembered to pay a particular bill.

You can move from transaction to transaction in the Register screen in two ways—you can use the keyboard or you can use the mouse. You learned about moving around the Register using both the keyboard and mouse earlier in this chapter.

To edit a transaction in the Register, move to the transaction you want to change, edit the fields you want to change, and re-record the transaction by pressing **Ctrl-Enter** or **F10**, by pressing **Enter** while the cursor is in the Category field, or by clicking **Ctrl ↵ Record** at the bottom of the screen in the information line.

If you decide you want to cancel changes that you have made to a transaction, you can do so any time before the changed transaction is recorded. To cancel the changes, choose **Esc**. Quicken displays the Leaving Transaction window, as shown in figure 5.10. Choose **2** to select the Cancel changes and leave option. Quicken enters the original information in the transaction and returns to the Main Menu.

Postdating Transactions

Postdating transactions means that you enter a future date for a check or deposit transaction. Traditionally, people use postdated checks as a way to delay a payment. The payee cannot or should not cash the check before the future date. With Quicken, you can use postdated transactions to delay checks being cashed. Perhaps more importantly, you can forecast your cash flows and balances by entering those checks and deposits that you know are in the future.

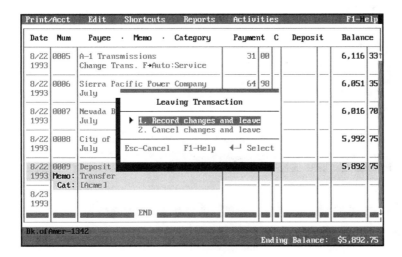

Fig. 5.10
The Leaving Transaction window.

The steps for entering postdated transactions mirror those for entering regular transactions. The only difference, of course, is that the check or deposit date is in the future. When you enter postdated transactions, Quicken calculates two account balances: the current balance, which is the account balance for the current date, and the ending balance, which is the account balance after the last postdated transaction. Quicken determines the current date by looking at the system date. If your computer's system date is incorrect, refer to your DOS user manual to learn how to set or reset the date in your system.

Figure 5.11 shows the 1stNatl Account Register with a postdated transaction. The ending balance, $5,701.41, incorporates all the transactions for the account, including postdated transactions. The current balance, $5,892.75, is the account balance at the current date.

Quicken identifies postdated transactions by drawing a double-dashed line between the current and previous transactions and the postdated transactions. In figure 5.11, notice the double-dashed line between the last two transactions.

Fig. 5.11

The Register
showing a
postdated
transaction.

```
 Print/Acct   Edit   Shortcuts   Reports   Activities              F1-Help

   Date  Num    Payee  ·  Memo  ·  Category    Payment  C  Deposit    Balance

   8/22 0006  Sierra Pacific Power Company       64 98             6,051 35↑
   1993       July              Utilities:Gas →

   8/22 0007  Nevada Bell                        34 65             6,016 70
   1993       July              Telephone

   8/22 0008  City of Reno                       23 95             5,992 75
   1993       July              Utilities:Water

   8/22 0009  Deposit to Savings                100 00             5,892 75
   1993                    [Acme]

   8/26 0010  American Express                  191 34             5,701 41
   1993 Memo: July
        Cat: Entertain

   8/26
   1993
                         END

 Bk.ofAmer-1342     (Alt+letter accesses menu)     Current Balance: $5,892.75
 Esc-Main Menu      Ctrl◄┘ Record                   Ending Balance:  $5,701.41
```

Using QuickReport for Instant Transaction Reports

New to Quicken 7 is a feature called *QuickReport*. Consider using QuickReport
if you would like to see a quick summary of information from the Register
without generating a full report. How to prepare full reports is discussed in
Chapter 12 "Creating and Printing Reports."

You may want to see a list of all checks written to your dentist or all checks
categorized "insurance." You can access this information instantly using
QuickReport.

To access QuickReport, follow these steps:

1. Choose Use **Register** from Quicken's Main Menu if the Register is not
   displayed already.

2. Move the cursor to the items for which you want a report. Quicken
   generates QuickReports for items in any field except Date or Balance.

3. Choose **QuickReport** from the Reports menu, or press **Alt-Z** (see fig. 5.12).
   Quicken displays the QuickReport for the items you want (see fig. 5.13).

4. Choose a transaction shown in the QuickReport, and press **F9** to go to
   it. Press **Esc** to return to the original transaction.

Fig. 5.12
The Reports menu.

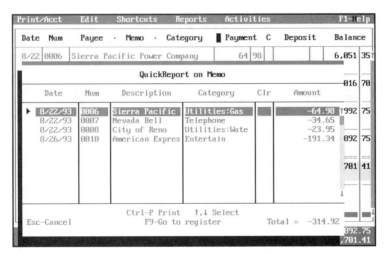

Fig. 5.13
The QuickReport.

Printing the Register

You will want to print a paper register each time you enter a group (perhaps more than five) of check and deposit transactions. A printed copy of the Register enables you to review checking account transactions without turning on your computer. It also can provide a way to recover your financial records if no backup files exist. (Chapter 19, "Managing Your Quicken Files," describes the steps for backing up your Quicken data files.)

To print the Register, follow these steps:

   1. From the Register, choose the Print/Acct menu. Quicken displays the Print/Acct menu (see fig. 5.14).

Fig. 5.14
The Print/Acct
menu.

2. Choose **Print Register**. Quicken displays the Print Register window
   (see fig. 5.15). You also can press **Ctrl-P** rather than first accessing
   the Print/Acct menu to display the Print Register window.

Fig. 5.15
The Print Register
window.

3. Verify that your printer is set to use regular paper, not check forms.

4. In the Print Transactions From field, enter the date of the first check or
   deposit transaction you want printed on the Register. If you are printing only the transactions for the day's batch of transactions, enter the
   Print Transactions From date as the current date. If you are printing a
   copy of the month's transactions, enter the Print Transactions From
   date as the first day of the month. (Remember that the + (plus) and –

(minus) keys change the date one day at a time, that the T letter key sets the date to the current system date, and that the M and H letter keys set the date to the first day and last day of the month.)

5. Move the cursor to the To field. Enter the date of the last check or deposit transaction that you want included in the printed Register. If you are printing only the transactions for the day's batch of transactions, enter the To date as the current date. If you are printing a copy of the month's transactions, enter the To date as the last day of the month.

6. Move the cursor to the Print To field. Use this field to specify which printer will print the Register. Quicken lists up to three printers you may have defined as part of the installation process, and it lists Disk as a fourth option. To specify the setting for the Print To field, enter the number that corresponds to the printer you want to use.

If you press **4** from the Print To field, you can create an ASCII file on disk. Quicken displays the Print To Disk window, which collects the file name you want to use for the ASCII file, the number of lines per page, and the page width. Enter the name you want Quicken to use for the ASCII file in the DOS File field. If you want to use a data directory different from the Quicken data directory, QUICKEN, you also can specify a path name. (See your DOS user's manual for information on path names.) Set the number of Register lines Quicken prints between page breaks in the Lines per Page field. If you are using 11-inch paper, the page length is usually 66 lines. Set the number of characters, including blanks, that Quicken prints on a line in the Width field. If you are using 8 1/2-inch paper, the Characters per Line figure usually is 80. Figure 5.16 shows the Print To Disk window.

7. (Optional) Move the cursor to the Title (optional) field. Enter a special title or description you want Quicken to print at the top of each page of the Register. You may, for example, enter **August Check Register** for August's Register.

8. (Optional) Move the cursor to the Print One Transaction per Line field. Choose **Y** if you want Quicken to print the Register in a compact form using only one line per transaction and using abbreviations for many of the fields.

Fig. 5.16
The Print To Disk
window.

9. (Optional) Move the cursor to the Print Transaction Splits field. If you *split* transactions (using more than one category for the transaction), you can instruct Quicken to print each of those categories by choosing **Y** from this field (see Chapter 6, "Automating the Register," to learn about split transactions).

10. (Optional) Move the cursor to the Sort by Check Number field. Usually, Quicken arranges the check and deposit transactions by date. You can, however, choose **Y** to arrange transactions by the check numbers. If a check deposit does not have a number or has the same number as another transaction, Quicken uses the date as a secondary sorting tool.

11. When the Print Register window is complete and you are ready to print, choose **Ctrl-Enter**.

CPA TIP

At the end of each month, print a copy of the Register for the transactions you entered in that month. Store the Register with the bank statement for the month. This way, if you ever have questions about a previous month—or the bad luck to lose your Quicken data file—you can reconstruct transactions from previous months. You can discard the now redundant individual Registers that show each of the groups of transactions for the month. You don't need these with a copy of the entire month.

Summary

This chapter introduces you to Quicken's Register—the central repository of all your checking account information. The basics include knowing the components of the Check Register screen; using the Register to record checks, deposits, and other checking account transactions; reviewing and editing Register transactions; and printing the Register.

The next chapter describes Quicken features that you can use to make working in the Register more efficient and easier.

Learning Quicken

Chapter 6

Automating the Register

This chapter can help you work more efficiently with Registers by describing the Quicken features you can use to enter transactions quickly and easily. These features can help you enter transactions quickly, search through your Register for specific transactions, or save and reuse information you record repeatedly in your Register. Editing features makes it easier for you to add, modify, and remove transactions; special shortcut options offer features that speed up the process of recording transactions.

Using QuickFill

You can enter transactions in the Register faster and easier than ever with the *QuickFill* feature in Quicken 7. When you type a few characters in a field, Quicken searches the various lists and the Register (the last three months of transactions is the default setting) to find a matching entry in that particular field. When Quicken finds a match, the QuickFill feature fills in the rest of the transaction with the transaction information it found.

QuickFill works while entering transactions when you make an entry in the Payee field or the Category field in the Register or Write Checks screen. QuickFill also works when you enter investment transactions in the Investment Register. This chapter, however, is limited to a discussion of using QuickFill in a Noninvestment Register. See Chapter 16, "Monitoring Your Investments," to see how QuickFill works when entering investment transactions. See Chapter 8, "Automating Check Writing," to see how QuickFill works when writing checks from the Write Checks screen.

In this chapter, you learn how to do the following:

■ Fill in transaction information

■ Delete and void transactions in the Register

■ Insert a transaction in the Register

■ Split transactions

■ Find transactions in the Register

■ Work with memorized transactions

■ Use the Scheduled Transactions feature

■ Switch between the Check Register and the Write Checks screen

Note

QuickFill does not work when you edit an existing transaction.

QuickFill is turned on or activated by default. When you first start to use Quicken 7, this feature should already be working. Refer to the *Deactivating QuickFill* section, later in this chapter, to learn how to turn on and off QuickFill.

Using QuickFill from the Payee Field

Quicken searches the Memorized Transaction List (you learn about memorized transactions later in this chapter) and the last three months of transactions in the Register when you type a few characters in the Payee field of a transaction, whether in the Register or the Write Checks screen. (You learn about using QuickFill from the Write Checks screen in Chapter 8, "Automating Check Writing.") When Quicken finds a transaction with the same payee name, QuickFill fills in the rest of the payee name from the transaction it found in the Memorized Transaction List or the previous transactions in the Register.

Follow these steps to use QuickFill from the Payee field:

1. In the empty transaction line of the Register, enter the date and transaction number as usual.

2. Type a few characters in the Payee field. Type **PS**, for example. Quicken searches the Memorized Transaction List and the last three months of transactions in the Register for a payee name that starts with *PS*. When Quicken finds the first transaction with the payee *PSI Utilities*, for example, QuickFill fills in the rest of the payee name.

3. If the payee name (*PSI Utilities*, in this example) is indeed the payee you want to enter in the transaction, press **Enter** and QuickFill fills in the rest of the transaction information for that payee: the transaction amount, the Memo field (if used), and the category or subcategory exactly like the transaction that Quicken found.

If Quicken finds the matching transaction in the Memorized Transaction List, it displays <MEM> next to the payee name. If Quicken finds the matching transaction in the Register, the month and day (<month/day>) appear next to the payee name.

If QuickFill doesn't fill in the payee information that you want, keep typing characters in the Payee field or press **Ctrl-+** (plus) or **Ctrl--** (minus) to keep searching the Memorized Transaction List or the transactions in the Register for the correct transaction.

> **Note**
>
> If more than one payee name exists in the Memorized Transaction List or previous transaction in the Register that begins with the characters that you type, QuickFill enters the transaction information for the first payee name found.

Figure 6.1 shows a transaction filled in by QuickFill from the Memorized Transaction List. Figure 6.2 shows a transaction filled from a transaction dated 8/23 in the Register.

Fig. 6.1
A transaction filled in by Quickfill from the Memorized Transaction List.

After QuickFill fills in the transaction, you can edit any of the transaction fields. When the transaction information is the way you want it, record the transaction by pressing **Ctr'·Enter** or **F10**.

Using QuickFill to Fill in the Category Field

QuickFill also works when you type a few characters in the Category field of a new transaction. (QuickFill does not work when editing an existing transaction.) QuickFill searches the Category and Transfer List for the first category or transfer account that begins with the characters you type. If you want to enter a subcategory or a class, you can type a colon (:) after the category name is filled in and Quicken searches the subcategories under that particular category and enters the first subcategory that it finds. If you want to enter a class, you can type a slash (/) and a few characters after the category or subcategory name is filled in. Quicken then searches the Class list and enters the first class it finds that begins with the characters you type. Classes were explained in Chapter 4, "Organizing Your Finances."

Fig. 6.2

A transaction filled in by QuickFill from a transaction in the register.

To use QuickFill to fill in the Category field, follow these steps:

1. From the Category field for a new transaction in the Register, type a few characters of the category name that you want to assign to the transaction. Quicken searches the Category and Transfer List for the first category or transfer account that matches the characters you type.

   When Quicken finds a matching category or transfer account, QuickFill fills in the rest of the category or transfer account name.

2. If this is the category or transfer account that you want to assign to the transaction, press **Enter** to accept it.

   If the category or transfer account name filled in by QuickFill is not the one that you want, type a few more characters or press **Ctrl-+** (plus) or **Ctrl--** (minus) until Quicken finds the right name.

3. To enter a subcategory after QuickFill fills in the category name, press **End** to go to the end of the category name and type : (colon). QuickFill fills in the first subcategory for the category that it just filled in. If the subcategory is not the one that you want, type a few more characters or press **Ctrl-+** (plus) or **Ctrl--** (minus) to find the next or preceding subcategory under the category. Press **Enter** to accept the subcategory.

4. To enter class information, type / (slash) after the category or subcat-
    egory name QuickFill filled in and type a few characters of the class
    name. QuickFill searches the Class list and fills in the first class that
    begins with the characters you type. To accept the class, press **Enter**.
    If the class is not the one that you want, type a few more characters or
    press **Ctrl-+** (plus) or **Ctrl--** (minus) to find the next or preceding class.
    To enter a subclass, type a colon after the class name and QuickFill fills
    in the first subclass for the class that it just filled in. Press **Ctrl-+** (plus)
    or **Ctrl--** (minus) to find the next or preceding subclass under the class.
    Press **Enter** to accept the subclass.

> **Note**
>
> If the category or class that you want to assign to a transaction is not in the
> Category and Transfer list or the Class List (because they're new), you can add
> a new category or class simply by typing the new name in the Category field.
> When you press **Enter** after the new category or class name, Quicken asks if
> you want to add it to the Category or Class list or choose a category or class
> from the existing list. To add the category or class, choose option 1, Add to
> Category List or Add to Class List, and go through the normal steps for adding
> categories and classes.

Deactivating QuickFill

If you don't want to use the QuickFill feature, perhaps because you have
varied transactions that are rarely the same or because you feel more comfortable typing transaction information on your own, you can deactivate or turn
off the QuickFill feature.

To deactivate QuickFill, follow these steps:

1. From the Quicken Main Menu, choose Set **Preferences**. The Set Prefer-
    ences menu appears.

2. Choose General Settings. Quicken displays the General Settings window
    (see fig. 6.3).

3. Move the cursor to the Activate QuickFill Feature field, and choose Y
    or N for this setting.

4. Choose Continue (or press **Ctrl-Enter**) to save the Activate QuickFill
    Feature setting.

5. Press **Esc** to return to the Main Menu.

Fig. 6.3

The General
Settings window.

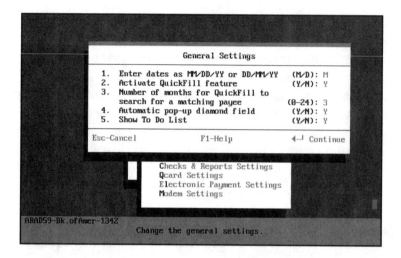

The QuickFill feature now is turned off. You can go back and activate it again if you decide that you want to use it by selecting Y from the Activate QuickFill Feature field.

Changing the Number of Months Quicken Searches for Transactions

Prior to Quicken 7, QuickFill only searched the last three months of transactions for a matching entry. In Quicken 7, you can search as far back as 24 months for a matching transaction. You should be aware, however, that if you set the feature to something greater than three months, it could slow down Quicken's performance.

To change the default setting of three months, follow these steps:

1. From the Quicken Main Menu, choose Set Preferences. The Set Preferences menu appears.

2. Choose General Settings. Quicken displays the General Settings window (refer to fig. 6.3).

3. Move the cursor to the Number of Months for QuickFill to Search for a matching payee option.

4. Enter a number between 0 and 24 for the number of months that you what QuickFill to search. If you enter 0, this is another method to deactivate QuickFill.

5. Choose Continue (or press **Ctrl-Enter**) to save your setting.

6. Press **Esc** to return to the Main Menu.

Deleting a Transaction from the Register

Quicken enables you to delete a transaction you inadvertently entered twice, entered in the wrong account Register, and so on. When you delete a transaction, it is removed permanently from the Register.

You should delete a recorded transaction only under the following conditions:

- *You inadvertently enter a transaction that should not be entered at all.* If you enter a deposit transaction in the Register and subsequently do not make the deposit, for example, you should delete the transaction. Or, if you enter a transaction for a bank fee in the Register that is later rescinded by the bank, delete the bank fee transaction.

- *You duplicate transaction information.* If you withdraw funds from an automatic teller machine and enter the transaction twice in the Register, for example, you should delete one of the two transactions.

- *You enter a transaction in the wrong Quicken Register.* (Quicken provides a Register for each account that you set up.) If you enter a credit card payment (that you make manually) in the Register for your checking account but want to track your credit card purchases in the Credit Card Register, you should delete the transaction from the Checking Account Register and enter the credit card information in the Credit Card Register.

In all other cases, you should void or reverse transactions in the Register so that you have complete records of all of your check numbers and have established a proper *audit trail* (a history of each and every transaction) in the Register.

To delete a transaction, follow these steps:

1. Access the Register for your checking account.

2. Highlight the transaction you want to delete.

3. Choose **Delete Transaction** from the **Edit** menu or press **Ctrl-D** (see fig. 6.4).

Tip

You should not delete transactions for manual checks or for checks that you have written with Quicken. When you delete a transaction, Quicken removes all record of the transaction. If the transaction involves a check, deleting the transaction removes the check information and leaves a gap in your check-numbering sequence. Information for voided transactions remains in the Register so that you can track each prenumbered check. You learn how to void a transaction in this chapter and how to void a check in Chapter 7, "Writing and Printing Checks."

Learning Quicken

Fig. 6.4

The Edit menu.

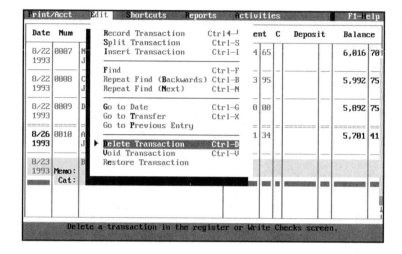

Quicken displays the OK to Delete Transaction? window shown in figure 6.5.

Fig. 6.5

The OK to Delete Transaction? window.

4. Choose 1 to delete the transaction or 2 if you don't want to delete the transaction.

When you delete a transaction, Quicken removes all transaction information from the Register.

> **Note**
>
> If you delete a transaction from one Quicken account that is part of a transfer transaction (where you transferred funds from one Quicken account to another), the corresponding transaction in the other account also is deleted.
>
> If you try to delete a transaction that is part of a split transfer transaction, you must delete the transaction from the account where the transaction originated. In other words, the account in which you entered the transfer transaction.
>
> To quickly find the corresponding transfer transaction, choose Go to Transfer from the Edit menu. See the *Using the Go to Transfer Option* section, later in this chapter.

Voiding a Transaction in the Register

You may need to void a check when you want to stop payment, when you lose a check and write another one to replace it, or when a check prints incorrectly and you need to print another. Note that you can choose to void a check from the Write Checks screen; however, when you choose the Void transaction option from the Write Checks screen, Quicken takes you to the Checking Account Register and enables you to void the check transaction from there.

If you void a transaction that is part of a transfer from one account to another, voiding any part of the transaction also voids the other parts of the transaction (those recorded in the other Registers).

To void a check from the Checking Account Register, follow these steps:

1. Access the Register.

2. Highlight the transaction for the check you want to void. If you are voiding a manual check you have not yet entered in the Register, enter the date and check number in the last empty transaction line. Keep this transaction highlighted as you move to the next step.

3. Choose Void Transaction from the Edit menu or press **Ctrl-V** (refer to fig. 6.4). Quicken displays the OK to Void Transaction? window shown in figure 6.6.

Fig. 6.6
The OK to Void
Transaction?
window.

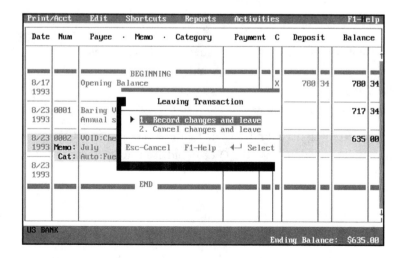

4. Choose **1** to void the transaction or **2** if you decide not to void the transaction.

   Quicken enters the word VOID: in the Payee field before the payee name and marks the transaction with an X in the Clear column so that the transaction is not considered an uncleared item when you perform your account reconciliation.

5. Quicken also gives you another chance to change your mind. When you attempt to move to the next transaction, Quicken displays the Leaving Transaction window shown in figure 6.7. Choose **1** and Quicken will void the transaction as shown in figure 6.8, or choose **2** and Quicken will leave the transaction intact in the Register.

Fig. 6.7
The Leaving
Transaction
window.

```
 rint/Acct    Edit    Shortcuts    Reports    Activities              F1-Help
 ┌─────┬────┬─────────────────────────────┬─────────┬─┬─────────┬─────────┐
 │Date │Num │ Payee  ·  Memo  ·  Category  │ Payment │C│ Deposit │ Balance │
 ├─────┼────┼─────────────────────────────┼─────────┼─┼─────────┼─────────┤
 │8/22 │0006│Sierra Pacific Power Company  │  64 98  │ │         │ 6,051 35│
 │1993 │    │July              Utilities:Gas →                            │
 │     │    │                             │         │ │         │         │
 │8/22 │0007│Nevada Bell                  │  34 65  │ │         │ 6,016 70│
 │1993 │    │July             Telephone   │         │ │         │         │
 │     │    │                             │         │ │         │         │
 │8/22 │0008│City of Reno                 │  23 95  │ │         │ 5,992 75│
 │1993 │    │July            Utilities:Water                              │
 │     │    │                             │         │ │         │         │
 │8/22 │0009│Deposit to Savings           │ 100 00  │ │         │ 5,892 75│
 │1993 │    │              [Acme]         │         │ │         │         │
 │═════│════│═════════════════════════════│═════════│═│═════════│═════════│
 │8/26 │0010│VOID:American Express        │         │X│         │ 5,892 75│
 │1993 │Memo│July                         │         │ │         │         │
 │     │Cat:│Entertain                    │         │ │         │         │
 │     │    │                             │         │ │         │         │
 │8/23 │    │                             │         │ │         │         │
 │1993 │    │                             │         │ │         │         │
 │     │    │          END                │         │ │         │         │
 ├─────┴────┴────────────────────────────┴────────┴─┴────────┴──────────┤
 │Bk.ofAmer~1342     (Alt+letter accesses menu)  Current Balance: $5,892.75│
 │Esc-Main Menu    Ctrl◄┘ Record                 Ending Balance:  $5,892.75│
 └──────────────────────────────────────────────────────────────────────┘
```

Fig. 6.8
The Register with
a voided check
transaction.

> **Note**
>
> When you void a check, Quicken erases the amount of the transaction and adjusts
> your checking account balance. Quicken also subtracts the amount of the voided
> check from the category that was originally assigned to the check transaction.

Inserting a Transaction in the Register

You can insert an empty transaction line anywhere in the Register. When you
insert a line, Quicken inserts the transaction line above the currently highlighted transaction line. You can use this empty transaction line to record
another transaction. Usually, transactions are recorded in the empty transaction line at the end of the Register, however.

To insert a transaction in the Register, follow these steps:

1. Access the Register.

2. Highlight the transaction line just below the place in which you want
   to insert a transaction.

3. Choose Insert Transaction from the Edit menu or press **Ctrl-I**. Quicken
   inserts an empty transaction line just above the highlighted line.

> **Note**
>
> When you enter and record a transaction in an inserted transaction line, Quicken sorts the transactions and moves it, if necessary, in proper date order. You therefore should not bother inserting transactions unless you insert them in the proper date order in the Register.

Splitting Transactions

In Chapter 5, "Using the Register," you learned how to enter transactions in the Register and how to assign a category to a single transaction. But what happens when you write a check for an expense that covers more than one category, such as the check you write to the bank to pay a mortgage payment that pays principal, interest, insurance, and property taxes? In this case, you need to *split the transaction*, or assign more than one category or subcategory to the transaction. (Subcategories further divide a category into second-, third-, fourth-level categories, and so on. You may want to divide the Utilities category so that you can track expenses for electricity, gas, and water, for example. Subcategories are explained in more detail in Chapter 4, "Organizing Your Finances."

> **Note**
>
> You can split transactions when you write a check from the Write Checks screen or enter a manual check in the Register. Quicken enables you to assign up to 30 categories or subcategories to a single transaction.

A transaction line in the Register screen provides one field to assign a category or subcategory. Occasionally, however, you need to be able to break down a transaction into multiple categories, such as in the mortgage payment example. Choosing Split Transaction from the Edit menu provides additional Category fields so that you can assign more than one category to a transaction or further describe a transaction.

To split a transaction, follow these steps:

1. From the Register, choose **Split Transaction** from the Edit menu, or press **Ctrl-S**. The Split Transaction window appears (see fig. 6.9).

```
 Print/Acct    Edit    Shortcuts    Reports    Activities        F1-Help
┌─────┬────┬──────────────────────────────┬─────────┬─┬─────────┬──────────┐
│ Date│ Num│  Payee  ·  Memo  ·  Category  │ Payment │C│ Deposit │ Balance  │
├─────┼────┼──────────────────────────────┼─────────┼─┼─────────┼──────────┤
│ 8/22│0006│Sierra Pacific Power Company   │   64 98 │ │         │ 6,051 35 │
│ 1993│Memo:│July                          │         │ │         │          │
│     │Cat:│Utilities:Gas & Electric        │         │ │         │          │
│ 8/22│0007│Nevada Bell                    │   34 65 │ │         │ 6,016 70 │
└─────┴────┴──────────────────────────────┴─────────┴─┴─────────┴──────────┘
                            Split Transaction                            ─
                                                                        5
            Category                        Memo              Amount
        1:Utilities:Gas & Electric                            64.98↑
        2:                                                        5
        3:                                                        │
        4:                                                        │
        5:                                                        5
        6:                                                        ↓
            Enter categories, descriptions, and amounts
    Esc-Cancel    Ctrl-D Delete    F9-Recalc Transaction Total    Ctrl◄─┘ Done

 Bk.of Amer-1342                        Current Balance:  $5,892.75
                                        Ending Balance:  $5,892.75
```

Fig. 6.9
The Split
Transaction
window.

2. Enter the category name in the Category field for the first line in the
   Split Transaction window. You use this field in this window the same
   way as the Category field in the Register screen. You also can use the
   Category field to record transfers to other accounts. The Split Transaction window provides 30 lines in which you can assign multiple
   categories to a transaction.

> **Note**
>
> Remember that Quicken provides defined Home and Business categories. You
> selected one of these lists when you set up your Quicken system (see Chapter
> 1, "Preparing To Use Quicken"). The Home Category list contains descriptions
> for most general household expenses, and the Business Category list has
> general business income and expense categories. Press **Ctrl-C** to view and
> select from a list of the defined categories for the Split Transaction window.

3. (Optional) Move the cursor to the Memo field in the first line of the
   Split Transaction window. Type a description of the category or the
   amount in this field. The Memo field provides a 27-character space for
   further description of a transaction or an explanation of your category
   choice.

4. Move the cursor to the Amount field. You use this field in two ways,
   depending on whether you choose Split Transaction before or after you
   enter the payment or deposit amount in the Register screen.

Tip
Usually, you want
to enter dollar
amounts in the
Split Transaction
window's Amount
fields. You also
can enter percent-
ages. Quicken
then uses these
percentages to
calculate the split
amount and enters
the result in the
Amount field. If
you enter a check
for $150 in the
Payment field of
the Register, for
example, and 30
percent of this
should be entered
in the first split
transaction
Amount field, you
can just type **30%**
in the Amount
field. When you
press **Tab** or **Enter**
to move to the
next field,
Quicken calculates
the number that
equals 30 percent
of $150 and enters
this resulting
value in the field.

■ If you select Split Transaction before you enter an amount in the Amount field, Quicken adds each of the amounts you enter in the Amount fields in the Split Transaction window. Quicken then takes the total of these amounts and enters that total in the Payment or the Deposit field of the Register screen. If the total of the split transaction amounts is negative, Quicken places the amount in the Payment field; if the total is positive, Quicken places the amount in the Deposit field.

■ If you choose Split Transaction after you enter the payment or deposit amount in the Register screen, Quicken copies the amount entered into the Split Transaction window into the first Amount field. When you enter the Register amount as a payment, Quicken copies the amount into the Split Transaction window as a negative number; when you enter the amount as a deposit, Quicken copies the amount into the Split Transaction window as a positive number. If you then overwrite the first Amount field in the Split Transaction window with another amount, Quicken calculates the difference between the Register screen amount and the amount you have entered and places this difference in the second Amount field in the Split Transaction window.

5. Move the cursor to the next line in the Split Transaction window. Repeat steps 3, 4, and 5 for each category and amount combination you want to record. You can record up to 30 category and amount combinations.

If you use all 30 of the Split Transaction Amount fields, the sum of the split transaction amounts may not equal the Register amount. In this case, you must adjust manually the Register screen amount or one of the Split Transaction window amounts. You also can press **F9** to recalculate the total of the amounts in the Amount fields in the Split Transaction window and to insert that total into the Payment or Deposit field in the Register.

6. When the categories and amounts in the Split Transaction window are complete, choose **Ctrl-Enter** to save the information in the Split Transaction window and return to the Register.

7. After you return to the Register from the Split Transaction window, choose **Ctrl-Enter** to record the split transaction in the Register. Quicken indicates that a transaction is split by displaying the word SPLIT below the check or transaction number (see fig. 6.10).

```
 Print/Acct    Edit    Shortcuts    Reports    Activities           F1-Help

  Date  Num    Payee  ·  Memo  ·  Category    Payment  C  Deposit   Balance

  8/22 0006   Sierra Pacific Power Company     64 98              6,051 35
  1993 SPLIT  July
       Cat:  Utilities:Gas & Electric
  8/22 0007   Nevada Bell                      34 65              6,016 70
  1993        July                  Telephone

  8/22 0008   City of Reno                     23 95              5,992 75
  1993        July              Utilities:Water

  8/22 0009   Deposit to Savings              100 00              5,892 75
  1993                       [Acme]

  8/26 0010   VOID:American Express               X               5,892 75
  1993        July              Entertain

  8/23
  1993
                          END

 Bk.of Amer-1342      (Alt+letter accesses menu)   Current Balance: $5,892.75
 Esc-Main Menu    Ctrl◄┘ Record                    Ending Balance:  $5,892.75
```

Fig. 6.10
Quicken identifies split transactions with the word SPLIT under the check or transaction number in the Num field.

If you split transactions, you may want to see the extra category names, memos, and amounts on the printed version of the Register. When you choose **Print Register** from the Acct/Print menu, the Print Register window includes a Print Transaction Splits field that you can use to indicate whether you want to print the category, memo, and amounts for each line in a split transaction. (See Chapter 5, "Using the Register," for more information on printing the Register.)

Entering Negative Amounts in Split Transactions

You can enter negative amounts in split transactions to represent withholdings for payroll checks or amounts deducted from a deposit, for example. To enter a negative amount in the Split Transaction window, just press the - (minus) key before you enter the amount. Figure 6.11 shows the Split Transaction window with negative amounts for a payroll check.

Fig. 6.11

The Split Transaction window with negative amounts.

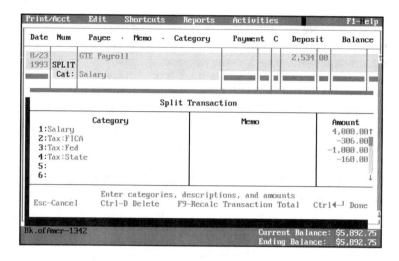

Calculating Transaction Amounts in Split Transactions

When entering a split transaction, you can have Quicken calculate the transaction amount as you are entering lines in the Split Transaction window. To have Quicken calculate the transaction amount, follow these steps:

1. Enter the transaction information (except for the amount) into the Register.

2. For check or payment transactions, position the cursor on the blank Payment field. For deposit transactions, position the cursor on the blank Deposit field.

3. Choose **Split** Transaction from the Edit menu, or press **Ctrl-S**. The Split Transaction window appears.

4. Enter the information in the Split Transaction window. As you enter amounts, Quicken fills in the Payment or Deposit field with the total amount in the Split Transaction window.

5. When you finish entering lines in the Split Transaction window, choose **Ctrl-Enter** to return to the transaction in the Register. If you need to return to the Split Transaction window to make a change, press **Ctrl-S** and make the necessary changes and then choose **Ctrl-Enter** again. Quicken does not record the split transaction until you return to the Register and record the transaction from there (as in step 6).

6. Choose **Ctrl-Enter** or **F10** to record the split transaction and the transaction amount in the Register.

Editing Split Transactions

You can change the information in the Split Transaction window just as you can change any other transaction. To edit a split transaction, follow these steps:

1. Highlight the split transaction in the Register.

2. Choose **S**plit Transaction from the Edit menu, or press **Ctrl-S**. The Split Transaction window appears.

3. Make any necessary changes to categories, memos, or amounts in the Split Transaction window. Move the cursor to the last line in the Split Transaction window. Note that if you change an amount, the Split Transaction window may not balance (the total amount in the Split Transaction window will not equal the transaction amount in the Register). If necessary, you can press **F9** to recalculate the transaction amount. Do not press F9 to recalculate if the amount in the Payment or Deposit field in the Register is the correct amount and you're just reallocating amounts to categories or subcategories in the Split Transaction window. To delete a line in the Split Transaction window, highlight the line you want to delete, and then press **Ctrl-D**. To delete all lines, press **Ctrl-D** at each line.

4. After making changes in the Split Transaction window, choose **Ctrl-Enter** to save the changes and to return to the split transaction in the Register.

5. Choose **Ctrl-Enter** to record the changed split transaction.

Deleting Split Transactions

Just as you can delete transactions with only one category or subcategory assigned to it, you also can delete split transactions. Use the same discretion when deleting a split transaction that you use for deleting a transaction assigned to only one category or subcategory as explained in the section *Deleting a Transaction from the Register*, earlier in this chapter.

You delete split transactions the same way you delete single-category transactions. To delete a split transaction, follow these steps:

1. Highlight the split transaction you want to delete.

2. Choose Delete Transaction from the Edit menu. Quicken displays the OK to Delete Transaction? window.

3. Choose **1** to delete the split transaction or choose **2** if you decide that you don't want to delete the split transaction.

When you want to track your income and expenses closely, enter split transactions for payments to department stores, discount stores, and so on where you purchase different types of items. If you don't split the transaction to record a check to Wal-Mart where you buy hardware, cleaning supplies, office supplies, and so on, for example, and lump the total check transaction into one category, your expenses are not reflected accurately.

> **Note**
>
> If you try to delete a transaction that is part of a split transfer transaction (where one part of the split transaction transfers funds from one Quicken account to another), you must delete the transaction from the account where the transaction originated; in other words, the account that you entered the split transfer transaction in. Use the Go to Transfer option to locate the split transfer transaction (see the *Using the Go to Transfer Option* section, later in this chapter). After you locate the split transfer transaction, press **Ctrl-S** to open the Split Transaction window, highlight the transfer transaction, and press **Ctrl-D** to delete the transaction. Quicken then deletes the corresponding transaction in the other account.

Undoing Split Transactions

After you split a transaction, you can go back, undo the split, and assign only one category or subcategory to the transaction. To undo a split transaction, follow these steps:

1. Highlight the split transaction you want to undo.

2. Choose **Split Transaction** from the Edit menu, or press **Ctrl-S**. The Split Transaction window appears.

3. Delete each line in the Split Transaction window by highlighting the line, and then pressing **Ctrl-D**.

4. After you delete all the lines you want, press **Esc** to return to the transaction in the Register. Notice that Quicken removes the word SPLIT from the Num field.

5. Enter one category or subcategory in the Category field.

6. Choose **Ctrl-Enter** or **F10** to record the transaction.

Finding Transactions

You may write only a handful of checks and make only one or two deposits a month. Even with such low volumes, however, you soon will have several dozen of transactions in a Register. As you write more checks and make additional deposits, searching through your Register for specific transactions becomes more and more difficult. You eventually may want to know whether you recorded a deposit or paid a bill, or when you last paid a vendor. Quicken provides the Find option to locate specific transactions.

You can use the Find option (on the Edit menu) to search through the Register for transactions using the following transaction fields: Num, Payee, Payment, C (Cleared), Deposit, Memo, or Category. Quicken provides another option—the **Go to Date** option (also on the Edit menu)—to locate transactions using the Date field. You learn about finding transactions with specific dates in the *Using the Go to Date Option* section, later in this chapter. You can look for transactions where the payee is *Stouffer's Office Supplies*, where the category is *Utilities*, or where the amount is *$88.44*, for example.

Using the Find Option

To locate quickly a specific transaction or group of transactions you recorded in the Register or Write Checks screen, follow these steps:

1. Choose Find from the Edit menu or press **Ctrl-F**. Quicken displays the Transaction to Find window shown in figure 6.12.

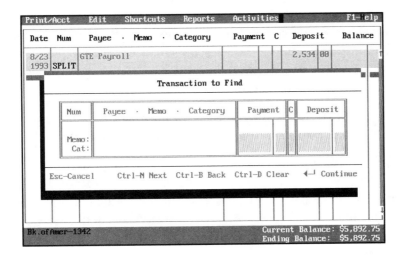

Fig. 6.12

The Transaction to Find window.

2. (Optional) To search through the Register for a transaction with a specific check or transaction number, enter that number in the Num field.

3. (Optional) To search through the Register for checks to a certain payee or a deposit from a particular source, type the payee or source name in the Payee field.

4. (Optional) To search through the Register for a transaction equal to a specific amount, enter the amount in the Payment or the Deposit field. The amount you look for is called a *search argument*.

   If you enter an amount in the Payment field in the Transaction to Find window, Quicken searches through the checks in the Register for that amount. If you enter an amount in the Deposit field, Quicken searches for that amount among the deposits in the Register. If Quicken finds a transaction that matches your search argument, it highlights that transaction on the Register screen.

5. To search through the Register C (cleared) field, type a period (.). To find uncleared transactions (for which the C field is blank), and to find reconciled transactions, enter an X. To find transactions that are cleared but not yet reconciled, enter an asterisk (*)

6. (Optional) To search through the Register for checks or deposits with a specific memo or description, type that memo or description in the Memo field.

7. (Optional) To search through the Register for checks or deposits assigned to a specific category or subcategory, enter the category or subcategory name in the Category field. Alternatively, you can press **Ctrl-C** to display the Category and Transfer list and select a category, subcategory, or transfer account from the list.

8. When you finish entering the search argument or arguments in the Transaction to Find window, choose Continue (**Ctrl-Enter**) or **F10**.

   Quicken asks in which direction you want to search by displaying the Search Direction? window shown in figure 6.13. Find backwards (**Ctrl-B**) searches through transactions with dates earlier than the transaction highlighted in the Register. Find next (**Ctrl-N**) searches through transactions with dates later than the date of the transaction highlighted in the Register.

9. Choose 1. Find backwards or 2. Find next.

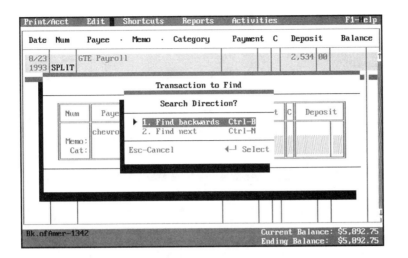

Fig. 6.13
The Search
Direction?
window.

Quicken searches for a transaction that matches exactly the information or search argument you entered in the Transaction to Find window. If you enter an asterisk (*) in the C field, for example, Quicken searches for those transactions in the Register that you marked as cleared with an asterisk. If you enter *Chris Katz* in the Payee field, Quicken searches for transactions with the payee *Chris Katz*. Quicken does not recognize case; *CHRIS KATZ*, *chris katz*, and *cHRIS kATZ* are all exact matches from Quicken's perspective. If the Payee field is *Christopher Katz*, *C. Katz*, or *Mr. Chris Katz*, however, Quicken does not find the transaction.

If Quicken does not find any matches, it will ask you if you want to continue the search to the end of the Register (if you had asked it to search backwards by pressing **Ctrl-B**).

If you asked Quicken to search forwards (by pressing **Ctrl-N**), and no matches are found, it will ask you if you want to continue searching from the beginning of the Register.

If Quicken then does not find a transaction that matches your search argument, the program displays the message No matching transactions were found, as shown in figure 6.14.

Tip
To clear the entries in the transaction to Find window, press **Ctrl-D**.

Fig. 6.14
The No matching transactions were found message.

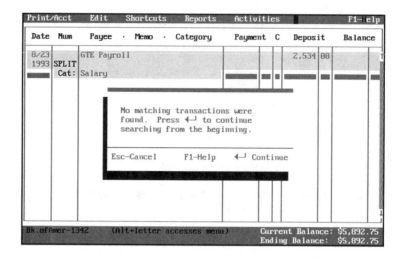

Using Key-Word Matches. *Key-word matches* enable you to search a field that includes or excludes certain letters, characters, or series of characters. Key-word matches use three characters: the period (.), question mark (?), and tilde (~). Periods are wild-card indicators that can represent any character, a group of characters, or even no characters. The question mark represents any character. The tilde identifies a word, character, or characters you want to exclude from your search. If you want to find transactions that don't include the word *Interest*, for example, enter the tilde character before the word interest (*~interest*) as the search argument. Table 6.1 in the following section summarizes what various search arguments do and do not find.

Table 6.1 Summary of Search Arguments Using Special Characters

Argument	What It Finds	What It Does Not Find
..interest	Interest Car loan interest Mortgage interest	Car loan Interest expense Mortgage expense War loan
interest..	Interest Interest expense	Car loan Car loan interest Mortgage expense Mortgage interest War loan
..interest..	Interest Car loan interest Interest expense Mortgage interest	Car loan Mortgage expense War loan

Argument	What It Finds	What It Does Not Find
~..interest	Car loan Interest expense Mortgage expense War loan	Interest Car loan interest Mortgage interest
~interest..	Car loan Car loan interest Mortgage expense Mortgage interest War loan	Interest Interest expense
~..interest..	Car loan Mortgage expense War loan	Car loan interest Interest Interest expense Mortgage interest
?ar loan	Car loan War loan	Car loan interest Interest Interest expense Mortgage expense Mortgage interest
~?ar loan	Interest Car loan interest Interest expense Mortgage expense Mortgage interest	Car loan War loan

Combining Exact and Key-Word Matches. You can search transactions using more than one exact match or key-word argument. Figure 6.15 shows the Transaction to Find window set to search for transactions with the phrase *Big National Bank* in the Payee field and an asterisk (*) in the Cleared field.

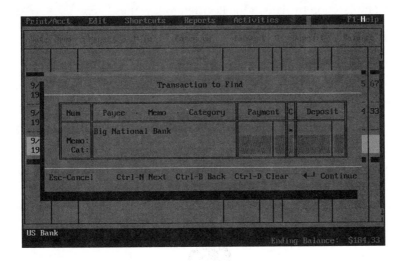

Fig. 6.15
Searching for transactions that include the phrase Big National Bank in the Payee field.

If you use more than one exact match or key-word argument, the Find option locates any transactions that meet all arguments. With the Transaction to Find window shown in figure 6.15, for example, Find does not locate transactions with the phrase *big national bank* used in the Payee field unless the asterisk character also is used in the C field. Find also does not locate transactions with the asterisk character used in the C field unless the phrase *big national bank* also is used in the Payee field.

Tip

Rather than thumbing through paid invoices, use the Quicken Find option to locate a transaction when a vendor is on the phone alleging nonpayment. Simply type the vendor's name in the Transaction to Find window and search backward or forward through the Register. Quicken finds and highlights each transaction to this particular vendor in seconds.

Repeating a Find Request. When Quicken executes a Find request, it selects the first transaction that meets the search argument or arguments you entered in the Transaction to Find window. If you were precise in specifying the exact match or key-word match, the first transaction Quicken finds may be the one you want. That transaction also could be similar to the one you want, but not an exact match, so Quicken gives you two additional Find options: Repeat Find backwards (Ctrl-B) and Repeat Find next (Ctrl-N). Repeat Find backwards (Ctrl-B) executes the find request already specified in the Transaction to Find window, and it looks through checks and deposits *before* the currently highlighted transaction. Similarly, Repeat Find next (Ctrl-N) executes the Find request already specified in the Transaction to Find window, but it looks through checks and deposits *after* the currently highlighted transaction.

Using the Go to Date Option

You may have wondered about the absence of a Date field in the Transaction to Find window with which you worked in the preceding section. Quicken provides the Go to Date option to search for transactions with a specific date.

To find a transaction by date in the Register, follow these steps:

1. From the Register, choose Go to Date from the Edit menu, or press **Ctrl-G**. The Go to Date window appears (see fig. 6.16).

   Quicken initially displays the current system date in the Go to Date field.

2. Change the date by typing the date you want over the default date. (You also can use the + (plus) and - (minus) special date entry keys to enter the date. If you don't remember how to use these keys, refer to Chapter 2, "Getting Around in Quicken."

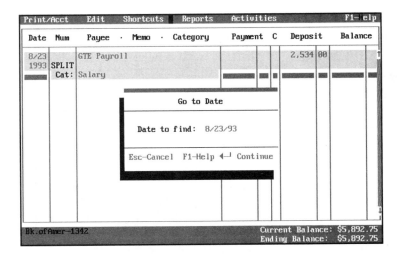

Fig. 6.16
The Go to Date window.

After you set the date you want, Quicken finds and displays the first transaction with the date you entered. If no transaction contains the date you entered, the transaction with the date closest to that date is displayed.

Because Quicken arranges transactions in the Register by date, you do not need to specify a search direction for the Go to Date option. By comparing the date of the currently highlighted transaction to the date in the Go to Date field, Quicken determines which direction it needs to search. If the Go to date is earlier than the date of the highlighted transaction, Quicken looks through the previous transactions; if the Go to date is later than the date of the highlighted transaction, Quicken searches succeeding transactions.

Using the Go to Transfer Option

If the currently highlighted transaction is a transfer transaction, you can switch quickly to the corresponding transaction by using the Go to Transfer option. A *transfer transaction* is a transfer from one Quicken account to another account. Figure 6.17, for example, shows that the Deposit to Savings transaction is selected. By looking at the Category field, which displays [Acme], you can see that this is a transfer transaction. The name of the account to which the transfer is taking place appears in brackets in the Category field.

Fig. 6.17

The Deposit to Savings transaction is part of a transfer.

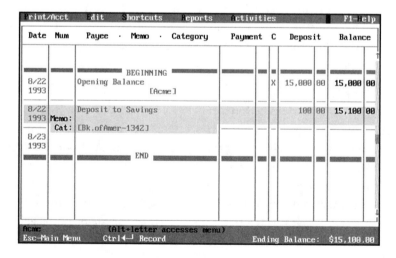

If you highlight the transfer transaction and choose Go to Transfer from the Edit menu (**Ctrl-X**), Quicken displays the Account Register with the corresponding transaction selected. Figure 6.18 shows the corresponding transaction in the Savings Account Register. In the first account, Bk.ofAmer-1342, the transaction is a payment because it reduces that account balance. In the second account, Acme, the transaction is listed as a deposit.

Fig. 6.18

The corresponding transfer transaction.

If you use the Go to Transfer option from a split transaction, Quicken asks you to identify the category to which you want to go. With a split transaction, you can make transfers to more than one account. If you try to change a split transaction from one of the other Registers, Quicken tells you that the transaction was created through a transfer, and you must return to the original transaction to make changes.

Working with Memorized Transactions

Quicken already may be fast enough for you. After all, it does not take that much time to type in the half dozen fields you enter to record a check or a deposit. But you can streamline your recordkeeping further by using *memorized transactions*. A memorized transaction is information you save from one transaction so that you can recall it for other transactions.

Many of the checks you write and the deposits you make are similar or identical to previous checks and deposits. A household, for example, may record the mortgage check, the car payment check, the utility bill check, and the payroll deposit each month. A business may write checks for the monthly rent, payroll, and expenses like supplies or insurance.

Because so many Register transactions are largely the same every month, Quicken gives you the capability to store transaction information in a memorized transaction list. Rather than entering the information over and over, you can recall it from the list of memorized transactions.

Quicken can memorize any transaction you enter into your system. You can memorize a transaction from any Quicken Account Register, including Investment Account Registers. Quicken stores memorized investment transactions in a separate memorized transaction list. In this section, you learn how to memorize and recall transactions in the Checking Account Register; you can use the same steps to memorize and recall transactions in any other Noninvestment Account Register. (You learn how to memorize check transactions in the Write Checks screen in Chapter 8, "Automating Check Writing," and how to memorize investment transactions in Chapter 16, Monitoring Your Investments.")

Quicken saves the memorized transactions to the Memorized Transaction List when you memorize the following types of transactions:

- Checks

- Deposits

- Banking fees

- Interest earned

- Automatic teller machine transactions

■ Any other transaction recorded in the following Account Registers: Bank, Credit Card, Cash, Other Asset, and Other Liability.

You can recall the memorized transaction from the Memorized Transaction List, and Quicken enters the transaction information in the Register. You can edit or delete a memorized transaction directly from the memorized lists.

Memorizing a Transaction

To memorize a transaction in a Register, follow these steps:

Tip

Memorized transactions provide a quick method to enter lengthy, split transactions you always assign to the same categories or subcategories. If you memorize a paycheck transaction and then recall it, Quicken enters the categories for you. You then simply change the amounts assigned to the categories, if necessary.

1. Enter the transaction you want to memorize in the Register. You can enter as little or as much of the transaction that you want to memorize. If you want to memorize the payee and the category only, for example, enter only that information and continue with steps 2 through 4.

2. With the transaction still highlighted, choose Memorize Transaction the Shortcuts menu, or press **Ctrl-M** (see fig. 6.19).

   Quicken displays a message telling you the program will memorize the highlighted fields (see fig. 6.20).

3. To memorize the transaction, press **Enter**. Quicken memorizes the transaction and adds it to the Memorized Transaction List shown in figure 6.21. Choose **Esc** if you do not want to memorize the transaction.

4. After Quicken memorizes the transaction information, you can complete the transaction, if necessary, and choose **Ctrl-Enter** or **F10** to record the transaction.

Tip

Quicken does not memorize the date of a transaction or the check or transaction number. When you recall a memorized transaction, Quicken enters the current date. You assign the check number when you enter or print a check transaction.

You do not need to record a transaction to memorize it. You can enter the transaction information, memorize it, and then press **Ctrl-D** to clear the transaction information from the Register. The memorized information remains in the Memorized Transaction List. You also can memorize transactions that you already have recorded.

To memorize a recorded transaction, follow these steps:

1. Highlight the transaction you want to memorize.

2. Choose Memorize Transaction from the Shortcuts menu, or press
Ctrl-M.

Quicken highlights the transaction information it is about to memorize. Quicken does not memorize the date, check number, or invoice
number.

3. Press **Enter** to memorize the transaction.

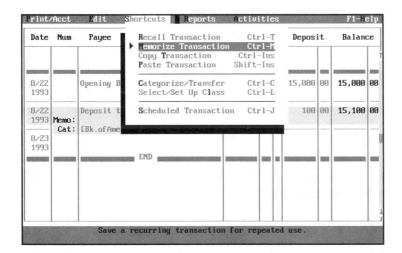

Fig. 6.19
The Memorize
Transaction option
on the Shortcuts
menu.

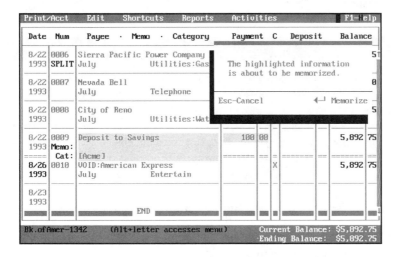

Fig.6.20
The Quicken
message telling
you that the
highlighted fields
will be memorized.

Fig. 6.21

The Memorized Transaction List.

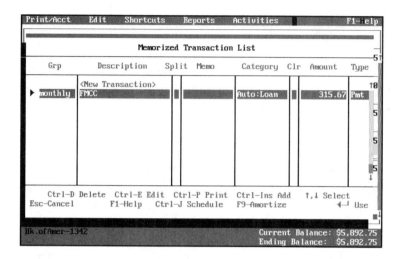

Recalling a Memorized Transaction

After you memorize a transaction, you can recall the transaction and record it in the Register. When you recall a transaction, Quicken enters the stored transaction information in the highlighted transaction.

To recall a memorized transaction in the Register, follow these steps:

1. From the Register, highlight the blank transaction line at the end of the Register.

> ### Caution
>
> If you recall a memorized transaction into a transaction line with a recorded transaction, Quicken replaces the existing transaction information with the recalled memorized transaction. You can set one of the transaction-setting options so that Quicken displays a confirmation message anytime you attempt to overwrite an existing transaction. To turn on this option, refer to Chapter 20, "Customizing Quicken," to learn about transaction-setting options.

2. Choose Recall Transaction from the Shortcuts menu, or press **Ctrl-T**.

   Quicken displays the Memorized Transaction List with a list of the transactions you have memorized.

3. Highlight the transaction you want to recall to the Register and press **Enter**.

Quicken enters the memorized transaction information into the Register.

4. Make any necessary changes to the transaction.

5. Choose **Ctrl-Enter** or **F10** to record the recalled transaction in the Register.

Editing a Memorized Transaction

You can change a memorized transaction at any time. You may want to do this if the amount of a memorized transaction changed, for example, or you want to change the category assigned to the memorized transaction.

To edit a memorized transaction, follow these steps:

1. From the Register, choose **Recall Transaction** from the Shortcuts menu, or press **Ctrl-T**. The Memorized Transaction List appears.

2. Highlight the memorized transaction you want to edit and press **Ctrl-E**. Quicken displays the Edit/Set Up Memorized Transaction window (see fig. 6.22).

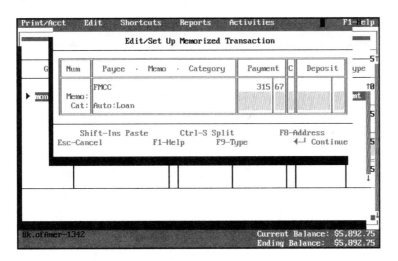

Fig. 6.22
The Edit Set Up Memorized Transaction window.

3. Change the fields in the memorized transaction as necessary, and then press **Enter**.

Deleting a Memorized Transaction

If you no longer use a memorized transaction, you can delete it from the list. You may want to delete a memorized transaction, for example, with the final payment on a house or car loan.

Follow these steps to delete a memorized transaction:

1. From the Register, choose **R**ecall Transaction from the **S**hortcuts menu, or press **Ctrl-T**. The Memorized Transaction List appears.

2. Highlight the memorized transaction you want to delete.

3. Press **Ctrl-D**. Quicken warns you that you are about to delete a memorized transaction (see fig. 6.23).

Fig. 6.23
Quicken's Warning that you are deleting a memorized transaction.

4. Press **Enter** to delete the memorized transaction, or press **Esc** if you do not want to delete the transaction from the memorized list.

Printing the Memorized Transaction List

Quicken also enables you to print a list of the transactions you have memorized. Most of the time, you will not need this feature. As long as Quicken is running, the Memorized Transaction List is at your fingertips simply by pressing **Ctrl-T**. One example of when you may want a printed list is for an annual review of transactions.

To print a copy of the Memorized Transaction List, follow these steps:

1. From the Register, choose **R**ecall Transaction from the **S**hortcuts menu, or press **Ctrl-T**. The Memorized Transaction List appears.

2. Press **Ctrl-P**. Quicken displays the Print Memorized Transaction List window, which you use to specify settings for printing the list.

3. Indicate which printer configuration you want to use (Rpt, Alt, Chk, or Disk). Quicken then prints the Memorized Transactions list, such as the following:

Payee/Memo/Category	Clr	Type	Amount
Indianapolis Power Company		Payment	-98.88
Utilities	28		
Inland Mortgage		Payment	-1,752.68
	SPLITS		
Mort Int			-1,300.00
Tax:Prop			-150.00
[Mortgage]			-302.68

Copying and Pasting Transactions

Memorizing transactions is a quick, easy way to enter recurring transactions. If you want to enter a transaction that is the same as another transaction in the Register, but you don't want to memorize it (perhaps because it may only be used once), you can copy the transaction and then paste it in the empty transaction line or in the Register. You can replace transactions by pasting a copied transaction over an existing transaction. You also can copy and paste transactions from the Write Checks screen (see Chapter 8, "Automating Check Writing").

When Quicken copies a transaction, it essentially is memorizing the transaction information. This information is stored in Quicken and can be pasted in the same Register or any other Noninvestment Account Register. You can repaste the same transaction more than once. Quicken will not save the stored transaction information after you copy another transaction or exit the program, however.

Tip
Consider each of the transactions you now record regularly as candidates for the Memorized Transaction List: rent, house payment, utility payment, school loans, payroll deposits, bank service fees, and so on. The easiest time to memorize transactions is when you initially record a transaction, so every time you enter a transaction, ask yourself whether the transaction is one you will enter repeatedly. You also can memorize split transactions.

Learning Quicken

To copy and paste a transaction in the Register, follow these steps:

1. Highlight the transaction in the Register you want to copy.

2. Choose Copy Transaction from the **Shortcuts** menu or press **Ctrl-Ins** (see fig. 6.24). Quicken flashes a message in the bottom right corner of your screen that it is memorizing the transaction.

Fig. 6.24

The Copy Transaction option on the Shortcuts menu.

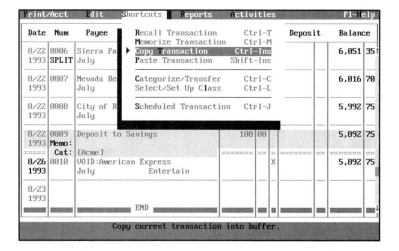

3. Move the cursor to the empty transaction line in the Register. Or, to replace an existing transaction with the copied transaction, highlight the transaction you want to replace.

4. Choose **P**aste Transaction from the **Shortcuts** menu, or press **Shift-Ins**. Quicken pastes a copy of the transaction information in the highlighted transaction.

If the transaction setting Confirm When Overwriting with a Memorized or Pasted Transaction is turned on, Quicken displays the OK to Overwrite Transaction? window before it replaces an existing transaction with the copied transaction (see fig. 6.25). To enter the copied transaction, press **Enter**. If you don't want to overwrite the existing transaction, press **Esc**. You learn how to work with transaction settings in Chapter 20, "Customizing Quicken."

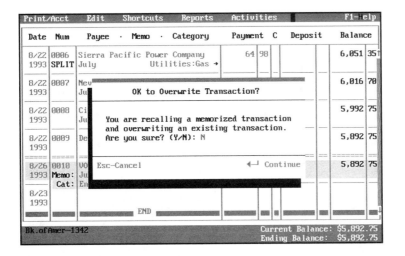

Fig. 6.25

The OK to Overwrite Transaction? window.

Using the Categories

You can assign a category or subcategory to a transaction by typing the category or subcategory name in the Category field or by using the Categorize/Transfer option on the Shortcuts menu. This option displays the Category and Transfer list so that you can find and assign a category, subcategory, or transfer account to a transaction. You also can use this option to add a new category or edit or delete an existing category. Adding, editing, and deleting categories and subcategories were described in Chapter 4, "Organizing Your Finances."

To find and assign a category or subcategory to a transaction, follow these steps:

1. From the Register, choose Categorize/Transfer from the Shortcuts menu, or press **Ctrl-C**.

Quicken displays the Category and Transfer List with predefined categories, subcategories, and any accounts you may have created (see fig. 6.26).

2. Select the category, subcategory, or account you want to assign to a transaction and press **Enter**. Quicken retrieves the category or account name from the list and enters it in the Category field.

Fig. 6.26

The Category and Transfer List.

You can use the PgUp, PgDn, Home, and End keys to move quickly through long lists of categories and accounts. Pressing PgUp displays the preceding page of categories in the list; pressing PgDn displays the next page of categories in the list; pressing Home displays the first page of categories, and pressing End displays the last page of categories. The Category and Transfer List also provides a scroll bar that mouse users can take advantage of for moving up and down the list. (For more information about using scroll bars, refer to Chapter 5, "Using the Register.")

> **Note**
>
> Quicken does not require you to assign categories to transactions. If you want to track your income and expense so that you know where your money comes from and where it goes, however, you should assign a category to each transaction that you enter in Quicken. To ensure that you do assign a category to each transaction, you can turn on the transaction-setting option Warn If a Transaction Has No Category. When this transaction setting is turned on, Quicken displays a warning message each time you record a transaction without an assigned category. To learn how to turn on this transaction setting, refer to Chapter 20, "Customizing Quicken."

Using Scheduled Transactions

You can plan ahead with Quicken by scheduling future transactions. You can schedule one-time transactions such as a vacation cruise plan to pay next month or recurring transactions, such as your cable TV bill, that you pay at the same time every month.

Once you schedule a transaction, Quicken can either remind you when it is due (and let you decide how you want to handle it), or simply enter it for you automatically in the specified account at the scheduled time.

Scheduling Future Transactions

To schedule a future transaction, follow these steps:

1. From the Register or the Write Checks screen, choose **Scheduled Trans-action** from the **Shortcuts** menu, or press **Ctrl-J**. Quicken displays the Scheduled Transactions List window (see fig. 6.27).

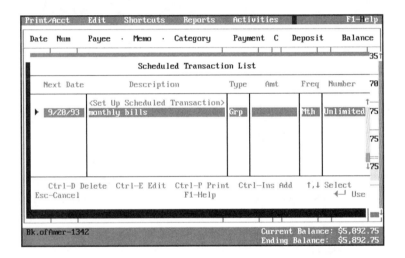

Fig. 6.27
The Scheduled Transaction List window.

2. Highlight the <Set Up Scheduled Transaction> line. If no other scheduled transactions have been set up, it will be the only line in the window. Choose **Enter**.

Quicken displays the Set Up Scheduled Transaction window as shown in figure 6.28.

3. In the Transaction Type field, press **1** for Payment, **2** for Deposit, **3** for Check, or **4** for Group.

4. Move the cursor to the Account field and enter the account to which this transaction relates. If the pop-up menu option is set to yes, a pop-up menu will appear with your choices for this field (see Chapter 20 "Customizing Quicken" for more information about pop-up menus).

Learning Quicken

Fig. 6.28

The Set Up
Scheduled
Transaction
window.

5. Move the cursor to the Frequency field and another pop-up menu will appear with nine choices. Select the one that is correct for this transaction.

6. Move the cursor to the Next Transaction Date field. Enter the date you want recorded in the transaction's Date field.

7. Move the cursor to the No. of transactions field and enter the number of times you want Quicken to enter the scheduled transaction, up to a maximum of 999. Quicken then determines the last transaction date based on what you entered in this field and the Next Transaction Date field. If you enter 999, Quicken assumes you want the transaction scheduled indefinitely.

8. Move the cursor to the Confirm before recording transaction field and choose **Y** if you want to view or edit the scheduled transaction just before Quicken records it in the Register. Choose **N** if you want Quicken to record the scheduled transaction automatically, as soon as you open the file on the next due date.

9. Move the cursor to the Days in advance to record field and enter the number of days before the next due date that you want Quicken to enter the scheduled transaction, up to a maximum of 99.

10. Choose Continue when you finish making the selection in the Set Up
Scheduled Transaction window.

11. If you specified a single transaction, Quicken displays the Scheduled
Payment Transaction window (see fig. 6.29). If you specified a group,
see the *Setting Up a Transaction Group* section later in this chapter. The
window contains the same fields as a transaction in your Register. Enter
the transaction information for the scheduled transaction and press
Enter to record the scheduled transaction.

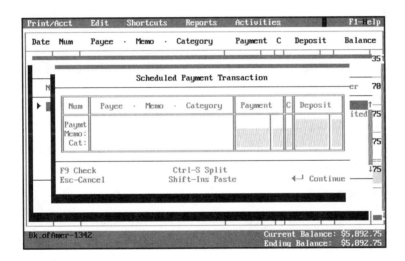

Fig. 6.29
The Scheduled
Payment Transaction window.

The first time you use Quicken either on or after the date a scheduled transaction is due, Quicken enters that transaction in the specified register (or reminds you that it is due).

If you entered a number other than zero in the Days in Advance to Enter field
when you set up the scheduled transaction, Quicken will enter the transaction in the Register as a postdated transaction (or remind you that it is due)
the specified number of days before the scheduled transaction date.

If you choose Yes in the Prompt before entering transaction field when you
set up the scheduled transaction, Quicken reminds you with The following
transaction is due window (see fig. 6.30).

Learning Quicken

Fig. 6.30
The following
transaction is due
window.

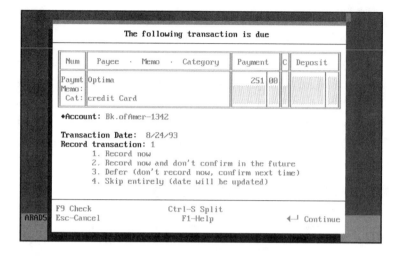

Changing a Scheduled Transaction Before It Is Entered

Quicken gives you the opportunity to edit the scheduled transaction *before* it is entered in the Register. To edit the scheduled transaction, see *Changing and Deleting Scheduled Transactions*, later in this chapter.

To tell Quicken how to handle the scheduled transaction, follow these steps:

1. From the Scheduled Transaction List window, highlight the transaction you want to change, and press **Enter**. Quicken displays the following window similar to the one in figure 6.31.

Fig. 6.31
The Record
the following
transaction
window.

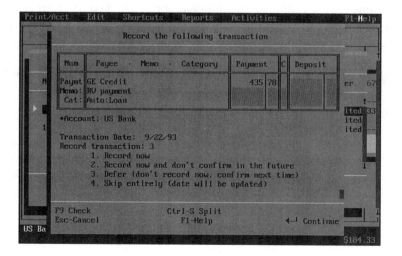

2. Move the cursor to the Record Transaction field and choose **1** to enter the transaction as scheduled.

3. Choose **2** to enter the transaction as scheduled and not be reminded in the future.

4. Choose **3** if you don't want to enter the transaction now. The next time you use Quicken, the same reminder will appear.

5. Choose **4** to skip the transaction entirely. This doesn't cancel the scheduled transaction and the reminder appears again the next time the transaction is due.

6. Press **Enter** after you make you choice and Quicken returns you to the Register.

Entering a Scheduled Transaction Before It Is Due

Sometimes you may want to record a scheduled transaction earlier than the date you originally scheduled. For example, you may have planned to write a check to pay your phone bill on September 14, but need to write it before you leave for vacation on September 10.

To change the payment date, follow these steps:

1. From the Register, choose **Scheduled Transaction** from the **Shortcuts** menu, or press **Ctrl-J**. Quicken displays the Scheduled Transaction List window that was shown in figure 6.30.

2. Highlight the transaction you want to pay early and press **Enter**.

3. Move the cursor to the Transaction Date field and change it to the current date (if you don't want to enter the transaction as a postdated transaction).

4. Move the cursor to the Record Transaction field and make your choice as explained previously.

5. Press **Enter** and Quicken records the transaction.

Quicken does not enter the transaction again until the next scheduled date. If you enter a check you regularly write on the 14th of every month on September 10 rather than September 14, for example, Quicken will not enter the transaction again until October 14th.

Editing Scheduled Transactions

To edit a scheduled transaction, follow these steps:

1. From the Register, choose Scheduled Transaction from the Shortcuts menu, or press **Ctrl-J**. Quicken displays the Scheduled Transaction List window.

2. Highlight the transaction that you want to edit, and then press **Ctrl-E**. Quicken displays the Edit Scheduled Transaction window.

3. Make the changes to the transaction information and press **Enter**. Quicken records the changes and returns you to the Register.

Deleting Scheduled Transactions

To delete a scheduled transaction, follow these steps:

1. From the Register, choose Scheduled Transaction from the Shortcuts menu, or press **Ctrl-J**. Quicken displays the Scheduled Transaction List window.

2. Highlight the transaction you want to delete and press **Ctrl-D**. Quicken displays the OK to Delete a Scheduled Transaction? window.

3. Choose **1** to delete the transaction or choose **2** to not delete it.

4. Press **Esc** and Quicken returns you to the Register.

> **Note**
>
> You don't need to delete a transaction to make it inactive. You can deactivate it temporarily by entering zero in the No. of transactions field in the Edit Scheduled Transaction window. The transaction remains in the list, but Quicken will not enter it again until you reactivate it.

Quicken's Calendar and Scheduled Transactions

Quicken's on-screen calendar was explained earlier (See Chapter 2 "Using Quicken's Calendar"), but there is one feature of the calendar that relates to Scheduled transactions.

When you enter a Scheduled Transaction, Quicken places a т in the calendar on each day that a future transaction is due. This gives you a visual reminder of due dates and can help you plan cash flow.

Using Transaction Groups

A transaction group contains recurring transactions that you simultaneously pay or add to a Register. Transaction groups can consist of one or many transactions. You may, for example, want to set up a transaction group for bills for which you don't receive invoices or statements, such as your rent or loan payments. You also may want to set up a transaction group for bills due at the same time each month, such as quarterly estimated tax payments and insurance premiums.

When you create a transaction group, you assign one or more memorized transactions to a group and then name it. You may, for example, set up a transaction group named *Monthly Bills*.

If you are using Billminder (see Chapter 20, "Customizing Quicken"), you'll be reminded at least three days before transaction groups are due by a message displayed at your computer's DOS prompt. Quicken also reminds you that you have transactions groups due by displaying a message at its Main Menu.

You will find Quicken's reminder system great for prompting you to pay bills for which you do not receive an invoice, such as your rent, payroll taxes, and loan payments.

After you set up a transaction group, you can add, delete, or change transactions in the group. You also can delete an entire transaction group.

Setting Up a Transaction Group

Before you can set up a transaction group, you must memorize the transactions that you want to include in the group. (You learned how to memorize transactions in *Memorizing a Transaction*, earlier in this chapter.) You can include one or several memorized transactions in a transaction group. You also can include the same transaction in more than one group.

To set up a transaction group, follow these steps:

1. From the Register, choose **S**cheduled Transaction from the **S**hortcuts menu, or press **Ctrl-J**. Quicken displays the Scheduled Transaction List window.

2. Highlight the <Set Up Scheduled transaction> line, and then press **Enter**.

3. Quicken displays the Set Up Scheduled Transaction window.

4. In the Transaction Type field, press **4** to instruct Quicken that you are setting up a group.

5. In the next field, enter the account name where the transactions should be recorded. A pop-up menu will appear to list your choices.

6. Move the cursor to the Frequency field. Set the frequency using one of the nine settings shown in the pop-up menu: Only Once, Weekly, Every two weeks, Twice a month, Every four weeks, Monthly, Quarterly, Twice a year, or Annually. Select the frequency you want. Quicken reminds you when transactions groups are due, based on your entry in this field and the Next transaction Date field.

7. Enter the date that the next transaction group is due in the Next Transaction Date field. If you're setting up a transaction group for checks that are due on the first of the month and today's date is October 15, for example, type **11/01/93**. Quicken enters the current date. Use the + (plus) and - (minus) keys to change the date one day at a time. Or, you can type a new date.

Tip
Create transaction groups for payroll tax payments, sales tax payments, federal and state estimated tax payments, and property tax payments. These transactions seem to creep up on you without warning and involve penalties if submitted just one day late!

8. When you complete the Set Up Scheduled Transaction window, press **Enter**. Quicken displays the Scheduled Transaction Group window. You now enter the Group name for the transaction group and press **Enter**.

9. Quicken displays the Assign Transactions to Scheduled Group window. Highlight each transaction you want to include in the new transaction group. Press the spacebar to include the transaction (Quicken enters the group name in the Grp field next to each transaction that you select). To unassign a transaction to a transaction group, highlight the transaction and press the spacebar again.

10. When you finish selecting transactions to include in the new transaction group, choose **Enter-Done**. Quicken enters the transaction group's name, the number of transactions in the group, frequency, and the next scheduled date in the Scheduled Transaction List window.

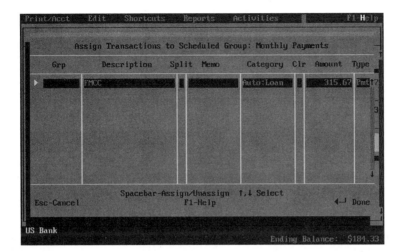

Fig. 6.32
The Assign
Transactions to
Scheduled Group
window.

Summary

In this chapter, you learn about Quicken features that make the Register easier and faster to work with. More specifically, you learned about Quicken 7's QuickFill feature; how to insert, delete, and void transactions; how to find transactions; how to split transactions; how to use memorized transactions, how to use scheduled transactions, and how to use transaction groups.

In the next chapter, you learn how to write and print checks at the Write Checks screen.

Chapter 7

Writing and Printing Checks

With Quicken's check-printing feature, you can write checks and pay bills faster and more efficiently than you ever thought possible. You can pay bills faster because Quicken provides a collection of shortcuts and timesaving techniques that automate and speed up check writing and bill paying. You can pay bills more efficiently because Quicken helps you keep track of the bills coming due and provides categories with which you can classify the ways you are spending your money.

The check-writing feature in Quicken is one of the program's most powerful tools. Writing checks with Quicken not only saves you valuable time, but spares you from having numerous opportunities to make clerical errors. When you write a check using Quicken, you simply enter the information in an on-screen check facsimile (the Write Checks screen), and Quicken takes it from there. The program records the check in the Checking Account Register, adjusts your account balance, and adds the transaction amount to the appropriate category, which you specify when you write a check. From this point, you only have to print the check, sign it, stick the check in an envelope (Intuit even provides window envelopes for checks), and mail it.

Accessing the Write Checks Screen

Access the Write Checks screen when you want to do the following:

- Write checks

- Postdate checks

This chapter describes the basics of writing and printing checks with Quicken. Included in this chapter are discussions of the following topics:

- Accessing and understanding the Write Checks screen

- Moving around the Write Checks screen

- Writing and recording checks

- Reviewing and editing checks

- Positioning checks in your printer

- Printing and reprinting checks

- Review checks that you have not printed

- Edit or delete checks that you have not printed

- Print checks

Before you access the Write Checks screen, you must select a bank account to use from the Select Account to Use window. You learned how to select accounts to use in Chapter 3, "Defining Your Accounts." You cannot write a check from any other type of account other than a bank account. The bank account that you use usually will be your checking account. If you attempt to access the Write Checks screen from an account other than a bank account, Quicken displays the message you see in figure 7.1. Press **Enter** from this message window and Quicken then takes you to the Select Account to Use window, where you can select a bank account.

Fig. 7.1

The message Quicken displays when you try to access the Write Checks screen from an account other than a bank account.

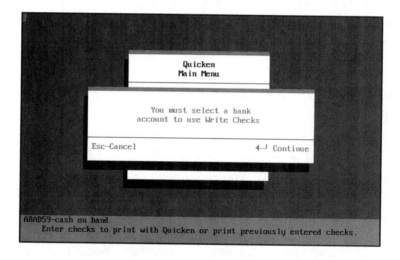

To access the Write Checks screen, choose **Write/Print Checks** from the Quicken Main Menu. Quicken displays the Write Checks screen (see fig. 7.2).

Understanding the Write Checks Screen

You use the Write Checks screen to collect the information you use to print checks. After collecting the information, Quicken records the check in the Register for the bank account that you're using.

The Write Checks screen can be broken down into three parts: the menu bar at the top of the screen, the actual check, and the information lines at the bottom of the screen.

Tip

You can access the Write Checks screen by pressing **Ctrl-W** from the Quicken Main Menu or by pressing **Ctrl-W** from a Bank Account Register.

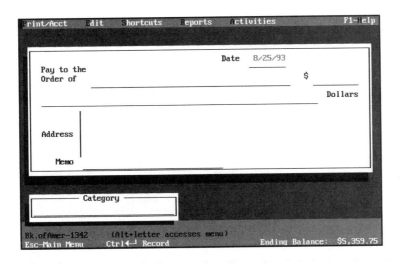

Fig. 7.2
The Write Checks
screen.

The menu bar shows the menus you use from the Write Checks screen to access commands. These menus should look familiar if you have worked with the Register screen: Print/Acct, Edit, Shortcuts, Reports, and Activities.

The second part of the screen is the actual check where you enter the date; payee; amount; memo (optional); and category, subcategory, or transfer account. Note that check numbers are not entered in the Write Checks screen; you specify the check numbers when you print checks. The steps for completing checks are described in the following section, *Writing a Check*.

The third part of the Write Checks screen includes the information lines at the bottom of the screen. These lines show several pieces of information, including the account you are using, descriptions of what the Esc and Enter keys do, the total amount of checks to print, and the current and ending balance in the account. The *current balance* represents the balance in your account as of the current date. The *ending balance* represents the balance, taking into account any postdated checks you have written.

Moving Around the Write Checks Screen

The following keys help you move around the Write Checks screen quickly and easily.

Press	To Move
Enter or Tab	Forward one field
Shift-Tab	Backward one field

(continues)

(continued)

Press	To Move
Home	Beginning of current field
Home, Home	Beginning of first field in current check
End	End of current field
End, End	End of last field in current check
Ctrl-→	Forward one word within a field
Ctrl-←	Backward one word within a field
PgUp	To the preceding check
PgDn	To the next check

Writing a Check

The mechanics of writing a check with Quicken closely resemble those for manually writing a check. The only real difference is that Quicken's Write Checks screen makes the process easier. With Quicken, writing a check means you simply complete the Write Checks screen. You fill in as many as seven fields: Date, Payee, Amount, Address, Message, Memo, and Category. After you write the check, you're ready to record and print the check.

Filling In the Check

To write a check, you take the following steps:

1. Choose Write/Print Checks from the Main Menu. Or, if you're already in the Register screen, choose **W**rite Checks from the Activities menu, or press **Ctrl-W** from the Register for the bank account that you want to use to write checks. Quicken displays the Write Checks screen.

2. Enter the date of the check in the Date field. Enter the date in the MM/DD/YY format (such as 12/11/93). The first time you write a check in the current Quicken session, the program fills the Date field with the system date (the current date according to your computer's internal memory). After you write your first check using the Write Checks screen, Quicken fills the Date field with the last date used. To edit the date, you have two choices. First, you can move the cursor to the part of the date (month, day, or year) you want to change and type over the

date already on-screen. Second, you can use the special date-editing keys.

> **CPA TIP**
>
> As mentioned in Chapter 6, businesses and individuals often receive discounts for paying bills early, so consider early payment in setting the check date. In effect, not taking early payment discounts is an extremely expensive way to borrow money from the vendor. Suppose that a vendor normally requires payment within 30 days but gives a two percent discount for payments received within 10 days. If you pay within 30 rather than 10 days, you pay the vendor a two percent interest charge for paying 20 days later. Because one year contains roughly 18 20-day periods, the two percent for 20 days equals approximately 36 percent annually.
>
> Although you may need to borrow this money, you probably can find a less-expensive lender. As a rule of thumb, if a vendor gives you a one percent discount for paying 20 days early, you are borrowing money from him at about an 18 percent annual interest rate if you do not pay early. A three percent discount works out to a whopping 54 percent per year.

3. Move the cursor to the Pay to the Order Of field. This field is where you enter the name of the person or business, called the *payee*, that the check pays. Type the name you want to appear on the check.

4. Move the cursor to the Amount field. The Amount field shows the amount of the check. You can use up to 10 characters to enter the amount. Quicken enables you to enter only numbers, commas, and decimal points in the Amount field. Quicken enters commas if you do not and if room is available for them. The largest value you can enter in the Amount field is 9999999.99. Because this number is difficult to read without commas (the number is $9,999,999.99), you probably will want Quicken to have enough room to insert commas. If you use some of the 10 characters for commas, the largest value you can enter is 999,999.99. When you complete the Amount field and press Enter, Quicken writes out the amount on the next line of the check-just as you do when writing a check manually. To save space, Quicken may abbreviate *hundred* as *Hndrd*, *thousand* as *Thsnd*, and *million* as *Mill*.

5. (Optional) Move the cursor to the next field—the first line of the address block. The optional Address field provides five 30-character lines. If you use envelopes with windows and enter the payee's address in this

Tip
Because you have space for up to 40 characters, you should not have any problem fitting in the payee's name. In fact, you should have room to enter *and* and *or* payees. An *and* payee, for example, is *Robert Southern and Ronald Hamilton.* Both Southern and Hamilton must endorse such a check to cash it. An *or* payee is entered as *Robert Southern or Ronald Hamilton* and requires Southern *or* Hamilton to endorse the check to cash it.

field, the address shows in the envelope window. You save time that otherwise is spent addressing envelopes.

Assuming that you are using the Address field, you need to type the payee's name on the first line. Quicken provides a shortcut for you. If you type ' (an apostrophe) or " (a quotation mark), Quicken copies the name from the Pay to the Order Of field. (Because the Pay to the Order Of field has space for 40 characters and the address lines have only 30 characters, this shortcut may cut off up to the last 10 characters of the payee's name.)

6. (Optional) If you set the check setting Extra Message Line on Check to Yes, press **Enter** or **Tab** to move the cursor to the Msg field. If this check setting is not Yes, no message line appears. To learn how to set the check setting so that the extra message line appears in the Write Checks screen, refer to Chapter 20, "Customizing Quicken."

The message field, if displayed as shown in figure 7.3, gives you another 24 characters for additional information you want printed on the check, such as an account number for a credit card or a loan number for a mortgage. Because this information does not show through an envelope window, do not use the line for address information.

Fig. 7.3
The Write Checks screen with the extra message (Msg.) line displayed.

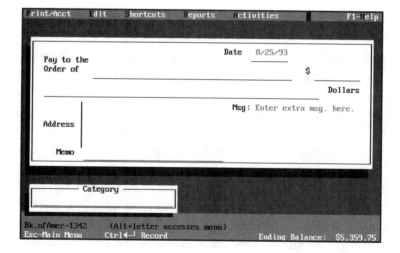

7. (Optional) Move the cursor to the second line of the address block. Enter the street address or post office box.

8. (Optional) Move the cursor to the third line of the address block. Enter the city, state, and ZIP code.

9. (Optional) Move the cursor to the other address lines (there are five altogether) and enter any additional address information.

10. (Optional) Move the cursor to the Memo field. You can use this field as you use the extra message line to further describe the check, such as November rent, or you can use the line to tell the payee your account number or loan number.

11. (Optional) Move the cursor to the Category field. You use this field to assign a category or subcategory to a transaction so that you know what the check covers, such as utilities expense, interest expense, or entertainment. You also can use the Category field to describe the class into which a check falls. (Categories and classes were described in Chapter 4, "Organizing Your Finances.") And, you can use the Category field to enter another Quicken account if the check that you are writing represents a transfer of funds between your checking account and another account. (Transfer transactions were explained in Chapter 5, "Using the Register.") Quicken provides a listing of the most typical categories for home or business use to enable you to quickly categorize your most frequent transactions. You access the defined list by pressing **Ctrl-C.**

Quicken 7 provides a feature called *QuickFill*, (explained in detail in Chapter 5). You can use QuickFill after you have learned a few of the category names. If you type enough characters of a category name to uniquely identify the category and then press Enter, Quicken searches the Category and Transfer list to find the first category that begins with the characters you type. Suppose that you have a category named *Entertainment*, and that it is the only category name that starts with the three letters *Ent*. If you type **Ent** and press **Enter**, Quicken searches the Category and Transfer list until it finds a category that begins with *Ent*. When Quicken finds *Entertainment*, the QuickFill feature fills in the remaining letters of the category name for you—*ertainment*. You also can use QuickFill to enter an account name in the Category field when transferring money to another account. You learn more about using QuickFill to write checks in Chapter 8, "Automating Check Writing."

Recording a Check

After the check is complete, record the check by pressing **Ctrl-Enter** or **F10.** Or, you can select Enter if the cursor is positioned in the last field in the Write Checks screen. When you select Enter to record a check, Quicken displays the OK to Record Transaction? window (see fig. 7.4). Choose **1** to record the check or choose **2** if you decide that you don't want to record the check.

Figure 7.5 shows a completed check at the Write Checks screen.

Fig. 7.4

The OK to Record
Transaction?
window.

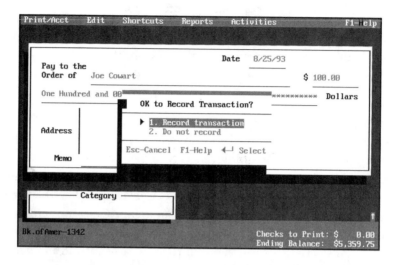

Fig. 7.5

A completed check
at the Write Checks
screen.

Whichever method you choose to record a check, you briefly see a flashing
message in the lower left corner of the screen that says RECORDING. (If you use
a very fast computer, you may not be able to read the message because it
appears and disappears so quickly.) After Quicken finishes recording the
check, your computer beeps, and the recorded check scrolls off-screen. A new,
blank check that was hidden by the preceding check is left on-screen, ready
to be completed.

Reviewing and Editing Checks

You can return to, review, and edit the checks you write with the Write/Print Checks option until you print them. You can correct errors in a payee's name, change the check amount, or change the category or subcategory assigned to the check, for example. Suppose that you write a check to pay several bills from the same person or business—perhaps the bank where you have your mortgage, your car loan, and a personal line of credit. If you receive another bill from the bank, you may need to change the check amount.

You can use the PgUp, PgDn, Home, and End keys on the Write Checks screen to move through the checks you have written but not yet printed:

PgUp	Displays the preceding check
PgDn	Displays the next check
Home	Displays the first check
End	Displays the last check

Quicken arranges by date the checks you have written at the Write Checks screen but have not printed. Those checks with the earliest dates are listed first, followed chronologically by later checks. Checks with the same date are arranged in the order you entered them. To edit a check you already have recorded, press PgUp or PgDn to move to the check you want to change and then edit the appropriate fields.

Note

Quicken does not store checks in the Write Checks screen after they have been printed. To review checks that have been printed, you must access the Register. Locate checks that you want to review in the Register by using the Find option or the Go to Date option you learned about in Chapter 6, "Automating the Register."

If you decide you don't want to print a check, you simply delete it. To delete the check, press **Ctrl-D** while the check is displayed. Or, you can choose Delete Transaction from the Edit menu in the Write Checks screen. Chapter 8, "Automating Check Writing," explains how to delete checks.

Postdating Checks

Chapter 5, "Using the Register," discusses using postdated transactions. All the same reasons described there also apply to postdated checks. When writing checks with Quicken, however, postdating takes on an added feature. Quicken can review postdated checks for those that you should print. To do this, Quicken uses a built-in program called the *Billminder*. Billminder looks for postdated checks it thinks you should print. You are reminded of postdated checks and of transaction groups every time you turn on your computer. Quicken uses a pop-up message window (see fig. 7.6).

If the To Do List feature set to Yes (you learn about this feature in Chapter 20, "Customizing Quicken"), a message willl appear reminding you of postdated checks (see fig. 7.7).

Fig. 7.6
The pop-up Billminder message window.

If you enter postdated checks, Quicken adds the current account balance in the information lines at the bottom of the Write Checks screen. The current balance is the checking account balance, not including postdated checks.

Printing Checks

When you have your Quicken checks, you need to position them in your printer properly before you start printing. Aligning checks in your continuous-feed printer is easy with Intuit's patented automatic alignment feature; you no longer have to align by trial and error. Aligning laser checks is a snap with Quicken 7's Vertical Check Adjustment feature.

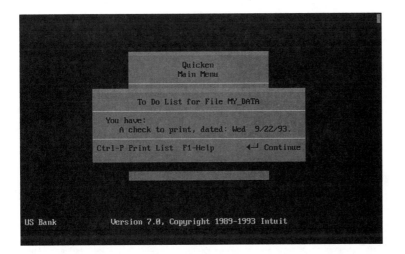

Learning Quicken

Fig. 7.7
The To Do List
window.

Before you begin to print checks with Quicken, make sure that your system
has been set up properly to print to your printer. Refer to Chapter 1, "Preparing To Use Quicken," to learn how to set up Quicken for your printer.

Positioning Checks in Your Printer

Before you start printing checks, you should print a sample check to ensure
that your checks are properly positioned and aligned in your printer and that
the vertical print settings are correct. If you're using continuous-feed checks,
use the sample checks that were enclosed in your Quicken software package
to print a sample check. If you're using a laser or page-oriented printer, it's
best to print a sample check on plain paper so that you don't waste any of
your checks. You can use the sample check printed on plain paper as an over-
lay on your laser checks to see how the print lines up. You learn how to print
both types of sample checks in this section.

> **Note**
>
> After you go through the process of aligning checks by entering the vertical print
> settings and determining the proper horizontal positioning for checks, your printer
> will stay aligned and you will not need to repeat this process each time you print
> checks.

Printing a Sample Continuous-Feed Check. To print a sample continuous-
feed check, follow these steps:

Tip
After you receive
your checks from
Intuit, review them
carefully to ensure
that they are free
of printing errors.
Most importantly,
examine the bank
account number to
make sure that it is
correct. If you find
an error, return the
checks immedi-
ately and have
them reprinted.
Unless the printing
error was caused by
wrong information
submitted by you,
your checks will be
reprinted at no
charge.

1. Be sure that you have at least one check to print. If not, you can write a sample check and then delete it later.

2. Insert the continuous-form checks into the printer as you would insert continuous-form paper.

3. From the Write Checks screen, choose Print Checks from the Print/Acct menu (see fig. 7.8). Quicken displays the Print Checks window that you see in figure 7.9.

Fig. 7.8
The Print/Acct menu.

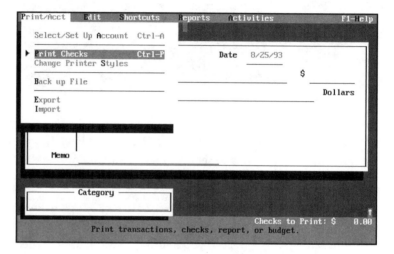

Fig. 7.9
The Print Checks window.

Tip
You can choose the **Print Checks** option by pressing **Ctrl-P** directly from the Write Checks screen.

5. With the cursor positioned in the Print To field, choosing the printer you want to use by selecting 1, 2, or 3. If you described your printer when installing Quicken, you should see your printer name here. If you don't see it, refer to Chapter 1, "Preparing to Use Quicken."

6. In the Type of Checks To Print On field, enter the number that corresponds to the continuous-feed check type you are using: 1 for Standard, 2 for Wallet, or 3 for Voucher.

7. Press **F9** to print a sample check with the fields filled so that you can see how the print on a check lines up—both vertically and horizontally for continuous-feed checks or just vertically for laser checks.

   Quicken displays a Note window that tells you not to adjust your printer after the sample check prints and to follow Quicken's on-screen instructions to adjust your printer.

8. Press **Enter** to remove the Note window and begin printing the sample check. Figure 7.10 shows the sample check printed by Quicken.

Fig 7.10
A sample check.

The Date field is filled as XX/XX/XX. The Pay to the Order of field is filled with Payee. The Amount field is filled with XX,XXX.XX. The Memo field is filled with the phrase This is a void check.

Quicken also prints a *pointer line*, as shown in figure 7.10. The pointer line enables you to tell Quicken how the check form is aligned vertically.

After the sample check is printed, Quicken displays the Type Position Number window that you see in figure 7.11, which you can use to align the check form vertically. If the sample check printed correctly, press **Enter**.

If the sample check did not print correctly, use Quicken's alignment feature by entering the number from the check form's pin-feed strips that the pointer line points to. (*Pin-feed strips* are the strips of holes on the sides of the check forms. Your printer uses these holes to move the check forms through the printer.) Only even numbers show on the pin-feed strips. The odd numbers are identified by hash marks. Press **Enter** after the pointer line number is entered and Quicken advances the checks in your printer and prints another sample check.

Fig. 7.11
The Type Position Number window to vertically align continuous-feed checks.

To align the check horizontally, manually adjust the check form in the printer to the right or left. You may decide, for example, that the print in the fields shown in figure 7.10 is a little too far to the left—perhaps an eighth of an inch. In that case, you manually move the check forms over to the left an eighth of an inch. Quicken prints the next check with its check form spaces filled an eighth of an inch to the right compared to the preceding check form.

Tip
When your continuous-feed checks are aligned properly, make note of their position in your printer so that you can align them correctly the next time you insert checks. Look for something on your printer that aligns with one of the position numbers on the edge of the checks (or mark your printer with a piece of tape to use as a guidepost).

When the checks are aligned properly in your printer, press **Enter** from the Type Position Number window to return to the Print Checks window.

Printing a Sample Laser Check. If you entered a test check, be sure to delete it after your continuous-feed checks are aligned properly. Refer to Chapter 8, "Automating Check Writing," to learn how to delete a check.

If you're using a laser printer, you will not use the F9 sample check feature to print a sample check. Rather, to print a sample laser check, use the Print command as if you are printing a check as usual.

To print a sample laser check, follow these steps:

1. Be sure that you have at least one check to print. If not, you can write a sample check and then delete it later.

2. Load regular paper into your laser printer.

3. From the Write Checks screen, choose Print Checks from the **Print/Acct** menu, or press **Ctrl-P**. The Print Checks window appears.

4. With the cursor positioned in the Print To field, choose the printer you want to use by selecting 1, 2, or 3. If you described your printer when

installing Quicken, you should see your printer name here. If you don't see it, refer to Chapter 1, "Preparing to Use Quicken."

5. Position the cursor in the Print All/Selected Checks field. Press **A** to print all checks if there is only one check to print. Press **S** if you have more than one check to print. (You don't want to print all of your checks until the check alignment is correct.)

6. In the Type of Checks To Print On field, enter the number that corresponds to the laser check type you are using: 4 for Laser Standard, 5 for Laser Voucher, or 6 for Laser Wallet.

7. Choose Print from the Print Check window.

8. (Optional) If you pressed **S** from the Print All/Selected Checks field, Quicken displays the Select Checks to Print window. Highlight the check you want to print and press the spacebar. To deselect a check to print, highlight the check and press the spacebar again. Choose Ctrl-Enter to continue.

Quicken displays the Enter Check Number window that you see in figure 7.12. You tell Quicken what your next check number is in this window.

Tip

Use plain paper to print a sample laser check so that you don't waste any of your pre-printed laser checks.

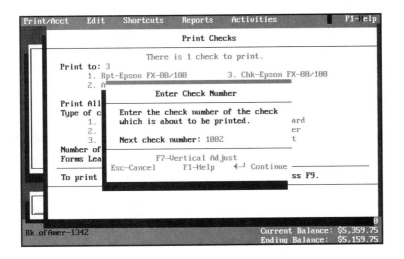

Fig. 7.12
The Enter Check Number window.

9. If the number that appears in the window is not the correct check number, press the + (plus) or - (minus) key to change the check number by one number at a time. When the check number is correct, press **Enter**.

Quicken prints the check information on the first sheet of blank paper in your laser printer and displays the Did Check # Print Correctly? window that you see in figure 7.13.

Fig. 7.13
The Did Check #
Print Correctly?
window.

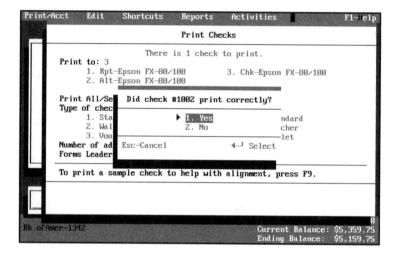

10. Place the printed sheet over one of your preprinted check forms to check the alignment of the print. You should be able to see through to the preprinted check form quite easily to determine if the printed text is placed properly. If so, select Yes by pressing **Enter** from the Did Check # Print Correctly? window. If your check printed correctly, don't print another sample check. Delete the check transaction that you just printed from the Register by going to the Register and highlighting the check that you just printed. Press **Ctrl-D** and then choose **Enter** to delete the transaction.

If your sample laser check did not line up properly, select the **No** option from the Did Check # Print Correctly? window by choosing 2. Quicken returns to the Print Checks window. You then need to adjust the vertical alignment by following these steps:

1. Choose **Ctrl-Enter** from the Print Checks window. Quicken displays the Enter Check Number window.

2. Press **F7** to display the Vertical Check Adjustment window that you see in figure 7.14.

3. If you printed a full check page, position the cursor in the Full Page Adj field. Enter the number of half lines that you want to adjust the text on

the check. Choose **Enter**. (If you printed a partial page of checks, use
the Partial Page Adj field to enter the number of half lines that you
want to adjust the text by.)

Fig. 7.14
The Vertical Check
Adjustment
window.

4. Position the cursor in the Higher/Lower field and press **H** if you want
   the text adjusted higher on the check or **L** if you want the text adjusted
   lower.

5. Choose **Ctrl-Enter** to save the vertical settings and return to the Enter
   Check Number window. Enter a check number and press **Enter** to print
   the second sample laser check.

Review the second sample check. If the vertical alignment is still off, choose
No from the Did Check # Print Correctly? window and perform steps 1
through 5. Be sure to delete any sample check transactions that Quicken
records in the Register after you finish printing sample laser checks.

> **Note**
>
> If you have printed at least three sample laser checks and still are having trouble with
> alignment, call Intuit's technical support staff to get help adjusting your printer
> control code settings.

Printing Checks

When your checks are positioned properly in your printer, you're ready to
print a check. Printing checks with Quicken is fast, easy, and even fun. Just

don't forget to sign your checks after they are printed. Signing checks is the one task that Quicken cannot perform for you.

To print checks, follow these steps:

1. Load the checks into your printer.

    If you are using a laser printer, place the check form sheets in the printer paper tray, as you would place regular sheets of paper. If your printer prints on the face-down side of the paper, for example, make sure that your laser checks are inserted face down. Be sure that your checks are positioned in the proper order according to check number (the sheet with check number 3456 comes before the sheet with check number 3459).

2. Choose Print Checks from the Print/Acct menu. Quicken displays the Print Checks window (see fig. 7.15). This window displays two messages that give you information about the checks ready to be printed and provides three fields for you to control the printing of your checks. The first two messages tell you how many checks you have to print, and, if relevant, how many checks are postdated. Figure 7.15 shows that you have one check to print.

Fig. 7.15

The Print Checks window.

3. With the cursor positioned in the Print To field, choose the printer you want to use by selecting 1, 2, or 3.

4. Move the cursor to the Print All/Selected Checks field. To print all the checks that you have written (but have not yet printed) at the Write

Checks screen, leave this field set to A for All. To print only some of the checks, press **S**.

5. If you have postdated checks to print, Quicken displays the Print Checks Dated Through field next. This field accepts a date through which you want Quicken to print postdated checks.

   Suppose that today is 11/15/93 and that the checks waiting to be printed are dated 11/15/93, 11/16/93, and 11/17/93. If you set the date of this field to 11/16/93, Quicken prints the checks dated 11/15/93 and 11/16/93. Quicken does not, however, print the check dated 11/17/93. Use the + (plus) and - (minus) keys to change the date in the Print Checks Dated Through field.

6. Move the cursor to the Type of Checks To Print On field. Then, specify the kind of check form:

Select	To Designate
1	Continuous-feed standard checks
2	Continuous-feed wallet checks
3	Continuous-feed voucher check
4	Laser checks
5	Laser voucher checks
6	Laser wallet checks

   If you are using a laser printer with multipart voucher checks, you need to specify the number of additional copies (up to 3) that should be printed in the Number of Additional Copies field.

7. (Optional) If you entered S in the Print All/Selected checks field, Quicken displays the Select Checks to Print window, from which you can select the checks you want to print (see fig. 7.16). To select a check you want to print, highlight a check. When the check that you want to print is highlighted, press the spacebar to select the check. To deselect a check previously marked for printing, highlight that check and press the space bar again.

8. After you select checks to print, press **Enter** to leave the Select Checks to Print window. Quicken then displays the Enter Check Number

window that prompts you for the number of the next check to print (see fig. 7.17). The number of the next check already appears the window.

Fig. 7.16
The Select Checks
to Print window.

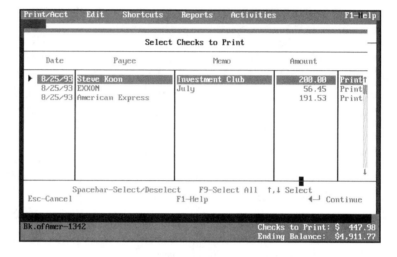

Fig. 7.17
The Enter Check
Number window.

9. If the number Quicken displays is the same as the number that appears in the upper right corner of the next check form, press **Enter** to print the check. If the number Quicken displays is incorrect, type the correct check number. You also can use the + (plus) and - (minus) keys to change the number.

If you're using a laser printer, you can print to a partial page of checks (one or two checks left on the page). You first must tell Quicken how many checks there are on the page, however. To print to a partial page of checks, press **F9** after you enter the correct check number in the Enter Check Number window. Quicken displays the Start Printing on Partial Page window that you see in figure 7.18.

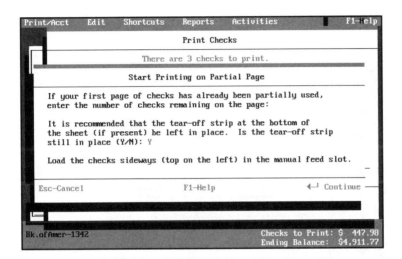

Fig. 7.18
The Start Printing on Partial Page window.

Type the number of checks remaining on the page in the first field (1 or 2). In the second field, indicate whether the strip at the bottom of the page is still intact by selecting **Y** or **N**. Follow the on-screen instructions for loading the partial page of checks into your printer and press **Enter**. Quicken returns to the Enter Check Number window.

> **Caution**
>
> If you are printing laser checks on a partial page, be sure to tell Quicken how many checks are left on the page by pressing **F9** from the Enter Check Number window. If you fail to do this, Quicken will assume that you are printing on a full page and your checks will not be printed correctly.

10. Press **Enter** to print the checks. Figure 7.19 shows a sample check to Jacobson's printed with the vertical and horizontal alignment correct. After Quicken finishes printing the checks, the program asks you if the checks printed correctly (see fig. 7.20). If each of your checks printed correctly, choose **Enter** or **1** to select Yes.

Fig. 7.19
A sample check
made payable to
Jacobson's.

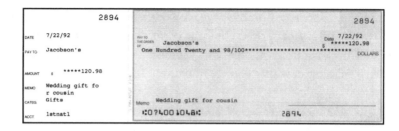

Fig. 7.20
Quicken asks
whether the check
printed correctly.

If one or more of your checks printed incorrectly—perhaps the alignment
was not right or the check forms jammed in the printer halfway through
printing—select 2 to answer No. Quicken asks for the number of the first
check that printed incorrectly. Quicken then returns to the Print Checks
window, and you repeat each of the Print Checks steps to reprint the checks
that printed incorrectly. Quicken records in the Register only those checks
that printed correctly.

> **CPA TIP**
>
> Write **VOID** in large letters across the face of checks that Quicken incorrectly prints.
> This precaution prevents you and anyone else from later signing and cashing the
> checks.

Reprinting a Check

If you decide later, even after leaving the Print Checks screen, that you want
to reprint a check, you can do so. Suppose that the original check somehow

gets lost or destroyed. You still have to pay the person, so you need to reprint the check. Rather than reenter all the same information, you can reprint the original information. (If you lose a check, consider placing a stop-payment order with your bank.)

When you describe checks you want to print using the Write Checks screen, Quicken actually records the checks in the Register. Because Quicken hasn't assigned check numbers, however, asterisks are entered in the check number field in the Register. These asterisks indicate that the check is one that you have set up to print using the Write Checks screen (see fig. 7.21). When Quicken prints the checks, it replaces the asterisks with the actual check number.

By itself, this bit of information isn't all that exciting, but it does enable you to trick Quicken into reprinting a check. All you need do is change a check's number to asterisks. Quicken then assumes that the check is one you want to print. To print the check after you have changed the number to asterisks, you follow the steps described earlier in *Printing Checks*.

Fig. 7.21

Quicken storing checks to be printed in the Register and identifying them by setting the check numbers to asterisks.

Summary

This chapter describes the basics of writing and printing checks with Quicken. These basics include the components of the Write Checks screen; how to use the Write Checks screen to record and postdate checks; and how to review, edit, and print checks.

The next chapter describes the Quicken features you can use to make check-writing even easier.

Chapter 8

Automating Check Writing

In Chapter 7, "Writing and Printing Checks," you learned how to write a check at the Write Checks screen. This chapter describes how you can use features in Quicken to make check writing faster and easier. Most of the features you learn about to automate check writing are the same as those for automating the Register (as you learned in Chapter 6). In fact, the only real difference between working with the Register and the Write Checks screen is that the screens are different; the menus and features are the same. If you're already familiar with the following Quicken features, you may want to skim this chapter.

If you're still not comfortable with the preceding Quicken features, read this chapter thoroughly so that you have the tools you need to make check writing fast and easy.

Using QuickFill

Writing checks is faster and easier with Quicken's *QuickFill* feature. When you type a few characters in a field, Quicken searches the various lists and the Register (the last three months of transactions only) to find a matching entry in that particular field. When Quicken finds a match, the QuickFill feature fills in the rest of the check with the transaction information that it found.

QuickFill works when you make an entry in the Payee field or the Category field in the Write Checks screen or the Register. To see how QuickFill works when entering transactions in the Register, see Chapter 6, "Automating the Register."

In this chapter,
you learn how to
do the following:

- Use QuickFill

- Delete and void transactions

- Split transactions

- Find transactions using the Find option, the Go to Date option, and the Go to Transfer option

- Memorize transactions

- Copy and paste transactions

- Use categories

- Use transaction groups

> **Note**
>
> QuickFill does not work when editing an existing check.

QuickFill is turned on or activated by default. When you first start to use Quicken 7, this feature already should be working. Refer to Chapter 6 to learn how to turn on QuickFill if it's not active when you start Quicken.

Using QuickFill at the Payee Field

Quicken searches the Memorized Transaction list and the last three months of transactions in the Register when you type a few characters in the Payee field of the Write Checks screen. When Quicken finds a transaction with the same payee name, QuickFill fills in the rest of the payee name from the transaction it found in the Memorized Transaction list or the previous transactions in the Register.

To use QuickFill at the Payee field, follow these steps:

1. At the Write Checks screen, enter the check date.

2. Type a few characters in the Payee field, such as **Ca**. Quicken searches the Memorized Transaction list and the last three months of transactions in the Register for a payee name that begins with *Ca*. When Quicken finds the first transaction with the payee *Carmel Boyscouts*, for example, QuickFill fills in the rest of the payee name.

3. If the payee name (or in this example, *Carmel Boyscouts*) is indeed the payee you want to enter in the transaction, choose Enter and QuickFill fills in the rest of the transaction information for that payee: the transaction amount, the memo field (if used), and the category or subcategory exactly like the transaction that Quicken found.

   If Quicken finds the matching transaction in the Memorized Transaction list, it displays <MEM> next to the payee name. If Quicken finds the matching transaction in the Register, it displays the month and day (<month/day>) next to the payee name.

   If QuickFill doesn't fill in the payee information that you want, keep typing characters in the Payee field or press **Ctrl-+** (plus) or **Ctrl--** (minus) to keep searching the Memorized Transaction list or the transactions in the Register for the correct transaction.

Note

If more than one payee name exists in the Memorized Transaction list or more than one previous transaction exists in the Register that begins with the characters you type, QuickFill enters the transaction information for the first payee name found.

Figure 8.1 shows the payee name filled in by QuickFill from the Memorized Transaction list. Figure 8.2 shows a check payee from a transaction dated 8/26 in the Register.

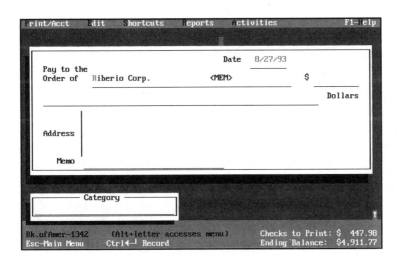

Fig. 8.1
A payee name filled in by Quickfill from the Memorized Transaction list.

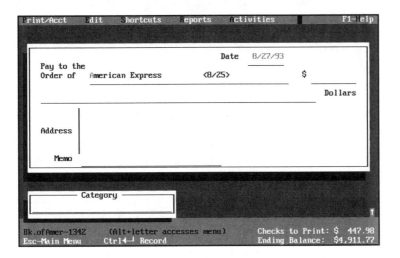

Fig. 8.2
A payee name filled in by QuickFill from a transaction in the Register.

4. After QuickFill fills in the check, you can edit any of the transaction fields. When the correct entries are made to all of the check fields, record the check by choosing **Ctrl-Enter** or **F10**. Quicken records the checks and displays a blank check next.

Using QuickFill to Fill In the Category Field

QuickFill also works when you type a few characters in the Category field of a new check. (QuickFill does not work when editing an existing check, however.) QuickFill searches the Category and Transfer list and searches for the first category or transfer account that begins with the characters you type. If you want to enter a subcategory or a class, you can type a colon (:) after the category name is filled in. Quicken searches the subcategories under that particular category and enters the first one that it finds. If you want to enter a class, you can type a slash (/) and a few characters after the category or subcategory name is filled in. Quicken then searches the Class list and enters the first class it finds that begins with the characters you type. For more information about classes, see Chapter 4, "Organizing Your Finances."

To use QuickFill to fill in the Category field, follow these steps:

1. At the Category field for a new check in the Write Checks screen, type a few characters of the category name you want to assign to the transaction. Quicken searches the Category and Transfer list for the first category or transfer account that matches the characters you type.

   When Quicken finds a matching category or transfer account, QuickFill fills in the rest of the category or transfer account name.

2. If this is the category or transfer account that you want to assign to the transaction, press **Enter** to accept it.

   If the category or transfer account name filled in by QuickFill is not the one that you want, type a few more characters or press **Ctrl-+** (plus) or **Ctrl--** (minus) until Quicken finds the right name.

3. To enter a subcategory after QuickFill fills in the category name, press **End** to go to the end of the category name and type a colon (:). QuickFill fills in the first subcategory for the category it just filled in. If the subcategory is not the one that you want, type a few more characters or press **Ctrl-+** or **Ctrl--** to find the next or preceding subcategory under the category. Press **Enter** to accept the subcategory.

4. To enter class information, type a slash (/) after the category or subcategory name that QuickFill filled in and type a few characters of the class name. QuickFill searches the Class list and fills in the first class that begins with the characters you type. To accept the class, press **Enter**. If the class is not the one you want, type a few more characters or press **Ctrl-+** or **Ctrl--** to find the next or preceding class. To enter a subclass, type a colon after the class name, and QuickFill fills in the first subclass for the class it just filled in. Press the **Ctrl-+** or **Ctrl--** to find the next or preceding subclass under the class. Press **Enter** to accept the subclass.

Note

If the category or class you want to assign to a check is not in the Category and Transfer list or the Class list (because they're new), you can add a new category or class simply by typing the new name in the Category field. When you press **Enter** after you enter a new category or class name in the Write Checks screen, Quicken displays the Category Not Found window and asks if you want to add it to the Category or Class list or select a category or class from the existing list. To add the category or class, choose **1**, Add to Category List or Add to Class List, and go through the normal steps for adding categories and classes.

Deactivating QuickFill

If you don't want to use the QuickFill feature, perhaps because you have varied checks that are rarely the same or because you feel more comfortable typing check information on your own, you can deactivate or turn off the QuickFill feature. Refer to Chapter 6, "Automating the Register," to learn how to deactivate QuickFill.

Deleting Checks

You can delete a check you have written at the Write Checks screen providing that you have not printed the check yet. After checks are printed, Quicken no longer stores them in the Write Checks screen. Printed check information is saved in the Register.

To delete a check from the Write Checks screen, follow these steps:

1. To display the check that you want to delete, use the PgUp and PgDn keys or the Home and End keys.

Tip
You should not delete a check you have written and printed with Quicken. When you delete a check, Quicken removes all record of the transaction. Deleting the check removes the check information and leaves a gap in your check-numbering sequence. Void a check transaction that you want to remove because of a lost check, a check that you have stopped payment on, or an improperly printed check, but do not delete such checks. Information for voided transactions remains in the Register so that you can track each prenumbered check.

2. Choose **D**elete Transaction from the Edit menu, or press **Ctrl-D** (see fig. 8.3).

Fig. 8.3
The Edit menu.

Quicken displays the OK to Delete Transaction? window that you see in figure 8.4.

Fig. 8.4
The OK to Delete Transaction? window.

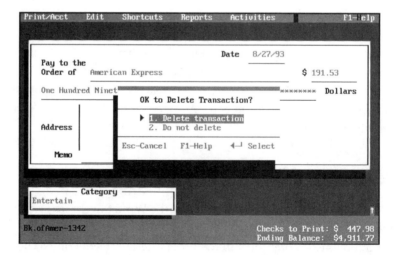

3. Press **Enter** to delete the transaction (the **D**elete Transaction option is highlighted), or choose 2 if you don't want to delete the transaction.

Voiding Checks

You may need to void a check when you want to stop payment, when you lose a check and write another one to replace it, or when a check prints incorrectly and you have to print another. Note that when you choose to void a check from the Write Checks screen, Quicken takes you to the Checking Account Register and enables you to void the check transaction from there.

If you void a check transaction that is part of a transfer from one account to another, voiding any part of the transaction also voids the other parts of the transaction—those recorded in the other Registers.

To void a check from the Write Checks screen, follow these steps:

1. To display the check you want to void, use the PgUp and PgDn keys or the Home and End keys.

2. Choose Void Transaction from the Edit menu, or press **Ctrl-V**.

   Quicken moves to the Register for the account from which you wrote the check and highlights the check you are voiding. The OK to Void Transaction? window appears (see fig. 8.5).

Fig. 8.5
The OK to Void Transaction? window.

3. Choose **Enter** to void the transaction (the Void Transaction option already is highlighted), or choose **2** if you decide not to void the transaction.

Learning Quicken

Quicken enters VOID: in the Payee field before the payee name and marks the transaction with an X in the Clear column so that the transaction is not considered an uncleared item when you perform your account reconciliation.

4. To return to the Write Checks screen, press **Ctrl-W**.

Splitting Check Transactions

The Write Checks screen provides a field for assigning a category or subcategory to the check transaction. A check written to the power company may be assigned to the Utilities category, for example. A check written to pay for office supplies may be assigned to the Supplies category. Many transactions, however, fit into more than one category. When you need to assign a check to more than one category, use the Split Transaction option on the Edit menu. This option provides additional category fields and more space to assign categories and subcategories to a check.

To split a check transaction, follow these steps:

1. Choose Split Transaction from the Edit menu, or press **Ctrl-S**. The Split Transaction window appears (see fig. 8.6).

Fig. 8.6

The Split Transaction window.

2. Enter the first category name in the Category field in line 1.

You can use the Category field in the Split Transaction window in the same way you use the Category field in the Write Checks screen. You also can use the Category field to record transfers to other accounts. Up to 30 lines are available on the Split Transaction window to assign categories, subcategories, or transfer accounts.

> **Note**
>
> Quicken provides defined Home and Business categories. The Home Category list provides categories for most general household expenses, and the Business Category list includes general business income and expense categories. To access these categories, press **Ctrl-C** from the Category field in the Split Transaction window.

3. (Optional) In the Memo field, type a description of the category or the amount. The Memo field provides a 27-character space you can use to describe a transaction, to explain why you selected a category, or to detail how you calculated the check amount.

4. Move the cursor to the Amount field. You can use the Amount field in two ways, depending on whether you select **S**plit Transaction before or after you enter the amount on the Write Checks screen.

   If you select **S**plit Transaction before you make an entry in the Amount field on the Write Checks screen, Quicken adds each of the amounts you enter in the Amount field in the Split Transaction window. Quicken then enters this total in the $ field in the Write Checks screen.

   If you select **S**plit Transaction after entering a check amount in the Write Checks screen, Quicken shows this amount in the first Amount field in the Split Transaction window. If you then enter a number in the first Amount field in the Split Transaction window, Quicken calculates the difference between the check amount in the Write Checks screen and the new amount you entered and then places this difference in the second Amount field in the Split Transaction window.

5. Move to the next line of the Split Transaction screen. Repeat steps 2, 3, and 4 for each category and amount combination you want to record. You can record up to 30 category and amount combinations. Figure 8.7 shows a completed Split Transaction window.

Fig. 8.7

A completed Split
Transaction
window.

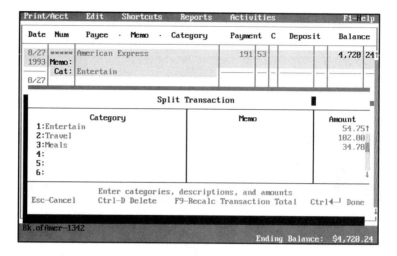

Tip

As noted in Chap-
ter 6, you also can
enter percentages
in the Split Trans-
action window's
Amount fields. If
you enter a check
for $1,200 and 25
percent of this
amount is to be
entered in the first
Split Transaction
field, move the
cursor to the field,
type **25%**, and
press **Enter**. When
you move to the
next field,
Quicken calculates
the number that
equals 25 percent
of $1,200 and
enters this value in
the Amount field.

If you use all 30 split transaction Amount fields, Quicken has nowhere
to make the Write Checks screen amount equal to the total Split Transaction amount. You must manually adjust the Write Checks screen
amount or one of the Split Transaction window amounts. You also can
choose **F9** to total the Amount fields in the Split Transaction window
and insert the total into the $ field in the Write Checks screen.

6. To leave the Split Transaction window and return to the Write Checks
screen, choose **Ctrl-Enter** or **F10**.

7. After returning to the Write Checks screen, record the check. Quicken
indicates a split transaction by displaying [SPLIT] below the Category
field (see fig. 8.8).

Calculating Check Amounts in Split Transactions

You can calculate the amount for which you want to write a check by using the
Split Transaction window. Perhaps you have several invoices from the same
vendor, but each invoice represents a different type of expense that you want
to assign to different categories. You can use the Split Transaction window to
assign the categories, enter the amounts, and calculate the total amount to
enter as the check amount in the Write Checks screen. (Calculating transaction
amounts in split transactions is explained in Chapter 6, "Automating the Register.) Use the same steps to calculate check amounts in split transactions in the
Write Checks screen.

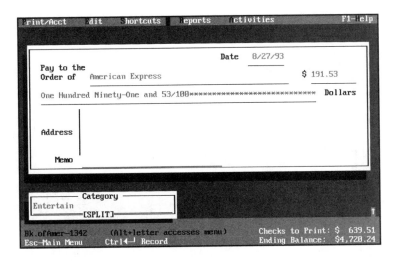

Fig. 8.8
Quicken identifies a split transaction with the word [SPLIT] below the Category field on the Write Checks screen.

Editing, Deleting, and Undoing Split Transactions

The procedures for editing, deleting, and undoing a split transaction in the Write Checks screen are the same as those for the Register. Refer to Chapter 6 to learn how to edit, delete, and undo a split transaction.

Finding Checks

After you write a large volume of checks, you may need to find a check to review or edit. Quicken's Find option enables you to locate a check you have written (but not printed) in the Write Checks screen quickly and easily.

Using the Find Option

One way to search through unprinted checks is to use an *exact match*. An exact match means that you look for a check that contains a payee, an amount, a category, or another piece of check information exactly equal to what you want. The amount for which you are searching is known as a *search argument*.

To search through checks you created but didn't print, follow these steps:

1. Choose Find from the Edit menu, or press **Ctrl-F**. The Transaction to Find window appears (see fig. 8.9).

2. Perform one or more of the following searches:

   To search through the Write Checks screen for checks with a specific entry in the Payee field, enter the name of the payee in the Payee field.

Tip
If you use check forms with vouchers and enter individual invoices and invoice amounts in the Split Transaction window, Quicken prints this information on the voucher. Vendors then can record your payments correctly, and you no longer have to spend time trying to explain which invoice a check pays. Remember that room is available on the voucher only for the first 15 lines in the Split Transaction window. If you use all 30 lines in the Split Transaction window, only half of the split transaction detail appears.

Fig. 8.9

The Transaction to
Find window.

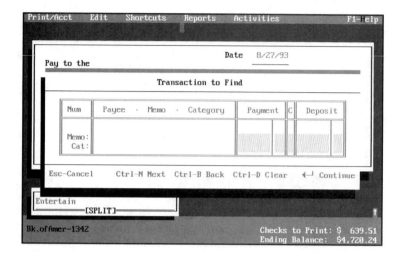

To search for checks equal to a specific amount, enter the amount in
the Payment field. Quicken searches through the unprinted checks for
the amount you entered. The amount for which you are searching is
the *search argument*.

To search for unprinted checks with a specific memo, enter the memo
for which you are searching in the Memo field.

To search for unprinted checks assigned to a specific category, enter the
category name assigned to the check for which you are searching in the
Category field.

Do not enter an amount in the Num, C, or Deposit fields. Although
these fields appear on the Transaction to Find screen, these amounts do
not appear in the Write Checks screen. Therefore, you cannot use these
fields to find checks written at the Write Checks screen.

3. After you enter the search arguments, press **Ctrl-Enter** or **F10**. Alternatively, press **Enter** when the cursor is in the Category field.

Quicken asks in which direction you want to search by displaying the
Search Direction? screen (see fig. 8.10). You have two options: Find
backwards and Find next. Find backwards (Ctrl-B) searches through
checks dated earlier than the check displayed in the Write Checks
screen. Find next (Ctrl-N) searches through checks dated later than the
check that appears in the Write Checks screen.

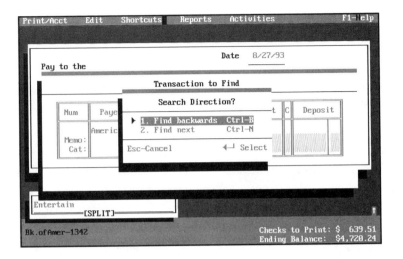

Fig. 8.10
Quicken prompts you to search through checks dated before or after the check that currently appears on-screen.

4. Choose Find backwards or Find next.

Quicken searches for the exact words you type. If you enter **75** in the Payment field, for example, Quicken searches for checks equal to $75.00. If you type **mortgage** in the Memo field, Quicken looks for checks with *mortgage* in this field. Because Quicken's search is not case sensitive, *Mortgage*, *MORTGAGE*, and *mortgage* all are exact matches from Quicken's perspective. If the Memo field reads *May mortgage*, however, Quicken does not find the check.

If Quicken finds a check that matches the search argument, it displays the check in the Write Checks screen. If Quicken does not find a check that matches the search argument, the program displays the message No matching transactions were found. (see fig. 8.11).

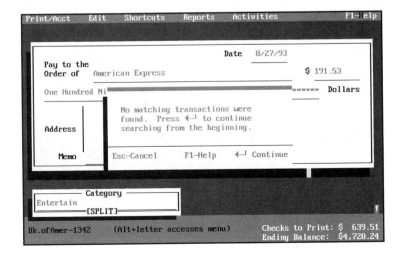

Fig. 8.11
The "No matching transactions were found." message.

If Quicken does not find any matches, it will ask you if you want to continue the search to the end of the Register (if you had asked it to search backwards by pressing **Ctrl-B**).

If you asked Quicken to search forwards (by pressing **Ctrl-N**), and no matches are found, it will ask you if you want to continue searching from the beginning of the Register.

Finding Key-Word Matches. Key-word matches enable you to search based on a field that includes or excludes certain letters, characters, or series of characters. Key-word matches use three special characters: periods (.), question marks (?), and tildes (~). Periods act as wildcard indicators that can represent any character, group of characters, or even no character. The question mark can represent any one character. The tilde character identifies a word, character, or group of characters to exclude from the search. For a summary of the special characters Quicken uses to find key-word matches in Write Checks screen fields, refer to Table 6.1 in Chapter 6.

Combining Exact Matches and Key-Word Matches. You can search by using more than one exact match or key-word search argument. Figure 8.12, for example, shows the Transaction to Find window to search for checks using *big national* in the Payee field and *mortgage* in the Memo field. The same techniques that work for searching through the Register also work for searching through unprinted checks. For more information about key-word matches, refer to Chapter 6, "Automating the Register."

Fig. 8.12
Using key-word matches in the Transaction to Find screen.

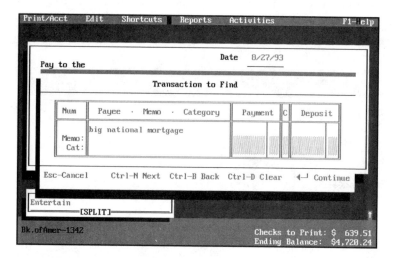

If you use more than one match test, Quicken locates only the checks that meet all the tests. In the example in figure 8.12, Quicken does not locate checks with the phrase *big national* in the Payee field unless the word *mortgage* is in the Memo field and vice versa.

Repeating a Search. When executing a Find request, Quicken selects the first check that matches the search arguments you entered. If you were precise in specifying the exact match or key-word match, the first check Quicken finds may be the one you want. Because the first check Quicken finds often is not the one you want, however, Quicken gives you two other Find options: Repeat Find (backwards) and Repeat Find (next). Repeat Find (backwards) executes the Find request already specified on the Transaction to Find window; it searches through checks dated earlier than the currently displayed check. Similarly, Repeat Find (next) executes the Find request already specified on the Transaction to Find window; it searches through checks dated later than the currently displayed check.

Using the Go to Date Option

To search for a specific day's checks, choose Go to Date from the Edit menu, or press **Ctrl-G**. Quicken displays the Go to Date window (see fig. 8.13).

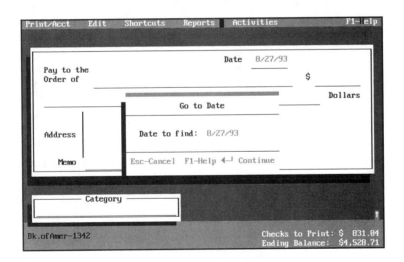

Fig. 8.13
The Go to Date window.

Initially, Quicken displays the current system date in the Go to Date window. To specify a date for the search, type the date you want over the default date. You also can use the + (plus) and – (minus) keys to move the date forward or backward one day at a time.

After you specify a date and press **Enter**, Quicken finds and displays the first check with the date you entered. If no check with the entered date is found, Quicken displays the check with the date closest to the entered date.

Because Quicken arranges all checks by the check date, you do not need to specify a search direction when using the Go to Date option. By comparing the date on the currently displayed check to the date you enter, Quicken determines the direction to search. If the date for which you want to search falls before the date on the current check, Quicken searches through the previous checks. If the date you want to search for falls after the date on the current check, Quicken looks through checks dated after the current check.

Using the Go to Transfer Option

You can choose Go to Transfer from the Edit menu, or press **Ctrl-X** to go to the transfer transaction related to the currently displayed check. If you entered the transfer account in the Category field, recorded the check, and then executed the Go to Transfer option, Quicken accesses the Account Register for the corresponding transaction and highlights the transfer transaction. Pressing **Ctrl-X** again returns you to the transaction in the Register for the account that you wrote the check from. Usually, you enter an account here because you're transferring money from a checking account to another bank account by writing a check. To review account transfers, see Chapters 5 and 6.

Using Memorized Check Transactions

To speed the check-writing process, you can memorize recurring check transactions from the Write Checks screen. Many checks you write probably are similar from week to week and month to month. For a household, you may write a mortgage check, a car loan check, a utility bill check, and so on. For a business, you may write weekly payroll checks to employees and monthly checks to major vendors. Because checks often are similar, Quicken enables you to store check information in a special list known as the *Memorized Transactions List*. Rather than re-entering the same information, you can reuse transaction information. The Memorize Transaction option is valuable if you address checks, because you do not have to re-enter the payee's address every time you write a check.

Memorizing a Check Transaction

If you have read Chapter 5, "Automating the Register," you already know about using memorized transactions in the Register. The Memorize Transaction option works similarly in the Write Checks screen. Therefore, if you feel well-versed in the mechanics of memorized transactions, skip or skim the next few paragraphs. The only substantive difference between memorized transactions in the Register and memorized transactions for unprinted checks in the Write Checks screen is that if you memorize an unprinted check, Quicken memorizes the address information. (Address information doesn't appear in the Register.)

To memorize a check transaction, follow these steps:

1. To display the check you want to memorize in the Write Checks screen, use the PgUp and PgDn keys or the Home and End keys (see fig. 8.14).

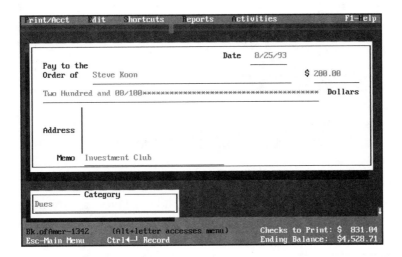

Fig. 8.14
Choosing a check to memorize.

2. Choose Memorize Transaction from the Shortcuts, or press **Ctrl-M**. Quicken alerts you that the marked information is about to be memorized (see fig. 8.15).

3. To complete the memorization process, press **Enter**. Quicken saves a copy of the check in the Memorized Transaction list.

Recalling a Check Transaction

You can select Recall Transaction by pressing **Ctrl-T** to complete the Write Checks screen by using information from memorized transactions. Suppose that you use the Memorize Transaction option to memorize the monthly contribution to an investment club shown in figure 8.15. When you need to pay Steve Koon again, choose Recall Transaction from the Shortcuts menu or press **Ctrl-T**. Either approach displays the Memorized Transaction List shown in figure 8.16. The Memorized Transaction list shows all memorized transactions (except memorized investment transactions). You want to recall, however, only those transactions that show Chk in the Type column. Chk indicates that the transaction was memorized from the Write Checks screen. Chk transactions include information that appears only in the Write Checks screen, such as the address data and the extra message line.

Fig. 8.15
Quicken tells you that the marked information is about to be memorized.

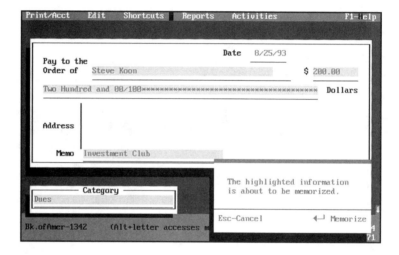

Figure 8.16 shows some of the information saved as part of the Memorize Transaction operation. The address information and message also are saved, but the address and message do not show in the Memorized Transaction list.

> **Note**
>
> If you memorize a split check transaction, Quicken displays a message window that asks if you want to memorize the split amounts as amounts or as percentages of the check amount. To answer the message, choose A if you want the actual amounts memorized or choose P to memorize the percentages. This feature is handy if a memorized check amount varies, but the split is always based on the same percentages.

```
 Print/Acct   Edit   Shortcuts   Reports   Activities          F1-Help

                        Memorized Transaction List

    Grp       Description    Split  Memo      Category  Clr  Amount   Type

            American Express  S              Entertain       191.53  Chk ↑
   monthly  FMCC                             Auto:Loan       315.67  Pmt
            Paula Yturbide           Apartment Rent          590.00  Pmt
            Riberio Corp.            Mini-wareho Rent         43.00  Pmt
  ▶         Steve Koon               Investment  Dues        200.00  Chk




    Ctrl-D Delete  Ctrl-E Edit  Ctrl-P Print  Ctrl-Ins Add  ↑,↓ Select
    Esc-Cancel        F1-Help  Ctrl-J Schedule F9-Amortize      ↵ Use

  Bk.of Amer-1342                        Checks to Print: $  831.04
                                         Ending Balance:  $4,528.71
```

Fig. 8.16

The Memorized
Transaction List.

The Memorized Transaction list is sorted by payee. For each payee, Quicken shows whether the transaction is a split transaction, the memo (if any), the category assigned to the memorized transaction, whether the memorized transaction has cleared the bank, the transaction amount, the transaction type (Chk, Pmt, Dep, and so on), and to which transaction group (if any) the memorized transaction belongs. Transaction groups are described in the *Using Check Transaction Groups* section, later in this chapter.

To recall a memorized check transaction, follow these steps:

1. To access the Write Checks screen, choose **Write/Print Checks** from the Main Menu, or press **Ctrl-W**.

2. Choose Recall Transaction from the **Shortcuts** menu, or press **Ctrl-T**. Quicken displays the Memorized Transaction List.

3. Highlight the memorized check you want to recall to the Write Checks screen.

4. Press **Enter**. Quicken uses the memorized transaction to fill the Write Checks screen.

5. Edit the information from the memorized check, if necessary.

6. Choose **Ctrl-Enter** or **F10** to record the check.

Editing a Memorized Check Transaction

Over time, you may need to update the check information you memorized. Updating check information, however, doesn't present a problem. To edit a memorized transaction, follow these steps:

1. Choose Recall Transaction from the Shortcuts menu, or press **Ctrl-T**. Quicken displays the Memorized Transaction list.

2. Highlight the transaction you want to edit and press **Ctrl-E**. Quicken displays the Edit/Set Up Memorized Transaction window (see fig. 8.17).

Fig. 8.17

The Edit/Set Up Memorized Transaction window.

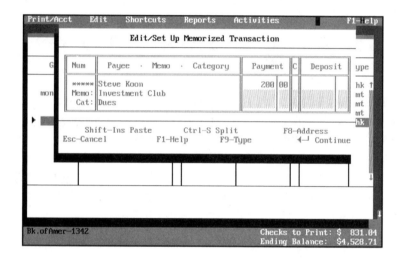

3. Change the fields as necessary and then choose **Ctrl-Enter** or **F10**.

Deleting a Memorized Check Transaction

At some point, the original reasons you had for memorizing a transaction may no longer apply. Eventually, you may pay off the mortgage or car loan, children may outgrow the need for day care, or you may choose to stop spending money on an item, such as club dues or cable television.

You can use the Recall Transaction option to delete memorized transactions from the Memorized Transaction list. To delete a transaction from the list, follow these steps:

1. Choose Recall Transaction from the Shortcuts menu, or press **Ctrl-T**. Quicken displays the Memorized Transaction List.

2. Highlight the transaction you want to delete and press **Ctrl-D**.

3. After you highlight the transaction to delete, press **Ctrl-D**. Quicken alerts you that you are about to delete a memorized transaction (see fig. 8.18).

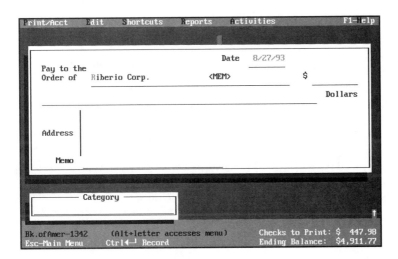

Fig. 8.18
Quicken warns you that you are about to delete a memorized transaction.

4. To delete the memorized check transaction, press **Enter**. If you decide not to delete the memorized transaction, choose **Esc**.

Printing the Memorized Transaction List

Quicken enables you to print lists of memorized transactions. Assuming that you entered payee addresses, a printed list of memorized transactions can act as a directory of the people and businesses to whom you write checks.

To print a list of memorized checks and other transactions, follow these steps:

1. Choose Recall Transaction from the Shortcuts menu, or press **Ctrl-T**. Quicken displays the Memorized Transaction list.

2. Choose **Ctrl-P**. Quicken displays the Print Memorized Transaction list window. Specify the printer settings you want to use to print the report.

3. Indicate the printer you want to use and press **Enter**. Quicken prints the list.

Tip

Consider as candidates for the Memorized Transaction List each check you regularly write using Quicken: rent, house payment, utility payment, school loans, and so on. Using the Memorized Transaction option saves you time you otherwise spend typing, finding addresses, and describing checks.

Copying and Pasting Check Transactions

If there is a single check you want to copy, but you don't feel the need to memorize it and make it part of the Memorized Transaction list, you can copy that check and paste it in a blank check or an existing check in the Write Checks screen.

When Quicken copies a check, it essentially is memorizing the check information. This information is stored in Quicken and can be pasted in a blank check or an existing check in the Write Checks screen. You can repaste the same check more than once. Quicken will not save the stored check information after you copy another check or exit the program, however.

To copy and paste a check in the Write Checks screen, follow these steps:

1. To display the check you want to copy, use the PgUp and PgDn keys or the Home and End keys.

2. Choose Copy Transaction from the Shortcuts menu, or press **Ctrl-Ins**. Quicken flashes a message in the bottom right corner of your screen that it is MEMORIZING the transaction.

3. Display a blank check or, to replace an existing check with the copied check, display the check you want to replace.

4. Choose Paste Transaction from the Shortcuts menu, or press **Shift-Ins**. Quicken enters (or pastes) the check information from the copied check into the currently displayed check.

If the Confirm When Overwriting with a Memorized or Pasted Transaction setting is turned on, Quicken displays the OK to Overwrite Transaction? message before it replaces an existing check with the copied check. To proceed and enter the copied check over the existing check, choose **Enter**. Otherwise, choose Esc. You learn how to work with transaction settings in Chapter 20, "Customizing Quicken."

Using Categories

You can assign a category or subcategory to a check by typing the category or subcategory name in the Category field or by choosing Categorize/Transfer from the Shortcuts menu. This option displays the Category and Transfer List so that you can find and assign a category, subcategory, or transfer account to a check. You also can use this option to add a new category or edit or delete an existing category. Adding, editing, and deleting categories and subcategories is described in Chapter 4, "Organizing Your Finances."

To find and assign a category or subcategory to a check, follow these steps:

1. From the Write Checks screen, choose Categorize/Transfer from the Shortcuts menu, or press **Ctrl-C**.

Quicken displays the Category and Transfer List with predefined categories, subcategories, and any accounts you may have created (see fig. 8.19).

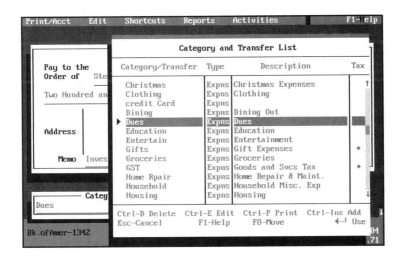

Fig. 8.19
The Category and Transfer List.

2. Highlight the category, subcategory, or account you want to assign to the check, and then press **Enter**. Quicken retrieves the category or account name from the list and enters it in the Category field.

Using Check Transaction Groups

The capability of recalling a single memorized check saves time, but Quicken provides you with another option: you can recall sets of memorized transactions, or *transaction groups*. Transaction groups enable you to recall several memorized checks at the same time. Rather than using Recall Transaction repeatedly to retrieve checks from the Memorized Transaction List, you can recall an entire group of checks in one step.

Tip
You also can use the PgUp, PgDn, Home, and End keys to move quickly through long lists of categories and accounts. The Category and Transfer List also provides a scroll bar that mouse users can take advantage of for moving up and down the list.

Using transaction groups is explained in Chapter 6, "Automating the Register," including setting up a transaction group, recalling a transaction group, editing and deleting transaction groups, adding a new transaction to a group, and deleting a transaction from a group. Using transaction groups at the Write Checks screen works the same way. In fact, when you're at the Write Checks screen and choose Scheduled Transaction from the Shortcuts menu, Quicken takes you to the Scheduled Transaction List with the Register in the background so that you can set up or recall a transaction group from there.

Summary

This chapter showed you how to speed up your check writing using QuickFill, memorized transactions, and transaction groups. You learned how to copy and paste a check transaction and how to quickly find transactions using the Find option, the Go to Date option, and the Go to Transfer option.

Chapter 9, "Reconciling Your Bank Account," shows you how to reconcile your bank account. The hours you have spent doing this task in the past will turn into minutes when you reconcile your account with Quicken!

Chapter 9

Reconciling Your Bank Account

Reconciling your bank account regularly is one of the most important steps you can take to protect your cash and the accuracy and reliability of your financial records; but most people probably don't reconcile—except out of a sense of guilt or frustration. The work is tedious and usually aggravating as you search, often futilely, for the transaction that explains the difference between the bank's records and your personal records. Fortunately, Quicken provides a fast and easy method of reconciliation.

Reviewing the Reconciliation Process

Reconciling a bank account is not difficult. You probably already understand the mechanics of the reconciliation process. For those readers who are a bit rusty with the process, however, the next few paragraphs briefly describe how reconciliation works.

To reconcile a bank account, you perform three basic steps:

1. Review the bank statement for new transactions and errors. You want to verify that you have recorded each transaction correctly.

2. Find the transactions not recorded by the bank (not cleared), and total these transactions.

3. Verify that the difference between your Quicken Register balance and the bank balance equals the total of the uncleared transactions. If the totals don't agree, you need to repeat steps 1 and 2.

In this chapter, you learn how to do the following:

- Reconcile a bank account using Quicken

- Mark transactions as cleared

- Print and use reconciliation reports

- Correct and catch reconciliation errors

Learning Quicken

I

Tip
If you still find the process confusing, examine your monthly bank statement. The back of your current bank statement probably explains the whole process step-by-step.

Reviewing the Bank Statement

The first step in reconciling an account is to review the bank statement. First, find any new transactions the bank recorded and that you now need to record. These transactions may include bank service fees, overdraft charges, and interest income. You need to record these transactions in the Register before you proceed with the reconciliation.

For each transaction, confirm that the checking account transaction recorded in the Register and on the bank statement are the same amount. If you find a transaction not recorded in both places for the same amount, review the discrepancy and identify the incorrect transaction.

CPA TIP

Carefully review each canceled check for authenticity. If a check forger successfully draws a check on your account, you can discover the forgery by reviewing canceled checks.

Checking Cleared Transactions

The second step in checking account reconciliation is to calculate the total dollar value of those transactions that have not cleared the bank. By adding all checks that have not cleared (usually known as *outstanding checks*) and also all deposits (usually known as *deposits in transit*), you calculate an amount that represents the logical difference between the bank's records and your records.

Usually, the mechanics of this step work in the following way: You look through the bank statement to identify checks and deposits that have cleared, and then mark cleared transactions in the Register. After you mark all the cleared transactions in the Register, adding all transactions that haven't cleared is a simple matter.

Verifying that Balances Correspond

The final step is a quick one: you verify that the difference between the Quicken Register balance and the bank statement balance is the total of the transactions that *have not* cleared. If you have correctly performed steps 1 and 2 in the reconciliation process, the balance in your Quicken Register and the ending bank balance should differ by the total of all transactions not yet cleared. If the two amounts don't differ by precisely this amount, you must repeat steps 1 and 2 until you locate and correct the error.

Using Quicken to Reconcile Your Account

Quicken makes reconciling a bank account easier by automating the steps and doing the arithmetic for you. To reconcile an account, follow these steps:

1. From the Write Checks or Register screen, choose Reconcile from the Activities menu.

> **Note**
>
> The first time you use Quicken to reconcile your account, a brief message appears telling you what the Reconcile option does and that you should read the chapter in the Quicken manual to learn about reconciling. Press **Enter** to remove the message and continue with the reconciliation process.

Quicken displays the Reconcile Register with Bank Statement window (see fig. 9.1).

Fig. 9.1

The Reconcile Register with Bank Statement window.

2. In the Bank Statement Opening Balance field, type the bank statement balance shown at the start of the period the statement covers if the balance differs from the one shown. This number appears on your bank statement. If this is your first time to reconcile your account with Quicken, the opening balance that you entered when you added the account to your system is entered as the bank statement opening balance.

> **Note**
>
> Quicken strongly recommends that you use the ending balance from your last
> bank statement as the opening balance in a new bank account. Therefore, if
> you used the ending balance as your opening balance, the opening balance
> that Quicken enters in the Bank Statement Opening Balance field should be
> correct.

If this is not your first time to use Quicken to reconcile your bank account, Quicken uses the ending balance per your bank statement from
the last time you reconciled your account as the opening bank statement balance.

If the opening bank statement balance that Quicken enters in the Reconcile Register with Bank Statement window does not agree with the
opening balance on your bank statement, be sure to read the section
Adjusting Opening Balance Differences, later in this chapter.

3. In the Bank Statement Ending Balance field, type the bank statement
   balance shown at the end of the period the bank statement covers. This
   number also appears on your bank statement.

4. In the Statement Opening Date field, type the date shown on your bank
   statement as the opening or starting date.

5. In the Statement Ending Date field, type the date shown on your bank
   statement as the ending date.

> **CPA TIP**
>
> If you normally keep a large account balance, you should have an interest-
> bearing checking account. You should not keep your money in an account
> that doesn't earn interest.
>
> Before you close your current account and open a new one, however, review
> the fees your bank charges for each type of account. Weigh the interest factor
> against the fee schedule to determine the most beneficial account type for
> your personal or business account. If your bank does not offer interest-bearing
> accounts to businesses, you may want to deposit excess cash into a savings or
> money market account. Remember that you can set up savings and money
> market accounts in your Quicken system and use the Reconcile feature to
> balance each account.

> **Note**
>
> After you have reconciled your account using Quicken, the next time you reconcile Quicken automatically enters dates in the Statement Opening Date and Statement Ending Date fields based on the dates you entered the first time you reconciled. If these dates differ, just change them by typing a new date or using the + (plus) or - (minus) keys to change the date one day at a time.

6. In the Service Charge field, if you have not recorded monthly service fees, record these fees now by entering the appropriate amount in the Service Charge field.

7. (Optional) Move the cursor to the Category field. If you entered an amount in the field and want to assign the charge to a category, enter the appropriate category name in the Category field. (Remember that you can access the Category and Transfer List by pressing **Ctrl-C**.)

8. Move the cursor to the Interest Earned field. If you have not recorded monthly interest income on the account, record the interest earned by entering the appropriate amount in the Interest Earned field.

9. (Optional) Move the cursor to the Category field. If you entered an amount in the Interest Earned field and want to assign the income to a category, enter the appropriate category name here.

10. (Optional) To print the last reconciliation report before you begin reconciling, choose **F9**. This is your last chance to print this report. After you start reconciling your account, the data from the last reconciliation report will be overwritten.

If you choose F9 to print a reconciliation report, Quicken displays the Print Reconciliation Report window. To learn how to complete this window and print a report, see the section *Printing a Reconciliation Report*, later in this chapter.

11. Choose **Enter** or **F10** when the Reconcile Register with Bank Statement window is complete. Quicken displays the Transaction List window, which shows each bank account transaction (see fig. 9.2).

Fig. 9.2

Bank account
transactions
shown in a list.

12. Mark checks and deposits that have cleared (were recorded by) the
    bank. To mark an item as cleared, highlight the transaction you want
    to mark. Choose **Enter** to mark the highlighted transaction as cleared
    and move to the next transaction. Quicken enters an asterisk (*) in the
    Cleared column. To unmark a transaction, highlight the transaction
    that you want to unmark and press the space bar to remove the asterisk.

    To mark a range of transactions as cleared, choose **F8**. The Mark Range
    of Check Numbers as Cleared window appears (see fig. 9.3). You use
    this screen to specify that all transactions with check numbers in the
    indicated range should be marked as cleared.

Fig. 9.3

The Mark Range of
Check Numbers as
Cleared window.

As you mark transactions, the reconciliation summary in the Transactions List window shows the numbers and dollar amounts of the check and deposit transactions you marked as cleared, the cleared transaction total, the ending balance, and the difference between the total and the balance. You are finished with the reconciliation when the difference between the cleared balance and the bank statement balance equals zero.

13. (Optional) To correct transactions you entered incorrectly in the Register, choose **F9** to redisplay the same information in an abbreviated form of the standard Register. Edit the transactions in the Register in the usual manner. To change the displayed screen back to the Transaction list, choose **F9** again. (Chapter 6 describes how to edit transactions in the Quicken Register.)

Figure 9.4 shows sample transactions as they appear in the Register.

Fig. 9.4

A Checking account transaction shown in the Register.

14. When the difference between the cleared balance and the bank statement balance is zero, choose **Ctrl-F10** to indicate that you are finished with the reconciliation. When you choose Ctrl-F10, Quicken changes each asterisk (*) in the C field to an X, and asks whether you want to print a reconciliation report (see fig. 9.5).

Fig. 9.5

Quicken congratu-
lates you when
your account
balances.

> **Note**
>
> If you understand double-entry bookkeeping, you probably recognize that Quicken uses the labels *debit* and *credit* incorrectly from your perspective. Do not be confused by this usage. The reconciliation summary uses the terms from the bank's perspective to help people who do not understand double-entry bookkeeping.

You can leave the reconciliation process at any time by choosing **Esc**. When you choose Esc, Quicken displays the Reconciliation is Not Complete window that you see in figure 9.6. Choose **2** to select the Leave reconciliation (your work will be saved) option. Quicken then returns to the Register you were in before you began the reconciliation. Any work you have done (entering balances, service charges, marking checks, and so on) is saved so that, when you return to the reconciliation, you can proceed at the point you left.

If you don't want to leave the reconciliation after you have selected Esc, just press **Enter** to select the Proceed to next reconciliation step option.

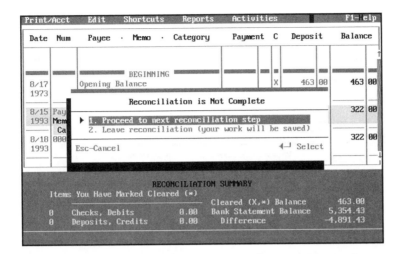

Fig. 9.6
The Reconciliation is Not Complete window.

Printing Reconciliation Reports

Many people like to keep printed records of their reconciliations. Printed copies of the reconciliation report show how you reconciled your records with the bank, indicate all checks and deposits still outstanding, and show all transactions that cleared the bank in a given month—information that may be helpful if you subsequently discover that the bank made an error or that you made a reconciliation error.

Printing the Report

To print a reconciliation report, follow these steps:

1. Choose **Y** (from the screen shown in figure 9.5) to print a reconciliation report. The Print Reconciliation Report window shown in figure 9.7 appears.

2. Complete the Print To field by choosing **1** for the report printer, **2** for the alternate report printer, **3** for the check printer, or **4** to print to a disk file. (If you used printer names on the Printer Settings screen, you see those printer names on the Print Reconciliation Report screen.)

    If you want to print an ASCII file to disk, choose **4** (Disk) from the Print Reconciliation Report window. Quicken then displays the Print to Disk window requesting three additional pieces of information: the file name, the number of lines per page, and the width (see fig. 9.8). In the DOS File field, enter the name you want Quicken to use for the created

ASCII file. To use a data directory other than QUICKEN, enter the drive and directory you chose, such as *C:\QUICKEN\PRNT_TXT*. Next, enter the number of lines per page—usually 66. Finally, enter the width of the page (80), or, if you are using a condensed mode, you may enter a larger number, such as 132.

Fig. 9.7

The Print Reconciliation Report window.

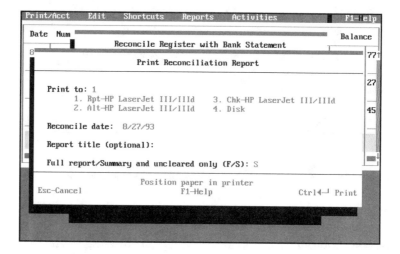

Fig. 9.8

The Print To Disk window.

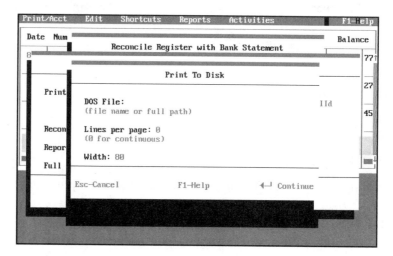

3. Move the cursor to the Reconcile Date field and enter the date you performed the reconciliation. Type the date or use the + (plus) or - (minus) key to change the date one day at a time.

4. (Optional) Move the cursor to the Report Title field, and then enter a report title for the reconciliation report. You may want to use the month and year to distinguish one report from another.

5. Move the cursor to the Full Report/Summary and Uncleared Only field. This field enables you to choose how much detail shows on the reconciliation report. The default is **Summary**, because **Full** includes all the details on every transaction you mark as cleared. Respond to the Full Report/Summary and Uncleared Only field by choosing **F** for Full or **S** for Summary.

6. Verify that the printer is turned on and loaded with paper. Choose **Ctrl-Enter** or **F10** to print the reconciliation report. Quicken warns you if the printer is not ready.

Reviewing the Reconciliation Report

The printed reconciliation report includes three distinct components: the Reconciliation Summary, the Cleared Transaction Detail, and the Uncleared Transaction Detail. (If you choose Summary, only the first and third parts of the reconciliation report print.)

The Reconciliation Summary report essentially restates the reconciliation summary shown at the bottom of the abbreviated Register screen that you saw in figure 9.2. The reconciliation summary contains two sections:

- Bank Statement-Cleared Transactions

- Your Records-Uncleared Transactions

The first section calculates the ending balance according to the bank statement by subtracting the cleared checks and adding the cleared deposits from the beginning bank balance. The second section calculates the ending Register balance by subtracting the outstanding checks and adding the deposits in transit from the ending bank balance.

The Reconciliation Summary report isn't a report you read—rather, the report documents how you reconciled the account. For this reason, you don't actually need to spend time reviewing this report unless, for some reason, you need to go back later and explain to the bank what the balance should be or you need to see which transactions were outstanding when you reconciled.

If you print a full transaction report, the Cleared Transaction Detail section of the reconciliation report shows each of the cleared checks and payment transactions and each of the cleared deposits and other credit transactions you marked with an asterisk as part of the most recent reconciliation. The report does not include transactions you marked as cleared in some prior reconciliation.

The Cleared Transaction Detail section includes most of the information related to a transaction, including the transaction date, the check or transaction number, the payee name or transaction description, any memo description, and the amount. Checks and payments appear as negative amounts because these amounts decrease the account balance. Deposits appear as positive amounts because these amounts increase the account balance. Because of space constraints, some Payee, Memo, and Category field entries are truncated on the right. The total amount and number of cleared transactions in the Cleared Transaction Detail section support the data shown in the first section of the Reconciliation Summary section.

The Uncleared Transaction Detail section of the reconciliation report is identical to the Cleared Transaction Detail report except that the still uncleared transactions for your checking account are summarized. The report is broken down into transactions dated prior to the reconciliation date and transactions dated subsequent to the reconciliation date.

Like the Cleared Transaction Detail section of the report, the Uncleared Transaction Detail section includes most of the information related to a transaction, including the transaction date, the check or transaction number, the payee name or transaction description, any memo description, and the amount. Checks and payments appear as negative amounts because they decrease the account balance. Deposits are appear as positive amounts because they increase the account balance. The total amount and total number of uncleared transactions in the Uncleared Transaction Detail section support the data shown in the second section of the Reconciliation Summary report.

Creating Balance Adjustment Transactions

If you cannot *reconcile* an account—that is, if the difference amount shown in the reconciliation summary equals any number other than zero—the difference may be due to a difference in the opening balance that Quicken shows in the Reconcile Register with Bank Statement window and the opening balance shown on your bank statement. Quicken handles these differences by adjusting the opening balance difference. Quicken handles any other differences (not arising from an opening balance difference) by creating a balancing adjustment.

Adjusting Opening Balance Differences

If you changed the amount in the Bank Statement Opening Balance field in the Reconcile Register with Bank Statement window to match the opening balance on your bank statement, Quicken shows the opening balance difference in the reconciliation summary (see figure 9.9).

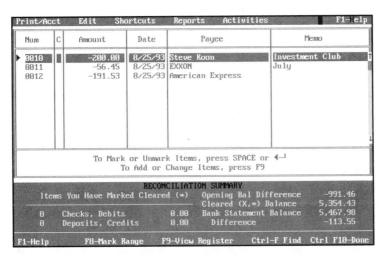

Fig. 9.9
The opening balance difference in the reconciliation summary.

The following three reasons can cause your Quicken opening balance to differ from your bank statement's opening balance:

■ You are reconciling your account with Quicken for the first time, so Quicken is using the opening balance you entered when you set up your checking account as the bank statement opening balance. If the opening balance that you entered when you set up your checking account did not account for uncleared checks written before you started your Quicken system (because you did not enter previous transactions), then your bank's opening balance differs from the opening balance in your account by the amount of uncleared checks.

Assume, for example, that you set up your checking account on November 1 and entered the opening balance shown in your manual checkbook register—$3,500. If, however, you had written three checks totaling $500 that had not cleared the bank by November 1, your opening bank statement balance would be $500 greater, or $4,000.

The opening balance difference remains until you enter all uncleared transactions and adjust Quicken's opening balance to agree with the amount that actually was in your checking account the day you started using Quicken (in this example, you adjust the opening balance to $4,000). You can enter uncleared transactions without leaving the reconciliation by pressing **F9** to access the Register. Note that Quicken can perform an automatic opening balance adjustment at the end of the reconciliation process; however, don't let Quicken make this adjustment unless you agree with the amount. In this section, you learn how to make opening balance adjustments when you complete the reconciliation process.

- You did not enter previous transactions before you began using Quicken. When you later entered these previous transactions, you changed the opening balance in the Checking Account or Bank Account Register to reflect your checking account's balance on the first day of the year. The opening balance difference remains until you mark previous transactions as cleared. To do this, leave the reconciliation and go to the Register.

  For each cleared transaction, type an **X** in the C (cleared) field. Because all previous transactions may not have cleared the bank, you should review your bank statements, beginning with the first of the year, to account for all numbered checks and deposits.

- You are not using the most current bank statement, or you have not reconciled a previous month's statement. Reconcile your account first against the earliest monthly statement, and then reconcile your account against each subsequent statement.

When you choose Ctrl-F10 to finish a reconciliation when there is an opening balance difference, Quicken displays the Create Opening Balance Adjustment window that you see in figure 9.10.

If you have exhausted all efforts at locating the opening balance difference, you can have Quicken create an adjustment to your opening balance. Press **Y** to create the adjustment; press **N** if you don't want to adjust the opening balance but want to finish the reconciliation.

To categorize an opening balance adjustment transaction (press **Ctrl-C** to display a Category and Transfer list), enter a category name in the optional Category field.

Press **Ctrl-Enter** or **F10** to create the opening balance adjustment.

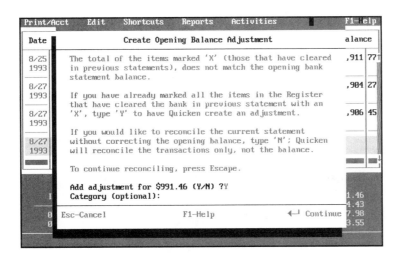

Fig. 9.10

The Create Opening Balance Adjustment window.

Adjusting for Other Differences

If other differences arise (other than an opening balance difference) at the completion of the reconciliation, as a last resort you may want to make a *balance adjustment*. A balance adjustment means that Quicken creates a transaction that forces the difference amount to zero. You can make a balance adjustment by pressing **Esc** from the Register screen before you have reduced the difference between the cleared balance and the bank statement balance to zero. Quicken then displays the Reconciliation is Not Complete window that you saw in figure 9.6.

The Reconciliation is Not Complete window identifies two options: **Proceed to next reconciliation step** and **Leave reconciliation (your work will be saved)**. If you choose the second option, Quicken returns to the Main Menu.

If you choose the first option, Quicken displays the window shown in figure 9.11. This window informs you of the magnitude of the problem and possible causes. If you still want to create an adjustment transaction, follow these steps:

1. Press **Enter** to adjust for the difference.

The Adding Balance Adjustment Entry window appears (see fig. 9.12). This window alerts you that the adjustment is about to be made and suggests that you may want to reconsider the decision.

2. To make the adjustment, choose **Y** for Yes. If you do not want to make the adjustment, choose **N** for No. To leave this screen and return to the abbreviated Register screen, choose **Esc**.

Fig. 9.11

The Problem:
Check Register
Does Not Balance
with Bank
Statement
window.

Fig. 9.12

The Adding
Balance Adjust-
ment Entry
window.

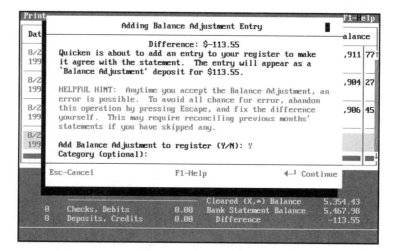

3. (Optional) To categorize an adjustment transaction (press **Ctrl-C** to display a Category and Transfer list), enter a category name in the optional Category field.

Quicken next tells you that the Register has been adjusted to agree with the bank statement balance and displays a window you can use to print the reconciliation report, as shown in figure 9.13. To print a reconciliation report, choose **Y** for Yes. The Print Reconciliation Report window appears, which you use as described previously in this chapter to print the reconciliation report. Figure 9.14 shows a sample adjustment transaction.

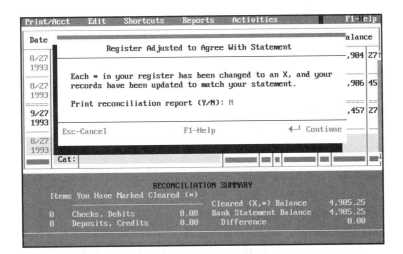

Fig. 9.13
The Register
Adjusted to Agree
With Statement
window.

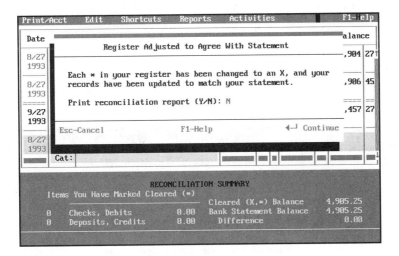

Fig.9.14
A sample adjust-
ment transaction
created by
Quicken.

Learning Quicken

CPA TIP

Although Quicken provides the adjustment feature, you probably should not use it because it camouflages errors in the Register. As a result, you never really can be sure where the error occurred. The difference amount equals a number other than zero because you are missing one or more transactions in the Register or because you incorrectly marked a transaction as cleared, or perhaps you transposed some num-bers (such as typing $87.00 as $78.00). The difference also may occur because some-one has forged checks or embezzled from your account. If you cannot reconcile the account, make sure that the previous month's reconciliation resulted in a difference equal to zero. If the previous month's reconciliation shows a difference other than zero, you must reconcile that month, and perhaps the months prior to that one, before you can get the current month's difference to be displayed as zero.

Catching Common Errors

You easily can make several errors when recording transactions in a checking account; these errors may make reconciling an account difficult or even impossible. At times, a general search for errors may not be as helpful as looking for certain kinds of errors; the next few sections identify (and explain tricks for catching) some of the more common errors.

Transposing Numbers

Transposing numbers is a frequent error in recording any financial transaction. People accidentally transpose two of the numbers in an amount. If the difference is divisible by 9, a transposition error is likely. You may write a check for $32.67, for example, and record the check as $23.67 or $32.76. This error appears obvious, but is surprisingly easy to make and often difficult to catch. When you review each transaction, you see all the correct numbers; however, the numbers are arranged in a slightly different order.

When searching for transposed numbers, you can focus on the decimal places of the transaction where the transposition error may have occurred. Table 9.1 summarizes by amounts where the transposition error may have occurred.

Table 9.1 Possible Locations of Transposition Errors	
Error Amount	**Decimal Places of Transposition**
$.09 to $.72	In cents. For example, $.12 versus $.21 or $1.19 versus $1.91.
$.90 to $7.20	Between the dollar decimal position immediately to the left of the decimal place and the cents decimal position to right of the decimal place. For example, $32.56 versus $35.26 or $2,004.56 versus $2,005.46.
$9.00 to $72.00	Between the two positions immediately to the left of the decimal place. For example, $1,423 versus $1,432 or $281 versus $218.
$90 to $720	Between the second and third positions immediately to the left of the decimal place. For example, $1,297 versus $1,927 or $1,124 versus $1,214.

Forgetting to Record Transactions

The most common mistake is forgetting to record transactions. In a personal checking account, these omissions often include decreases in the account (for example, automated teller machine withdrawals) and increases in the account, such as interest income. In a business checking account, manual checks seem to be a common culprit; you tear out a blank check for a purchasing trip and subsequently forget to record the check.

If the amounts differ because of one transaction, identifying the missing transaction can be as easy as finding a transaction on the bank statement that equals the difference. Also, examine the sequence of checks to see whether any are missing.

Entering Payments as Deposits or Deposits as Payments

Another error is to enter a payment transaction as a deposit transaction or a deposit transaction as a payment transaction. This error, until found, can be particularly frustrating. If you look at the Register, you see that every transaction is recorded, and every number is correct.

An easy way to find such an error is to divide the error by half and see whether the result equals some transaction amount. If the result does match a transaction amount, you may have incorrectly recorded the transaction. Suppose that you currently have a difference of $1,234.56 between the Register and the bank statement balances. If you divide $1,234.56 by 2, you get $617.28. If you see a $617.28 transaction in the Register, verify that you recorded this transaction in the correct column. If you recorded a $617.28 payment as a deposit or if you recorded a $617.28 deposit as a payment, the difference will equal twice the transaction amount, or $1,234.56.

Offsetting Errors

You may have more than one error in your account, and these errors may partially offset each other. Suppose that you forgot to record an automated teller machine withdrawal of $40, and then made a transposition error in which you recorded a deposit as $216 rather than the correct amount of $261. The difference equals $5, which is the combined effect of both transactions and is calculated as the following:

$$- 40 + (261 - 216) = \$5$$

Although the difference seems small, you actually have two large errors in the account.

With offsetting errors, remember that when you find one of the errors, you may feel that you are moving further away from the goal of a zero difference. Do not get discouraged if one minute you are $5 away from completing the reconciliation, and the next minute, you are $50 away from completing the reconciliation. Clearly, you are making progress if you find errors—even if the difference grows larger.

Summary

This chapter explains how to reconcile your account with Quicken. You learn about the reconciliation process, how to mark transactions that have cleared, how to print a reconciliation report, how to adjust for differences, and how to detect errors.

The next chapter begins Part II of *Using Quicken 7 for DOS*, "Getting the Most from Quicken." In Part II, you learn how to track your net worth, manage your credit cards, create and print reports, pay bills electronically, and use Quicken to prepare for income taxes.

Part II

Getting the Most

Quicken
Main Menu

Use Register
Write/Print Checks
Create Print/Acct   Edit   Shortcuts   Reports   Activities
View G
Select
File A
Set Pr
Use Tu
Exit

                                              Date   8/23/93
          Pay to the   _____
          Order of $
                    _____

                    |
          Address |
                    |
                    |
          Memo

                    ┌──────── Category ────────┐
                    │   │
                    └──────────────────────────┘

Bk.ofAmer-1342   (Alt+letter accesses menu)
Esc-Main Menu   Ctrl◄┘ Record   Ending Balance:

Dollars   ▶ Record Transaction   Ctrl◄┘
                   Split Transaction   Ctrl-S
cuts   Reports   Activities   F1-Help
                                                    Ctrl-F
o · Category   Payment C   Deposit   Balance (Backwards) Ctrl-B
                                                   (Next)   Ctrl-N
s   191 53   4,720 24↑
                                                    Ctrl-G
                                                 er Ctrl-X

                                       Delete Transaction   Ctrl-D
                                       Void Transaction   Ctrl-V
                                       Restore Transaction

Tracking Your Net Worth, Other Assets, and Liabilities

Quicken was originally designed as an electronic check register for writing and recording checks. The newer releases of Quicken can do much more than keep track of your checking account. You can maintain financial records for any asset or liability by using Quicken's familiar check-register format.

Assets are personal or business resources that have lasting value. For individuals, assets include such items as a house, cars, furniture, and investments. For businesses, assets include money owed by customers (accounts receivable), inventory held for resale, and any fixtures or equipment used in the business. *Liabilities* are debts—any money you owe others. For individuals, liabilities include mortgages, car loans, credit card debts, and income taxes. For businesses, liabilities include amounts owed suppliers (accounts payable), wages payable to employees, and loans from banks and leasing companies.

The benefits of using Quicken to track your other assets (in addition to bank accounts) and your liabilities are similar to the benefits derived from tracking bank accounts. By carefully tracking your other assets, you know what those assets currently are worth and why they may have changed in value. By carefully tracking your liabilities, you maintain a firmer control over your debts, which helps you make regular payments, and you have concrete records showing why the amounts of your debts have changed. With both your assets and your liabilities carefully documented this way, you can use Quicken to generate a report that states your personal or business financial net worth.

(The only drawback to tracking your other assets and your liabilities is the additional effort you expend keeping track. In many cases, however, the benefits you realize more than merit this effort.)

In essence, using Quicken to track all your assets, as well as your liabilities, gives you a complete picture of your entire financial state in one place. You not only have a powerful record-keeping tool for your cash inflows and outflows, but also all the information you need to determine your overall financial health, or *net worth*, within easy access.

This chapter describes generally how to use Quicken to keep records of your other assets and your liabilities. You are told why and how to use Quicken to generate net-worth reports, or *balance sheets*, also. (If Quicken's record-keeping possibilities intrigue you, read Chapters 16, 21, and 22 for more information.)

Specifically, this chapter teaches you how to do the following:

- Set up accounts for other assets and liabilities

- Record assets and liabilities and track their values

- Record assets and liabilities using transfer transactions

- Use Quicken's Loan Calculator to calculate loan payments or principal balances

- Amortize memorized loan payments on fixed-rate loans, variable-rate loans, or balloon payment loans.

- Recall memorized loan payments

- Update Cash Account balances

- Measure your net worth by creating a net-worth report, or balance sheet

Setting Up Accounts for Other Assets and Liabilities

You must set up a Quicken account for each asset or liability for which you want to keep computer records. You can track any asset or liability you want. Only one limit or restriction exists: You can keep a maximum of only 255 accounts within a single Quicken file. You must remember, however, that any accounts you want grouped on a single balance sheet must be set up within the same file. Typically, this restriction means that all your business accounts must be kept in one file and all your personal accounts in another file.

After you create a Quicken file, follow these steps to set up your accounts:

1. Choose Select Account from the Main Menu. Quicken displays the Select Account to Use window (see fig. 10.1).

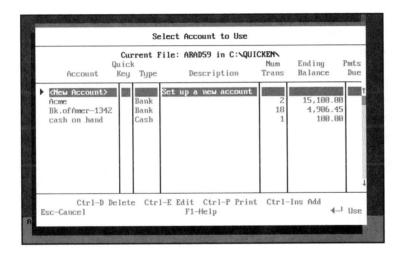

Fig. 10.1
The Select Account to Use window.

2. To add a new account, select <New Account> from the Select Account to Use window. Quicken displays the Set Up New Account window (see fig. 10.2).

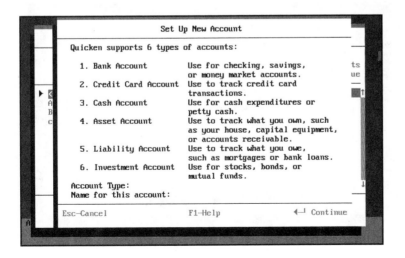

Fig. 10.2
The Set Up New Account window.

II

Getting the Most

3. In the Account Type field, type the number of the account type you are adding. This can be in an asset account or a liability account.

Quicken lists four asset account types: Bank Account, Cash Account, Asset, and Investment Account. If the asset is a bank account, choose account type **1** (you learned about bank accounts in Chapter 3). If the asset is cash, such as that in your wallet or in the petty cash box, choose account type **3**. If the account is an investment, choose account type **6**. (Refer to Chapter 16 for specifics on defining an investment account.) For any other asset—accounts receivable, real estate, and so on—choose account type **4**.

Quicken lists two liability account types: Credit Card and Liability. If the liability is the balance on your VISA or MasterCard account, choose account type 2 (you learn about credit card accounts in the next chapter); otherwise, choose account type 5.

4. In the This Account field, enter a description of the account. The Name field can contain up to 15 characters and can include any character except the following:

[ ] / :

You also can use spaces.

5. Choose **Enter** or **F10** to display the Starting Balance and Description window (see fig. 10.3).

Fig. 10.3
The Starting Balance and Description window.

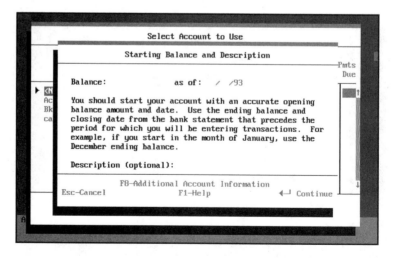

6. In the Balance field, enter the starting balance for the account. (You learned how to enter the starting balance for a bank account in Chapters 1 and 3.) To set up a starting balance for an asset or liability, enter the amount here. Assets can be listed at their original costs or their current fair market values. Liabilities are listed at their current balances. If the starting balance is zero, you must enter **0** in the Balance field; you cannot leave the Balance field blank.

7. Move the cursor to the As Of field. Enter the date on which the balance you entered is correct.

8. (Optional) When you set up a credit card account, Quicken displays the IntelliCharge field. See Chapter 11 for complete information about setting up credit card accounts and IntelliCharge.

9. (Optional) Move the cursor to the Description field. Fill in the Description field with up to an additional 21 characters of account description.

10. (Optional) When you set up a credit card account, Quicken asks for the credit limit on your card.

After you enter the information for your new asset or liability account, Quicken adds the account to the Select Account to Use window. Quicken then organizes all accounts alphabetically within each account type. The account types are listed in the same order as on the Set Up New Account window. Thus, the first accounts listed are Bank Accounts, followed by Credit Card, Cash, Other Asset, and Other Liability accounts; Investment Accounts are listed last.

Recording Assets and Liabilities

After you initially set up an account—whether an asset or a liability account—you can maintain it in one of two ways: record transactions directly in the Register, or use transfer transactions.

Recording Transactions in the Register

Select an account by choosing Select Account from the Main Menu. Quicken displays the Select Account to Use window. Highlight the account you want to update or revise and choose **Enter**. After you select an account, you can use the Register to enter transactions that increase or decrease your balance, just as you do in your Quicken checking account.

II

Getting the Most

Figure 10.4 shows how the Register may look for a major real-estate asset (a personal residence). This Other Assets Register almost is identical to the regular Bank Account Register and is used the same way. Transaction amounts that decrease the asset account balance are recorded in the Decrease field of the Register (the Payment field on the bank-account version of the Register screen). Transaction amounts that increase the asset account are recorded in the Increase field of the Register (the Deposit field on the bank-account version). The total Real Estate account balance appears in the bottom right corner of the screen. If you have *postdated transactions*—transactions with dates in the future—the current balance also is shown.

Fig. 10.4

A Real Estate Account Register used to record the value of a personal residence.

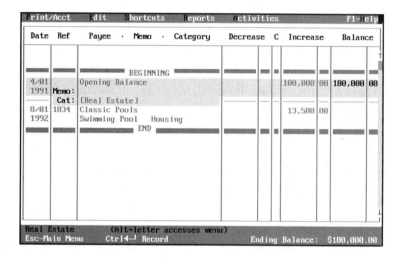

In the example in figure 10.4, the opening balance of $100,000 shows what you may originally have paid for your home. The two subsequent transactions—one for the addition of a new family room and the other for a new backyard swimming pool—show what changed the value of your home. By keeping these records, you can better keep track of the value of your home and any reasons for changes in its value.

When working with an Other Assets Register, you can access the same menu options as from the Bank Account Register, except that **Update Account Balances** replaces **Reconcile** on the Activities menu. (See *Updating Account Balances*, later in this chapter.)

Figure 10.5 displays a Register for tracking what you owe on a loan, such as a business credit line or a home mortgage. The Other Liability Register also mirrors the Bank Account Register in appearance and operation. Transaction amounts that increase the amount owed are recorded in the Increase field of the Register. (On the bank-account version of the Register screen, this field is labeled Payment.) Transaction amounts that decrease the amount owed are recorded in the Decrease field of the Register. (On the bank-account version of the Register, this field is labeled Deposit.) The total liability balance is shown in the bottom right corner of the screen. If you have postdated transactions, the current balance also is shown. You do not use the C field when tracking a liability account.

Fig. 10.5
The Register used to track the outstanding balance on a mortgage loan.

In the example in figure 10.5, the opening balance of $80,000 shows what you may have borrowed originally on a mortgage. The subsequent transaction—the July mortgage payment—shows the reduction in the outstanding loan balance stemming from the principal portion of the July loan payment.

When working with the Other Liability Register, the menu options available are the same as when you work with the Bank Account Register, except that the **Update Account Balance** option from the Activities menu replaces the **Reconcile** option for bank accounts.

> **Note**
>
> Only the principal reductions are recorded in the Register for a loan or mortgage. The interest portion is reported as interest expense and should be assigned to a category set up for mortgage interest (Mort Int).

Using Transfer Transactions to Maintain Correct Balances

Entering transactions directly into a Register is one way to maintain correct account balances for another asset or liability account. You can, however, choose a second way to maintain correct account balances for other assets and liabilities. Quicken enables you to enter an account name in the Category field on the Write Checks and Register screens. Quicken then uses the information from the checking-account transaction to record the appropriate transaction in one of the other asset or liability accounts.

If you write a check to the bank or company that holds your mortgage and enter the account name for your mortgage (for example, *Mortgage*) in the Category field (in the Write Checks screen or the Checking Account Register) to show the principal portion of the payment, Quicken records a corresponding decrease in your mortgage liability account. This decrease is equal to the principal portion of the payment made from your checking account. When you enter an account name in the Category field for a transaction, Quicken places that account name in brackets ([Mortgage]) to show that the transaction is a transfer transaction. The portion of your payment that pays interest is assigned to the mortgage interest category (see fig. 10.6).

Fig. 10.6

A $1,000 check written for a mortgage payment.

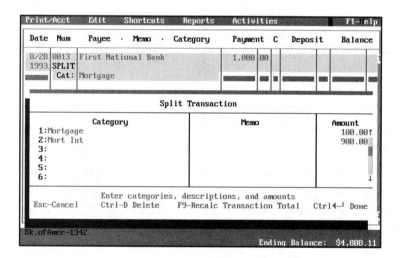

Figure 10.6 shows a $1,000 check written to First National Bank for a mortgage payment. The transaction is split to allocate a portion of the payment to the mortgage liability account ([Mortgage]) and mortgage interest (Mort Int). (You learned about split transactions in Chapters 6 and 8.) The principal amount of this payment that is applied to the current mortgage balance is

$100. (The remainder of the payment is mortgage interest.) When you record the check, Quicken records a corresponding $100 decrease in your Mortgage account.

A convenient way to move between different parts of the same transfer transaction is to use the Go to Transfer option on the Edit menu. You also can use the shortcut key **Ctrl-X** to go to a transfer transaction. After you record a mortgage payment in the Check Register, you may want to look at the liability account for your mortgage to see how much your outstanding balance is.

Using QuickReport

Quicken 7 has a new feature called *QuickReport* that you can use for most of the activities in this chapter. To learn more about how to use QuickReport, see Chapter 5, "Using the Register."

Using the Loan Calculator

Quicken includes a tool for loan payment and balance record-keeping: a Loan Calculator. You can use this calculator in two ways: to calculate loan payments and to calculate the interest and principal portions of memorized loan payments.

Calculating Fully Amortized Loans

Probably the simplest use of the Loan Calculator is to calculate loan payments. If you know the loan amount, annual interest rate, number of years the loan will be outstanding, and the number of payments made annually, Quicken can calculate the payment amount. The Loan Calculator also can produce a payment, or *amortization*, schedule. An amortization schedule shows what portion of your payments goes to paying interest and what portion goes to reducing the principal balance of the loan.

You can select the type of calculation to make with the Loan Calculator. You can calculate the principal amount outstanding when you know the annual interest rate, number of years the loan will be outstanding, the number of payments made annually, and the payment amount.

To calculate loan payments or the principal amount of a loan, and to produce a payment schedule (amortization schedule), follow these steps:

1. From any Register or Write Checks screens, choose the Activities menu (see fig. 10.7).

Fig. 10.7
The Activities
menu.

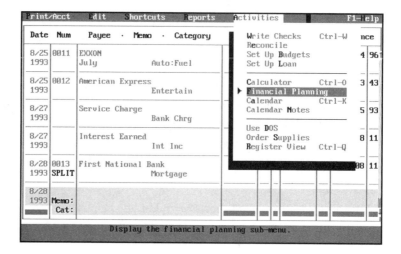

2. Choose Financial Planning from the Activities menu. Quicken displays the Financial Planning menu (see fig. 10.8).

Fig. 10.8
The Financial
Planning menu.

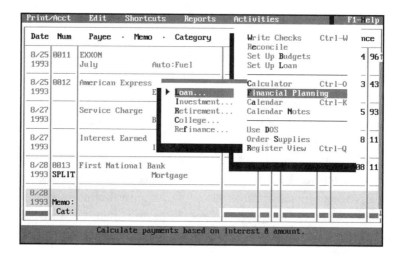

3. From the Financial Planning menu, choose Loan.... Quicken displays the Loan Calculator and places a check mark next to the variable to be calculated (Principal or Regular Payment), as shown in figure 10.9. (In the figure, the check mark appears next to the Regular Payment field. To instruct Quicken to calculate the principal amount of the loan rather than the regular payment, choose **F8** to move the check mark to the Principal field. Choose **F8** again to re-mark the Regular Payment field.)

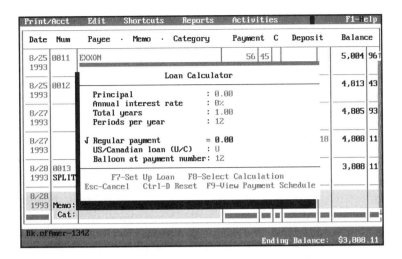

Fig. 10.9
The Loan
Calculator.

4. *Important:* Skip this step if you are calculating the principal amount of a loan. To calculate a loan's regular payment (the check mark appears next to the Regular Payment field), start with the cursor in the Principal field. Enter the amount of the balance of the loan in the Principal field. If you are calculating the principal amount of a loan (the check mark appears next to the Principal field), Quicken does not accept an entry in the Principal field; go to step 5.

5. In the Annual Interest Rate field, enter the annual interest rate. If the annual loan interest rate is 12.5 percent, for example, type **12.5**.

> **Caution**
>
> Don't mistake the annual percentage rate (APR) for the annual interest rate. The APR encompasses all the costs of obtaining credit and includes not only interest charges but loan fees and other borrowing costs as well. The APR, which is required by truth-in-lending laws, provides a way to compare the overall cost of obtaining a loan. The APR, however, shouldn't be used to calculate the loan payment.

6. Move the cursor to the Total Years field. Enter the number of years you must make payments. If the loan is a 5-year car loan, for example, type **5**. If the loan is a 30-year mortgage, type **30**.

7. Move the cursor to the Periods per Year field. Enter the number of payments you must make each year. Typically, because most payments must be made monthly, this number is *12* and is already entered.

Getting the Most

II

8. *Important:* Skip this step if you are calculating the regular payment of a loan. To calculate the principal amount of the loan (the check mark appears next to the Principal field), move the cursor to the Regular Payment field. Enter the amount of your loan payment in the Regular Payment field. If you are calculating the regular payment amount (the check mark appears next to the Regular Payment field), no entry is allowed in the Regular Payment field; go to step 9.

9. Move the cursor to the US/Canadian loan field and choose **U** for a loan originating in the US or choose **C** for a loan originating in Canada. Canadian lenders use a different method to compute interest which results in slightly lower payments for a Canadian loan.

10. Move the cursor to the Balloon at payment number field and enter a number between 1 and 5200. You learn about balloon payment loans later in this chapter. For a fixed payment loan, enter a number equal to the total number of payments for the entire loan. For a 30 year loan with monthly payments, you would enter **360** (30 x 12 = 360). If your loan doesn't amortize exactly into 360 payments, Quicken adds the necessary amount to the last payment (usually a few cents).

11. Choose **Enter** after you enter the value for the last field on the Loan Calculator. Quicken calculates the loan payment amount in the Regular Payment field or the principal amount in the Principal field. Figure 10.10 shows the monthly payment on a $12,000 loan with 12.5 percent interest and 4 years of monthly payments to be $318.96. Figure 10.11 shows the principal amount of a loan to be $228,828.28 when the regular loan payment is $1,600.00 per month for 30 years and the annual interest rate is 7.5 percent.

12. (Optional) To produce a payment schedule (amortization schedule) for the loan, choose **F9** after you finish calculating the Regular Payment or Principal amount. Quicken displays the Approximate Payment Schedule window (see fig. 10.12). The Approximate Payment Schedule window shows the approximate interest and principal portions of each loan payment and the loan balance after the payment. To move up and down in the payment schedule, use the PgUp and PgDn keys, or click the scroll bar. You also can use the Home and End keys: Home displays the first page of the payment schedule, and End displays the last page of the payment schedule.

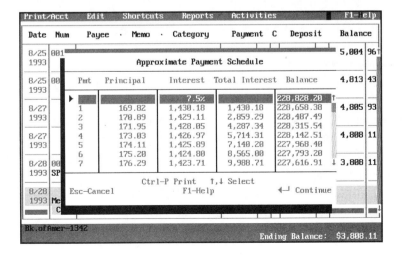

```
 Print/Acct    Edit    Shortcuts    Reports    Activities          F1-Help
 Date  Num    Payee  ·  Memo  ·  Category    Payment  C   Deposit    Balance
 8/25 0011   EXXON                              56 45            5,004 96
 1993
              ╔════════════ Loan Calculator ════════════╗    4,813 43
 8/25 0012   ║                                          ║
 1993        ║   Principal              : 12,000.00     ║
              ║   Annual interest rate   : 12.5%         ║    4,805 93
 8/27        ║   Total years            : 4.00          ║
 1993        ║   Periods per year       : 12            ║
              ║                                          ║
 8/27        ║ √ Regular payment        = 318.96     18 ║    4,808 11
 1993        ║   US/Canadian loan (U/C) : U             ║
              ║   Balloon at payment number: 48          ║
 8/28 0013   ║                                          ║    3,808 11
 1993 SPLIT  ║      F7-Set Up Loan   F8-Select Calculation║
              ║ Esc-Cancel   Ctrl-D Reset  F9-View Payment Schedule║
 8/28        ╚══════════════════════════════════════════╝
 1993 Memo:
      Cat:

 Bk.ofAmer-1342
                                    Ending Balance:   $3,808.11
```

Fig. 10.10
The Loan
Calculator
showing a regular
payment calcula-
tion.

```
 Print/Acct    Edit    Shortcuts    Reports    Activities          F1-Help
 Date  Num    Payee  ·  Memo  ·  Category    Payment  C   Deposit    Balance
 8/25 0011   EXXON                              56 45            5,004 96
 1993
              ╔════════════ Loan Calculator ════════════╗    4,813 43
 8/25 0012   ║                                          ║
 1993        ║ √ Principal              = 228,828.20    ║
              ║   Annual interest rate   : 7.5%          ║    4,805 93
 8/27        ║   Total years            : 30.00         ║
 1993        ║   Periods per year       : 12            ║
              ║                                          ║
 8/27        ║   Regular payment        : 1,600.00   18 ║    4,808 11
 1993        ║   US/Canadian loan (U/C) : U             ║
              ║   Balloon at payment number: 360         ║
 8/28 0013   ║                                          ║    3,808 11
 1993 SPLIT  ║      F7-Set Up Loan   F8-Select Calculation║
              ║ Esc-Cancel   Ctrl-D Reset  F9-View Payment Schedule║
 8/28        ╚══════════════════════════════════════════╝
 1993 Memo:
      Cat:

 Bk.ofAmer-1342
                                    Ending Balance:   $3,808.11
```

Fig. 10.11
The Loan Calcula-
tor showing a
principal amount
calculation.

```
 Print/Acct    Edit    Shortcuts    Reports    Activities          F1-Help
 Date  Num    Payee  ·  Memo  ·  Category    Payment  C   Deposit    Balance
 8/25 001                                                        5,004 96
 1993        ╔═══════════ Approximate Payment Schedule ═══════════╗
 8/25 00    ║  Pmt   Principal    Interest  Total Interest  Balance ║ 4,813 43
 1993        ║ ▶              7.5%                   228,828.20      ║
              ║  1     169.82    1,430.18    1,430.18   228,658.38  ║ 4,805 93
 8/27        ║  2     170.89    1,429.11    2,859.29   228,487.49  ║
 1993        ║  3     171.95    1,428.05    4,287.34   228,315.54  ║
              ║  4     173.03    1,426.97    5,714.31   228,142.51  ║ 4,808 11
 8/27        ║  5     174.11    1,425.89    7,140.20   227,968.40  ║
 1993        ║  6     175.20    1,424.80    8,565.00   227,793.20  ║
              ║  7     176.29    1,423.71    9,988.71   227,616.91 ↓║ 3,808 11
 8/28 00     ║                                                     ║
 1993 SP     ║        Ctrl-P Print    ↑,↓ Select                   ║
              ║ Esc-Cancel          F1-Help          ↵ Continue     ║
 8/28        ╚═════════════════════════════════════════════════════╝
 1993 Me
      C

 Bk.ofAmer-1342
                                    Ending Balance:   $3,808.11
```

Fig. 10.12
The Approximate
Payment Schedule
window.

II

Getting the Most

13. (Optional) To print a copy of the payment schedule, choose **Ctrl-P**. Quicken displays the Print Payment Schedule window, which is similar to the Print Checks window described in Chapter 7. Indicate the printer you want to use and choose **Enter**. Quicken prints the schedule.

CPA TIP

If you are uncertain how large a mortgage you can afford when buying a home, use the Loan Calculator to help you determine what amount you actually can afford. To calculate the principal amount, enter into the appropriate Loan Calculator fields the amount you decide that you can spend for housing from your monthly income (Regular Payment) and the current annual interest rate. Then, if you want to pay less interest over the life of the mortgage and pay off the mortgage balance sooner, use 15 years as the total years to pay. If you cannot afford the monthly mortgage payments for a 15-year loan, use 30 years. With this information, you can calculate the total principal amount, which gives you a better idea of what to look for in a mortgage.

Quicken normally calculates an arrangement known as a *payment in arrears*, or an *ordinary annuity*. These terms mean that the payment is made at the end of the payment period, as is the case with loan payments. With some loans, however, payments are made at the beginning of the period. This beginning-of-the-month arrangement is known as a *payment in advance*, or an *annuity due*. To convert a payment-in-arrears payment to a payment-in-advance payment, divide the payment amount Quicken calculates by the following factor:

$$(1 + (\text{annual interest rate}/\text{periods in a year}))$$

To convert the $318.96 payment in arrears to a payment in advance on a 12.5 percent loan (.125), perform the following calculation:

$$\$318.96/(1 + (.125/12))$$

This calculation produces a result of $315.67.

Calculating Loans with Balloon Payments

New to Quicken 7 is a feature that enables you to compute loan payments and principal balances for loans with *balloon payments*. In a loan with a balloon payment, the principal is not fully repaid when the regular payments stop, so that the balance of the loan (the *balloon payment*) is due at the end of the payment period. The loan actually is amortized over a longer period than the period of the payments. If you have a "30 due in 7" loan, for example, your payment is amortized over 30 years. At the end of seven years, however, you must pay off the balance or refinance the loan.

In some balloon payment loans, each payment covers only the accrued interest (no principal), and the original loan amount is due at the end of the repayment period. For such an *interest-only* loan, do not use Quicken's loan tracking feature. Instead, create a regular memorized transaction for the payment and categorize the entire payment amount as interest.

To calculate loan payments or the principal amount of a balloon payment loan, follow these steps:

1. To calculate fully amortized loans, follow steps 1 through 9 in the preceding section.

2. Move the cursor to the Balloon at payment number field and enter a number between 1 and 5200. This number represents the point at which the entire principal balance becomes due (*balloons*). If the loan shown in figure 10.10 were changed to a loan with a balloon payment after two years, for example, you would enter **24** (12 x 2) and choose **Enter**. The monthly payment amount would remain the same.

3. To view the Approximate Payment Schedule, choose **F9**. Highlight payment 24 to see the balloon payment as shown in figure 10.13.

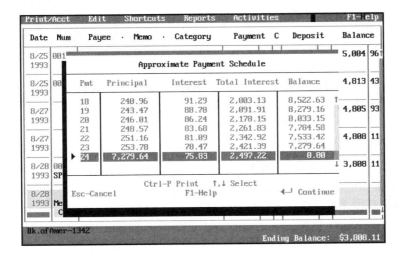

Fig. 10.13

The Approximate Payment Schedule window showing a balloon payment.

4. (Optional) To print a copy of the payment schedule, choose **Ctrl-P**. Quicken displays the Print Payment Schedule window, which is similar to the Print Checks window described in Chapter 7. Indicate the printer you want to use and choose **Enter**. Quicken prints the schedule.

Amortizing Memorized Loan Payments

You also can use the Loan Calculator with memorized loan payments. In effect, using the payment schedule information, you can memorize not only the loan payment amount, but also the loan interest expense and loan principal reduction associated with each payment.

You also can amortize and memorize the payment schedule information for loans with variable interest rates and prepayments. The interest rate on a fixed-rate loan remains constant throughout the loan period and cannot be adjusted unless you refinance the loan. The interest rate on a *variable-rate* loan, however, fluctuates throughout the loan period to correspond with another factor, such as Treasury Bill interest rates or the prime lending rate. Loan *prepayments* are payments you make in addition to required payments. If your mortgage payment is $850 per month, for example, and you pay $900 every month, you're making a $50 prepayment of principal each month that you pay $900 rather than the required $850.

If you want some additional assistance with amortizing loan payments, Quicken provides the Amortize Loan Assistant, to help. To use the assistant, choose Use Tutorials/Assistants from the Main Menu. Then choose More Assistants to display the Select Tutor/Assistant window. From here, just highlight the Amortize assistant and choose **Enter**. Follow the Amortized Loan Assistant's on-screen instructions to set up a loan for amortization and to learn how to record payments on a loan.

Amortizing and Memorizing a Loan Payment on a Fixed-Rate or Balloon Payment Loan. To amortize and memorize the payment-schedule information for a fixed-rate or balloon payment loan, follow these steps:

1. Record a loan payment in the Register for the account from which you write your loan payment or the Write Checks screen. Loan payments are recorded as split transactions because you allocate a portion of the payment to a liability account (to decrease the principal balance of the loan) and a portion to the interest category. There may be other allocations made for loan payments, such as property taxes, insurance, and so on. You learned how to split transactions in Chapters 6 and 8.

2. Press **Ctrl-S** to display the Split Transaction window to assign the liability account and the interest expense category to the transaction.

   The first item in the Split Transaction window must be the liability account you use to track the principal balance (such as *[Mortgage]*).

The second item must be the expense category you use to track interest expense (such as *Mort Int* for mortgage interest). You can use all other lines in the Split Transaction window to allocate the remainder of the loan payment to property taxes, insurance, and so on. Figure 10.14 shows the Split Transaction window for a loan payment, broken down into the principal amount, mortgage interest, property taxes and insurance. Chapter 6 shows you how to split a transaction.

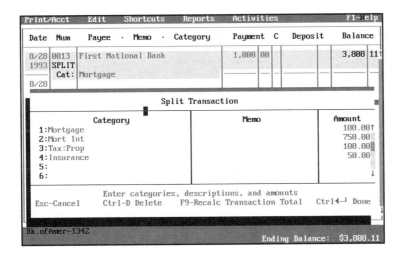

Fig. 10.14
The Split Transaction window for a mortgage payment.

3. Memorize the loan payment by pressing **Ctrl-M**. (You learn about memorizing transactions in Chapters 6 and 8. The procedure is the same when memorizing loan payments.)

4. Choose **Recall** Transaction from the **Shortcuts** menu to display the Memorized Transaction List (see fig. 10.15).

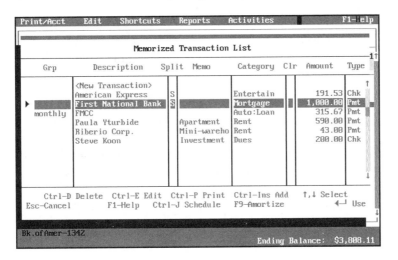

Fig. 10.15
The Memorized Transaction List.

5. Highlight the loan payment transaction you memorized in step 3.

6. Choose **F9**. Quicken displays the Set Amortization Information window (see fig. 10.16).

Fig. 10.16

The Set Amortization Information window.

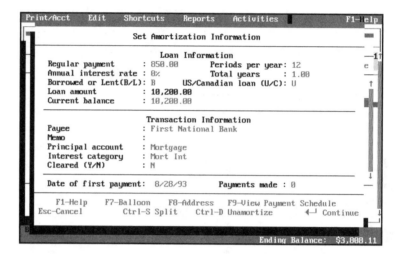

7. In the Regular Payment field, enter the usual loan payment amount if it is different than the amount shown. (Quicken enters the regular payment amount from the memorized transaction.)

8. In the Periods per Year field, enter the number of payments you must make each year if different than 12.

9. In the Annual Interest Rate field, enter the annual interest rate.

10. In the Total Years field, enter the number of years you must make payments.

11. Move the cursor to the Borrowed or Lent field. If you are paying back this loan, enter **B**. If you are holding the loan note and receive payments for it, enter **L**.

12. Move the cursor to the US/Canadian loan field. Enter **U** if the loan originated in the US, enter **C** if the loan originated in Canada.

13. If this is a balloon payment loan, choose **F7** to display the Set Balloon Payment window. Enter the payment number at which the loan balloons. For example, enter 84 if it is a 30 year loan due in 7 years (12 x 7 = 84).

14. After the appropriate information is entered in all the fields, choose **Enter**. Quicken calculates the loan balance and displays this amount in the Loan Amount field. Figure 10.17, for example, shows each payment on a $121,564.98 loan at 7.5 percent interest with 30 years of monthly payments to be $850.00.

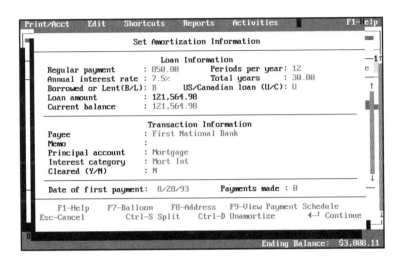

Fig. 10.17

The loan amount, given an $850 monthly payment on a 30-year, 7.5 percent loan.

> **Note**
>
> A slight rounding error of a penny or two may occur when performing calculations with the Loan Calculator.

15. If you have already made payments on this loan, enter the current outstanding principal balance in the Current Balance field. The current, or outstanding principal, balance is not the same as the original loan amount (the amount in the Loan Amount field) if any payments have been made.

> **Note**
>
> You can use the Loan Calculator to determine the current outstanding principal balance of a loan. Use the calculator as explained in the preceding sections, and choose **F9** to view the Approximate Payment Schedule (refer to fig. 10.12). Use the up- and down-arrow keys to move through the Approximate Payment Schedule until you come to the payment number of the loan you currently are paying. The amount shown in the Balance field is the outstanding principal balance after the current payment has been made.

16. To change any fields in the Transaction Information section, move the cursor to the field you want to change and type the new entry. (The Transaction Information section of the Set Amortization Information window already is filled in for you based on the categories and accounts you assigned in the Split Transaction window for the memorized loan payment.)

17. In the Date of First Payment field, enter the date you made or will make the first loan payment.

18. In the Payments Made field, enter the number of payments you have made (0 if you have not yet made any payments). As you make payments on the loan, Quicken updates the number of payments listed in the Payments Made field.

19. Choose **Ctrl-Enter** or **F10** to return to the Memorized Transaction List. An A (for *amortized*) appears in the Split column of the memorized loan payment in the Memorized Transaction List.

20. Choose **Esc** to return to the Register or the Write Checks screen.

Amortizing and Memorizing a Loan Payment on Variable-Rate Loans and Prepayments. Amortizing a memorized loan payment on a variable-rate loan differs only slightly from amortizing a memorized loan payment on a fixed-rate loan. The difference lies in how you set up the amortization. For variable-rate loans, you set up the amortization as if payments for the loan were starting today, with no previous payments made. (You set up the amortization this way regardless of how many payments you have actually made.)

To amortize and memorize the payment schedule information for a variable-rate loan and prepayments, follow these steps:

1. To amortize a memorized fixed-rate loan payment, follow steps 1 through 12 in the preceding section.

2. After you enter the appropriate information in all the fields, choose **Enter**. Quicken calculates the loan balance and displays this amount in the Loan Amount field. If you already have made payments on this loan, the current, or outstanding principal, balance is not the same as the original loan amount (the amount in the Loan Amount field).

3. In the Current Balance field, enter the current outstanding principal balance in the Current Balance field if it is different from what Quicken displays in the Loan Amount field.

4. To change any of the fields in the Transaction Information section, move the cursor to the field you want to change, and type the new entry. (The Transaction Information section of the Set Amortization window is filled in for you based on the categories and accounts you assigned in the Split Transaction window for the memorized loan payment.)

5. Move the cursor to the Date of First Payment field. Enter the date of the next payment you will make.

6. Move the cursor to the Payments Made field and enter zero (**0**). (Regardless of the number of payments you may already have made, you always enter zero in the Payments Made field when amortizing a memorized loan payment on a variable-rate loan or a loan on which you have made prepayments.)

7. Choose **Ctrl-Enter** or **F10** to return to the Memorized Transaction List. An A (for *amortized*) appears in the Split column of the memorized loan payment in the Memorized Transaction List.

8. Choose **Esc** to return to the Register or the Write Checks screen.

Recalling Amortized Loan Payments. After you amortize a memorized loan payment, you can recall your record of the loan whenever you want to record a new payment. Quicken keeps track of which payment is being made—the first payment, the second payment, the third payment, and so on. Quicken then uses the payment schedule information to split the payment amount between the loan's principal re-duction and the interest expense. After you have recalled a memorized loan payment and recorded new payments as many times as you initially indicated that payments were left, Quicken removes the loan from the Memorized Transaction List.

To recall an amortized loan payment, follow these steps:

1. From an empty transaction line in the Register or a blank check in the Write Checks screen, press **Ctrl-T**. The Memorized Transaction List appears.

Tip
If QuickFill is activated, type only the first few characters of the payee name in the Payee field. Quicken searches the Memorized Transaction List for a transaction with a payee name that begins with the characters you type. QuickFill then fills in the rest of the memorized transaction for you. Refer to Chapter 6, "Automating the Register," to learn more about QuickFill.

II

Getting the Most

2. Highlight the memorized loan payment and choose **Enter**.

Quicken displays the Use Amortize Transaction window for the memorized loan payment, as shown in figure 10.18.

Fig. 10.18

The Use Amortize Transaction window.

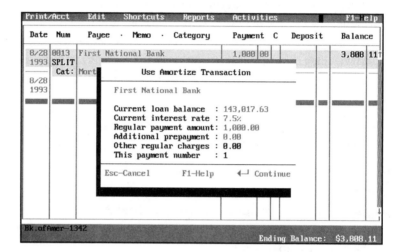

3. To change any of the information in the Use Amortize Transaction window, move the cursor to the field you want to change, and type a new entry. Here, you tell Quicken whether you're making additional prepayments on the loan (in the Additional Prepayment field) or whether the interest rate has changed on a variable-rate loan (in the Current Interest Rate field). When you change the current interest rate, Quicken recalculates the payment amount for you and enters the result in the Regular Payment Amount field.

4. After you enter the appropriate information in all the fields of the Use Amortize Transaction window, choose **Ctrl-Enter**. Quicken enters the transaction information in the Register or the Write Checks screen.

5. Choose **Ctrl-Enter** or **F10** to record the transaction.

CPA TIP

When Quicken prepares an approximate payment schedule, the program makes certain necessary assumptions. Quicken assumes, for example, that you always make the payment on the same day of the month; that each month has the same number of days; and that interest on your loan is calculated, or *compounded*, only at the time each payment is made. Obviously, however, these assumptions do not always match reality. You may not always remember to pay a loan on the same day each month, for example. Or the mail may be delayed. The fact that not every month has the same number of days also can alter your payment schedule. Your bank may even have some special way of calculating interest. The result of such discrepancies is that the split between interest and principal turns out to be slightly incorrect—perhaps by a few pennies or perhaps even by several dollars. To deal with this problem, update the loan account balance at the end of each year by using the Update Account Balances option on the Activities menu. Any such discrepancies should be assigned to a category for interest expense.

Undoing Recalled Loan Payments. If you make a mistake and record a loan payment you didn't actually make, you must reverse the payment so that Quicken keeps an accurate count of the loan payments you have made. (Remember that every time you recall a memorized loan payment, Quicken increases the number in the Payments Made field by one.)

To undo a recalled loan payment, follow these steps:

1. From the Register or the Write Checks screen, press **Ctrl-T**. The Memorized Transaction List appears.

2. Highlight the memorized loan payment you mistakenly recalled.

3. Choose **F9** to display the Set Amortization Information for the memorized loan payment.

4. In the Payments Made field, enter the number of payments made before you mistakenly recalled the memorized loan payment.

5. Position the cursor in the Current Balance field and type the correct current balance. (If you changed the interest rate or entered a prepayment in the Use Amortize Transaction window when you mistakenly recalled the memorized loan payment, you must change the Current Balance amount back to that of the outstanding principal balance before you recalled the memorized loan payment.)

Getting the Most

6. Choose **Ctrl-Enter**. Quicken displays a warning that you are about to change the amortization information. Choose **Enter** to change the amortization information, or choose **Esc** to cancel the changes.

7. After you change the amortization information, go to the recalled transaction in the Register or the Write Checks screen and delete the transaction for the memorized loan payment you mistakenly recalled. You learn how to delete transactions from the Register in Chapter 6.

Reviewing Tips for Working with Other Assets and Liabilities

All Quicken Registers work essentially the same way, regardless of account type. A few tips and techniques, however, can help you in using Quicken to account for your other assets and liabilities. These tips and techniques include hints on dealing with the nuances and subtleties of cash accounts. They also cover using the Update Account Balances option with cash accounts. (Credit card accounts have their own nuances and subtleties, but these account types are not explained in this chapter. Chapter 11, "Managing Your Credit Cards," describes how to use credit card accounts in Quicken to manage your credit card debts.)

Dealing with Cash Accounts

Tip

The cash account type is a convenient way for businesses to keep track of petty-cash expenditures and reimbursements. Even very large businesses can benefit by using Quicken for petty-cash accounting.

The Cash Account option works well when you want to keep complete, detailed records of miscellaneous cash outlays. (*Miscellaneous cash outlays* are all those paid out of pocket with actual currency rather than with a check, such as $5 for stamps, $12 for lunch, $7.50 for parking, and so on.) Often, you don't really need this level of control or detail. But when you do want such detailed records, the cash account type gives you just the tool you need for the job. (As Quicken warns you with an on-screen message, however, you cannot use the Write/Print Checks option with this type of account.)

Figure 10.19 shows a Cash Account Register (called *Petty Cash*), which is almost identical to the Bank Account Register. Money flowing out of the account is recorded in the Spend field and money flowing in is recorded in the Receive field. In the Bank Account Register, money flowing out of the account is recorded in the Payment field and money flowing into the account is recorded in the Deposit field. In the Other Assets and Other Liability Account Registers, money flowing into and out of the account is recorded in the Increase and Decrease fields.)

Fig. 10.19
A Cash Account
Register (Petty
Cash).

As with the Other Assets and Other Liability Account Registers, the C field usually is not used. You can use this column, however, to match receipts against entries to indicate that you have backup records. Press **C** in this field to show that you have entered a cash transaction from an actual receipt.

Updating Account Balances

The Update Account Balance option replaces Reconcile on the Activities menu at the Registers for Cash Accounts and for Other Asset and Other Liability accounts. The Reconcile option is explained in Chapter 9, "Reconciling Your Bank Account." (On the Activities menu at the Credit Card Account Register, the Pay Credit Card Bill option replaces the Reconcile option. The Pay Credit Card Bill option is described in Chapter 11.) Figure 10.20 shows the Cash Account Activities menu.

Choosing **Update Account Balance** from the Activities menu on a Register gives you a window with which to reconcile, or adjust, an account. Suppose that the Register you use to keep track of your petty cash or pocket cash shows $68.50 as the on-hand cash balance, but the actual balance is $61.88. To update your account, use the Update Account Balance window to record an adjustment, as shown in figure 10.21.

To update or adjust an account balance, follow these steps:

1. From the Cash Account Register, choose **Update Account Balance** from the Activities menu. Quicken displays the Update Account Balance window.

Fig. 10.20

The Cash Account
Activities menu.

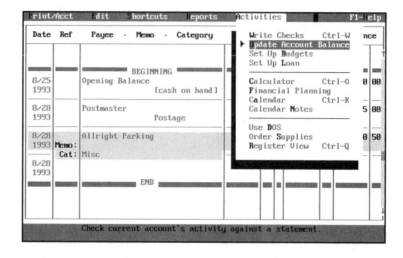

Fig. 10.21

The Update
Account Balance
window.

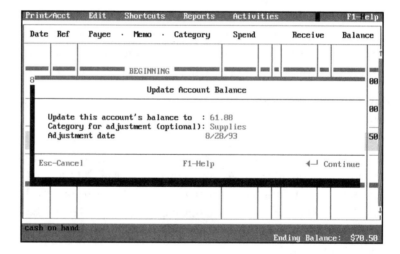

2. Enter the amount to which the account balance should be adjusted in the Update this Account's Balance To field.

3. (Optional) Move the cursor to the Category for Adjustment field. Enter the category to which you want to assign the difference between the old and new account balances. You can use a miscellaneous category or, if you know exactly what the difference stems from, use that category.

4. Choose **Enter**. Quicken makes the adjustment transaction to update the account balance. (Remember that you can press **Ctrl-C** to see the Category and Transfer list.) Figure 10.22 shows the adjustment transaction created by the Update Account Balance transaction so that the account balance is now $61.88.

```
 Print/Acct    Edit    Shortcuts    Reports    Activities              F1-Help
┌─────────────────────────────────────────────────────────────────────────┐
│  Date  Ref    Payee  ·  Memo  ·  Category    Spend      Receive    Balance│
│                                                                           │
│                    ═══ BEGINNING ═══                                      │
│  8/25         Opening Balance                            100 00    100 00 │
│  1993                    [cash on hand]                                   │
│                                                                           │
│  8/28         Postmaster                     25 00                 75 00  │
│  1993                    Postage                                          │
│                                                                           │
│  8/28         Allright Parking               6 50                 68 50   │
│  1993                    Misc                                             │
│                                                                           │
│  8/28         Balance Adjustment             6 62                 61 88   │
│  1993 Memo:                                                               │
│       Cat:                                                                │
│  8/28                                                                     │
│  1993                    ═══ END ═══                                      │
│                                                                           │
│ cash on hand        (Alt+letter accesses menu)                           │
│ Esc-Main Menu    Ctrl◄─┘ Record              Ending Balance:   $61.88     │
└─────────────────────────────────────────────────────────────────────────┘
```

Fig. 10.22

The adjustment transaction in the Register.

II

Getting the Most

Caution

You cannot guess or estimate tax-deduction amounts. *Do not*, therefore, use the method described in the preceding tip to increase your tax deductions. The Internal Revenue Service may disallow deductions that cannot be supported with evidence as to the exact type and amount of the deduction.

Dealing with Credit Card Accounts

Chapter 11, "Managing Your Credit Cards," explains how to use credit card accounts to track your credit card activity, reconcile your credit card accounts, and pay your credit card bills.

Measuring Your Net Worth

A balance sheet is one traditional tool individuals and businesses use to measure net worth. The balance sheet lists all your assets and liabilities. The difference between assets and liabilities is called *owner's equity*, or *net worth*. A balance sheet differs from reports such as income statements and cash-flow reports, which summarize financial activity occurring over a certain period of time. A balance sheet provides a "snapshot" of your personal or business finances at a particular moment in time.

Creating a balance sheet with Quicken is a two-step process. First, you must set up an account for each of your assets, with a beginning balance amount for each asset that is equal to the asset's cost or value. Generally, *assets* are items you have paid for that have lasting value. *Personal assets* include such items as the cash in your wallet, the surrender value of a life insurance policy, any investments, your home, and durable personal items such as your car and furniture. *Business assets* usually include cash, accounts receivable, inventory, and other property and equipment.

> **Note**
>
> Often you don't really know which category explains the difference between the old and new account balances. The discrepancy may be caused by transactions you forgot to record or recorded incorrectly. Essentially, what you are trying to do at the Update Account Balance window is to correct or record erroneous or missing transactions. If you cannot decide which category to record in the Category for Adjustment field, enter the category that you use most frequently with this Register. If most of your petty-cash transactions involve postage payments, for example, enter *postage* in the Category for Adjustment field.

The second step in creating a balance sheet is to set up accounts for all your liabilities, recording the balance owed on each liability. *Liabilities* are amounts you currently owe other people, banks, or businesses. *Personal liabilities* encompass such items as credit card balances, income taxes, car loans, and mortgages. *Business liabilities* usually include accounts payable, wages and salaries owed employees, income and payroll taxes, and bank credit lines and loans.

Tip
Before you create a balance sheet, make certain that all your asset and liability accounts are located within the same Quicken file.

Figure 10.23 shows an example of a personal balance sheet, or net-worth statement, created by Quicken. At the top of the page, Quicken lists each asset account and its balance as of a specific date. Below the asset accounts, Quicken lists each liability account and its balance as of a specific date. The difference between total assets and total liabilities is *total net worth*. In figure 10.23, the net-worth amount is $34,068.33

A business balance sheet looks essentially the same, although the assets and liabilities listed usually are different. Chapter 12, "Creating and Printing Reports," describes how to print a business balance sheet, as well as each of Quicken's other reports.

```
                          Net Worth Report
                           As of 9/22/93
ARAD59-All Accounts                                          Page 1
9/22/93
                                             9/22/93
                       Acct                  Balance
            ───────────────────────────────────────────
            ASSETS
              Cash and Bank Accounts
                Acme                       15,100.00
                Bk.ofAmer-1342              3,351.44
                cash on hand                   61.88
                                           ──────────
              Total Cash and Bank Accounts 18,513.32

              Assets
                Real Estate               100,000.00
                                          ───────────
              Total Assets                100,000.00
                                          ───────────
            TOTAL ASSETS                  118,513.32

            LIABILITIES
              Liabilities
                Fleet Mortgage             84,901.66
                                          ──────────
              Total Liabilities            84,901.66
                                          ──────────
            TOTAL LIABILITIES              84,901.66
                                          ──────────
            TOTAL NET WORTH                33,611.66
                                          ══════════
```

Fig. 10.23

An example of a personal balance sheet.

CPA TIP

Determine the cost or market value of all your assets and liabilities as of the same date. The cost or market value information must be accurate for your net worth calculation also to be accurate. Use only one method for appraising your assets or liabilities: either original cost or fair market value. Mixing the different methods can yield inaccurate results. Note also on your opening balances whether you used original cost or fair market value to determine these appraisals. If you use fair market value, be sure to document the source you used to make your estimate of fair market value.

After you enter the costs or market values of all your assets and liabilities, you can generate a report that calculates your net worth by subtracting your liabilities from your assets. The desired result, of course, is for the difference to be a positive one. Whether you are determining your net worth as a business or an individual, you want the net worth amount to grow larger in time, because this amount acts as a financial cushion should you ever experience fiscal difficulties.

Summary

In this chapter, you learn how easy it is to use Quicken for nearly all your personal or small-business accounting needs. This chapter describes how Quicken can help you keep records on such assets as real estate or accounts receivable and on liabilities such as mortgage loans. For more information on Quicken's accounting capabilities, refer to Chapters 16, 21, and 22.

Chapter 16, "Monitoring Your Investments," describes Quicken features that can help you monitor your investments. Chapter 21, "Using Quicken for Home Finances," describes how to use Quicken for your home finances. Chapter 22, "Using Quicken in Your Business," describes how to use Quicken as a business accounting package.

Chapter 11, "Managing Your Credit Cards," describes how to set up, use, reconcile and pay a credit card account. If you use Quicken's VISA card, you also will learn how to track your credit card activity through statements received on disk or through a modem.

Managing Your Credit Cards

If you're like most people, you use several credit cards to purchase merchandise. Now that many service providers such as doctors, lawyers, and dentists are accepting credit as payment, you may be making even more credit purchases.

The more you purchase on credit and the more credit cards you use, the more important managing your credit becomes. With Quicken, you can set up individual credit card accounts that help you record and keep track of purchases, payments, and finance charges. Credit card accounts also can help you track a line of credit from your bank.

Now with Quicken, you can set up an IntelliCharge account to use with your Quicken VISA card. *IntelliCharge* is a service that updates your Credit Card Register automatically by disk or modem. When you use IntelliCharge, you avoid entering credit transactions in your Credit Card Register; IntelliCharge does that for you. In this chapter, you learn how to set up an IntelliCharge account and receive your statement on disk or by modem. You also learn how to review and categorize your credit transactions.

If you pay the balance on your credit card bills each month, you probably don't need to set up a credit card account. Instead, enter the payment transaction in the Register for the account that you use to pay your credit card bill and split the transaction to assign multiple categories to the transaction (see Chapters 6 and 8 to learn how to split transactions). If you don't pay your credit card balance each month, setting up a credit card account will help you manage your credit transactions.

In this chapter, you learn how to do the following:

- Set up a credit card account

- Track credit card activity in a credit card account

- Reconcile your credit card account

- Pay your cre-dit card bills

- Set up an IntelliCharge account

- Update your IntelliCharge account with statements received on disk or by modem

II

Getting the Most

Using a Credit Card Account

Tip

If you're interested in obtaining a Quicken credit card, fill out the application form enclosed in your Quicken 7 package.

If you always pay your credit card in full every month, you do not need to use the Credit Card Register, unless you want to track exactly where and when charges are made. You don't need to use the Credit Card Register because you usually can record the details of your credit card spending when you record the check payment to the credit card company. Also, because the credit card balance always is reduced to zero every month, you do not need to keep track of the balance.

Tip

The balance carried on your credit cards is a liability. If you want all liabilities reflected in your net worth, set up a credit card account so that these liabilities appear in Net Worth or Balance Sheet reports.

The steps involved in using the Credit Card Register to perform record-keeping for your credit cards parallel the steps for using any other Register: set up an account, enter transactions, and then reconcile the account.

Setting Up a Credit Card Account

First, you set up the account and record the beginning balance. (Because you are working with a liability, the beginning balance is what you owe.)

To set up a credit card account, follow these steps:

1. Choose Select Account from Quicken's Main Menu. Quicken displays the Select Account to Use window shown in figure 11.1.

Fig. 11.1

The Select Account to Use window.

2. To add a new credit card account, select <New Account> from the Select Account to Use window. Quicken displays the Set Up New Account window shown in figure 11.2.

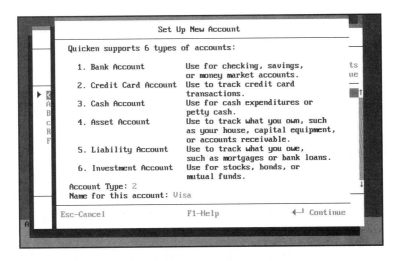

Fig. 11.2
The Set Up New
Account window.

3. In the Account Type field, choose **2** to select the Credit Card account
   type.

4. In the Name for This Account field, enter the name of the credit card,
   such as MasterCard, VISA, Discover, and so on. The Name for This Account field can contain up to 15 characters, and you can use any character except the following:

   [ ] / :

   You can include spaces.

5. Choose **Ctrl-Enter** or **F10** to display the Starting Balance and Description window (see fig. 11.3).

Fig. 11.3
The Starting
Balance and
Description
window.

6. In the Balance field, enter the outstanding credit card balance as of the date you are setting up the credit card account. If the credit card balance is zero, you must enter **0** in the Balance field (you cannot leave the Balance field blank).

7. In the As of field, enter the date on which the balance you entered is correct.

8. (Optional) If you use Quicken's VISA card and want to set up the credit card account to receive statements by disk or modem, choose **Y** in the IntelliCharge field. Refer to *Using the IntelliCharge Account*, later in this chapter, to learn more about setting up IntelliCharge accounts.

9. (Optional) In the Description field, fill in the Description field to provide an additional 21 characters of account description. Here, you may want to enter the credit card account number.

10. Choose **Ctrl-Enter** when the Starting Balance and Description window is complete.

11. Quicken next displays the Specify Credit Limit window and prompts you for the credit limit on your card (see fig. 11.4). Enter your credit limit, if desired, and press **Enter**.

Fig. 11.4
The Specify Credit
Limit window.

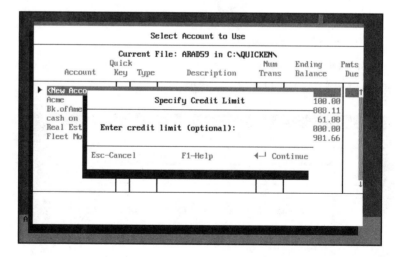

After you enter the information for the new credit card account, Quicken adds the account to the Select Account to Use window.

Tracking Credit Card Activity

To track your credit card activity, you simply enter all credit card transactions into your Credit Card Register. Credit card purchases are entered directly into your credit card account. Credit card payments are entered into the Bank Account Register you use to pay bills when you reconcile your credit card statement.

As with the Other Asset and Liability Registers, some minor differences exist between the Bank Account Register and menu options and the Credit Card Register and menu options. The Charge field in the Credit Card Register is where you record each use of your credit card. The Payment field is where payments to the credit card company are recorded. If you fill in the Credit Limit field when you set up the credit card account, Quicken shows the credit remaining in the lower right corner of the screen above the Ending Balance field. Figure 11.5 shows the Credit Card Register.

Fig. 11.5

The Credit Card Register.

Enter credit card transactions the same way that you enter transactions in the Bank Account Register. Refer to Chapters 5 and 6 to review the techniques for entering transactions into the Bank Account Register.

Reconciling Your Credit Card Account

When you receive your credit card statement each month, you should review it carefully to make sure that you have entered all credit purchases in the Credit Card Register. It also is a good idea to review your statement in order to uncover unauthorized uses of your credit card. You may find that the statement contains credit purchases that you or your spouse did not make.

Before you pay your credit card bill, you should reconcile your statement balance with the balance in your Quicken Credit Card Register. After you successfully reconcile your credit card statement, Quicken gives you the option of paying the entire credit card account balance or making a partial payment.

To reconcile your credit card account, follow these steps:

1. From the Credit Card Register, choose the Activities menu (see fig. 11.6).

Fig. 11.6

The Activities Menu.

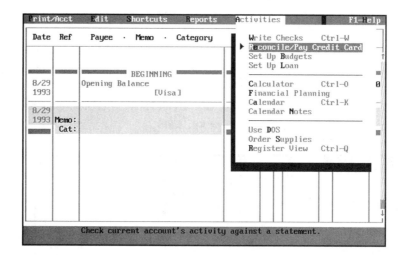

2. From the Activities menu, choose the Reconcile/Pay Credit Card. Quicken displays the Credit Card Statement Information window (see fig. 11.7).

Fig. 11.7

The Credit Card Statement Information window.

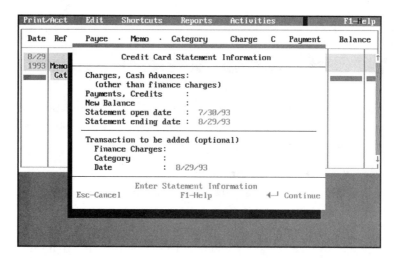

> ### CPA TIP
>
> If your credit card allows for cash advances, don't make the mistake of assuming that the cash you receive avoids interest charges for 30 days. Cash advances begin accruing interest on the day the cash is advanced to you. If you are in a bind for cash, take out the cash advance, but pay it back as soon as possible to avoid excessive interest charges.
>
> If you receive a cash advance from your credit card, record the advance in the Charge field. If you also use a cash account to track your cash expenditures (as explained in Chapter 10), enter the name of that account in the Category field for the transaction. Then, the cash advance that you receive also is entered in your cash account.

3. Enter the charges plus cash advances shown on your statement in the Charges, Cash Advances field and choose **Enter**.

4. In the Payments, Credits field, enter the amount of payments plus credits shown on your credit card statement and choose **Enter**.

5. In the New Balance field, enter the balance due as shown on your credit card statement and choose **Enter**. This is the balance due after charges plus cash advances, minus payments plus credits.

6. In the Statement Open Date field, enter the opening date on the credit card statement and choose **Enter**.

7. In the Statement Ending Date field, enter the closing date on the credit card statement and choose **Enter**.

8. (Optional) In the Transactions to be Added section of the Credit Card Statement Information window, enter any finance charges that appear on your credit card statement in the Finance Charges field. Quicken will enter a credit card transaction in your Credit Card Register for finance charges.

9. In the Category field, enter the category you want to assign to the finance charge transaction that Quicken enters, such as *Int Exp* (for *interest expense*). Choose **Enter**.

   You can press **Ctrl-C** to display the Category and Transfer list to select a category from the list. Quicken's QuickFill feature also works from the Category field when you type the first few characters of the category name (see Chapter 6 for more information on QuickFill).

II

Getting the Most

10. In the Date field, enter the date that the finance charges were charged to your credit card account.

11. When you complete the Credit Card Statement Information window, choose **Ctrl-Enter** to continue with the reconciliation.

Quicken displays the Transaction List window, which shows each credit card account transaction (see fig. 11.8).

Fig. 11.8

Credit card account transactions shown in a list.

12. Mark charges and payments that have *cleared* (were recorded by) the credit card company. To mark an item as cleared, highlight the transaction you want to mark. Choose **Enter** to mark the highlighted transaction as cleared and move to the next transaction. Quicken enters an asterisk in the cleared column. To unmark a transaction, highlight the transaction that you want to unmark, and press the space bar to remove the asterisk.

To mark a range of transactions as cleared, choose **F8**. The Mark Range of Dates as Cleared window appears. You use this window to specify that all transactions with dates within the indicated range should be marked as cleared.

As you mark transactions, the Reconciliation Summary in the Transactions List window shows the number and dollar amount of the charge and payment transactions you marked as cleared, the cleared transaction total, the statement balance, and the difference between the two. You are finished with the reconciliation when the difference between the Cleared Balance and the Statement Balance equals zero.

CPA TIP

Avoid credit card interest and finance charges. Deductions for consumer or personal interest are no longer allowed for federal and most state income tax returns. What's more, credit card annual interest rates are usually 18 percent to 21 percent (or if you are considered a high risk, even more). Consequently, with the lost tax deduction and high interest costs, carrying credit card balances that accrue interest doesn't make sense.

---

13. (Optional) To correct transactions you entered incorrectly in the Credit Card Register, choose **F9** to redisplay the same information in an abbreviated form of the standard Register. Edit the transactions in the Register in the usual manner. To change the screen back to the Transaction list, choose **F9** again.

14. When the difference between the Cleared Balance and the Statement Balance is zero, choose **Ctrl-F10** to indicate that you are finished with the reconciliation. Quicken displays the Make Credit Card Payment window shown in figure 11.9. The next section explains how to pay your credit card bill after you have reconciled your credit card statement.

Fig. 11.9
The Make Credit Card Payment window.

If the difference does not equal zero and you choose **Ctrl-F10** to complete the reconciliation, Quicken displays an Adjusting Register To Agree with Statement window. To accept Quicken's adjustments, enter a category to assign to the adjustment transaction in the Category field and choose **Enter**. To cancel, choose **Esc**.

> **Note**
>
> Chapter 9, "Reconciling Your Bank Account," gives tips on finding and correcting reconciliation errors for a bank account. These tips also apply to reconciling a credit card statement.

You can leave the reconciliation process at any time (even when the difference between the cleared balance and the statement balance *is not* zero) by choosing **Esc**. When you choose Esc, Quicken displays the Reconciliation is Not Complete window. Choose **2** to select the Leave reconciliation (your work will be saved) option. Quicken then returns to the Credit Card Register. Any work you have done (entering balances, finance charges, marking transactions, and so on) is saved so that when you return to the reconciliation you can proceed from the point you left.

If you don't want to leave the reconciliation after you select Esc, just choose **Enter** to select the Proceed to next reconciliation step option.

Paying Your Credit Card Bill

Now that you have reconciled your credit card statement, you're ready to pay your credit card bill. You can choose to pay the entire balance, to make a partial payment, or to pay nothing at all.

To pay your credit card bill, follow these steps:

1. From the Make Credit Card Payment window shown in figure 11.9, in the Bank Acct field, enter the bank account that you want to use to pay your credit card bill.

2. Choose **Ctrl-C** to display the Account list you see in figure 11.10.

3. Highlight the bank account that you want to use to pay your credit card bill and choose **Enter** to select the account. Quicken returns to the Make Credit Card Payment window.

> **Note**
>
> If you don't want to pay your credit card bill, choose **Esc** from the Make Credit Card Payment window. Quicken returns to the Credit Card Register.

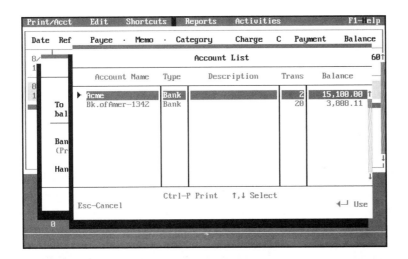

Fig. 11.10
The Account list.

2. Move the cursor to the Computer Check/Manual Check/Electronic Payment field. Choose **C** if you want to write a check at the Write Checks screen and print a check using Quicken. Choose **M** if you want to write a manual check and have Quicken enter the check transaction in the Register, or choose **E** to pay your credit card bill electronically through CheckFree (see Chapter 13 to learn how to make electronic payments through CheckFree).

CPA TIP

Balancing your credit card account keeps you alert to unauthorized credit transactions. Your credit card number can be used for purchases made by telephone because no signature is required. All that an unauthorized user needs is your account number, expiration date, and your current address to make a credit purchase by telephone.

If you do not monitor your credit card statements on a timely basis, you may not be aware of violated usage until several thousands of dollars have been charged. Most credit card companies protect you against unauthorized credit transactions. You must inform them within a certain time period for their safeguards to take effect, however.

3. Choose **Ctrl-Enter** or **F10**. If you selected to write a computer check, Quicken displays the Write Checks screen and fills in the check with the outstanding balance amount in the Amount field and the category that you assigned in the Category field. You fill in the credit card company name in the Payee field.

If you want to make a partial payment rather than paying the outstanding balance, move to the Amount field and change the amount to whatever you want to pay. Choose **Ctrl-Enter** or **F10** to record the check in the Write Checks screen.

If you selected to write a manual check, Quicken displays the Register and fills in the transaction with the outstanding balance amount in the Payment field and the category that you assigned in the Category field.

If you want to make a partial payment rather than paying the outstanding balance, move to the Payment field and change the amount to the amount you want to pay. Choose **Ctrl-Enter** or **F10** to record the transaction in the Register.

If you selected to pay your credit card bill electronically, Quicken displays the Write Checks screen and fills in the outstanding balance in the Amount field and the category that you assigned to the transaction in the Category field. As with computer checks, you can change the Amount field to make a partial payment rather than paying the outstanding balance. Choose **Ctrl-Enter** or **F10** to record the electronic check in the Write Checks screen.

Using QuickReport

Quicken offers a new feature, called *QuickReport*, that enables you to zoom out from an individual field in your Credit Card Register to see historical transaction information about the entry in that field. You can do this without setting up a report or modifying your Register layout. See Chapter 5, "Using QuickReport for Instant Transaction Reports," for more information about using QuickReport.

Using the IntelliCharge Account

IntelliCharge is a service that you can use in Quicken to track your Quicken VISA card activity. (If you don't have a Quicken VISA card, don't set up an IntelliCharge account; IntelliCharge accounts only work with Quicken credit cards.) With IntelliCharge, you receive your monthly credit card statements on disk or by modem. With your credit card statement on disk or downloaded by modem, your credit card activity is instantly recorded in your IntelliCharge account. Credit transactions are not only recorded, but also are assigned automatically to categories according to Intuit's standard credit card category list.

Setting Up an IntelliCharge Account

Before you can begin using IntelliCharge to record your credit card transactions, you must set up a credit card account as an IntelliCharge account. Setting up an IntelliCharge account is similar to setting up a regular credit card account.

To set up an IntelliCharge account, follow these steps:

1. Choose Select Account from Quicken's Main Menu. Quicken displays the Select Account to Use window.

2. To add a new credit card account, choose <New Account> from the Select Account to Use window. Quicken displays the Set Up New Account window.

3. In the Account Type field, choose 2 to select the Credit Card account type.

4. In the Name for This Account field, enter the name of the credit card, such as Quicken VISA, Quicken, or just VISA. The Name for This Account field can contain up to 15 characters, and you can use any character except the following:

   [ ] / :

   You can include spaces.

5. Choose **Ctrl-Enter** or **F10** to display the Starting Balance and Description window.

6. In the Balance field, enter zero (0). Enter zero even if you have an outstanding credit card balance.

7. Move to the As Of field and enter the date that you are setting up your IntelliCharge account.

8. In the IntelliCharge field, choose **Y** to set up the credit card account as an IntelliCharge account. When you select Y in the IntelliCharge field, Quicken changes the Description field in the Starting Balance and Description window to the Account Number field.

9. In the Account Number field, enter the account number of your Quicken VISA card (enter the 16-digit account number). Be sure to enter the correct account number from your card or your latest Quicken VISA statement.

II

Getting the Most

10. When the Starting Balance and Description window is complete, choose **Ctrl-Enter** or **F10**.

   Quicken next displays the IntelliCharge Account Information window shown in figure 11.11.

Fig. 11.11
The IntelliCharge Account Information window.

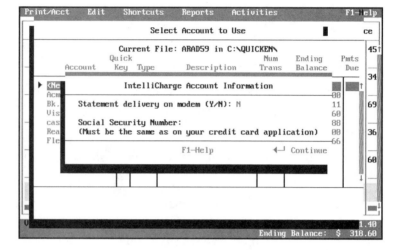

11. In the Statement Delivery on Modem field, choose **Y** if you want to download your Quicken VISA statements by modem. Leave the setting at N if you want to receive your statements on disk. Choose **Enter**.

12. Enter your Social Security number in the Social Security Number field and choose **Enter**. Be sure this is the same number that you entered when you filled out your Quicken VISA application.

13. If you chose to receive your statements on disk, skip to step 17. If you chose to receive your statements by modem, Quicken displays the IntelliCharge Phone Number and Password window shown in figure 11.12.

14. In the Enter the IntelliCharge Phone Number field, enter the local access number for the CompuServe network through which IntelliCharge downloads your statements. Choose **Enter**. If you don't have this number, call 1-800-848-8980 and choose **2** at the prompt. The system will ask for the speed of your modem and your telephone number (from which you are calling). The system then gives you the CompuServe network number nearest you.

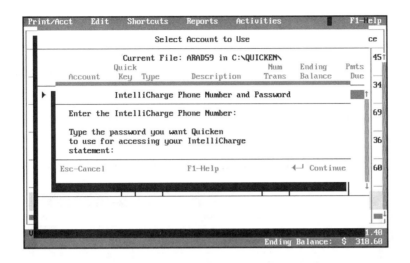

Fig. 11.12
The IntelliCharge
Phone Number
and Password
window.

> **Note**
>
> You do not need a CompuServe membership in order to use IntelliCharge.

15. (Optional) In Type the Password... field, enter a password to prevent unauthorized access to your Quicken VISA statement file. Passwords can be eight characters in length, but must include at least four, nonblank characters.

16. When the IntelliCharge Phone Number and Password window is complete, choose **Ctrl-Enter**. Quicken displays the Specify Credit Limit window.

17. Enter your Quicken VISA card limit, if desired, and choose **Enter**. If you don't want to enter your limit, choose **Enter** to continue.

Quicken adds your IntelliCharge account to the Select Account to Use window.

Converting a Credit Card Account to IntelliCharge

If you already have a credit card account set up in Quicken for your Quicken VISA card, you will need to convert the account to an IntelliCharge account if you want to receive your statements on disk or downloaded by modem.

Once you convert your regular credit card account to an IntelliCharge account, transactions are reconciled as they are imported into the Register, with an X in the C (Cleared) field.

II

Getting the Most

To convert a regular credit card account to an IntelliCharge account, follow these steps:

1. Choose Select Account from Quicken's Main Menu. Quicken displays the Select Account to Use window.

2. Highlight the regular credit card account you want to convert to an IntelliCharge account and choose **Ctrl-E**.

   Quicken displays the Edit Account Information window (see fig. 11.13).

Fig. 11.13

The Edit Account Information window.

3. In the IntelliCharge field, choose **Y**.

4. When you change the IntelliCharge field to Y, Quicken replaces the Description field with the Account Number field. If you had not entered your Quicken VISA card account number in the Description field before, enter the account number of your Quicken VISA card (enter the 16-digit account number) in the Account Number field. Be sure to enter the correct account number from your card or your latest Quicken VISA statement.

5. Choose **Ctrl-Enter** or **F10**. Quicken displays the IntelliCharge Account Information window.

6. To complete the IntelliCharge Account Information window and subsequent windows, follow steps 11 through 17 in the preceding section.

> **Note**
>
> When you update your new IntelliCharge account the first time, the asterisks (*) in the C (Cleared) field of any old transactions will be changed to Xs.

Updating Your IntelliCharge Credit Card Account

Updating your IntelliCharge credit card account is the same as entering credit card transactions in a regular credit card account, except that IntelliCharge enters the transactions for you, either from a disk file or by modem. Every month, Intuit sends you your Quicken VISA card statement. If you choose to receive your statements on disk, Intuit mails a disk or file that contains your credit card activity (credit card purchases, cash advances, finance charges, credit, and payments) during the current statement period. If you choose to download your statement information by modem, Intuit makes an electronic statement available each month for you to download by modem to your Quicken system. After credit card transactions from the IntelliCharge statement are read by Quicken, they appear in the IntelliCharge Statement window so that you can review them and mark any transactions for edit or further review in the Register. After your review, transactions are recorded in the Credit Card Register.

The following sections explain how to receive your Quicken VISA card statements on disk and by modem, how to review transactions in the IntelliCharge Statement window, and how to record credit card transactions in the Register.

Receiving Your Statement on Disk. The disk file that Intuit sends you each month contains the current period activity for your Quicken VISA card. Information included in the disk file includes current credit purchases, cash advances, finance charges, credits, and payments. Normally, you enter these transactions yourself in the Credit Card Register. When you receive this information on disk, however, you quickly can import the credit card transactions into your IntelliCharge credit card account.

To receive your statement on disk and update your IntelliCharge account, follow these steps:

1. Access the Register for your IntelliCharge credit card account.

2. Choose Get IntelliCharge Data from the Activities menu. Quicken displays the Get IntelliCharge Data window (see fig. 11.14).

Fig. 11.14

The Get IntelliCharge Data window.

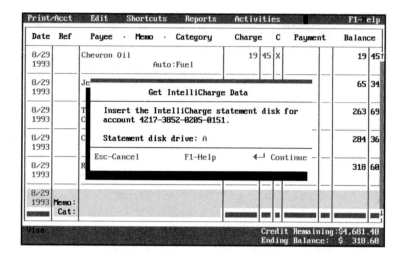

3. Insert the disk that contains your Quicken VISA card statement file into drive A: or B:.

4. In the Statement Disk Drive field, type the drive into which you inserted your disk into (A or B) and choose **Enter**. Quicken displays the Updating Account window. Each of your credit card transactions appear as Quicken reads them from the disk. You cannot make changes to any of these transactions as they are being read from the disk. After the transactions are entered in the IntelliCharge Statement window, however, you can review them and mark transactions that you want to edit. (You also can edit them after they are recorded in the Credit Card Register.)

5. As you learn later in this chapter, IntelliCharge assigns categories to your credit card transactions. If IntelliCharge determines that a category should be assigned to a transaction that you do not have set up in the Category and Transfer list, you are given the following options:

   Option 1: Add it to the Category List

   Option 2: Select from Category List

If you select Option 1, Quicken displays the Set Up Category window so that you can enter the information for the new category. If you select Option 2, Quicken displays the Category and Transfer list so that you can choose another category to assign to the transaction.

6. After all credit card transactions are read from the disk file, Quicken displays the IntelliCharge Statement window that shows the date, payee, amount, and category for each credit card transaction.

The next step in updating your IntelliCharge account is to review all the transactions in the IntelliCharge Statement window to make sure that they match your records and that the category assigned to each transaction is appropriate. For more information on reviewing the transactions in the IntelliCharge Statement window, see *Reviewing Credit Card Transactions*, later in this chapter.

Receiving Your Statement by Modem. Receiving your Quicken VISA card statement by modem is similar to receiving your statement on disk, except that you download the statement file rather than manually inserting a disk file into your computer's disk drive. The file you download contains the current period activity for your Quicken VISA card. Information included in the file includes current credit purchases, cash advances, finance charges, credits, and payments. Normally, you enter these transactions yourself in the Credit Card Register. When you download this information, however, you quickly can import the credit card transactions into your IntelliCharge credit card account.

To receive your statement by modem and update your IntelliCharge account, follow these steps:

1. Access the Register for your IntelliCharge credit card account.

2. Choose Get IntelliCharge Data from the Activities menu. Quicken displays the Get IntelliCharge Data window as shown in figure 11.15.

3. Turn on your modem and make sure your telephone line is plugged in. Choose **Enter** to initialize your modem and download your statement file.

4. Quicken displays the Updating Account window. Each credit card transaction appears as Quicken reads it from the downloaded file. You cannot make changes to any of these transactions as they are being downloaded from the disk. After the transactions are entered in the IntelliCharge Statement window, however, you can review them and mark transactions that you want to edit. (You can edit them after they are recorded in the Credit Card Register.)

Fig. 11.15

The Get IntelliCharge Data window.

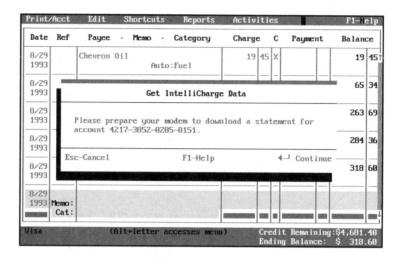

5. As you learn later in this chapter, IntelliCharge assigns categories to your credit card transactions. If IntelliCharge determines that a category should be assigned to a transaction that is not set up in the Category and Transfer list, you are given the following options:

   Option 1: Add it to the Category List

   Option 2: Select from Category List

   If you select Option 1, Quicken displays the Set Up Category window so that you can enter the information for the new category. If you select Option 2, Quicken displays the Category and Transfer list so that you can choose another category to assign to the transaction.

6. After all credit card transactions are read from the downloaded file, Quicken displays the IntelliCharge Statement window that shows the date, payee, amount, and category for each credit card transaction.

The next step in updating your IntelliCharge account is to review all the transactions in the IntelliCharge Statement window to make sure they match your records and that the category assigned to each transaction is appropriate. For more information on reviewing the transactions in the IntelliCharge Statement window, see the following section.

Reviewing Credit Card Transactions. After you receive your IntelliCharge statement, whether on disk or by modem, you need to review your credit card transactions to ensure that they match your records and that the categories assigned by IntelliCharge are appropriate. You can review credit card transactions in the IntelliCharge Statement window, which appears after transactions are read from the disk file or the downloaded file.

From the IntelliCharge Statement window, you can mark items for further review. When you mark a transaction for further review, Quicken places five question marks (?????) in the Ref field of the transaction in the Credit Card Register. To mark a transaction for further review, use the up- and down-arrow keys to highlight the transaction and mark it in the IntelliCharge Statement window and press the space bar. Press the space bar again to unmark the transaction.

IntelliCharge assigns categories to your credit card transactions according to Intuit's standard Credit Card Category list (for more information on how IntelliCharge assigns categories, see *Assigning Categories to IntelliCharge Transactions*, later in this chapter). You can change the category that IntelliCharge assigned to a transaction in the IntelliCharge Statement window. To change the category, highlight the transaction that contains the category you want to change and choose **Ctrl-C**. Quicken displays the Category and Transfer list that you can use to select a category for the credit card transaction.

To delete a category assigned to a transaction, highlight the transaction that contains the category you want to delete and choose **Ctrl-D**.

Recording Credit Card Transactions in the Register. When you finish reviewing the credit card transactions in the IntelliCharge Statement window, you're ready to record the transactions in the Credit Card Register.

To record the credit card transactions, choose **Ctrl-Enter**. Quicken records the transactions in the Credit Card Register and displays the Make Credit Card Payment window. To complete the Make Credit Card Payment window and pay your Quicken credit card bill, follow the steps in the section *Reconciling Your Credit Card Account*. If you don't want to make a credit card payment at this time, choose **Esc**.

II

Getting the Most

> **Note**
>
> If a transaction appears in your IntelliCharge statement that does not match your records, you can dispute the item by contacting Primerica Bank immediately (1-800-772-2221). You also must notify the bank, in writing, of any disputed item.
>
> Mark disputed items in the IntelliCharge Statement window. After you record the credit card transactions from the IntelliCharge Statement window to your Credit Card Register, use the Find feature (**Ctrl-F**) to locate the disputed transaction in the Register. Quicken inserts five question marks (?????) in the Ref field of marked transactions, so you can use ????? as your search argument in the Num field (this corresponds to the Ref field in a Credit Card Register) of the Transaction to Find window.

Assigning Categories to IntelliCharge Transactions

This section explains how IntelliCharge assigns categories to your credit card transactions. Because you don't assign the categories yourself, you should understand how IntelliCharge assigns categories.

The first time you use IntelliCharge to update your credit card account, transactions are categorized by IntelliCharge according to Intuit's standard Credit Card Category list. (The standard Credit Card Category list is contained in the file INTELLIC.CAT on your Quicken 7 program disks and copied to your hard disk when you install Quicken.) After the first time you update your credit card account, if you change any of the assigned categories (by pressing **Ctrl-C** from the IntelliCharge Statement window), IntelliCharge learns how you prefer your transactions to be categorized by scanning the Credit Card Register. IntelliCharge looks for a payee that matches the payee in the transaction in the current statement. When it finds a matching payee, it assigns the category assigned to the previous transaction (the one you changed) to the current transaction. IntelliCharge copies the category from the most recent transaction with a matching payee.

If IntelliCharge finds a matching payee in a split transaction, it copies the category information from the first line in the Split Transaction window.

If IntelliCharge does not find a matching payee in the Credit Card Register, it assigns a category to the new credit card transaction from its own list of credit card categories.

> **Note**
>
> Remember that you can change the category that IntelliCharge assigns to a credit card transaction by highlighting the transaction in the IntelliCharge Statement window and pressing **Ctrl-C** to display the Category and Transfer list.

Summary

In this chapter, you learn how to use Quicken's credit card accounts to manage your credit card activity. You learn how to set up a credit card account, how to enter credit transactions, and how to reconcile your credit card account and pay your credit card bill. You also learn about Quicken's IntelliCharge account, how to receive your IntelliCharge statements on disk or by modem, and how to review and categorize IntelliCharge transactions.

The next chapter shows you how to create and print Quicken reports. All of the work you have done so far in Quicken is meaningless unless you create reports that show you the results of your work. Quicken provides you with several types of reports that can help you assess your financial condition.

II

Getting the Most

Chapter 12

Creating and Printing Reports

When you collect information about your finances in a Quicken file, you essentially construct a database. With a database, you can arrange, retrieve, and summarize the information that database contains. With a financial database, you can determine your cash flows, net income or loss, tax deductions, and net worth. You do need a way to arrange, retrieve, and summarize the data, however, and within Quicken, this need is met with the variety of reports the program provides.

This chapter describes the ten report options available from the Reports menu.

You access the **R**eports menu by choosing Create Reports from the Main Menu or **R**eports from the Activities menu at any Register or the Write Checks screen. Figure 12.1 shows the Reports menu.

The first four options on the Reports menu display menus of different types of reports that you can create. Figure 12.2 shows the Home Reports menu. Figure 12.3 shows the **B**usiness Reports menu. Figure 12.4 shows the Investment Reports menu. Figure 12.5 shows the Other Reports menu.

The fifth option, **M**emorized Reports, enables you to memorize reports that you have created so that you can easily go back and regenerate the report again. The sixth option from the Reports menu, **R**edo Last Report, enables you to regenerate the last report you created.

The last four options on the Reports menu enable you to create custom reports, as discussed later in the section *Creating Custom Reports*.

In this chapter, you learn how to do the following:

- Create and print Quicken reports

- Use the QuickZoom feature

- Redo the last report created

- Edit reports

- Change the layout of reports

- Memorize reports

- Create customized reports

- Print reports to a disk file

II

Getting the Most

Fig. 12.1
The Report menu.

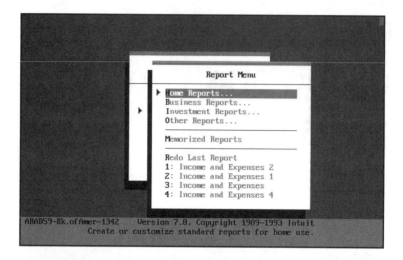

Fig. 12.2
The Home Reports menu.

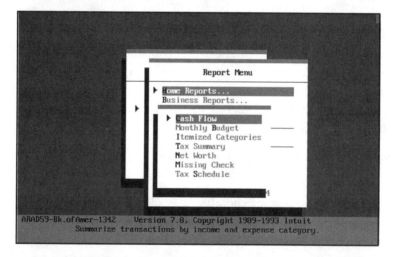

Fig. 12.3
The Business Reports menu.

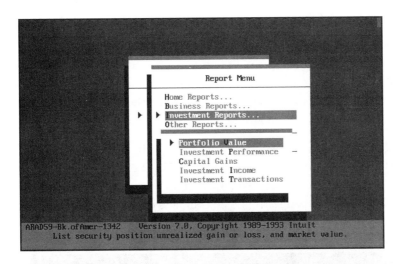

Fig. 12.4
The Investment
Reports menu.

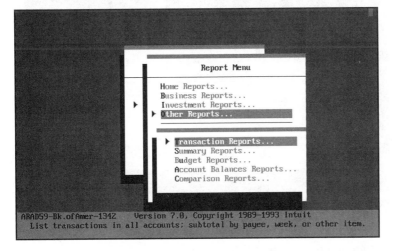

Fig. 12.5
The Other Reports
menu.

Reviewing Report Printing Basics

No matter which Quicken report you want to print, you need to follow the same basic steps. To print any report, follow these steps:

1. From Quicken's Main Menu, choose Create Reports. Quicken displays the Reports menu. You also can access the Reports menu by pressing **Alt-R** from any Register or the Write Checks screen.

2. From the Reports menu, choose the menu option for the report you want to print. If, for example, you want to print a personal cash flow report, choose Home Reports from the Reports menu. If you want to print a profit and loss statement, choose Business Reports.

When you select Home Reports, Business Reports, Investment Reports, or Other Reports from the Reports menu, Quicken displays a second menu that lists the types of reports you can print. If you select Home Reports, for example, Quicken displays the Home Reports menu (refer to fig. 12.2). From this second menu, choose the report you want to print, and then choose **Enter**.

Quicken displays the window you use to create the report. The Cash Flow Report window is shown in figure 12.6, but this window closely resembles other windows you use to print several of the reports. (Later in this chapter, you learn how to complete the individual report window for each report.)

Fig. 12.6

The Cash Flow Report window.

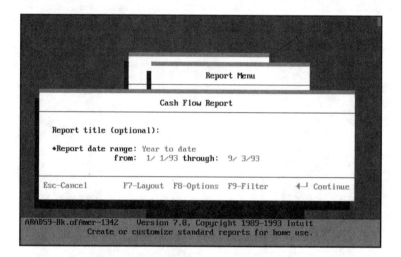

3. (Optional) Enter a report title.

If you don't enter a report title, Quicken names the report using the menu option. The report produced when you chose Cash Flow, for example, is named *Cash Flow Report*. The report created when you choose Monthly Budget is named *Monthly Budget Report*.

4. New to Quicken 7 is a *named date range list* pop-up menu that enables you to pick 1 of 11 predefined date ranges (see figure 12.7). If none of the predefined ranges are appropriate, you can choose Custom Date that enables you to enter any date you want.

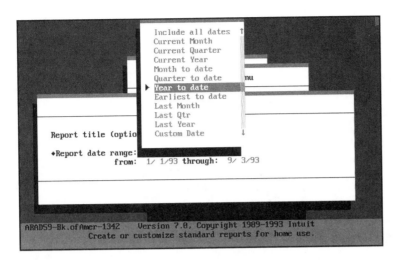

Fig. 12.7
The Report Date
Range menu.

To use this feature, move the cursor to the Report date range field. Choose the time frame the report should cover by highlighting the date range you want in the named date range list. If none of these time periods suit you, choose Custom Date and enter a date range manually. If you don't choose a date range, the report covers January 1 of the current year through the current date.

5. Choose **Enter** or **F10**. Quicken creates the report you selected and displays it on-screen.

6. When you are ready to print the report, choose the File/Print menu (**Ctrl-P**). Quicken displays the Print Report window shown in figure 12.8. This window enables you to specify where you want the report printed.

7. In the Print To field, choose **1** for printer 1, **2** for printer 2, and so on. If you choose printer 1, 2, or 3 in the Print Report window, choose **Enter** or **F10** to begin printing the report.

Tip
You can use the cursor-movement keys to see different portions of the report. You also can use the Home and End keys to see the first and last pages of the report. Or, you can use the mouse to scroll through the report by clicking the vertical or horizontal scroll bar. (See Chapter 2, "Getting Around in Quicken," to learn how to use a mouse to scroll report screens.)

Getting the Most

Note

After you create a report and the report appears on-screen, you can remove the report without printing it by pressing **Esc** or clicking the right mouse button. Quicken returns to the report window.

Fig. 12.8

The Print Report window.

If you choose 4 in the Print To field, Quicken prints an ASCII file. *ASCII files* are standardized text files you can use to import a Quicken report into a word processing program, such as WordPerfect or Microsoft Word. Before creating the ASCII file, Quicken uses the Print To Disk window to request three pieces of information (see fig. 12.9).

Fig. 12.9

The Print To Disk window.

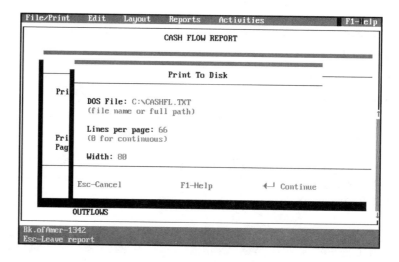

To print to disk, complete the following steps while in the Print to Disk window:

1. (Optional) In the DOS File field, enter a name for Quicken to use for the ASCII file. To use a data directory other than the Quicken data directory, QUICKEN, you can specify a path name. (See your DOS users' manual for information on path names.)

2. (Optional) In the Lines Per Page field, set the number of report lines between page breaks. If you are using 11-inch paper, the page length usually is 66 lines.

3. (Optional) In the Width field, set the number of characters (including blanks) that Quicken prints on a line. If you are using 8 1/2-inch paper, the characters-per-line setting usually is 80. Figure 12.9 shows the completed Print To Disk window with the file name cashfl.txt. Choose **Enter** or **F10** from the Print to Disk window to begin printing the selected report to the disk file you specified.

If you choose **5** to select the Disk (1-2-3 file) option from the Print To field in the Print Report window, Quicken displays the Print to Lotus File window. (1-2-3 is a popular spreadsheet program published by Lotus Development Corporation.)

To create a 1-2-3 file, Quicken requests the name of the file you want to create using the Print to Lotus File window. As with the ASCII file creation option, if you want to use a data directory other than QUICKEN, you can specify a path name. (You don't have to worry about the correct file extension. Quicken adds the extension for you.)

Choose **Enter** from the Print to Lotus File window to begin printing the selected report to the disk file that you specified.

II

Getting the Most

Note

You can customize all reports that you create to include transactions for certain payees, with certain memos, assigned categories, or classes. This is called *filtering* a report. Choose **F9** from the report window to access the Filter Transactions window. Filtering reports is explained later in this chapter.

You also can change the appearance of reports by setting report options such as the report organization (income and expense basis or cash-flow basis), whether transfers are included, whether unrealized gains from investment accounts are included, how amounts appear (rounded to the nearest dollar or including cents), and so on. Choose **F8** from the Report window to access the Report Options window. You learn how to set report options in the section *Setting Report Options*, later in this chapter.

You can change the layout of a report by choosing **F7** from the report window to access the Create Summary or Create Transaction Report windows. You can change the report title, date range, row headings, column headings, and the accounts used in the report. Changing the report layout is covered in the section *Changing the Report Layout*, later in this chapter.

Tracking Personal Finances with Home Reports

You can choose from seven reports in the Home Reports menu. To create any of these reports, you need to complete the window that appears when you select a report from the Home Reports menu.

The Cash Flow Report

Figure 12.10 shows an example of a personal cash flow report. The *cash flow* report shows the total cash inflows and outflows, by category. The personal cash flow report can show transfers to and from other accounts (however, the report in figure 12.10 does not show transfers). The report includes transactions from all the bank, cash, and credit card accounts in the current Quicken file.

Fig. 12.10

The personal cash flow report.

```
                            CASH FLOW REPORT
                        1/ 1/93 Through 9/22/93
         ARAD59-Bank, Cash, CC Accounts                          Page 1
         9/22/93
                                                     1/ 1/93-
                         Category Description         9/22/93
                         ─────────────────────      ──────────

         INFLOWS
            Interest Income                               2.18
            Professional Fees                         6,000.00
            Inflows - Other                              20.00
                                                     ──────────
         TOTAL INFLOWS                                6,022.18

         OUTFLOWS
            Automobile Expenses:
               Auto Fuel                      131.33
               Auto Loan Payment              631.34
               Auto Service                    31.00
                                             ────────
            Total Automobile Expenses                    793.67
            Bank Charge                                    7.50
            credit Card                                  674.00
            Dues                                         200.00
            Education                                    198.35
            Entertainment                               271.66
            Insurance                                     50.00
            Miscellaneous                                  6.50
            Mortgage Interest Exp                        750.00
            Mortgage                                     100.00
            Postage                                       25.00
            surcharge                                     20.00
            Taxes:
               Property Tax                   100.00
                                             ────────
            Total Taxes                                  100.00
            Telephone Expense                             34.65
            Water, Gas, Electric:
               Gas and Electricity             64.98
               Water                           23.95
                                             ────────
            Total Water, Gas, Electric                    88.93
            Outflows - Other                               6.62
            TO Fleet Mortgage                             98.34
                                                     ──────────
         TOTAL OUTFLOWS                                3,425.22
                                                     ──────────
         OVERALL TOTAL                                2,596.96
                                                     ══════════
```

The cash flow report can be extremely valuable. This report shows the various categories of cash flowing into and out of your personal banking accounts, cash accounts, and credit card accounts. If you question why you seem to have a bigger bank balance than usual or you always seem to run out of money before the end of the month, this report provides some answers.

The Monthly Budget Report

The *monthly budget* report shows actual income and expenses and budgeted income and expenses over a specified period. The monthly budget report also shows the comparison between the actual and budgeted amounts and calculates the difference (how much over or under budget you are, by category). This report includes transactions from all the bank, cash, and credit card accounts within the current Quicken file.

To produce a monthly budget report, you need to have first set up your budget. For information about setting up a monthly budget, refer to Chapter 15, "Budgeting with Quicken."

The Itemized Category Report

The *itemized category* report shows each transaction in the current Quicken file, sorted and subtotaled by category. This type of report provides a convenient way to see the detailed transactions that add up to a category total. The Itemized Category Report window works like the other report windows.

You can replace the default report title, *Itemized Category Report*, with a more specific title, such as *Personal Itemized Category Report*, by using the optional Report Title field. You also can specify a range of months to be included on the report. Figure 12.11 shows part of a sample itemized category report. (The defaults have been changed in this figure to customize the report titles.)

The itemized category report resembles the cash flow report in purpose and information, except that the itemized category report does not include account transfers. If you want to see your cash inflows and outflows grouped and summarized by category, this is the report you want.

Fig. 12.11

A sample itemized category report.

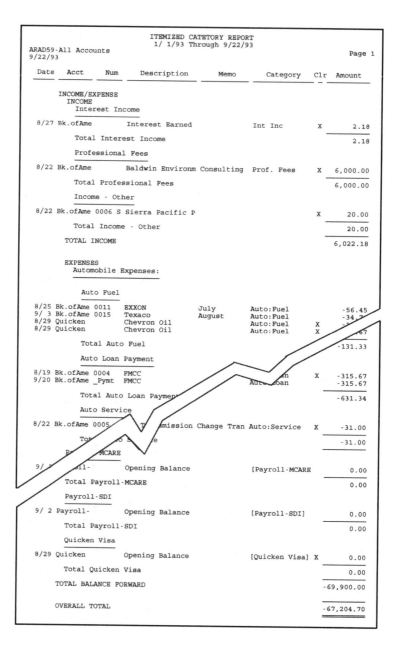

```
                          ITEMIZED CATETORY REPORT
                            1/ 1/93 Through 9/22/93
ARAD59-All Accounts
9/22/93                                                          Page 1

  Date  Acct    Num    Description    Memo    Category   Clr  Amount


        INCOME/EXPENSE
          INCOME
            Interest Income
  8/27 Bk.ofAme       Interest Earned          Int Inc    X    2.18
              Total Interest Income                            2.18
            Professional Fees
  8/22 Bk.ofAme       Baldwin Environm Consulting  Prof. Fees  X  6,000.00
              Total Professional Fees                        6,000.00
            Income - Other
  8/22 Bk.ofAme 0006 S Sierra Pacific P                   X     20.00
              Total Income - Other                            20.00
            TOTAL INCOME                                    6,022.18

          EXPENSES
            Automobile Expenses:

            Auto Fuel
  8/25 Bk.ofAme 0011  EXXON           July    Auto:Fuel       -56.45
  9/ 3 Bk.ofAme 0015  Texaco          August  Auto:Fuel       -34.
  8/29 Quicken        Chevron Oil             Auto:Fuel   X
  8/29 Quicken        Chevron Oil             Auto:Fuel   X    67
              Total Auto Fuel                                -131.33
            Auto Loan Payment
  8/19 Bk.ofAme 0004  FMCC                            n   X   -315.67
  9/20 Bk.ofAme _Pymt FMCC                    Aut  oan        -315.67
              Total Auto Loan Paymen                         -631.34
            Auto Service
  8/22 Bk.ofAme 0005   T  mission Change Tran Auto:Service X  -31.00
              To        e                                     -31.00
        B        MCARE
  9/           11-      Opening Balance        [Payroll-MCARE  0.00
              Total Payroll-MCARE                              0.00
            Payroll-SDI
  9/ 2 Payroll-        Opening Balance         [Payroll-SDI]   0.00
              Total Payroll-SDI                                0.00
            Quicken Visa
  8/29 Quicken        Opening Balance          [Quicken Visa] X  0.00
              Total Quicken Visa                               0.00
            TOTAL BALANCE FORWARD                         -69,900.00

            OVERALL TOTAL                                 -67,204.70
```

The Tax Summary Report

The *tax summary* report shows all the transactions assigned to categories you marked as tax-related. Transactions are sorted and subtotaled by category. The Tax Summary Report window works like the other report windows, enabling you to give the tax summary report a more specific title or to include only transactions from specified months. Figure 12.12 shows a page from a sample tax summary report.

```
                              TAX SUMMARY REPORT
                             1/ 1/93 Through 9/22/93
      ARAD59-Selected Accounts                                Page 1
      9/22/93

       Date   Acct    Num     Description     Memo    Category   Clr Amount


            INCOME/EXPENSE
              INCOME
                Interest Income
        8/27 Bk.ofAme          Interest Earned         Int Inc     X      2.18

                  Total Interest Income                                   2.18

                Professional Fees
        8/22 Bk.ofAme          Baldwin Environm Consulting  Prof. Fees  X  6,000.00

                  Total Professional Fees                             6,000.00

              TOTAL INCOME                                           6,002.18


              EXPENSES
                Mortgage Interest Exp
        8/28 Bk.ofAme 0013 S First National B       Mort Int        -750.00

                  Total Mortgage Interest Exp                        -750.00

                Taxes:


                  Property Tax
        8/28 Bk.ofAme 0013 S First National B       Tax:Prop        -100.00

                    Total Property Tax                              -100.00

                  Total Taxes                                       -100.00

                TOTAL EXPENSES                                      -850.00


              TOTAL INCOME/EXPENSE                                 5,152.18
```

Fig. 12.12
A sample tax summary report.

The tax summary report is a handy tax-preparation tool to use at the end of the year. This report summarizes the taxable income items and the tax deductions you need to report on your federal and state income tax returns. (The report, however, summarizes only tax deductions paid with those bank accounts, cash accounts, and credit card accounts you choose to track with Quicken. If you have two checking accounts, write tax-deductible checks using both accounts, and track only one of the accounts with Quicken, you are missing half of your deductions.)

The Net Worth Report

A *net worth* report shows the balance in each of the accounts in your Quicken file on a particular date. If the file includes all your assets and liabilities, the resulting report is a balance sheet that provides one estimate of your financial net worth. *Net worth* is the difference between your total assets and total liabilities. If you own more assets than liabilities, you have a positive net worth. If you own fewer assets than liabilities, you have a negative net worth. (For more information about balance sheets, see Chapter 10, "Tracking Your Net Worth, Other Assets, and Liabilities.") Figure 12.13 shows the Net Worth Report window.

Fig. 12.13
The Net Worth
Report window.

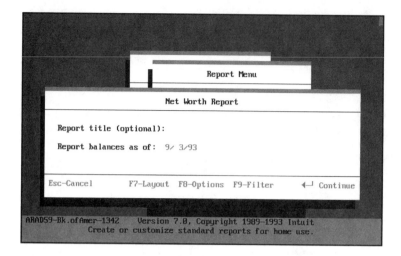

The Net Worth Report window differs from other personal report windows because you cannot enter a range of dates; you can enter only one date. The net worth report does not report on activity for a period of time but provides a snapshot of certain aspects of your financial condition—the account balances in your Quicken file—at a point in time. Figure 12.14 shows a sample net worth report.

Fig. 12.14
A sample net
worth report.

```
                              NET WORTH REPORT
                               As of 9/22/93
ARAD59-All Accounts                                                   Page 1
9/22/93
                                              9/22/93
                        Acct                  Balance

              ASSETS
                Cash and Bank Accounts
                  Acme                         15,100.00
                  Bk.ofAmer-1342                3,316.68
                  cash on hand                     61.88

                Total Cash and Bank Accounts   18,478.56

                Assets
                  Real Estate                 100,000.00

                Total Assets                  100,000.00


              TOTAL ASSETS                    118,478.56

              LIABILITIES
                Credit Cards
                  Quicken Visa                    318.60

                Total Credit Cards               318.60

                Liabilities
                  Fleet Mortgage              84,901.66
                  Payroll-FICA                     0.00
                  Payroll-FWH                      0.00
                  Payroll-MCARE                    0.00
                  Payroll-SDI                      0.00

                Total Liabilities            84,901.66


              TOTAL LIABILITIES              85,220.26


              TOTAL NET WORTH                 33,258.30
```

Monitoring your net worth probably is more important than most people realize. Over the years you work, one of your financial goals may be to increase your net worth. During your retirement years, you probably will look to your net worth to provide income and security. Your net worth, for example, may include investments that produce regular interest or dividend income. Your net worth also may include your personal residence, completely paid for by the time you retire.

The Missing Check Report

The *missing check* report displays a list of all checking account transactions in check number order with any gaps in the check number sequence identified. To request a missing check report, you use the Missing Check Report window shown in figure 12.15. The Missing Check Report window works just like the other report windows. Figure 12.16 shows a sample missing check report on-screen with a missing check (number 0014) identified.

Fig. 12.15

The Missing Check Report window.

The Tax Schedule Report

The *tax schedule* report summarizes tax-related categories in a way that makes it easy to prepare every common income tax schedule. Using category information, Quicken adds up the transactions that go on each line of each tax schedule. To create a tax schedule report, fill in the Tax Schedule Report window, which works like the other report windows. Chapter 14, "Using Quicken to Prepare for Income Taxes," describes and illustrates this handy report.

Fig. 12.16

The Missing Check Report displayed.

Tracking Your Business Finances with Business Reports

The Business Reports menu, shown in figure 12.3, provides eight reports. To create a business report, choose the report you want to create from the Business Reports menu, and then complete the report window with an optional title and the date range that you want the report to cover. (The eighth report in the Business Reports menu is the missing check report. This report mirrors the missing check report from the Personal Reports menu already described in *The Missing Check Report*.)

The P & L (Profit and Loss) Statement

The *P & L* (*profit and loss statement*) shows the total income and expenses by category for all accounts on a monthly basis. Data from transactions from any of the accounts in the current Quicken file are included, but transfers between accounts are not. Figure 12.17 shows the Profit & Loss Statement window. Like most of the report windows, you have two options: to use your own report title or the default title and to specify the months to be included in the report or to use the default (from January of the current year to the current date). Figure 12.18 shows a sample profit and loss statement.

Unless a business makes money (profits), it cannot keep operating for very long. Accordingly, business owners and managers must monitor profits. The profit and loss statement provides the means to do so.

Fig. 12.17
The Profit & Loss
Statement
window.

Fig. 12.18
A sample profit &
loss statement.

```
                        PROFIT & LOSS STATEMENT
                        1/ 1/93 Through 9/22/93
ARAD60-All Accounts                                              Page 1
9/22/93
                                        1/ 1/93-
            Category Description         9/22/93

INCOME/EXPENSE
   INCOME
      Gross Sales                       23,546.76
      Dividend                             100.00
      Income - Other                     7,626.28

   TOTAL INCOME                         31,273.04

   EXPENSES
      Auto Lease                           623.00
      Water, Gas, Electric                 296.76
      Merch.Pur.                        17,438.43
      Office Expenses                      342.89
      Payroll:
         Comp FICA            54.03
         Comp MCARE           12.63
         Gross              871.50

      Total Payroll                        938.16
      Rent Paid                         2,000.00
      Telephone                           137.36
      Expenses - Other                      0.00

   TOTAL EXPENSES                       21,776.60

   TOTAL INCOME/EXPENSE                  9,496.44
```

II

Getting the Most

CPA TIP

The profit and loss statement is one of your business's most used and important financial reports. It reports your net income or net loss for a specific time period (month, quarter, year, and so on). Remember that the sales revenue shown on the profit and loss statement is not the same as cash inflow from sales for the period and that the expenses shown do not necessarily reflect the cash outflows of your business for the period. Create a cash flow report to show the cash position of your business.

The Cash Flow Report

A *cash flow* report resembles a profit and loss statement. This report includes all bank, cash, and credit card accounts and shows the money received (*inflows*) and the money spent (*outflows*) by category for each month. The cash flow report also shows transfers between accounts.

Like the Profit & Loss Statement window, the Cash Flow Report window provides fields for you to enter the range of months that you want the cash flow report to cover. You can enter your own report title for Quicken to print on the cash flow report in place of the default title, *Cash Flow Report.*

Figure 12.19 shows a sample cash flow report. The difference between this report and the profit and loss statement is that transfers to other accounts are shown on the cash flow report and the cash flow report groups cash inflows together and cash outflows together. The difference between cash inflows and outflows is the overall total, which may be positive or negative.

Cash flow is just as important as profits—particularly over shorter time periods. Besides making money, businesses need to have cash to purchase inventory or equipment, to have as working capital while they wait for customers to pay their bills, and to pay back loans from banks and vendors. The cash flow report, which summarizes your cash inflows and outflows by category and account, provides a method for monitoring your cash flow—and for pinpointing problems that arise.

Fig. 12.19

A sample business cash flow report.

```
                           CASH FLOW REPORT
                         1/ 1/93 Through 9/22/93
ARAD60-US BANK1234                                                Page 1
9/22/93
                                         1/ 1/93-
                  Category Description    9/22/93
                  ---------------------  ---------

                  INFLOWS
                    Gross Sales                     23,546.76
                    FROM Payroll-FICA                  108.06
                    FROM Payroll-FWH                    72.00
                    FROM Payroll-MCARE                  25.26
                    FROM Payroll-SDI                    12.20
                                                   ---------
                  TOTAL INFLOWS                     23,764.28

                  OUTFLOWS
                    Auto Lease                         623.00
                    Water, Gas, Electric               296.76
                    Merch.Pur.                      17,438.43
                    Office Expenses                    342.89
                    Payroll:
                      Comp FICA          54.03
                      Comp MCARE         12.63
                      Gross             871.50
                                       --------
                    Total Payroll                      938.16
                    Rent Paid                        2,000.00
                    Telephone                          137.36
                    Outflows - Other                     0.00
                                                   ---------
                  TOTAL OUTFLOWS                    21,776.60
                                                   ---------
                  OVERALL TOTAL                      1,987.68
                                                   =========
```

The A/P by Vendor Report

Because Quicken uses what is called *cash-basis accounting*, expenses are recorded only when you actually pay the bill. By not paying bills, or even paying bills late, your net income or profit and your net cash flow may look better. The problem, of course, is that this concept is clearly illogical. Just because you haven't paid a bill by the end of the month doesn't mean that the bill shouldn't be considered in assessing the month's financial performance. To partially address this shortcoming, Quicken provides the A/P (Unprinted Checks) by Vendor report, which enables you to see which bills have not been paid.

The *A/P by vendor* report lists all the unprinted checks, sorted and subtotaled by payee. (*A/P* is an abbreviation for *accounts payable*—the unpaid bills of a business.) Figure 12.20 shows the A/P (Unprinted Checks) by Vendor window. You do not enter a date or a range of dates in this window, but you can enter a substitute report title for Quicken to use rather than the default report title, *A/P (Unprinted Checks) by Vendor Report.*

Fig. 12.20

The A/P (Unprinted Checks) by Vendor window.

Quicken subtotals unprinted checks with the exact payee names. If you type the payee name differently for different checks, the payee is not recognized by Quicken as the same payee, and the amounts are not subtotaled. If you plan to use this report (or the A/R by customer report described next), use the Memorized Transaction feature. When you use this feature, the payee name is identical for each transaction.

The A/R by Customer Report

The *A/R by customer* report shows the transactions in all of the other asset accounts, sorted and subtotaled by payee. The report, however, does not include transactions marked as cleared—those transactions marked with an asterisk (*) or X in the C field of the Register. (*A/R* is an abbreviation for *accounts receivable*—the amounts your customers owe.) The A/R by Customer window is very similar to the A/P by Vendor window shown in figure 12.20. You can enter a title to replace the default report title, *A/R by Customer Report*.

After you enter a report title in the A/R by Customer window, press **Enter**. Quicken displays the Select Accounts to Include window (see fig. 12.21).

Fig. 12.21

The Select Accounts to include window.

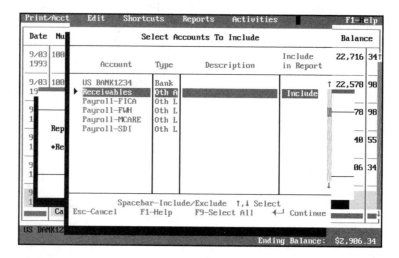

Quicken lists all of your accounts in the Select Accounts to Include window. You should include only receivable accounts in the A/R by customer report. To include or exclude accounts, follow these steps:

1. Highlight the account you want to include or exclude, and then press the space bar.

   The space bar acts as a toggle switch, alternately marking the account for inclusion or exclusion.

2. (Optional) To select all the accounts, choose **F9**.

For businesses that extend customer credit—which is what you do anytime you allow a customer to "buy now, pay later"—monitoring the amounts the customers owe is essential to profits and cash flows. Unfortunately, some customers don't pay unless you remind them several times, some customers frequently lose invoices and then forget that they owe you, and sometimes customers never receive your bill. To ensure that these small problems don't become big cash-flow problems, you can use the A/R by customer report.

CPA TIP

Good collection procedures usually improve cash flows dramatically, so consider using the customer-aging report as a collection guide (see Chapter 22 to learn how to create an aging report). You may, for example, want to telephone any customer with an invoice 30 days past due, and you may want to stop granting additional credit to any customer with invoices more than 60 days past due, and—in the absence of special circumstances—you may want to initiate collection procedures for any customer with invoices more than 90 days past due.

The Job/Project Report

The *job/project* report shows category totals by month for each month in the specified date range. The report also shows account balances at the end of the last month. (If you are using classes, the report shows category totals by class in separate columns across the report page.) The Job/Project Report window is just like many of the other report windows, such as the Profit & Loss Statement window shown in figure 12.17. Refer to Chapter 22 for more information on job costing and a sample job/project report.

The Payroll Report

The *payroll* report shows the total amounts paid to individual payees when the transaction category starts with payroll. (The search argument used is *payroll*. See the discussions of exact and key-word matches in Chapters 6 and 8 for more information.) The payroll report includes transactions from all accounts. The Payroll Report window works just like the other report windows.

Figure 12.22 shows a sample payroll report. Refer to Chapter 22 for more information on preparing payroll with Quicken and to Appendix B "Using QuickPay with Quicken."

Fig. 12.22

A sample payroll report.

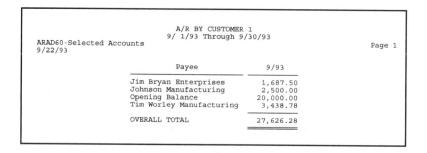

```
                                  A/R BY CUSTOMER 1
                                9/ 1/93 Through 9/30/93
    ARAD60-Selected Accounts                                        Page 1
    9/22/93


                             Payee             9/93

                  Jim Bryan Enterprises        1,687.50
                  Johnson Manufacturing        2,500.00
                  Opening Balance             20,000.00
                  Tim Worley Manufacturing     3,438.78

                  OVERALL TOTAL               27,626.28
```

CPA TIP

At the end of the calendar year, create a payroll report to help you complete your W-2 forms. Make sure that the time period covered by the report is for the full calendar year (1/1/93 to 12/31/93, for example). The payroll report shows the total gross wages paid to each employee and his or her total withholdings (federal, social security, state, local, and so on).

A W-2 form must be sent by January 31 of the following calendar year to each person that you employed at any time during the previous calendar year.

The Balance Sheet

The *balance sheet* report shows the account balances for all accounts in the current Quicken file at a specific point in time. If the file includes accounts for all your assets and liabilities, the resulting report is a balance sheet that shows the net worth of your business. (Chapter 10 describes balance sheets in more detail.) Figure 12.23 shows the Balance Sheet window.

CPA TIP

The balance sheet report measures the value of your business as of one moment in time the date you entered in the Report Balances As Of field in the Balance Sheet window. *Asset amounts* represent values based on original cost—not replacement costs or earning power (unless you entered any amount other than original costs for assets in Quicken). *Liabilities* represent the legal claims of creditors who have loaned you money or goods or services that have been provided to you that you have not yet paid for. *Owner's equity*, or *net worth*, represents a claim resulting from the capital invested by the owners of the business and past profits retained in the business.

Even for small businesses, balance sheets are important reports. Because a balance sheet shows what a business owns and what it owes, balance sheets give an indication of the financial strength or weakness of a business. The smaller the total liabilities amount in relation to the total assets amount, for example, the stronger the business. Alternatively, the larger the total liabilities in relation to the total assets, the weaker the business. As a result of these and similar financial insights, banks usually require a balance sheet in order to evaluate loan applications from businesses.

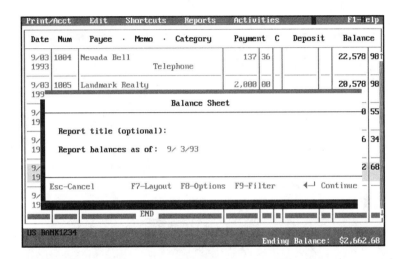

Fig. 12.23
The Balance Sheet window.

Tracking Your Investments with Quicken's Investment Reports

The Investment Reports menu provides five report options (refer to fig. 12.4). As with personal and business reports, the basic steps for printing an investment report are straightforward. To print any of the five reports, choose the report that you want to print from the Investment Reports menu, complete the appropriate report window, and then print the report. You may want to review Chapter 16 before you attempt to print investment reports.

The Portfolio Value Report

A *portfolio value* report shows the estimated market values of each of the securities in your Quicken investment accounts on a specific date. To estimate the market values, Quicken uses each security's individual *price history* (a list of prices on certain dates). Quicken determines which price to use by comparing the date that you enter in the report window to use as the value date to the dates that have prices in the price history. Ideally, Quicken uses a price for the same date as the date you specify. When the price history does not contain a price for the same date specified, Quicken uses the price for the date closest to that date.

To create a portfolio value report, complete the Portfolio Value Report window shown in figure 12.24. You can enter a report title, and you need to enter a date in the Report Value As Of field. You can specify that the information on the report be summarized by account, security type, and investment goal. You also can specify whether the report should include the current account, all accounts, or only selected accounts, by using a window.

Fig. 12.24
The Portfolio Value Report window.

The Investment Performance Report

Investment performance reports help you measure how well or how poorly your investments are doing. These reports look at all the transactions for a security and calculate an annual rate of return (in effect, the interest rate) an investment has paid you. To generate an investment performance report, you use the report window shown in figure 12.25.

The report window enables you to use a custom title for the report. The window also requires that you enter dates into the Report Performance From and To fields. These dates tell Quicken for which time frame you want to calculate investment returns. The report window also enables you to subtotal rates of return by different time periods, by account, by security, by security type, or by investment goals. You also can specify whether you want rates of return calculated for just the current account, for all accounts, or for selected accounts. Quicken notifies you if one or more of the total return calculations cannot be completed and displays the value as NA.

Fig. 12.25
The Investment
Performance
Report window.

The Capital Gains (Schedule D) Report

The *capital gains* report attempts to print all the information you need to complete the federal income tax form, Schedule D. Taxpayers use Schedule D to report capital gains and losses. To generate a capital gains report, use the Capital Gains (Schedule D) Report window shown in figure 12.26.

Fig. 12.26
The Capital Gains
Report window.

Most of the fields in the Capital Gains Report window should be familiar to you, and the fields that also appear on the other investment report windows are not described here. Two fields do deserve mention, however: the Subtotal by and the Maximum Short-Term Gain Holding Period (Days) fields. Although income tax laws currently in effect treat short-term capital gains the same as long-term capital gains, Congress may change this treatment. Accordingly, Quicken enables you to subtotal by short-term and long-term gains and losses.

Currently, gains and losses that stem from the sale of capital assets held for more than one year are considered long-term. The Maximum Short-Term Gain Holding Period field enables you to change the default number of days Quicken uses to determine whether a gain or loss is long-term should the law change.

The Investment Income Report

The *investment income* report summarizes all the income transactions you recorded in one or more of the investment accounts. To generate the report, use the report window shown in figure 12.27.

Fig. 12.27

The Investment Income Report window.

Realized gains and losses result when the investment is actually sold and cash is received. A realized gain or loss is calculated by comparing the proceeds of the sale with the original cost of the investment. *Unrealized gains and losses* result when the cost of the investment is compared with the market value to determine what the gain or loss would have been if the investment had been sold.

The Investment Transactions Report

The *investment transactions* report lists each of the investment transactions in the Register. To create the report, use the Investment Transactions Report window. As with many of the other report windows, Quicken enables you to enter an optional title, specify the time frame the report should cover, indicate whether you want transactions subtotaled according to some convention, and to decide which accounts you want included in the report.

Creating Custom Reports

The Reports menu includes five custom reports that you can create in Quicken; transaction, summary, budget, account balances, and comparison (see fig. 12.5). You can use any one of these custom report options as a template to create a specific report to meet your needs. You can create a summary report by using the Reports menu's custom Summary option, which doesn't have a specific purpose the way other Quicken reports have. The profit and loss statement, for example, is a summary type report because it summarizes transactions and shows account totals rather than individual transactions. The custom Transaction report option on the Reports menu lists transactions in the current account, all accounts, or selected accounts. Quicken can list transactions by payee; category; class; account; or a time period such as week, month, quarter, and so on. You can create a custom budget report by using the Budget report option. This option enables you to compare actual amounts by category against monthly budget amounts. The custom Account Balances report enables you to list balances for all your accounts, selected accounts, or just the current account. Balances are listed based on intervals that you specify. The new Comparison Reports option enables you to compare dollar or percentage amounts between two defined time periods.

When you choose a custom report option, such as Transaction, Quicken displays the Create Transaction Report window. Quicken displays the Create Summary Report window when you choose the Summary report option. These create report windows are the same windows that appear when you choose F7 (to change the report layout) from the report windows that you saw when you learned to create standard reports earlier in this chapter. If you choose the **F7-Layout** option by choosing **F7** from the personal Cash Flow Report window, Quicken displays the Create Summary Report window. Because the cash flow report is a summary report (because it summarizes transactions rather than listing individual transactions), you use the Create Summary Report window to change the layout of the cash flow report.

Likewise, if you choose **F7-Layout** from the personal Itemized Categories Report window, Quicken displays the Create Transaction Report window. Because the itemized categories report is a transaction report (because it lists

II

Getting the Most

individual transactions rather than summarizing transactions and showing totals only), you use the Create Transaction Report window to change the layout of the itemized cash flow report. You learn more about changing report layouts later in this chapter in the section *Changing the Report Layout*. For now, remember that the custom reports that you are about to read about are the basis for all other Quicken reports.

Creating Transaction Reports

You may want to view your Register transactions in some order other than chronologically by date. You may find value in sorting and summarizing transactions by the payee or by time periods such as a week or month, for example. The transaction report enables you to see your account transactions in any of these ways.

To create a transaction report, follow these steps:

1. Choose **Other Reports** from the **Reports** menu. The Other Reports menu appears.

2. Choose **Transaction Reports** from the Other Reports menu. Quicken displays the Create Transaction Report window (see fig. 12.28.)

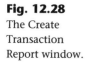

Fig. 12.28
The Create
Transaction
Report window.

3. (Optional) Enter a report title. If you don't enter a report title, Quicken names the report *Transaction Report*.

4. (Optional) Move the cursor to the Report date range field. Enter the time frame you want the report to cover by choosing from the pop-up menu

the starting and ending dates. If you don't enter these dates, the report covers from January 1 of the current year through the current date.

5. (Optional) Move the cursor to the Subtotal By field. Choose one of the 12 subtotal options by selecting the number that appears to the left of the option.

6. (Optional) Move the cursor to the Use Current/All/Selected Accounts field. Here, you determine whether to include just the current accounts' transactions, just the selected accounts' transactions, or all the accounts' transactions. If you choose selected accounts only, Quicken displays the Select Accounts to Include window.

7. (Optional) Choose **F8** (Options) to access the Report Options window. Complete the Report Options window as described later in this chapter in the section *Setting Report Options*.

8. (Optional) Choose **F9** (Filter) to access the Filter Report Transactions window. Complete the Filter Report Transactions window as described later in this chapter in the section *Filtering Reports*.

9. When the Create Transaction Report window is complete, choose **Enter** or **F10**. Quicken generates and displays the report on-screen.

10. When you are ready to print the report, choose **Ctrl-P**. Quicken displays the Print Report window shown in figure 12.8. The Print Report window enables you to specify to where you want the report printed. Follow the steps outlined in the section *Reviewing Report Printing Basics*, earlier in this chapter, to learn how to complete the Print Report window.

Creating Summary Reports

Like a transaction report, a summary report extracts information from the financial database you create using Quicken's Registers. A summary report, however, gives you totals by category, class, payee, or account, in addition to any of the other subtotals you request. With this type of report, you also can choose the accounts to include.

To create a summary report, you follow essentially the same steps you follow to create a transaction report, except that you choose the Summary report option from the Other Reports menu. Quicken then displays the Create Summary Report window, which you use to specify how the custom report should appear (see fig. 12.29). Refer to the steps for completing the Create Transaction Report window in the preceding section, *Creating Transaction Reports*, to learn how to complete the Create Summary Report window.

Fig. 12.29
The Create
Summary Report
window.

```
                    Create Summary Report          ▮              e

        Report title (optional):                                 55

        ◆Report date range: Earliest to date
                   from: 12/31/92 through:  9/ 3/93               34

        Row headings (down the left side): 1
              1. Category          3. Payee                       68
              2. Class             4. Account

        Column headings (across the top): 1                       18
              1. Don't Subtotal   5. Month          9. Category
              2. Week             6. Quarter       10. Class
              3. Two Weeks        7. Six Months    11. Payee      82
              4. Half Month       8. Year          12. Account

        Show percentage column(Y/N): N

        Use Current/All/Selected accounts (C/A/S): C

     Esc-Cancel             F8-Options   F9-Filter      ←┘ Continue
                                                                   82
```

Creating Budget Reports

Chapter 15, "Budgeting with Quicken," describes budgeting as a fundamental tool that businesses and individuals can use to better manage their finances. One of the ongoing steps in using a budget as a tool is to compare the amount you spent with the amount you planned to spend, or budgeted. Quicken's Option report option on the Reports menu enables you to create customized budget reports tailored to your business or personal needs.

To print a budget report, follow the same steps you use when creating transaction, summary, or account balances reports. Choose Other Reports from the Reports menu, and then choose Budget Reports from the Other Reports menu.

Quicken displays the Create Budget Report window, which you use to specify how the custom report should appear. Refer to the steps for completing the Create Transaction Report window in the preceding section to learn how to complete the Create Budget Report window.

Creating Account Balances Reports

You can use the eighth option on the Reports menu to create customized account balances reports. If you have extensive investments with several brokers, for example, and you want a report that specifies only those accounts, you can create this report (or a specialized version of this report).

Figure 12.30 shows the Create Account Balances Report window that you use to construct customized account balances reports.

Fig. 12.30
The Create
Account Balances
Report window.

The basic steps you follow for creating an account balances report are the same as for any of the other custom reports. Choose Other Reports from the Reports menu, and then choose Account Balances Reports from the Other Reports menu and Quicken displays the Create Account Balances Report window.

To create an account balances report, follow these steps:

1. In the Report Title field, enter a report title of up to 39 characters and choose **Enter**. If you leave this field blank, Quicken supplies the title *Account Balances Report.*

2. The Report Balances on Dates From and Through fields are slightly different from the Report date range fields in other custom report windows. The account balances report shows the account balances at a specific point in time. This field sets a boundary around the points in time for which an account balances report is generated. Enter the dates that cover the time period to show account balances, and then choose **Enter**.

3. The Report at Intervals Of field determines the points in time for which an account balances report is generated. The start of the first interval is the first day of the year. Assuming that the Report Balances on Dates From field is 1/1/93, the first account balances column is for 1/1/93.

The next date depends on the interval. If the interval is weekly, the second column is 1/7/93. If the interval is biweekly, the second column is 1/14/93. If the interval is by half month, the second column is 1/15/93, and so on. The report shows account balances for each interval between the From and Through dates. The last column of the report shows the account balances on the Through date. In the Report at Intervals Of field, enter the number that corresponds to the interval you want to use, and then choose **Enter**.

If the Report at Intervals Of field is set to 1 for **None**, the only point in time for which the account balances report is generated is the date entered in the Through field.

4. As with the other custom reports, the Use Current/All/Selected Accounts field enables you to determine which account balances are reported on the account balances report. Choose **C** to designate just the current account; choose **S** to designate only the selected accounts; choose **A** to designate all accounts. If you choose only selected accounts, Quicken displays the Select Accounts to Include window. Highlight the accounts you want to include in the report and press the space bar to mark the account as included. Use the space bar as a toggle to designate **Include** or **Detail** next to the account. If you choose **Detail**, Quicken shows the class or security detail for that account. Choose **Enter** when you are finished selecting accounts. Quicken returns to the Create Account Balances Report window.

5. When the Create Account Balances Report window is complete, choose **Enter** or **F10** to display the report on-screen.

Creating Comparison Reports

New to Quicken 7 are comparison reports. A *comparison report* compares your income and expenses during one period with your income and expenses during another period. For example, you can compare this year with last year or this quarter with last quarter. The comparison can be shown as either a dollar amount or a percentage or both.

To create a comparison report, follow these steps:

1. Choose Other Reports option from the **Reports** menu, and then choose Comparison Reports from the **Other Reports** menu. Quicken displays the Create Comparison Report window (see fig. 12.31).

Fig. 12.31
The Create
Comparison
Report window.

2. In the Report Title field, enter a report title of up to 39 characters, and then choose **Enter**. If you do not enter a title, Quicken supplies the title *Comparison Report*.

3. Move the cursor to the Compare field. From the pop-up Named Date list, choose a named date for the range of transactions to be included in the report. This range specifies the left column in each pair of columns to be compared.

4. Move the cursor to the With field. From the pop-up Named Date list, choose a named date for the range of transactions to be included in the report. This range specifies the right column in each pair of columns to be compared.

5. Move the cursor to the Column headings (across the top) field. Enter the number of the item that corresponds to how you want Quicken to subtotal the report. Quicken includes a separate column for each Column Heading item.

6. Move the cursor to the Row headings (down the left side) field. Enter the number of the item that corresponds to what you want to report on: categories, classes, payees, or accounts. The names of these appear down the left side of your report.

7. Move the cursor to the Show differences column and choose **Y** if you want the report to show the differences between the compared amounts as a dollar amount. The report lists a *$ Difference* column for each pair of compared columns. Enter **N** if you don't want the report to show dollar differences.

8. Move the cursor to the Show percentage column and choose **Y** if you want the report to show the difference between the compared amounts as a percentage of the total difference. The report lists a *% Difference* column for each pair of compared columns. Press **N** if you don't want the report to show percentage differences.

> **Note**
>
> You can have the dollar differences and percentage differences set to yes to display both comparisons on the same report.

9. Move the cursor to the Use Current/All/Selected Accounts field. Here, you determine whether to include just the current accounts' transactions, just the selected accounts' transactions, or all the accounts' transactions. If you choose just selected accounts, Quicken displays the Select Accounts to Include window.

10. (Optional) Choose **F8** (Options) to access the Report Options window. Complete the Report Options window as described later in this chapter in the section *Setting Report Options*.

11. (Optional) Choose **F9** (Filter) to access the Filter Report Transactions window. Complete the Filter Report Transactions window as described later in this chapter in the section *Filtering Reports*.

12. When the Create Comparison Report window is complete, choose **Ctrl-Enter** or **F10**. Quicken generates and displays the report on-screen.

Viewing Reports On-Screen

You have learned how to create Quicken reports so that they are appear on-screen. Most reports you display, however, are too wide or too long to fit entirely within the boundaries of your screen. Table 12.1 lists the keys you can use to view reports on your screen.

Table 12.1 Report-Viewing Keys	
Press	**To View**
Tab or →	Next column to the right
Shift-Tab or ←	Preceding column to the left
Ctrl-→	One screen to the right
Ctrl-←	One screen to the left
PgUp	Up one screen
PgDn	Down one screen
Home	Far left column, current row
End	Far right column, current row
Home Home	Top left corner of report
End End	Bottom right corner of report

> **Note**
>
> You can use the Full Column Width option from the report Layout menu to display transaction reports in full-width columns so that you can see more transaction detail. Refer to *Changing the Report Layout*, later in this chapter, for more information on displaying full-width columns.

You also can use your mouse to scroll report screens by clicking the scroll box on the vertical or horizontal scroll bar. See Chapter 2, "Getting Around in Quicken," to learn more about using a mouse to scroll report screens.

Re-creating the Last Report

The last item on the Reports menu is the Redo Last Report option. This option enables you to display the last report you created without having to select the report from the menu. This option is particularly useful if you last created a customized report by changing the layout, setting report options, and filtering report transactions. By selecting the Redo Last Report option, Quicken displays the last report, as you created it.

To re-create the last report, follow these steps:

1. Create any Quicken report. Exit the report screen by choosing **Esc**. Continue with your work in Quicken.

2. From the Main Menu, choose Create Reports to display the Reports menu, or from the Register or the Write Checks screen, display the Reports menu.

3. From the Reports menu, choose Redo Last Report or press **Ctrl-Z**. Quicken completes the appropriate report window and displays the report that you last created.

Customizing Reports

You learned how to create standard reports by selecting the report option from the Reports menu and completing the report's Create Report window. What if, for example, you want to report over different dates than you're allowed to enter in the Create Report window, or if you want to restrict transactions to those with a particular payee or assigned to certain categories? You can customize each standard Quicken report. The available options vary among report types.

You can customize reports so that Quicken provides the exact information that you want and exactly how you want to see this information. You can use the following Quicken options to customize a report from the report window (see fig. 12.32):

- F7-Layout

- F8-Options

- F9-Filter

Quicken displays all available customizing options at the bottom of the window that you use to create the report. Remember that report windows appear when you choose the report that you want to create from the Personal, Business, or Investment Reports menu. When you choose **F7-Layout**, Quicken displays one of the four custom report windows (Transaction, Summary, Budget, or Account Balances), depending on the type of report that you are creating. When you choose **F7** from the Net Worth Report window, for example, Quicken displays the Create Account Balances Report window because the net worth report is a report that shows account balances as of some point in time.

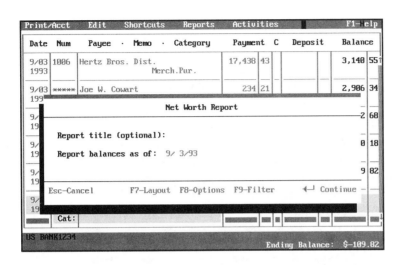

Fig. 12.32

The Net Worth Report window with customizing options.

When you choose **F8-Options**, Quicken displays the Report Options window like the one you see in figure 12.33. The report options Quicken enables you to change depend on the type of report you are creating.

Fig. 12.33

The Report Options window.

The last customizing option, **F9-Filters**, also can be selected from the report window you use to create the report. When you choose **F9-Filters**, Quicken displays the Filter Transactions window (see fig. 12.34). Filtering transactions enables you to limit the transactions included in the report. You can restrict reports to transactions meeting specific criteria; choose which accounts and classes to include in reports; and include only those transactions with amounts below, equal to, or above certain amounts.

II

Getting the Most

Changing the Report Layout

You can change the report layout by changing titles, the date range of transactions to include, the row and column headings, and the accounts used in the report. To change the report layout, choose **F7-Layout** from the report window that you use to create the report. When you choose **F7**, Quicken displays the Create Summary Report window like the one you saw in figure 12.29. The Create Report window that appears will be the same Create Report window that appears to create custom reports (Summary, Transaction, Budget, or Account Balances).

Fig. 12.34

The Filter Transactions window.

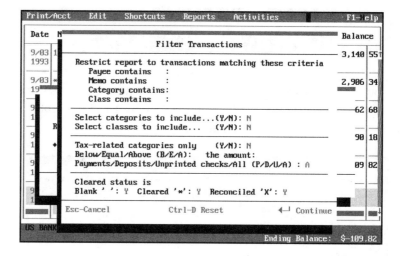

Depending on the type of report you are customizing, Quicken enables you to change the layout of the report by changing the following settings:

Report Title: You can enter the title that you want to appear at the top of the report. The title can include numbers, letters, and other characters (up to 39 characters). If you don't enter a title, Quicken uses the report type title, such as *Cash Flow Report* or *Net Worth Report.*

Restrict to Transactions From and Through: By entering dates, you determine the transactions covered by the report. If you want the report to cover transactions for August 1993 only, for example, type **8/1/93** in the From field and **8/31/93** in the Through field. You can use the + (plus) and - (minus) keys in these fields to change the date one day at a time.

Row Headings: You can choose the item on which you want to report. Press the number that corresponds to the item on which you want to report. Choose 1 for **Category**, 2 for **Class**, and so on. The item you select determines the text that appears down the left side of the report. If you choose to report on categories, for example, Quicken includes all the category names as row headings in the report.

Column Headings: You choose how the report is subtotaled. When the report is created, Quicken includes a separate column for each column heading you choose. Choose the number that corresponds to the column heading you want to use. Choose 1 for **Don't Subtotal** (Quicken includes a single column), 2 for **Week**, 3 for **Two Weeks**, and so on.

Use Current/All/Selected Accounts: You can determine which accounts you want to include in the report. Choose **C** to include only the current account. Choose **A** to include all accounts in the current Quicken file. For investment reports, selecting all accounts includes all investment accounts only. Or, choose **S** to select the accounts that you want to include. When you choose to select the accounts to include, Quicken displays the Select Accounts to Include window. You learned how to complete the Select Accounts to Include window in the section *The A/P by Vendor Report*, earlier in this chapter.

> **Note**
>
> All the options to change the report layout are not included in every Create Report window. Options available depend on the type of report you are creating. When you are creating an investment report, the **F7-Layout** option is not available from the report window used to create the report.

After you complete the Create Report window, choose **Enter** or **F10** to return to the original report window. From the report window, you can choose to set report options (by choosing **F8**) or filter transactions (by choosing **F9**). Or, you can go ahead and create the report on-screen by choosing **Enter** or **F10**.

When the report is displayed on-screen, you can use the following options from the Edit menu to change some of the options you set to change the report layout:

II

Getting the Most

- Set Title & Date Range

- Accounts

You can use the Layout menu to change other options you set to change the report layout:

- Row Headings

- Column Headings

Setting Report Options

Quicken enables you to set report options to change the appearance of reports, including report organization and what transaction information is included. To set report options, choose **F8-Options** from the report window you use to create the report. When you select **F8-Options**, Quicken displays the Report Options window (refer to fig. 12.33).

Depending on the type of report you are customizing, Quicken enables you to design the report by changing the following settings:

Report Organization: You can organize reports on an income and expense basis or a cash flow basis. If you select **Income and expense** by choosing **1**, the report totals income, expenses, and transfer transactions in separate sections of the report. If you select **Cash flow basis** by choosing **2**, the report groups and totals inflows (including transfers into the accounts) and outflows (including transfers out of the accounts).

Transfers: For summary and transaction reports, you can select to include all transfers from and to the accounts included in the report by choosing **1**, to exclude all transfers by selecting **2**, or to include external transfers only by selecting **3** (where the corresponding transfer transaction is recorded in an account that is not included in the report).

Include Unrealized Gains: You can include (by choosing **Y**) or exclude (by choosing **N**) unrealized gains from investment accounts in the report. Unrealized gains result when the cost of the investment is compared with the market value to determine what the gain or loss would have been if the investment had been sold.

Show Totals Only: In transaction reports, enables you to show the totals for transactions, not the detail. Choose **Y** for totals only or **N** to show transaction detail.

Show Split Transaction Detail: In transaction reports, you can include the detail from split transactions in the report by choosing **Y**. Note that transaction reports automatically show split transaction detail if you set transaction filters or total the report by category or class.

Memo/Category Display: In transaction reports, you can choose to include columns for the memo only by choosing **1**, for the category only by choosing **2**, or for both the memo and category by choosing **3**. By default, Quicken includes a column for both.

Show Cents When Displaying Amounts: By choosing **N**, you can round report totals to the nearest dollar.

Normal/Suppressed/Reversed Subcategory Display: These options control how subcategories and subclasses are appear in reports. Choose **N** for **Normal** to indent subcategories under their main category. Choose **S** for **Suppressed** to omit subcategories and subclasses in reports. The amounts from subcategories and subclasses then are combined into the total for the main category and class. Choose **R** for **Reversed** to group the items in the report first by subcategory or class, with the main category and class grouped under them.

Note

All the report options are not included in every Report Options window. Report options available depend on the type of report that you are creating. Some investment reports include fewer report options.

After you complete the Report Options window, choose **Enter** or **F10** to return to the original report window. From the report window, you can choose to change the report layout (by choosing **F7**) or filter transactions (by choosing **F9**). Or, you continue to create the report on-screen by choosing **Enter** or **F10**.

When the report appears on-screen, you can use the following options from the Layout menu to change any of the report options you set in the Report Options window:

Getting the Most

II

- Show/Hide Cents

- Show/Hide Split

- Other Options

Filtering Report Transactions

Quicken report filters enable you to specify which transactions to include in a report. To filter transactions, choose **F9-Filter** from the report window that you use to create the report. When you choose **F9-Filter**, Quicken displays the Filter Transactions window (refer to fig. 12.34).

You can use a variety of fields in the Filter Transactions window to include or exclude transactions in or from a report. To filter transactions, follow these steps:

1. From the Filter Transactions window, move the cursor through the various fields on-screen.

   The Payee Contains field enables you to instruct Quicken to include or exclude a certain payee or transaction description from a transaction report based on exact or key-word matches. (Chapters 6 and 8 describe the mechanics of exact and key-word matches.) If you leave this field blank, you do not affect transactions being included or excluded from the report.

   The Memo Contains field works like the Payee Contains field, except that Quicken compares the Memo Contains field entry to the transactions' Memo field entries. This field affects the transactions included or excluded on the report, as does the Payee Contains field. Using this field is optional.

   The Category Contains field enables you to instruct Quicken to include or exclude transactions assigned to certain categories based on exact or key-word matches. If you leave this field blank, the transactions being included or excluded from the report are not affected.

   The Class Contains field works like the Category Contains field, except that Quicken compares the Class Contains field entry to entries in the transactions' classes. Like the Category Contains field, this optional field affects the transactions included or excluded on the report.

   The Select Categories to Include field enables you to specify an entire set of categories to be included in a report. Choose **Y** to select categories.

Quicken displays the Select Categories to Include window (after you choose **Enter** or **F10** from the Filter Transactions window) shown in figure 12.35. (Leave the setting at N if you don't want to select categories to include in the report.)

Fig. 12.35
The Select Categories To Include window.

When you first access the Select Categories to Include window, Quicken marks all categories to include in the report. To select specific categories to include, first choose **F9** to unmark all categories. Highlight the categories that you want to mark or include in the report, and press the space bar. The space bar acts as a toggle switch, alternately marking the category for inclusion or exclusion.

The Select Classes to Include field enables you to specify an entire set of classes to be included in a report. If you choose **Y** from this field, Quicken displays the Select Classes To Include window (after you choose Enter or F10 from the Filter Transactions window) that you can use to mark individual classes you want included in a report (see fig. 12.36).

To include a class, highlight the class you want to include and press the space bar. The space bar acts as a toggle switch, alternately marking the class for inclusion and exclusion. To select all classes, choose **F9**.

The Tax-Related Categories Only field enables you to include each of the categories you marked as tax-related when initially defining the category. (Chapter 4 describes how to identify a category as tax-related.)

Fig. 12.36

The Select Classes To Include window.

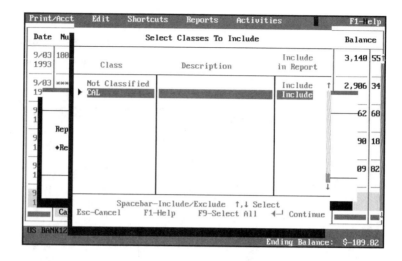

The Below/Equal/Above field and the The Amount field enable you to include transactions in a report based on the transaction amount. Using these two fields, you tell Quicken that you want transactions included in your report only when the transaction amount is less than, equal to, or greater than some amount. Choose **B** to indicate below, **E** to indicate equal, or **A** to indicate above. Enter the amount you want transaction amounts compared to in the The Amount field. If you want to include only transactions over $25, for example, choose **A** for above and type **25** in the The Amount field.

The Payments/Deposits/Unprinted Checks/All field enables you to include only certain types of transactions. To include only payments, choose **P**; to include only deposits, choose **D**; to include only unprinted checks, choose **U**; to include all transactions, choose **A**. You can use this report filter to determine your cash flow requirements. If you have entered all your bills and want to know the total, choose **U** for unprinted checks. Your report tells you the total cash required for all unpaid bills.

The Cleared Status Is field enables you to include transactions on a report based on the contents of the C field in the Register. The C field shows whether a transaction has been marked as cleared. Three valid entries exist for the C field: *, X, and nothing. As the Filter Report Transactions window shows, you include transactions in a report by choosing **Y** in the Blank, *, or X fields. You also can exclude transactions by choosing **N** for No next to the same three fields.

2. (Optional) If you start modifying these fields and then want to reset them to the original values, choose **Ctrl-D**.

3. When you complete the Filter Transactions window, choose **Enter** or **F10** to return to the report window. (If you selected **Y** in the Select Categories To Include or the Select Classes To Include field, the Select Categories To Include or the Select Classes To Include windows appear next.)

Using QuickZoom

QuickZoom enables you to examine the transaction detail behind an amount in a report while the report appears on-screen. If, for example, you create a cash flow report and want to see the transaction detail behind the amount shown for the category *Charity* (for charitable donations), you can use QuickZoom to search the Register for all transactions that make up the total amount shown in the report. QuickZoom then displays a list of those transactions. After you examine the transaction detail, you can return to the report.

> **Note**
>
> You can use the QuickZoom option in noninvestment reports only. You cannot use QuickZoom in account balances type reports, such as the net worth report or the balance sheet.

To use QuickZoom to examine transaction detail in a report, follow these steps:

1. With the report displayed on-screen, highlight the report amount you want to examine. If, for example, you just displayed a report and want to know the detail behind the salary amount shown highlight the amount in the Salary line.

2. From the File/Print menu, choose QuickZoom or press **Ctrl-Z**.

   For summary or budget type reports, Quicken displays a Transaction List window (see figure 12.37). For transaction type reports, Quicken goes to the Register and highlights the Register entry for the transaction.

3. To see the Register entry for a transaction listed in the Transaction List window, highlight the transaction and choose **F9**. Quicken goes to the Register and highlights that transaction. From here, you can make any necessary changes or return to the report.

4. To return to the report, choose **R**edo Last Report from the **R**eports menu or press **Ctrl-Z**.

Fig. 12.37
The Transaction
List window.

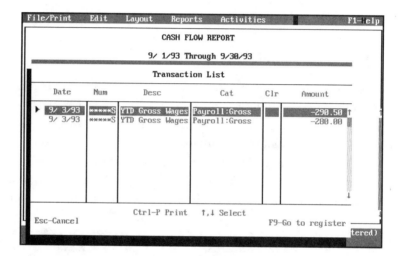

Editing Reports On-Screen

If you already have created a report and it is displayed on-screen, you don't have to go back to the report window to change the report layout, set report options, or filter transactions. You can change the report on-screen by using the menu options that appears at the top of the report screen. Following are the menu options available from report screens:

File/Print. Includes options to print reports, memorize reports, and use QuickZoom. The File/Print menu is shown in figure 12.38.

Edit. Includes options to set the report title and date range; filter transactions; and select which accounts, categories, and classes are included in the report. The Edit menu is shown in figure 12.39.

Layout. Includes options to change the appearance and format of the report, such as the row and column headings, whether amounts are rounded, whether the detail in split transactions is shown, which transactions appear and which are hidden, and so on. Figure 12.40 shows the Layout menu.

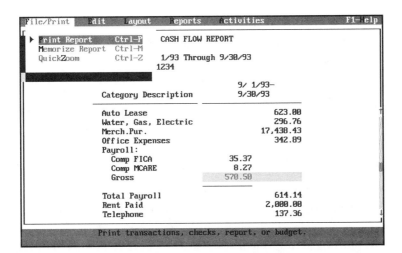

Fig. 12.38
The File/Print menu.

Fig. 12.39
The Edit menu.

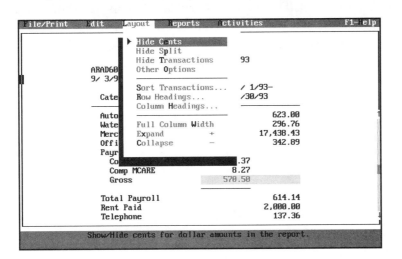

Fig. 12.40
The Layout menu.

Two other menu options are included in the report screen; Reports and Activities. The Reports menu is the same one that you see in figure 12.1, except that it does not include the Redo Last Report option. You can choose to create any other type of report from the report screen currently displayed.

The Activities menu enables you to go to the Register or the Write Checks screen from the report screen or to use the Quicken Calculator while the report is still displayed.

You already have learned how to customize reports by using the **F7-Layout**, **F8-Options**, and **F9-Filter** options from the report window. Many of the options available from the menu at the top of the on-screen report enable you to set the same report settings that you set using F7, F8, or F9. The menu makes customizing and editing reports easier because you can do it directly from the report screen rather than going back to the various windows to change the layout, set options, and filter transactions. Because you have learned about most of these options in previous sections in the chapter, not every menu option is explained here. Menu options that you have not learned about are explained in the following sections.

Hiding/Showing Transactions in Reports

If you are creating a noninvestment transaction report, such as the itemized category report or the tax summary report, you can choose to omit or display transaction detail. In transaction reports, Quicken displays the date, account, transaction number, description, memo, category, whether the transaction has cleared, and the amount for each transaction included in the report. If you choose to hide transaction detail, Quicken displays only the description and the amount for each transaction. You easily can switch your report back to full transaction detail by choosing Show Transactions. The Hide Transactions option is useful if you want a more concise transaction report that still lists the individual amounts and overall totals of transactions.

> **Note**
>
> The Hide Transactions and Show Transactions options shown in the Layout menu alternate, depending on the option last chosen. If transaction detail is shown in your report, for example, the option that appears in the Layout menu is Hide Transactions. If you select the Hide Transactions option to hide transaction detail, Quicken changes the option in the Layout menu to Show Transactions.

To hide transaction detail, follow these steps:

With the transaction report displayed on-screen, choose Hide Transactions from the Layout menu.

Quicken searches transactions and displays only the description and amount of each transaction.

To show transaction detail again, follow these steps:

With the transaction report with hidden transactions displayed on-screen, choose Show Transactions from the Layout menu.

Quicken searches transactions and redisplays detail for each transaction.

Sorting Transactions in Reports

For noninvestment transaction reports, you can change how transactions are ordered in the report. You can sort transactions by account, date, check number, or amount. If you chose to have the report subtotaled (if you selected **F7-Layout** when you were creating the report), you can change the way that transactions are sorted within each subtotaled group.

To sort transactions in a report, follow these steps:

1. With the transaction report that you want to sort displayed on-screen, choose Sort Transactions from the Layout menu.

Quicken displays the sort options shown in figure 12.41.

Getting the Most

Fig. 12.41

The sort options available to sort transactions in a report.

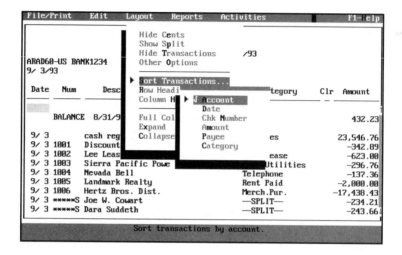

2. Highlight the sort option you want to use to sort transactions and choose **Enter**. Quicken searches transactions and redisplays the report in the sort order you selected.

Changing Report Columns

Full Column Width on the Layout menu controls whether Quicken uses full-width columns or half-width columns for reports that list transactions. By default, Quicken displays reports in half-width columns so that you can see all transaction detail on-screen. The basic rule is to use columns wide enough to display the information you want to see. If, for example, the descriptions or memos in a report are cropped because the columns are too narrow, use full column widths.

To display a report with full-width columns, follow these steps:

With the transaction report displayed on-screen, choose Full Column Width from the Layout menu.

Quicken uses full-width columns and changes the option name to Half Column Width.

To change the report back to half-width columns, simply perform the steps above and choose Half Column Width.

Summarizing Rows in Reports

The Expand and Collapse options on the Layout menu work together and enable you to change the way that report rows are summarized. Collapse summarizes the detail for a row heading in summary, budget, or account balance reports without changing the report totals. If you want to present Total Inflows in a cash flow report as just one line, for example, you can collapse the row heading and Quicken reduces the Total Inf lows section of the report to a single line.

> **Note**
>
> You cannot use the Collapse option to summarize report rows in transaction reports.

To summarize a row in a report, follow these steps:

1. With the report displayed on your screen, highlight the row heading you want to summarize.

2. Choose Collapse from the Layout menu. Or, press the - (minus) key to select the Collapse option. Quicken displays one line for the row heading that you selected.

To return any detail in a report that is summarized or collapsed, use the Expand option. To expand report detail, follow these steps:

1. Highlight the row heading you previously collapsed and want to expand.

2. Choose Expand from the Layout menu, or press the + (plus) key to choose the Expand option. Quicken displays the detail for the row in the report.

> **Note**
>
> When you collapse a category within a section of a report, Quicken moves the category to the end of the section, removes the category name, and replaces it with a hidden title. If you collapse the Salary Income category in the Inflows section of a cash flow report, for example, Quicken moves the category to the end of the Inflows section and replaces the *Salary Income* title with the title *Inflows - Hidden*.

Memorizing Reports

If you have spent considerable time customizing a report to include the specific information in a particular format, you will want to save the report

II

Getting the Most

settings so that you don't have to customize the report again. Quicken enables you to memorize a customized report so that you simply can select it from a list the next time you want to use it.

When you memorize a report, Quicken saves all report settings and transaction filters, but doesn't save dates or data. If you customize your January profit and loss statement to include certain accounts and categories and show the report information in a certain order, when you memorize the report, Quicken stores only the report settings that indicate which accounts and categories to include and how to format the information. The program does not save the January dates or data in the memorized report. You therefore can recall the memorized report and create your February profit and loss statement, using the same report settings you specified for the January report. In essence, the memorize report option prevents you from having to reinvent the wheel every time you need a report.

Memorizing a Report

You memorize a report after you customize the report and the report is displayed on-screen. You can, however, memorize a report from the report window, the Create Report window, the Report Options window, or the Filter Transactions window.

To memorize a report, follow these steps:

1. Create the report you want to memorize.

2. Choose Memorize Report from the File/Print menu, or press **Ctrl-M**. Quicken displays the Memorizing Report window shown in figure 12.42.

3. Enter a unique title for the report in the Title field, which Quicken uses to identify the report, but does not display as the report's title.

4. Move the cursor to the Dates to use when running report field and choose one of the three options.

5. Choose **Enter** to memorize the report.

Recalling a Memorized Report

You easily can recall a memorized report with the exact report settings you specified before you memorized it. To recall a memorized report, follow these steps:

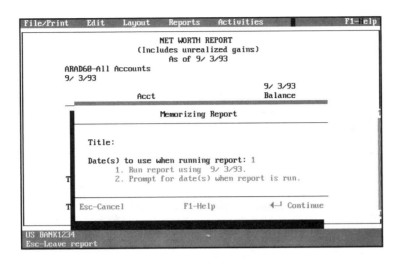

Fig. 12.42
The Memorizing
Report window.

1. Choose **Memorized Reports** from the **Reports** menu. Quicken displays
   the Memorized Reports list shown in figure 12.43.

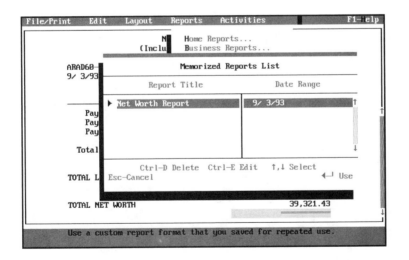

Fig. 12.43
The Memorized
Reports List
window.

2. Highlight the memorized report you want to recall to the screen and
   choose **Enter**. Quicken displays the Memorized Report window as
   shown in figure 12.44. Quicken enters the memorized report title.

3. Type over the title if you want to change it.

4. Change the Report on Months From or Through field in the Memorized
   Report window as necessary.

5. Choose **Enter** or **F10** to display the memorized report.

Fig. 12.44
The Memorized
Report window.

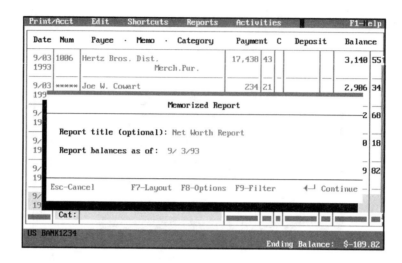

Editing and Deleting Memorized Reports

You can change a memorized report's title or delete a memorized report at any time. To change the title of a memorized report, follow these steps:

1. Choose **M**emorized Reports from the Reports menu. Quicken displays the Memorized Reports List window.

2. Highlight the memorized report you want to edit and choose **Ctrl-E**. Quicken displays the Rename Memorized Report window (see fig. 12.45).

Fig. 12.45
The Rename
Memorized Report
window.

3. Type the new title in the Report Title field and choose Enter to save the changes.

To delete a memorized report, follow these steps:

1. Choose **M**emorized Reports from the **R**eports menu. Quicken displays the Memorized Reports List window.

2. Highlight the memorized report that you want to delete and choose **Ctrl-Del**. Quicken displays a warning that you are about to permanently delete a memorized transaction.

3. Choose **Enter** to delete the memorized report or choose **Esc** if don't want to delete the memorized report.

Summary

This chapter reviews the basics of printing any Quicken report and details the steps and tricks for printing each of Quicken's home, business, investment, and custom reports. These reports use the information stored in your Quicken file to provide you with a wealth of financial information that you can use to better manage your personal or business finances.

In the next chapter, you learn how to pay your bills electronically through CheckFree. If you have a modem and are ready to give up the process of hand-writing or printing checks, you will benefit by Quicken's electronic bill-payment feature and CheckFree.

Getting the Most

Chapter 13

Paying Bills Electronically

Quicken enables you to use CheckFree, an electronic bill payment service, to pay bills. By using Quicken and a modem, you can send payment instructions to CheckFree Corporation. Your payment instructions include all the information CheckFree needs to actually pay the bill: who you owe the money to, when the bill needs to be paid, how much you owe, and so on. CheckFree Corporation then either draws a check on or electronically transfers funds from your bank account to whomever you owe the money.

Paying bills electronically isn't for everyone. By getting one more party involved in the bill-paying process, you just may make this process more complicated. For Quicken users who have a modem and who want to stop printing checks, however, electronic payment is appealing.

Setting Up Your System for Electronic Payment

To begin using electronic bill paying, you need to complete three steps. First, you need to complete the CheckFree paperwork. Second, you need to activate the electronic payment feature in Quicken so that Quicken knows that you want to use CheckFree. When you activate the electronic payment feature, you also must configure the modem and select the account(s) you use to pay bills electronically. Third, you need to set up the payees (the persons or companies that you will pay electronically). Performing these steps is easy. Completing this part of the work should take no more than a few minutes.

This chapter explains how to perform the following tasks:

- Set up your system for electronic payment through the CheckFree service

- Set up payees

- Set up fixed payments

- Pay bills electronically

- Issue stop-payments

- Make payment inquiries

- Send and receive electronic mail to or from CheckFree

II

Getting the Most

Completing the CheckFree Paperwork

Before you begin using the CheckFree service, you need to complete the CheckFree service form (see fig. 13.1). The form is self-explanatory. You need to tell CheckFree Corporation how much memory your computer has; give CheckFree some personal information, including your Social Security number, name, address, and so on; and provide CheckFree with a credit card account number so that CheckFree can charge your credit card account if it—acting on your payment instructions—overdraws the account. (For security reasons, use a security code—similar to what you use for automated teller machines—to gain access to your account.)

After you provide this basic information, you also need to tell CheckFree which phone lines you are using, specify which account number/security code you plan to use to gain access to the CheckFree system, and sign an authorization so that CheckFree can deduct funds from your bank account. (If you don't choose an account number or security code, CheckFree creates one for you.)

After you complete the CheckFree service form, attach a voided check to the form and then mail the form to Intuit. To mail the form, use the business reply envelope included for returning the CheckFree service form. Intuit forwards the service form to CheckFree Corporation. In a few days, CheckFree sends you a confirmation letter that confirms or assigns the account number/ personal security code, gives you the telephone number to use for CheckFree transmissions, and the fastest *baud rate*—the transmission speed—you can use for sending payment information.

Activating the Electronic Bill Payment Feature

After you receive the confirmation letter from CheckFree, you can activate Quicken's electronic bill payment feature, which basically tells Quicken that you are going to use the CheckFree service.

You need to do two things when activating the electronic bill payment feature: configure the modem and set up the bank accounts you plan to use to make the payments.

Configuring Your Modem. You must configure your modem so that you can transmit information to CheckFree through your modem and so that CheckFree can transmit confirmations and other information back to you.

Fig. 13.1
The CheckFree service form.

CONFIDENTIAL

CHECKFREE SERVICE FORM

(To receive CheckFree service, please complete this form and return the top copy in the enclosed postage paid envelope as soon as possible. As with all CheckFree data, the information on this form is handled with the strictest security. Please print all information.)

IMPORTANT

PLEASE ATTACH A VOIDED CHECK FROM YOUR PAYMENT ACCOUNT TO THE TOP OF THIS FORM.

YOUR EQUIPMENT AND SOFTWARE

How much RAM does your computer have? _____ 384 _____ 512 _____ more than 512
What disk size do you require? _____ 3½ _____ 5¼
With what type of software will you be using CheckFree? _____ Quicken 5.0 for DOS _____ Quicken for Windows

PERSONAL IDENTIFICATION

Your social security number _____ _____ - _____ - _____
(CheckFree Systems Identification Number)

Name _____
           Last   First   Middle

Current Address _____
           Street   City   State   Zip

CREDIT CARD INFORMATION

CheckFree requires an account number for at least one credit card, should an overdraft occur. CheckFree reserves the right to charge the account only for the purpose of overdraft protection.

MasterCard or Visa Account Number _____ Exp. _____

COMMUNICATIONS INFORMATION

Home Phone (_____) _____ - _____   Work Phone (_____) _____ - _____
Circle number from which you will be transmitting.

CHECKFREE PERSONAL SECURITY CODE

Your CheckFree personal security code is a four digit number which you may choose yourself. You will need to enter this number in your Quicken software and use it as a password to run your software. My number is |___|___|___|___| . If you have no number preference, leave the space provided blank and CheckFree will assign a number for you. We will give you this number at the same time you receive your CheckFree network access telephone number.

Date _____ Signature _____
Your use of the CheckFree service signifies that you have read and accepted all of the terms and conditions of the CheckFree service printed on the back of this form.

CHECKFREE BANK REGISTRATION

Note: Checking accounts with credit unions and money markets occasionally require special handling. If your account is with either type of institution, please call 1-800-882-5280 before you send in this form and ask for a "Financial Institution Check." We'll advise you if any special action is required.

I, _____
    (Last Name)   (First Name)   (Middle Initial)
authorize my bank to post my bill payment transactions from CheckFree to my account as indicated below.
I understand that I am in full control of my account. If at any time I decide to discontinue service, I will simply call or write CheckFree to cancel service.

_____
(Bank Name)

_____
(Street Address)

_____
(City)   (State)   (Zip)

_____
Customer Signature

Return the top copy of this entire form to CheckFree in the postage paid envelope provided and retain the bottom copy for your records. Also,

DON'T FORGET TO PROVIDE A VOIDED CHECK WITH THIS FORM AND RETURN BOTH ITEMS TO CHECKFREE.

Return to CheckFree in the enclosed postage paid envelope.

CheckFree®

Q50/Q51

II

Getting the Most

To configure the modem, complete these steps:

1. From the Quicken Main Menu, choose Set Preferences. The Set Preferences menu appears.

2. Choose Modem Settings (see fig. 13.2). Quicken displays the Modem Settings window shown in figure 13.3.

Fig. 13.2
The Modem
Settings option.

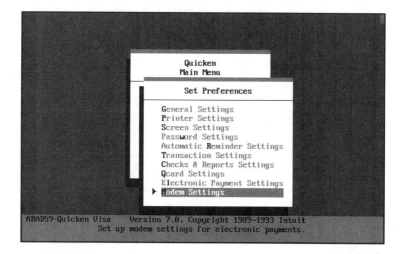

Fig. 13.3
The Modem
Settings window.

3. With the cursor positioned in the Serial Port Used by Modem field, enter the number of the serial port that the modem uses: 1 for serial communications port 1; 2 for serial communications port 2; and so on.

If you don't know the serial communications port the modem uses, follow the cable that connects the modem to the computer and see whether the socket in which the modem cable plugs is labeled. The socket may be labeled with *COM1* or *Serial 1.*

4. Move the cursor to the Modem Speed field. Choose the fastest modem speed setting that both CheckFree and your modem support. The CheckFree confirmation letter gives the modem speed settings that CheckFree supports. The modem users' manual indicates the transmission speeds the modem is capable of running.

5. Move the cursor to the Tone or Pulse Dialing field. Choose **T** if the telephone service is tone; choose **P** if the telephone service is pulse. If you aren't sure, refer to your monthly telephone bill or call the telephone company.

6. Move the cursor to the Telephone Number to Dial field. Enter the telephone number given in the confirmation letter you receive from CheckFree. Include any special characters you want to dial. If you have call waiting, for example, *70* may turn off call waiting. You can start the dialing with *70* so that the beep a call-waiting call makes doesn't interfere with data transmission. You can use a comma to insert a pause. Quicken ignores any spaces and parentheses you enter.

7. At the Turn on Electronic Payment Capability field, choose **Y** for Yes.

8. (Optional) If the modem is not Hayes-compatible, you need to give Quicken the initialization codes the modem uses to access the telephone line and get a dial tone. The odds are that the modem is Hayes-compatible, so you probably don't have to worry about the codes. If the modem isn't Hayes-compatible, choose **F8** from the Modem Settings window. The Custom Modem Initialization window appears (see fig. 13.4). Enter the initialization code that Quicken needs to send to the modem to access the telephone line and get a dial tone. The modem users' manual gives this initialization code.

Identifying CheckFree Bank Accounts. After you complete the Modem Settings window, you are ready to identify the CheckFree bank account or accounts. Essentially, here you identify only the bank accounts to use for electronic payment. You cannot use a credit card, asset, liability, or investment account for electronic payment-only bank accounts.

Fig. 13.4

The Custom
Modem Initializa-
tion window.

In Quicken, you cannot select an account to use for electronic payment until
the Modem Settings window is filled out and the Turn on Electronic Payment
Capability field is set to Y.

To set up a bank account for electronic payment, follow these steps:

1. From the Set Preferences menu, choose Electronic Payment Settings.
   Quicken displays the Set Up Account for Electronic Payment window
   shown in figure 13.5. Because you can set up only bank accounts for
   electronic payment, Quicken lists only bank accounts in the window.

Fig. 13.5

The Set Up
Account for
Electronic
Payment window.

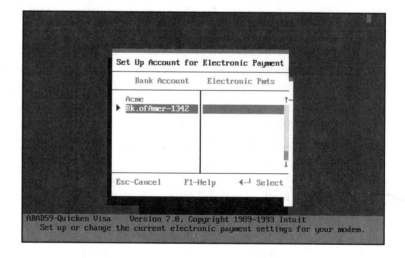

2. Highlight the bank account that you want and choose **Enter**.

   For each account that you select, Quicken displays a message that asks whether you want to set up the account for electronic payment.

3. Choose **Y** for Yes and choose **Enter**. Quicken displays the Electronic Payment Account Settings window (see fig. 13.6).

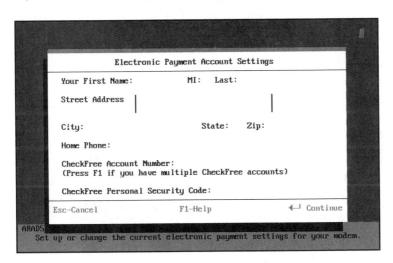

Fig. 13.6
The Electronic Payment Account Settings window.

4. With the cursor positioned in the Your First Name field, enter your first name.

5. Move the cursor to the MI field and enter your middle initial.

6. Move the cursor to the Last field and enter your last name.

7. Move the cursor to the Street Address field and enter the appropriate information.

8. Move the cursor to the City field and enter the name of the city or town in which you live.

9. Move the cursor to the State field and enter the two-character abbreviation for your state. If you don't know the two-character abbreviation, enter the first letter of the state name and choose **Enter**. Quicken displays a list of valid state abbreviations from which you can choose the state's abbreviation.

10. Move the cursor to the Zip field and enter your ZIP code. Quicken validates the entry against a list of valid ZIP codes. If Quicken doesn't recognize what you enter, but you know the code is correct anyway, choose **Ctrl-Z** to force Quicken to accept the ZIP code.

11. Move the cursor to the Home Phone field and enter your home phone number, including the area code. You don't have to include the punctuation characters, such as hyphens and parentheses; Quicken adds these characters after you choose **Enter**.

12. Move the cursor to the Social Security Number field and enter your Social Security number, or the alternative identification number assigned by CheckFree. If you previously set up more than one bank account for electronic bill paying, which means that you filled out more than one CheckFree Service Agreement form, CheckFree gives you identifying numbers based on your Social Security number for each account. Enter this identifying number here.

13. Move the cursor to the CheckFree Personal Identification Number field and enter the account number/security number or PIN number from the CheckFree confirmation letter.

14. After the Electronic Payment Account Settings window is complete, choose **Ctrl-Enter**. Quicken redisplays the Set Up Account for Electronic Payment window. The account you set up now is marked as *enabled* for electronic payment. When you subsequently select the enabled account to use, Quicken adds several more menu options that you can use for processing electronic payments.

Setting Up Your Payees

To pay a bill electronically, you need to collect and store information about each person or company you plan to pay so that CheckFree Corporation can process payments to the appropriate person or business. To set up a payee, just add the payee to the electronic payee list. From the Electronic Payee list, you can edit a payee or delete a payee to whom you no longer make payments.

Adding a Payee. Before you can make an electronic payment to a payee, you must add the payee to the Electronic Payee list. To add a payee, follow these steps:

1. From the Main Menu, choose **Write/Print Checks**. Quicken displays the electronic payment version of the screen (see fig. 13.7).

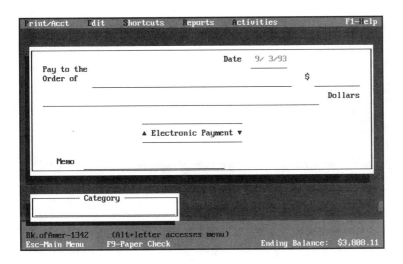

Fig. 13.7
The electronic payment version of the Write/Print Checks screen.

2. Access the **Shortcuts** menu and then choose the Electronic Payee List option from this menu. Quicken displays the Electronic Payee list shown in figure 13.8.

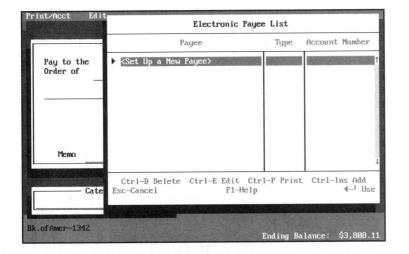

Fig. 13.8
The Electronic Payee List.

3. To add a payee to the list, highlight the <Set Up a New Payee> line and choose **Enter**. The Set Up Electronic Payee window appears (see fig. 13.9).

Fig. 13.9
The Set Up
Electronic Payee
window.

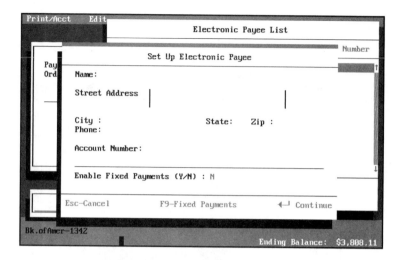

4. Move the cursor to the Name field and enter the complete name of the person or company you want to pay. In this field, you can add up to 28 characters.

5. Move the cursor to the Street Address field and enter the mailing address for sending payments to the payee.

6. Move the cursor to the City field and enter the name of the payee's city or town.

7. Move the cursor to the State field and enter the two-character abbreviation for the payee's state. If you don't know the two-character abbreviation, enter the first letter of the state name and press **Enter**. Quicken displays a list of valid state abbreviations from which you can pick the correct abbreviation.

8. Move the cursor to the Zip field and enter the payee's ZIP code. Quicken validates the entry against a list of valid ZIP codes. If Quicken doesn't recognize the code you enter even though you know the code is correct, choose **Ctrl-Z** to force Quicken to accept the ZIP code.

> **Note**
>
> Entering the payee name, address, phone number, and account number accurately is important because CheckFree uses this information to make payments to the payee.

9. Move the cursor to the Phone field and enter the person's or company's phone number, including the area code. You do not need to include punctuation, such as hyphens and parentheses; by default, Quicken adds these characters when you choose **Enter**.

10. Move the cursor to the Account Number field and enter the account number the person or business uses to identify you.

11. (Optional) If you want to set up a fixed payment to the payee that you are setting up, move the cursor to the Enable Fixed Payments field and choose **Y**. Fixed payments are explained in *Setting Up Fixed Payments*, later in this chapter.

12. After the Set Up Electronic Payee window is complete, check to ensure that the information is correct, and then choose **Enter**. The Electronic Payee List appears. To define additional electronic payees, repeat steps 3 through 12.

Editing and Deleting Payees. As in other lists in the Quicken system, you can choose **Ctrl-D** to delete a payee from the Electronic Payee list, you can choose **Ctrl-E** to edit a payee on the Electronic Payee list, and you can choose **Ctrl-P** to print a list of electronic payees. The only difference between working with electronic payees and accounts, categories, classes, and so on, is that you cannot edit or delete an electronic payee if an untransmitted transaction exists for this payee. You learn more about untransmitted transactions later in this chapter.

Setting Up Fixed Payments

You can set up a payee to receive fixed payments from CheckFree. You also can edit an existing payee to receive fixed payments. *Fixed payments* are recurring payments, to the same payee, for the same amount, at a fixed interval (weekly, monthly, quarterly, and so on). After you set up a fixed payment to a payee, CheckFree makes the payment for you, based on the intervals that you specify. You may want to set up fixed payments, for example, for your mortgage, rent payment, insurance premiums, and so on. After you set up a fixed payment, you don't need to remember to transmit payment information to CheckFree; CheckFree remembers to make the payment for you.

Getting the Most

Setting Up a Fixed Payment

To set up a fixed payment, follow these steps:

1. Access and complete the Set Up Electronic Payee window from the account Register that you want CheckFree to use to make payments. Or highlight an existing payee from the Electronic Payee list and choose **Ctrl-E** to display the Edit Electronic Payee window.

2. Move to the Enable Fixed Payments field of the Set Up Electronic Payee or the Edit Electronic Payee window, choose **Y**, and then choose **Enter**. You also can choose **F9** to set up a fixed payment. Quicken displays the CheckFree Fixed Payments window shown in figure 13.10.

Fig. 13.10
The Checkfree
Fixed Payments
window.

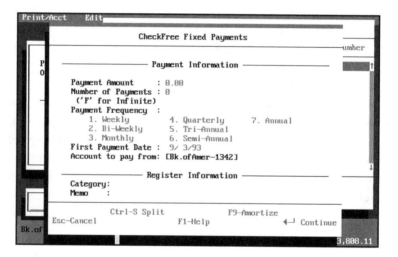

3. In the Payment Amount field, enter the amount of the fixed payment and press **Enter**.

4. Enter the number of payments (1 to 500) due to the payee in the Number of Payments field. If you owe 48 payments on your car loan, for example, and have already made 5, enter **43** in the Number of Payments field.

5. Move to the Payment Frequency field and choose the number that corresponds to how frequently payments are made (**1** for weekly, **2** for biweekly, **3** for monthly, and so on).

6. Move to the First Payment Date field and enter the date that you want CheckFree to make the first payment. Use the + (plus) or - (minus) key to change the date one day at a time.

Caution

Because many persons or businesses are not set up to handle electronic funds transfers, these kinds of payments are mailed by CheckFree from Ohio. If the payee's location is your home town, then the payment may take an extra day or two to reach the payee from Ohio. Schedule all CheckFree payments early enough to allow for delays in the mail system.

Quicken enters the account that you selected to pay this payee from in the Account to Pay From field. Quicken does not allow you to change this field.

7. Move to the Category field and enter the category you want to assign to the fixed payment transaction. If necessary, press **Ctrl-C** to display the Category and Transfer list and select a category from the list. To assign more than one category to the fixed payment transaction, press **Ctrl-S** to open the Split Transaction window. Fill in the Split Transaction window as usual (see Chapters 6 and 8 to learn how to split transactions). If you are setting up a fixed payment for an amortized loan (see step 10), be sure that you enter the principal category on the first line in the Split Transaction window and the interest category on the second line.

8. (Optional) If you want to enter a memo to the fixed payment transaction, move to the Memo field and enter the additional information.

9. (Optional) If the fixed payment you are setting up is a payment on a fixed-rate loan, you may want to memorize the amortized payment schedule so that Quicken allocates the proper principal and interest amounts to each payment. To set up a fixed payment for an amortized loan, choose **F9**. Quicken displays the Set Amortization Information window. Fill in the Set Amortization Information window as you do for any other loan payment. To learn about amortizing loan payments, see Chapter 10, Tracking Your Net Worth, Other Assets, and Liabilities."

10. After the CheckFree Fixed Payments window is complete, choose **Ctrl-Enter** to return to the Set Up Electronic Payee window.

11. Choose **Ctrl-Enter** or **F10**. A note appears that tells you Quicken first must connect to CheckFree to make fixed payments. To authorize CheckFree to begin making fixed payments to the payee you just set up,

II

Getting the Most

choose **Enter**. Quicken initializes the modem and transmits fixed payment information immediately to CheckFree. CheckFree, however, cannot make a payment until the first payment date that you specified in the CheckFree Fixed Payments window.

When you set up a fixed payment to a payee, Quicken enters the transaction in the Register and inserts the word FIXED in the Num field. After CheckFree makes the fixed payment and Quicken receives confirmation from CheckFree that the payment was made, the word FIXED is replaced with E-PMT (for electronic payment).

Editing a Fixed Payment

If you want to change the payment information for a fixed payment, you can do so from the Electronic Payee list.

To edit fixed payment information, follow these steps:

1. From the Register for the account that you use to make electronic payments, press **Ctrl-Y** to display the Electronic Payee list.

2. Highlight the payee for the fixed payment and choose **Ctrl-E**. The Edit Electronic Payee window appears (see fig. 13.11).

Fig. 13.11
The Edit Electronic Payee window.

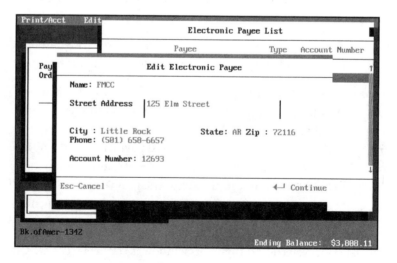

3. From the Edit Electronic Payee window, choose **F9** to display the CheckFree Fixed Payments window.

4. Move to the field you want and make the necessary changes.

5. After the changes are complete, choose **Ctrl-Enter**. Quicken initializes the modem and immediately transmits to CheckFree the changes to the fixed payment information.

Deleting a Fixed Payment

If you no longer want to make fixed payments to a payee, you can delete the fixed payment information at any time. You cannot delete a fixed payment, however, that was already made and confirmed (E-PMT appears in the Register for these transactions). To delete a payment that was already made, use a stop payment request, as explained later in this chapter.

To delete a fixed payment, follow these steps:

1. From the Register for the account that you use to make electronic payments, press **Ctrl-Y** to display the Electronic Payee list.

2. Highlight the payee for the fixed payment and choose **Ctrl-E**. Quicken displays the Edit Electronic Payee window.

3. Move to the Enable Fixed Payments field and choose **N** to disable fixed payments.

4. Quicken displays a message that prompts you to confirm that you want to cancel fixed payments. Choose **Enter** to confirm.

5. Quicken initializes the modem and immediately transmits instructions to CheckFree to cancel fixed payments to the payee. Quicken also deletes from the Register all transactions (for the payee that you set up the fixed payment to) that show the FIXED message in the Num field.

Paying Bills and Transmitting Mail

Paying bills electronically closely resembles the process of writing and printing checks with Quicken. For this reason, this chapter doesn't repeat the discussions of Chapters 7 and 8, which cover how you write and print checks with Quicken. Instead, this section concentrates on different parts of the process. (If you haven't used the Quicken Write/Print Checks feature, you may want to review Chapters 7 and 8 before continuing in this chapter.)

After you set up for electronic payment and identify the people you want to pay, you can begin paying bills electronically.

For each bill you want to pay, follow these steps:

1. From Quicken's Main Menu, choose **Write/Print Checks**. (Before you choose this option, be sure to select the bank account you use to make electronic payments). Quicken displays the electronic payment version of the Write Checks screen.

2. Complete the electronic payment version of the Write Checks screen in the same way you complete the regular version of the screen, except for the following differences:

   ■ Rather than typing the payee's name, choose the payee from the electronic payee list. To display the electronic payee list, press **Ctrl-Y**. To use one of the electronic payees shown on the list, highlight the payee you want to pay and choose **Enter**. You also can use Quicken's QuickFill feature to enter an electronic payee (see Chapter 8 for more information about QuickFill).

   ■ Rather than track unprinted checks, Quicken shows the checks to transmit in the lower right corner of the screen.

3. After you complete the Write Checks screen, choose **Ctrl-Enter** or **F10**.

The check that contains the electronic payment scrolls off-screen, leaving behind an empty check that you can use to complete another electronic payment. Until you begin transmitting the electronic payments, you can edit these payments just as you do any other check you write at the Write Checks screen.

You also can enter and edit electronic payments by using the Quicken Register. Quicken identifies electronic payment transactions in the Quicken Register with >>>>> in the Num field.

Transmitting Payment Information to CheckFree

After you enter the electronic payments, you can transmit the electronic payments so that CheckFree Corporation can pay them.

To transmit the electronic payments, follow these steps:

1. Turn on the modem.

   Quicken first attempts to initialize the modem and then retries the modem twice. If a problem is encountered, a message appears that says Quicken was unable to initialize the modem. Be sure that your modem is connected properly and turned on. If Quicken continues to have a problem initializing your modem, refer to the users' manual for your modem or call Intuit's technical support staff.

2. From the Write Checks screen, choose Transmit Payments from the Print/Acct menu (see fig. 13.12).

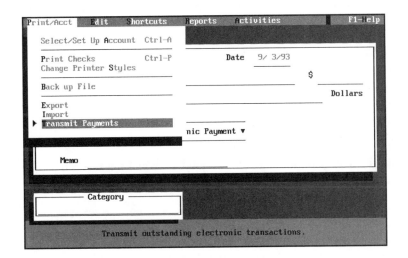

Fig. 13.12
The electronic payment version of the Print/Acct menu.

Quicken displays the window shown in figure 13.13, which tells you how many payments you have to transmit.

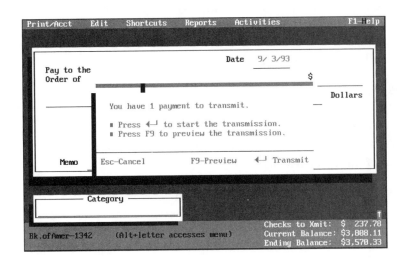

Fig. 13.13
The window that tells you how many payments you have to transmit.

3. If you are ready to transmit, choose **Enter**. Or, if you want to review the payments that are ready to be transmitted, choose **F9**. Quicken displays the Preview Transmission to CheckFree window.

This window lists the payments Quicken will transmit. After you do transmit the payments, CheckFree sends confirmation numbers back to Quicken for each transmitted payment. Confirmation numbers are stored in the Memo field of each transaction.

Issuing a Stop Payment Request

You can use Quicken to issue stop payment requests on electronic payments you transmitted previously. To issue a stop payment request, follow these steps:

1. Turn on the modem.

2. Access the Register for the account you use to make electronic payments.

3. Highlight the transaction in the Register on which you want to stop payment.

4. Choose Transmit Stop Payment Request from the Edit menu.

5. Quicken asks you to confirm the stop payment. Choose **Y** for Yes. Quicken immediately transmits the request to CheckFree. If the transmission is successful, Quicken marks the transaction as VOID.

As with stop payment requests issued directly to the bank, you need to make the request before the transaction is processed.

Making an Electronic Payment Inquiry

You can ask about a payment you transmitted previously. Suppose that you receive a telephone call from someone who wants to know whether you have sent them a check yet. You can make an electronic payment inquiry to check the status of this particular payment.

To make an electronic payment inquiry, follow these steps:

1. Turn on the modem.

2. Access the Register for the account that you use to make electronic payments.

3. Highlight the transaction in the Register that you want to inquire about. Electronic payments are marked with >>>>> in the Num field.

4. Choose Electronic Payment Inquiry from the Edit menu. Quicken displays the details of the transmitted payment, including the account number, the payment date, the date the transaction was transmitted to CheckFree, and the confirmation number you received from CheckFree. This window also indicates whether you can stop payment (if at least five days still remain between the transmission date and the payment date). Quicken also asks whether you want to send an inquiry message to CheckFree regarding the transaction.

5. Choose **Y** to send a payment inquiry to CheckFree. Quicken displays the Transmit Inquiry to CheckFree window.

6. Complete the Transmit Inquiry to CheckFree window and choose **Ctrl-Enter** to send the payment inquiry to CheckFree.

Sending Electronic Mail to CheckFree

You also can send an electronic message to CheckFree. You may want to send a message to inquire about your CheckFree account or to respond to an inquiry from CheckFree.

To send an electronic mail message to CheckFree, follow these steps:

1. Turn on the modem.

2. Choose Send Electronic Mail from the Activities menu. The Transmit Inquiry to CheckFree window appears (see fig. 13.14).

3. Type the message to CheckFree just as you type a message in a word processing application. You can type messages up to five lines in length. CheckFree wraps the end of the line to the following line so that you don't need to press **Enter** at the end of each line.

4. After you type the message, choose **Ctrl-Enter**. Quicken initializes the modem and transmits the message to CheckFree.

Receiving Electronic Mail from CheckFree

You can receive electronic mail from CheckFree that you can read from the Register or the Write Checks screen.

Fig. 13.14

The Transmit
Inquiry to
CheckFree
window.

To receive electronic mail messages from CheckFree, follow these steps:

1. Turn on the modem.

2. Choose Check Electronic Mail from the Activities menu.

3. Quicken initializes the modem and transmits instructions to check your electronic mailbox for messages.

4. Quicken displays all messages in chronological order. Choose **F10** to read the next page or **F9** to read the previous page. Press **PgUp** or **PgDn** to move up or down one message screen at a time.

Summary

This chapter describes Quicken's electronic payment capability. You learn how to set up your system to make electronic payments, how to set up payees, how to use the fixed payment feature, and how to pay bills electronically. You also learn how to transmit electronic messages to CheckFree and how to receive electronic mail from CheckFree.

In the following chapter, you learn how to make tax time less hectic by using Quicken to accumulate tax data in reports that you can use easily to prepare your return. You also learn how to export tax data to tax preparation programs, such as TurboTax and TaxCut.

Chapter 14

Using Quicken to Prepare for Income Taxes

A basic accounting requirement for businesses and individuals is to complete the required Federal Income Tax forms at the end of the year to report income and expenses. Although everyone knows that taxes are inevitable, not everyone organizes financial activities so that tax time is not a surprise. With Quicken, you can designate categories and subcategories as tax-related and accumulate your tax information in seconds. Whether you prepare your own income tax return or hand your tax information to a paid tax accountant, Quicken alleviates the burden of gathering tax data.

This chapter explains how to organize your Quicken data for income tax purposes. Some Quicken users also want to know how to export the income tax data inside Quicken to external income tax preparation packages, such as TurboTax. The mechanics of exporting income tax data also are covered in this chapter.

Using Quicken to Organize Income Tax Data

Quicken is not a tax preparation program, but it is an excellent tax data organization program. Quicken provides the following three reports to assist you in preparing your Federal Income tax: Tax Summary, Capital Gains (Schedule D), and Tax Schedule. The Tax Summary and the Capital Gains reports are discussed in Chapter 12 "Creating and Printing Reports." The Tax Schedule report is discussed in the section *Creating the Tax Schedule Report* later in this chapter.

Utilizing the benefits of Quicken in organizing your tax data is a two-step process. You first must record your income and expenses in categories that parallel IRS income and expense (deduction) categories. You do this by using categories as discussed in the next section. The second step is to relate the data to the appropriate IRS form so that it can be used to prepare a manual return or exported to a tax preparation program, such as TurboTax.

Using Categories

The basic rule for using categories (and subcategories) to accumulate your tax data is to set up a category or subcategory for each taxable income item or tax deduction you have. The best way to do this is by reviewing your last two income tax returns to determine which of these items you have. If you make charitable contributions each year and itemize your deductions, you will want to be sure to have a category set up (and designated as tax-related) to assign to charitable contribution transactions. If you want to track a taxable income item or tax deduction item in more detail, you can use subcategories and designate the subcategories as tax-related. Chapter 4, "Organizing Your Finances," describes how to create and use categories and subcategories and how to designate a category or subcategory as tax-related.

If you don't itemize your deductions (because the total of your itemized deductions does not exceed the standard deduction amount), then it's not necessary to designate the charitable contribution category as tax-related.

The following examples may help you to better understand how to use categories and subcategories. Real estate investors, royalty holders, S corporation shareholders, Estates and Trusts, and members of a partnership complete IRS Form 1040, Schedule E. Farmers complete Form 1040, Schedule F, and sole proprietors complete Form 1040, Schedule C (now there is a Schedule C-EZ for very small businesses that is easier to prepare).

Partnerships complete Form 1065 which is known as an information return since no tax is paid by the partnership. Individual partners receive a Form 1065, Schedule K-1 which has the amounts they use to report on their Form 1040s, Schedule E.

Corporations complete one of the three corporate income tax forms: 1120A for small corporations, 1120S for S Corporations, and 1120 for all other corporations.

> **CPA TIP**
>
> *S Corporations* are corporations that have elected to be treated as partnerships for income tax purposes. The income from the S Corporation is not taxed to the S Corporation, but rather to its shareholders.

If you live in a state with income taxes, you also may need to complete an equivalent state income tax form. Make sure that you or an accountant can easily prepare the tax return with the information Quicken produces.

You also can work with categories that you need to combine with other categories to calculate an entry on a tax form. Suppose that you are a sole proprietor and own a restaurant. Although total wages is entered on one line of the Schedule C tax form, you may want to track several categories of wages (subcategories), including servers, dishwashers, cooks, bartenders, and so on. Here, you have several wage subcategories that must be added to calculate the wages amount that goes on the tax form. The Tax Schedule report can help you accumulate data from more than one subcategory.

If you are using Quicken for a sole proprietorship and you hold and resell inventory, you need Part III of the Schedule C form to calculate the cost of goods sold and the inventory balances. You can use the periodic inventory approach described in Chapter 22, "Using Quicken in Your Business," to produce the information for Part III of the Schedule C form.

If you are using Quicken for a partnership or a corporation, you must report asset and liability amounts (a balance sheet) on the tax return. You also want to verify that Quicken provides the data necessary to complete these lines of the tax return. The easiest approach probably is to set up accounts to track each asset and liability that appears on the tax return. Another approach is to use accounts that you can combine to calculate the total asset or liability figure that needs to be entered on the tax return.

Sole proprietors must consider one other thing: You may need to complete more than one Schedule C form. You cannot aggregate a series of dissimilar businesses and report the consolidated results on one Schedule C. If you own a tavern, practice law, and run a small manufacturing business, you must complete three Schedule C forms: one form for the tavern, one form for the law practice, and still another form for the manufacturing firm. Quicken can handle this situation, but you need to account for each business that needs a separate Schedule C in a separate Quicken file. (Chapter 19, "Managing Your Quicken Files," explains how to set up and select different Quicken files.)

II

Getting the Most

> **CPA TIP**
>
> Although tax forms give most of the general information about the types of expenses, the instructions and regulations made by the IRS may require that you gather additional information. One example is that the business usage of a vehicle owned by a business is subject to different limitations, which are not necessarily found in Quicken. Consult a tax advisor when you encounter questionable areas.

Creating the Tax Schedule Report

Whether you prepare your tax return manually or export it to a tax preparation program (see "Exporting Quicken Data into Tax Preparation Programs" later in this chapter), an adequately prepared Tax Schedule Report is the way to save the most time and money in preparing your Federal Income Tax Return.

> **CPA TIP**
>
> The tax schedule report only supports IRS Form 1040 (personal tax returns) and its related schedules and forms. If you are preparing data for a partnership or corporation, use the tax summary report.

To prepare the Tax Schedule Report, follow these steps:

1. Assign a category (or subcategory) to each transaction in Quicken as discussed earlier in this chapter and in Chapter 4, "Organizing Your Finances."

2. From the Register or Write Checks screen, choose Categorize/Transfer from the Shortcuts menu. The Category and Transfer List appears (see fig. 14.1).

   Notice the column at the right side of the window titled *Tax*. Some of the categories have a diamond in this field. Quicken has helped you by designating certain categories (denoted by the diamond) as tax-related. However, as the tax laws are very complicated, no predetermined list could be right for everybody.

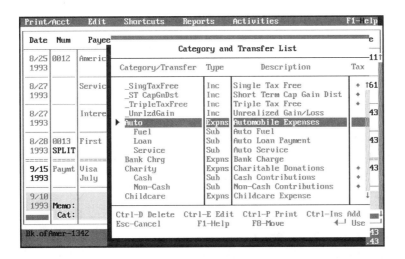

Fig. 14.1

The Category and Transfer List window.

Caution

Quicken has designated some categories as tax-related only and some as also assigned to a tax schedule. A category assigned only as tax-related will appear on the tax summary report but not on the tax schedule report.

---

3. Highlight a category that you want to add or delete from the tax-related option and choose **Ctrl-E**.

Quicken displays the Edit Category window as shown in figure 14.2.

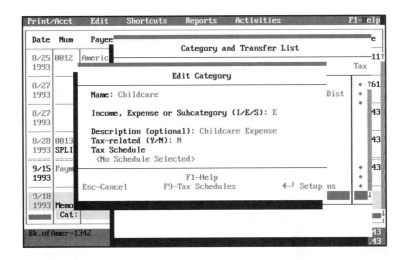

Fig. 14.2

The Edit Category window.

4. Move the cursor to the Tax-related field and choose **Y** to add the category, or **N** to delete a category. Categories with a Yes in this field will be included in the tax summary report.

5. Choose **F9** to display the Tax Schedule window and highlight the tax schedule that relates to your category (see fig. 14.3).

Fig. 14.3

The Tax Schedule window.

6. Choose **Enter** and Quicken displays the Tax Line window as shown in figure 14.4. Choose the item that relates to your category and Quicken will include on the tax schedule report the correct line of the tax form to enter the information.

Fig. 14.4

The Tax Line window.

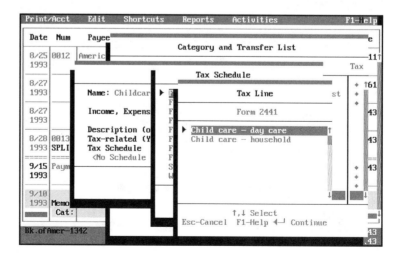

For some forms where multiple copies are possible (such as schedule C), Quicken displays a Schedule Copy Number window. If this applies to the form you need, choose the correct copy number and choose **Enter**. Quicken adds this category to the tax schedule report, returns you to the Edit Category window and displays your selection in the Tax Schedule field.

CPA TIP

This is where using the tax schedule report gets complicated as most people don't know what the various IRS schedule and form numbers relate to. Looking at a copy of your last year's tax return is one way to overcome this hurdle. Another way is to guess at a schedule or form number and choose **Enter**. Quicken displays additional information that might tell you if you have the right form. Suppose that you spent money on child care and know that it's deductible (actually it's a credit against your income tax, not a deduction) but notice that Quicken didn't show it as tax-related in the Childcare category. You have reached this step and think Form 2441 sounds familiar. Choose **Form 2441** and Quicken displays the Tax Line window (see fig. 14.4) showing Child care-day care, which should tell you that you guessed right. A third method is to call the IRS.

---

7. Choose **Esc** twice to return to the Register or Write Checks screen.

8. (Optional) Enter a report title. If you don't enter a report title, Quicken names the report Tax Schedule Report.

9. Choose **Home Reports...** from the Reports menu. Quicken displays the Home Reports menu.

10. Choose the Tax Schedule report option you want. Quicken displays the Tax Schedule Report window shown in figure 14.5.

11. (Optional) Move the cursor to the Report date range field. Enter the time frame the report should cover by selecting from the pop-up menu the starting and ending dates you want included in the report (for most taxpayers, it should be 1/1/*xx* to 12/31/*xx*). If you don't enter these dates, the report covers from January 1 of the current year through the current date.

12. (Optional) Choose **F8** (Options) to access the Report Options window. Complete the Report Options window as described in Chapter 12 in the section "Setting Report Options."

II

Getting the Most

Fig. 14.5

The Tax Schedule
Report window.

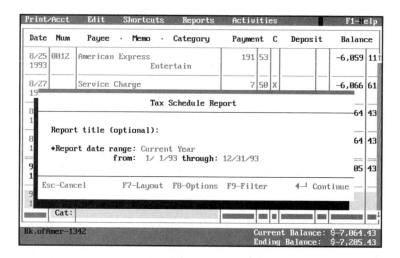

13. (Optional) Choose **F9** (Filter) to access the Filter Report Transactions window. Complete the Filter Report Transactions window as described in Chapter 12 in the section *Filtering Report Transactions*.

14. Choose **Enter**. Quicken displays the Select Accounts to Include window. Initially, all the accounts in the Select Accounts to Include window are marked to be included in the Tax Schedule report. To exclude an account, highlight the account you want to exclude and press the space bar. The space bar acts as a toggle switch to mark transactions to include or exclude.

15. After you select the accounts you want Quicken to include in the tax schedule report, choose **Enter**. Quicken generates and displays the report on-screen.

Exporting Quicken Data into Tax Preparation Programs

You can import the financial data you collect and store in Quicken directly into several popular income tax preparation packages. TurboTax, for example, imports Quicken data if you follow general steps. Even if you don't have TurboTax, you still may be able to apply the same general steps discussed in this section to export Quicken data to other tax preparation packages.

It's easy to export your Quicken data to a file that you can use in TurboTax, Taxcut, or other tax preparation packages. Quicken provides the Export Tax Schedule assistant, which you use to create a Tax Schedule report, and then to export the information from the report to a file you can import into your tax preparation program.

To export your Quicken data to a tax preparation program using the Export Tax Schedule assistant, follow these steps:

1. From the Quicken Main Menu, choose Use Tutorials/Assistants.

   Quicken displays the Use Tutorials/Assistants menu, as shown in figure 14.6.

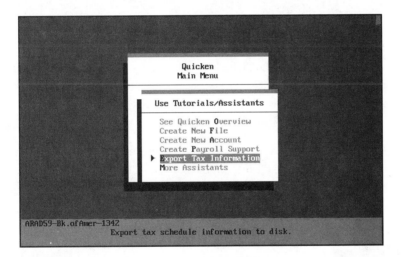

Fig. 14.6
The Use Tutorials/
Assistants menu.

2. Choose Export Tax Information. Quicken displays the Export Tax Assistant window, shown in figure 14.7. Read the message that appears and choose **Enter** to continue.

3. In the assistant's next window, you're asked to enter the year that you want the Tax Schedule report to cover. When you enter a year, Quicken includes transactions through and including 1/1/*xx* to 12/31/*xx*. In the next field, the assistant asks for the beginning date for the capital gains information that you want to export. This date tells Quicken the earliest purchase date of any stock that you may have sold during the year. Choose **Enter** or **F10** to continue.

Fig. 14.7
The Export Tax
Schedule Assistant
window.

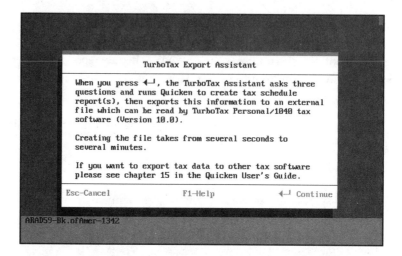

Fig. 14.7
The Export Tax
Schedule Assistant
window.

4. Enter the DOS file name you want Quicken to use to name the file to which it exports the Tax Schedule report data. You can include a full path in the DOS File field. Be sure that your file name meets the criteria for DOS file names (consult your DOS manual if you need help). Choose **Enter** to continue with the exporting process.

   Quicken's Export Tax Schedule assistant sets up the transaction dates for the Tax Schedule report and displays the Choose Accounts to Include window superimposed over the Select Accounts to Include window (see fig. 14.8).

Fig. 14.8
The Choose
Accounts to
Include and the
Select Accounts to
Include windows.

5. Choose **Enter** to remove the Choose Accounts to Include window so that you can choose the accounts you want Quicken to use to accumulate tax data. You will want to include all your bank, cash, and credit card accounts so that Quicken picks up tax-related transactions from these accounts. You should not include your IRA or retirement account, however, because IRA and retirement contributions are tax deferred and are not reported at this time.

Initially, all the accounts in the Select Accounts to Include window are marked to be included in the Tax Schedule report. To exclude an account, highlight the account you want to exclude and press the space bar. The space bar acts as a toggle switch to mark transactions to include or exclude.

6. After you choose the accounts you want Quicken to include in the Tax Schedule report, choose **Enter**. Quicken's Export Tax Schedule assistant goes through some steps to include those accounts in the Tax Schedule report, and then displays the Export Capital Gains window as shown in figure 14.9.

Fig. 14.9
The Export Capital Gains window.

7. If you don't have capital gains to report (if you didn't sell any investments during the year) press **Esc** twice and quit the assistant.

8. If you sold investments and need capital gains exported, choose **Enter** and Quicken displays the Choose Investment Accounts to Include window superimposed over the Select Accounts to Include window (see fig. 14.10) Quicken includes only investment accounts in this window.

Choose **Enter** to remove the Choose Investment Accounts to Include window.

Fig. 14.10

The Choose Investment Accounts to Include and the Select Accounts to Include window.

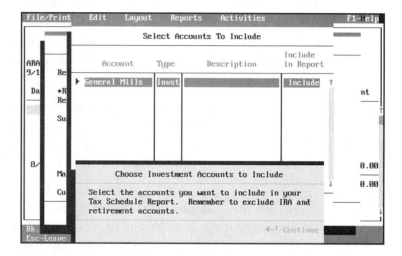

Highlight the investment account you want to include in the Tax Schedule report and press the space bar to include or exclude transactions. After you select the investment accounts you want to include, choose **Enter**.

9. The assistant searches through the investment accounts that you selected to include tax-related transactions. If no transactions are found, a message to that effect appears. Choose **Enter** to remove the message, and the assistant continues with the exporting process.

   The assistant continues to accumulate tax-related data and create and export the Tax Schedule report to an external file that can be used by TurboTax or other tax preparation programs. When the process is complete, the Quicken Export Tax Schedule Assistant displays an ending message telling you that the Tax Schedule report was exported and is ready to be imported into TurboTax, Taxcut, or other tax preparation programs (see fig. 14.11).

10. After the Tax Schedule report is exported to an external file, exit Quicken and follow the instructions in your TurboTax or other tax preparation software manual for importing the data contained in the disk file that you just created.

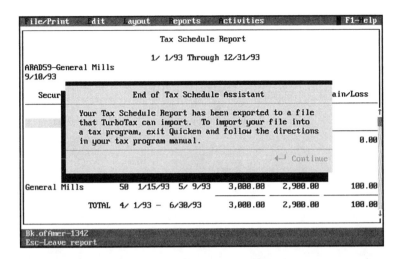

Fig. 14.11

The End of Tax Schedule Assistant window.

> **Note**
>
> You don't have to use the Export Tax Schedule assistant to export tax data. You can create the Tax Schedule report (as explained in Chapter 12, "Creating and Printing Reports"), and then choose the Disk (tax file) option from the Print Report window by choosing **6**.

Summary

This chapter describes the basic steps to take to ensure that Quicken produces the data necessary to complete federal and state income tax returns. The steps are neither complex nor difficult. You are required from the very beginning, however, to use categories that enable you to summarize income and expense data correctly.

The next chapter begins Part III of *Using Quicken 7 for DOS*, "Analyzing Your Finances with Quicken." In this part, you learn how to create a budget and how to use investment accounts to monitor your investments in securities. You also learn about graphs and financial calculators.

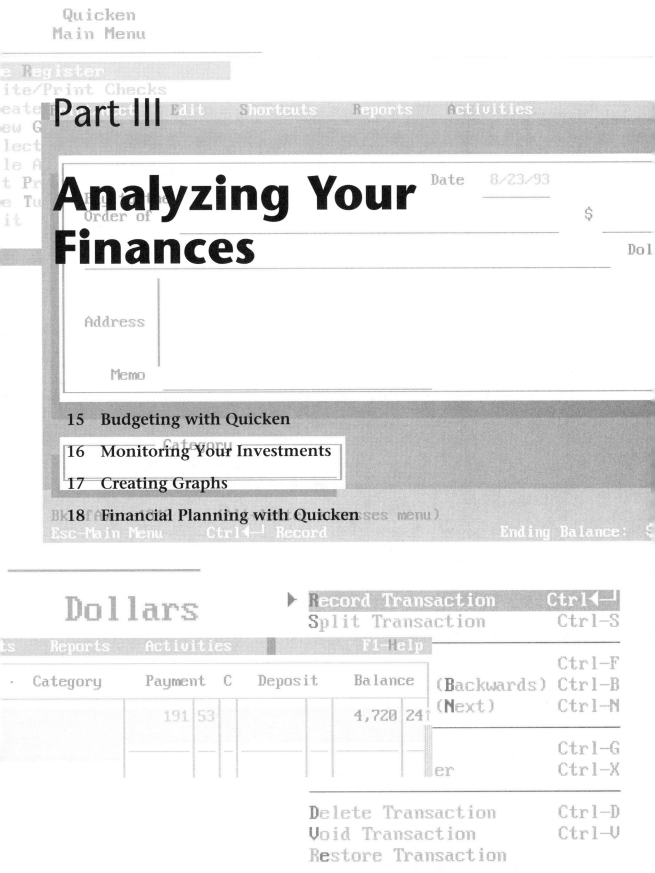

Part III

Analyzing Your Finances

Quicken
Main Menu

Use Register
Write/Print Checks
Create Print/Acct   Edit   Shortcuts   Reports   Activities
View G
Select
File A
Set Pr
Use Tu
Exit

Pay to the
Order of

Date   8/23/93

$

Address

Memo

─── Category ───

Bk.ofAmer-1342   (Alt+letter accesses menu)
Esc-Main Menu   Ctrl◄─┘ Record   Ending Balance:

Dollars   ▶ Record Transaction   Ctrl◄─┘
                     Split Transaction   Ctrl-S

:cuts   Reports   Activities   │   F1-Help
                                                        Ctrl-F
no · Category   Payment C Deposit   Balance   (Backwards) Ctrl-B
                                                      (Next)   Ctrl-N
ss   191 53   4,720 24↑
                                                        Ctrl-G
                                                  er   Ctrl-X

                                      Delete Transaction   Ctrl-D
                                      Void Transaction   Ctrl-V
                                      Restore Transaction

Chapter 15

Budgeting with Quicken

Budgeting has an undeserved bad reputation because people tend to think of a budget as financial handcuffs, an obstacle to enjoyment and a drag on financial freedoms. Actually, nothing is further from the truth. Budgeting is a simple tool with astonishingly positive benefits for businesses and households. Budgets represent game plans that calibrate, or specify, what you need to do to succeed in business or personal financial life.

Because one of Quicken's most significant benefits is the capability of monitoring your financial success through budgeting, this chapter reviews the three steps of budgeting, describes how Quicken helps budget more effectively, and provides some tips on how to budget successfully.

Defining Budgeting

Budgeting consists of the following three steps:

1. Setting business or personal financial goals.

2. Using the list of goals as a guide to developing a financial game plan, or *budget*.

3. Using the budget to monitor your spending to determine how closely you are progressing toward your business or personal goals.

Setting Your Goals

Budgeting begins with identifying goals in business or life. You are on your own here. When building a list of goals, however, keep the following two things in mind:

In this chapter you learn the definition of budgeting and how to do the following tasks:

■ Set financial goals

■ Enter and edit budget data in Quicken's budgeting spreadsheet

■ Change the spreadsheet layout

■ Print, export, and import budget data

III

Analyzing Your Finances

- Keep the goals general.

- Involve other people, particularly those who have to live within the budget, in setting the goals.

By stating the goals in more general terms, you don't start with built-in constraints and conflicts. Suppose that your goal is to live in an opulent fashion where the weather is warm and sunny. With this goal, you have a world of choices and an incredible range of prices. If the goal is to live in a mansion in Beverly Hills, you are limiting yourself. Living in a Beverly Hills mansion is one way—but not the only way—to live in an opulent fashion where the weather is warm and sunny. Keep your options open as you build a list of life goals, and you are more likely to get more of the things you want out of life and to achieve more in your business.

A second point about setting goals is to involve other people, because people who work together to build a list of goals later also work together to achieve the goals. Working together also produces better goal lists.

The United States Air Force and many businesses play a game called *desert survival*. This game demonstrates the results of a group that works to make decisions. You pretend that a plane on which you are a passenger crashes in the desert. You are 30 miles off course and at least that far from civilization; the temperature is over 100 degrees in the shade, and you can salvage about 15 or 20 items before the plane bursts into flames. First, you decide by yourself whether to stay with the wreckage or start toward civilization and which of the items you want to keep. Next, you repeat the analysis in groups of four or five people, and this time the entire group must agree on the plan and which items to keep. An interesting point about the game—and the reason that this whole issue applies to budgeting—is that in almost every case, when people make the decisions together, they dramatically increase the chance of survival of all the members of the group.

Making the wrong budgeting decision may not cost you your life or your business, but the moral of the desert survival game still applies. Whether you budget personal or business finances, you build better goal lists when you involve more people. Your spouse may end up discovering an option not previously considered. A daughter may announce that she is no longer interested in piano lessons or business school. A partner may point out a subtle flaw you overlooked.

After you finish setting your goals, write them down. Don't limit yourself to just financial goals. You may have financial goals, such as accumulating the down payment for a new car or taking a special vacation. You also may have nonfinancial goals, such as spending more time with the family or beginning a recreational or charitable activity.

Designing a Game Plan

After you build a list of goals, you are ready to create a game plan to achieve these goals. As you work through the details, you undoubtedly will modify the goals and make compromises. If you describe the goals in general terms and include everybody's good ideas, you come up with a detailed list of the costs of pursuing and achieving your business or personal goals.

At this stage, you decide how much money you are going to spend on entertainment or a vacation, how much you can spend on housing, and other issues. As a rough yardstick to use to build a detailed game plan, Table 15.1 summarizes, on the average, what percent of income most people spend in various spending categories. This list comes from the July 1990 issue of *Survey of Current Business*, which is published by the U.S. Department of Commerce. The survey is dated, but because the results show as percentages of total income, the data is still valid for planning and comparison purposes.

Table 15.1 Average Spending Based on After-Tax Income	
Spending Category	**Percent**
Durable Goods	
Motor vehicles and parts	5.43
Furniture and household equipment	4.50
Other durables	2.29
Nondurable goods	
Food	15.74
Clothing and shoes	5.38
Gasoline and oil	2.13
Other nondurables	6.57

(continues)

III

Analyzing Your Finances

Table 15.1 Continued	
Spending Category	**Percent**
Services	
Housing	14.34
Utilities	5.46
Transportation	3.47
Medical care	12.12
Other Services	14.71
Interest	2.74
Savings	5.12

If you are budgeting for a business, you can visit the local public library to obtain similar information. Dun and Bradstreet and Robert Morris Associates annually publish financial information on businesses grouped by industry and business size. For business or personal budgeting, however, don't interpret the averages as anything other than general guidelines. Seeing other companies spending numbers can provide a useful perspective on your spending but your goals should determine the details of your financial game plan.

After you finish setting your goals, write your spending game plan. Now that you know how much time and money you can allocate to each goal, you often can expand the list of goals to include estimates of costs and time. Table 15.2 lists a set of sample personal goals, and Table 15.3 lists a set of sample business goals. Table 15.4 shows an example of an annual personal budget with monthly breakdowns supporting the goals from table 15.2. Table 15.5 shows an example of an annual business budget that supports the goals from Table 15.3.

Table 15.2 Sample Personal Budget Goals		
Goal	**Cost**	**Timing**
Visit Egypt	$5,000	1995
Start fishing again	$50	ASAP
Prepare for retirement	$100,000	2025
Spend time with family	$0	ASAP

Table 15.3 Sample Business Budget Goals

Goal	Cost	Timing
Generate 20% more annual sales	$20,000	Over year
Pay down credit line	$5,000	Year-end
Make profits of $25,000	$25,000	Over year
Provide higher quality service	$0	ASAP

Table 15.4 Sample Budget To Support Personal Goals

Personal Budget	Annual	Monthly
Income	$25,000	$2,083
Outgo		
Income taxes	$1,750	$146
Social Security	$1,878	$156
Rent	$6,000	$500
Other housing	$3,000	$250
Food	$4,800	$400
Transportation	$2,500	$208
Vacation, recreation	$1,200	$100
Fishing gear	$50	$4
Clothing	$1,250	$104
Savings-IRA	$500	$42
Other	$1,200	$100
Total Expenses	$24,628	$2,052
Leftover/Contingency	$373	$31

III

Analyzing Your Finances

Table 15.5 Sample Budget To Support Business Goals		
Business Budget	**Annual**	**Monthly**
Sales	$125,000	$10,417
Expenses		
Materials	$30,000	$2,500
Labor	$30,000	$2,500
Rent	$12,000	$1,000
Transportation	$12,500	$1,042
Supplies	$12,000	$1,000
Legal/Accounting	$1,200	$100
Other	$2,100	$175
Total Expenses	$99,800	$8,317
Profits	$25,200	$2,100

Notice a few things about the relationships between the goals and budget. First, some goals represent plateaus you can achieve almost immediately; other goals may take longer to achieve. Second, some goals on the list don't directly affect the budget. Third, some expenditures don't tie to formal, or stated, goals but still represent implied goals. You do not, for example, list feeding the children or staying in business, but these actions may be your most important goals.

Monitoring Your Progress

The third and final step in budgeting relates to monitoring your progress in achieving personal or business goals. On a periodic basis—every month or quarter—compare the amount you budgeted to spend with the amount you actually spent. Often, people view these comparisons as negative, but the idea is that, when following a budget, you are moving toward your goals. If you get through the first month of the year and are operating under the budget shown in Table 15.4, for example, you can compare what you spent with your budget. If you see from the numbers on the budget that you are having difficulty setting aside extra money for the trip to Egypt and to contribute to an individual retirement account, you know that your spending or your goals need to change.

Using Quicken to Budget

Quicken provides three features that enable you to budget more effectively
for personal finances and for small businesses: categories, the budget spreadsheet, and reporting.

Using Categories

With categories, you can assign each check that you record a spending category, such as housing, contribution, entertainment, or taxes. You also can
assign an income category to each of the deposits you record, such as wages,
gross sales, or interest income. The steps and benefits of using categories are
discussed in greater detail in Chapter 4, "Organizing Your Finances." By assigning the category into which every check and deposit you record belongs, you
can produce reports that summarize and total the inflows and outflows (by
category) for a specific period, such as a cash flow report shown in figure 15.1.

```
                          Cash Flow Report 1
                         8/ 1/93 Through 8/31/93
ARAD59-Bank, Cash, CC Accounts                                    Page 1
9/22/93
                                              8/ 1/93-
                    Category Description       8/31/93

             INFLOWS
                Interest Income                     2.18
                Professional Fees              6,000.00

             TOTAL INFLOWS                     6,002.18

             OUTFLOWS
                Automobile Expenses:
                   Auto Fuel            96.57
                   Auto Loan Payment   315.67
                   Auto Service         31.00

                Total Automobile Expenses        443.24
                Bank Charge                         7.50
                Credit Card                       533.00
                Dues                              200.00
                Education                         198.35
                Entertainment                     271.66
                Insurance                          50.00
                Miscellaneous                       6.50
                Mortgage Interest Exp             750.00
                Mortgage                          100.00
                Postage                            25.00
                Taxes:
                   Property Tax        100.00

                Total Taxes                       100.00
                Telephone Expense                  34.65
                Water, Gas, Electric:
                   Gas and Electricity  64.98
                   Water                23.95

                Total Water, Gas, Electric         88.93

             TOTAL OUTFLOWS                     2,808.83

             OVERALL TOTAL                      3,193.35
```

Fig. 15.1

A sample cash flow
report, by category.

III

Analyzing Your Finances

If you decide to tap the power of budgeting, reports are invaluable. The report
shows what you actually spent. What you actually spent can be compared
to what you budgeted. When the actual spending matches the budgeted

spending, you know you are following your financial game plan. When the spending doesn't match the budget, you know you are not following the game plan.

Creating Budgeting Reports

Quicken also enables you to enter any amount budgeted for a category. With this information, Quicken calculates the difference, or *variance*, between the total spent on a category and the budgeted amount for a category. Quicken performs the arithmetic related to monitoring how closely you follow the budget and how successfully you are marching toward your life goals. To generate a budget report such as the one shown in figure 15.2, refer to Chapter 12, "Creating and Printing Reports."

Fig. 15.2

A sample budget report in whole dollars.

Tip

You can create and print graphs of the actual and budgeted data with Quicken's View Graphs option on the Main Menu. Refer to Chapter 17, "Creating Graphs," to learn how to create on-screen graphs to compare the actual data to budgeted data.

```
                              Budget Report
                       8/ 1/93 Through 8/31/93
ARAD59-All Accounts                                              Page 1
9/22/93
                                    8/ 1/93      -        8/31/93
              Category Description  Actual     Budget      Diff

  INCOME/EXPENSE
    INCOME
      Interest Income               2.18        10.00      -7.82
      Professional Fees          6,000.00    5,000.00    1,000.00

    TOTAL INCOME                  6,002.18    5,010.00      992.18

    EXPENSES
      Automobile Expenses:
        Auto Fuel                   96.57       50.00       46.57
        Auto Loan Payment          315.67      316.00       -0.33
        Auto Service                31.00       25.00        6.00

      Total Automobile Expenses    443.24      391.00       52.24
      Bank Charge                    7.50        0.00        7.50
      Credit Card                  533.00      300.00      233.00
      Dues                         200.00        0.00      200.00
      Education                    198.35      100.00       98.35
      Entertainment                271.66      200.00       71.66
      Insurance                     50.00        0.00       50.00
      Miscellaneous                  6.50        0.00        6.50
      Mortgage Interest Exp        750.00      900.00     -150.00
      Mortgage                     100.00      100.00        0.00
      Postage                       25.00        0.00       25.00
      Taxes:
        Property Tax               100.00        0.00      100.00

      Total Taxes                  100.00        0.00      100.00
      Telephone Expense             34.65       50.00      -15.35
      Water, Gas, Electric:
        Gas and Electricity         64.98      100.00      -35.02
        Water                       23.95       25.00       -1.05

      Total Water, Gas, Electric    88.93      125.00      -36.07

    TOTAL EXPENSES               2,808.83    2,166.00      642.83


  TOTAL INCOME/EXPENSE           3,193.35    2,844.00      349.35

  TRANSFERS
    TO Acme                       -100.00        0.00     -100.00
    TO Fleet Mortgage             -98.34        0.00      -98.34
    FROM Bk.ofAmer-1342            198.34        0.00      198.34

  TOTAL TRANSFERS                   0.00        0.00        0.00


  OVERALL TOTAL                  3,193.35    2,844.00      349.35
```

Setting Up Budgets

To create budget reports, you first need to enter the budget amounts that Quicken uses for actual-to-budget comparisons. Quicken provides a spreadsheet screen in which you enter budgeted amounts for each category and subcategory.

To use Quicken's budgeting spreadsheet to set up a budget, follow these steps:

1. From the Register or the Write Checks screen, choose Set Up Budgets from the Activities menu (see fig. 15.3).

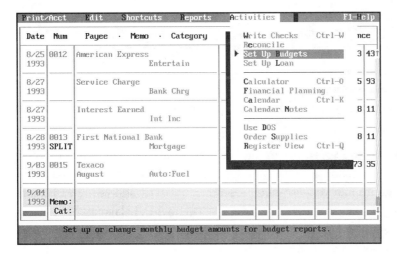

Fig. 15.3

The Set Up Budget option on the Activities menu.

Quicken displays the budgeting spreadsheet screen you see in figure 15.4. The budget spreadsheet shows a menu at the top of the screen that includes the File, Edit, Layout, Percent View, and Activities names.

2. Enter monthly budgeted amounts for each category and, optionally, subcategories and account transfers on the category list. Use the mouse or use the up- and down-arrow keys to move up or down a monthly column, or use the Tab key to move right across the category rows. Pressing Shift-Tab moves you to the left in a category row. See *Entering and Editing Budget Data*, later in this chapter, to learn how to enter or edit budgeted amounts in the budgeting spreadsheet.

3. After you enter the budgeted amounts, choose **Esc** to leave the budgeting spreadsheet. The budget data then is saved.

III

Analyzing Your Finances

Fig. 15.4

The budgeting spreadsheet screen.

Customizing the Spreadsheet

Quicken enables you to customize a spreadsheet by changing the layout and the view.

Changing the Spreadsheet Layout. By default, Quicken assumes that you want to budget on a monthly basis, so the spreadsheet displays a column for each month, but you also can budget on a quarterly and yearly basis by displaying the Layout menu (see fig. 15.5). Highlight the layout you want (Quarter or Year), and then choose **Enter**. Quicken changes the spreadsheet to the layout you select.

Fig. 15.5

The Layout menu from the budgeting spreadsheet screen.

The Layout menu also gives you the option of displaying your budgets in dollars and cents or whole dollars. The default is in dollars and cents. To change to whole dollars, choose Hide Cents from the Layout menu. The screen display changes to whole dollars and the Layout menu displays Show Cents the next time you access it so that it acts as a toggle switch.

CPA TIP

You may find that a budget is easier to work with in whole dollars.

Changing the Budget View. When you open the Set Up Budget window, Quicken displays the budget spreadsheet in Normal View where each field contains a dollar amount. Quicken 7 offers a new feature that enables you to view the budget spreadsheet in percentages.

To view the budget spreadsheet using percentages, follow these steps:

1. From the Register or the Write Checks screen, choose Set Up Budgets from the Activities menu (see fig. 15.1). Quicken displays the budgeting spreadsheet screen.

2. From the budgeting spreadsheet, access the Percent View menu (see fig. 15.6).

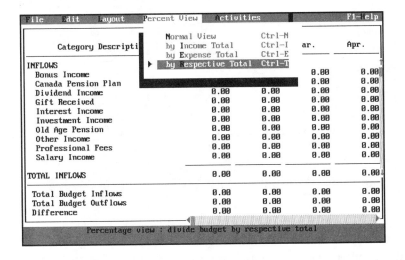

Fig. 15.6
The Percent View menu from the budgeting spreadsheet screen.

3. (Optional) Choose by Income Total to show a value in each field that is a percentage of the total income in the same column. The value in the Total Budget Inflows field for each column always is 100% and the value in the Total Budget Outflows field for each column shows your expense total as a percentage of your income total.

4. (Optional) Choose by Expense Total to show a value in each field that is a percentage of the total expenses in the same column. The value in the Total Budget Outflows field for each column always is 100% and the value in the Total Budget Inflows field for each column shows your income total as a percentage of your expense total.

5. (Optional) Choose by Respective Total to show a value in each income field that is a percentage of the total income in that column, and a value in each expense field that is a percentage of the total expenses in that column. The value in both the Total Budget Inflows field and the Total Budget Outflows field for each column is always 100%.

6. Quicken displays the Budgeting spreadsheet in the format you selected (see fig. 15.7). You can toggle back and forth between Normal View and the last Percent View you selected by pressing F9.

Fig. 15.7

The budgeting spreadsheet showing the Percentage view by Respective Total.

File Edit Layout Percent View Activities				F1-Help
Percentage view by Respective Total				
Category Description	Aug.	Sept.	Oct.	Nov.
Other Income	0%	0%	0%	0%
Professional Fees	99.80%	0%	0%	0%
Salary Income	0%	0%	0%	0%
TOTAL INFLOWS	100.00%	0%	0%	0%
OUTFLOWS				
Automobile Expenses:				
Auto Fuel	2.31%	0%	0%	0%
Auto Loan Payment	14.59%	0%	0%	0%
Auto Service	1.15%	0%	0%	0%
Automobile Expenses - Other	0%	0%	0%	0%
Total Budget Inflows	100.00%	0%	0%	0%
Total Budget Outflows	100.00%	0%	0%	0%
Difference	2,844.00	0.00	0.00	0.00
ARAD59				
Esc-Cancel	F9-Toggle View		F10-Save Budget	

Entering and Editing Budget Data

One way to enter budgeted amounts is directly into the spreadsheet by moving the cursor to the budget amount you want to enter, such as childcare expenses for January, and then typing the new budget figure. A second way to enter budget amounts is to copy amounts into the spreadsheet by using one of the Edit menu options. Figure 15.8 shows the Edit menu available on the budget spreadsheet screen. Using the Edit menu options, you can enter budget data in a variety of ways. You can enter budget data based on your actual income and expenses over a specified period of time, for example. Or, you can fill in one column or row and have Quicken copy the budget data that you entered into other columns or rows. You also can specify whether you want to enter budget data for subcategories and transfer accounts. The following sections describe the options from the Edit menu that you can use to enter data into the budgeting spreadsheet.

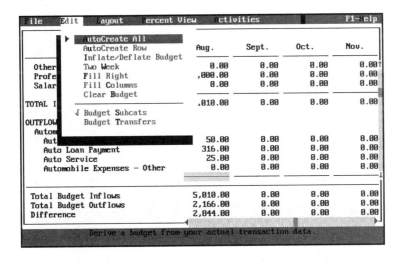

Fig. 15.8
The Edit menu from the budgeting spreadsheet screen.

Entering Budget Data from Actual Data. If you want to set up a budget based on actual income and expense amounts, you can use one of the AutoCreate options from the Edit menu. AutoCreate copies actual data from a specified time period into the budgeting spreadsheet. You can tell Quicken to enter rounded values in the budget or to use averages for the period that you specify.

To enter budget data from actual data, follow these steps:

1. Access the budgeting spreadsheet screen, as explained in the previous section, *Setting Up Budgets*.

2. Choose AutoCreate All or the AutoCreate Row from the Edit menu.

   The AutoCreate All command fills in budget amounts for all income and expense categories.

The AutoCreate Row command is a new feature of Quicken 7. The AutoCreate Row command fills in budget amounts (across the spreadsheet for one category) for the currently selected category only. This gives you more flexibility in preparing your budget.

Be sure to select the category for which you want Quicken to fill in budget amounts before you choose AutoCreate Row from the Edit menu.

Quicken displays the Automatically Create Budget window that is identical for either option (see fig. 15.9).

Fig. 15.9

The Automatically Create Budget window.

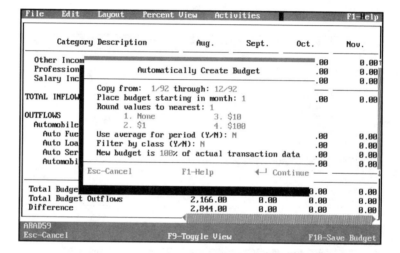

3. Enter the date range of the actual monthly figures you want to copy in the Copy From and Through fields.

4. Move the cursor to the Place Budget Starting in Month (or period) field. Identify the first budgeting month or period in which you want to place the first copied number.

5. To indicate how Quicken rounds copied values before using them as the new budgeted amounts, move the cursor to the Round Values to Nearest field, and choose a rounding option: **1** for no rounding, **2** to round to the nearest dollar, **3** to round to the nearest 10 dollars, and **4** to round to the nearest 100 dollars.

6. To tell Quicken to calculate the average for the copied actual amounts and use the result as the budgeted amount, move the cursor to the Use Average for Period field and choose **Y**.

7. Move the cursor to the Filter by class field and choose **Y** if you want to use the amounts from only selected classes in your budget.

8. Move the cursor to the New budget is % of actual transaction data field and enter a number between 1 and 999. The number indicates what percentage of the actual transaction amounts that the budget amounts will be. (A number below 100 decreases the actual amounts; a number above 100 increases them).

This field enables you to adjust your budget figures for changing circumstances. For example, you might want to deflate your budget if you go back to school and take a cut in income, so you can make a plan for scaling down your expenses appropriately.

This feature represented in the New budget is % of actual transaction data field is known as *Inflate/Deflate Budget* and also can be accessed by choosing Inflate/Deflate Budget from Edit menu.

9. To enter the budgeted amounts in the budgeting spreadsheet from the actual data, choose **Enter** or **F10**.

Budgeting for Items that Occur Every Two Weeks. The Edit menu's Two Week option enables you to budget amounts that occur every two weeks, such as salary paid biweekly. To use this handy option, take the following steps:

1. Access the budgeting spreadsheet screen.

2. Highlight the amount field for the category for which you want to set up a two-week budget amount.

3. Choose Two Week from the Edit menu. Quicken displays the Set Up 2 Week Budget window that you see in figure 15.10. In the Category field, Quicken enters the category name for the amount field you selected in step 2.

4. Enter the dollar amount you want to budget in the Enter the Amount field, and then choose **Enter**.

5. Enter the starting date for the first two-week interval in the Every 2 Weeks Starting field.

6. Choose **Enter** or **F10** to set up the two-week budget amount.

III

Analyzing Your Finances

Fig. 15.10

The Set Up 2 Week
Budget window.

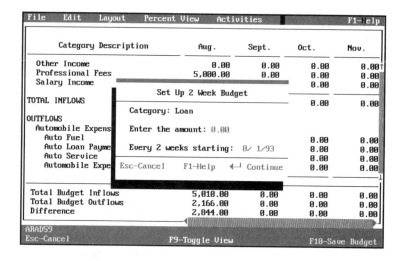

Filling in Rows and Columns. Fill Right from the Edit menu copies the
highlighted budget amount to each field to the right in the current row.
If you highlight, for example, the January entertainment expense budget
amount field, which is set to $25, and then you select the Fill Right option,
Quicken copies 25 to the entertainment expense budgets fields for February,
March, April, May, and so on.

Fill Columns from the Edit menu works like the Fill Right option except that
Fill Columns doesn't copy a single budget amount. Fill Columns copies a
column of budget amounts to the columns to the right of that column. If you
highlight one of the budget amounts in the July column, for example, and
then choose Fill Columns, Quicken copies the budgeted figures in the July
column to the August, September, October, November, and December budget
columns.

Clearing the Budget Spreadsheet. If you want to clear all data from the
budget spreadsheet and start over, you can select Clear Budget from the Edit
menu. When you select Clear Budget, Quicken displays a warning that you
are about to clear all budget amounts. To clear budget amounts, choose **Enter**. If you decide that you don't want to clear the budgeted amounts from
the budget spreadsheet, choose **Esc**.

Budgeting Subcategories and Transfers. The last two options on the Edit
menu—Budget Subcats and Budget Transfers—control whether rows for budgeting subcategories and budgeting account transfers appear in the budget
spreadsheet. Both the Budget Subcats and Budget Transfers options are toggle

switches that alternately turn on and turn off the display of these extra sub-category and account transfer rows. If the budget spreadsheet doesn't show subcategories, for example, just choose Budget Subcats to display subcategories. If you later decide that you want the subcategories hidden, choose Budget Subcats again.

Creating Multiple Budgets

Quicken enables you to create and save multiple budgets that can be used with any Quicken file. These budgets can be used to try out different scenarios to help in planning your income and expenses.

Each Quicken file has one default budget associated with it that loads automatically each time you choose Set Up budgets from the Activities menu. You may, however, create additional budgets, save them, and use them again at any time.

To save and retrieve a budget, follow these steps:

1. Create a budget as explained at *Setting Up Budgets* earlier in this chapter.

2. When you finish creating the budget you want to save, choose Save As from the File menu. Quicken displays the Save Budget To File window (see fig. 15.11).

```
 File    Edit    Layout    Percent View    Activities            F1-Help

      Category Description        Aug.      Sept.     Oct.     Nov.

   Other Income                    0.00      0.00      0.00      0.00
   Professional Fees           5,000.00      0.00      0.00      0.00
   Salary Income                                       0.00      0.00
                          Save Budget To File
 TOTAL INFLOWS                                         0.00      0.00
                     Current budget:  ARAD59
 OUTFLOWS
   Automobile Expense    Save budget as:
     Auto Fuel             (8 character DOS filename)   0.00      0.00
     Auto Loan Paymen                                   0.00      0.00
     Auto Service       Esc-Cancel   F1-Help  ←┘ Continue  0.00   0.00
     Automobile Expen                                   0.00      0.00

   Total Budget Inflows        5,010.00      0.00      0.00      0.00
   Total Budget Outflows       2,166.00      0.00      0.00      0.00
   Difference                  2,844.00      0.00      0.00      0.00
 ARAD59
 Esc-Cancel                   F9-Toggle View          F10-Save Budget
```

Fig. 15.11
The Save Budget to File window.

3. Enter an eight character DOS filename, and then choose **Enter**. Quicken adds a .BGT extension to the filename, saves the file in the current directory, and returns you to the budgeting spreadsheet screen.

4. To retrieve a budget you have saved, choose Load Budget from the File menu.

   Quicken displays the Load Budget From File window that lists the names of all budget files in the current directory.

5. Highlight the name of the budget you want to retrieve and choose **Enter** or **F10** and Quicken displays the selected budget.

Printing, Exporting, and Importing Budget Data

The budget spreadsheet's File menu provides three options: Print Budgets, Export Budget, and Import Budget. The first File menu option, Print Budgets, prints a copy of the budget spreadsheet. When you select this option, Quicken displays a Print Budget window that looks like and works like the Print Register window described in Chapter 5.

The second and third File menu options, Export Budget and Import Budget, enable you to move data between Quicken and other application programs. Export Budget creates a QIF file that stores the information contained in the budget spreadsheet. Import Budget imports a QIF file that stores budget information and uses the information to fill in the budget spreadsheet screen. When you select the Export Budget or Import Budget option, Quicken displays a window you use to name the QIF file. Exporting, importing, and QIF files are discussed in greater detail in Chapter 19, "Managing Your Quicken Files."

Reviewing Tips for Successful Budgeting

Even if you started out listing personal or business goals, involved the entire family or company in the process, and created a budget compatible with stated and implied goals, you can take other precautions to succeed in budgeting. These precautions include paying yourself first, recognizing after-tax shares, providing for unplanned or emergency events, and using zero-based budgeting.

Paying Yourself First

Families need savings to provide cushions for financial emergencies, money for major expenditures, such as a home or a child's education, and the means for financial support during retirement. Small businesses need savings to provide funds for expanding the business, for replacing assets, and for unexpected delays in collecting from customers.

You always have bills to pay, however, and you have to resist a great number of financial temptations. Reaching the end of the month with extra money is difficult—which is why you need to pay yourself first. For many people, paying yourself first is the only way to successfully save money.

Figure 15.12 shows the amount you ultimately accumulate if you put away $25 a month and earn 8 percent interest, assuming various income tax rates. (The logic behind including income taxes is that if you earn $100 in interest and are taxed on the money at the 28 percent tax rate, for example, you need to withdraw $28 of the $100 to pay income taxes.)

Ultimate Savings accumulated at $25 of savings per month assuming 8% annual interest				
Years	Marginal Income Tax Rates			
	0%	15%	28%	31%
5	$1,837	$1,781	$1,734	$1,723
10	4,574	4,280	4,044	3,992
15	8,651	7,788	7,124	6,980
20	14,726	12,711	11,228	10,916
25	23,776	19,622	16,699	16,100
30	37,259	29,323	23,990	22,926
35	57,347	42,938	33,709	31,917

Fig. 15.12
Saving $25 a month adds up.

If you save $50 a month, double the amounts shown in the figure. If you save $100, quadruple the amounts shown in the table, and so on.

III

Analyzing Your Finances

CPA TIP

If you save money for retirement, try to use options such as individual retirement accounts (IRAs) and 401K plans. Figure 15.10 shows that when you save $25 a month for 35 years in one of these investment vehicles where you pay 0 percent income tax, you end up with roughly twice as much as you would if you were paying a 28 or 31 percent income tax on the interest income. (If you are saving for retirement, refer to Chapter 18, "Financial Planning with Quicken," which discusses how to estimate how much you should save for retirement.)

Eventually, you do pay income taxes on the money you contributed to a 401K or IRA if you received a tax deduction for the contribution. The tax becomes due in the year that you withdraw funds from the retirement plan. You also pay income taxes on earnings accumulated in the account over the years. You don't need to begin withdrawing money, however, until you're 70 1/2 years old and, even if you begin withdrawing at the earliest possible date—age 59 1/2—you have a good chance of paying at a lower rate.

Recognizing After-Tax Shares of Bonuses and Raises

A second important budgeting consideration in personal and business situations is recognizing that if you receive an extra $1,000 as a bonus, raise, or windfall, you cannot spend the entire $1,000. You must pay Social Security and Medicare taxes, (either deducted by your employer or in the form of self-employment taxes if you are self employed). You also must pay all federal and state income taxes. You may even have other expenses that, like income taxes, decrease your take-home share of any bonus or windfall, such as an automatic contribution to a deferred compensation plan or charity to which you have made a donation commitment. Totaled, you typically need to deduct at least 20 percent and as much as 60 percent from any bonus or windfall to figure out what you have available for spending.

Allowing for Unplanned and Emergency Expenses

Unfortunately, people lose jobs, cars break down, and children get sick. Over the time period a budget covers, all kinds of unforeseen and unplanned events occur that can cost you money. If you can afford to, the best approach is to budget and set aside a little money each month to cover these unexpected expenses.

Budget planners use several rules of thumb in determining how much emergency savings is enough. If your primary reason for emergency savings is in case you lose a job—because you are well-insured for medical, disability, and life claims—the following is an approach you should use:

- Consider the length of time you need to find a new job. (A traditional rule of thumb says that you need a month for every $10,000 of annual salary. If, for example, you make $10,000 a year, figure on one month. If you make $50,000 a year, figure on five months.)

- Take the salary you would have earned over the period of unemployment and subtract any unemployment benefits or severance pay you receive.

■ Reduce that remainder by the income taxes you do not pay and all amounts you do not save because you have no income.

To illustrate, suppose that you take as long as six months to find a job. You currently earn $2,500 a month; you get half a month's severance pay if you lose your job; unemployment amounts to $100 a week; and you pay 6.2 percent Social Security tax, 1.45 percent Medicare tax, and a 15 percent income tax. You then can calculate the emergency savings as:

$$((6*\$2{,}500) - (26*\$100) - \$1{,}250)*(1 - 6.2\% - 1.45\% - 15\%) = \$8{,}625$$

Using Zero-Based Budgeting

Large businesses and some governments use zero-based budgeting with success. Individuals and smaller businesses also can use this method successfully. Basically, *zero-based budgeting* means that although you spent money on some category last year, you should not necessarily spend money on the same category this year.

Looking at what you spent last year can provide a valuable perspective, but determine the present year's spending by this year's goals. Saying, "Well, last year I spent $500 on furniture, and therefore I should spend $500 this year," is dangerous. Your house or apartment may not have room for more furniture. What about the dues for the athletic club you haven't used for months or years or the extra term life insurance you bought when the kids were living at home? What about the advertising money you spent to attract your first customers? Budgeting and spending amounts as you have in the past is easy to do, even when new goals, lifestyles, or businesses have meanwhile made the expense unnecessary.

Summary

This chapter outlines the budgeting process, explains why budgeting is important in managing personal and business finances, describes how Quicken helps with the process, and provides some tips on how to budget and manage finances more successfully. With this information as a background, you should be able to decide whether you want to use the budgeting tools that Quicken provides.

III

Analyzing Your Finances

In the next chapter, you learn how to use investment accounts to track investments in stocks, bonds, mutual funds and so on. Quicken's investment accounts are an advanced feature in the program, so, if you want to use Quicken to monitor investments, pay particular attention to Chapter 16.

Chapter 16

Monitoring Your Investments

Quicken provides features that enable you to monitor and report on your investments. Quicken provides a Register specifically for investments. You enter all of your security holdings and transactions in the Register for each investment account that you set up. The Register not only provides a way to track your investment transaction but also shows you how your investments are performing and the market value of your investments.

And now in Quicken 7, investment transactions such as buying and selling securities, recording dividends and interest, option trades, and so forth, are entered in new forms that prompt you for the information that Quicken needs to record the transaction. You still can enter investment transactions directly into the Register; however, the new investment forms ensure that your transaction information is complete. When selling securities from multiple lots, you can now specify which lots you are selling. Another new investment feature in Quicken 7 is the Portfolio View window for investment accounts. From the Investment Register, you can change to the Portfolio View so that you see snapshots of your security portfolio that shows the current market value, return on investment, price changes, and other important data.

Quicken's investment accounts show you more information about your securities. Quicken 7 includes 18 measures of investment performance and value. For example, you can now determine a security's estimated income, investment yield, return on investment, internal rate of return, and so forth. Quicken 7 also enables you to designate the tax status of an investment account as you set it up. You can designate an account as tax deferred if you're

In this chapter, you learn how to do the following:

■ Set up an investment account

■ Work with mutual fund accounts

■ Work with investment accounts that track brokerage accounts or individual securities

■ Use securities lists

■ Update investment accounts for market values

■ Reconcile an investment account

III

Analyzing Your Finances

setting up a 401K or 403K, IRA, annuity, or Series EE and HH U.S. Savings Bond account. When you designate an account as tax-deferred, Quicken includes transactions from the accounts in tax reports.

This chapter describes how to prepare to monitor your investments with Quicken and how to track mutual funds and other investments using the Quicken Investment Register, the new investment forms, and the Portfolio windows. To save you from reviewing material you already know, the chapter does not explain the parts of the Investment Register that also are part of the other Quicken Registers that you have examined in previous chapters. If you are not well-acquainted with the basics of using Quicken, refer to the first section of this book, "Learning Quicken."

Preparing to Monitor Investments

To monitor investments with Quicken, you need to set up an investment account. When you set up an investment account in Quicken, you must specify whether the account is a mutual fund. If the account is not a mutual fund account, you can use the account to track a variety of securities or to have it maintain a cash balance. The *mutual fund account* is a simplified investment account that you use for a single mutual fund. The *securities and cash account* is a more powerful investment account that you use for other investments and investment groups.

The mutual fund account keeps track of the market value and the number of shares you hold of a single fund. The securities and cash account keeps track of the market value of multiple securities, the shares, and the cash balance. (The cash balance usually represents the money with which you buy additional stocks, bonds, and so on.)

Given these distinctions, the easiest approach is to set up a mutual fund account for each mutual fund investment you hold, set up a securities and cash account for each brokerage account you hold, and set up a securities and cash account for any collection of individual investments that you want to track and manage together in one Register (for example, if you just want to track your investment in IBM stock, set up a securities and cash investment account named *IBM*). As you work with the Quicken investment options, you will be able to fine-tune these suggestions.

CPA TIP

A *mutual fund* is an open-end management company that pools the money of many investors and uses it to establish a portfolio of securities. The securities of the investors are managed by an investment advisor or portfolio manager.

If you don't want to manage your own portfolio by making decisions as to which securities to buy and sell, invest in a mutual fund. Large mutual funds usually hire the best investment advisors available.

If you want to diversify your portfolio, a mutual fund is an excellent vehicle for spreading your money to a variety of securities. When a single company's stock held in the fund declines, the impact on the total value of the mutual fund's portfolio is less because the fund's portfolio is made up of many securities. Also, security values that decline are offset by those securities that are appreciating in value.

Transaction costs when buying and selling shares in a mutual fund are often less than commission costs when buying and selling individual securities through a broker.

Note

Because Quicken's investment accounts are one of the more advanced features in the program, Quicken includes assistants that help you set up your investment accounts and enter transactions in the Investment Register. To use the investment assistants, choose the Use Tutorials/Assistants option from the Main Menu. Then choose the More Assistants option from the Use Tutorials/Assistants menu. Next, you see options to choose two investment related assistants: one for setting up investment accounts and the other for entering transactions. Highlight the assistant you want to use and choose **Enter**. Follow the investment assistant's on-screen instructions to move through the steps in the tutorials.

III

Analyzing Your Finances

Setting Up Investment Accounts

As you learned earlier in this chapter, you can set up two kinds of investment accounts in Quicken: a regular investment account and a mutual fund account.

To set up either type of investment account, follow these steps:

1. Choose Select Account from Quicken's Main Menu. Quicken displays the Select Account to Use window, shown in figure 16.1.

Fig. 16.1

The Select Account to Use window.

2. Highlight the <New Account> line in the Select Account to Use window and choose **Enter**. Quicken displays the Set Up New Account window, shown in figure 16.2

Fig. 16.2

The Set Up New Account window.

3. Choose **6** in the Account Type field to indicate that this is an investment account.

4. Move the cursor to the Name for This Account field and enter a description of the account. The account name can be up to 15 characters and can contain any characters except the following: [ ] / : . You can include spaces in the account name.

5. Choose **Enter** to display the Investment Account Type and Description window, shown in figure 16.3.

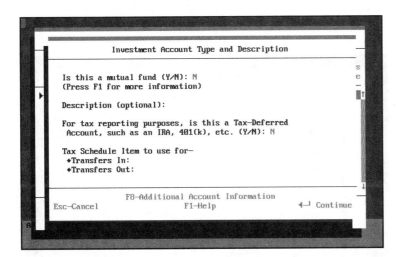

Fig. 16.3
The Investment Account Type and Description window.

6. In the first field, choose **Y** if the account is a mutual fund. Leave the setting at N if the account is a securities and cash account.

7. (Optional) Move the cursor to the Description field. The Description field provides 21 spaces for additional investment description.

8. Move the cursor to the tax-Deferred Account field and choose **Y** if the account is tax-deferred (such as an IRA, 401K, 403K, Keogh, Series EE and HH U.S. Savings Bonds), or choose **N** if the account is not tax-deferred.

9. (Optional) Move the cursor to the Tax Schedule to use for Transfers In field and enter the appropriate source of funds for this account. See the *Creating a Tax Schedule Report* section in Chapter 14 for more information.

10. (Optional) Move the cursor to the Tax Schedule to use for Transfers Out field and enter the appropriate tax schedule item for this account. See the *Creating a Tax Schedule Report* section in Chapter 14 for more information.

11. When you complete the Investment Account Type and Description window, choose **Enter** or **F10**. Quicken returns you to the Portfolio window.

III

Analyzing Your Finances

If you are setting up a mutual fund account and have set the Is This a Mutual Fund field to Y, Quicken displays the Set Up Mutual Fund Security window (see fig. 16.4). The account name appears in the Name field.

Fig. 16.4

The Set Up Mutual Fund Security window.

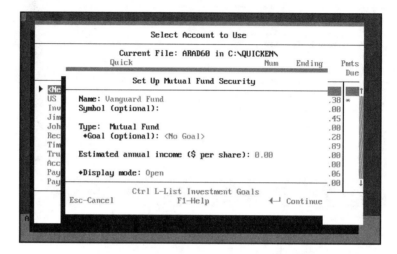

If you set the Is This a Mutual Fund field to N, you don't need to complete steps 12 through 15.

12. (Optional) Enter the mutual fund symbol in the Symbol field if you plan to import price data from another file. You can import stock prices from Prodigy to a file that you can import to your investment account.

The symbol that you enter in the Symbol field should be whatever you use to identify the mutual fund in the other file. For more information on this process, refer to *Updating Your Investment Records for Market Values* and *Importing Stock Prices*, later in this chapter.

13. Choose **Enter**. Quicken has placed Mutual Fund in the Type field and moves the cursor to the Goal field.

14. (Optional) Specify an investment goal in the pop-up menu for the Goal field: College Fund, Growth, High Risk, Income, or Low Risk. If the goal that you have for your investment does not appear on the list, you can add a new goal by selecting the <Set Up New Goal> line and typing the new goal description (up to 15 characters) in the Set Up Investment Goal window.

The Type and Goal fields don't significantly affect the way Quicken processes information. (The Type field does dictate whether share prices are recorded using decimal or fractional numbers.) Quicken uses the Type field to sort securities alphabetically within type in the Update Prices window when you enter security prices from the newspaper. When securities are sorted by type, it's much easier for you to enter prices. You can use the Type and Goal fields to sort and organize information on reports. How to define different investment types and goals is discussed later in the chapter.

15. (Optional) Move the cursor to the Estimated annual income ($ per share) field and enter an amount.

16. Move the cursor to the Display mode field and choose from the pop-up menu that appears. See *Hiding a Security* later in this chapter for more information on this field.

17. After you complete the Set Up Mutual Fund Security screen, choose **Enter** or **F10**. Quicken returns you to the Portfolio window.

Repeat steps 1 through 11 for each securities and cash account you choose to set up. For each mutual fund account you establish, repeat steps 1 through 17.

After you create an investment account, you are ready to use the Register to record initial balances, changes in the investment balance due to purchases or sales, and fluctuations in the market value. The following section explains the Portfolio View feature new to Quicken 7.

Using the Portfolio View of an Investment Account

Quicken enables you to change the view of the Investment Register so that you can see each of your security holdings (listed alphabetically by security type), the number of shares, current price, market value, and return on investment. When you change the view of the Register to the Portfolio View, not only can you see your securities listed in one place, but you can update security prices, create a QuickReport listing all transactions associated with a security, and graph the price history of a security. You also can record investment transactions and edit your list of securities in the Portfolio View of the Register.

To switch to the Portfolio View of an investment account, follow these steps:

1. Display the Register for the investment account for which you want to see the Portfolio View.

2. Press **Ctrl-R**. Quicken displays the Portfolio View window for the investment account, as shown in figure 16.5

Fig. 16.5

The Portfolio View of an investment account.

```
Print/Acct    View    Shortcuts    Reports    Activities                F1-Help

              Portfolio Valuation for Wal-Mart as of 9/13/93
         Security      Type  Market    Shares       $         $        Market
         Name                Price                Invested   Return    Value

  ▶ Vanguard Fund      Mut  5                0.00      0.00      0.00
    Reno Air           Sto  16 7/8    *      0.00      0.00      0.00
    Sears              Sto  56.675    *↑     0.00      0.00      0.00
    Wal-Mart           Sto  25 1/2    *↑     0.00   2,475.00    35.00
    —Cash—                                                              2,510.00




    Total Market Value                                                  2,510

Wal-Mart
Esc-Main Menu    Ctrl-B Buy   Ctrl-S Sell   F8-Show Detail    F9-All Accounts
                                            Ctrl-N Reinvest   Ctrl-L Other Action
```

Changing the View of Your Investments

Quicken enables you to change the view of your investments so that you can see up to seven different views that each contain different information about your securities. If you choose to view the Portfolio View window by Holdings, for example, Quicken assesses the market value of each security, its estimated income, and its market value as a percentage of the total value of all of your investments in the selected account(s).

To change the view of your investments, access the View menu and choose from the following options:

View Menu Option	What You See
Holdings	Market value of each security, estimated income, and market value as a percentage of the total market value of all investments
Performance	Dollar amount invested in each security, earnings in dollars for each security, and the ROI (return on investment) percentage

View Menu Option	What You See
Valuation	Dollar amount invested in each security, earnings in dollars for each security, and the market value of each security
Price Update	Last price of each security, market value of each security, and the market value change
Summary	Average cost per share, percent gain, and market value of all securities in an account
Gains	Unrealized dollar gain and unrealized percent gain
Detail	Complete transaction history for each security

Working with Mutual Fund Accounts

Using Quicken to monitor a mutual fund investment consists of recording your starting balance and periodically recording changes in the balance due to the purchase of additional shares or the redemption of shares. To put things in perspective, you record the same information that appears on your mutual fund statements. By recording the information in the Quicken Register, however, you can use the information in several calculations that show how you really are doing with your investments.

The first step in working with a mutual fund is to record the initial purchase. To record the initial purchase of a mutual fund, follow these steps:

1. From the Quicken Main Menu, choose Select Account to display the Select Account to Use window.

2. Highlight the mutual fund for which you want to record an initial balance and choose **Enter**. Quicken displays the Create Opening Share Balance window (see fig. 16.6). The easiest way to set up a mutual fund balance is to follow steps 1 through 5. If, however, you want reports that accurately summarize the complete history of a mutual fund investment, skip steps 3 through 5 and enter each of the mutual fund transactions you make.

3. Enter the date you want to begin recording the opening share balance in the Create Opening Balance As Of field.

4. Move the cursor to the Number of Shares field and enter the number of shares that you now own.

Fig. 16.6

The Create
Opening Share
Balance window.

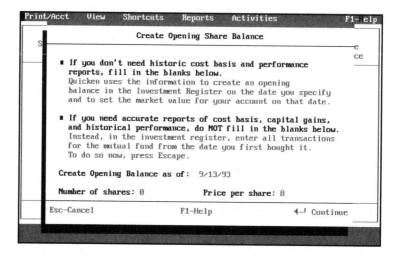

```
Print/Acct    View    Shortcuts    Reports    Activities            F1-Help
                          Create Opening Share Balance
    S                                                                   e
                                                                        ce
        ▪ If you don't need historic cost basis and performance
          reports, fill in the blanks below.
          Quicken uses the information to create an opening
          balance in the Investment Register on the date you specify
          and to set the market value for your account on that date.

        ▪ If you need accurate reports of cost basis, capital gains,
          and historical performance, do NOT fill in the blanks below.
          Instead, in the investment register, enter all transactions
          for the mutual fund from the date you first bought it.
          To do so now, press Escape.

        Create Opening Balance as of:   9/13/93

        Number of shares: 0            Price per share: 0

    Esc-Cancel                  F1-Help                 ←┘ Continue
```

5. Move the cursor to the Price per Share field and enter today's price per share for the mutual fund. You don't need to enter a dollar sign. If the price happens to be a whole number, you don't need to enter a decimal point and two zeros after the price. (You can find price per share information in many local newspapers and in daily financial newspapers, such as *The Wall Street Journal*.)

By default, stock and bond prices use fractions. A stock price may be 7 1/8 and a bond price may be 97 1/8. Other investment prices, such as mutual funds and certificates of deposit, use decimals. A mutual fund price, for example, may be 14.02.

6. When the Create Opening Share Balance window is complete, choose **Enter** or **F10**. Quicken displays the Portfolio window into which you can record investment transactions (see fig. 16.7).

After you set up the initial mutual fund investment balance, you are ready to record a wide variety of transactions: purchases, sales, dividends, and so on. The basic process of recording each type of investment transaction is the same.

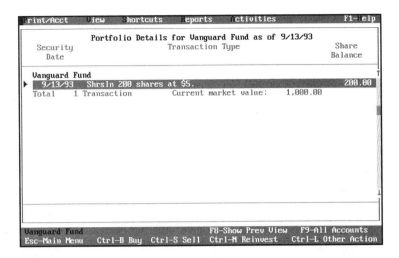

Fig. 16.7
The Portfolio View window with the opening mutual fund balance.

CPA TIP

If you buy mutual fund shares, you should know the difference between *load funds* and *no load funds*. You usually purchase load funds through a broker, who charges an up-front commission that can run from 3 percent to as high as 10 percent. The commission is compensation for the salesperson who placed the order and helped you choose the fund. Even though you may need the help of a broker in selecting a fund and placing an order, you should be aware that you can save yourself the commission (which means you're ahead from the start) by choosing a no-load (no sales commission) mutual fund.

Research shows that on the average, load funds perform no better than no-load funds. Therefore, many investors see no reason to choose a load fund over a no-load fund. To find a no-load mutual fund, flip through *The Wall Street Journal* and look for mutual fund advertisements that specify no load. T. Rowe Price, Vanguard, and Scudder are large investment management companies that offer families of no-load mutual funds.

Using the Investment Register

Now that your investment accounts are set up, you're ready to start using the Investment Register to track the activity in your account. For each real-life transaction that occurs in your investment account, you will enter a transaction in the Investment Register so that all investment activity is accounted for. When you receive dividends on a stock that you own, you must enter a transaction to record the receipt of dividends. When a stock splits so that you now own more shares, you must record the stock split so that the number of shares in your Register reflects the actual number of shares now held.

In previous chapters in this book, you learn about and work with Quicken Registers. You probably use the checking account Register most of all. Investment Registers work in a similar manner, however, the few differences are discussed in this section.

Although you can enter investment transactions directly into the Investment Register, it's much easier to access the appropriate investment form and enter the transaction data in the form. When you save a form by choosing **Enter**, Quicken enters the transaction, in the proper fields, in the next empty transaction line in the Register. Because you use forms to enter transactions, change the view of the Investment Register to Portfolio View before entering transactions.

Entering Investment Transactions

Each time you buy or sell a security in your investment account, receive dividends or interest, buy or redeem Treasury bills, and so forth, you should enter a transaction to reflect the activity. Quicken provides new forms that make it easy to enter investment transaction information. Table 16.1 summarizes the general and specific actions for investment accounts necessary for different investment transactions. These actions are recorded in the Action column of the Register.

Table 16.1 Actions for Investment Accounts	
Action	**Description**
Add/Remove shares	
ShrsIn	Investment shares transferred into the account
ShrsOut	Investment shares transferred out of the account
Buy shares	
Buy	Purchase investment shares with cash in the investment account
BuyX	Purchase investment shares with cash transferred into the account

Action	Description
Capital Gains distr	
CGLong	Cash representing a long-term capital gain received into the account
CGLongX	Cash received from a long-term capital gain transferred out of the account
CGShort	Cash representing a short-term capital gain received into the account
CGShortX	Cash received from a short-term capital gain transferred out of the account
Dividend	
Div	Cash received representing a dividend
DivX	Cash received from a dividend transferred out of the account
Interest	
IntInc	Cash received representing interest income
MargInt	Cash paid on margin loan interest using cash in account
Other transactions	
MiscExp	Pay for expenses, using cash from the account
MiscInc	Receive miscellaneous income
Reminder	Reminder note tied to future date (Billminder reminds you about these notes)
RtrnCap	Cash received that represents return of initial capital investment
StkSplit	Increase or decrease in number of shares because of a stock split
Reinvest	
ReinvDiv	Reinvest cash dividends or other income interest by purchasing more shares
ReinvInt	Reinvest interest by purchasing more shares
ReinvLg	Reinvest long-term capital gains distribution by purchasing more shares
ReinvSh	Reinvest short-term capital gains distribution by purchasing more shares

(continues)

III

Analyzing Your Finances

Table 16.1 Continued

Action	Description
Sell shares	
Sell	Sell investment shares and leave cash received in the investment account
SellX	Sell investment shares, but transfer cash received out of the investment account
Transfer cash	
XIn	Cash transferred into the investment account
XOut	Cash transferred out of the investment account. (If you don't want to record a transfer account, use ShrsIn or ShrsOut, because these options don't require you to enter an account.)

Note

If you're a previous user of Quicken and are comfortable with the Investment Register, you can enter investment transactions directly into the Register as you are used to doing. Entering investment transactions is similar to entering other types of transactions in Quicken Registers.

Buying Securities. When you purchase a security, you enter the transaction in the appropriate investment account in Quicken. If you use a brokerage firm to buy, sell, and manage securities for you, and have an investment account set up for your broker account, enter security purchases in this account. If you buy, sell, and manage securities yourself, you may have an investment account set up for each security that you own. If so, enter purchases of additional shares of a security that you already own in that security's investment account. For purchases of new securities, set up an investment account for the security and then enter the purchase in that account. (You learned how to set up an investment account earlier in this chapter).

To enter a transaction to buy securities, follow these steps:

1. In the Investment Register, press **Ctrl-R** to change to the Portfolio View window.

Fig. 16.8
The Buy Shares form.

2. Choose **Ctrl-B**. Quicken displays the Buy Shares form shown in figure 16.8.

3. Enter the date you purchase the security and then enter the number of shares you are purchasing in the Buy field.

4. Move the cursor to the shares of field. A pop-up menu appears and lists all securities that you have set up. If this is a security you haven't set up, highlight the <New Security> field and choose **Enter**. Quicken displays the Set Up Security window. Complete the Set Up Security window as explained later in this chapter at *Adding a Security*.

5. Enter the price paid per share, and the commission or fees charged to you (if explicit). Quicken calculates the total amount of the purchase. If you don't know the commissions or fees charged, leave the Commission/Fees field blank and enter the total you paid for the shares in the Total Purchases field. Quicken calculates the commissions or fees.

CPA TIP

When you buy a bond after its original date of issue and on any date other than an interest payment date (coupon date), you pay accrued interest to the previous owner of the bond at the time of purchase. (This is because you will receive the full coupon amount, usually six months' interest, as the owner of record at the next payment date.) Enter the accrued interest portion of the purchase price as a separate transaction in the Miscellaneous Expense form.

III

Analyzing Your Finances

6. (Optional) Enter a memo that describes the transaction.

7. Move the cursor to the Source of funds field and highlight your choice from the pop-up menu that appears.

8. When the Buy Shares form is complete, choose **Enter**. Quicken displays the Confirm Buy window and asks you to confirm the transaction by choosing Y. Review the information shown on the screen and if it's correct, choose **Y**. Quicken records the transaction in the Register and returns you to the Portfolio View window. If it's not correct, choose **N** and Quicken returns you to the Buy window for you to make corrections.

CPA TIP

Use the Buy Shares form for purchases of securities with money you already have. If you receive shares of a security by gift, use the Add Shares to Account form. You learn how to enter gifts of securities later in this section.

Selling Securities. When you sell shares of a security, enter the transaction in the investment account where you recorded their purchase. With Quicken 7, you can now identify the shares that you sell if you have purchased shares in different lots. For example, if on 1/1/90 you bought 100 shares of IBM, then on 6/30/91 you bought 200 shares, and then again on 5/15/92 you bought 100 more shares, you have three different lots of shares in IBM stock. If you then sell 50 shares of IBM on 1/1/94, you can choose which shares of the stock you are selling. Quicken keeps track of the number of shares remaining and their cost basis in each lot. If you do not specify which shares you are selling, Quicken uses the FIFO (first in, first out) rule, which assumes that the first shares purchased are the first shares sold.

CPA TIP

To minimize the capital gain resulting from the sale of securities whose market value has increased, identify the highest per share cost basis as the shares you are selling. Suppose that you bought 100 shares of Electronic Arts at $20 and then bought another 100 shares at $25. If you later sell 100 shares for $30 per share, you should specify the second lot (or the shares purchased at $25) as the shares you are selling because the resulting capital gain is less. If you need to generate a capital loss to offset other capital gains in your portfolio, then specify the shares with the lowest per share cost basis.

Fig. 16.9
The Sell Shares form.

To enter a transaction to sell shares of a security, follow these steps:

1. In the Investment Register, press **Ctrl-R** to change to the Portfolio View window.

2. Choose **Ctrl-S**. Quicken displays the Sell Shares form shown in figure 16.9.

3. Enter the date that you sell the security and then enter the number of shares you are selling in the Sell field.

4. Move the cursor to the shares of field. A pop-up menu appears and lists all securities that you have set up. If this is a security you haven't set up, highlight the <New Security> field and choose **Enter**. Quicken displays the Set Up Security window. Complete the Set Up Security window as explained in *Adding a Security*, later in this chapter.

5. Enter the price received per share, and the commission or fees charged to you (if explicit). Quicken calculates the total amount of the purchase. If you don't know the commissions or fees charged, leave the Commission/Fees field blank and enter the total you received for the shares in the Net of Sale. Quicken calculates the commissions or fees.

6. (Optional) Enter a memo that describes the transaction in the Memo field.

7. Move the cursor to the Destination of funds field and highlight your choice from the pop-up menu that appears.

III

Analyzing Your Finances

8. To specify which lots of securities that you are selling, choose **F9**. Quicken displays the Open Lots for (*name*) window as shown in figure 16.10.

Fig. 16.10

The Open Lots for (name) window.

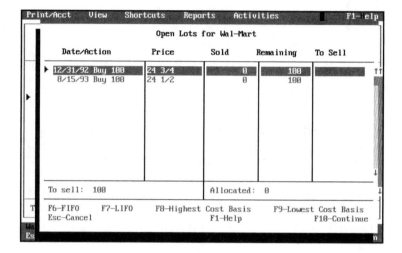

Quicken shows each security lot in the Open Lots for (*name*) window. Each lot is identified by the date purchased, price per share, and the number of shares within each lot that you still own. Highlight the lot you want to sell and enter the quantity in the To Sell field. Quicken keeps track of the number of shares specified as sold in the Allocated field. When the total selected is equal to the number of shares shown in the To Sell field (entered by Quicken from the number of shares sold in the Sell field of the Sell window), you're finished allocating shares to lots. Choose **Enter** to return to the Sell Shares form.

9. When the Sell Shares form is complete, choose **Enter**. Quicken displays the Confirm Sell window and asks you to confirm the transaction by choosing Y. Review the information shown on the screen and if it's correct, choose **Y**. Quicken records the transaction in the Register and returns you to the Portfolio View window. If it's not correct, choose **N** and Quicken returns you to the Sell window for you to make corrections.

CPA TIP

You should try to plan your security transactions to minimize the amount of taxable net capital gain realized each year. If you are in a net capital gain position, consider selling other securities that are in a loss position. You can offset capital gains with capital losses to minimize, or eliminate, your net gain position. Capital losses offset capital gains dollar for dollar. You may not, however, deduct more than $3,000 of capital losses against ordinary income. Be mindful of your net capital loss position before entering into transactions resulting in losses. Capital losses can be carried over to future years.

Recording Investment Income. If you receive dividends, interest income, miscellaneous income, or capital gains distributions from a security, enter the receipt as investment income in the investment register.

To enter a transaction to record investment income, follow these steps:

1. In the Investment Register, press **Ctrl-R** to move to the Portfolio View window.

2. Choose **Ctrl-L** to display the pop-up Other Actions menu. Highlight the Record Income option and choose **Enter**. Quicken displays the Record Income form as shown in figure 16.11.

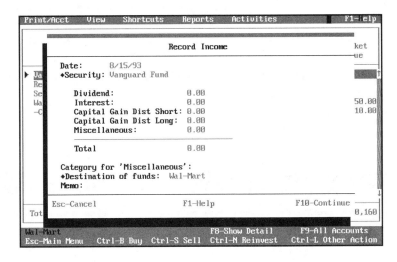

Fig. 16.11
The Record
Income form.

III

Analyzing Your Finances

3. Enter the date the income is received and select the security associated with the income in the Security pop-up list.

4. In the appropriate field, enter the income received as dividends, interest, capital gains (short-term), capital gains (long-term), or miscellaneous income. A capital gains distribution is money paid to shareholders by a mutual fund from the sales by the fund of its underlying securities for more than the security's cost. Distributions received are a distribution of the fund's own capital gains. The fund usually informs you as to the nature of capital gains; long term or short term. Assume a capital gains distribution is long term if the mutual fund does not inform you of the nature of the gains.

5. If you enter an amount in the Miscellaneous field, enter a Category (**Ctrl-C**) in the Category for Miscellaneous field and choose **Enter**.

6. If the income is retained in the current investment account, highlight the name of the current account in the Destination of funds field from the pop-up menu that appears. Otherwise, highlight the account to which the income is to be transferred and choose **Enter**.

7. (Optional) Enter a memo that describes the transaction in the Memo field.

8. When the Record Income form is complete, choose **Enter**. Quicken displays the Confirm Income window and asks you to confirm the transaction by choosing Y. Review the information shown on the screen and if it's correct, choose **Y**. Quicken records the transaction in the Register and returns you to the Portfolio View window. If it's not correct, choose **N** and Quicken returns you to the Sell window for you to make corrections.

Note

Do not enter reinvestment of dividends, interest income, or capital gains distributions in the Record Income form. Instead, use the Reinvest Income form to record the reinvestment of income to purchase additional shares of a security.

Note

If you have interest income from a tax-free bond, set up a category to assign to the tax-free interest. When you receive interest income on the bond, record the interest in the Record Income form as Miscellaneous income. Then assign it to the tax-free category at the Category for Miscellaneous field.

Recording Reinvestments. When you reinvest the dividends, interest income, or capital gains distributions to purchase additional shares of a security, you record a reinvestment transaction as follows:

1. In the Investment Register, press **Ctrl-R** to move to the Portfolio View window.

2. Choose **Ctrl-N** to display the Reinvest Shares form shown in figure 16.12.

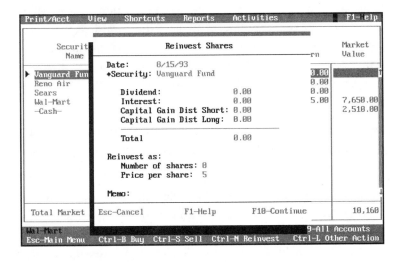

Fig. 16.12
The Reinvest Shares form.
Figure 16.12.

3. Enter the date that additional shares were purchased and choose the security associated with the income in the Security pop-up list.

4. In the appropriate field, enter the dividends, interest income, or capital gains distributions (short or long term) amounts used to purchase additional shares.

5. In the Reinvest as: Number of shares field, enter the number of new shares you are receiving. Quicken calculates the per share price of the new shares based on the information that you enter in the proper field.

III

Analyzing Your Finances

6. (Optional) Enter a memo describing the reinvestment transaction.

7. When the Reinvest Shares form is complete, choose **Enter**. Quicken displays the Confirm Reinvest window and asks you to confirm the transaction by choosing Y. Review the information shown on the screen and if it's correct, choose **Y**. Quicken records the transaction in the Register and returns you to the Portfolio View window. If it's not correct, choose N and Quicken returns you to the Sell window for you to make corrections.

Entering Stock Splits and Stock Dividends. Occasionally, you may receive additional shares of stock if a company declares a stock split. Suppose that the ABC Company declares a stock split that entitles shareholders to one new share for every share that they currently hold. If you own 100 shares, you will be issued 100 new shares, for a total of 200. When you receive additional shares of a security from a stock split, your total cost basis remains the same (because you cannot have a cost basis more than the amount you actually invested); however, the per share price is adjusted downward. In the preceding example, if you paid $10 per share for the 100 shares that you purchased for a total investment of $1,000 ($10 x 100), and you receive 100 shares in a stock split, your total investment is still $1,000, however, your per share cost is now $5 ($1,000/200).

Stock splits are entered based on the ratio of new shares issued to existing shares. In the above example, the ratio is 2:1 (two shares for every one share held).

A stock dividend occurs when a dividend is issued in the form of shares rather than cash. Most stock dividends are nontaxable. For nontaxable stock dividends, enter the transaction as a stock split for the ratio of dividend shares given per shares held. Taxable stock dividends are entered as reinvestment transactions (see the preceding section).

To enter a stock split or nontaxable stock dividend, follow these steps:

1. In the Investment Register, press **Ctrl-R** to move to the Portfolio View window.

2. Choose **Ctrl-L** to display the Other Actions menu.

3. Highlight Stock Split and choose **Enter**. Quicken displays the Stock Split form shown in figure 16.13.

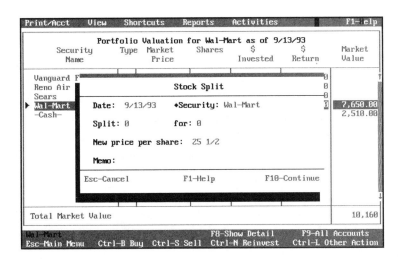

Fig. 16.13
The Stock Split form.

4. Enter the date of the stock split and choose the security to which the stock split relates in the Security pop-up list window.

5. In the Split field, enter the number of new shares you own.

6. In the for field, enter the number of old shares you own. Quicken calculates the new per share price after the split.

7. (Optional) Enter a memo describing the stock split transaction.

8. When the Stock Split form is complete, choose **Enter**. Quicken displays the Confirm Stock Split window and asks you to confirm the transaction by choosing Y. Review the information shown on the screen and if it's correct, choose **Y**. Quicken records the transaction in the Register and returns you to the Portfolio View window. If it's not correct, choose N and Quicken returns you to the Sell window for you to make corrections.

Entering Gifts and Receipts of Securities. When you give shares of stock as a gift, or receive shares of stock as a gift, you must enter these activities in the Investment Register so that it reflects the correct number of shares held. Because there is not a transfer of funds when you give shares or receive shares, you use the Add Shares to Account form and the Remove Shares from Account forms to enter gift transactions. (You learn how to complete the Add Shares to Account form earlier in this chapter in the section, "Entering Opening Share Balances for Securities.")

III

Analyzing Your Finances

Enter a gift of securities the same way that you create an opening balance transaction in a new investment account. When you enter the receipt of shares as a gift, Quicken increases your number of shares without subtracting cash from your investment account or any other bank account. The rules for determining the cost per share of gifted stock are complicated. For now, enter the price per share paid by the giver when the shares were originally purchased. Then consult your tax advisor to determine the cost per share that you should use. (You may be eligible for a "stepped-up basis" that reduces the tax.)

For gifts of stock that you make, follow these steps to record the gift:

1. In the Investment Register, press **Ctrl-R** to move to the Portfolio View window.

2. Choose **Ctrl-L** to display the Other Actions menu.

3. Highlight Move Shares Out and choose **Enter**. Quicken displays the Move Shares Out form shown in figure 16.14.

Fig. 16.14

The Move Shares Out form.

4. Enter the date of the gift and move the cursor to the Move field.

5. In the Move field, enter the number of shares that you are gifting and choose **Enter**.

6. Choose the security you are gifting in the shares of field from the pop-up list that appears.

7. (Optional) Enter a memo describing the transfer of shares. You might want to enter here the recipient's name, the reason for the gift, or any other pertinent information about the gift.

8. When the Move Shares Out form is complete, choose **Enter**. Quicken displays the Confirm Shares Out window and asks you to confirm the transaction by choosing Y. Review the information shown on the screen and if it's correct, choose **Y**. Quicken records the transaction in the Register and returns you to the Portfolio View window. If it's not correct, choose **N** and Quicken returns you to the Sell window for you to make corrections.

Recording Margin Loans. Brokerage firms allow their clients to borrow money to purchase securities. This is called a *margin loan* and the brokerage firm charges interest (margin interest) on the loan as a bank or other lending institution would do. The cash balance in your brokerage account will be negative when you borrow money on margin.

To record interest you pay on the margin loan, access the Expense form by choosing **Ctrl-L** and choosing the Expense from the Other Actions list. Enter the date, choose the security from the pop-up list, enter the amount of interest, and enter **_IntExp** in the Expense category field. (The *_IntExp* category identifies the interest as investment related which is handled a special way for tax purposes.)

Alternatively, you can set up a loan in Quicken to record a margin loan. (Refer to Chapter 10, "Tracking Your Net Worth, Other Assets, and Liabilities" to learn how to set up a loan.) You then transfer the proceeds of the loan to your investment account with the Move Cash In form shown in figure 16.15. Access the Move Cash In form by choosing **Ctrl-L** and choosing Move Cash In from the Other Actions list. Enter the amount of the margin loan and then enter the liability account at the Source of funds field.

When you pay off the margin loan, use the Move Cash Out form (see fig. 16.16). Access the Move Cash Out form by choosing **Ctrl-L** and choosing Move Cash Out from the Other Actions list. Enter the amount of the margin loan and then enter the liability account at the Destination of funds field.

Fig. 16.15
The Move Cash In
form.

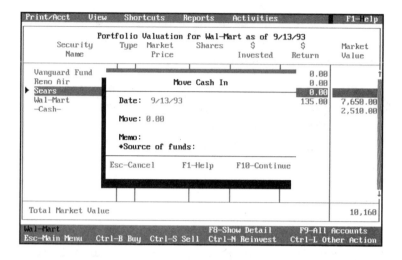

Fig. 16.16
The Move Cash
Out form.

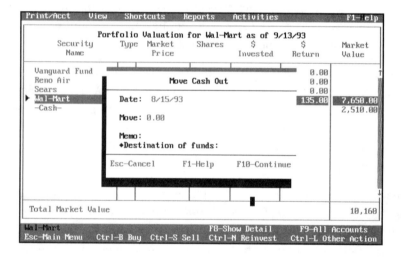

Recording Returns of Capital. A return of capital takes place when you receive money as a total or partial repayment of the money that you invested in a security. A return of capital is similar to a sale, however, the investor is not the initiator of the return of capital. If you invest in a mortgage backed securities, for example, you receive a return of capital when the underlying mortgages are paid off.

To record a return of capital, follow these steps:

1. In the Investment Register, press **Ctrl-R** to move to the Portfolio View window.

2. Choose **Ctrl-L** to display the Other Action menu.

3. Highlight Return of Capital and choose **Enter**. Quicken displays the Return of Capital form shown in figure 16.17.

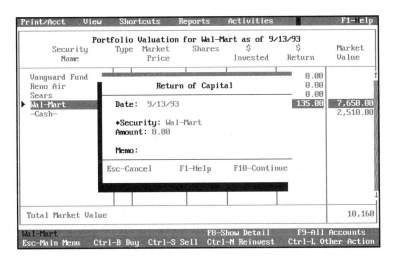

Fig. 16.17
The Return of Capital form.

4. Enter the date you receive payment and then choose the security to which you receive a return of capital in the Security pop-up list.

5. Enter the total or partial repayment amount.

6. (Optional) Enter a memo describing the transaction.

7. When the Return of Capital form is complete, choose **Enter**. Quicken displays the Confirm Return of Capital window and asks you to confirm the transaction by choosing Y. Review the information shown on the screen and if it's correct, choose Y. Quicken records the transaction in the Register and returns you to the Portfolio View window. If it's not correct, choose **N** and Quicken returns you to the Sell window for you to make corrections.

Recording Zero-Coupon Bonds. *Zero-coupon* bonds are bonds that do not pay interest until the bond is sold or matures. Zero-coupon bonds are purchased at a discount, and while you hold the bond, it increases in value due to the accruing of interest. Unfortunately, you must report accrued interest each year as taxable interest (even though you don't receive it). Accrued interest on zero-coupon bonds is reported to you on Form 1099-OID by the issuer.

III

Analyzing Your Finances

To record accrued interest on a zero-coupon bond, enter the amount as interest in the Record Income form (refer to fig. 16.11).

To record the increase in value of a zero-coupon bond, enter the accrued interest amount as a negative amount in the Return of Capital form (refer to fig. 16.17). Negative amounts in the Return of Capital form increase your cost basis in the bond.

Recording Short Sales. A *short sale* is a sale of a security that you do not actually own, but that you borrow from your broker.

CPA TIP

You would make this transaction when you expect the price of the security to decline; however, this is a very risky transaction and should be undertaken with caution. Quicken recognizes short sales as such because you enter the sale of the security before the actual purchase.

To record a short sale, follow these steps:

1. Access the Sell Shares form (refer to fig. 16.9) as explained previously in this chapter.

2. Complete the Sell Shares form for the security you are selling short. Choose **Enter**.

3. When Quicken searches the Investment Register and finds that you do not already own the security, a warning message appears telling you that this transaction is being entered as a short sale. Choose **Enter** to confirm the transaction.

4. Quicken records the short sale in the Investment Register and returns you to the Portfolio View window.

Later, when you actually purchase the security (hopefully at a lower price), enter the purchase in the Buy Shares form (refer to fig. 16.8). Quicken closes the short sale and calculates the gain or loss. Gains from short sales do not appear in the Capital Gains Report but do appear in the Investment Income Report.

> **Caution**
>
> Quicken closes out a short sale before it opens a new position in a security. Therefore, if you record two short sales in the same security before buying the security, you must specify which short sale you are closing when you enter the purchase. Choose **F9** in the Sell Shares form to specify short sale lots. (You learned how to specify lots earlier in this chapter.)

Entering Option Trades. A *stock option* is a contract that represents your right or obligation to buy or sell 100 shares of stock at a specified price (called the strike price) at any time during a specified period. There are two types of options: *calls* and *puts* and. A call option gives you the right to buy shares at a fixed price for a fixed period of time. A put option gives you the right to sell shares at a fixed price for a fixed period of time.

Enter the purchase or sale of options as you would any other security in the Buy Shares and Sell Shares forms. (When you set up the security for an option, use a distinctive name so that you can identify options in your Security List.) When you buy calls, for example, use the Buy Shares form to enter the number of calls and the call price. When you exercise calls (buy the shares), enter the exercise price in the Sell Shares form for the original purchase price of the calls (this transaction clears the option position from your investment account). Then, enter the purchase of the shares in the Buy Shares form. Enter the exercise price as the price per share and include in the call price the fee paid or commission. This adjusts the cost basis of the shares to include the price of the calls.

Recording Miscellaneous Expenses. If you incur expenses in an investment account (perhaps fees charged by your broker) that are paid from your investment account, enter a miscellaneous expense transaction in the account.

To enter a miscellaneous expense in the Investment Register, follow these steps:

1. In the Investment Register, press **Ctrl-R** to move to the Portfolio View window.

2. Choose **Ctrl-L** to display the Other Actions menu.

3. Highlight Expense in the pop-up list and choose **Enter**. Quicken displays the Record Expense form shown in figure 16.18.

III

Analyzing Your Finances

Fig. 16.18

The Record
Expense form.

```
Print/Acct    View    Shortcuts    Reports    Activities          F1-Help

            Portfolio Valuation for Wal-Mart as of 9/13/93
        Security    Type  Market    Shares      $         $        Market
         Name             Price                Invested   Return    Value

    Vanguard
    Reno Air             Record Expense
    Sears
►   Wal-Mart   Date:  9/13/93                                     7,650.00
    —Cash—                                                        2,510.00
               ◆Security: Wal-Mart
               Amount:   0.00
               Expense category:

               Memo:

               Esc-Cancel          F1-Help          F10-Continue


    Total Market Value                                            10,160

Wal-Mart                                F8-Show Detail    F9-All Accounts
Esc-Main Menu   Ctrl-B Buy  Ctrl-S Sell  Ctrl-N Reinvest  Ctrl-L Other Action
```

4. Enter the date the expense is incurred and choose the security associated with the expense in the Security pop-up list.

5. In the Expense category field, enter the amount of the expense and assign a category to the expense transaction.

6. (Optional) Enter a memo describing the expense.

7. When the Expense form is complete, choose **Enter**. Quicken displays the Confirm Expense window and asks you to confirm the transaction by choosing Y. Review the information shown on the screen and if it's correct, choose **Y**. Quicken records the transaction in the Register and returns you to the Portfolio View window. If it's not correct, choose **N** and Quicken returns you to the Sell window for you to make corrections.

Editing and Deleting Investment Transactions. You can edit or delete an investment transaction in the Portfolio View window. You can edit the fields within a transaction or choose Edit from the Shortcuts menu (**Ctrl-E**). Delete a transaction by accessing the Shortcuts menu and choosing the Delete option (**Ctrl-D**).

Memorizing Investment Transactions. If you have transactions that you enter in the Investment Register on a regular basis, you can memorize the transaction to have Quicken save the transaction data in the Memorized

Investment Transaction list. Each time you need to record the transaction, you simply recall it and Quicken enters the memorized transaction in the Investment Register.

> **Note**
>
> Memorizing investment transactions is similar to memorizing regular transactions in the check Register or any other account Register; however, Quicken stores memorized transactions in their own list; the Memorized Investment Transaction list. Regular memorized transactions are stored in the Memorized Transaction list.

To memorize an investment transaction, follow these steps:

1. In the Investment Register, highlight the investment transaction that you want to memorize.

2. Choose the Memorize Transaction option from the Shortcuts menu or press **Ctrl-M**.

3. Quicken displays a message that the transaction is about to be memorized. Choose **Enter** to memorize the transaction.

When you're ready to enter a memorized investment transaction in the Investment Register, follow these steps:

1. In the Investment Register, press **Ctrl-End** to move to the next empty transaction line.

2. Choose Recall Transaction from the Shortcuts menu. Quicken displays the Memorized Investment Transactions list as shown in figure 16.19.

3. Highlight the memorized investment transaction that you want to enter, and choose **Enter**. Quicken enters the memorized transaction in the Investment Register.

4. Review the transaction and choose **Enter** to record the memorized investment transaction in the Register.

III

Analyzing Your Finances

Fig. 16.19

The Memorized
Investment
Transactions list.

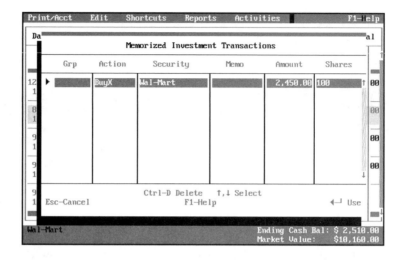

Using Investment Reminders

You can set up investment reminders so that Quicken alerts you to actions that you want to take with regard to your investment portfolio. You can use investment reminders to help you remember when a bond or CD is maturing or to remind you to look at a stock's price to determine if it's time to sell.

You can use the investment reminders in two ways: to make notes in the Investment Register and to remind yourself about certain investment transactions through the Quicken Billminder and Reminder feature. Investment reminders are displayed in the Billminder window each time you start your computer and in the Quicken Reminder window each time that you start Quicken. (Refer to Chapter 20, "Customizing Quicken," to learn more about how Quicken Reminders work.)

> **Note**
>
> Quicken Reminders are associated with the Billminder feature. Quicken Reminders, and therefore investment reminders, do not appear if you have not installed Billminder in Quicken. See Chapter 20, "Customizing Quicken," to learn how to install Billminder if you didn't install it during installation of Quicken 7.

To enter an investment reminder, follow these steps:

1. In the Investment Register, press **Ctrl-R** to move to the Portfolio View window.

2. Choose **Ctrl-L** to display the Other Action menu.

Fig. 16.20
The Reminder
form.

3. Highlight Reminder and choose **Enter**. Quicken displays the Reminder form shown in figure 16.20.

4. Enter the date that you are reminding yourself to take action in your investment account. Quicken displays investment reminders every time that you turn on your computer or start Quicken, regardless of the date that you enter.

5. (Optional) Enter additional information in the Memo field. An entry in this field will generate an entry in the To Do list.

6. In the Description field, type the text of your reminder, using up to 19 characters.

7. In the Display in To Do List field, choose **Y** if you want Quicken to display the message you entered in the Memo field. Choose **N** if you don't want Quicken to display this message.

8. Choose **Enter**. Quicken displays the Confirm Reminder window. Choose **Y** if you want Quicken to enter the investment reminder in the transaction line in the Register. Choose **N** if you don't and Quicken returns you to the Reminder window to make corrections.

Quicken displays investment reminders in the Billminder or Quicken Reminder windows until you turn off the reminder.

9. To turn off an investment reminder, return to the Register by choosing View Register from the View menu.

III

Analyzing Your Finances

10. Choose Delete Transaction from the Edit menu, or press **Ctrl-D**. Quicken displays the OK to Delete Transaction? window. Choose **1** or **Enter** and Quicken deletes the reminder.

Working with the Securities Lists and the Investment Register

In the remaining sections of this chapter, you learn how to define your own investment types and goals; how to update your investment records because of changes in market values; and how to reconcile your investment records with those provided by the mutual fund company, brokerage house, or bank. The last section in the chapter offers tips on investments and investment record keeping that may save you headaches and money.

Working with the Security Lists

When working with the Securities and Cash Account Register, you can add securities to the list that Quicken maintains. Although this approach may be all you ever need, Quicken's Security List option enables you to work with the securities list before entering transactions in the Register. This option is helpful when, for example, you know that over the coming months you will be purchasing shares of several companies. The Security List option saves you time by enabling you to define the securities before you purchase them.

You can access the security list from either the Investment Register or the Portfolio View window by choosing Security List from the **Shortcuts** menu, or press **Ctrl-Y**. Either method produces the Security List window, shown in figure 16.21. From this list, you can add, edit, delete, and print lists of securities. You also can use the security list to access windows that enable you to add, edit, and delete investment types and goals.

Adding a Security. To add a security to the securities list, follow these steps:

1. To display the Security List window from the Investment Register or the Portfolio View window, choose Security List from the **Shortcuts** menu, or press **Ctrl-Y** (refer to fig. 16.21).

2. Highlight the <New Security> line, and then choose **Enter**. Quicken displays the Set Up Security form as shown in figure 16.22.

3. Enter the security name in the Name field. You can enter a maximum of 18 characters.

Fig. 16.21
The Security List window.

Fig. 16.22
The Set Up Security form.

4. (Optional) Enter the security symbol in the Symbol field. (You use security symbols for importing price data from a separate ASCII file—a process described later this the chapter.) You can enter a maximum of 12 characters.

5. To define the investment type, move the cursor to the Type field, highlight the investment type in the pop-up Security Type list, and choose **Enter**.

   Alternatively, if you want to define a new investment type, move the cursor to the Type field, and choose the <Set Up New Type> line from the pop-up Security Type list. Quicken displays the Set Up Security Type window. To define a new security type, describe the security type in the Type field and indicate whether you want the price calibrated in fractional or decimal units. You can have up to 16 security types. Only six security types fit in the Security Type list at one time, so if you use more than six security types, press **PgUp** and **PgDn** or use the scroll bar to see the first and last parts of the type list.

The Type field is optional and has no effect on recordkeeping, other than determining the form in which a security price is shown. The Type field enables you to enter another piece of information about your investment. Quicken provides several investment types that you may find valuable: Bond, CD, Mutual Funds, and Stock. You may, however, have another piece of data that is more important to collect and store. If you are investing money based on the advice of several investment advisors, for example, you can keep track of which advisor suggested which security. Or, if you invest in several different industries, such as utilities, transportation, banking, and computers, you can keep track of the industry of individual issuers.

You also can edit and delete security types. To delete a security type, choose **Ctrl-D** when the security you want to delete is highlighted in the Security Type list. Quicken warns you that a security type is about to be deleted and alerts you if the type is in use. If you want to delete the security type, choose **Enter**. Choose **Esc** if you don't want to delete the security type.

To edit a security type, choose **Ctrl-E** when the security you want to edit is highlighted in the Security Type list. Quicken displays the Edit Security Type window, which you use as described in the earlier paragraphs to change the security type name or the price calibration.

6. To define the investment goal, move the cursor to the Goal field in the Set Up Security window and the pop-up Goal list appears. Highlight your choice from the Goal list, and choose **Enter**. Investment goals describe the purpose of an investment, such as retirement, college fund, down payment, and so on.

To define a new investment goal, move the cursor to the Goal field, and highlight the <Set Up New Goal> line and choose **Enter**. Quicken displays the Set Up Investment Goal window. To define a new investment goal, describe the goal in the Goal field. As is the case with the Security Type list, only six goals fit on the Goal list at one time. Use the PgUp and PgDn keys or the scroll bar to view the first and last parts of the goal list. You can have up to 16 investment goals.

The Goal field is optional and has no effect on the way that you track or monitor a particular investment. Like the Type field, the Goal field enables you to record another piece of information about your investment. Quicken provides several investment goals that you may find valuable. You may, however, have another piece of information that is more important to collect and store. Rather than using the Goal field to describe the investment, for example, you can use the Goal field to categorize how you want to spend the money you make on the investment. In that case, you can choose other goals, such as Retirement, Vacation, Emergency, and so on.

You also can edit and delete investment goals. To delete an investment goal, choose **Ctrl-D** when the goal you want to delete is highlighted on the Goal list. Quicken warns you that a goal is about to be deleted and alerts you if the goal is in use.

To edit a goal (to change the title of a goal), choose **Ctrl-E** when the goal is highlighted in the Goal list. Quicken displays the Edit Investment Goal window, which you use to edit the name. After you edit the goal name, choose **Enter** to return to the Goal list.

7. (Optional) Move the cursor to the Estimated annual income ($ per share) field and enter an amount.

8. Move the cursor to the Display Mode field and choose from the pop-up list one of three options: Always, Open, and Never. See the section *Hiding a Security* later in this chapter for an explanation of these options.

9. When the Set Up Security window is complete, choose **Enter** or **F10**. Quicken adds the new security to the Security List window.

Deleting a Security. Even if you are a long-term investor, you eventually will decide to sell a certain stock or bond and never purchase that security again. Because there is no reason to clutter your securities list, Quicken enables you to delete securities in which you no longer invest.

To delete a security from the Security List window, follow these steps:

1. To display the Security List window from the Investment Register or the Portfolio View window, Security List from the **Shortcuts** menu, or press **Ctrl-Y**.

III

Analyzing Your Finances

2. Highlight the security you want to delete and then choose **Ctrl-D**. Quicken alerts you that the security is about to be deleted permanently. Choose **Enter** to delete the security or choose **Esc** if you don't want to delete the security.

When a security is in use, Quicken presents a message that the security is in use and cannot be deleted at this time.

Editing a Security. Quicken stores six pieces of information about a security in the Securities list: name, symbol, type, goal, estimated annual income, and display mode. Over time, one or more of these elements may change. When changes in any of these items occur, you can edit the security.

To edit a security on the securities list, follow these steps:

1. To display the Security List window from the Investment Register or the Portfolio View window, choose Security List from the Shortcuts menu, or press **Ctrl-Y**.

2. Highlight the security you want to edit, and then choose **Ctrl-E**. Quicken displays the Set Up Security window (refer to fig. 16.22). The process for editing a security mirrors the process of adding a new security. If you have questions about how to complete the Set Up Security window, refer to the steps that describe how to add a new security.

Printing the Security List. To print a list of the securities on the securities list, follow these steps:

1. To display the Security List window from the Investment Register or the Portfolio View window, choose Security List from the Shortcuts menu, or press **Ctrl-Y**.

2. When the Security List window appears, choose **Ctrl-P**. Quicken displays the Print Security List window, which is similar to the Print Register window.

3. Complete the Print Security List window as you would the Print Register window: Indicate which printer setting you want to use, and then choose **Enter**.

Hiding a Security. You also can hide certain securities so that they don't appear on Quicken's investment reports. Suppose that you don't want your children (who print out reports of investments for their college education) to see your retirement savings balance. You can hide the investments that you don't want them to see.

To hide a security, follow these steps:

1. To display the Security List window from the Investment Register or the Portfolio View window, choose Security List from the Shortcuts menu, or press **Ctrl-Y**.

2. Highlight the security you want to hide and press the space bar. Quicken changes the display setting to **Never**.

Follow the same process to "unhide" the security. The space bar acts as a toggle between three choices: **Open**, **Never**, and **Always**. **Always** causes a security to appear in the Update Prices and Market Value window (even if you no longer own the security). **Open** causes a security to appear as long as you own it. **Never** causes the security to never appear in the Portfolio Update Prices window. (You learn about the Portfolio Update Prices window in the next section of this chapter.)

Updating Your Investment Records for Market Values

One of the most common investment recordkeeping activities is tracking the market value of your investments. Quicken provides several tools that enable you to update your investment records and determine the overall market value of your investments.

To record the market value of an investment manually, follow these steps:

1. Access the Register that records the transactions for an investment. (The Register may be a Mutual Fund Account Register or a securities and Cash Account Register, depending on the investment.)

2. Choose Update Prices from the Activities menu, or press **Ctrl-U**. Quicken displays the Portfolio Update Prices screen (see fig. 16.23).

3. Alternatively, from the Portfolio window, choose Update Prices from the View menu. Quicken displays the Portfolio Update Prices screen shown in figure 16.23.

4. Highlight the security whose price you want to update.

5. With the cursor positioned on the Market Price field, enter the current market price. You also can use the + and - keys to increase or decrease the price by 1/8 or .125.

Fig. 16.23

The Portfolio Update Prices screen.

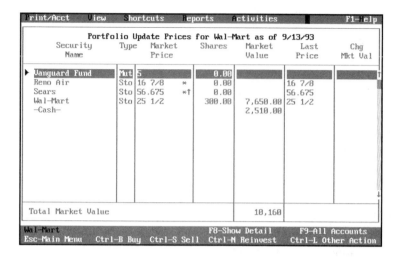

```
 rint/Acct    View    Shortcuts    Reports    Activities              F1- elp

              Portfolio Update Prices for Wal-Mart as of 9/13/93
          Security    Type   Market      Shares    Market     Last      Chg
           Name              Price                  Value     Price    Mkt Val
  ▶ Vanguard Fund     Mut  5                 0.00
    Reno Air          Sto  16 7/8       *    0.00              16 7/8
    Sears             Sto  56.675       *↑   0.00              56.675
    Wal-Mart          Sto  25 1/2          300.00   7,650.00  25 1/2
    -Cash-                                           2,510.00


    Total Market Value                              10,160

  Wal-Mart                            F8-Show Detail      F9-All Accounts
  Esc-Main Menu    Ctrl-B Buy  Ctrl-S Sell   Ctrl-N Reinvest   Ctrl-L Other Action
```

6. Repeat steps 3 and 4 for each security in the Portfolio Update Prices screen. If you want to update investments in your other accounts, choose **F9** to display a complete list of your securities in all investment accounts.

After you record the change in the market price, Quicken asks you whether it is OK to record the new prices and whether the system date is appropriate. If so, choose **Enter**. To change the date, use the + and - keys to change to the date of record. Otherwise, F9 acts as a toggle between the current Investment Register and all accounts. Choose **Esc** to return to the Investment Register from the Portfolio Update Prices screen.

Tip

To view a date other than the current date in the Portfolio Update Prices screen, choose **Go to Date** from the **Shortcuts** menu, or press **Ctrl-G**. Quicken displays the Go to Date window in which you can enter a new date to use to view the market value of securities.

Creating a Price History for a Security. When you record security prices using the Update Prices and Market Value screen, you create a price history for each security.

To see the price history for the currently selected security when you are in the Portfolio Update Prices screen, follow this step:

Choose View Price History from the Shortcuts menu, or press **Ctrl-H**. (You learn about graphing price history in the Chapter 17, "Creating Graphs.") Quicken displays the Price History for: window which lists each of the price updates you entered for the security (see fig. 16.24). The dates shown in the price history are the system dates on which you recorded new security prices.

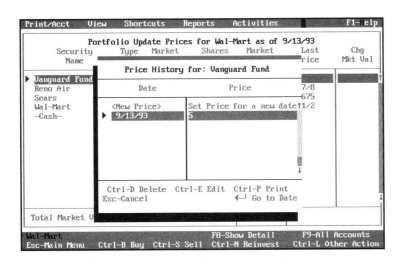

Fig. 16.24

The Price History for: window.

You can request reports that show the market value of your investments on different dates. (Chapter 12, "Creating and Printing Reports," discusses Quicken's reports in detail.) Quicken uses the security prices from the price history to prepare these reports. If you want to see market values as of June 1, for example, Quicken uses the securities prices from the price history that are on or before June 1. For this reason, you may want to update security prices regularly. With the Portfolio Update Prices screen, however, you add a price to the price history for the current date.

To add to the price history a price for some date other than the current system date, choose the <New Price> line in the Price History for: window. Quicken displays the New Price for: window, shown in figure 16.25, with the date filled in as the current system date. Enter the correct date and price. To record the date and price combination, choose **Enter**.

You likewise can edit or delete a price from the price history of a particular investment. Choose **Ctrl-D** to delete and **Ctrl-E** to edit. The changes you make will be reflected on the Portfolio Update Prices screen after you complete the entry of new or updated information.

Importing Stock Prices

You also can import price history data from an ASCII text file. The steps aren't difficult, as long as the ASCII text file looks the way Quicken expects it to. The file needs to contain at least two pieces of information: the security symbol and the price in decimal form. You also can (optionally) include a third piece of information: the date. The three pieces of information that make up a price must be together on a single line, must be separated by

III

Analyzing Your Finances

commas, and must not contain any embedded spaces. Quicken can import the data even if one or more of the elements are enclosed in quotation marks. If the price history does not include a date, Quicken uses a default date that you specify as part of the import operation. All of the following, for example, can be imported as price history data:

TIMEW,105.25,8/06/93

TIMEW,105.25

"TIMEW",105.25,"8/06/93"

"TIMEW","105.25","8/06/93"

Fig. 16.25

The New Price for: window.

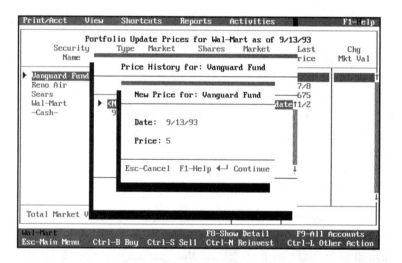

To import price history data, access the Portfolio Update Prices screen and follow these steps:

1. Choose Import from the Print/Acct menu. Quicken asks you to choose between Import Transactions and Import Prices.

2. Highlight **Import Prices** and choose **Enter**. Quicken displays the Import Price Data window (see fig. 16.26).

Fig. 16.26
The Import Price Data window.

3. In the DOS File field, enter the file name and extension of the ASCII text file that contains the price history information you want to import. If the ASCII file is not in the current directory, also specify the drive and directory in which the ASCII file can be found.

4. Move the cursor to the Date field. Enter the date that should be used as the default price date in case a date is not specified in the ASCII text file.

5. When the Import Price Data window is complete, choose **Enter**. Quicken imports the price history data contained in the ASCII text file and updates the appropriate security price histories.

Note

You also can export security prices from the Portfolio Update Prices screen to an ASCII file for use in other programs. To export prices, choose Export from the Print/Acct menu, or press **Ctrl-X**. Quicken enables you to export prices for all securities listed in the Update Prices and Market Value screen or selected securities.

III

Analyzing Your Finances

Reconciling Your Investment Accounts

Quicken enables you to reconcile mutual fund and securities and cash accounts. For the most part, the steps for reconciling these account types parallel the steps for reconciling other Quicken accounts. There are, however, a few minor differences.

In a mutual fund account, you reconcile the shares in the account—not the dollars. The basic process of reconciling a mutual fund account closely resembles the process described in Chapter 9 for reconciling bank accounts.

To reconcile a mutual fund account, follow these steps:

1. From the Investment Register or the Portfolio View window, choose Reconcile from the Activities menu. The Reconcile Mutual Fund Account window appears (see fig. 16.27).

Fig. 16.27

The Reconcile Mutual Fund Account window.

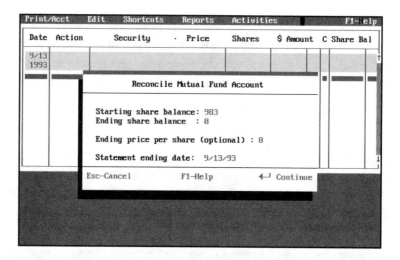

2. Enter the starting and ending shares balance from your mutual fund statement.

3. (Optional) Move the cursor to the Ending Price per Share field and enter the ending share price that appears on your statement. Choose **Enter**.

4. In the Statement Ending Date field, type the ending date that appears on your statement.

5. Choose **Enter** or **F10** when the Reconcile Mutual Fund Account window is complete. Quicken displays the abbreviated Mutual Fund Transaction list with the Reconciliation Summary at the bottom of the screen (see fig. 16.28).

Fig. 16.28

The Mutual Fund Account Transaction list window.

6. Mark the transactions in the transaction list that correspond to the transactions appearing on the mutual fund statement.

   You can mark transactions individually by using the space bar to toggle the * character in the C field. Alternatively, choose **F8** to mark a range of transactions, and Quicken asks you to indicate cleared transactions between two dates. Choosing **F9** toggles between the Reconcile option and the Investment Register that you are reconciling. Quicken records a balance adjustment in the Investment Register to balance the account.

7. When the difference between the Cleared Balance and the Statement Balance equals zero, choose **Ctrl-F10**.

As with the process of reconciling bank accounts, the basic idea is that the difference in shares between your records and the mutual fund's records should stem only from transactions that (for reasons of timing) have not yet appeared on the mutual fund statement.

In a securities and cash account, you reconcile the cash balance. Predictably, this process parallels that for reconciling a bank account. (The cash balance in a securities and cash account also may be a bank account.) To reconcile the cash balance, enter the beginning and ending statement balances in the Rec-

III

Analyzing Your Finances

oncile Investment Account window (see fig. 16.29). Just as for a bank account, mark the transactions that have cleared the cash account, using an abbreviated transaction list (see fig. 16.30). Use the space bar to toggle, and mark transactions that have cleared with an asterisk.

Fig. 16.29

The Reconcile Investment Account window.

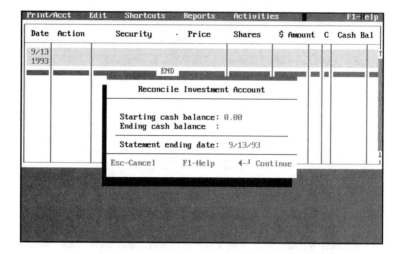

Fig. 16.30

The Securities and Cash Account Transaction list window.

If you want to reconcile an account but have questions about the mechanics of the reconciliation process, refer to Chapter 9, "Reconciling Your Bank Account." The basic principles described in that chapter also apply to investment accounts.

Adjusting Investment Account Balances

If you don't want to reconcile your account, you may want to use the Adjust Balance option that appears on the Activities menu from the Investment Register or the Portfolio View window. If the investment is a securities and cash account, Quicken displays the Adjust Balance menu, which lists options for adjusting the cash balance or the share balance. Choose the balance you want to adjust. Figure 16.31 shows the Adjust Cash Balance window.

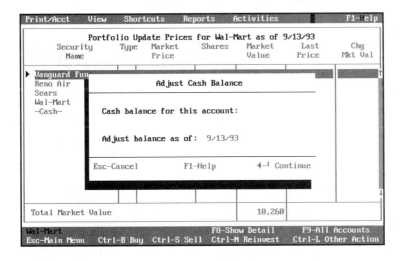

Fig. 16.31
The Adjust Cash Balance window.

To update the cash balance in the account, follow these steps:

1. Access the Adjust Cash Balance window.

2. In the first field, enter the current cash account balance.

3. Move the cursor to the Adjust Balance As Of field and enter the date for which the cash adjustment transaction should be recorded.

4. When the Adjust Cash Balance window is complete, choose **Enter** or **F10** to update the cash balance.

Figure 16.32 shows the Adjust Share Balance window accessed by choosing the Adjust Share Balance option from the Adjust Balance menu.

III

Analyzing Your Finances

Fig. 16.32

The Adjust Share Balance window.

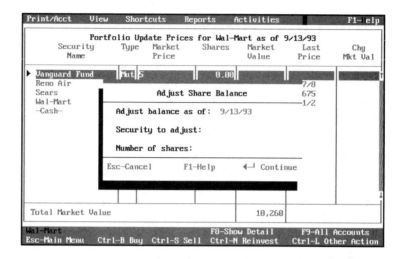

To update the share balance for a specific security, follow these steps:

1. At the Adjust Share Balance window, enter the date for which the share adjustment transaction should be recorded in the Adjust Balance As Of field.

2. Move the cursor to the Security to Adjust field and enter the name of the security whose share balance needs to be adjusted. You also can press **Ctrl-Y** to select the security from the security list.

3. Move the cursor to the Number of Shares field and enter the number of shares of the security as of the date in the Adjust Balance As Of field.

4. When the Adjust Share Balance window is complete, choose **Enter** or **F10** to update the share balance.

If the investment is a mutual fund account, Quicken does not display the Adjust Balance menu. Quicken displays the mutual fund version of the Adjust Share Balance window (see fig. 16.33).

Mutual funds sometimes reinvest the interest on dividend income. Accordingly, with each interest or dividend payment, you may need to update or adjust the share balance.

Fig. 16.33

The mutual fund version of the Adjust Share Balance window.

To update the share balance for a specific mutual fund security, follow these steps:

1. In the Adjust Share Balance window, enter the date for which the share balance adjustment transaction should be recorded.

2. Move the cursor to the Number of Shares field. Enter the current share balance of the mutual fund.

3. When the Adjust Share Balance window for the mutual fund is complete, choose **Enter** or **F10** to update the share balance.

Although the Adjust Balance option enables you to forgo the work of reconciling an account, this option has disadvantages. As Chapter 9 points out, the purposes of reconciling include catching errors, recording forgotten transactions, and discovering fraudulent transactions. By not reconciling an account, you miss out on significant benefits.

Tips on Investments and Investment Recordkeeping

Earlier sections of this book explained the procedural details of using Quicken; this section covers three additional tips.

III

Analyzing Your Finances

First, you should know that Quicken applies the *first-in, first-out* (often called FIFO) method of recordkeeping. This means that when you sell shares of Apple Computer, for example, Quicken assumes that the shares you sell are the first shares that you bought.

The FIFO assumption conforms with Internal Revenue Service regulations. The problem with FIFO is that often the first shares you bought were the least expensive. This means that when you calculate the actual taxable gain by subtracting the original purchase price from the sales price, you end up calculating the largest possible gain and, as a result, you incur higher income taxes.

You can use another method, called *specific identification*, to record the sales and purchases of investments. Specific identification requires that you record all purchases of a particular stock as different investments, or lots. When you sell shares of Apple Computer, for example, you actually sell the shares from a specific lot. The obvious tax-saving opportunity results from picking the lot with the highest purchase price, because doing so minimizes your gain or maximizes your loss. See your tax advisor for specific details. Quicken 7 helps you by keeping your investments in separate lots.

Second, if you record meticulously the transactions that affect an investment, you can use one of Quicken's investment reports (the performance report) to measure the actual rate of return an investment produces. Although most individual investors are not accustomed to measuring the performance of their investments, you will find doing so an invaluable exercise. Too often, individual investors don't get to measure the performance of stocks a broker recommends, of a mutual fund an advertisement touts, or the bonds a financial planner suggests. But with the Quicken performance report, which is described in Chapter 12, you have a convenient way to calculate precisely how well or how poorly an investment has performed. Investment performance information can help you make better investment decisions.

Finally, there is more to investing than just recordkeeping. Despite the fact that Quicken provides an excellent recordkeeping tool, understanding how the tool works is not the same as understanding investments. To better understand investments, read *A Random Walk Down Wall Street*, by Burton G. Malkiel, a Princeton economics professor. You should be able to find the most recent edition in any good bookstore.

Summary

This chapter describes how to monitor your investments using Quicken's investment accounts. The chapter lists the steps for tracking mutual funds with Quicken and the steps for tracking other investments, such as stocks, bonds, and certificates of deposit. You also learn how to import stock prices from ASCII files and how to reconcile your investment accounts.

In the next chapter, you learn about graphing. You learn how Quicken analyzes your financial data and puts it into graph format so that you can view your income and expenses, assets and liabilities, actual and budget amounts, and your investments on a relative basis.

III

Analyzing Your Finances

Chapter 17

Creating Graphs

In previous chapters, you learn how to enter transactions and write checks, track your assets and liabilities, create budgets, and monitor your investments. In Chapter 12, "Creating and Printing Reports," you learn how to produce reports so that you can analyze the information and data you enter in Quicken. Creating reports is an excellent way to summarize your financial information, but not the only way. With Quicken, you can create on-screen graphs to show relationships between your income and expenses, assets and liabilities, actual and budget amounts, and individual investments and total portfolio. With Quicken 7, you also can print these graphs if you have a graphical printer. If you have an installed graphics card, you can create any one of 18 different graphs. You can create graphs in just seconds based on the transactions you enter and categorize, the account balances, budgeted data, and investment transactions entered.

In the case of your finances, it sometimes is easier to assess your financial situation when you can see a graph (picture) that shows an overview or summary of your finances. Graphs show you, for example, the relationship of individual expense categories to your total expenditures. You therefore can quickly see what percentage each individual expense category is to your total expenses. Although reports show you information in a format that is useful in financial analysis, graphs are a visual means for analysis that sometimes have more effect than a list of categories or accounts in a report.

Overview of Quicken Graphs

Depending on the type of graph you select to create, Quicken displays the following graph formats:

In this chapter, you learn how to do the following:

- Identify each graph format that Quicken creates (double-bar graphs, line graphs, pie charts, and stacked bar graphs)

- Set up Quicken to display and print graphs

- Create income and expense, net worth, budget, and investment graphs

- Filter graph transactions

III

Analyzing Your Finances

- Double-bar graphs

- Line graphs

- Pie charts

- Stacked bar graphs

Quicken decides which graph format to create when you select a graph type.

Each of these graph formats compares financial information or shows information in a different way. In the following sections, you learn about the different graph formats and what they represent. Each graph you create includes a *legend* (the box located in the upper right corner of the graph screen) that tells you what each line, bar, or piece of pie represents.

Double-Bar Graphs

Quicken creates *double-bar graphs*, like the one you see in figure 17.1, to compare data. The items the graphs compare appear as bars and are shown on the horizontal axis, side by side. The dollar amounts or values of the items being compared are shown on the vertical axis. In figure 17.1, you see the comparison of income to expenses. Income for the month is about $6,000, and is greater than expenses for the month, which are about $3,000. The box in the upper right corner of the graph shows that one bar in the graph represents income and the other represents expenses.

Fig. 17.1
A sample double-bar graph.

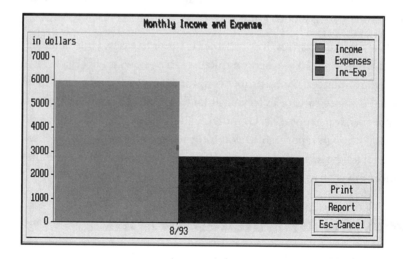

Line Graphs

The *line graph* shows net values over time. Net values result when you select graph options, such as monthly assets and liabilities, monthly income and expenses, and monthly budget and actual. For some graph formats, Quicken doesn't create line graphs as a separate graph, but incorporates them into stacked bar graphs. Figure 17.2 is an example of a line graph that shows the price history of a security.

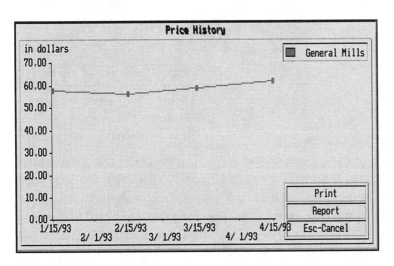

Fig. 17.2
A sample line graph.

III

Analyzing Your Finances

CPA TIP

You can use line graphs to analyze trends over a period of time. If, for example, you are *overspending* (your expenses are greater than your income on a monthly basis), the line graphs show the trend of overspending over a specified period of time. Perhaps in January the deficit is $200, in February it's $300, and in March it's up to $500. A line graph shows an upward moving line that quickly tells you your overspending problem is not dissipating but rather accelerating. News presented to you in this format, hopefully, will cause you to act to solve the problem.

Pie Charts

Pie charts show the composition of each individual item to the whole. Pie charts show you what the composition of an individual item is to the total items. If you graph your income composition, for example, you see the percentage your salary contributes to your total income from all sources. You can use a pie chart like the one shown in figure 17.3 to help you determine whether you are spending too much in a particular expense category or earning too little as compared to your total income.

Fig. 17.3
A sample pie chart
graph.

Stacked Bar Graphs

A *stacked bar graph* shows trends (as does the line graph). Stacked bar graphs
show two trends simultaneously (see fig. 17.4). First, the graph shows the
composition of items in the stacked bar, such as the composition of total
expenses. In this case, each income item is represented by a different color or
pattern within each bar. That's why this graph format is called *stacked bar*—it
stacks the items that comprise the whole in a single bar. Stacked bar graphs
also show how items are comprised to the whole, over time. In figure 17.4,
you see how the composition of expense changes over a period of eight
months.

Fig. 17.4
A sample stacked
bar graph.

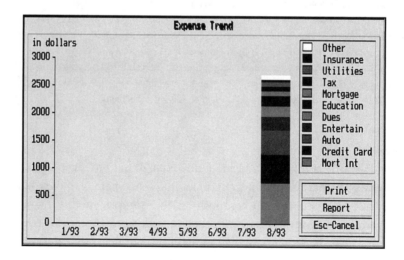

Setting Up Quicken to Display Graphs

Before you can create and display graphs with Quicken, you must tell Quicken the graphics driver that you are using. If you forget to set up Quicken for your graphics driver, the first time you attempt to create a graph, Quicken displays the appropriate window for you to select the graphics driver you are using.

To set up Quicken to display graphs, follow these steps:

1. From the Quicken Main Menu, choose Set **P**references. Quicken displays the Set Preferences menu.

2. From the Set Preferences menu, choose **S**creen Settings. Quicken displays the Screen Settings menu.

3. From the Screen Settings menu, choose Screen **G**raphics. Quicken displays the Graphics Drivers Options window you see in figure 17.5.

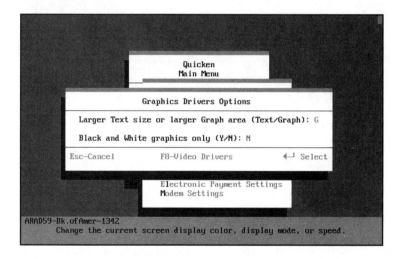

Fig. 17.5
The Graphics Drivers Options window.

You first must tell Quicken whether to make the text in a graph larger or the graph area larger.

4. Choose **T** to make the text larger or **G** to make the graph area larger, and then choose **Enter**. Quicken enables you to change this setting from the graph window you use to create a graph.

If you have a color monitor but want to show graphics in black and white only, choose **Y** from the Black and White Graphics Only field. When you display graphics in black and white, Quicken uses patterns rather than colors to distinguish different bars, lines, or pie pieces in graphs. Choose **N** if you want Quicken to display graphics in color.

5. Choose **F8** to display the Select Graphics Driver window shown in figure 17.6. Highlight the graphics driver you have installed, and then choose **Enter** to return to the Graphics Drivers Options window.

Fig. 17.6
The Select
Graphics Driver
window.

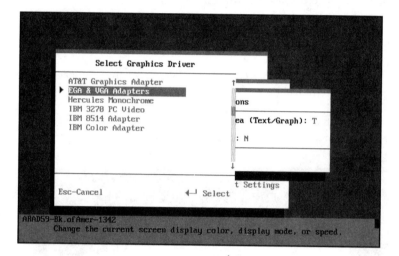

6. When the Graphics Drivers Options window is complete, choose **Enter** or **F10**. Quicken returns to the Screen Settings menu. Press **Esc** twice to return to the Main Menu.

Creating Graphs

This section explains how to create and display graphs, in general. You learn how to access the View Graphs menu, select a graph option, display the graph, and remove the graph from your screen. The next section in this chapter explains how to create each individual graph to analyze your income and expenses, net worth, budget versus actual data, and investments.

To create a graph, follow these steps:

1. From the Quicken Main Menu, choose View **G**raphs.

Quicken displays the View Graphs menu shown in figure 17.7.

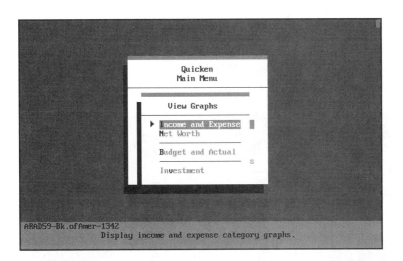

Fig. 17.7
The View Graphs menu.

2. Highlight the type of graph you want to create and choose **Enter**.

   Quicken displays the Income and Expense Graphs menu, the Net Worth Graphs menu, the Budget and Actual Graphs menu, or the Investment Graphs menu. Figure 17.8 shows the Income and Expense Graphs menu.

3. Highlight the graph option you want and press **Enter**. From the Income and Expense Graphs menu you see in figure 17.8, for example, you can choose one of five graph options: Monthly Income and Expense, Income Composition, Income Trend, Expense Composition, and Expense Trend.

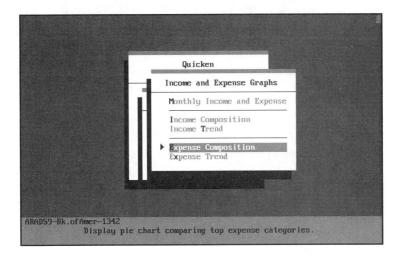

Fig. 17.8
The Income and Expense Graphs menu.

III

Analyzing Your Finances

After you choose a graph option, Quicken displays the graph window labeled with the option you selected. In figure 17.9, Quicken displays the Income Composition window that appears if you chose Income Composition from the Income and Expense window.

Fig. 17.9

The Income Composition window.

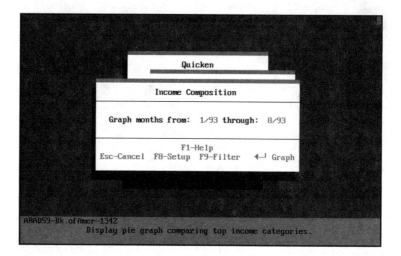

4. In the graph window, enter the dates to which you want to limit transactions. If you want to see only your income composition for the first six months of the year, for example, enter **1/93** in the Graph Months From field and **6/93** in the Through field. You can use the + (plus) and - (minus) keys to change the day or month by one.

Other graph types you select present other graph settings such as whether to include unrealized gains; the date to use to graph balances as of; whether to show only income categories, only expense categories, or both; or whether to display balances by security, account, type, or goal. Graph settings are explained in more detail later in this chapter when you learn to create each type of Quicken graph.

5. (Optional) From the graph window, choose **F8-Setup** to display the Graphics Drivers Options window. Here, you can tell Quicken whether to make the text in a graph larger or the graph area larger. Choose **T** to make the text larger or **G** to make the graph area larger. You probably will not need to set this option until after you display a graph to see whether the text or graph area needs to be adjusted.

If you have a color monitor but want to show graphics in black and white only, choose **Y** from the Black and White Graphics Only field. When you display graphics in black and white, Quicken uses patterns rather than colors to distinguish different bars, lines, or pie pieces in graphs. Choose **N** if you want Quicken to display graphics in color.

If you haven't already set up Quicken for your graphics driver, from the Graphics Drivers Options window, you can choose **F8-Video Drivers** to display the Select Graphics Driver window. Highlight a graphics driver and choose **Enter** to return to the Graphics Drivers Options window.

When the Graphics Drivers Options window is complete, choose **Enter** or **F10** to return to the graph window.

6. (Optional) If you want to filter graph transactions, choose **F9-Filter** from the graph window. *Filtering transactions* enables you to restrict the transactions included in the graph; to include certain categories and classes; to include the current account, all accounts, or select accounts; and so on. You learn about filtering graph transactions later in this chapter.

7. When the graph window is complete, choose **Enter** or **F10** to display the graph on-screen.

8. When you are finished reviewing the graph, choose **Esc** to remove the graph from your screen and return to the graph window used to create the graph.

Creating Income and Expense Graphs

You can use *income* and *expense graphs* to analyze the items that make up your total income, expense items that make up your total expenses, spending habits, and your spending and earning trends. You also can use these graphs to compare your total income to expenses. Following are common questions you can answer by creating income and expense graphs:

- By what margin is my income more than my expenses?

- Am I overspending?

- What sources make up my total income?

- Has my income increased over time?

- What expenses make up my total expenses?

- Have my expenses increased or decreased over time?

III

Analyzing Your Finances

After you create each income and expense graph, you will be able to answer these questions, and more.

Quicken provides five different graphs you can create to analyze your income and expenses:

Graph	Description
Monthly Income and Expense	A bar graph of your monthly income and monthly expenses over a specified period of time.
Income Composition	A pie chart showing each individual income source as a pie piece that makes up your total income (the pie) over a specified period of time.
Income Trend	A stacked bar graph of your monthly income categories over a specified period of time.
Expense Composition	A pie chart (like the Income Composition graph) showing each expense that makes up your total expenses over a specified period of time.
Expense Trend	A stacked bar graph of your monthly expense categories over a specified period of time.

Income and expense graphs are created from the categories you assign to transactions. Subcategories are not included in graphs. If you assigned categories to transactions, Quicken includes the subcategory totals within the categories it graphs.

This section shows you how to create each type of graph. You can change the transactions Quicken includes in graphs by using the Filter option (see *Filtering Graph Transactions*, later in this chapter).

The Monthly Income and Expense Graph. The *Monthly Income and Expense graph* helps you to determine how your income compares to your expenses, on a monthly basis, over time.

To create a Monthly Income and Expense graph, follow these steps:

1. Choose Monthly Income and Expense from the Income and Expense menu.

   Quicken displays the Monthly Income and Expense window, which is similar to the Income Composition window shown in figure 17.9.

2. In the Graph Months From field, type the starting month and year you want the graph to cover. Type the ending month and year in the

Through field. You can use the + (plus) and - (minus) keys to change the dates by one month at a time.

3. Choose **Enter** or **F10** to display the Monthly Income and Expense graph.

The Monthly Income and Expense graph compares income and expenses over time and tells you if you aren't earning enough to cover expenses or vice versa (spending too much in relation to your income).

The Income Composition Graph. The *Income Composition graph* helps you see from what sources your total income is derived.

To create an Income Composition graph, follow these steps:

1. Choose Income Composition from the Income and Expense menu. Quicken displays the Income Composition window.

2. In the Graph Months From field, type the starting month and year you want the graph to cover. Type the ending month and year in the Through field. You can use the + (plus) and - (minus) keys to change the dates by one month at a time.

3. Choose **Enter** or **F10** to display the Income Composition graph, which is similar to the graph shown in figure 17.3.

The Income Composition graph, displayed as a pie chart, is fairly self-explanatory. From this graph, you can see the relative contribution of each income source to your total income. Perhaps you see that your salary is the greatest contributor to your income or that you have no sources of income other than your salary. If that's the case, you may want to find a way to supplement your income to hedge against job loss or a layoff.

The Income Trend Graph. The *Income Trend graph* is a stacked bar graph that shows you two things: the composition of your income and the growth trend of your income over time.

To create an Income Trend graph, follow these steps:

1. Choose Income Trend from the Income and Expense menu. Quicken displays the Income Trend window.

2. In the Graph Months From field, type the starting month and year you want the graph to cover. Type the ending month and year in the Through field. You can use the + (plus) or - (minus) key to change the dates by one month at a time.

III

Analyzing Your Finances

3. Choose **Enter** or **F10** to display the Income Trend graph, which is similar to the graph shown in figure 17.4.

The Income Trend graph shows how your income is comprised and your income trend over time. The composition of your income is represented by each stacked bar that appears in the graph. Each item of income is shown in a different color or pattern within the bar. With the Income Trend graph, you easily can see your income patterns over a specified period of time. If you see that your income is decreasing, you should investigate the reasons. The stacked bar will show you if the decrease is a result of a salary decrease, declining investment income, such as interest, dividends, and so on.

The Expense Composition Graph. Use the *Expense Composition graph* to see what items make up your total expenses and the relationship of each expense to the total.

To create an Expense Composition graph, follow these steps:

1. Choose Expense Composition from the Income and Expense Graphs menu. Quicken displays the Expense Composition window.

2. In the Graph Months From field, type the starting month and year you want the graph to cover. Type the ending month and year in the Through field. You can use the + (plus) and - (minus) keys to change the dates by one month at a time.

3. Choose **Enter** or **F10** to display the Expense Composition graph, which is similar to the graph shown in figure 17.3.

The Expense Composition graph shows each individual expense as it comprises your total expenses. From this graph, you can see how you are spending your money. This is a quick way to see just which expenses are out of line with other expenses. You may find that some *discretionary* expenses (expenses that are not fixed, such as your mortgage, rent, insurance premiums, and so on) make up a greater portion of your total expenses than they should. These types of expenses are the easiest to modify—you can eat out less, rent a movie rather than going to the theater, buy fewer clothes, watch for sales, and so on.

The Expense Trend Graph. An *Expense Trend graph* shows you the trend in your spending over time. You can see if spending is increasing at a rapid, steady, or declining rate.

To create an Expense Trend graph, follow these steps:

1. Choose Expense Trend from the Income and Expense menu. Quicken displays the Expense Trend window.

2. In the Graph Months From field, type the starting month and year you want the graph to cover. Type the ending month and year in the Through field. You can use the + (plus) and - (minus) keys to change the dates by one month at a time.

3. Choose **Enter** or **F10** to display the Expense Trend graph.

The Expense Trend graph shows how your expenses are comprised and your spending trend over time. The composition of your expenses is represented by each stacked bar that appears in the graph. Each expense category is shown in a different color or pattern within the bar. With the Expense Trend graph, you easily can see your spending patterns over a specified period of time. If you see that your spending is increasing, you should investigate the reasons. The stacked bar will show you if the increase is a result of a fixed expense increase (like an increased mortgage payment due to a variable-rate change) or an increase in discretionary expenses such as clothing, entertainment, dining out, and so on.

Creating Net Worth Graphs

You can use *net worth graphs* to analyze the assets that make up your total assets, the liabilities that make up your total liabilities, and how your assets and liabilities have changed over time. You also can use net worth graphs to compare your total assets to your total liabilities. Following are common questions you can answer by creating net worth graphs:

- Do I have more assets than liabilities?

- How has my *net worth* (assets minus liabilities) changed over time?

- What assets make up my total assets?

- Have my assets increased over time?

- What liabilities make up my total liabilities?

- Have my liabilities increased or decreased over time?

After you create each net worth graph, you will be able to answer these questions, and more.

III

Analyzing Your Finances

Net worth graphs are created from the account balances in your Quicken file.

This section shows you how to create each type of graph. You can change the transactions Quicken includes in graphs by using the Filter option. (For more information, see *Filtering Graph Transactions*, later in this chapter,)

Quicken provides five different graphs you can create to analyze your net worth:

Graph	Description
Monthly Assets and Liabilities	A bar graph of your monthly asset balances and monthly liability balances over a specified period of time.
Asset Composition	A pie chart that shows each individual asset as a pie piece that makes up your total assets (the pie) as of a specified date.
Asset Trend	A stacked bar graph of your total asset balances, by month, over a specified period of time.
Liability Composition	A pie chart (like the Asset Composition graph) that shows each liability that makes up your total liabilities as of a specified date.
Liability Trend	A stacked bar graph of your total liability balances, by month, over a specified period of time.

The Monthly Assets and Liabilities Graph. The Monthly Assets and Liabilities graph compares your total assets to your total liabilities over time.

To create the Monthly Assets and Liabilities graph, follow these steps:

1. Choose Monthly Assets and Liabilities from the Net Worth Graphs menu shown in figure 17.10.

   Quicken displays the Monthly Assets and Liabilities window shown in figure 17.11.

2. In the Graph Ending Balances for Months field, type the starting month and year you want the graph to cover. Type the ending month and year in the Through field. You can use the + (plus) and – (minus) keys to change the dates by one month at a time.

3. Move the cursor to the Include Unrealized Gains field. Choose **N** if you don't want Quicken to include the unrealized gains and losses from changes in the value of your securities in your investment accounts. Keep the setting at **Y** if you do want to include unrealized gains and losses in the graph.

4. Choose **Enter** or **F10** to display the Monthly Assets and Liabilities graph (see fig. 17.12).

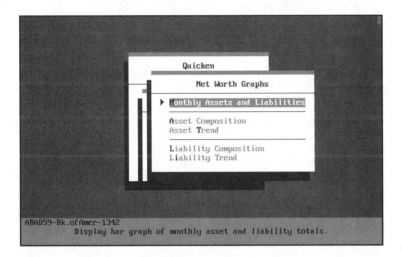

Fig. 17.10
The Net Worth Graphs menu.

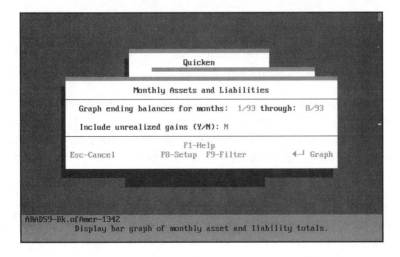

Fig. 17.11
The Monthly Assets and Liabilities window.

Fig. 17.12
The Monthly
Assets and
Liabilities graph.

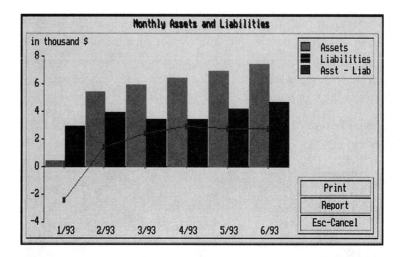

The Monthly Asset and Liabilities graph compares assets and liabilities over time. Hopefully, you will see that your assets are greater than your liabilities so that you have a positive net worth. If your liabilities are greater than your assets, you have a negative net worth and will find it difficult to decrease your liabilities without some future infusion of income or other funds.

The Asset Composition Graph. The *asset composition graph* is a pie chart that shows how your assets are composed and the relationship of each asset to the total assets.

To create an asset composition graph, follow these steps:

1. Choose Asset Composition from the Net Worth Graphs menu. Quicken displays the Asset Composition window.

2. In the Graph Balances As Of field, type the date you want to use to show balances. Quicken uses this date to look for account balances and uses the balances found on that particular date in the graph. You can use the + (plus) and - (minus) keys to change the dates by one day at a time.

3. Move the cursor to the Include Unrealized Gains field. Choose **N** if you don't want Quicken to include the unrealized gains and losses from changes in the value of your securities in your investment accounts. Keep the setting at **Y** if you do want to include unrealized gains and losses in the graph.

4. Choose **Enter** or **F10** to display the asset composition graph.

The asset composition graph, displayed as a pie chart, is fairly self-explanatory. From this graph, you can see the relative contribution of each of your assets to your total assets.

The Asset Trend Graph. Hopefully, the value of your assets grows over time. Creating an *Asset Trend graph* helps you see if your assets are increasing, remaining steady, or decreasing. You also can see how your assets are comprised.

To create an Asset Trend graph, follow these steps:

1. Choose Asset Trend from the Net Worth Graphs menu. Quicken displays the Asset Trend window.

2. In the Graph Ending Balances for Months field, type the starting month and year you want the graph to cover. Type the ending month and year in the Through field. You can use the + (plus) and - (minus) keys to change the dates by one month at a time.

3. Move the cursor to the Include Unrealized Gains field. Choose **N** if you don't want Quicken to include the unrealized gains and losses from changes in the value of your securities in your investment accounts. Keep the setting at Y if you do want to include unrealized gains and losses in the graph.

4. Choose **Enter** or **F10** to display the Asset Trend graph (see fig. 17.13).

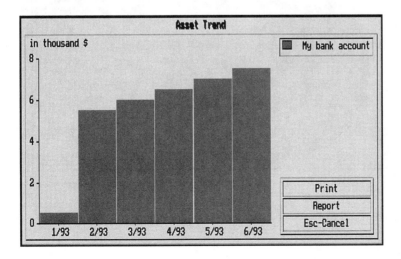

Fig. 17.13
The Asset Trend graph.

The Asset Trend graph shows how your assets are comprised and your Asset Trend over time. The composition of your assets is represented by each stacked bar that appears in the graph. Each asset is shown in a different color or pattern within the bar. With the Asset Trend graph, you easily can see how the value of your assets changes over time.

The Liability Composition Graph. To see how your liabilities are comprised, you can create a *Liability Composition graph* displayed as a pie chart. With this graph, you see the relationship between each of your liabilities to your total liabilities.

To create a Liability Composition graph, follow these steps:

1. Choose Liability Composition from the Net Worth Graphs menu. Quicken displays the Liability Composition window.

2. In the Graph Balances As Of field, type the date you want to use to show balances. Quicken uses this date to look for account balances and uses the balances found on that particular date in the graph. You can use the + (plus) and - (minus) keys to change the dates by one day at a time.

3. Choose **Enter** or **F10** to display the Liability Composition graph (see fig. 17.14).

Fig. 17.14
The Liability Composition graph.

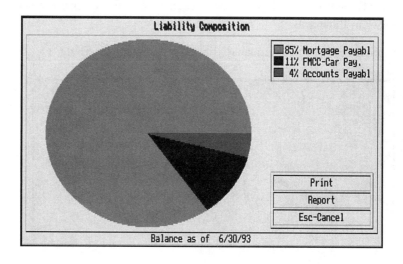

The Liability Composition graph shows each individual liability as it comprises your total liabilities.

The Liability Trend Graph. The *liability trend graph* not only shows how your liabilities are comprised, but also how your liabilities have increased or decreased over time.

To create a liability trend graph, follow these steps:

1. Choose Liability Trend from the Net Worth Graphs menu. Quicken displays the Liability Trend window.

2. In the Graph Ending Balances for Months field, type the starting month and year you want the graph to cover. Type the ending month and year in the Through field. You can use the + (plus) and - (minus) keys to change the dates by one month at a time.

3. Choose **Enter** or **F10** to display the liability trend graph.

The liability trend graph shows how your liabilities are comprised and any increases or decreases in liabilities over time. The composition of your liabilities is represented by each stacked bar that appears in the graph. Each liability account is shown in a different color or pattern within the bar. With the Liability Trend graph, you easily can see how your debts fluctuate over a specified period of time. If you see that your liabilities are increasing, you should investigate the reasons. The stacked bar will show you if the increase is a result of new loan (such as a new car loan or a home improvement loan) or increased credit card debt.

Creating Budget versus Actual Data Graphs

You can use net budget and actual graphs to compare your actual income and expenses to your budgeted income and expenses. The budget reports you learn how to create in Chapter 12 also tell you how your budget compares to your actual income and expense. The budget and actual graphs provide a visual comparison that enables you to quickly assess how successful (or unsuccessful) you are in sticking to your budget.

You can use budget and actual graphs to compare actual amounts to budgeted amounts, identify areas where you are over budget, identify areas where you are under budget, show the relative contribution of budgeted amounts to your whole budget, and see how your budget has changed over a period of time.

III

Analyzing Your Finances

Following are common questions you can answer by creating budget and actual graphs:

■ Am I sticking to my budget?

■ How much more can I spend and still stay within my budget?

■ In which areas am I over budget?

■ In which areas am I under budget?

■ What income and expense items make up my budget?

■ How has my budget changed over time?

After you create each budget and actual graph, you will be able to answer these questions, and more.

Quicken provides five different graphs you can create to analyze your budget versus actual data:

Graph	Description
Monthly Budget and Actual	A bar graph of your monthly budget and monthly budget categories over a specified period of time.
Categories Over Budget	A double-bar graph of only the categories that were over budget over a specified period of time.
Categories Under Budget	A double-bar graph of only the categories that were under budget over a specified period of time.
Budget Composition	A pie chart that shows each budget category as a pie piece that makes up your total budget (the pie) over a specified period of time.
Budget Trend	A stacked bar graph of your monthly budget categories over a specified period of time.

You cannot display budget and actual graphs unless you have first created your budget. Refer to Chapter 15, "Budgeting with Quicken," to learn how to create a budget. Budget and actual graphs are created from the categories that you assign to transactions and the categories you establish budget amounts for. Quicken graphs categories only. Any subcategories you assign to transactions or enter a budget amount for are included within the categories in the budget and actual graphs.

This section shows you how to create each type of graph. You can change the transactions Quicken includes in graphs by using the Filter option (see *Filtering Graph Transactions*, later in this chapter).

The Monthly Budget and Actual Graph. The *Monthly Budget and Actual graph* appears as a double-bar graph that compares your budgeted expenses to your actual expenses. Note that you also can compare budgeted income to actual income using this graph.

To create the Monthly Budget and Actual graph, follow these steps:

1. Choose Monthly Budget and Actual from the **B**udget and Actual Graphs menu shown in figure 17.15. Quicken displays the Monthly Budget and Actual window.

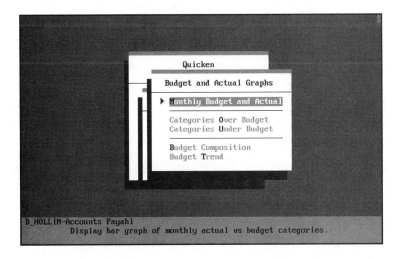

Fig. 17.15
The Budget and Actual Graphs menu.

2. In the Graph Months From field, type the starting month and year you want the graph to cover. Type the ending month and year in the Through field. You can use the + (plus) and - (minus) keys to change the dates by one month at a time.

3. Move the cursor to the Show Income, Expense, or Both Categories field. By default, Quicken graphs expense categories only (the setting is E). However, if you want to graph both income and expense categories, choose **B**. If you want to graph only income categories, choose **I**.

4. Choose **Enter** or **F10** to display the Budget and Actual: Income graph (see fig. 17.16).

Fig. 17.16

The Budget and Actual: Income graph.

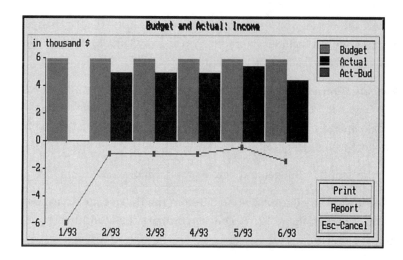

The Budget and Actual Income: graph compares budgeted amounts to actual amounts over a period of time. If you're sticking to your budget, you should see that the budget bar is higher in the graph than the actual bar. If you graph expense categories only, the Budget and Actual: Income graph helps you pinpoint which months you were over budget so that you can go back and look at expenses for those months to determine why spending was so high.

The Categories Over Budget Graph. The *Categories Over Budget graph* helps you quickly see which areas of spending you're having problems with.

To create a Categories Over Budget graph, follow these steps:

1. Choose Categories Over Budget from the Budget and Actual Graphs menu. Quicken displays the Categories Over Budget window shown in figure 17.17.

2. In the Graph Months From field, type the starting month and year you want the graph to cover. Type the ending month and year in the Through field. You can use the + (plus) and - (minus) keys to change the dates by one month at a time.

3. Move the cursor to the Show Income or Expense Categories field. By default, Quicken graphs expense categories only (the setting is E). If you want to graph only income categories, choose I.

4. Choose **Enter** or **F10** to display the Categories Over Budget: Expense graph (see fig. 17.18).

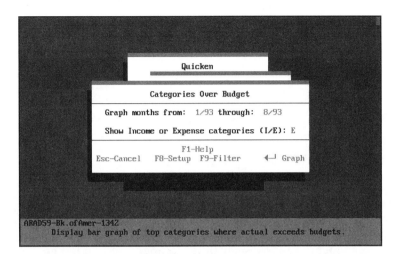

Fig. 17.17
The Categories Over Budget window.

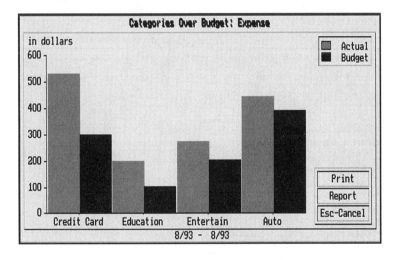

Fig. 17.18
The Categories Over Budget: Expense graph.

The Categories Over Budget: Expense graph shows you the categories that were furthest over budget for the time period you specify (Quicken cannot include every category over budget in the graph because there is not enough space). The farther away from zero an over-budget category is on the graph, the more attention you need to pay to that particular category to determine whether your budget amount is not realistic or whether actual spending or income needs to be brought into line.

The Categories Under Budget Graph. To see the categories in which you are under budget over a specified time, you can create the *Categories Under Budget graph*. This graph appears as a double-bar graph that compares budgeted amounts to actual amounts for under-budget categories.

To create a Categories Under Budget graph, follow these steps:

1. Choose the Categories Under Budget from the **Budget and Actual Graphs** menu. Quicken displays the Categories Under Budget window.

2. In the Graph Months From field, type the starting month and year you want the graph to cover. Type the ending month and year in the Through field. You can use the + (plus) and - (minus) keys to change the dates by one month at a time.

3. Move the cursor to the Show Income or Expense Categories field. By default, Quicken graphs expense categories only (the setting is E). If you want to graph only income categories, choose **I**.

4. Choose **Enter** or **F10** to display the Categories Under Budget graph.

The Categories Under Budget graph shows you the categories that were furthest under budget for the time period you specify (Quicken cannot include every category under budget in the graph because there is not enough space). If you graph income categories only, negative values in the graph indicate that you earned more than you thought you would when you created your budget.

The Budget Composition Graph. The *Budget Composition graph* appears as a pie chart that shows what expenses (or income items) make up your total budget.

To create a Budget Composition graph, follow these steps:

1. Choose **Budget Composition** from the **Budget and Actual Graphs** menu. Quicken displays the Budget Composition window.

2. In the Graph Months From field, type the starting month and year you want the graph to cover. Type the ending month and year in the Through field. You can use the + (plus) and - (minus) keys to change the dates by one month at a time.

3. Move the cursor to the Show Income or Expense Categories field. By default, Quicken graphs expense categories only (the setting is E). If you want to graph only income categories, choose **I**.

4. Choose **Enter** or **F10** to display the Budget Composition: Expense graph (see fig. 17.19).

Fig. 17.19
The Budget
Composition:
Expense graph.

The Budget Composition: Expense graph, displayed as a pie chart, shows the relative contribution of each of your budgeted income or expense categories to your total budget.

The Budget Trend Graph. To see which expense categories make up your total budget and how your total budgeted expenses increase or decrease over time, you can create the *Budget Trend graph.*

To create a Budget Trend graph, follow these steps:

  1. Choose Budget Trend from the Budget and Actual Graphs menu. Quicken displays the Budget Trend window.

  2. In the Graph Months From field, type the starting month and year you want the graph to cover. Type the ending month and year in the Through field. You can use the + (plus) and - (minus) keys to change the dates by one month at a time.

  3. Move the cursor to the Show Income or Expense Categories field. By default, Quicken graphs expense categories only (the setting is E). If you want to graph only income categories, choose **I**.

  4. Choose **Enter** or **F10** to display the Budget Trend: Expense graph (see fig. 17.20).

The Budget Trend: Expense graph shows how your budget is comprised and your budgeting trend over time. The composition of your budget is represented by each stacked bar that appears in the graph. Each budgeting category is shown in a different color or pattern within the bar.

III

Analyzing Your Finances

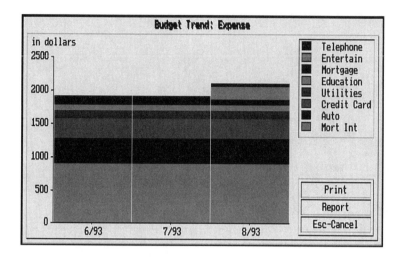

Creating Investments Graphs

You can use *investment graphs* to analyze your investment portfolio. With investment graphs, you can see how your portfolio is distributed (stocks, bonds, options, Treasury Bills, and so on), see the changes in your portfolio value over time, and analyze the price trends of your security holdings.

> **Note**
>
> If you don't track your investments using Quicken's investment accounts, you will not be able to create investment graphs. Refer to Chapter 16, "Monitoring Your Investments," to learn how to use Quicken's investment accounts.

Following are common questions you can answer by creating investment graphs:

- Is my investment portfolio value increasing?

- How diversified is my investment portfolio?

- Are the prices of my individual holdings increasing?

- Should I sell a security because the price trend of the security is downward?

After you create each investment graph, you will be able to answer these questions, and more.

This section shows you how to create each type of graph. You can change the transactions that Quicken includes in graphs by using the Filter option (see *Filtering Graph Transactions*, later in this chapter).

Quicken provides three different graphs that you can create to analyze your income and expenses:

Graph	Description
Portfolio Composition	A pie chart showing each individual security as a pie piece that makes up your investment portfolio (the pie) over a specified period of time.
Portfolio Value Trend	A stacked bar graph that shows the total market value of your investment accounts (or if you filter transactions, the market value of specific securities, types, or goals), by month, over a specified period of time.
Price History	A line graph showing the price trend of securities that you have updated in the Update Prices and Market Value window. Refer to Chapter 16, "Monitoring Your Investments," to learn about updating security prices.

The Portfolio Composition Graph. The *Portfolio Composition graph* displays as a pie chart and shows you just how your portfolio is comprised and the relationship of each of your investments to your total investments.

To create a Portfolio Composition graph, follow these steps:

1. Choose Portfolio Composition from the Investment Graphs menu shown in figure 17.21.

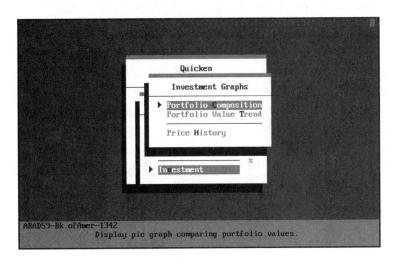

Fig. 17.21
The Investment Graphs menu.

Quicken displays the Portfolio Composition window shown in figure 17.22.

Fig. 17.22
The Portfolio
Composition
window.

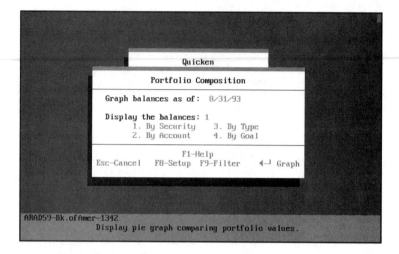

2. In the Graph Balances As Of field, type the date you want to use to show balances. Quicken uses this date to look for investment account balances and uses the balances found on that particular date in the graph. You can use the + (plus) and - (minus) keys to change the dates by one day at a time.

3. Move the cursor to the Display the Balances field. Choose the number that corresponds to the balances you want to display in the graph. Choose **1** to display your portfolio allocation by security, **2** to display your portfolio allocation by account, **3** to display your portfolio allocation by type, or **4** to display by goal.

   If you want to see how your total investment portfolio is allocated, create a Portfolio Composition graph displayed by security (choose **1**). When you display the graph by account, Quicken combines all your investment accounts and shows the relationship of each individual account to your total accounts. Displaying the graph by type shows the relationship of each type of security you hold to your total portfolio. When you display the graph by goal, Quicken shows the relationship of each security goal to your total portfolio.

4. Choose **Enter** or **F10** to display the Portfolio Composition by Security graph (see fig. 17.23).

Fig. 17.23
The Portfolio
Composition by
Security graph.

The Portfolio Composition Security graph shows you some valuable information about your investments. You can see how diversified your investments are by displaying the graph by security type (stocks, bonds, CDs, mutual funds, unit trusts, and so on). You also can use the Portfolio Composition graph to show the allocation of securities to meet investment goals (such as funding college, retirement, growth, income, and so on), by displaying the graph by goal.

The Portfolio Value Trend Graph. You can create a *Portfolio Value Trend graph* to help you see how your investments are increasing or decreasing over time and which investments comprise your total portfolio.

To create a Portfolio Value Trend graph, follow these steps:

1. Choose Portfolio Value Trend from the Investment Graphs menu. Quicken displays the Portfolio Value Trend window.

2. In the Graph Ending Balances for Months field, type the starting date you want Quicken to use to graph security or investment account balances. In the Through field, type the date you want balances graphed through. You can use the + (plus) and - (minus) keys to change the dates by one month at a time.

3. Move the cursor to the Display the Balances field. Choose the number that corresponds to the balances you want to display in the graph. Choose **1** to display your portfolio allocation by security, **2** to display your portfolio allocation by account, **3** to display your portfolio allocation by type, or **4** to display by goal.

III

Analyzing Your Finances

If you want to see how the value of your individual securities have changed over time, create a Portfolio Value Trend graph displayed by security (choose **1**). When you display the graph by account, Quicken combines all your investment accounts and shows the value of your accounts over time. Displaying the graph by type shows the value of securities, grouped by type, over a period of time. When you display the graph by goal, Quicken shows the value of securities, grouped by goal, over time.

4. Choose **Enter** or **F10** to create the Portfolio Value Trend by Security graph (see fig. 17.24).

Fig. 17.24

The Portfolio Value Trend by Security graph.

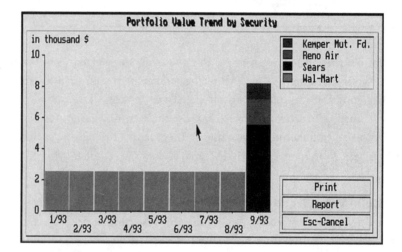

The Portfolio Value Trend graph shows you how your portfolio is growing (or not growing) over a period of time. Within this graph, you also can see how each individual security (if you display the graph by security) is moving. If your total portfolio value is not moving upward, the Portfolio Value Trend graph helps you determine which securities are holding down the value of your portfolio.

The Price History Graph. The *Price History graph* helps you see how the prices of securities you hold in your portfolio have increased or decreased over time.

To create a Price History graph, follow these steps:

1. Choose Price History from the Investment Graphs menu. Quicken displays the Price History window.

2. In the Graph Price From field, type the starting date you want Quicken to use to graph security prices. In the Through field, type the date you want security prices graphed through. You can use the + (plus) and - (minus) keys to change the dates by one day at a time.

3. Move to the Adjust Prices for Splits field. Choose **Y** if you had stock splits and want Quicken to adjust the prices to take the split into account.

If you bought 100 shares of stock and paid $10 per share (for a total price of $1,000), and subsequently the stock split 1 for 1 (you received one share for every one share that you held), for example, you now have 200 shares of the stock. The per share price of the stock you now have is $5, which is determined by dividing the total price of the stock ($1,000) by the total shares (200).

4. (Optional) If you want to select which securities Quicken graphs in the Price History graph, choose **F9**. Quicken displays the Select Securities to Include window. Highlight the security you want and press the space bar to include the security in the Price History graph. Press the space bar again to exclude a security from the graph, or choose **F9** to select all securities in the Select Securities to Include window. When you are finished selecting securities to include, choose **Enter** to return to the Price History window.

5. Choose **Enter** or **F10** to create the Price History graph (see fig. 17.25).

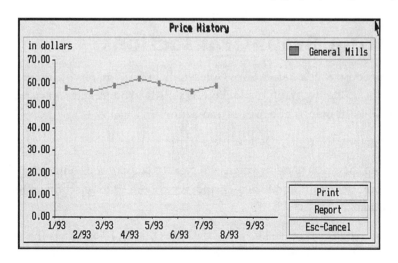

Fig. 17.25
The Price History graph.

III

Analyzing Your Finances

Using QuickZoom for Graphs

Tip
When you see the cursor turn into a miniature magnifying glass, you're in a field that supports QuickZoom.

Another new feature in Quicken 7 is *QuickZoom* for graphs. QuickZoom has been available in previous versions of Quicken, but only for reports. Refer to *Using QuickZoom* in Chapter 12 for more information on using QuickZoom for reports.

To use QuickZoom for graphs, follow these steps:

1. With a graph displayed on-screen, choose a pie slice, bar, or legend item in the graph and choose **Enter**.

   Quicken displays a QuickZoom graph that shows more detail about the item you selected.

2. To examine an item in a QuickZoom graph further, select the item and choose **Enter**.

   Quicken displays a report that shows more detail about the item you selected.

3. To examine an item in the QuickZoom report, select the item and choose QuickZoom from the File/Print menu, or press **Ctrl-Z**.

   Quicken displays a list of the transactions that make up the item.

4. When you are finished reviewing the QuickZoom items, choose **Esc** and Quicken returns you to the window used to create the graph.

Filtering Graph Transactions

You can choose which transactions Quicken includes in graphs by filtering transactions. Filtering graph transactions is similar to filtering report transactions (you learn how to filter report transactions in Chapter 12).

To filter graph transactions, follow these steps:

1. From the graph window you use to create a graph (for example, the Monthly Income and Expense window), choose **F9** to select the **Filter** option.

   Quicken displays the Filters window. Note that Quicken enters the title of the report option in the Filters window. If you select the **Filter** option from the Monthly Income and Expense window, Quicken displays the Income and Expense Filters window because this type of graph is an income and expense graph.

2. Move the cursor to the field where you want to set a filter option. Because each graph you create presents different filtering options, Table 17.1 describes the available options.

3. When the Filters window is complete, choose **Enter** or **F10**. If you chose to select categories, classes, accounts, securities, security types, or investment goals, Quicken displays the appropriate window next so that you can make your selections. When you are finished making your selections, choose **Enter** to return to the graph window you are using to create a graph.

Table 17.1 Filtering Options

Filtering Option	Function
Restrict to Transactions Below/Above the Amount	Enables you to include only those transactions that fall below (B) or above (A) the amount you enter.
Category Contains Class Contains	Enables you to specify which categories or classes to include in graphs. You can enter partial words or phrases and also use special match characters for Quicken to search.
Select Categories to Include Select Classes to Include	Enables you to select which categories or classes to include in graphs. When you select to include categories or classes, Quicken displays the Select Categories to Include window or the Select Classes to Include window so that you can make your selections.
Use Current/All/Selected Accounts	You can tell Quicken which accounts to use in graphs: the current account (C), all accounts (A), or selected accounts (S). If you want to select accounts, Quicken displays the Select Accounts to Include window so that you can make your selections.
Display the (2-12)	By default, Quicken displays 10 items in a graph. If you want to display a different number of items, enter a number from 2 to 12.
Categories with Accounts with Budget Categories with	Enables you to include categories, accounts, or budget categories with the highest balance (1) or the lowest balance (2).

(continues)

Analyzing Your Finances

Table 17.1 Continued	
Filtering Option	**Function**
Summarize Remaining Categories or Accounts into "Other"?	Balances for categories that are not displayed are lumped into an Other category in graphs. Press **N** if you don't want to show the Other category in the graph.

For investment graphs, other filtering options are available as follows:

Filtering Option	**Function**
Select Securities to Graph	Enables you to select the securities to include in the graph. If you want to select securities, Quicken displays the Select Securities to Include window so that you can make your selections.
Select Security Types to Graph	Enables you to select the security types to include in the graph. If you want to select security types, Quicken displays the Select Security Types to Include window so that you can make your selections.
Select Investment Goals to Graph	Enables you to select the investment goals to include in the graph. If you want to select investment goals, Quicken displays the Select Investment Goals to Include window so that you can make your selections.

Printing Graphs

A new feature in Quicken 7 is the capability to print a graph after you create it on-screen. You must, however, have a graphical printer to utilize this feature.

To print a graph, follow these steps:

1. Refer to the *Setting Your Printer* section in Chapter 1 to set your printer for printing graphs.

2. Make sure the printer is turned on, on-line, and loaded with paper.

3. Create the graph you want to print.

4. With the graph displayed on-screen, choose **Print** in the lower right corner of the screen.

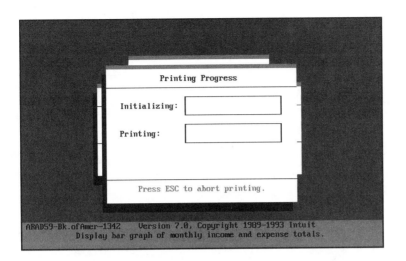

Fig. 17.26
The Printing
Progress window.

Quicken displays a Printing Progress window (see fig. 17.26) to let you know how printing is progressing. To stop printing at any time, choose **Esc**.

5. Quicken finishes printing the graph and returns you to the setup window for the graph you just printed.

Summary

In this chapter, you learn about Quicken's graphing feature. You learn about the different types of graphs Quicken creates (double-bar, line, pie, and stacked bar) and how to create graphs to analyze your income and expenses, net worth, budget versus actual data, and investments. You also learn how to filter graphs to include only the categories or accounts you want and then to print your graphs. Graphing your financial information sometimes provides more insight to help you make decisions about your finances.

The next chapter describes more Quicken features: the financial planning calculators. You learn about planning your investments, planning for retirement, planning for college, and refinancing your mortgage.

III

Analyzing Your Finances

Chapter 18

Financial Planning with Quicken

You already know how to use Quicken to write checks, keep your Register, reconcile your bank account, track your assets and liabilities, manage your credit cards, create a budget, prepare for income taxes, monitor your investments, and create graphs to show comparative data. But what about using Quicken for financial planning? And what is financial planning?

Financial planning is the process of setting future goals and developing plans to meet those goals. For example, in order to retire with enough money to meet expenses (and have a little fun) through the remainder of your life, you first must determine how much money you will need, and then develop and implement a financial plan so that you have that amount of money at retirement age. You also need to develop a financial plan for the things you would like to acquire, such as a first home, new car, vacation home, trip to Europe, and so on. And if you have children, you will want to plan for college expenses *now*, even though your children are young.

With Quicken, you don't need other software programs to help you with planning your financial needs for the future. Quicken includes financial planning calculators that are convenient and easy to use. Quicken's financial planning calculators are easy to access from the Register or the Write Checks screen and make calculations as quickly as you can enter the data. Financial planning calculators include the following:

> *Loan Calculator:* Amortizes fixed-rate and variable-rate loans. You learn about this calculator in Chapter 10.

In this chapter, you learn how to do the following:

- Use each of the financial planning calculators described (except the Loan Calculator, which is covered in Chapter 10)

- Change the calculation that Quicken makes in each financial planning calculator

- Display payment schedules based on the calculations that the financial calculators make

- Print payment schedules

III

Analyzing Your Finances

Investment Planning Calculator: Calculates the expected growth of an investment, how much money you need now to have a certain amount in the future, or how much money you need to contribute periodically to an investment to have a certain amount in the future. You learn about the Investment Planning Calculator in this chapter.

Retirement Planning Calculator: Calculates how much your current retirement account will yield in annual, after-tax income at retirement age given your estimated tax rate, yearly contributions, predicted inflation rate, and the expected annual yield. With the Retirement Planning Calculator, you also can determine how much you need to have now or how much you need to contribute to your retirement account on a yearly basis so that you have the money you need when you retire. This chapter explains how to use the Retirement Planning Calculator.

College Planning Calculator: Calculates how much money you need to have today, or how much you need to save each year, to send your kids to college in the future. You can even use this tool to help you determine how much annual tuition you can afford—state supported school, Ivy League, or other. You learn about the College Planning Calculator in this chapter.

Refinance Calculator: The Refinance Calculator is somewhat different from the other financial planning calculators. It helps you determine the benefits of refinancing your existing mortgage. You can calculate the difference in your monthly payment at various interest rates and how long it will take to recover the closing costs incurred when you refinance your mortgage. This chapter shows you how to use the Refinance Calculator.

Planning Your Investments

Most of us have some amount of money saved or invested (no matter how large or small) that we would like to see grow. Whether you're saving for a new car, a down payment, or a European vacation, you want your money to grow quickly so that you don't have to wait so long to acquire the things you want. Although Quicken can't make your money grow any quicker than the investment vehicle it's currently maintained in, you can monitor your investment growth and play out "what-if" scenarios using Quicken's new Investment Planning Calculator. You can see how much your investment will grow given different interest rates, inflation rates, and yearly contributions.

Using the Investment Planning Calculator

With the Investment Planning Calculator, you can calculate the following variables:

- The expected growth of the money that you currently have saved or invested over a certain time period and based on a specific interest rate and expected inflation rate.

- How much money you need *now* to accumulate a certain amount of money in the future.

- How much money you need to save on a yearly basis to accumulate a certain amount of money in the future.

To access the Investment Planning Calculator, follow these steps:

1. From the Register or the Write Checks screen, access the Activities menu.

2. Choose Financial Planning from the Activities menu to display the Financial Planning menu (see fig. 18.1).

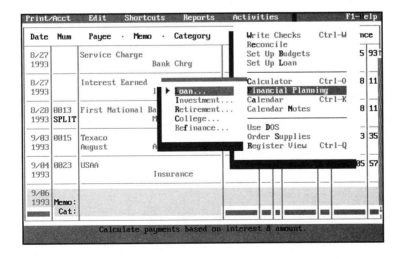

Fig. 18.1
The Financial Planning menu.

3. Choose Investment... from the Financial Planning menu. Quicken displays the Investment Planning Calculator, shown in figure 18.2.

Fig. 18.2

The Investment Planning Calculator.

Notice the calculation check mark in the far left column of the Investment Planning Calculator. The calculation check mark determines which calculation the calculator will perform when you enter data. In figure 18.2, the check mark appears next to the Future Value field. When you enter data in the other fields in the Investment Planning Calculator, Quicken calculates the future value, or the amount that your investment grows to or is worth in the future.

To change the calculation Quicken makes, choose **F8** to move the check mark to the Present Value field, the Additions Each Year field, or the Future Value field.

Performing Investment Planning Calculations

To calculate the future value of an investment based on the amount that you have invested today, follow these steps:

1. Access the Investment Planning Calculator (follow the preceding steps).

2. Choose **F8**, if necessary, to move the calculation check mark to the Future Value field.

3. Move the cursor to the Present Value field, and enter the current value of your investment or your savings account.

4. Move the cursor to the Additions Each Year field. Enter the amount of additional investments or savings that you plan to make each year.

5. Move the cursor to the Number of Years field. Enter the number of years you plan to make contributions to your investment account or savings account. If you want to change the time period from yearly to quarters, months, or weeks, choose **F7** until the time period you want appears. If you change the time period, be sure to enter the amount of additional investments or savings (in step 4) based on the new time period.

6. Move the cursor to the Annual Yield field. Enter the rate of return that you expect from this investment (do not type a percent sign). If, for example, you're calculating the future value of a savings account, enter the interest rate that the account currently pays.

7. Move the cursor to the Predicted Inflation field and enter the current or expected inflation rate. Do not type a percent sign.

8. In the Inflate Payments Yearly field, choose **Y** to adjust the additions made to your investment or savings account based on the inflation rate. Choose **N** if you want the additions to remain constant.

After you enter all variables in the Investment Planning Calculator, Quicken calculates the future value of the investment and enters the result in the Future Value field. Quicken converts the future value amount to today's dollars (the amount that your investment is worth today) and enters the result under the Future Value field. Figure 18.3 shows that a savings account worth $10,000 today is worth $16,288.94 10 years from now if the savings account earns 5 percent annually and inflation is 4 percent.

Fig. 18.3
Calculating the future value of an investment using the Investment Planning Calculator.

To calculate how much money you need *now* to accumulate a certain amount of money in the future, follow these steps:

1. Access the Investment Planning Calculator.

2. Choose F8, if necessary, to move the calculation check mark to the Present Value field.

3. Except for the Present Value field, fill in all other fields in the Investment Planning Calculator as explained for calculating the future value of an investment.

4. Move the cursor to the Future Value field and enter the amount of money that you would like to have in the future (your financial goal). If your goal is to have one million dollars in 10 years, enter **1000000** in the Future Value field. (Quicken converts the amount you enter in the Future Value field to today's dollars and enters the result under the Future Value field.)

Based on the variables you enter in the Investment Planning Calculator, Quicken calculates the amount of money that you need today to reach your financial goal and enters the result in the Present Value field. Figure 18.4 shows that you need to have $613,913.25 invested now (at 5 percent with 4 percent inflation) if you want to have one million dollars in 10 years.

Fig. 18.4
Calculating the amount of money you need to have invested now to meet your future financial goal.

To calculate how much money you need to save on a periodic (yearly, quarterly, monthly, or weekly) basis to accumulate a certain amount of money in the future, follow these steps:

1. Access the Investment Planning Calculator.

2. Choose **F8**, if necessary, to move the calculation check mark to the Additions Each Year field (this field may be labeled Additions Each Year, Quarter, Month, or Week based on the period that you are using. Remember, choose **F7** to change the periods used in the calculation).

3. Except for the Additions each Year field, fill in all other fields in the Investment Planning Calculator to calculate the future value of an investment. Leave the Present Value field blank if you have no current savings or investments.

When you're finished entering all variables in the Investment Planning Calculator, Quicken calculates the amount of money you need to save or invest each period. Figure 18.5 shows that to have $50,000 in five years (with no current savings), you need to save or invest $8,869.82 each year.

Fig. 18.5
Calculating the periodic savings or investments required to accumulate a certain amount in the future.

Planning for Your Retirement

Most people aspire to stop working someday so that they can enjoy their later years. However, just because you stop working doesn't mean your expenses also stop. So how do you plan to pay for living expenses after the paycheck stops? You may believe this topic to interest only readers who are retiring soon, but this is not the case. The irony is that the easiest time to prepare for retirement is when the time you stop working is still a long way off, and the hardest time to prepare for retirement is when retirement is right around the bend.

Preparing a Living Expenses Budget

The first step in planning for retirement is to estimate living expenses. Obviously, the further away your retirement, the less precise are the estimates. Even if retirement is 20 years away, however, your current spending can provide a useful benchmark for estimating future expenses. The general rule of thumb is that retirement expenses are roughly 80 percent of current living expenses. Generally, three reasons account for this calculation:

- Housing expenses may go down, either because you owned a home and paid off your mortgage or you moved to a smaller house or apartment.

- Children grow up and, usually, cease to be financial responsibilities.

- Work expenses, such as special clothing, transportation, tools, dues, and so on, stop because you stop working.

Be careful, however, that you don't drastically reduce your planned living expenses. Remember that certain expenses also may increase because you age or retire. Medical expenses—such as the insurance an employer paid previously—may increase. Entertainment and vacation expenses may increase because you have more free time on your hands. Consider also that retirement may mean new hobbies or activities with attendant costs.

In any event, the reports that Quicken provides should prove immensely helpful. In particular, Quicken's Itemized Category report should be useful because the report shows the ways you currently are spending money. (Refer to Chapter 12 if you have questions about how to print a particular report.) Figure 18.6 provides a worksheet you can use to estimate the living expenses you may have during retirement. You can fill in the first column, the one that records your current expenses, using the Itemized Category report.

Using this information and the ideas already touched on, you can fill in the second column to come up with an estimate of retirement expenses. Remember that Quicken's calculator provides a convenient way to compute the total expenses for retirement.

Estimated Living Expenses Worksheet		
Expense	Current	Retirement
Housing		
Mortage or rent		
Property taxes		
Property insurance		
Maintenance		
Food		
Transportation		
Work		
Hobby		
Vacation		
Recreation		
Healthcare/Insurance		
Clothing		
Other		
Total Expenses		

Fig. 18.6
A worksheet you can use to estimate living expenses.

Once you determine your estimated retirement living expenses, you have the number you need to enter as your after-tax income for retirement in the Retirement Planning Calculator.

Keep in mind two more things about estimating retirement living expenses. First, don't adjust the expense estimates for the inflation that probably will occur between now and the time you retire, because the Retirement Planning Calculator addresses the ravages of inflation by factoring an inflation rate into its calculations. Second, don't worry about taxes in your worksheet, the Retirement Planning Calculator also factors a tax rate into its calculations.

Estimating Tentative Retirement Income

Estimating tentative retirement income is the second step in planning a retirement income. In general, a person's retirement income essentially consists of three components: Social Security, investment income, and pension income. To tally these three sources, you need to do the following:

1. Contact the local Social Security office and ask for the form called *Request for Earnings and Benefit Estimate Statement.*

2. Complete the Request for Earnings and Benefit Estimate Statement by following the directions on the form. You need to enter your Social Security number, information about your earnings, and when you plan to retire. After you complete the form, send it to the address given. In a few weeks, you will receive an estimate of what you may receive in Social Security benefits when you retire.

III

Analyzing Your Finances

3. If you qualify for an employer's pension, contact the pension fund administrator or trustee and ask for whatever information you need to estimate your future retirement benefits. The administrator should be more than happy to give this information to you. In fact, the pension fund trustee is required to give you the information.

4. Add any other income sources that you may have when you retire, such as rental income from properties, annuities, and so on.

Now you have the information you need to determine your estimated retirement income. Add the amounts from steps 2, 3, and 4. This is your total retirement income. You use this number in the Retirement Planning Calculator.

Using the Retirement Planning Calculator

Now you're ready to use the Retirement Planning Calculator to calculate any of the following variables:

- How much your current retirement account will yield annually when you retire based on yearly contributions, expected annual yields, and estimated income tax rates.

- How much money you need *now* to accumulate the money you will need when you retire.

- How much you need to contribute each year to your retirement account to ensure that you have enough money when you retire.

To access the Retirement Planning Calculator, follow these steps:

1. From the Register or the Write Checks screen, access the Activities menu.

2. Choose Financial Planning from the Activities menu to display the Financial Planning menu.

3. Choose Retirement... from the Financial Planning menu. Quicken displays the Retirement Planning Calculator, shown in figure 18.7.

Notice the calculation check mark in the far left column of the Retirement Planning Calculator. The calculation check mark determines which calculation the calculator will perform when you enter data. In figure 18.8, the check mark appears next to the After-Tax Income field. Therefore, when you enter data in the other fields in the Retirement Planning Calculator, Quicken calculates the amount you will have after taxes. (You first must enter the amount you currently have saved in the Present Savings field, or the amount you plan to contribute in the yearly payments field.)

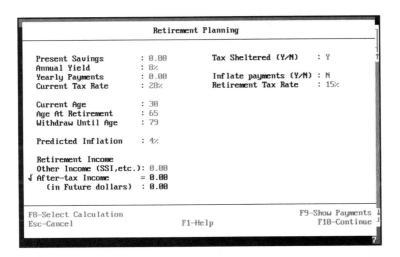

Fig. 18.7

The Retirement Planning Calculator.

To change the calculation that Quicken makes, choose **F8** to move the check mark to the Yearly Payments field, the After-Tax Income field, or the Present Savings field.

```
                        Retirement Planning

    Present Savings      : 25,000.00   Tax Sheltered (Y/N)   : Y
    Annual Yield         : 5%
    Yearly Payments      : 2,000.00    Inflate payments (Y/N) : Y
    Current Tax Rate     : 28%         Retirement Tax Rate    : 15%

    Current Age          : 35
    Age At Retirement    : 62
    Withdraw Until Age   : 80

    Predicted Inflation  : 4%

    Retirement Income
    Other Income (SSI,etc.): 18,000.00
  √ After-tax Income      = 22,447.46
      (in Future dollars) : 64,724.30


  F8-Select Calculation                      F9-Show Payments
  Esc-Cancel  ▌              F1-Help              F10-Continue
```

Fig. 18.8

Calculating after-tax retirement income using the Retirement Planning Calculator.

Performing Retirement Planning Calculations

Now you're ready to perform the various retirement calculations with the Retirement Planning Calculator.

To calculate how much your current retirement account, plus annual contributions, will yield annually when you retire, follow these steps:

1. Access the Retirement Planning Calculator.

2. Choose **F8**, if necessary, to move the calculation check mark to the After-Tax Income field.

3. Position the cursor on the Present Savings field. If you have a retirement account or a savings account established, enter the amount in the account(s).

4. Move the cursor to the Tax Sheltered field. If your current retirement account is tax-sheltered—not subject to federal income taxes due to a tax law provision, such as a 401K plan or IRA, choose **Y**. Otherwise, choose **N**.

5. Move the cursor to the Annual Yield field and type the rate of return that you expect from your retirement or savings account. Don't enter percentages as decimals. To enter 5 percent, for example, just press **5**.

CPA TIP

As a frame of reference in picking appropriate real rates of return, you may find several pieces of data helpful. Over the last 60 years or so, inflation has averaged a little more than 3 percent, common stocks have averaged 10 percent return, long-term bonds have averaged around 5 percent yield, and short-term treasury bills have averaged roughly 3.5 percent yield. Therefore, when you subtract inflation, stocks produced real returns of 7 percent, long-term bonds produced real returns of about 2 percent, and treasury bills essentially broke even. Accordingly, if half of the retirement savings is invested in long-term bonds yielding 2 percent and the other half invested in common stocks yielding 7 percent, you may want to guess the return as somewhere between 4 and 5 percent.

---

6. Move the cursor to the Yearly Payments field. Enter the amount you plan to contribute to your retirement or savings account on a yearly basis. Typically, for an IRA account, the yearly contribution is $2,000. For 401K plans, you can contribute a maximum (in 1993) of $8,994.

7. Move the cursor to the Inflate Payments field. Here is where Quicken factors in rates so that your yearly contributions keep up with inflation.

The *inflation rate* is the annual percentage rate that prices increase. The $2,000 that you contribute this year will not be the same as contributing $2,000 10 years from now. Choose **Y** if you want Quicken to increase your yearly contributions for inflation, or choose **N** to keep your contributions constant.

8. Move to the Current Tax Rate field. Quicken uses this rate to calculate the income tax effect on the earnings from your yearly contributions if your retirement account is not tax sheltered. Type your current maximum tax rate without the percent sign. Because tax rates continually change, be mindful that you may need to modify retirement planning results to take into consideration higher or lower tax rates.

9. Move to the Retirement Tax Rate field. Type your estimated tax rate when you retire. This may be tough to project because you really don't know where tax rates will be in the future. The best estimate, however, is today's tax rates given your future level of income.

10. Move the cursor to the Current Age field and type your age.

11. Next, move the cursor to the Age At Retirement field and enter the age that you're eligible or would like to retire.

12. Then, in the Withdraw Until Age field, enter the age to which you hope to live. Use some common sense here. If your family history shows a long life span for men, be positive and enter an older age than the average here. If your family history shows just the opposite, be realistic and enter the average life span age here.

13. Move the cursor to the Predicted Inflation field. Type the current inflation rate without the percent sign.

14. Move the cursor to the Other Income field in the Retirement Income section of the Retirement Planning Calculator. This is where you enter your estimated retirement income (Social Security, pensions, other income) that you determined in the last section. Enter your annual retirement income and choose **Enter**.

After you enter all the variables, Quicken's Retirement Planning Calculator calculates the unknown variable, or in this case, the after-tax retirement income (in today's dollars and future dollars). Figure 18.8 shows after-tax income of $22,447.46 in today's dollars and $64,724.30 in future dollars based on the following variables:

Present savings	$25,000 (tax-sheltered)
Annual yield	5%
Yearly payments	$2,000 (inflated)
Current tax rate	28%
Retirement tax rate	15%
Current age	35
Age at retirement	62
Withdraw until age	80
Predicted inflation	4%
Other Income	$18,000

You also can calculate the amount of present savings you need to yield the desired after-tax retirement income. To calculate how much money you need *now* to accumulate the money you will need when you retire, follow these steps:

1. Access the Retirement Planning Calculator.

2. Choose **F8**, if necessary, to move the calculation check mark to the Present Savings field.

3. Except for the Present Savings field, fill in all other fields in the Retirement Planning Calculator as explained in the previous steps for calculating after-tax retirement income.

4. Move the cursor to the After-Tax Income field and enter your projected retirement income goal. (When you enter your income goal in today's dollars, Quicken converts today's dollars to future dollars and enters this amount under the After-Tax Income field.)

Figure 18.9 shows that if you want to have $50,000 in after-tax retirement income ($144,168.42 in future dollars), you must have present savings of $747,485.42 with yearly contributions of at least $2,000 (granted, of course that you're 35 now, retire at age 62, and live to be 80).

```
                      Retirement Planning
  ┌─────────────────────────────────────────────────────────────┐
  │ √ Present Savings     = 747,485.42   Tax Sheltered (Y/N)   : Y │
  │   Annual Yield        : 5%                                     │
  │   Yearly Payments     : 2,000.00    Inflate payments (Y/N) : Y │
  │   Current Tax Rate    : 28%         Retirement Tax Rate    : 15%│
  │                                                               │
  │   Current Age         : 35                                    │
  │   Age At Retirement   : 62                                    │
  │   Withdraw Until Age  : 80                                    │
  │                                                               │
  │   Predicted Inflation : 4%                                    │
  │                                                               │
  │   Retirement Income                                           │
  │   Other Income (SSI,etc.): 0.00                               │
  │   After-tax Income    : 50,000.00                             │
  │     (in Future dollars) : 144,168.42                          │
  │                                                               │
  ├─────────────────────────────────────────────────────────────┤
  │ F8-Select Calculation                     F9-Show Payments    │
  │ Esc-Cancel               F1-Help              F10-Continue     │
  └─────────────────────────────────────────────────────────────┘
```

Fig. 18.9
Calculating present savings required to yield a desired after-tax retirement income using the Retirement Planning Calculator.

Lastly, you can use the Retirement Planning Calculator to calculate how much you need to contribute each year to your retirement account to ensure that you have enough money when you retire. To perform this calculation, follow these steps:

1. Access the Retirement Planning Calculator.

2. Choose **F8**, if necessary, to move the calculation check mark to the Yearly Payments field.

3. Except for the Yearly Payments field, fill in all other fields in the Retirement Planning Calculator as explained in the previous steps for calculating after-tax retirement income.

4. Move the cursor to the After-Tax Income field and enter your projected retirement income goal. (When you enter your income goal in today's dollars, Quicken converts today's dollars to future dollars and enters this amount under the After-Tax Income field.)

Quicken calculates the amount you need to contribute yearly to your retirement account to yield the desired after-tax retirement income.

More Tips on Retirement Planning

Planning for retirement can be frustrating and difficult. Before you decide that you can never quit working, however, consider the following suggestions and observations.

III

Analyzing Your Finances

First, invest retirement money in tax-deferred investments, such as individual retirement accounts, 401Ks, annuities, and so on. Consider these kinds of investments even if you don't receive an immediate tax deduction because paying income taxes on the interest or investment income you earn greatly reduces the real interest rate you enjoy.

Suppose that you choose to invest in a mutual fund you expect will return around 7.5 percent annually. If you don't have to pay income taxes on the interest, you may be left with a real interest rate of around 4.5 percent (calculated as the 7.5 percent minus the 3 percent historical inflation rate).

If you have to pay income taxes, however, the story is different. Suppose that your highest dollars of income are taxed at the 28 percent tax rate. To subtract the income taxes you pay, multiply the 7.5 percent by (1 - 28 percent). This means that the real *adjusted-for-income-taxes* interest rate is 5.4 percent. When you calculate the real interest rate by taking this 5.4 percent interest rate and subtracting the 3 percent inflation rate, the annual real interest rate amounts to a measly 2.4 percent-less than half the amount you receive if you use an investment option that allows you to defer income taxes.

In this example, using investment options in which you can defer the taxes more than doubles the return, which makes a huge difference in the amounts you accumulate over the years you save.

A second consideration is that the longer you postpone retirement, the more retirement income you typically enjoy when you do retire. This tactic isn't much of a revelation, of course, because it makes intuitive sense. However, the difference postponed retirement makes may surprise you. If you postpone retirement, you have several things working in your favor.

Social Security benefits may increase because you begin drawing benefits later or because the average earnings are higher. Any retirement savings you accumulate have a few more years to earn interest, and you probably can save more money. Finally, pension plans usually pay benefits based on years of service, so working a little longer can increase this source of retirement income. You can rework the numbers by using the Retirement Planning Calculator described in this chapter to see specific results for your case.

A third and final point to consider relates to a fundamental assumption of the Retirement Planning Calculator. The calculator assumes that you live off only the annual investment income, Social Security, and pensions. This means that you never actually spend the money you save, only the interest those savings earn. If you have $100,000 in savings that earns $5,000 in annual interest, for example, you spend only the $5,000, and you leave the $100,000 intact. As a practical matter, however, you probably can spend some of the $100,000. The trick is to make sure that the $100,000 doesn't run out before you do.

Planning for College

Financing a college education is no small investment. You can no longer wait until your kids are in high school to start thinking about where you're going to get the money to send them to college. With rising tuition costs, most people must save and invest for several years to have enough money to pay for college.

With Quicken's new College Planning Calculator, you can determine how much you need to save each year for college, as well as how much tuition you can afford in the future based on the amount that you can afford to save today. You also can calculate how much you need to have invested or saved currently to have enough to pay tuition when your child reaches college age.

Note

Quicken's College Planning Calculator assumes that you will continue to save until your child graduates from college. If, for example, your child is 8 years old, there are approximately 10 years remaining until he or she starts college. But, there are 14 years until your child graduates from college. Therefore, the College Planning Calculator calculates present savings, current tuition, and yearly payments based on 14 years of savings, not 10.

Using the College Planning Calculator

To access the College Planning Calculator, follow these steps:

1. From the Register or the Write Checks screen, access the Activities menu.

2. Choose Financial Planning from the Activities menu to display the Financial Planning menu.

3. Choose College... from the Financial Planning menu. Quicken displays the College Planning Calculator, shown in figure 18.10.

III

Analyzing Your Finances

Fig. 18.10

The College Planning Calculator.

Notice the calculation check mark in the far left column of the College Planning Calculator. The calculation check mark determines which calculation the calculator will perform when you enter data. In figure 18.10, the check mark appears next to the Yearly Payments field. Therefore, when you enter data in the other fields in the College Planning Calculator, Quicken calculates the yearly savings, or the amount that you need to have yearly to meet tuition costs when your child reaches college age.

To change the calculation that Quicken makes, choose **F8** to move the check mark to the Yearly Payments field, the Current Tuition field, or the Present Savings field.

Performing College Planning Calculations

To calculate how much you money you need *now* to have enough to fund your child's college education, follow these steps:

1. Access the College Planning Calculator.

2. Choose **F8**, if necessary, to move the calculation check mark to the Present Savings field.

3. Move the cursor to the Current Tuition field and enter the current annual tuition for the school that your child plans to attend. Check with the school's bursar's office to find out the current cost of tuition.

4. Move the cursor to the Years Until Enrollment field. Type the number of years between now and the time your child reaches college age.

5. Move the cursor to the Number of Years Enrolled field. Type the number of years you will be funding your child's education. Normally, this is four; however, if your child plans to get a graduate degree and you plan to pay for that, enter the total undergraduate years and graduate years.

6. Move the cursor to the Annual Yield field. Enter the annual rate of return you expect to receive on your investment or college savings. Do not enter the percent sign.

7. Move the cursor to the Yearly Payments field and type the amount, if any, that you will invest or save each year.

8. Move the cursor to the Predicted Inflation field and enter the expected inflation rate from now until your child begins college. This is tough to estimate, so you can just use the current inflation rate unless you have some source that estimates inflation in the future.

9. In the Inflate Payments Yearly field, choose **Y** if you want to inflate the yearly payment or choose **N** if you want the payments to remain constant.

When you have entered all variables in the College Planning Calculator, Quicken calculates the amount you need to have now to fund your child's education based on the current tuition level, the annual yield, and the number of years from now until your child starts college. Figure 18.11 shows that you need to have $74,451.65 today to pay for your four-year-old's annual tuition of $25,000 (in today's dollars).

Fig. 18.11

Calculating present savings for college using the College Planning Calculator.

To calculate the amount that you need to set aside each year to fund your child's college education, follow these steps:

1. Access the College Planning Calculator.

2. Choose **F8**, if necessary, to move the calculation check mark to the Yearly Payments field.

3. Except for the Yearly Payments field, fill in all other fields in the College Planning Calculator for calculating the present savings needed.

4. Move the cursor to the Present Savings field and enter the amount, if any, that you have saved or invested for college.

Quicken calculates the amount that you need to set aside each year and enters the result in the Yearly Payments field. Figure 18.12 shows that if you have no other savings for college, you need to save $9,955.57 each year to send your 10-year-old to a $25,000 (in today's dollars) per year college.

Fig. 18.12

Using the College Planning Calculator to calculate annual savings for college.

You can use the College Planning Calculator to determine how much tuition you can afford based on the amount that you can afford to save each year. To make this calculation, follow these steps:

1. Access the College Planning Calculator.

2. Choose **F8**, if necessary, to move the calculation check mark to the Current Tuition field.

3. Except for the Current Tuition field, fill in all other fields in the College Planning Calculator for calculating the present savings needed.

4. Move the cursor to the Yearly Payments field and enter the amount you currently can afford to save for college each year.

Quicken calculates the annual tuition amount you can afford based on the yearly payments you entered. Figure 18.13 shows that you could afford a $5,784.34 per year school if you save $2,000 each year for 10 years.

```
 Print/Acct    Edit    Shortcuts    Reports    Activities          F1-Help

  Date  Num    Payee  ·  Memo  ·  Category    Payment  C   Deposit   Balance

  8/27  ┌──────────────────────────────────────────────────────┐ 4,805 93
  1993  │                  College Planning                    │
        │                                                      │
  8/27  │ √ Current Tuition (annual)        = 5,784.34         │
  1993  │   Years Until Enrollment          : 10            8  │ 4,808 11
        │   Number of years enrolled        : 4               │
  8/28  │   Present Savings                 : 0.00            │
  1993  │   Annual Yield                    : 6%             │ 3,808 11
  0013  │                                                      │
  SPLIT │   Yearly Payments                 : 2,000.00         │
  9/03  │   Predicted Inflation             : 4%              │ 3,773 35
  1993  │   Inflate Payments Yearly (Y/N)   : N               │
  0015  │                                                      │
  9/04  │ All calculations assume saving until student        │ 3,605 57
  1993  │   graduates from college.                           │
  0023  │                                                      │
  9/06  │ F8-Select Calculation  Ctrl-D Reset  F9-Show Payments│
  1993  │ Esc-Cancel             F1-Help       F10-Continue    │
  Memo: └──────────────────────────────────────────────────────┘
  Cat :

 Bk.of Amer-1342

                                        Ending Balance:  $3,605.57
```

Fig. 18.13

Using the College Planning Calculator to determine the tuition you can afford.

Tips on Saving for College

Tuition and fees at state colleges have risen an average of 9 percent a year since 1980. Costs have risen 10 percent at private schools. At these rates, it's estimated that a four-year degree for a newborn will cost between $95,000 and $290,000, or even more. So there's no question that you must think about saving for college *now* (when your children are young) so that you can keep up with these rising costs. The following are some things to consider to help you decide how you're going to meet rising college costs head on.

■ If you're funding college for a young child, consider a multiphase investment plan. Phase 1, when your children are young, should include mutual funds that invest in stocks. Stocks are your best bet for growth at a level that exceeds the high rate of increasing college costs. Although the stock market can drop, it usually bounces right back and over the long run, stock values rise.

III

Analyzing Your Finances

Begin phase 2 of your college investment plan as your child becomes closer to college age (12 to 14 years old, for example). You will not want the volatility of the market to impact your capital or earnings at this point. Consider gradually moving your money into capital preservation investments, such as Series EE Savings Bonds, Treasury securities, and certificates of deposit (CD). You also could switch to a mutual fund that divides your money between stocks and bonds.

Phase 3 should begin when your child reaches age 14 or so (then you know college is only four years away). At this time, preserving your investment becomes more important. Begin moving a portion of your funds (maybe 25 percent to cover the first year of college) into a guaranteed four-year investment like a CD. The next year, move another 25 percent, and so on.

- Automated savings plans are available that take money directly from your bank account each month and deposit it into a savings plan or investment account. This makes saving a little less painful and virtually effortless. Consider the amount withdrawn from your bank account a fixed payment, like your mortgage or car loan payment. That way, you will not be tempted to think of other ways to spend it.

- Don't get hooked into investing your money in bonds that don't mature until after your child reaches college age. If you buy a 30-year bond when your child is born, for example, you will be forced to sell it after only 18 years and risk losing some of your capital. Make sure that bond maturity dates coincide with the dates you will need the money for college.

- Some states (about half) are offering special college savings bonds, also known as *baccalaureate bonds*. These bonds are *zero-coupon bonds*, which means that they don't pay interest over the life of the bond, but sell at a large discount from their maturity value. The face value of college savings bonds increases from year to year. College savings bonds usually come in maturities of 5 to 21 years and are exempt from federal income tax and from state and local taxes if you live in the issuing state. Check with your state's finance department to see if these bonds are being issued in your state and which brokerage firm you can call to place an order.

- Remember that you can take out a home-equity loan to pay for college when the time comes. Hang on to your home, rather than trading up. The longer you keep it, the more equity you will have.

Refinancing Your Mortgage

In this day and age of rising and falling mortgage interest rates, refinancing has become quite popular. Although refinancing your mortgage may save on your monthly payment, refinancing is rarely achieved without incurring additional costs (closing costs and mortgage points). Don't be fooled into thinking that refinancing is the answer just because you can secure a lower interest rate. Mortgage lenders usually charge closing costs and points to refinance a mortgage. If your existing mortgage is not very old and you incurred closing costs to obtain your mortgage, it may not be prudent to refinance unless the refinance rate is significantly less than your current rate. Quicken's Refinance Calculator can help you determine if it's cost effective for you to refinance your current mortgage. The Refinance Calculator shows you your new monthly payment amount (based on the refinance rate), how much you save per month by refinancing, the total closing costs you will incur if you refinance, and the amount of time it will take to recoup those closing costs with your monthly savings from refinancing.

CPA TIP

Many mortgage lenders will refinance only 80 percent of your home's current market value or less. If the value of your home has not appreciated and your current mortgage balance is greater than 80 percent of the market value of your home, you may not be able to find a lender willing to refinance your mortgage.

Using the Refinance Calculator

Use the Refinance Calculator if you're considering refinancing your existing mortgage; it may save you some wasted time spent with mortgage companies if you find that the refinance rate they are offering isn't cost effective. You may also find, though, that refinancing makes a lot of sense and results in significant savings.

To use the Refinance Calculator, follow these steps:

1. From the Register or the Write Checks screen, access the Activities menu.

2. Choose Financial Planning from the Activities menu to display the Financial Planning menu.

3. Choose Refinance... from the Financial Planning menu. Quicken displays the Refinance Calculator, shown in figure 18.14.

Fig. 18.14

The Refinance Calculator.

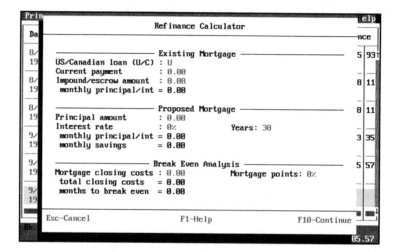

4. In the Existing Mortgage section of the Refinance Calculator, enter **U** if your loan originated in the U.S. or a C if your loan originated in Canada (Canadian lenders use a slightly different method to compute interest). Enter your current payment amount in the Current Payment field and the escrow amount for insurance, property taxes, and so on in the Impound/Escrow Amount field. Quicken subtracts the escrow amount from your current payment and enters the result in the monthly Principal/Int field. This is the portion of your monthly payment that relates to the principal balance of your mortgage loan and the mortgage interest due.

5. Move the cursor to the Proposed Mortgage section of the Refinance Calculator. This is where you enter the data for the new mortgage. In the Principal Amount field, enter the amount that you would be refinancing and choose **Enter**. Remember that this amount is not the same amount as your original mortgage because you have paid down some principal since the time the mortgage originated.

In the Interest Rate field, enter the refinancing rate and choose **Enter**. Don't enter a percent sign. Type 8.75% as *8.75*, for example. Next, in the Years field, enter the number of years that you plan to extend the refinanced mortgage loan and choose **Enter**. This is usually 30 or 15 years.

Quicken calculates the new monthly principal and interest payment and your monthly savings (your old monthly principal and interest payment minus the new monthly principal and interest payment).

6. In the last section of the Refinance Calculator, Break Even Analysis, enter any cost you will incur by refinancing. In the Mortgage Closing Costs field, enter the amount that the mortgage bank is charging to refinance your mortgage and choose **Enter**. Move to the Mortgage Points field and enter the percentage point(s) you are being charged. Usually this is anywhere from 1 percent to 4 percent, but this can vary from lender to lender and also is based on the size of the loan.

Quicken calculates the total closing costs to refinance and determines how many months it will take you to break even (how many months it will take you to recover the closing costs using the monthly savings from refinancing).

Figure 18.15 shows a monthly savings of $118.37 when refinancing a mortgage of $125,000 at 7 percent. With closing costs of $2,250, it will take exactly 19 months to break even or recover the closing costs using the monthly savings.

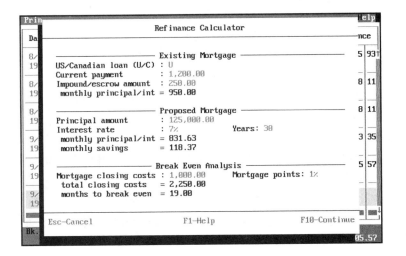

Fig. 18.15

Using the Refinance Calculator to determine monthly savings and recovery of closing costs when refinancing a mortgage.

CPA TIP

When you refinance your mortgage, in essence, you're giving up deductible interest by refinancing at a lower interest rate. Currently, mortgage interest on up to two residences is generally fully deductible (subject to the 3 percent reduction for itemized deductions if your adjusted gross income is greater than $100,000-$50,000 if filing separately). You may end up paying more in taxes a few years down the road than you would if you hadn't refinanced. Consider the income tax implications before you make the decision to refinance.

Tips on Refinancing

Use the Refinance Calculator to help you determine whether refinancing is a viable option for you. Also consider the following:

- Although the Refinance Calculator shows that you will save on your monthly payment by refinancing your mortgage, in the long run, refinancing could cost you more. If you extend your current mortgage over a longer time period than it is originally set to come due, you may end up paying more in interest than you would have had you stayed with the original mortgage at the higher rate. If you currently have a 30-year mortgage at 10.5 percent, for example, but have made payments for 6 years, your mortgage matures in 24 years. If now, you refinance for another 30 years, even though the refinance interest rate is lower, you have in effect created a 36-year loan with an interest rate change in year 6. Many times, this scenario results in lower monthly payments, but more interest paid over the term of the loan. You can prevent this result, however, by refinancing at a lower rate and shortening the mortgage term. Just continue to make your old payment and apply the excess (the amount of the old payment that exceeds the new payment) to the principal. Your loan will be paid off quicker and you will avoid paying more in interest.

- When you're shopping for mortgage interest rates, be sure that you lock in the rate or have the rate guaranteed by the mortgage company or bank. Just one-half point rise in interest rates could make a difference in your decision to refinance. Most lenders, however, require that you file an application before they will give you a locked-in rate.

- Mortgage points charged to refinance are not fully tax deductible in the year you refinance. Deductions for points paid to refinance a mortgage (unlike points paid up front when you purchase a home) must be spread over the life of the loan. Therefore, if you paid $2,400 in mortgage refinancing points for a 30-year loan, you can deduct only $80 each year. Two exceptions exist for deducting points on refinancing. If part of the loan is used for renovations, the points attributable to that part of the loan are fully deductible. Also, if you refinanced previously and did not fully deduct the points incurred to refinance, you can deduct them in the year that you pay off the loan (you pay off the existing loan when you refinance a loan).

■ Carefully scrutinize mailings you receive from mortgage brokers. On the surface, it may sound like they're offering a great deal, but what you don't know is how much they charge in *up-front fees* (fees that are charged even though the loan never closes). Be suspicious if you read or hear about up-front money for appraisals, credit checks, and application fees that are greater than $500. And be sure that your money is refundable if the loan doesn't close and that this provision is stated clearly in writing.

Displaying and Printing Payment Schedules

Each financial calculator, except the Refinance Calculator, enables you to display the payment schedules based on the current calculation. To display payment schedules, simply choose **F9** from the Financial Calculator. Quicken displays a window like to the one you see in figure 18.16 which shows a calculation from the Investment Planning Calculator for the scenario shown at figure 18.5.

To remove the payment schedule from the screen, just choose **Esc** and Quicken returns to the financial calculator currently in use.

You can print a payment schedule if you want a hard copy of Quicken's calculations. You might want to show payment schedule data to your financial planner, estate planner, or your accountant.

To print a payment schedule, follow these steps:

1. From the financial calculator you currently are using and that you want to see payment for, choose **F9** to display the Payment Schedule window.

Fig. 18.16

The Investment
Planning Payment
Schedule window.

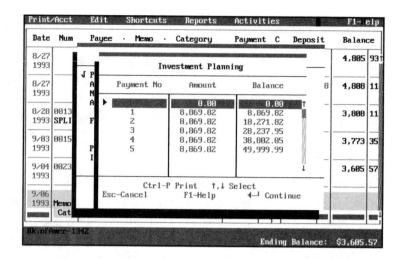

2. Choose **Ctrl-P** to display the Print window. The Print window is similar to the Print Register window.

3. Select the number that corresponds to the printer you want to print to or the **Print To Disk** option and choose **Enter**. If you select to print to a disk file, Quicken displays an additional window for you to enter the DOS file name, lines per page, and width.

Summary

This chapter concludes Part III of *Using Quicken 7 for DOS*, "Analyzing Your Finances with Quicken." In this chapter, you learn how to use Quicken's financial calculators to plan your investments, plan for your retirement, plan for college, and analyze mortgage refinancing options.

The next chapter begins Part IV, "Managing Quicken." You learn how to manage your Quicken files and customize the Quicken program in this part of the book. Chapter 19 deals with managing Quicken files. You learn how to add, edit, and delete files, back up and restore files, shrink the size of files, import and export data, and assign and use passwords to prevent unauthorized access to your Quicken files.

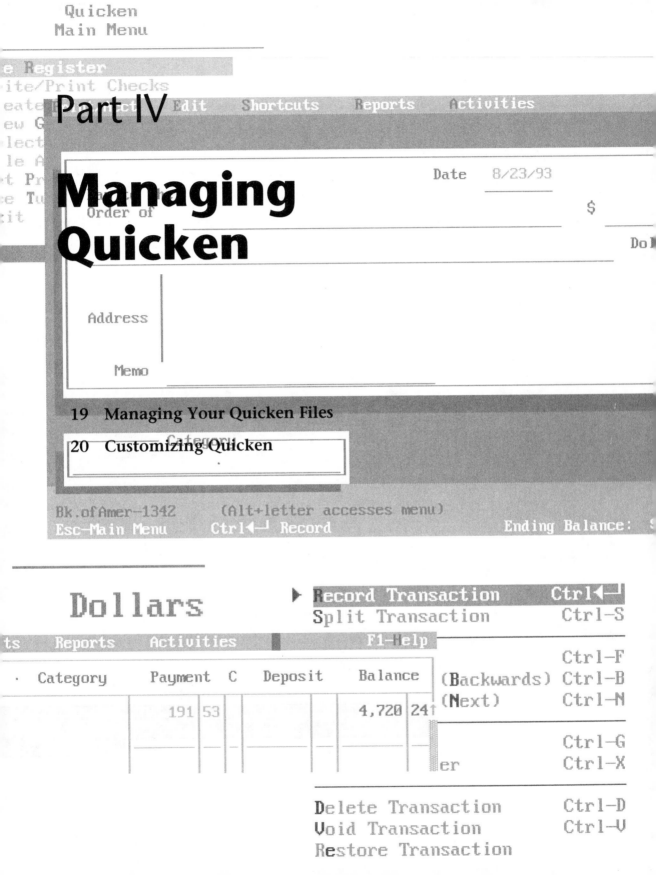

Part IV

Managing Quicken

Quicken
Main Menu

Use Register
Write/Print Checks
Create Print/Acct   Edit   Shortcuts   Reports   Activities
View G
Select
File A
Set Pr   Date   8/23/93
Use Tu   Pay to the
Exit   Order of $

              Address
                    |

              Memo

        ┌──────── Category ────────┐
        │   │
        └──────────────────────────┘

    Bk.ofAmer-1342   (Alt+letter accesses menu)
    Esc-Main Menu   Ctrl⏎ Record   Ending Balance:

        Dollars   ▶ Record Transaction   Ctrl⏎
                           Split Transaction   Ctrl-S
cuts   Reports   Activities │   F1-Help
                                                      Ctrl-F
o · Category   Payment C Deposit   Balance   (Backwards) Ctrl-B
s   191 53   4,720 24↑ (Next)   Ctrl-N

                                                      Ctrl-G
                                                er   Ctrl-X

                                   Delete Transaction   Ctrl-D
                                   Void Transaction   Ctrl-V
                                   Restore Transaction

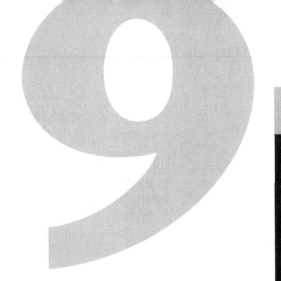

Chapter 19

Managing Your Quicken Files

Up to now, you worked with only one Quicken file. Quicken enables you to add additional files so that you can maintain separate accounts for more than one household or business. With multiple files in the Quicken system, you can work easily with several different sets of accounts by switching from one file to another. With Quicken, however, you can work with only one file at a time.

Working with Quicken Files

Quicken assigns a DOS file name to each file. As you learned in Chapter 1, the name for the first file added to the Quicken system is based on the name you enter when you install Quicken. Each Quicken file consists of four data files with the same DOS file name, but with different extensions—QDT, QNX, QMT, and QDI. You can find these data files in the directory where you store Quicken data (C:\QUICKEN). Quicken stores in files the financial information you enter in the Register. You can delete unneeded files to free memory and make Quicken even more efficient.

Quicken stores accounts you define in files and enables you to have more than one file. The obvious question, then, when you begin defining new accounts is to which file an account should be added. You usually find these decisions fairly easy to make.

The general rule is that you store related accounts together in a separate file. Accounts are related when they pertain to the same business or the same household. If you use Quicken for home accounting and for a commercial

In this chapter, you learn how to perform the following tasks:

- Add, select edit, and delete a new Quicken file

- Change the location of Quicken files

- Search for Quicken files in other directories

- Back up and restore your Quicken data

- Shrink Quicken files

- Export and import file data

- Assign, change, and eliminate passwords

printing business, you use two files: one for home and one for business. If you use Quicken for three businesses—a consulting practice, a small publishing business, and a restaurant—you use three files, a file for each business.

Adding a New File

As part of installing Quicken, you create at least one file by using the Create New File option on the Use Tutorials and Assistants menu or the Select/Set Up File option on the File Activities menu. Chapter 1, "Preparing to Use Quicken," explains how you use both these options to create the first Quicken file. You may, however, need to add new files even after the installation.

To add a new file to the Quicken system, follow these steps:

1. From Quicken's Main Menu, choose File Activities. Quicken displays the File Activities menu as shown in figure 19.1.

Fig. 19.1
The File Activities menu.

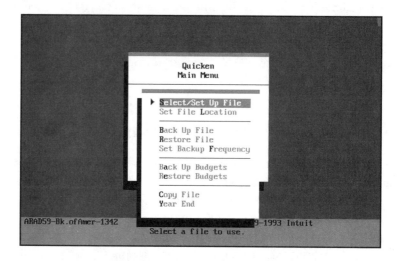

2. Choose Select/Set Up File from the File Activities menu. Quicken displays the Select/Set Up New File window (see fig. 19.2).

Tip
You can press **Ctrl-G** from the Main Menu to access the Select/Set Up New File window.

3. Highlight the <Set Up New File> line and choose **Enter** to display the Set Up New File window shown in figure 19.3.

4. Enter the name for the new file you want DOS to use. The name you enter must be a valid DOS file name. Refer to the DOS user's manual if you have questions about DOS file-naming conventions.

5. When the file name is correct, move the cursor to the Location for File field. By default, Quicken stores data files in the Quicken program

directory. If you want the file stored in a different directory, enter the new directory path name.

Fig. 19.2
The Select/Set Up New File window.

Fig. 19.3
The Set Up New File window.

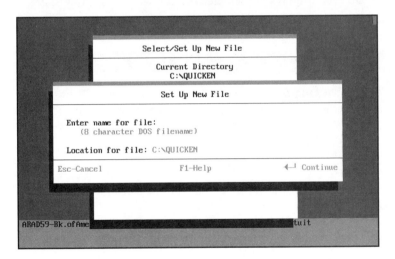

6. When the file location is correct, choose **Enter**. Quicken displays the Standard Categories window in which you select the standard category list that you want to use in the new file.

From here, you select the standard categories to use in the new Quicken file and then set up an account to use. Refer to Chapter 1 to learn how to select categories and set up an account.

Editing File Names

You also can use the Select/Set Up File option to edit the names of existing files. You may want to edit a file name, for example, if you named the file incorrectly. If you name files based on the business name, changing the name of the business also may mean that you want to change the name of the file. Suppose that the file name for the business Acme Manufacturing is ACME_MFG. If the business name changes to Acme, Incorporated, you can change the file name to ACME_INC.

To edit a file name, follow these steps:

1. From the Quicken Main Menu, choose File Activities. Quicken displays the File Activities menu.

2. From the File Activities menu, choose Select/Set Up File. The Select/Set Up New File window appears.

3. (Optional) To edit a file in a directory other than C:/QUICKEN, choose **F9**. Quicken displays the Set File Location window for specifying another location for Quicken's files. Choose **Enter**.

> **Note**
>
> If you don't know the name of the directory that contains a file, you can search all directories by pressing **F7** and Quicken searches the drive that you specify. See *Searching for Data Files*, later in this chapter, to learn how to search for data files.

4. Highlight the file you want to edit from the Select/Set Up New File window.

5. Choose **Ctrl-E**. The Rename a File window appears.

6. Edit the file name in the Enter New File Name field. Be sure that you enter a valid DOS file name.

7. Choose **Enter** to save the name change and return to the Select/ Set Up New File window. To edit additional file names, repeat steps 1 through 7.

Deleting a File

Quicken enables you to delete files that you added inadvertently or that you no longer use. Usually, never delete a file because when you do, you essentially are deleting all the accounts in the file. If you are no longer track-ing any of the accounts in the file, you can delete the entire file. This may be the case if you set up a special file for learning to use Quicken and you no longer use the file. You also no longer need the file used for a business if you sell the business.

To delete a file, display the Select/Set Up New File window and follow these steps:

1. (Optional) To delete a file in some directory other than C:\QUICKEN, choose **F9**. Quicken displays the Set File Location window, which you can use to specify some other directory as the location in which to look for Quicken files. Choose **Enter**.

2. In the Select/Set Up New File window, highlight the file you want to delete.

3. Choose **Ctrl-D**. Quicken displays the Deleting File window (see fig. 19.4). This window gives the name of the file that Quicken is ready to delete and asks you to confirm the deletion.

Fig. 19.4
The Deleting File window.

4. Type **yes** to delete the file. If you don't want to delete the file, choose **Esc**.

5. To complete the deletion and return to the Select/Set Up New File win-dow, choose **Enter**. To delete additional files, repeat steps 1 through 5.

Selecting a File

When you work with more than one file, you need to tell Quicken the file in which you want to work. To select a Quicken file, follow these steps:

1. In the Select/Set Up New file window, highlight the file you want to use.

2. Choose **Enter**. Quicken displays the Select Account to Use window so that you can select an account to use to begin your work in the selected file.

Locating Files

If you accept the program defaults, Quicken stores data files in the C:\QUICKEN directory. You have the option, however, of having Quicken locate the files somewhere other than the default location when you specify where the files for a data file are to be located (when you are setting up or shrinking a data file). If you locate Quicken files in a place other than the default directory, you need to tell Quicken where these files are.

To inform Quicken of the location of a data file that you have relocated, follow these steps:

1. Choose File Activities from Quicken's Main Menu. The File Activities menu appears.

2. Choose Set File Location from the File Activities menu. Quicken displays the Set File Location window shown in figure 19.5.

Fig. 19.5

The Set File Location window.

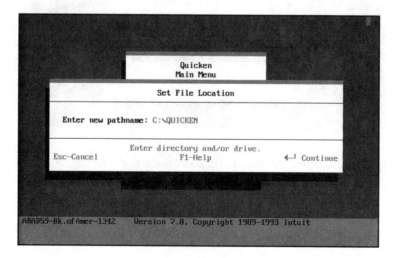

IV

Managing Quicken

3. Enter the drive and directory where the Quicken data files are located.

The drive and directory you enter must be a valid DOS path name. The drive letter must be valid and followed by a colon. (The Quicken 7 installation program creates the directory QUICKEN.) If you use a directory and subdirectory together, the combination must constitute a valid path name. The subdirectory specified must be in the directory specified. (For more information on directories, subdirectories, and path names, see the DOS user's manual.)

4. Choose **Enter** to save the file location.

Searching for Data Files

Quicken provides a feature, Search, that you can use to search for and open a Quicken data file from any drive (including a floppy disk drive). This is useful if you want to locate a data file that you know is somewhere on your hard disk but you don't know which directory it's in.

To search for a Quicken data file and open the file, follow these steps:

1. From the Quicken Main Menu, choose the File Activities option. The File Activities menu appears.

2. From the File Activities menu, choose **S**elect/Set Up File. Quicken displays the Select/Set Up New File window.

3. From the Select/Set Up New File window, choose **F7** to display the Search for Quicken Files window shown in figure 19.6.

Fig. 19.6
The Search for Quicken Files window.

4. Enter the drive in which you want Quicken to search for your Quicken data files. Choose **Enter**.

Quicken searches the drive that you specify and, in the Existing Quicken Files window, lists all Quicken data files found in the drive (see fig. 19.7).

Fig. 19.7
The Existing Quicken Files window.

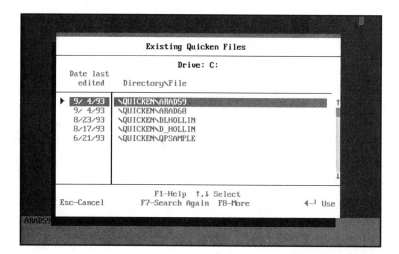

5. (Optional) To see the size or complete path of any file in the list, highlight the file and choose **F8**. Quicken displays the File window that shows the date of the last entry into the file, the file's size, and the full path where the file is located. Choose **Esc** to return to the Existing Quicken Files window.

6. To open a file Quicken finds in the specified drive, highlight the file that you want to open and choose **Enter**. Quicken opens the file and displays the Select Account to Use window so that you can select an account on which to work.

Backing Up and Restoring Files

You need to understand the importance of backing up files. Although you may be a careful computer user, everyone loses data at one time or another. Avoid losing important financial data by backing up your files regularly.

Backing up means that you make a second copy of all Quicken data files (including Q3.DIR). Back up these files so that if the original Quicken data files are damaged, you can use the backup copies to restore the damaged files to original condition. You can back up and restore by using DOS file commands or one of the popular hard disk management programs. For convenience, you may find the Quicken backup and restore options easier to use. This section discusses these backup and restore options.

Backing Up Files

You need to make two important decisions about backing up files. First, you must decide how often you need to perform a backup. Although opinions on the subject vary, a good habit to form is to back up data files after completing a session in which you enter or change financial data. When you finish entering the first set of account transactions, for example, back up all the data files.

Most people back up financial records daily, weekly, or monthly. After you spend time working with Quicken and become familiar with data file restoration procedures, you can estimate more accurately how often you need to back up files.

Second, decide how many old backup copies to keep. Usually, two or three copies are adequate. (This rule of thumb is the grandfather, father, and son scheme.) Suppose that you back up the data files every day. On Thursday, a co-worker deletes the data file accidentally. If you keep two old backup copies besides the most recent backup copy, you have backups from Wednesday, Tuesday, and Monday. If the Wednesday copy is damaged (an unlikely but possible situation), you still have the Tuesday and Monday copies. The more recent a backup copy, the easier data is to recover, but using an old backup copy still is easier than reentering all the data from the original documents.

Store these data file backup copies in a safe place. Do not keep all backup copies in the same location. If you experience a fire or if someone burglarizes your business or house, you may lose all the copies—no matter how many backups you keep. Store at least one copy at an off-site location. If you use Quicken at home, you can keep a backup copy in your desk at work; if you use Quicken for business, keep a backup copy at home.

To back up your Quicken files, follow these steps:

1. From Quicken's Main Menu, choose File Activities. The File Activities menu appears.

2. From the File Activities menu, choose Back Up File. Quicken displays the Select Backup Drive window shown in figure 19.8. Insert the backup

disk into drive A: or B: and type the appropriate drive letter in the Drive Letter of Backup Disk field.

Fig. 19.8
The Select Backup Drive window.

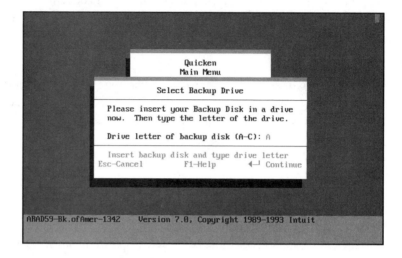

3. Choose **Enter**. Quicken displays the Select File to Back Up window. This window is similar to the Select/Set Up New File window shown in figure 19.2—only the title is different.

4. Highlight the file you want to back up and choose **Enter**.

   The message Backing Up appears as Quicken copies the selected file to the backup disk. When Quicken finishes backing up, the message File backed up successfully appears.

5. Remove the backup disk from the disk drive and store the disk in a safe place.

> **Note**
>
> If the file you are trying to back up cannot fit on the disk, an error message alerts you that the disk is full, and you must choose **Esc** to cancel. The warning message File not backed up appears. If the disk is full, choose **Esc**, insert a different backup disk, and repeat steps 1 through 5.

Tip
You can press **Ctrl-B** from the Main Menu to display the Select Backup Drive window. Then continue with steps 3 through 5 to back up a selected file.

To back up the current Quicken file, follow these steps:

1. From the Register or the Write Checks screen, choose **Back Up File** from the Print/Acct menu. Quicken displays the Select Backup Drive window.

2. Insert the backup disk into drive A: or B: and type the appropriate drive letter in the Drive Letter of Backup Disk field.

3. Choose **Enter** to begin the backup process.

4. When Quicken finishes backing up, the message `File backed up successfully` appears.

5. Remove the backup disk from the disk drive and store the disk in a safe place.

Restoring Backed-Up Files

Eventually, someone or something may accidentally delete or destroy a data file. A computer can malfunction; a co-worker may spill the contents of the pencil sharpener or a cup of coffee on the floppy disk that contains the Quicken data files. If you recently backed up these files and if you were diligent about printing copies of the Register, you should experience no serious problems. You can restore the Quicken files by using the backup copies.

To retrieve the data you copied with the Back Up File option, follow this procedure:

1. From Quicken's Main Menu, choose File Activities. The File Activities menu appears.

2. Choose **R**estore File from the File Activities menu. Quicken prompts you to identify the backup disk drive and to insert the backup disk.

3. After you insert the backup disk, choose **Enter**. Quicken displays the Select File to Restore window. Quicken reads the files from the backup disk that you inserted into drive A: or B: and displays the files in the Select File to Restore window.

4. In the Select File to Restore window, highlight the file you want to restore and choose **Enter**.

> **Note**
>
> Quicken alerts you that the restoration operation will overwrite the existing file (see fig. 19.9). To continue with the restoration, choose **Enter**.

Fig. 19.9
The Overwrite
Existing File?
message.

When the file is restored, Quicken displays the File restored successfully
message.

> **Note**
>
> You cannot restore the currently selected file. If you try to restore the currently
> selected file, the message shown in figure 19.10 alerts you to this error. If you
> originally set up only one file, you need to set up a second, dummy file that
> you can select as the current file before you use the restore option.

Fig. 19.10
The Cannot
Restore the
Current File
message.

5. Using the most recent printed copy of the Register, reenter each transaction that you entered between the time you backed up and the time
you lost the data. You need to reenter transactions for each account.

6. Back up these files in case another accident causes you to lose the Quicken files again.

Using the Backup Reminder

Without regular backups, you may lose financial records. Obviously, backing up files is important. Because backing up is this important, Quicken provides a backup reminder feature that you can set so that Quicken periodically reminds you to back up a specified file.

To use the backup reminder feature, first choose the file for which you want to be reminded to back up. You need to take this step because backup reminders attach to specific files. To continue, follow these steps:

1. From Quicken's Main Menu, choose File Activities. The File Activities menu appears.

2. Choose Set Backup Frequency from the File Activities menu. The Backup Reminder Frequency window appears (see fig. 19.11).

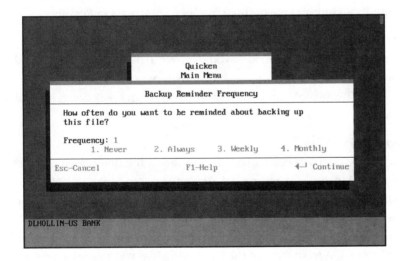

Fig. 19.11
The Backup Reminder Frequency window.

3. Indicate how often you want to be reminded to back up the current file. Choose **1** if you never want to be reminded to back up. Choose **2** to be reminded every time you exit the Quicken program (and you have entered transactions or changed the data file in any way). Choose **3** to be reminded once a week. Choose **4** to be reminded once a month. After you make your selection, choose **Enter**.

After you set a backup frequency reminder, Quicken monitors backups you make of a particular file. If the time arrives for you to again back up a file, Quicken displays a message upon exiting the program that tells you to back up a particular file.

> **Note**
>
> Remember that the backup reminders attach to specific files. Accordingly, if you decide to use this handy feature, you probably want to set backup frequencies for each file so that you don't forget to back up a file.

Shrinking Files

Tip
If disaster strikes data files you didn't back up, you must reenter each Register transaction. Up-to-date printed copies of each Register can show what you need to reenter. If you don't have up-to-date copies of each of the Registers, you need to reenter each transaction, using the original source documents, such as checks, deposits receipts, and so on. Of course, you don't want to reenter data from original documents, so back up the files regularly and store the backup disks in a safe place.

Theoretically, Quicken enables you to store up to 65,353 transactions in a file's Registers. Practically, these limitations are much lower. Using a hard disk, you may not be limited by disk space, but you probably do not want to work with thousands or tens of thousands of transactions in Registers.

Quicken provides a twofold solution for dealing with the problem of ever-growing data files: Quicken enables you to create archive copies of files and to create fresh copies of files that include only transactions that fall after a certain date. This twofold solution means that you can break down large files into smaller, more manageable files.

When to Shrink Files

For most users, the most convenient time to shrink the files is after completing the annual income tax return and after any year-end reporting. At this time, all transactions from the prior year should have cleared the bank, and you have printed all necessary Quicken reports. Now, an archive copy of the files can provide a permanent copy of the data you used to prepare the year's financial reports. A fresh copy of the file also enables you to start a new year without a load of old, unnecessary data.

How to Shrink Files

Because you can shrink only the currently selected file, you need to use the Select/Set Up File option to select a file to shrink. If you don't select a file before attempting to shrink files, Quicken warns you before shrinking the files.

When you are ready to shrink files, take the following steps:

1. From Quicken's Main Menu, choose File Activities. The File Activities menu appears.

IV

2. From the File Activities menu, choose Year End. The Year End window appears (see fig. 19.12).

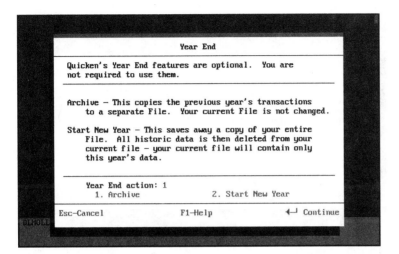

Fig. 19.12
The Year End window.

```
                              Year End

   Quicken's Year End features are optional.  You are
   not required to use them.


   Archive - This copies the previous year's transactions
       to a separate File.  Your current File is not changed.

   Start New Year - This saves away a copy of your entire
       File.  All historic data is then deleted from your
       current file - your current file will contain only
       this year's data.


       Year End action: 1
         1. Archive                    2. Start New Year

   Esc-Cancel              F1-Help              ←┘ Continue
```

3. Identify the year-end action you want to take. Choose **1** (Archive) to create a year-end archive copy of the current file. Choose **2** (Start New Year) to create a fresh copy of the file that includes only transactions from the current year. After you enter your selection, choose **Enter**.

> **Note**
>
> If you select **2** to create a fresh file copy, Quicken may include some transactions from previous years, such as investment transactions and any uncleared transactions. You need to keep these transactions in a working copy of a file because the investment transactions are needed for investment recordkeeping and the uncleared transactions are needed for bank reconciliations.

4. If you select the Archive option in step 3, the Archive File window shown in figure 19.13 appears. By default, Quicken names the archive file with the current file name and the previous year, locates the file in the Quicken program directory, and includes transactions only through the end of the previous year. If any of these default settings are incorrect, move the cursor to the incorrect field, and then make the necessary corrections. When the Archive File window is complete, choose **Enter** or **F10**. Quicken creates the archive file copy and then displays a message that asks if you want to work with the archive file or the

Tip

If you create a separate set of Quicken data files for each year, consider including the year number in the account group name. You can name the data files from 1993 as QDATA93, the data files from 1994 as QDATA94, and so on. Including the year number in date file names enables you to easily determine which year's records are contained in a particular data file.

current file. Choose **1** to use the current file; choose **2** to use the archive file.

Fig. 19.13
The Archive File window.

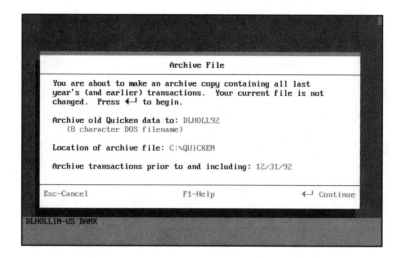

```
                          Archive File

      You are about to make an archive copy containing all last
      year's (and earlier) transactions.  Your current file is not
      changed.  Press ← to begin.

      Archive old Quicken data to: DLHOLL92
         (8 character DOS filename)

      Location of archive file: C:\QUICKEN

      Archive transactions prior to and including: 12/31/92


   Esc-Cancel                    F1-Help                ←  Continue

DLHOLLIN-US BANK
```

5. If you select the Start New Year option in step 3, the Start New Year window appears (see fig. 19.14). Enter the file name you want Quicken to use for the new file in the Copy All Transactions to File field. Indicate the date that, if a transaction date falls before, controls the transactions that get deleted from the file in the Delete Transactions from Current File Older Than field. If you only want the file to contain transactions dated from 1/1/93 to 12/31/93, for example, enter 1/1/93 in this field. All transactions dated before 1/1/93, such as 11/2/92 or 4/15/92, are deleted from the file. When the Start New Year window is complete, choose **Enter** or **F10**. Quicken creates the new file copy and then displays a message that asks if you want to work with the old file or the file for the new year. Choose **1** to use the old file; choose **2** to use the new year file.

Copying Quicken Files

You can make a copy of your Quicken file, perhaps to give to your accountant to use with his Quicken program. Before you begin to copy a file, choose the file to copy from the Select/Set Up New File window to make this file the current file.

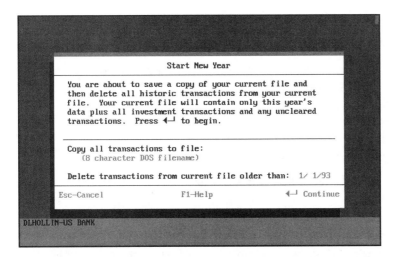

Fig. 19.14
The Start New Year window.

IV

Managing Quicken

To copy the current Quicken file, follow these steps:

1. From Quicken's Main Menu, choose **F**ile Activities. The File Activities menu appears.

2. From the File Activities menu, choose Copy File. Quicken displays the Copy File window shown in figure 19.15.

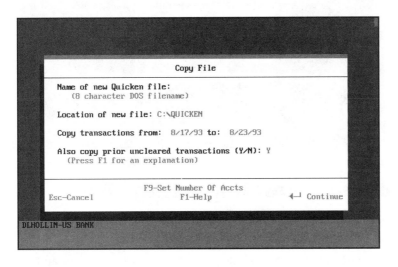

Fig. 19.15
The Copy File window.

3. Type the DOS file name for the new Quicken file in the first field and choose **Enter**.

4. In the Location of New File field, type the path (drive and/or directory) in which you want to locate the new file, and then choose **Enter**.

5. In the Copy Transactions From and To fields, enter the beginning and ending dates for transactions to be copied, and then choose **Enter**.

6. In the next field, choose **Y** to copy prior uncleared transactions or **N** if you do not. Choose **Enter**.

7. (Optional) Choose **F9** to set the maximum number of Quicken accounts that can be created in the new file (up to 255). Quicken sets the maximum amount to 64.

8. Choose **Enter** or **F10** from the Copy File window to start copying the file.

When the copy procedure is complete, Quicken displays the File Copied Successfully window, shown in figure 19.16. To reload the original file, choose **1**; to load the new file copy, choose **2**.

Fig. 19.16
The File Copied Successfully window.

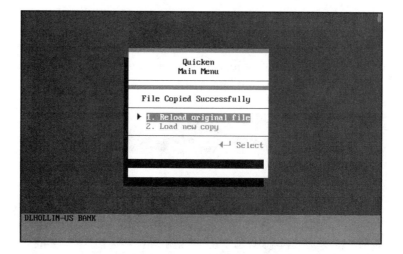

Exporting and Importing Files

Exporting is the process by which a software program makes a copy of a file in a format that another program can read. You may want to export the information stored in the Quicken Register so that you can retrieve and use the information in a database program, such as dBASE, or in a spreadsheet program, such as 1-2-3.

Importing is the process by which information created by one software program is retrieved by a second software program. You may want to import into

Quicken the information created by an accounting program, such as DacEasy, so that you can use Quicken's reports to summarize the information.

Exporting and importing represent two sides of the same coin: exporting creates a file by using the information stored in the Quicken Register, and importing retrieves information from another file into the Quicken Register. Although most Quicken users never need to export or import files, Quicken provides the tools to do both. The Export and Import options are available from any Register or the Write Checks screen.

Exporting Files

The Export option enables you to create an ASCII text file from Register transactions. You then can use this ASCII file in another software program. Most word processing, spreadsheet, and database applications commonly enable you to import ASCII text files from Quicken.

To execute an export operation, follow these steps:

1. At the Register or the Write Checks screen, display the Print/Acct menu (see fig. 19.17).

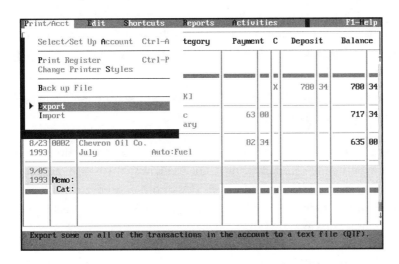

Fig. 19.17
The Print/Acct menu.

2. Choose Export from the Print/Acct menu. Quicken displays the Export Transactions to QIF File window shown in figure 19.18. *QIF* stands for Quicken Interchange Format, which describes the special format in the ASCII file.

3. In the DOS File field, enter the DOS file name to use for the new ASCII file. You also can include a path name.

Fig. 19.18

The Export
Transactions to
QIF File window.

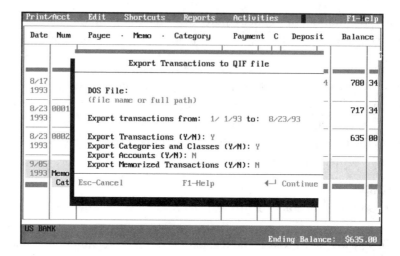

4. (Optional) To limit exported transactions to within a certain range of dates, fill in the Export Transactions From and To fields. You can use the + (plus) and - (minus) keys to change the date one day at a time.

5. (Optional) Quicken enables you to export transactions, categories, classes, accounts, and memorized transactions. To change the default settings for these items, move the cursor to the Y/N answer fields in the Export Transactions to QIF File window, and then choose **Y** for Yes or **N** for No.

6. To start the export operation, choose **Enter** or **F10** after you complete the Export Transactions to QIF File window.

Quicken creates an ASCII file that contains the exported transactions. At the beginning of the file, Quicken prints a line to identify the type of account from which transactions were exported. This information begins with an exclamation point and the word type, and is followed by the actual type name. Transactions exported from a bank account, for example, show Bank as the first line.

The following example is the actual ASCII information that Quicken uses to record each transaction in the Register:

```
D7/24/93
T-1,000.00
CX
N*****
PBig National Bank
L[Savings]
^
```

The first line begins with D and shows the transaction date. The second line begins with T and shows the transaction amount as -1,000.00. (The amount is negative because the transaction is a payment.) The third line begins with a C and shows the cleared status. The fourth line shows the transaction number set to asterisks because the check isn't yet printed. The fifth line begins with P and shows the payee. The sixth line begins with L and shows the Category field entry. If you split a transaction, Quicken creates several L lines. The last line shows only a caret (^), which designates the end of a transaction.

Other types of exported data, such as categories, classes, accounts, and memorized transactions, work in a similar way. Each kind of data starts with a header to identify the exported data: *!Type:Cat* for category list, *!Type:Class* for class list, *!Account* for account list, *!Type:Memorized* for memorized transaction list, and so on. Then, each field in the data type that describes an item starts with a code. Suppose that you want to export the class name *West* and the description *Western*. The ASCII file looks like the following example:

```
!Type:Class
N West
D Western
^
```

Note

The codes for category, account, and memorized transactions are not mentioned here. You easily can obtain this information from the Quicken user's manual.

The Export option doesn't produce the same ASCII file as the Print to Disk option described in Chapters 5, 7, and 12. The Export option creates an ASCII file with each transaction field on a separate line. You can use this option if you are trying to import the Quicken data into another software program, such as an accounting program, that uses the information. The Print Register's Print to Disk setting creates an ASCII text file that looks like a printed Check Register. You may use this option to create a list of certain Quicken transactions that you can retrieve by a word processing program, edit with the word processor, and then print or use in a document.

Importing Files

The Import option retrieves files stored in the Quicken QIF format. This format is the same one Quicken uses when exporting data. The steps for importing parallel those for exporting data.

To import files, follow these steps:

1. At the Register or the Write Checks screen, choose Import from the Print/Acct menu. The Import from QIF file or CheckFree window appears, as shown in figure 19.19.

Fig. 19.19

The Import from QIF file or CheckFree window.

2. Enter the DOS file name of the file you want Quicken to import. You also can include a path name.

3. Move the cursor to the Import Transactions field. To import transactions, choose **Y** for Yes and then choose **Enter**.

4. Move to the Ignore Duplicate Transactions field. If you are importing data you previously exported, choose **Y** to prevent duplicating transfer transactions when importing from multiple accounts.

5. (Optional) Move the cursor to the Special Handling for Transfers field. To import transactions with account transfers included in the Category field, choose **N** for No and then choose **Enter**. If you are importing from CheckFree, press **Y** here to include transfers, such as credit card bill payments.

6. (Optional) Move the cursor to the Import Categories and Classes field. To import categories and classes, choose **Y** for Yes and then choose **Enter**.

7. (Optional) Move the cursor to the Import Accounts field. To import accounts, choose **Y** for Yes and choose **Enter**.

8. (Optional) Move the cursor to the Import Memorized Transactions field. To import memorized transactions, choose **Y** for Yes and then choose **Enter**.

9. To import the file, choose **Enter** or **F10** when the Import from QIF file or CheckFree window is complete. Quicken imports the file and records the transactions in the Register.

10. If the imported file does not contain categories, you may be prompted to add categories.

11. On completion, Quicken tells you that the import was successful.

Using Passwords

Anytime you deal with financial information, you must maintain the integrity of the information and safeguard the system that stores the information from unauthorized entry. Using passwords in Quicken enables you to control the access or restrict transactions from being modified in your Quicken files.

Passwords represent an internal control mechanism. With Quicken, you can use passwords to limit access to the data files in which you store financial records.

Assigning Passwords

You can use two kinds of passwords in Quicken: *file* and *transaction* passwords. The file password that you assign to the current file provides access to the Registers, Write Checks screen, Reports menu, and the View Graphs menu in a Quicken file. If you want each file in your Quicken system to use a password, you need to set up a password for each file. The transaction password restricts anyone without access to the password from changing or deleting transactions prior to the date that you specify.

Assigning a File Password. File passwords prevent unauthorized users from accessing any Register, the Write Checks screen, the Reports menu, and the View Graphs menu. To assign a file password to the current file, follow these steps:

1. From the Quicken Main Menu, choose **Set** Preferences. Quicken displays the Set Preferences menu.

2. From the Set Preferences menu, choose Password Settings. The Password Settings menu appears, as shown in figure 19.20.

3. Choose File Password from the Password Settings menu. Quicken displays the Set Up Password window shown in figure 19.21.

Fig. 19.20

The Password
Settings menu.

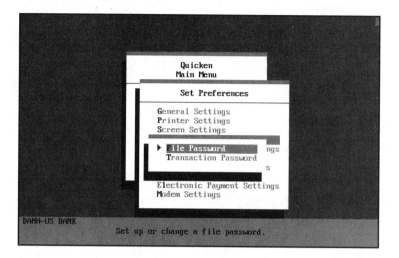

4. To define a file password, type the combination of letters and numbers you want to use as a password. You can use up to 16 characters. Then choose **Enter**.

> **Note**
>
> Quicken doesn't distinguish between the use of upper- and lowercase letters in establishing or using passwords.

5. Quicken prompts you to retype the password to confirm what you entered in the Confirm Password window (see fig. 19.22). Type the password, exactly as you entered it in the Set Up Password window, and choose **Enter**.

Quicken returns to the Password Settings menu. Choose **Esc** twice to return to the Main Menu. After assigning the file password, Quicken asks you for the password before enabling you to view or modify transactions in any of the accounts within the data file that you assigned the password to. Figure 19.22 shows the file password set to SNF86. The next time you try to access the Write Checks, Register, or Reports screen in the data file with the password *SNF86*, Quicken requires that you enter this password. Figure 19.23 shows the

Password Required window in which you type the password. As an additional precaution, Quicken doesn't display the password as you type.

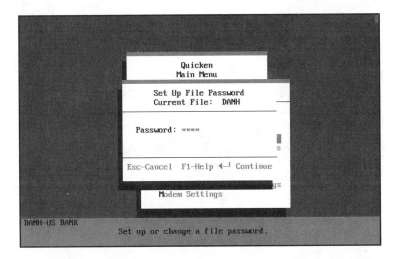

Fig. 19.21
The Set Up
Password window.

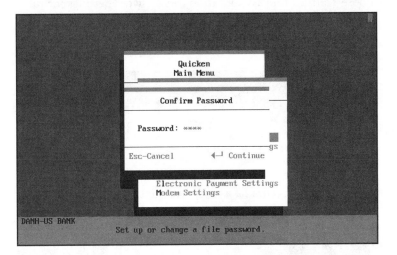

Fig. 19.22
The Confirm
Password window.

Assigning a Transaction Password. Transactions passwords prevent unauthorized users from changing or deleting transactions dated prior to a date that you specify when you assign the password.

To assign a transaction password to the current file, follow these steps:

1. From the Quicken Main Menu, choose Set Preferences. Quicken
   displays the Set Preferences menu.

Fig. 19.23
The Password
Required window.

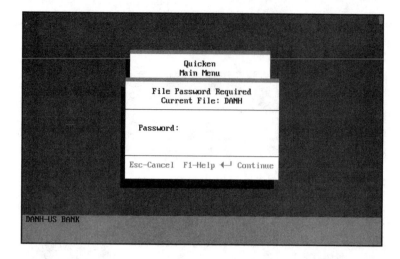

2. Choose Password Settings from the Set Preferences menu. Quicken displays the Password Settings menu.

3. Choose Transaction Password from the Password Settings menu. The Password to Modify Existing Transactions window appears (see fig. 19.24).

Fig. 19.24
The Password to
Modify Existing
Transactions
window.

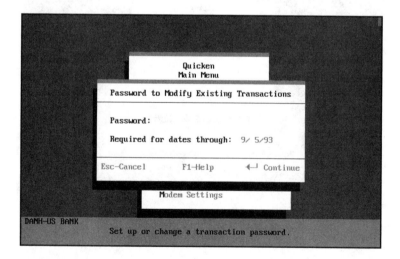

4. Enter the password you want to assign to transactions in the Password field. You can enter up to 16 characters, including spaces. Then choose **Enter**.

5. In the Required for Dates Through field, enter the date through which the transaction password is required.

6. Choose **Enter** to assign the password and display the Confirm Password window. Type the password to confirm the password that you entered in the Password to Modify Existing Transactions window. Be sure that you type the password exactly as you entered it the first time and choose **Enter**.

7. Quicken returns to the Password Settings menu. Choose **Esc** twice to return to the Main Menu.

If you want to record a transaction dated earlier than the date specified when you assigned the transaction password, Quicken requires that you enter the transaction password in the Transaction Password Required window, shown in figure 19.25. As with file passwords, Quicken doesn't display the transaction password as you type.

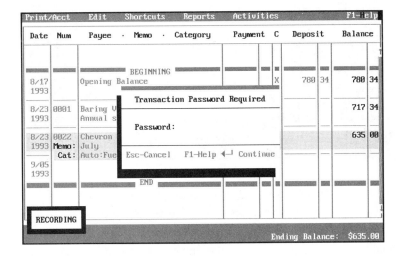

Fig. 19.25

The Transaction Password Required window.

Changing or Eliminating a Password

You can change the assigned password. You must enter the existing password, however, before Quicken enables you to change it. This precaution prevents unauthorized persons from entering the Quicken system and changing the password and then accessing your data file. You also can remove passwords to eliminate password protection from your file and transaction data.

To change or eliminate a password, follow these steps:

1. From the Quicken Main Menu, choose **Set Preferences**. Quicken displays the Set Preferences menu.

2. Choose Password Settings from the Set Preferences menu. Quicken displays the Password Settings menu.

3. Choose File Password or Transaction Password (whichever password you want to change or eliminate) from the Password Settings menu. Quicken displays the Change File Password window or the Change Transaction Password window (see fig. 19.26).

Fig. 19.26
The Change Password window.

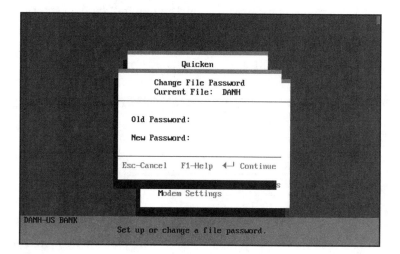

4. To change the file password, type the old and new passwords in the Change Password window and choose **Enter**. You now can use the new password. To eliminate the file password, type the old password in the Old Password field in the Change Password window and leave the New Password field blank. Choose **Enter** to eliminate the file password.

5. To change the transaction password, type the old and new passwords in the Change Transaction Password window and choose **Enter**. You also can change the date through which the transaction password is required. To eliminate the transaction password, type the old password in the Old Password field in the Change Transaction Password window and leave the New Password field blank. Choose **Enter** to eliminate the transaction password.

IV

Managing Quicken

> **Note**
>
> When using passwords, consider the following precautions:
>
> Make sure that you do not lose or forget the password. If you lose the password, you lose your data. Record the password in a safe place.
>
> If you are worried about someone accessing Quicken and then writing computer checks, initiating electronic payments, or modifying the account information, use nonsensical passwords of at least six characters. The passwords you create with this procedure are extremely difficult to guess.
>
> Be sure that you don't use a seemingly clever password scheme, such as month names or colors, as passwords. If you set the transaction password to *blue*, the curious user may not take long to figure out the main password.

Summary

This chapter describes the steps and the logic for taking care of Quicken data files. This chapter identifies the Quicken files and explains how to back up and restore files, how to shrink files, and how to tell Quicken where the files are located. This chapter also describes how to export information from Quicken and how to import information from other programs into a Quicken Register. And finally, this chapter covers the use of passwords to protect your Quicken data from unauthorized access.

In the following chapter, you learn how to customize Quicken to work the way you want the system to work. You learn how to change screen colors, background patterns, how Quicken displays the Register, and how to set transaction, check, and report settings. You also learn how to use Quicken's built-in reminder system called Billminder to help you remember checks that you need to print or transaction groups that become due.

Chapter 20

Customizing Quicken

When you install Quicken, the program sets the transaction, check, and report options that control how transactions and checks are entered, how items in reports are listed, and how the program works. You can change these options, however, so that Quicken works to suit your needs. If you don't want to assign a category to every transaction, for example, you can turn off the transaction setting that warns you if a transaction has no category. If you don't want the extra message line to appear on checks in the Write Checks screen, you can turn off the check and report setting that controls whether the extra message line appears.

If you have a color monitor and are tired of the default screen colors, you also can change to five other color schemes, and now with Quicken 7, you even can change the on-screen background patterns.

Quicken enables you to use another option, Billminder, which is a reminder system displayed each time you start the computer, even before you start Quicken. Billminder reminds you of actions you need to take, such as printing checks or recalling transaction groups.

Customizing General Settings

Quicken includes five general settings you can change so that the program processes data in the way you find most helpful. The general settings in Quicken are described in the following section.

To change general settings, perform these steps:

1. From Quicken's Main Menu, choose **S**et Preferences. Quicken displays the Set Preferences menu.

In this chapter, you learn how to perform the following tasks:

- Customize general settings

- Customize transaction settings

- Customize check and report settings

- Change screen settings, including screen colors, background patterns, the register display, menu access, monitor speed, and screen graphics

- Use Billminder

- Deactivate Billminder

- Start Quicken with parameters

2. From the Set Preferences menu, choose General Settings. Quicken displays the General Settings window (see fig. 20.1).

Fig. 20.1
The General
Settings window.

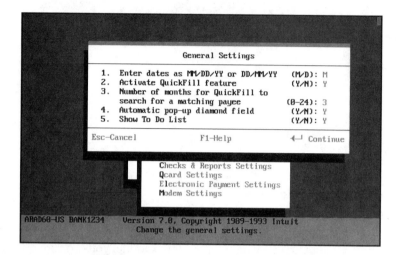

3. (Optional) Move the cursor to the Enter Dates as MM/DD/YY or DD/MM/YY setting. If you want dates to appear in month/day/year format—August 21, 1993 appears as 8/21/93, for example—press **M** for month first. If you want the dates to appear in day/month/year—August 21, 1993 appears as 21/8/93—press **D** for day first.

4. (Optional) Move the cursor to the Activate QuickFill Feature setting. If you don't want Quicken's QuickFill feature to search through the memorized transaction list of transactions in the register when you make an entry in the Payee field or the Category field and fill in the transaction for you, press **N** to turn off QuickFill. Refer to Chapter 6, "Automating the Register," and Chapter 8, "Automating Check Writing," to learn more about the QuickFill feature.

5. (Optional) Move the cursor to the Number of Months for Quickfill to search for a Matching Payee field. This is an option new to Quicken 7. In prior versions, three months was the only time period that QuickFill used to search for a matching payee. Now you can set the number of preceding months that QuickFill will search the Register from 0 up to a maximum of 24.

6. (Optional) Move the cursor to the Automatic Pop-up Diamond Field option. Press **Y** if you want Quicken to automatically display pop-up lists for fields marked with a diamond (see fig. 20.2). Press **N** if you don't want pop-up lists to appear.

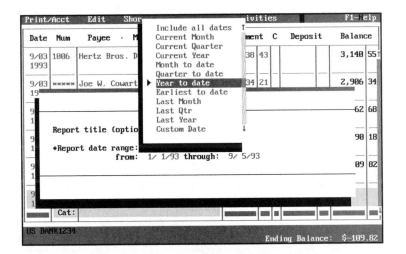

Fig. 20.2
The Pop-up menu at a Diamond Field.

7. (Optional) Move the cursor to the Show To Do List field. Press **Y** if you want Quicken to display the TO Do List whenever you open a data file that has tasks which need to be done (see figure 20.3).

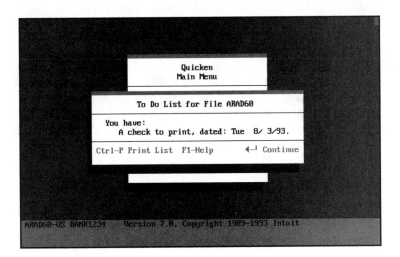

Fig. 20.3
The To Do List window.

The To Do List provides information about tasks such as dates of checks to be printed, accounts from which electronic payments need to be transmitted, and accounts in which investment reminders are due.

Customizing Transaction Settings

Quicken includes nine transaction settings you can change so that the program processes transactions in the way you find most helpful. The transaction settings in Quicken are described in the following section.

To change transaction settings, follow these steps:

1. From Quicken's Main Menu, choose **Set Preferences**. Quicken displays the Set Preferences menu.

2. From the Set Preferences menu, choose Transaction Settings. Quicken displays the Transaction Settings window (see fig. 20.4).

Fig. 20.4
The Transaction Settings window.

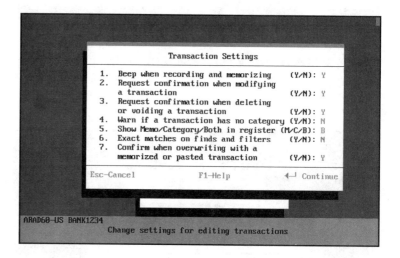

```
                      Transaction Settings

          1.  Beep when recording and memorizing      (Y/N): Y
          2.  Request confirmation when modifying
              a transaction                            (Y/N): Y
          3.  Request confirmation when deleting
              or voiding a transaction                 (Y/N): Y
          4.  Warn if a transaction has no category (Y/N): N
          5.  Show Memo/Category/Both in register (M/C/B): B
          6.  Exact matches on finds and filters    (Y/N): N
          7.  Confirm when overwriting with a
              memorized or pasted transaction          (Y/N): Y

     Esc-Cancel              F1-Help            ◄┘ Continue


 ARAD60-US BANK1234
              Change settings for editing transactions
```

3. (Optional) The cursor should already be positioned on the Beep When Recording and Memorizing setting. Choose **N** to turn off the beep that Quicken tells the computer to make when the program records and memorizes transactions; leave the setting at Y to keep the beep. (You may want to consider this option if you enter many transactions. You also use this setting to turn on the beep if you previously turned off the beep.)

4. (Optional) Move the cursor to the Request Confirmation When Modifying a Transaction setting. To turn off the confirmation messages, choose **N**. This setting turns on and off the pop-up confirmation messages that Quicken displays before you record a modified transaction.

5. (Optional) Move the cursor to the Request Confirmation When Deleting or Voiding a Transaction setting. To turn off the confirmation message, choose **N**. This setting turns on and off the pop-up confirmation messages that Quicken displays before you delete or void a transaction.

6. (Optional) Move the cursor to the Warn if a Transaction Has No Category setting. If you want Quicken to display a reminder message that asks you to confirm transactions you enter without a valid category, choose **Y**. You do not need to use categories if this switch is set to Y, but you do need to confirm that you do not want to use a category. If you plan to assign categories to all transactions, set this switch to **Y** for Yes. (Chapter 4, "Organizing Your Finances," describes how to use categories in greater detail.)

7. (Optional) Move the cursor to the Show Memo/Category/Both in Register setting. This setting determines the information that appears on the memo line of the register when the transaction isn't selected. Choose **M** to tell Quicken that you want only the memo to appear; choose **C** to designate that only the category should appear; choose **B** to designate that both the memo and category should appear. Because you do not have enough room to fully display both the Memo and Category fields, if you select B, Quicken abbreviates the two fields.

8. (Optional) Move the cursor to the Exact Matches on Finds and Filters setting. If you want Quicken to search only for the exact data you specify as a search argument when using the Find option or to include items on a report that exactly match a filter, choose **Y**. (Refer to Chapter 6, "Automating the Register," for more on the Find option. Report filters are described in Chapter 12, "Creating and Printing Reports.")

9. (Optional) Move the cursor to the Confirm When Overwriting with a Memorized or Pasted Transaction setting. To turn off the confirmation message, choose **N**. This setting turns on and off the pop-up confirmation messages that Quicken displays before recording a memorized or pasted transaction over an existing transaction.

10. After the transaction settings are the way you want them, choose **Enter** or **F10**. Quicken returns you to the Set Preferences menu.

Customizing the Checks and Reports Settings

Quicken includes seven checks and reports settings you can change so that the program prints checks and reports to best fit your needs. The checks and reports settings in Quicken are described in the following section.

If you want to change any of the checks and reports settings, first perform the following steps:

1. From Quicken's Main Menu, choose **Set Preferences**. Quicken displays the Set Preferences menu.

2. From the Set Preferences menu, choose **Checks & Reports Settings**. Quicken displays the Checks and Reports Settings window shown in figure 20.5.

Fig. 20.5

The Checks and Reports Settings window.

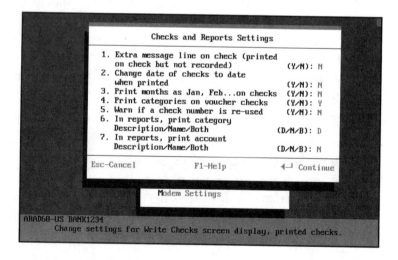

3. (Optional) The cursor should be positioned on the Extra Message Line on Check setting. To see and use the extra message line that appears to the right of the address box on the checks, choose **Y**. To remove the extra message line, choose **N**. The extra line message is explained in Chapter 7, "Writing and Printing Checks."

4. (Optional) Move the cursor to the Change Date of Checks to Date When Printed setting. If you want Quicken to print the current system date as the check date when printing checks, choose **Y**. When the check date you enter differs from the check printing date, the check's date changes.

5. (Optional) If you want Quicken to print the three-character abbreviation for the month on checks, move the cursor to the Print Months as Jan, Feb...on Checks setting, and then choose **Y**.

6. (Optional) Move the cursor to the Print Categories on Voucher Checks setting. If you want what you enter in the Category field or in the Split Transaction window fields to appear on the voucher portion of checks, choose **Y** for Yes.

You don't need to print the Category field information on the voucher stub unless someone to whom you pay a check needs to know the income and expense categories you assigned to the check transaction. If you decide not to use the Category fields to record categories, and instead use the fields for information, such as the invoices a check pays, you can print this information on the check stub. This setting doesn't apply unless the checks have voucher stubs.

7. (Optional) Move the cursor to the Warn If a Check Number is Re-used setting. If you want Quicken to display a pop-up message when you use a check number you have used previously, set this field to **Y** for Yes.

8. (Optional) Move the cursor to the In Reports, Print Category Description/Name/Both setting. This field determines whether the category name, category description, or both appear on reports. You have three choices: selecting D designates that only the description appears; selecting N designates that only the name appears; selecting N designates that both the name and description appear. D is the default setting and the one you probably want to use.

9. (Optional) Move the cursor to In Reports, Print Account Description/Name/Both. Choose **D** if you want the account description to appear on reports. Choose **N** if you want the account name to appear. Choose **B** if you want both pieces of information to appear.

10. When the checks and reports settings are as you want, choose **Enter** or **F10**. Quicken returns you to the Set Preferences menu.

Changing the Screen Settings

You can change the "look and feel" of Quicken by changing the screen settings. Quicken enables you to change the following screen settings:

- Screen colors

- Screen patterns

- EGA/VGA 43-line display (displays Registers and reports in compressed format)

- Monitor speed

- Menu access (changes the method for choosing menus and menu options)

- Screen graphics (specifies the graphics driver)

- Register view (changes the number of text lines displayed in an unselected transaction)

The following sections explain how to change each of these screen settings.

Changing Screen Colors

Quicken gives you control over the colors the program uses on menus and screens. If the monitor is monochrome, you can choose monochrome, reverse monochrome, or shades of gray. If the monitor is color, you can choose a navy and azure combination, white and navy, red and gray, purple and white, or green and yellow. Go ahead and have fun experimenting with the various color combinations. When you change screen colors, your data file is not affected in any way.

To change the screen colors Quicken uses, take the following steps:

1. From Quicken's Main Menu, choose Set Preferences. Quicken displays the Set Preferences menu.

2. From the Set Preferences menu, choose Screen Settings. Quicken displays the Screen Settings menu (see fig. 20.6).

3. From the Screen Settings menu, choose Screen Colors. Quicken displays the Change Color Scheme window, as shown in figure 20.7.

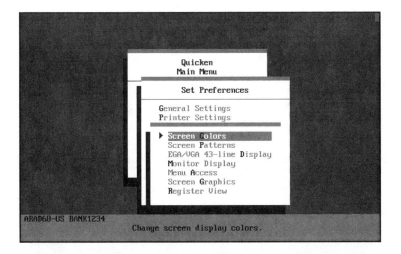

Fig. 20.6
The Screen Settings menu.

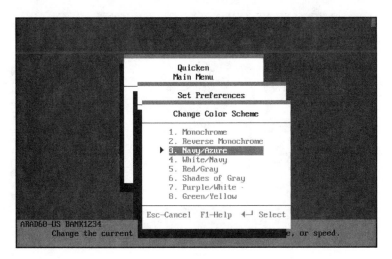

Fig. 20.7
The Change Color Scheme window.

4. Highlight the color combination you want to use and choose **Enter**. Alternatively, choose the number of the color scheme you want to use: **1** for Monochrome, **2** for Reverse Monochrome, **3** for Navy/Azure, **4** for White/Navy, and so on.

The default color option for a monochrome monitor is Monochrome, but also try **Shades of Gray** to find the combination that works best. If you have a monochrome monitor and the screen display is unclear or portions of the screen don't show, you probably defined the monitor type as color. The default color scheme for a color monitor is Navy/Azure, but try each of the other color schemes to find the combination that works best. If you are color-blind, for example, one of the other color schemes may be easier to see.

Changing Screen Patterns

If you have a color monitor or a one-color monitor that can display shades of gray, you can change the background pattern that appears at the Main Menu.

To change the screen patterns, follow these steps:

1. From Quicken's Main Menu, choose **S**et Preferences. Quicken displays the Set Preferences menu.

2. Choose **S**creen Settings from the Set Preferences menu. Quicken displays the Screen Settings menu (refer to fig. 20.6).

3. From the Screen Settings menu, choose Screen **P**atterns. Quicken displays the Change Background Patterns window, as shown in figure 20.8.

Fig. 20.8

The Change Background Patterns window.

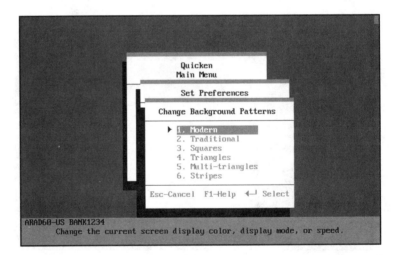

4. Highlight the background pattern you want to display and choose **Enter**. Alternatively, press **1** for Modern, **2** for Traditional, **3** for Squares, and so on.

The default background pattern is Modern, but you can try the other patterns to find the selection you like best. Changing screen patterns has no effect on the Quicken data.

Changing the Number of Lines Displayed

If the computer uses an Enhanced Graphics Adapter (EGA), you can display 43 transaction lines in the Register by changing the EGA/VGA 43-line Display screen setting. If you have a Video Graphics Adapter (VGA) monitor and card, by changing the setting you can display 50 transaction lines in the Register. By default, Quicken displays only 25 transaction lines in the Register. If you have an EGA or VGA monitor, try this option. Having more Register information on-screen is helpful. If the compressed version of the Register strains your eyes, set the EGA/VGA 43-line Display screen setting back to **N**.

To change the Register line display from 25 to 43/50 lines, take the following steps:

1. From Quicken's Main Menu, choose **S**et Preferences. Quicken displays the Set Preferences menu.

2. From the Set Preferences menu, choose **S**creen Settings option. Quicken displays the Screen Settings menu.

3. From the Screen Settings menu, choose EGA/VGA 43-line Display. Quicken displays the Display Mode window shown in figure 20.9.

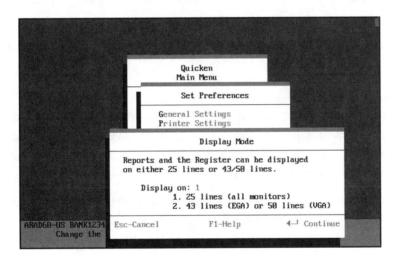

Fig. 20.9
The Display Mode window.

4. Choose **2** and then choose **Enter**.

When you return to the Register, Quicken displays 43 transaction lines in the Register if you have an EGA monitor or 50 lines if you have a VGA monitor. You can change the display back to 25 lines by following the preceding list of steps, except choose the 25 lines option rather than the 43/50 lines option.

Changing Monitor Speed
The Monitor Display option on the Set Preferences menu enables you to choose between slow and fast for the screen-update speed. Quicken initially

assumes that you want the fast option. If Quicken ascertains that your monitor can handle the fast update speed, the program doesn't enable you to change the setting to slow. If Quicken determines that the monitor cannot handle the fast speed, Quicken enables you to change the speed to slow.

If the monitor cannot handle the fast-speed setting, you may see little flecks and patches—sometimes known as *snow*—on-screen. If you notice snow on the monitor, set the monitor speed to slow.

To set the monitor speed to slow, follow these steps:

1. From Quicken's Main Menu, choose the Set Preferences. Quicken displays the Set Preferences menu.

2. From the Set Preferences menu, choose Screen Settings to display the Screen Settings menu.

3. From the Screen Settings menu, choose Monitor Display. Quicken displays the Monitor Display window.

4. Choose the number of the speed setting you want: **1** for Slow and **2** for Fast. Choose **Enter**.

Changing Menu Access

Before Version 5, Quicken used the function keys rather than Alt-letter key combinations to display menus that appear on the Write Checks and Register screens. If you are a former Version 3 or 4 user and want to continue using the function keys, Quicken Version 7 enables you to do so.

Changing the way that menus and menu options are selected is explained in Chapter 2, "Getting Around in Quicken." Refer to Chapter 2 to learn how to change the menu access from the Alt-key style to the function-key style.

Specifying Graphics Options

You learn how to create graphs in Chapter 17, "Creating Graphs." To display graphs, however, you must tell Quicken which graphics driver you installed, whether you want the text area of the graph larger, and whether you want graphs displayed in black and white rather than in color.

To specify graphics options so that you can create graphs with Quicken, take the following steps:

1. From Quicken's Main Menu, choose **Set Preferences**. Quicken displays the Set Preferences menu.

2. From the Set Preferences menu, choose Screen Settings to display the Screen Settings menu.

3. From the Screen Settings menu, choose Screen Graphics. Quicken displays the Graphics Drivers Options window, as shown in figure 20.10.

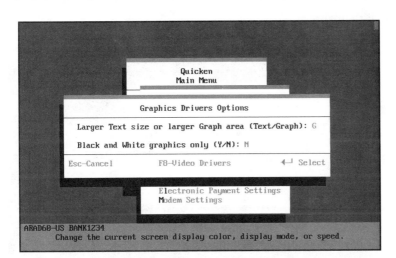

Fig. 20.10
The Graphics Drivers Options window.

4. In the first field, choose **T** to display the text in graphs in a larger size. Quicken displays graph labels in larger text but with coarser resolution overall. Choose **G** to display a larger graph area with labels in smaller text. Choose **Enter**.

5. In the Black and White Graphics Only field, choose **Y** if you want graphs to appear in black and white. Otherwise, leave the setting at N to display graphs in color.

6. Choose **F8** to display the Choose Graphics Driver window shown in figure 20.11. Highlight the graphics driver installed on the computer. Choose **Enter** to select the highlighted graphics driver.

7. Quicken returns to the Graphics Drivers Options window. Choose **Enter** or **F10** to save the option settings.

Changing the Number of Text Lines in Transactions

You can change the number of text lines Quicken displays for unselected transactions in the Register. Usually, the Register shows unselected transactions on two lines; selected transactions are shown on three lines. To compress the data in the Register screen so that you see more transactions, change the number of text lines in unselected transactions to one line per transaction by changing the Register View screen setting. Changing this setting is the same as selecting the Register View option from the Activities menu at a Noninvestment Account Register (see Chapter 6, "Automating the Register," for more information about the **Register View** option from the Activities menu).

Fig. 20.11
The Select Graphics Driver window.

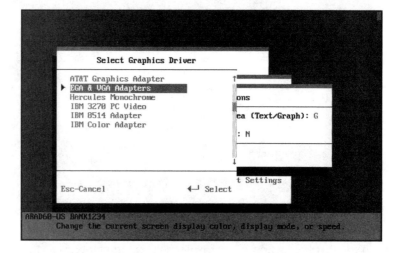

Note

Changing the number of text lines in unselected transactions by changing the Register View Screen setting doesn't yield the same results as changing the number of lines that appear by changing the EGA/VGA 43-line Display Screen setting. When you set the display to 43 or 50 lines, unselected transactions appear on two lines in the Register but in smaller print. Therefore, more transactions appear in the Register screen at one time. When you change the number of text lines in unselected transactions with the Register View Screen setting, only one line of text appears for each unselected transaction in the Register. The print size remains the same. When transactions appear on one line only, the memo or category assigned to the transaction doesn't appear.

To change the number of text lines in unselected transactions, follow these steps:

1. From Quicken's Main Menu, choose **Set Preferences**. Quicken displays the Set Preferences menu.

2. From the Set Preferences menu, choose **S**creen Settings to display the Screen Settings menu.

3. From the Screen Settings menu, choose **R**egister View. Quicken displays the Register View Mode window as shown in figure 20.12.

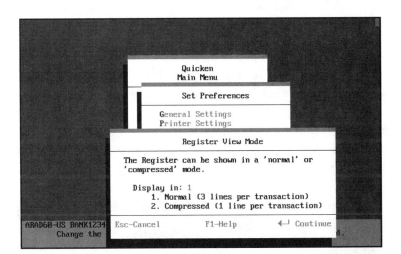

Fig. 20.12
The Register View Mode window.

4. Choose 2 to compress transactions to display only one line in the Register when the transaction is not selected or highlighted. Choose **Enter**.

Quicken returns to the Screen Settings menu. When you return to the Register, all transactions—except for the selected transaction—appear on one line.

Using Billminder

Billminder is Quicken's reminder system that checks the data files and displays messages each time you start the computer. Billminder reminds you about actions you need to take, such as printing checks, recalling transaction groups that are due, and so on.

When you install Quicken, the program asks whether you want to also install Billminder (see Appendix A, "Installing Quicken"). If you answer Yes, the program adds an additional line to the computer's AUTOEXEC.BAT file so that Billminder executes each time you turn on the computer. When you turn on the computer, Billminder knows where to look to check the data files (unless you subsequently move the Quicken program).

Tip
To change the Register view back to normal (noncompressed) mode so that unselected transactions again appear on two lines, select the **Register View** option from the Activities menu or press **Ctrl-Q**.

> ### Note
>
> If you didn't install Billminder when you installed Quicken, you can perform a reinstallation and install Billminder. When you reinstall Quicken, the program files are overwritten, but data files are not disturbed. When Quicken displays the Use Billminder window during the reinstall process, press **1** to install Billminder.

Getting Billminder Messages

If you installed Billminder when you installed the Quicken program, you simply turn on the computer, and Billminder loads and then searches the Quicken data files for checks to print, transaction groups that are due, electronic payments to transmit to CheckFree, and actions to take in investment accounts. Billminder displays a message similar to the one you see in figure 20.13 each time you turn on the computer.

Fig. 20.13
A Billminder message.

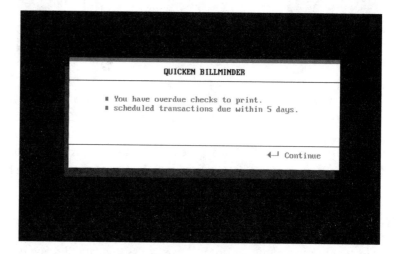

To remove the Billminder message, choose **Enter** and the DOS prompt appears.

Changing the Directory

If you moved Quicken files from the directory where you initially installed Quicken, you must tell Billminder where to look for these files. Billminder cannot recognize a directory that doesn't contain the Quicken configuration file (Q.CFG), and, therefore, cannot check data from within the directory. Be sure that the directory that holds the Quicken program files also contains the

Q.CFG file. To check the directory from the DOS prompt, change to the directory in which you moved the Quicken program files, type **dir**, and then press **Enter** to display the list of files contained in the directory.

To change the directory in which Billminder looks for Quicken files, change the Billminder line in the AUTOEXEC.BAT file to include the new directory. To learn how to edit AUTOEXEC.BAT files, consult your DOS manual. The Billminder line differs between DOS Versions 3.0 and higher and DOS Versions lower than 3.0.

Changing Automatic Reminder Settings

Quicken enables you to control how many days in advance Billminder reminds you of postdated checks, scheduled transactions, transaction groups that are due, electronic payments to be transmitted, and actions to be taken in investment accounts. By default, Billminder reminds you three days in advance of items you need to take action on. You can change the advance notice time period from 0 to 30 days.

To change the automatic reminder settings in Billminder, follow these steps:

1. From Quicken's Main Menu, choose **S**et Preferences. The Set Preferences menu appears.

2. From the Set Preferences menu, choose Automatic **R**eminder Settings. Quicken displays the Automatic Reminder Settings window shown in figure 20.14.

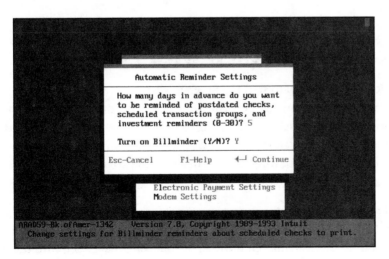

Fig. 20.14
The Automatic Reminder Settings window.

3. Enter the number of days in advance that you want to be reminded of postdated checks, scheduled transactions, electronic payments, and investment actions. You can enter any number of days from 0 to 30.

4. Be sure that the Turn on Billminder field is set to **Y** so that Billminder is active and ready. To return to the Set Preferences menu, choose **Enter** or **F10**.

Disabling Billminder

If you don't want to use the Billminder feature, you can disable (or turn off) this feature at any time.

To disable Billminder, follow these steps:

1. From Quicken's Main Menu, choose **S**et Preferences. The Set Preferences menu appears.

2. From the Set Preferences menu, choose Automatic **R**eminder Settings. Quicken displays the Automatic Reminder Settings window shown in figure 20.14.

3. Move the cursor to the Turn on Billminder field and choose **N**.

4. Choose **Enter** or **F10** to disable Billminder.

You can turn on Billminder again by returning to the Automatic Reminder Settings window and changing the N setting in the Turn on Billminder field to **Y**.

Starting Quicken with Parameters

Quicken enables you to start the program with parameters. (*Parameters* are codes you type following the *q* you type to start the program.) These parameters enable you to select an account and to select the menu-access method. Although the parameters may sound complicated, these parameters really are not difficult. The following sections describe how to use the parameters that Quicken provides.

Selecting an Account

To start Quicken, type **q** at the DOS prompt. You can specify the account to select from the last Quicken file used by following the letter *q* with the name of this account. To start Quicken and simultaneously select the account named CHECKING, for example, at the DOS prompt type the following text:

Q CHECKING

If an account isn't in the current file, you also can identify the file as a second parameter. If you want to select the account CHECKING in the file named QDATA, type the following text at the DOS prompt:

Q CHECKING QDATA

Leave a space between the Q and *CHECKING* and between *CHECKING* and *QDATA*.

Selecting an account when you start Quicken isn't difficult and can be quite handy. You do need to remember one trick, however. If the account name is two words, you need to enclose the account in quotation marks so that Quicken doesn't think one part of the name is the file name. In the case of an account named *1st National* in the QDATA file, you enter the parameter in the applicable one of the two following forms:

Q "1ST NATIONAL"
Q "1ST NATIONAL" QDATA

You also can specify the path of the file, which you need to do if the file is not in the Quicken program directory.

Selecting Menu Access

You also can start Quicken with a parameter that selects the menu-access method. As noted in *Changing Menu Access*, earlier in this chapter, in early versions of Quicken, you used function keys to access the menus; in the current version, you use Alt-letter key combinations. One way to control menu access is by using the Menu Access option on the Screen Settings menu (see fig. 20.6). You also can control menu access by using the /f and /i command parameters. To start Quicken with function-key access, for example, type **q /f**.

Using Versions 4.0 and 3.0 Key Definitions

Quicken Version 4 and later versions use slightly different key definitions of the Home and End keys than earlier versions of Quicken use. Table 20.1 summarizes the different definitions.

Table 20.1 Key Definitions

Key(s)	Versions 4, 5, 6, 7	Versions 3 and earlier
Home	First character in field in the Register	First transaction
End	Last character in field in the Register	Last transaction
Home Home	First field on-screen	Not used
End End	Last field on-screen	Not used
Ctrl-Home	First transaction in the Register	Same as Home
Ctrl-End	Last transaction in the Register	Same as End

Although Version 7 key definitions are more consistent with the standard uses of the two keys, you may want to use Version 3 key definitions and the /a parameter. To use the Version 3 key definitions for the Home and End keys, for example, type the following command at the DOS prompt:

> **Q /A**

Leave a space between the letter *q* and the character sequence */a*.

After you start Quicken by using the /a parameter, Quicken continues to use the Version 3 key definitions until you tell Quicken to stop. To tell Quicken to stop using the Version 3 key definitions and return to the Version 7 definitions, use the /s parameter. For example, type the following command at the DOS prompt:

> **Q /S**

One other command-line parameter exists. However, you probably never will need to use this parameter. The /e parameter tells Quicken not to use the computer's expanded memory. Usually, Quicken uses the computer's expanded memory for overlays and reports. If you have problems with expanded memory, however you can use this command-line parameter until you fix the problems.

Summary

You can customize the Quicken program so that transactions are recorded the way you want and checks and reports are printed to best fit your needs. In this chapter, you learn how to change transaction settings and checks and reports settings to get Quicken to work the way you want. You also learn how to change screen settings, such as screen colors, background patterns, menu access, and so on. And finally, you learn how to use Quicken's built-in reminder system, Billminder, to help you remember to take actions such as printing checks that you have written or recalling transaction groups that are due.

The following chapter begins the final part of *Using Quicken 7 for DOS*: "Putting Quicken to Use." In this part, you learn how to use Quicken for home finances or in small business. The next two chapters provide helpful hints for using Quicken to meet your needs.

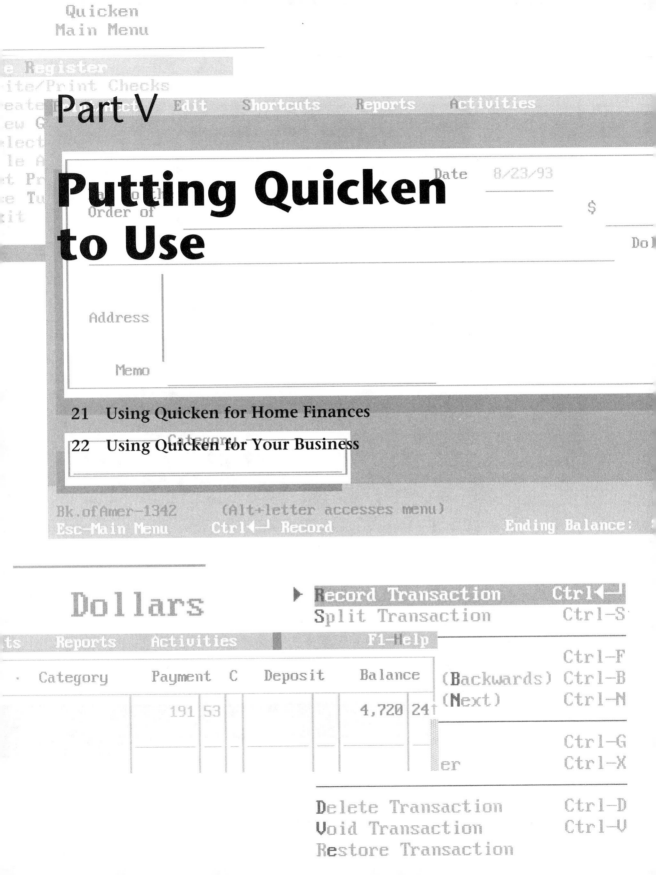

Part V

Putting Quicken to Use

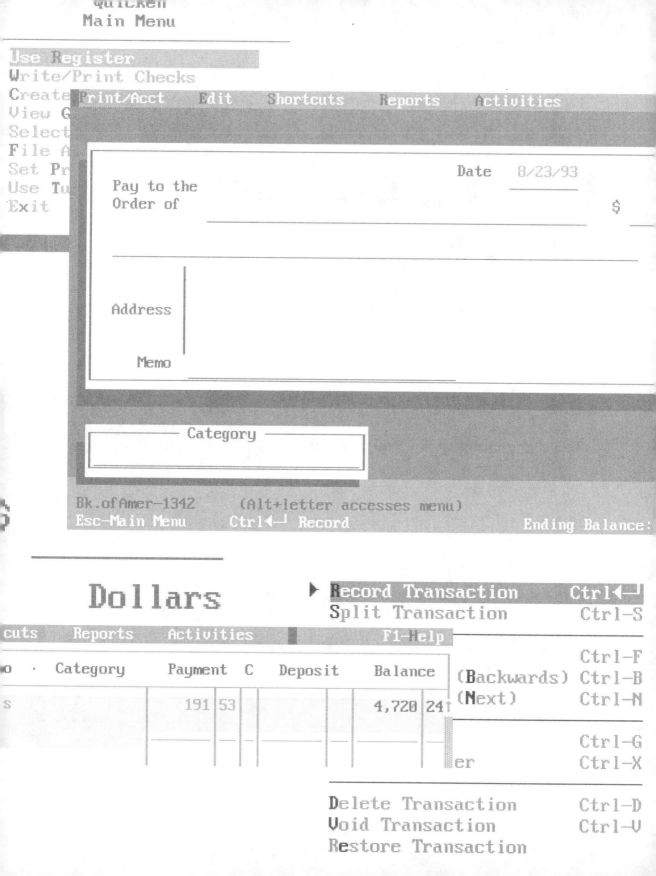

Quicken
Main Menu

Use Register
Write/Print Checks
Create
View G
Select
File A
Set Pr
Use Tu
Exit

Print/Acct   Edit   Shortcuts   Reports   Activities

Date   8/23/93

Pay to the
Order of
                                                    $

Address

Memo

Category

Bk.of Amer—1342   (Alt+letter accesses menu)
Esc—Main Menu   Ctrl↵ Record   Ending Balance:

Dollars   ▶ Record Transaction   Ctrl↵
                             Split Transaction   Ctrl-S

cuts   Reports   Activities   F1-Help
                                                        Ctrl-F
o · Category   Payment C Deposit   Balance   (Backwards) Ctrl-B
                                                    (Next)   Ctrl-N
s   191 53   4,720 24↑
                                                                Ctrl-G
                                                    er   Ctrl-X

                             Delete Transaction   Ctrl-D
                             Void Transaction   Ctrl-V
                             Restore Transaction

Chapter 21

Using Quicken for Home Finances

If you read the first four parts of this book, you know the mechanics of using Quicken. Using any software—particularly an accounting program—takes more than understanding how the software works, however. Like most people, you probably have questions about where Quicken fits in, how Quicken changes the way you keep financial records, and when to use different Quicken options. This chapter answers these kinds of questions.

Where Quicken Fits In

Where Quicken fits into personal financial management or home finances depends on what you want to get from Quicken.

Tracking Income-Tax Deductions

When tracking income-tax deductions, you need to make sure that transactions that produce an income-tax deduction are entered into one of the Quicken Registers. You also need to be sure that you use a category marked as tax-related.

This process is not as difficult as it sounds. First, although you currently may make payments that represent income-tax deductions from a variety of accounts, often you can change the way you make payments so that every transaction that produces an income-tax deduction is recorded in one or two accounts. If you currently make charitable contributions in cash and with a credit card, rather than set up a cash account and a credit card account, you can change the way you do things and start writing checks on an account

You can use Quicken for your home finances in the following ways:

- To track income tax deductions

- To automate recordkeeping

- To monitor how closely you are following a budget

- To calculate what-if scenarios, such as how much you will save if you refinance your home mortgage or how much you need to save each year to send your two-year-old to Harvard you are tracking with Quicken. In this way, if you use Quicken for tracking income-tax deductions only, you need to set up only one account—a bank account is probably the easiest method—and use this bank account only for charitable contributions.

Second, you may not need the power of Quicken to track and tally income-tax deductions. The organization to which you make a tax-deductible payment may track and tally the tax deduction for you. Consider the case of a home mortgage. At the end of the year, the bank sends you a statement (Form 1098) that identifies how much you have paid over the year in interest, principal, and, if applicable, for items such as property taxes and insurance. Similarly, a charity may send a statement that shows all contributions for the year. A bank or brokerage firm also may indicate the total individual retirement account contributions. Although you may need to track and tally certain income-tax deductions, you may not want to go to all this work if an organization tracks these deductions for you.

See Chapter 14, "Using Quicken to Prepare for Income Taxes," for a more thorough discussion of income taxes.

Automating Recordkeeping

As a rule, any financial recordkeeping you now perform manually probably is a candidate for Quicken. People go to different lengths in their efforts to keep clean, precise accounting records. The obvious candidate for Quicken is tracking activity in bank accounts—particularly checking accounts. You may be someone, however, who also tracks investments carefully, tracks personal spending in a precise manner, or keeps records of personal assets or liabilities. In all these cases, Quicken can make the job easier.

Consider the following three cautions when automating financial recordkeeping. First, as with income-tax deductions, don't go to a great deal of effort to account for items that someone else already tracks for you. You probably don't need to use Quicken if all your investments appear on the same monthly statements from a broker or a mutual fund manager. You probably don't need to track other items, such as a monthly pension fund or 401K contributions, when your employer pays professional accountants to track these finances.

The second caution to consider is that keeping financial records isn't fun. Keeping records is tedious, requires attention to detail, and can take much time. For these reasons, carefully consider whether you need to keep financial records for a specific asset or liability. You can track the value of a home or car, but often, tracking these values isn't worth the effort. Whenever you go to the work of keeping a detailed, transaction-by-transaction record of an asset or liability, the resulting information should enable you to better manage your personal finances. If the information doesn't help you manage your finances, the data isn't worth collecting and storing.

The third caution to consider is to remember that in a Quicken Register, you record transactions that change the balance of an asset or liability. The values of possessions, such as a home, stocks, or bonds, can change without a transaction occurring. Therefore, you cannot point to an event and say, *This event needs to be recorded*. Not surprisingly, you usually have difficulty tracking changes in the value of something when you don't have actual transactions to which you can point and then record. Accounts that you most likely will want to track are your bank accounts (including checking, savings, and money market accounts), your credit card accounts if you don't pay the balance each month, and cash accounts if you use cash a lot of the time to pay for expenses.

Monitoring a Budget

As suggested in Chapter 15, "Budgeting with Quicken," one of the most powerful home accounting uses for Quicken is to monitor how closely you are following a budget. Although the budgeting tools that Quicken provides are superb, the process of using Quicken to monitor monthly spending can be a challenge. Because you probably spend money in several ways—using checks, credit cards, and cash—the only way to really track your monthly spending is to record all three spending groups in registers. Otherwise, you see only a piece of the picture. Recording all three groups can involve a great deal of work.

To simplify monitoring a budget, consider several budgeting ideas:

- Focus on discretionary items

- Aggregate spending categories

- Consider the spending method

Focusing on Discretionary Items. In Chapter 15, budgeting is described as a three-step process:

1. Setting financial goals.

2. Using financial goals as a guide to developing a financial game plan or budget that covers how you want to spend your money.

3. Using the financial game plan or budget to monitor spending in order to track how closely you are progressing toward your business goals.

Quicken helps you with the third step, using the budget to monitor spending. You then need to monitor only discretionary spending and not spending fixed by contract or by law. Keep this spending difference in mind when you define categories and set up accounts. Some spending may not need to be monitored at all. Consider a mortgage payment or a rent payment: Although you certainly want to include these major expenditures in a budget, you probably don't need to monitor whether you are spending money on these payments. The spending is fixed by a mortgage contract or a rental agreement. You cannot, therefore, spend less than the budgeted amount unless you want to be evicted from your home. You also will not spend more than the budgeted amount because you have no reason to do so (unless you're trying to pay down your mortgage over an accelerated time schedule).

Note

The Quicken monthly budget report is the principal tool you use to monitor a budget. (Refer to Chapter 15, "Budgeting with Quicken," for more information.)

Other examples of fixed spending are loan or lease payments for a car, income and Social Security taxes, and child care. Which spending categories are fixed in this case depends on the specifics of the situation. In general, you probably don't need to closely monitor categories already fixed—or locked in—by a contract, by law, or by the terms of employment. You do need to include fixed spending in the budget because you want to make sure that you have enough money for the item, but this kind of spending doesn't need to be monitored. The rule is that for purposes of monitoring a budget, focus on monitoring discretionary spending.

Aggregating Spending Categories. When you monitor discretionary spending, working with a handful of categories rather than a big clump of specific categories is the easier method. Take the case of spending on entertainment. You can choose to track spending on entertainment by using just one category, which you name *Entertainment*. You also can break down the spending into all the various ways you spend entertainment dollars, as shown in the following list:

- Eating at restaurants

- Going to the movies

- Renting videos

- Seeing plays at the theater

- Playing golf

- Attending sporting events

Tracking exactly how you spend entertainment dollars takes a certain precision and usually takes effort for two reasons. The first reason is that you end up recording more transactions. A credit card bill that contains charges for only the six spending groups listed needs to have one transaction recorded if only one general category is used, but a split transaction with six separate amounts must be recorded if all six specific categories are used.

The second reason is that you budget by category, so the more categories you use, the more budgeted amounts you need to enter. If you feel you must have the detail that comes with using many, specific categories, consider using subcategories that at least minimize the work of entering budgeted amounts.

Consider these general rules for aggregating spending categories:

- Lump together items that are substitutes for each other.

- Lump together items of similar importance, or priority, to you and the other members of the family.

Both rules stem from the idea that if you overspend in a category, you should consider reducing further spending in this category. A couple of examples may help you use these rules in budgeting. Suppose that you lump together the six spending groups listed previously into one general category. Suppose that you go golfing with friends over three straight weekends so that you also have no money left for restaurants and the theater (favorite activities of your spouse), or no money left for movies, videos, and sporting events (the favorite activities of your kids). In this case, don't lump all six categories together because not spending money in one category may not be a practical remedy for overspending in another category. A sensible solution is to budget for golf as one category, for the theater and restaurants as a second category, and for the movies and sporting events as a third category. You then can make sure that overspending on golf doesn't occur. If your spouse overspends on the theater, a reasonable response is to minimize or curtail spending on restaurants. If the children insist on seeing two videos, they must forego a trip to the ballpark and the movie theater.

Considering the Spending Method. Researchers have proven that the method people use to spend money—credit cards, checks, or cash—affects how they spend. In general, people spend more when they use a credit card than they do when spending cash or writing a check, and people often spend less when they use cash than when they write a check. This phenomenon doesn't directly affect how you work with Quicken but, in terms of monitoring a budget, consider this information before you decide which accounts you set up to monitor spending.

You can find a budget more manageable if you choose an easily controlled spending method. The accounts you set up to monitor spending should recognize this reality. Remember that Quicken enables you to set up special accounts for bank accounts, credit cards, and cash. For monitoring the spending categories you want to watch, choose a spending method that makes staying within a budget easier.

Reviewing What-If Scenarios

With the financial calculators in Quicken, you can use the program to review what-if scenarios for investments, retirement, refinancing, or college. Use the Investment Calculator to calculate the growth of an investment using various interest rates, over various time periods, and making various contributions each year.

The Retirement Calculator can show you how soon (or how long) you can retire. You can calculate the growth of your "nest egg" using various interest rates over various time periods. You also can vary the contributions you make each year until retirement. This feature is particularly useful in calculating the future value of an IRA or Keogh account in the year you retire.

And if you have children, you're probably concerned about saving money for college. Not only do we want our kids to go to college, we want them to go to an academically outstanding college (which means expensive!). Use the College Calculator to determine how much you need to save each year, given various interest rates, time periods, and tuition levels.

The Refinance Calculator helps you make the decision of whether to go through the hassles and expense of refinancing your home mortgage or staying with your current mortgage. The Refinance Calculator shows you what your savings will be, based on the refinance rate, and how long it will take you to recover the closing costs and points you have to pay.

How to Use Quicken

With the information covered so far, you are in a good position to know when and where to use Quicken for your home finances. This section covers a few tips that elaborate on the preceding discussion and covers bank-account reconciliation, tracking credit card spending, and recording tax-deductible cash outlays.

Using Quicken for Bank Accounts

Usually, you can use Quicken for any bank accounts you want to reconcile on a monthly basis. You also can use Quicken for checking accounts for which you want to print checks. Finally, you may want to track certain bank accounts used for income-tax deductions or budget-monitoring reasons.

You probably don't need to use Quicken (unless you want to) for bank accounts that don't need to be reconciled. You probably don't need to use Quicken for certificates of deposit or for savings accounts with no activity other than monthly interest or fees. If you want to reflect your net worth accurately in Quicken net worth reports, however, you must set up an account for each bank account that has money in it.

Using Quicken for Credit Cards

You don't need to use Quicken to track credit card spending for credit cards for which you pay off the balance at the end of the month. When you write the monthly check to pay off the credit card company, you can record the spending categories by splitting the transaction.

For credit cards that you don't pay off on a monthly basis, but still need to track income-tax deductions or monitor spending, you can set up and use Quicken accounts. For credit cards for which you want to use the reconcile feature, you also need to set up and use Quicken accounts.

If you set up accounts for credit cards, you need to enter each credit card transaction into the Register. Therefore, you need to collect the credit card slips, and then periodically enter the amounts into the Register.

If you have a Quicken VISA card and want to use the IntelliCharge feature to track credit card activity (see Chapter 11, "Managing Your Credit Cards"), you must set up a credit card account and designate the account as an IntelliCharge account.

Using Quicken for Cash

If you spend cash on items that are tax deductible, you can use Quicken to track these deductions. If you are using Quicken to monitor cash spending so that you can compare actual spending with budgeted spending, you also can use Quicken to track this information. Essentially, every time you withdraw cash from the bank, you increase cash (and decrease your bank account balance). Every time you spend money, you need to collect a receipt for the expense. You then periodically enter these cash transactions into the Register.

One practical problem with tracking cash spending is that you cannot get a receipt for small items, such as candy, a newspaper, or tips to a bellhop. Therefore, you need to keep a record of these small transactions, or you need to adjust the register's cash balance periodically to match the actual cash on hand. You can give this kind of adjustment category a descriptive name, such as *Sundries* or *Misc.*

For credit card and cash transactions, collect in an envelope the credit card and cash receipts you need to enter. On a periodic basis (such as once a week or month), enter the receipt amounts in the appropriate Register, mark the receipts as entered, and label the outside of the envelope with a descriptive name, such as *credit card and cash receipts from week beginning 11/1/93.* If you have a large number of receipts, number the receipts, and then use these numbers as the transaction numbers in the Register so that you can specifically tie a transaction in the Register to a receipt.

Tracking the Adjusted Basis of Your Home

By law, the gain on the sale of a home is taxable unless you purchase another home of equal or greater value within a certain time frame, or unless you can use the one-time $125,000 (by being over age 55) exclusion to eliminate the gain. The gain on the sale of a home is calculated roughly as:

(sale price - costs of sale) - (original cost + cost of improvements) = gain

The sales price and the original cost are set and are connected to the purchase and to the sale. One way to reduce the calculated gain, however—and therefore to minimize the income tax on the gain—is to track the cost of improvements.

Improvements don't include repairs or maintenance, such as fixing a roof, painting the walls, or sealing an asphalt driveway. These are simply repairs and don't increase the value of the asset, your home. Over the years, however, you probably will make a series of improvements that, if tracked, may reduce the gain. These improvements may include the landscaping you put in after you buy the house, bookshelves you add to the family room, and the extra bathroom a remodeler puts in upstairs. Figure 21.1 shows an example of a Register used to collect this kind of information. (Remember that the account-transfer feature means you may never need to access the Register for the asset, House, because you can record the cost of the improvement when you write the check to pay for the improvement.)

Fig. 21.1
A Quicken Register being used to track the tax basis of a home.

Tracking the Nondeductible Portions of an IRA

One of the record-keeping nightmares from the last decade's ever-changing tax laws is the nondeductible individual retirement account (IRA) contribution. Essentially, although you may not qualify for an IRA deduction, you still may have the option of contributing to an IRA. An IRA contribution can be beneficial financially because without the income taxes on the investment earnings, the account grows faster.

Over long periods, you can accumulate a great deal more money—even though the original contribution didn't generate a tax deduction. If, for example, you contribute $25 a month over 35 years, you may accumulate $94,916 if you pay no taxes, but $47,231 if you pay the 28 percent federal income tax (these calculations assume a 10 percent annual yield). In other words, you may accumulate almost twice as much money by not paying income taxes on the earnings. Nondeductible IRA contributions enable you to defer income taxes on money earned until you withdraw the money.

The complication with nondeductible IRA contributions is that the nondeductible portion of your contributions is not taxed when you withdraw the money; you need a way to track the nondeductible contributions. This calculation is reported to the IRS each year on Form 8606.

For most people, Quicken is an excellent solution. The basic process is to set up an investment account for nondeductible IRA contributions. Whenever you make a nondeductible contribution, record the payment as a transfer to the account you use to track nondeductible IRA contributions. Over the years, you build a detailed record of all the nondeductible contributions you make. Figure 21.2 shows an example of an Investment Register that tracks the asset *Nondeduct IRA*.

Fig. 21.2
Using Quicken to track nondeductible IRA contributions.

When to Perform Quicken Tasks

One final question that you often have with using Quicken is when to perform the various Quicken tasks. Table 21.1 divides these tasks into three groups: tasks to perform on a daily and weekly basis, tasks to perform on a monthly basis, and tasks to perform on an annual basis. Consider the information in Table 21.1 as a rough guideline; as you use Quicken, you learn what works best for you.

Table 21.1 When To Perform Quicken Tasks

Daily and Weekly Tasks

Record transactions in the Registers

Print checks

Print a temporary copy of the month's Register

Back up the files

Monthly Tasks

Print monthly reports, including a budget report so that you can analyze actual versus budget results

Reconcile accounts

Print a final copy of the month's Register

Throw away the daily or weekly copies of the Register because all this information is contained on the final copy of the month's Register

Back up the files

File or store the month's bank statement, Register, reports, and backup files

Annual Tasks

Print annual reports

Print a permanent copy of the transaction report that subtotals by tax-deduction category. (This report is your permanent record for income-tax purposes.)

Back up files for the year

Create new year's budget and enter the budget

Shrink the file*

V

Putting Quicken to Use

* When you shrink the file, you don't want to lose the transaction detail in accounts that you maintain on a long-term basis for income tax purposes, such as for ultimately calculating the gain on the sale of a home or for determining the total nondeductible IRA contributions. So that you do not lose detail in the shrink file operation, do not mark transactions in these Registers as cleared, and set the Include Only Cleared Transactions switch to Yes. Chapter 19, "Managing Your Quicken Files," describes how to shrink files.

Summary

This chapter covers information you ultimately learn on your own through trial and error. It also discusses where Quicken fits into your home finances, how to use Quicken for home accounting, and when to use the various Quicken options and features. You now can more easily incorporate Quicken into your personal financial management activities.

The next chapter shows you how you can use Quicken for business accounting.

Chapter 22

Using Quicken in Your Business

You may be surprised to learn that more people use Quicken as a business accounting package than as a home finance package. The reasons for this usage are logical: you don't need to know double-entry bookkeeping (as you do for many other small-business accounting packages), and you use a simple and familiar tool, the Check Register. Because Quicken isn't a true full-fledged business accounting package, however, this chapter covers some of the special techniques and procedures for using Quicken in business.

The procedures for using Quicken are well-documented in this book. For this chapter you are better armed if you know how to enter transactions into a Register, set up accounts, define categories, and print reports. If you are not familiar with these features of Quicken, review the material covered in the first four sections of the book.

This chapter is not intended to be an exhaustive list of all the business uses of Quicken. Different types of businesses require different accounting procedures, accounts, and reports. You need to modify your accounts, categories, subcategories, and so on to fit the needs of your particular business situation.

This chapter begins by discussing the overall approach for using Quicken in a business. In this chapter, you learn how to do the following:

■ Track receivables

■ Track payables

■ Account for fixed assets

■ Prepare payroll

■ Track inventory

■ Job costing

V

Note

With the tools that you have been provided so far in this book, you should be able to create a Quicken system that works for you. Notice, however, that Quicken is not designed to track inventory on an item-by-item basis. If your business requires specific inventory tracking, you will need a more advanced accounting software package.

When you combine basic bill paying and check writing (described through-out this book's chapters) with the details of the six basic accounting tasks described in this chapter, you should have the information you need to per-form business accounting with Quicken. If you find that you need something more than Quicken to handle your business finances, read *An Introduction to QuickBooks*, later in this chapter. QuickBooks is a program, also published by Intuit, that is specifically designed to meet the needs of small business users.

Understanding the Basics

Using Quicken for business accounting is easier if you understand the follow-ing three basic concepts: what Quicken accounts track, what should be re-corded in a Register, and how categories are used.

Knowing What Quicken Accounts Track

You can use Quicken accounts to track the values of business assets or liabili-ties. You need to set up one account for each business asset or liability you want to track.

A *business asset* is anything you own. Common examples of business assets include the cash in a checking account, the receivable a customer or client owes you, an investment in stock, inventory you resell, a piece of furniture, a piece of equipment, real estate, and so on.

A *business liability* is a debt that you owe. Common examples of business liabilities include the loan on a car or delivery truck, payroll taxes you owe the government, the mortgage on the building, the balance on a bank credit line, and so on.

Assets and liabilities have something in common: at any time, you can calcu-late the value of the asset or liability. Usually, you are not interested in the day-to-day or week-to-week change in a particular asset but rather the value at a specific time.

All the accounts you set up for a business must be included in the same Quicken file. If you perform accounting for several businesses, each business needs a separate file. If you use Quicken at business and at home, you need to create a file for each (see Chapter 19, "Managing Your Quicken Files," to learn how to create multiple Quicken files).

Defining a Transaction

A *transaction* is any activity that affects the balance in an account or the value of an asset or liability. No change ever affects only one asset or liability, however, so each time you record the change in the value of some asset or liability, you also need to record how the change affects other accounts, or income or expenses categories. You actually perform double-entry bookkeeping without thinking or worrying about debits and credits.

When you transfer money from a checking account to a savings account, for example, you record the decrease in the checking account balance with one transaction and the increase in the savings account balance with another transaction. Similarly, when you write a check to pay for utilities, you record the decrease in the bank account that the check is written from, and you assign an expense category to classify the transaction, such as *Utilities*. To accurately reflect all your transaction activity, you must assign a category or a transfer account to all transactions.

This discussion of transactions may seem redundant, but you need to verify that all assets and liabilities are true assets and true liabilities. You also need to verify that items you want to record as transactions in a Register are true transactions and not assets or liabilities.

Suppose that you want to track receivables and record customer payments on these receivables. You must set up an account each time you create an individual receivable. If you bill Johnson Manufacturing $1,000 for a service, you must set up an account for this receivable. The temptation with a group of similar assets, such as receivables, is to group all receivables as one asset by using one account. Using the grouping approach, however, obscures information on specific accounts. You cannot tell whether Johnson Manufacturing still owes the $1,000 or how the $1,000 original receivable value has changed. Changes in the value of this asset, such as when you receive the customer's payment, need to be recorded as transactions in the Register.

The key to using Quicken as a small-business accounting system is knowing your assets, liabilities, and transactions. Throughout this chapter, you find many tips and suggestions to assist you in this analysis.

Knowing How Categories Are Used

The term *bottom line* refers to the figure at the bottom of a profit and loss statement that shows whether you made a profit or lost money in business. The reason you use categories in Quicken is to calculate the bottom line to determine whether you are making or losing money. You use two kinds of categories to perform this calculation: *Income* and *Expense*. Income categories are assigned to business revenues, or *inflows*. Common income categories include sales of products or services, income from rental properties, interest and dividends from investments, and so on. Expense categories are assigned to the costs of doing business, or *outflows*. Examples of expense categories include the cost of advertising, insurance, utilities, and employee wages.

Income and expense categories have something in common: both categories enable you to accumulate business inflows and outflows over a period of time, such as for the week, month, or year. You can use the income and expense category information to tell whether you made or lost money during the last week, month, or year. (Income minus expenses equals net income or net loss.)

When you use Quicken categories to track only cash inflows and outflows (bank and cash accounts), you are using *cash-basis* accounting. Cash-basis accounting means that you record income only when you receive money, and you record expenses only when you pay money. This system makes sense. When you make the bank deposit or write a check, you are categorizing the transaction as income or expense.

When you use Quicken categories to track other assets and liabilities, however, you move toward *accrual-* or *modified accrual-basis* accounting. Accrual-basis accounting means that you record income when you earn it, and you record expenses when you use the goods or services from which the expenses stem. If you use Quicken to account for customer receivables, you recognize the sale transaction as income when you record the receivable. If you use Quicken to account for fixed assets and depreciation, you categorize the expense of using the asset when you record depreciation.

CPA TIP

Accrual-basis accounting gives you better estimates of income and expenses to better measure profits. Accrual-basis accounting also results in better record keeping because you keep Registers for all assets and liabilities, not just cash. If accurately measuring profits is important to the business, try to use accrual-basis accounting. If you use this method, you have a better idea of whether you're making money.

Also, if you meet certain criteria, the IRS requires that you use accrual accounting in preparing your tax return.

Tracking Receivables

To track customer payments and receivables, you first need to set up an asset account for receivables. You can set up just one receivables account and aggregate all receivable activity or you can set up a receivables account for each customer or client. If you set up separate receivable accounts, it will be easier to track receivable balances by customer or client and to generate an aging report that gives you useful information as to the outstanding balances for each customer or client at any given time. You may name an aggregate receivable account *Receivables* or *Acc Rec*, for example. For separate receivable accounts, you could use the customer name in the account name, such as *Jones Rec* or *Smith Rec*.

Each time you make a sale to a customer on credit (the customer does not pay for the goods or services at the time of sale), you must record an increase in the receivables account. Figure 22.1 shows the Receivables Register with a transaction for a sale to Johnson Manufacturing for $2,500.

Fig. 22.1
A sale transaction in the Receivables Register.

After you record the receivable, you can record customer payments on the receivable and monitor receivables-topics covered in the following sections.

Recording Customer Payments

To record customer payments, choose the bank account you use to deposit the check and record the deposit in the usual way. To categorize the transaction, record the deposit as a transfer from the actual receivable account. If you receive a $500 check from Johnson Manufacturing for partial payment of the $2,500 receivable created by Invoice 93-01 (see fig. 22.1), for example, you enter the deposit in the Register for the bank account into which you are depositing the money, as shown in figure 22.2. (Remember that Quicken lists the categories and transfer accounts in the Category and Transfer list and displays the list when you press **Ctrl-C**, when you choose Categorize/Transfer from the **Shortcuts** menu, or when you click **Cat:** in the Register or Write Checks screen).

CPA TIP

Although businesses prefer that customers pay cash at the time of sale (to the extent that they sometimes extend discounts for cash payments), business owners find that extending credit to their customers increases sales and is therefore good for business. Be cautious, however; one major cause of business failure is lack of control over accounts receivable. If you extend credit to everyone without investigating their credit history, you may get stuck with many bad debts and a large amount of receivables on your hands. Remember: Receivables are an asset but are of no value if they are uncollectible!

Fig. 22.2

Recording a $500 partial payment on the $2,500 receivable.

Date	Num	Payee · Memo · Category	Payment	C	Deposit	Balance
9/03 1993	1004	Nevada Bell / Telephone	137 36			22,578 98
9/03 1993	1005	Landmark Realty / Rent Paid	2,000 00			20,578 98
9/03 1993	1006	Hertz Bros. Dist. / Merch.Pur.	17,438 43			3,140 55
9/03 1993	***** SPLIT	Joe W. Cowart / Payroll:Gross	234 21			2,906 34
9/03 1993	***** SPLIT	Dara Suddeth / Payroll:Gross	243 66			2,662 68
9/08 1993	Memo: Cat:	Receipt from Johnson Mfg. / [Receivables]			500 00	

US BANK1234   (Alt+letter accesses menu)
Esc-Main Menu   Ctrl⏎ Record   Ending Balance: $2,662.68

Quicken records a $500 reduction in the account you use to track the $2,500 receivable. Figure 22.3 shows the Receivables Register after you record the $500 partial payment from Johnson Manufacturing as a deposit to the bank account. Quicken records the transaction as a decrease in the receivables account.

Fig. 22.3
Quicken records
the second half of
the transfer
transaction.

Tracking Customer Receivables

Another basic receivables accounting task is tracking how much customers owe you and how long customers have owed you. The age of a receivable usually determines the collection efforts you make. You probably don't worry about receivables that aren't yet due. You may call customers with receivables more than 30 days past due. You may even turn over to a collection agency or an attorney receivables more than 90 days past due.

To create a summary report that shows accounts receivable balances grouped by age, follow these steps:

1. Choose Create Reports from the Main Menu or access the Reports menu from the Register or Write Checks screen.

2. From the Reports menu, choose Other Reports and then the Summary Reports. Quicken displays the Create Summary Report window (see fig. 22.4).

3. To complete the screen to show receivables balances only, enter a report title (such as *Accounts Receivable Aging*) and a range of dates in the Report date range field that begins with the date of the oldest receivable and ends with the current date.

4. In the Set the Row Headings field, choose 4 for Account.

5. In the Column Headings field , choose the time intervals you want to use to age receivables. (Usually, businesses age receivables on a monthly basis.)

Fig. 22.4
The Create Summary report window completed for a receivables aging report.

CPA TIP

An *aging* refers to segregating receivables into different age groups. Aging receivables tells you how long receivable balances have been outstanding. Ages are calculated as the difference between the invoice date and the current date.

6. In the Use Current/All/Selected Accounts field, choose **S** for Selected, and then choose **Enter**.

Quicken next displays the Select Accounts To Include window (see fig. 22.5). Exclude all accounts that are not receivables.

Fig. 22.5
The Select Accounts To Include window.

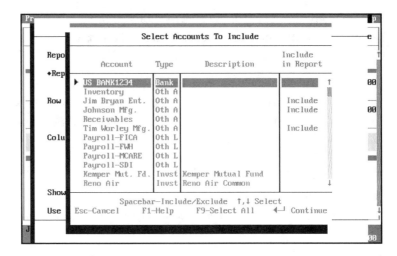

7. To exclude these accounts, highlight the account you want to exclude and press the space bar. The space bar acts as a toggle to select between include and exclude.

8. After you complete the Select Accounts To Include window, choose **Enter**, and Quicken displays the Accounts Receivable Aging report summary (see fig. 22.6).

```
 ile/Print   dit    ayout   eports   ctivities              F1- elp

                      Accounts Receivable Aging

                       6/ 1/93 Through 8/31/93
         ARAD60-Selected Accounts
         9/ 8/93
                                                       OVERALL
           Account Description    6/93      7/93      8/93      TOTAL

           Jim Bryan Ent.          0.00      0.00   3,267.45   3,267.45
           Johnson Mfg.            0.00  1,000.00    -500.00     500.00
           Tim Worley Mfg.     2,364.89      0.00       0.00   2,364.89

           OVERALL TOTAL       2,364.89  1,000.00   2,767.45   6,132.34



         Tim Worley Mfg.
         Esc-Leave report
```

Fig. 22.6

The Accounts Receivable Aging report.

The summary report shows how much money each of the receivables customers owes you and also the ages of the receivables. Johnson Manufacturing, for example, shows a receivable balance of $1000 in July because the date of this account's first transaction is in July, and as $500 at the end of August because you received a partial payment on the receivable in August.

Tracking Accounts Payable

Accounts payable are liabilities to vendors for goods and services used in a business, and any other liabilities the business owes but remain unpaid. To record your payables, you must set up a separate accounts payable account in Quicken. Because an accounts payable account is a liability of your business, it should be set up as a Liability Account (account type 5 in the Set Up New Account window). If you're not using the accrual system of accounting discussed earlier in this chapter, don't worry about setting up accounts payable accounts.

Note

The Quicken user's manual offers another approach for recording receivables and two other approaches for recording payments on the receivables. The manual suggests that you record all receivables, or at least all of a specific customer's receivables, in one account. Regarding recording payments, the manual suggests that you enter the payment as a decrease transaction in a large Receivables Register or as a negative transfer amount for a specific receivable transaction by using the Split Transaction window. (If you have more questions about these approaches, refer to the user's manual.) The benefit of the manual's two approaches is that you don't use as many accounts—the limit is 255. These suggestions, however, have the following problems:

- If you record invoices and payment transactions in a large Register, you have difficulty determining how much money a customer owes you or has paid you on a specific invoice.

- If you use the Split Transaction window to record payments on an invoice, a second problem arises. To apply a payment to five invoices, you must go into the Receivables Register and edit five transactions to show the payment. Bank reconciliation also is more difficult because you recorded the payment as five deposits rather than as one payment.

To set up an accounts payable account, add a liability account, name it *Accounts Pay* or *A/P*, and enter zero as the starting balance. Because the accounts payable account is a liability, it will be shown in the Liabilities section of the Balance Sheet.

CPA TIP

Take advantage of all early payment discounts by paying invoices on the early payment date. Pay all other invoices so that the payment is received on the due date. You may even consider using aggressive accounts-payable management by taking a 2 percent discount on any early payment, even if the vendor offers no such discount. Most vendors will be glad to receive 98 percent of the invoice amount early, rather than waiting for 100 percent in 30 or more days.

After you establish your accounts payable account, you can begin entering transactions for purchases or services.

To track your accounts payable, follow these steps:

1. Access the Register for the accounts payable account.

2. Enter a transaction for each credit purchase or service. Use the purchase invoice to enter this information. Use the same dates as the purchase date shown on the invoice. Enter the amount of the purchase or service in the Increase field. Use the Memo field to enter descriptive information about the credit transaction, such as invoice number, payment terms, and so on. Then, assign a category or subcategory to the transaction and record the transaction.

Figure 22.7 shows the Accounts Payable Register with a credit transaction entered.

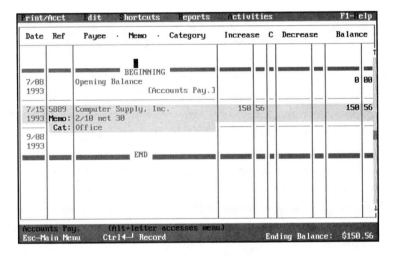

Fig. 22.7

The Accounts Payable Register with a credit purchase transaction.

To record the transaction when you pay for credit purchases you entered in the accounts payable account, follow these steps:

1. Choose the bank account you use to write checks, and access the Register.

2. Enter the payment transaction as usual. In the Category field, enter the accounts payable account. Quicken enters the account in brackets to show that this is a transfer transaction (you're transferring funds from your bank account to decrease the balance in the accounts payable account). Record the transaction. Quicken enters the corresponding transaction in the Accounts Payable Register. Figure 22.8 shows the Accounts Payable Register after a payment is made. (Remember, you can press **Ctrl-X** to go directly to the corresponding transfer transaction.)

Fig. 22.8

The Accounts Payable Register after a payment is made.

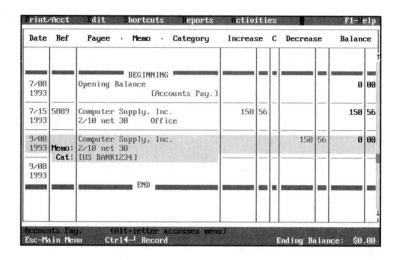

Often, vendors provide incentives to their customers to pay their invoices early. Such incentives can include a 2 percent discount from the invoice amount if paid within 10 days of the invoice date. Otherwise, vendors require the full amount paid within 30 days. (Note that there are many other discount terms provided by vendors.) If you take advantage of an early payment discount, split the transaction for the payment to the vendor and assign the discount to a subcategory called *Discounts* under the Category *Purchases* (you will need to add this subcategory to the Category and Transfer List). The check that you write will be less than the amount of the payable (by the 2 percent discount), so to clear the payable, put the difference in the Discounts account. When you prepare your income statement, the discounts taken will become a deduction from the cost of goods purchased.

Accounting for Fixed Assets

Accounting for fixed assets represents another activity most businesses need to address. You may own furniture, equipment, and even real estate that needs to be depreciated. Although you can depreciate different assets, the mechanics of recording depreciation are consistent.

> **Note**
>
> If you need to record depletion for natural resources, such as timber, or if you need to record amortization expenses for intangible assets, such as copyrights or patents, the procedures are the same as those described for depreciation.

Understanding Depreciation

Suppose that you purchase a delivery truck for $12,000. You plan to use the truck for five years and then sell the truck for $2,000 (its salvage value). The rationale for depreciating the truck is that over the five years, you need to include the expense of the truck when measuring profits. *Depreciation* is a way of allocating the cost (not assigning the value) of an asset over two or more years. Several methods are available to make this allocation, but a common method is *straight-line* depreciation. Straight-line depreciation works in the following manner: If you buy the truck for $12,000, intending to sell the truck five years later for $2,000, the overall cost of using the truck over the five years is $10,000. To calculate the yearly cost, divide the $10,000 by five years, and $2,000 is the annual depreciation expense to include in the calculations of profits.

On balance sheets, assets are listed at their adjusted basis (an amount equal to the original cost, minus the depreciation already taken). Continuing with the delivery truck example, at the end of year one the balance sheet lists the truck at $10,000—calculated as $12,000 original cost minus $2,000 of depreciation. Similarly, at the end of years two, three, four, and five, the balance sheet lists the truck at the original cost minus the depreciation taken to date. After the end of year five, when the truck is listed at $2,000—calculated as $12,000 minus $10,000 of depreciation—you stop depreciating the asset because you don't depreciate the asset below its salvage value.

CPA TIP

Other depreciation methods exist, and the methods the federal tax laws prescribe often are confusing. In essence, however, how you use Quicken to record depreciation works the same way no matter what depreciation method you use. This chapter cannot give you complete information about how to calculate the depreciation on assets, but if you want more information on the tax laws, call the Internal Revenue Service and ask for Internal Revenue Service Publication 534. For more information on how to calculate depreciation according to generally accepted accounting principles (GAAP), which is different from depreciation calculated for the tax laws, consult a certified public accountant.

Recording Fixed Assets and Depreciation

To record fixed assets and the depreciation expense related to fixed assets, set up an account for each asset that must be depreciated. Enter a descriptive account name, set the account type to 4 for Assets account, and enter the purchase price as the initial balance. Figure 22.9 shows the Set Up New Account window with the $12,000 delivery truck entered as an Other Asset account.

Fig. 22.9

The Set Up New Account window to add a new account for a $12,000 delivery truck.

If you have groups of similar assets with similar life spans, you usually can depreciate these assets as a group. You probably don't need to depreciate individually each piece of furniture you buy during the year; you can aggregate and depreciate all the furniture together, as one asset. If you do maintain a detailed list of your depreciable assets, it is known as a depreciation schedule; a term you are probably use to hearing from your accountant.

To record depreciation, you can enter a decrease transaction for $2,000 each year and assign the Depreciation Expense category to the transactions. If you did not set up a category for depreciation, Quicken prompts you to add the category when you try to assign it to the depreciation transaction. Remember that Quicken does not use a transaction in calculating net income unless the date is within the range you specify on the Create Report screens. Therefore, you can enter all five years of depreciation at one time by using transaction dates in each of the five years. Figure 22.10 shows the fixed Asset Account's Register for the delivery truck with depreciation expense recorded for 1993, 1994, and 1995.

Remember that you can record transactions in the future. Notice the different color in the date field for the future transactions. The balance column shows the reduction of $2000 each year, but these entries won't be posted anywhere else (the balance sheet, for example) until the future date has occurred.

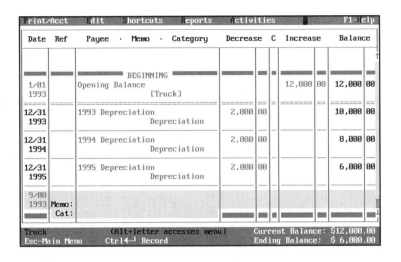

Fig. 22.10
The Delivery Truck Register.

Preparing Payroll

One of the more common business applications of Quicken is to prepare employee payroll checks and reports. Suppose that you want to prepare a payroll check for an employee who earns $1,000 every two weeks. The employee's Social Security tax is $62, the Medicare tax is $14.50, the federal income tax withholding amount is $100, and the state income tax withholding amount is $40. You also can assume that the employer's matching share of Social Security is $62, the matching share of Medicare is $14.50, and the employer must pay $10 for federal unemployment tax. There also is an employer paid state unemployment tax, but it is omitted for this example.

Getting Ready for Payroll

To record this payroll transaction, set up a liability account for each of the payroll tax payable accounts. In the Set Up New Account window, enter the account type as 5, for Other Liability, and enter the initial amount (the amount you already owe) as the starting balance in the account. In this example, the amount includes the federal income tax withholding, state income tax withholding, the employee's Social Security and Medicare amount, your matching Social Security and Medicare taxes, and the federal unemployment tax. To define each of the payroll tax accounts, use the Set Up New Account window.

You also need to set up a category for each of the employer's payroll expenses: the employee's gross wages, the employer's matching share of the Social Security and Medicare tax, and the federal unemployment tax.

Tip
If your payroll is becoming burdensome, consider using Quicken's add-on utility program called QuickPay. QuickPay calculates and processes your payroll and even enters the employee's paycheck information in the Write Checks screen for you. Refer to Appendix B, "Using QuickPay with Quicken," to learn more about this payroll-preparation utility.

You don't set up expense categories for the employee's withholding for Social Security tax, Medicare tax, federal income tax, or state income tax, however, because these amounts are expenses of the employee—not the employer.

CPA TIP

Be sure to keep up with the changing FICA (Federal Insurance Contribution Act) tax rates and the unemployment tax rates for your state. You also should be aware of limitations on 401K plan contributions each year. At the beginning of the year, consult with your accountant or tax advisor for this information.

Paying Employees

To record the payroll check, enter the payroll transaction in the Write Checks screen or the Register (see fig. 22.11). If you write payroll checks using the same bank account you use to write other checks, enter the Memo description as *payroll*, or payroll and the pay date, so that you can use the Memo field as the basis for including transactions on reports. Choose **S**plit Transaction by pressing **Ctrl-S** to assign multiple categories and accounts to the payroll transaction. You don't need to fill in the net paycheck amount in the Amount field in the Write Checks screen because Quicken calculates the net amount for you by subtracting any negative amounts that you enter in the Split Transaction window for withholding from the positive amount that you enter for wages. If you use checks with vouchers—a good idea for payroll— the employee's gross wages and the employee's deductions should appear on the first 16 lines of the Split Transaction window so that the payroll transaction is detailed on the voucher. The employee then can see how much of his gross pay was withheld for federal, state, Social Security, and Medicare taxes.

Note

You can turn on the Print Categories on Voucher Checks setting (from the Checks and Reports settings) so that Quicken prints voucher information on checks. To learn how to turn on this setting, see Chapter 20, "Customizing Quicken."

Enter the other wages expenses (such as the employer's matching share of Social Security, Medicare, and federal unemployment tax) starting on line 17 of the Split Transaction window so that these expenses don't appear on the payroll check's voucher (see fig. 22.12). (Entries made to lines 16 through 30 of the Split Transaction window are not printed on check vouchers.)

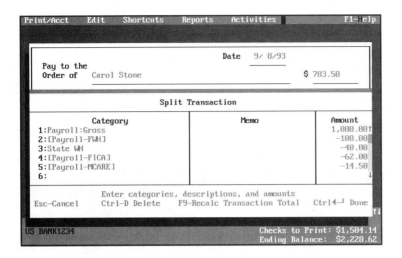

Fig. 22.11
The Split Transaction window showing the employee portion of the payroll calculation.

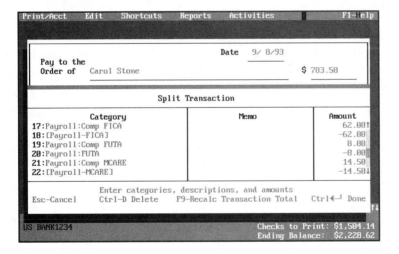

Fig. 22.12
The Split Transaction window showing the employer portion of the payroll calculation.

V

Putting Quicken to Use

After you complete the Split Transaction window, choose **Enter** or **F10** to return to the Write Checks screen or the Register. Figure 22.13 shows a completed payroll check. The net wages amount is $783.50, which is $1,000 in gross wages minus $100 in federal withholding, minus $40 in state tax withholding, minus $62 in Social Security, and minus $14.50 in Medicare.

Using the Create Payroll Support Assistant

As you may recall from Chapter 1, the Use Tutorials/Assistants menu, which you access from Quicken's Main Menu, provides several utilities that make working with Quicken easier. One of these utilities, the Create Payroll Support option, makes setting up payroll quick and easy. In essence, the Create

Fig. 22.13

The completed payroll check.

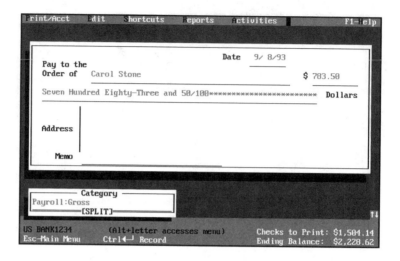

Payroll Support option sets up the categories and accounts you need to pre-pare payroll in your state. When you choose this option, Quicken displays a message screen that tells you what the Create Payroll Support option does. To continue, choose **Enter**. Next, Quicken prompts you for the state's two-letter abbreviation, such as NV for Nevada or NY for New York. (If you don't know the state's two-letter abbreviation, choose **Enter** without making an entry. Quicken displays a window that lists state names and abbreviations, and you can select one of the states on the list.) After you enter or identify the state's two-letter abbreviation, Quicken creates each of the accounts and categories needed in your state.

> **Note**
>
> The accounts and categories that Quicken sets up differ from the generic accounts and categories used for illustrating payroll. Quicken sets up accounts and categories specific to the state that you enter.

Paying Payroll Taxes

When you pay the government, you already have recorded the expense of the taxes and are carrying as a liability the payroll taxes you still owe. When you write the check to the government, the entry made in the Category field should be the payroll tax liability account. If you write a check to pay the $10 in federal unemployment taxes, you enter the category as **[Payroll-FUTA]** because Payroll-FUTA is the name of the liability account you use to track the amount you owe in federal unemployment tax.

CPA TIP

You may know that most payroll deductions and taxes are calculated as a percentage of gross wages. Social Security deductions and matching payroll taxes are calculated as 6.2 percent, and up, of the gross wages to a ceiling amount ($57,600 in 1993). Medicare deductions and matching payroll taxes are 1.45 percent of the gross wages amount to a ceiling amount ($135,000 in 1993). With this feature of payroll preparation, you often can have Quicken calculate most of the payroll deductions and payroll taxes by using the percentage-split feature.

To use the percentage-split feature to calculate payroll deductions and taxes, enter the transaction as usual, except enter the gross wages amount in the Check Amount field in the Write Checks screen or the Payment field in the Register. Then, open the Split Transaction window. Enter a line for each payroll deduction or payroll tax item. In the Amount field, enter the percentage used to calculate the deduction or tax (such as **6.2%** for Social Security tax and **1.45%** for Medicare). Enter the Payroll:Gross amount as **100%**.

After you enter the percent and choose **Enter**, Quicken calculates the amount by multiplying the percentage by the amount entered in the Check Amount field or the Payment field. Enter the exact amounts in the Split Transaction window for any deductions or taxes that you derive from withholding tables, such as Employer's Circular E for federal income tax withholding.

A minor problem with this approach, however, is that the check amount isn't really the gross wages amount that you entered. The check amount should be the net of the gross wages amount minus payroll deductions and taxes. This problem isn't difficult to fix. You may recall from Chapter 8 that to make the split transaction lines equal the check amount, Quicken adds another split transaction line to balance the transaction. Just delete this line by highlighting it and choosing **Ctrl-D**. Then, choose **F9** to direct Quicken to recalculate the check amount. The amount that Quicken calculates should be equal to the net payroll or paycheck.

Finally, Quicken enables you to create memorized transactions that use percentages rather than amounts. If you use the previously described approach, you can use this capability to make preparing payroll checks even easier.

V

Putting Quicken to Use

You also use the same approach to record paying all the other payroll tax liabilities you owe. You write a check to the government agency and categorize the transaction as a transfer from the payroll taxes liability account.

In real life, of course, you may have several more payroll tax expenses and liabilities for items, such as state and local income taxes, state unemployment insurance, and disability insurance. The accounting procedures you follow to record and pay each of these liabilities, however, are the same as the procedures described in the preceding paragraphs.

CPA TIP

You should segregate the payroll taxes that you withhold from your employees' gross wages. The best approach is to set up a separate bank account to collect and disburse payroll taxes. Do not, for any reason, *borrow* money from the payroll taxes bank account. Although the act may seem innocuous, this money is not yours to spend. This money belongs to your employee or the federal government; you only hold the money in trust.

Completing Quarterly and Annual Tax Reports

The final aspect of preparing payroll relates to the filing of the quarterly and annual payroll forms and reports to federal, state, and local government. A series of federal reporting requirements exists for W-2s, W-3s, 940s, and 941s. Depending on where you live, you also may have several state and local payroll forms and reports to complete. You may be able to retrieve the numbers for these forms by printing a summary report based on the bank account you use to write payroll checks.

To print the summary report, choose Summary Reports from the Other Reports menu. You may want to subtotal the report by category. If you write payroll checks on the same account you use to write other checks and include **payroll** in the Memo field, you can use the **F9-Filter** option to specify that only transactions with `payroll` appear in the summary report.

Completing the W-2 and W-3

You use the gross wages figures as the total wages amounts on the employees' W-2s. You use the transfers from withholding figures as the federal income tax withholding amounts. You use the transfers from employees' FICA as the Social Security and Medicare taxes withheld amounts.

The W-3 summarizes the W-2 forms you complete. You enter the employer totals for the individual amounts from each employee's W-2. You can use the totals from the summary report for these employer totals.

Note

One difference between the transaction report shown in figure 22.14 and the one you use to prepare the W-2 and W-3 forms is that the range of transaction dates encompasses the entire calendar year.

Completing Other Forms and Reports

The federal and the state governments have other tax forms and reports you must complete. You use the 940 form to calculate and report annual federal unemployment tax liability. You also use the 941 form each quarter to calculate and report federal income and Social Security taxes withheld and the employer's share of the Social Security taxes. Again, you may be able to use a summary report similar to the report shown in figure 22.14 to complete the quarterly return.

> **CPA TIP**
>
> For the Employer's Annual Unemployment Tax (form 940), the range of transaction dates must encompass the entire year. For the Employer's Quarterly Federal Tax (form 941), the range of transaction dates must cover the quarter.

> **Note**
>
> Typically, the Internal Revenue Service provides a great deal of help and information about federal payroll taxes. You may want to take advantage of the IRS help guides. Specifically, you need the Employer's Tax Guide (also known as Circular E). If you don't already have this document, call the nearest IRS office and request a guide. If you are a sole proprietor, you also may want to request the information packet "Your Business Tax Kit for Sole Proprietor," which provides information about the taxes you pay as a sole proprietor. The IRS also has toll-free 800 numbers you can call that can answer many of your questions. Some IRS locations provide free small-business tax education seminars. You also can call the state revenue office and request all information they have on the state income and payroll taxes.

Preparing Inventory Accounting

A good inventory accounting system answers two questions: How much inventory do you currently hold and how much inventory did you sell over the year? A perpetual inventory system can answer both questions. Unfortunately, Quicken does not provide the tools to maintain a perpetual system. A perpetual inventory system tracks every change in inventory as the changes occur, in dollars and in units. As a result, you always know exactly how much inventory you hold, in dollars and in units. Because Quicken tracks only dollars, not units, you can answer only the second question: How much inventory did you sell over the year? You can answer this question with a simple periodic inventory system.

Understanding Periodic Inventory Systems

A periodic system works in the following way: At the end of every year, you count the inventory you are holding and add up the cost of the inventory. Calculate the cost of the goods, or inventory, you sold by taking the inventory purchases you made over the year and subtracting the change in inventory.

Suppose that you sell antique cars and each car costs $10,000. You held 3 cars in inventory at the beginning of the year, purchased 10 cars over the year, and have 4 cars in inventory at the end of the year. Using the equation described previously, you can calculate the value of the inventory you sold over the year as follows:

Car purchases: ($10,000 * 10) = $100,000

Change over year:

Ending: ($10,000 * 4 cars) = $40,000

Beginning: ($10,000 * 3 cars) = $30,000

Minus change over year: -$10,000

Cost of inventory sold over year: $90,000

You know that during the year you bought $100,000 of cars and that you are holding $10,000 more inventory than you held at the end of the previous year, which means that you did not sell all the cars you bought.

Implementing a Periodic Inventory System

If you want to enjoy the benefits of a periodic inventory system, you can use Quicken to construct a simple inventory system.

The following steps describe how you implement a periodic inventory system using Quicken:

1. Set up an Asset account for the inventory you buy and sell. The name can be *Inventory*. Choose **4** as the account type. The starting balance is the starting inventory balance. (If you are just starting a business, the starting inventory balance can be zero if you have not yet begun to purchase inventory.)

2. When you purchase inventory, don't categorize the purchase as an expense; transfer the total purchase amount to the inventory account (enter the inventory account in the Category field; Quicken enters it like this: [Inventory]).

3. At the end of your fiscal year, choose the inventory account and use the Update Account Balance option from the Activities menu to reset the inventory account balance to whatever the physical count shows at the end of the year. Assign the Cost of Goods Sold category to the adjustment transaction. You may have to add the category Cost of Goods Sold as an expense category.

Figure 22.14 shows an Inventory Account Register after a month of purchases and the adjustment transaction that calculates the actual Cost of Goods Sold amount.

Fig. 22.14

An Inventory Account Register.

Reviewing the Problems of a Periodic System

As you know, a periodic inventory system is not without problems. Make sure that you can live with the problems of a periodic inventory system before you spend a great deal of time and energy to implement this kind of system.

Although you have accurate measures of cash flow, you have an accurate measure of profits only through the last adjustment transaction. If you need to measure profits frequently, you must take frequent physical counts of the inventory and make the inventory adjustment transaction.

You don't know the details or components of the cost of goods sold because you get the cost of goods sold from an adjustment transaction. As a result, you don't know the portion of cost of goods sold that stems from sales to specific customers or the portion that stems from breakage, shoplifting, or spoilage. This loss of information can be especially troublesome if the business has more than one kind of item sold, such as books, tapes, and CDs. You may have to set up separate accounts for each kind of item in your inventory and be sure that you segregate all purchases by using the Split Transaction option.

Except when you make physical counts of inventory, you also never know how much inventory you actually have on hand. You cannot use this inventory system, therefore, to see the items you need to reorder or how many units of a specific item are presently in stock.

Job Costing

Job costing refers to tracking the costs of a specific project, or job, and comparing these costs to the amount you planned to spend. Home builders, advertising agencies, and specialty manufacturers are examples of businesses with projects you must monitor for actual and planned costs.

The Quicken user's manual suggests one approach for job costing: Categorize each expense into a category and a class. When you print a transaction or summary report, you can choose to subtotal by the classes. If you use classes to represent jobs, for example, the total for a class is the total for a job. This approach, however, is not strong. The following paragraphs describe alternative approaches that help you avoid two problems you encounter when categorizing expenses into categories and classes. (See Chapter 4, "Organizing Your Finances," for a detailed discussion of categories and classes.)

The first problem with using classes as the basis for a job-costing system is that within Quicken, you budget by categories, not by classes. If you use the class approach, you omit one of the basic job-costing tasks: comparing the amount you planned to spend with the actual amount spent. Fortunately, you can solve this problem by setting up a group of categories that you use only for a specific job. You may even include a code or an abbreviation in the category name to indicate the job.

Suppose that you are a home builder constructing a house on Lot 23 in Deerfield subdivision and that you use three rough categories of expenses on all the homes you build: land, material, and labor. You can create three special categories: *D23 land*, *D23 material*, and *D23 labor*, which you can use exclusively to budget and track the costs of the house under construction. Figure 22.15 shows the budgeting report that you can generate to monitor job costs if you follow the approaches described in the preceding paragraph.

```
 ile/Print   dit   ayout   eports   ctivities        F1- elp

                    BUDGET REPORT BY MONTH

                    8/ 1/93 Through 8/31/93
     ARAD60-All Accounts
     9/ 9/93
                            8/ 1/93    -      8/31/93
       Category Description  Actual   Budget    Diff

     INCOME/EXPENSE
       EXPENSES
         D23 Labor          16,753.00  20,000.00  -3,247.00
         D23 Land           30,400.00  30,000.00     400.00
         D23 Materials      23,456.00  25,000.00  -1,544.00

       TOTAL EXPENSES       70,609.00  75,000.00  -4,391.00


       TOTAL INCOME/EXPENSE -70,609.00 -75,000.00  4,391.00



 US BANK1234                                     (Filtered)
 Esc-Leave report
```

Fig. 22.15
A budget report for a job.

A second problem with using classes as the basis for a job-costing system is that you don't always have to categorize as expenses the costs you incur on a job. Often, you need to treat these costs as assets. The costs of building the home on Lot 23 in the Deerfield subdivision should be carried as inventory until the home is sold. When the home is sold, the total costs of the home may be categorized as the cost of goods sold.

During the job, if you categorize the costs of building the home as expenses when you pay the costs, you overstate expenses (which understates profits), and you understate assets (which understates net worth). These understatements of profits and net worth can become a real problem if you have investors or lenders looking carefully at your financial performance and condition. To solve this problem, create a transaction in which you move cost dollars out of the job-cost categories into an asset account.

An Introduction to QuickBooks

If you like using Quicken but find that it just doesn't fit the needs of your small business (because you cannot print invoices and statements, track accounts receivable and payable adequately, or create customer and vendor lists), you may want to look into Intuit's small business package called *QuickBooks*. You easily can convert your Quicken data to QuickBooks, so don't worry about having to re-enter anything in a new system. Even though you may decide to convert to QuickBooks and convert your Quicken data, after the conversion process, your Quicken data still is intact if you want to use Quicken to perform activities that QuickBooks doesn't do, such as amortize loans and track investments.

Although Quicken fully accommodates the individual user for home finances and many small business users, Quicken does not offer some of the features that you may need to track your business finances adequately. QuickBooks offers small-business owners the ease of use that they're accustomed to in Quicken, as well as features that relate more specifically to business, such as invoicing and accounts payable tracking.

You write checks and enter transactions in your Check Register in QuickBooks just like in Quicken. You also can use QuickBooks to reconcile your bank account using almost the same steps that you use in Quicken. QuickBooks can do several other things just like Quicken; however, QuickBooks does a lot of things that Quicken cannot do, such as the following:

- Initiates most transactions from the Accounts Receivable or Accounts Payable Register because that's where most small-business activities begin. Transactions entered the Accounts Receivable or Accounts Payable Register are entered by QuickBooks in the appropriate checking account. When you record and pay a bill the Accounts Payable Register, for example, QuickBooks enters the payment in the Check Register.

- Tracks your accounts receivable so that you know at any given time how much your customers owe.

- Applies customer payments to invoices and calculates early payment discounts.

- Prepares a deposit summary that you can take to the bank when you deposit customer payments.

■ Offers complete invoice writing capabilities that enable you to enter line items with item codes that link invoice transactions to accounts.

■ Determines when your bills are due and gives you the opportunity to pay outstanding bills directly from the Accounts Payable Register.

■ Uses your chart of accounts to track income, expenses, and balance sheet accounts, rather than the categories and subcategories that are used in Quicken.

■ Uses company lists to store data about your customers, customer types, vendors, vendor types, employees, invoice-line items, projects, shipping methods, payment methods, and payment terms. You can even store invoice memos so that you don't need to retype them each time you write an invoice. Company lists speed up entry in many fields through-out the program. Any time a small black diamond appears in a field, you can display the appropriate list and select an item, and QuickBooks immediately enters the items that you select in the field. Company lists also serve as a database of your customers, vendors, and employees, and you can use these lists to print mailing labels for your customers and vendors.

■ Uses balance sheet accounts that are more representative of business, such as fixed asset and equity accounts.

■ Enables you to define projects or jobs and assign transactions to them so that you can track closely each project, job, client, and so on. (In Quicken, projects are called *classes*.)

■ Enables you to assign password protection to 13 QuickBooks activities. If you assign a password to the check printing activity, for example, QuickBooks requires a password before printing that first check.

■ Uses terminology with which small-business people are familiar. Famil-iar, however, does not mean that you must be an accounting expert to understand the terminology in QuickBooks. On the contrary—Intuit strived for a program that does not intimidate the nonaccounting user. In QuickBooks, you don't even see common accounting terms, such as debit or credit. You *do* see accounts receivable and payable, invoice, voucher, and so on—the terms that you use or hear on a daily basis.

■ Offers business reports that are designed to appear in the usual and customary business format.

- Creates an aging status schedule for each customer that shows the portion of the customer's balance that is current and the portion that is 0 to 30 days past due, 31 to 60 days past due, 61 to 90 days past due, and more than 90 days past due.

- Generates an accounts payable aging report that shows the status of your unpaid bills.

- Generates an IRS Form 099 report that you can use to fill out 1099 forms at the end of the calendar year for those vendors to whom you pay more than $600.

- Tracks the sales tax that you collect for each government agency and accumulates sales tax data in a report that you can use when it's time to file sales tax returns and pay sales tax.

- Displays a transaction history for transactions that you select in accounts receivable and accounts payable. A transaction history shows each transaction related to the selected transaction.

- Enables you to enter notes about customers, vendors, or employees in the QuickBooks program so that the notes are readily available.

As you can see, QuickBooks is designed to handle most small-business activities (with the exception of inventory control). If your small business has significant investments, however, you should know that QuickBooks is not set up to do the following:

- Track individual investments, their market values, and their gains or losses. If it's important that you closely track your investments, use the investment feature in Quicken, and use QuickBooks for everything else.

- Look at transaction detail in reports. QuickBooks does not include the QuickZoom feature that Quicken has that enables you to highlight a line in a report to see the transactions that make up the amount shown on that line. If you want to see transaction detail in a QuickBooks report, you must exit the report screen and search through the Registers for transactions.

- Specify accounts as tax-related. However, this feature is not as important in QuickBooks because most all business accounts and subaccounts are tax-related.

Summary

This chapter provides you with a basic approach to accounting for any business asset or liability and gave specific suggestions and tips for performing basic accounting tasks. You now have the necessary information to use Quicken as the basis of a business accounting system. If, however, you still feel that you cannot adequately track your business finances with Quicken, this chapter introduced you to QuickBooks, a software product very similar to Quicken but modified to handle most small-business tasks.

This chapter is the last of *Using Quicken 7 for DOS*. In the appendixes that follow, you learn how to install Quicken (which you probably already have done), and how to use QuickPay with Quicken.

V

Putting Quicken to Use

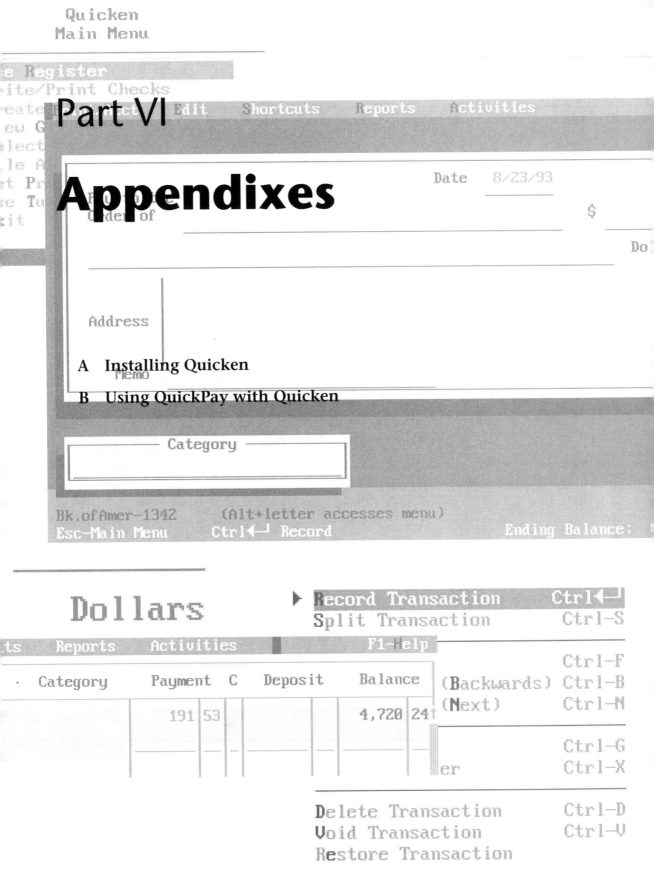

Part VI

Appendixes

QUICKEN
Main Menu

Use Register
Write/Print Checks
Create Print/Acct   Edit   Shortcuts   Reports   Activities
View G
Select
File A
Set Pr
Use Tu
Exit

                                          Date   8/23/93
        Pay to the
        Order of $
        _____

        _____

        Address

        Memo

                        ─ Category ─

Bk.ofAmer-1342   (Alt+letter accesses menu)
Esc-Main Menu   Ctrl↵ Record   Ending Balance:

Dollars   ▶ Record Transaction   Ctrl↵
                           Split Transaction   Ctrl-S
cuts   Reports   Activities   ▌   F1-Help
                                                     Ctrl-F
o · Category   Payment C Deposit   Balance   (Backwards) Ctrl-B
                                                  (Next)   Ctrl-N
s   191 53   4,720 24↑

                                                             Ctrl-G
                                                  er   Ctrl-X

                           Delete Transaction   Ctrl-D
                           Void Transaction   Ctrl-V
                           Restore Transaction

Appendix A

Installing Quicken

Before you can use Quicken, you must install the program on your hard disk. This appendix provides the steps to install Quicken and explains software and hardware requirements.

Reviewing the Program Requirements

The following sections review some of the software and hardware requirements of Quicken.

Hardware Requirements

To use Quicken, you must have the following hardware:

- An IBM PC, XT, AT, PS/1, PS/2, Tandy, or 100 percent compatible computer.

- At least 512K of memory (640K if you plan to use IntelliCharge with a modem).

- A hard drive.

- At least one floppy disk drive, one of which is a high-density 1.2Mb or 1.44Mb drive.

- An 80-column color or monochrome monitor. You will need a monitor with a graphics card if you are planning to use the View Graphs feature.

- (Optional) Any printer (except one that uses thermal paper if using checks from Intuit).

- ■ (Optional) A modem if you plan to pay bills electronically or use IntelliCharge.

- ■ (Optional) Intuit checks (if you plan to print checks).

Software Requirements

To use Quicken, you must have the following software:

- ■ MS-DOS or PC DOS Version 3.0 or higher (use the VER DOS command to determine the DOS version installed on your computer).

- ■ Quicken Install Disks 1 and 2 (3.5 inch) or Install disks 1, 2, 3, and 4 (5.25 inch).

Installing Quicken

INSTALL (for Quicken 7) creates a directory named QUICKEN on your hard disk, in which the program files are stored. Your data files also are stored in the QUICKEN directory, unless you change the system settings (described in Chapter 19, "Managing Your Quicken Files"). *Program files* refer to the files that contain the actual Quicken software instructions, and *data files* refer to the files that contain your financial information.

INSTALL also creates a batch file named Q.BAT so that all you need to do is press **Q** at the C:> prompt to run Quicken. If you already have a Q.BAT file—if you have been using Quicken Version 6, for example—INSTALL renames the old file Q2.BAT.

INSTALL also verifies that the CONFIG.SYS file's BUFFERS statement equals or exceeds 10 and that the FILES statement equals or exceeds 10. INSTALL resets these statements because Quicken runs with several files open and performs many reads from the hard disk. For more information on the CONFIG.SYS file and the BUFFERS and FILES statements, see your DOS manual. If you do not have a CONFIG.SYS file, INSTALL creates one with the appropriate BUFFERS and FILES statements. If the CONFIG.SYS file you currently have does not have these statements, INSTALL adds them. If the statements exist but are set to less than 10, INSTALL increases the statement settings to 10. INSTALL does not cause any problems by changing your computer's CONFIG.SYS file.

To install Quicken, follow these steps:

1. Turn on your computer and monitor. Be sure that the correct system date and time are set. (Type **date** or **time** at the C:> prompt.) DATE is the DOS command for setting the system date. TIME is the DOS command for setting the system time. Refer to your DOS user's manual if you need help using the DATE or TIME command.

2. Insert the Quicken Install Disk 1 into drive A: or B:. Type **a:install** or **b:install** (depending on which drive you placed your Quicken Install disk into) and press **Enter**.

3. Quicken displays the Welcome to Quicken Install window as shown in figure A.1.

Fig. A.1
The Welcome to Quicken Install window.

4. Choose the appropriate number to identify your screen type and press **Enter**.

   Quicken displays the Choose Install Method window as shown in figure A.2.

VI

Appendixes

Quicken gives you the choice of Express Install or Custom Install installation methods. The Express Install method is the easiest to use. If you
choose Express Install, Quicken makes decisions for you on the choice
of drives and directories, the type of printer to set up, and to not install
Billminder (see the *Using Billminder* section in Chapter 20).

Fig. A.2
The Choose Install
Method window.

5. If you want to use Quicken's Express Install feature, choose Express
Install, and then press **Enter**. Follow the instructions on-screen, and
then skip to step 11.

6. If you want to specify the drive and directory, set up a particular
printer, or install Billminder, choose Custom Install, and then press
Enter. Quicken displays the Drive and Directory window to specify
where you want to install Quicken, as shown in figure A.3. The default
directory that Quicken creates and installs itself into is QUICKEN.

If you previously used Version 6 of Quicken and stored the program
and data files in \QUICKEN6, installing Quicken Version 7 in the
\QUICKEN6 directory will not damage the Quicken Version 6 data files.

If you want to use some other directory, you specify it here by typing
a new drive and directory. When the correct directory appears, press
Enter. Quicken displays the Choose a Printer window (see fig. A.4).

7. Use the list of printers at the Choose a Printer window to identify your
printer. To select a printer from the list, use the up- and down-arrow
keys to highlight the printer you want to select. If you cannot find your
printer, select another printer that your printer emulates.

Fig. A.3
The Drive and
Directory window.

Fig. A.4
The Choose a
Printer window.

You should be able to find which printers your printer emulates by checking the printer's users' manual. If you cannot find your printer on the list and also cannot find a printer your printer emulates, choose the <Other Dot-Matrix> or <Other Laser> options. Later, you can define printer settings for printers not found in the Choose a Printer list. Chapter 1, explains how to define printer settings.

After you select the printer, press **Enter**.

Quicken next asks whether you want the Billminder feature installed, as shown in figure A.5.

Fig. A.5

The Use
Billminder
window.

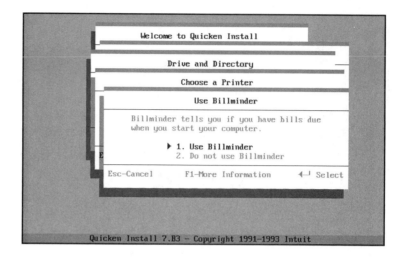

Tip

To move quickly
through the
Choose a Printer
list, press the first
letter of the name
of your printer.
Quicken takes you
to the first printer
in the list that
begins with that
letter. Then use
the down-arrow
key to move to
your printer. To
select an HP
LaserJet IIp printer,
for example, press
H to move to the
first printer in the
list that begins
with the letter H
(HP DeskJet), and
then use the
down-arrow key to
scroll through the
Hs until you get to
HP LaserJet IIp/
IIIp.

8. Press **Enter** to use Billminder, or press **2** and then **Enter** to tell Quicken
   not to use Billminder. The Billminder feature reminds you of bills you
   should pay. When you turn on your computer or when you enter
   Quicken, you are reminded that bills must be paid. This handy feature
   can save you the price of Quicken and this book many times over by
   eliminating or minimizing late-payment fees.

   Quicken displays the Confirm Settings window with all your installation settings listed (see fig. A.6).

9. To accept the settings, press **Enter**. If one of the settings is incorrect,
   press **Esc** one or more times to return to that setting's window. Then,
   make the necessary changes.

   When you press Enter from the Confirm Settings window, Quicken
   starts the file-copying part of the installation. As Quicken installs the
   program, you see a message on-screen that says Installing Quicken and
   a few Welcome to Quicken 7 messages. When necessary, Quicken
   prompts you to insert additional Quicken Install Disks into drive A:
   or B:.

   If Quicken finds data files in an old directory, such as QUICKEN6, a
   message appears and asks you whether you want these files moved to
   your new directory. Press **Enter** to move the data files to the QUICKEN
   directory or press **2** for the data files to remain in the old directory.
   Then press **Enter**.

Fig. A.6
The Confirm
Settings window.

If the INSTALL program does not find a mouse installed on your hard
drive, a message appears telling you that you must have a mouse
installed if you plan to use a mouse with Quicken. Press **Enter** to
continue.

10. Quicken tells you when the installation is complete by displaying a
screen with the message Installation Complete (see fig. A.7). To return
to the C:> prompt, press **Enter**.

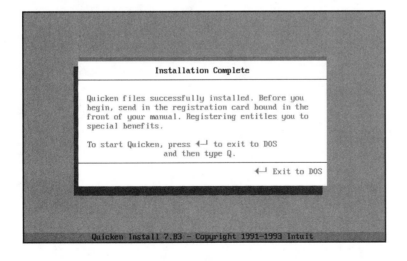

Fig. A.7
The Installation
Complete window.

To learn how to start Quicken for the first time, see Chapter 1, "Preparing To
Use Quicken."

Using QuickPay with Quicken

If you're a business user of Quicken and the payroll tricks and tips described in Chapter 22, "Using Quicken in Your Business," don't give you the payroll horsepower you need, don't despair. Still another option is available that works seamlessly with Quicken: the QuickPay payroll utility. At the time of this printing, QuickPay 3.0 is the latest version of the program.

QuickPay is a payroll program that works with Quicken. In essence, the QuickPay program calculates the amounts you usually have to calculate out-side the Quicken program—including the gross wages and the federal, state, and local taxes—and uses these amounts to prepare and record payroll checks.

Payroll preparation requires a tremendous number of calculations and auto-mation of this function is an excellent computer application. You probably will find that the modest cost of the QuickPay program will repay itself many times over in time savings as well as a lower frustration level.

The following paragraphs describe briefly how to use the QuickPay utility. Quicken users considering the QuickPay utility and new QuickPay users may find the ensuing discussion useful in deciding whether to acquire QuickPay and in getting started with the program.

Installing and Starting QuickPay

Installing QuickPay is easy. You need just two other items: an installed copy of Quicken Version 3 or later and at least 82K of memory more than the

minimum amount Quicken requires. Assuming that you meet these two requirements, follow these steps to install and start QuickPay:

1. Insert the QuickPay disk in drive A:.

2. Type **a:** at the C:> prompt to make the A drive active.

3. Type **install**. QuickPay's installation program displays a screen that
prompts you for the type of monitor you use (see fig. B.1).

Fig. B.1
The Do You Have
a Color Monitor?
window.

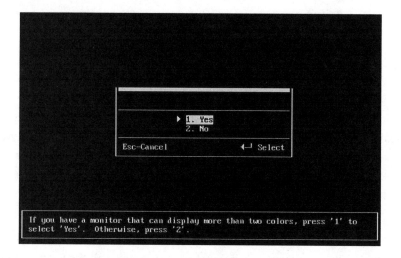

4. Choose **1** if you have a color monitor or **2** if you don't.

5. QuickPay next displays a screen telling you where it found Quicken (see
fig. B.2). QuickPay then asks you to confirm its discovery. If the identified directory is the correct Quicken program directory, press **Enter**.

6. If the identified directory is incorrect, enter the correct path name, and
then press **Enter**. QuickPay's installation program next copies the
QuickPay program files to the Quicken program directory. When it
finishes, it returns you to the DOS prompt.

7. To start Quicken and the QuickPay program, type **qp** at the DOS
prompt. Quicken starts and the Main Menu appears and displays the
message

```
With QuickPay - Version 3.0
```

at the top of the screen to show that the QuickPay utility is loaded and
available.

When With QuickPay - Version 3.0 appears at the Main Menu, the QuickPay program is available. Be certain to choose the Quicken file that you want to use for QuickPay (you may have one file for your home accounts and a different file for your business accounts). You learned how to select a Quicken file in Chapter 19, "Managing Your Quicken Files."

Using QuickPay

To begin using QuickPay, follow these steps:

1. Choose the Quicken file you want to use for the QuickPay utility by selecting File Activities from the Main Menu. The File Activities menu appears.

2. Choose Select/Set Up File from the File Activities menu. Quicken displays the Select/Set Up New File window.

3. Highlight the file that contains the bank account on which your payroll checks will be drawn, and then press **Enter**. Quicken displays the Select Account to Use window.

4. Highlight the bank account that the payroll checks will be drawn on and press **Enter**. Quicken displays the Register screen.

5. From the Register or the Write Checks screen, choose QuickPay from the Activities menu. Quicken displays the QuickPay Main Menu (see fig. B.3).

Tip
You also can write payroll checks from the Write Checks screen.

VI

Appendixes

Fig. B.3
The QuickPay
Main Menu.

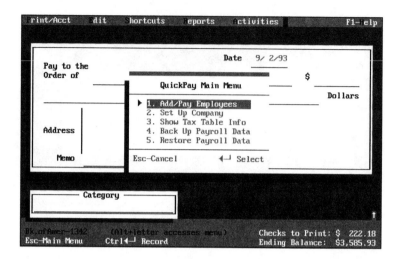

6. Once you access the QuickPay Main Menu, you can enter the information for your company and for your employees so that QuickPay can process your payroll as discussed in the next section.

Setting Up QuickPay

Just two steps are necessary to set up QuickPay to process your payroll; describing the employer and describing the employees.

To describe the employer, follow these steps:

1. Choose Set Up Company from the QuickPay Main Menu. QuickPay displays the Set Up Company window (see fig. B.4).

2. In the Set Up Company window, enter all the employer information that you may use to prepare an employee's payroll check or that you may use to prepare any employer payroll tax returns. You enter such information as your company name and address, your federal and state tax identification numbers, how your state's SDI (disability insurance) is calculated, and if you are using voucher checks.

3. After you complete the Set Up Company window, choose **Ctrl-Enter** or **F10** to return to the QuickPay Main Menu.

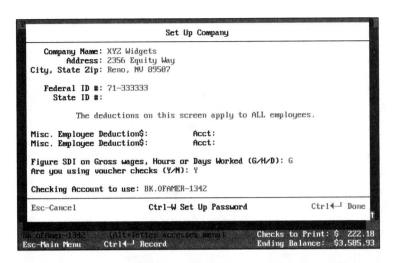

Fig. B.4
The Set Up
Company window.

Note

Most menus and screens work the same way in QuickPay as they do in Quicken.

The second step for setting up QuickPay to process payroll is entering
information for the employees whom you will pay. To enter employee
information, follow these steps:

1. Choose Add/Pay Employees from the QuickPay Main Menu.

2. QuickPay displays the Add/Pay Employees window (see fig. B.5). This
window lists all existing employees and enables you to add a new employee to the list, edit or delete existing employees, or sort employees.

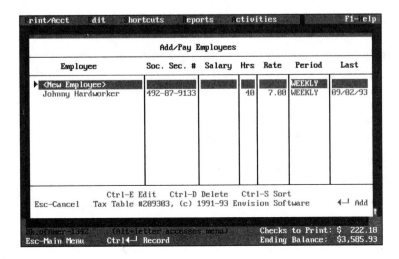

Fig. B.5
The Add/Pay
Employees
window.

VI

Appendixes

3. Highlight <New Employee> and press **Enter**. QuickPay displays the Add New Employee window (see fig. B.6).

Fig. B.6
The Add New
Employee
window.

4. In the Add New Employee window, enter information necessary to prepare a payroll check and to calculate an employee's gross wages, any deductions, and any payroll taxes. This information includes items such as the employee's name and address, salary or hourly pay rate, and Social Security number.

5. After you complete the Add New Employee window, choose **Ctrl-Enter** or **F10** to return to the Add/Pay Employees window. To add other employees, repeat steps 3 and 4 for each employee.

Processing Payroll with QuickPay

After you describe the employer and the employees, you're ready to begin preparing payroll checks. To process payroll for an employee, follow these steps:

1. From the Register or Write Checks screen, choose QuickPay from the Activities menu. The QuickPay Main Menu appears.

2. Choose Add/Pay Employees. QuickPay displays the Add/Pay Employees window.

3. Highlight the employee you want to pay and choose **Enter**. QuickPay displays the Compute Payroll window (see fig. B.7).

4. In the Compute Payroll window, enter any information specific to the payroll check being prepared. This usually is just the hours worked because QuickPay already knows the standard hourly pay rate.

Fig. B.7
The Compute Payroll window.

5. After you complete the Compute Payroll window, choose **Ctrl-Enter**. QuickPay computes the paycheck and enters it in the Register. QuickPay then returns you to the Add/Pay Employees window for the next payroll calculation. Figure B.8 shows a payroll check filled in by QuickPay.

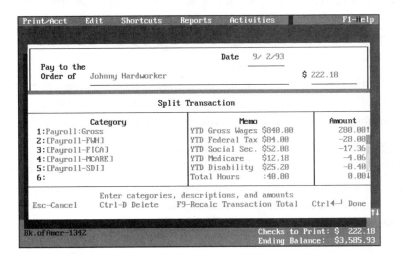

Fig. B.8
A sample payroll check filled in by QuickPay.

VI

Appendixes

Tips and Suggestions for Using QuickPay

If QuickPay sounds like something you would benefit from using, following are two suggestions for making your use of this tool as easy as possible:

- Use the Create Payroll Support Assistant, described in Chapter 22, "Using Quicken in Your Business," to create the categories and accounts you will need. QuickPay requires that certain categories and accounts exist. If they don't exist, QuickPay will not work correctly. The Create Payroll Support Assistant is the easiest way to be certain that your payroll categories and accounts have the right names.

- Recognize that QuickPay isn't the same thing as a payroll accountant or tax attorney. You cannot expect the QuickPay program or the QuickPay documentation to provide payroll tax knowledge or to answer your questions about how state unemployment taxes are calculated, for example.

Like every other payroll program, the QuickPay program automates payroll processing only. If you need to prepare payroll but don't understand how the basic process works, you first need to acquire an understanding of payroll processing.

Several options are available if you need to acquire payroll processing knowledge. The Internal Revenue Service and many state taxing authorities offer tax workshops that explain how to calculate federal and state payroll taxes.

The Internal Revenue Service also provides, free to small businesses, several well-written books and booklets that explain all kinds of accounting requirements, including those related to payroll processing. Finally, in a pinch, you always can use outside service bureaus, such as ADP or PayChex, until you feel confident about tackling payroll on your own.

Index

A Powerful Dose of DOS
for the Everyday User!

Count on Que for the Latest in DOS Information!

Using MS-DOS 6, Special Edition

Que Development Group

Version 6

$29.95 USA

1-56529-020-8, 1,000 pp., $7^3/_8$ x $9^1/_4$

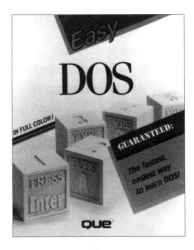

Easy DOS, 2nd Edition

Shelley O'Hara

Through Version 6

$16.95 USA

1-56529-095-x, 200 pp., 8 x 10

More DOS Titles from Que

I Hate DOS

Bryan Pfaffenberger

Version 6

$16.95 USA

1-56529-215-4, 384 pp., $7^3/_8$ x $9^1/_4$

MS-DOS 6 Quick Reference

Que Development Group

Version 6

$9.95 USA

1-56529-137-9, 160 pp., $4^3/_4$ x 8

MS-DOS 6 QuickStart

Que Development Group

Version 6

$21.95 USA

1-56529-096-8, 420 pp., $7^3/_8$ x $9^1/_4$

Find It Fast with Que's Quick References!

Que's Quick References are the compact, easy-to-use guides to essential application information. Written for all users, Quick References include vital command information under easy-to-find alphabetical listings. Quick References are a must for anyone who needs command information fast!

Que—The Leader in Spreadsheet Information!

Using Quattro Pro 4, Special Edition

Patrick T. Burns

This complete, easy-to-follow introduction to Quattro Pro includes in-depth tutorials, tips, and a tear-out Menu Map.

Versions 3 & 4

$27.95 USA
0-88022-931-4, 1,000 pp., 7³/₈ x 9¹/₄

More Spreadsheet Titles From Que

Using Quattro Pro for Windows, Special Edition

Version 1.0 for Windows

$27.95 USA
0-88022-889-X, 900 pp., 7³/₈ x 9¹/₄

Excel 4 for Windows QuickStart

Version 4 for Windows

$21.95 USA
0-88022-925-X, 400 pp., 7³/₈ x 9¹/₄

Excel 4 for Windows Quick Reference

Version 4

$9.95 USA
0-88022-958-6, 160 pp., 4³/₄ x 8

Quattro Pro 4 Quick Reference

Version 4

$9.95 USA
0-88022-939-X, 160pp., 4³/₄ x 8

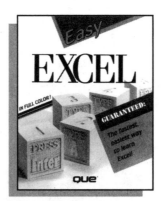

Quattro Pro 4 QuickStart

Versions 3 & 4

$21.95 USA
0-88022-938-1, 500 pp., 7³/₈ x 9¹/₄

Quattro Pro for windows Quick Reference

Versions 3 & 4

$9.95 USA
0-88022-956-X, 160 pp., 4³/₄ x 8

Easy Excel

Shelley O'Hara

This revolutionary text provides ideal coverage for beginners. 4-color illustrations, step-by-step instructions, and before-and-after screen shots make learning easy.

Version 4

$19.95 USA
0-88022-820-2, 200 pp., 8 x 10

Easy Quattro Pro

Version 3

$19.95 USA
0-88022-798-2, 200 pp., 8 x 10

Using Excel 4 for Windows, Special Edition

Through Latest Version

$29.95 USA
0-88022-916-0, 1,034 pp., 7³/₈ x 9¹/₄

To Order, Call: (800) 428-5331 OR (317) 573-2500